S0-FDJ-334

श्रीः ☎ 26507590
VEDANTA BOOK HOUSE
CHAMRAJPET, BANGALORE-560 018.
E.mail: vedantabooks@vsnl.net.

CHĀNDOGYA UPANIṢAD

Translated and with notes based on Śaṅkara's commentary

SWAMI LOKESWARANANDA

THE RAMAKRISHNA MISSION INSTITUTE OF CULTURE
GOL PARK, CALCUTTA 700 029

Published by
Swami Sarvabhutananda
Secretary
The Ramakrishna Mission Institute of Culture
Kolkata-700 029, India

First Published in April 1998
Second reprint : December 2010

Price in India : Rupees Two hundred and thirty only

ISBN 81-85843-91-0

Printed in India

Computer typeset at the Ramakrishna Mission Institute of Culture
Photo-offset at Rama Art Press
Kolkata - 700 030

PUBLISHER'S NOTE

This edition of the Chāndogya Upaniṣad is based on Swami Lokeswarananda's weekly discourses. It is the ninth in a series of Upaniṣads being published by the Institute. Readers will find this Upaniṣad simple and lucid. It is also authentic in that it follows Śaṅkara's interpretation.

February 1998

INVOCATION

ॐ आप्यायन्तु ममाङ्गानि वाक्प्राणश्चक्षुः श्रोत्रमथो बलमिन्द्रियाणि च सर्वाणि। सर्वं ब्रह्मौपनिषदं माऽहं ब्रह्म निराकुर्यां मा मा ब्रह्म निराकरोदनिराकरणमस्त्व-निराकरणं मेऽस्तु। तदात्मनि निरते य उपनिषत्सु धर्मास्ते मयि सन्तु ते मयि सन्तु।

ॐ शान्तिः शान्तिः शान्तिः॥

Om Āpyāyantu mamāṅgāni vākprāṇaścakṣuḥ śrotramatho balamindriyāṇi ca sarvāṇi; Sarvaṁ brahmaupaniṣadaṁ mā'haṁ brahma nirākuryāṁ mā mā brahma nirākarodanirākaraṇamastvanirākaraṇaṁ me'stu; Tadātmani nirate ya upaniṣatsu dharmāste mayi santu te mayi santu. Om Śāntiḥ Śāntiḥ Śāntiḥ.

Om, the word Om is always used at the beginning and end of anything said or done; *Mama,* my; *aṅgāni,* organs; *vāk,* the organ of speech; *prāṇaḥ,* the organ of breathing; *cakṣuḥ,* the eyes; *śrotram,* the ears; *atho,* and; *balam,* strength; *ca,* and; *sarvāṇi indriyāṇi,* all the organs; *āpyāyantu,* may be well nourished; *sarvam,* all things; *aupaniṣadam brahma,* are Brahman, the subject-matter of the Upaniṣads; *aham mā,* may I never; *brahma nirākuryām,* deny Brahman; *brahma mā mā nirākarot,* may Brahman never deny me; *anirākaraṇam,* no rejection; *astu,* may be [from Brahman—i.e., may Brahman never reject me]; *me,* by me; *anirākaraṇam astu,* may [Brahman] never be disowned [i.e., may I never feel that I am separate from Brahman]; *upaniṣatsu,* in the Upaniṣads; *ye dharmāḥ,* those good things [that are spoken of]; *te,* they; *tat-ātmani nirate,* which are said to be in the Self; *mayi,* in me; *santu,* may they be; *te mayi santu,* may they be in me. *Om śāntiḥ,* peace [relating to the body and mind]; *śāntiḥ,* peace [relating to animals]; *śāntiḥ,* peace [relating to the elements].

May all my limbs grow strong, so also my breath, speech, eyes, ears, and all my organs. All is Brahman, of which the Upaniṣads speak. May I never turn away from Brahman. May Brahman never turn me away. Let there be no turning away, no turning away at least on my side. I am engaged in the study of the Self. The Upaniṣads speak of qualities that one must possess to succeed in such a study. May I acquire those qualities. Om Peace! Peace! Peace!

This is a prayer for strength. Why do we need strength? We need strength so that we can understand the Upaniṣad—so that we can understand Brahman, the Truth, which is discussed in the Upaniṣad. I want the Truth; I want the knowledge that is in the Upaniṣad. As the Muṇḍaka Upaniṣad (III.ii.4) says, '*Nāyamātmā balahīnena labhyaḥ*—this knowledge is not attained by the weak.' It is for those with strength—physical strength, intellectual strength, and moral strength. The Upaniṣads are difficult and very subtle. The weak cannot understand Brahman. So this is a very significant prayer to begin the study of an Upaniṣad.

CHĀNDOGYA UPANIṢAD

The Chāndogya Upaniṣad is found in the Chāndogya Brāhmaṇa of the Sāma Veda. The Chāndogya Brāhmaṇa has ten chapters altogether, the last eight of which constitute the Upaniṣad. The name of this Upaniṣad is derived from the word *chandas.* A person who sings the Sāma Veda (*chandas*) is called a *Chandoga.* And the beliefs and practices of the Chandogas are set forth in the Chāndogya Upaniṣad.

Each of the chapters of the Chāndogya Upaniṣad is important. The first five chapters are about worship and meditation (that is, they are dualistic); whereas from the sixth chapter on, they are about Brahman (and in that sense they are more or less non-dualistic). The purpose of the meditation chapters is to emphasize the need for a pure heart. Only when the heart is pure can instructions about Brahman be effective.

The Chāndogya Upaniṣad occupies a high place among the extant Upaniṣads. Its language is simple and it tells many stories, but its subject-matter is profound. It takes care of the needs of ordinary people as well as those who are highly intellectual. It is like a loving mother, leading her child by the hand.

The Upaniṣad begins by telling people what they have to do to maintain spiritual progress, and it offers two options: either ritualistic worship as prescribed by the scriptures, or meditation on the sublime

Brahman, again as prescribed by the scriptures. The Chāndogya concedes that for most people the first option is the best. They are people incapable of thinking of anything beyond the reach of sense perception. Brahman, beyond thought and speech, means nothing to them. They have many desires and they would be happy to have those desires fulfilled. Ritualistic worship offers them the opportunity to attain just those things they desire.

But the Upaniṣad makes no secret of the fact that everything that ritualistic worship offers—money, health, beauty, power, even heaven—is short-lived. If a person wants permanent peace and happiness, he has to have liberation—liberation from the bondage of desires. And this is attainable only through Self-knowledge. As the Śvetāśvatara Upaniṣad (III.8) says: *'Tameva viditvā'timṛtyumeti nānyaḥ panthā vidyate'yanāya*—If you know that [Brahman], you overcome death. There is no other way [for liberation].' This is a warning to those who engage in ritualistic worship, thinking they will get everything they want through it. The Śvetāśvatara Upaniṣad says that the only way to attain permanent peace and happiness is through knowledge of Brahman—that is, through Self-knowledge.

The Chāndogya Upaniṣad sounds the same warning, and having done this, it tries to draw our attention to Self-knowledge. As a first step in this direction, it gives an instruction on the *udgītha,* the recitation of Om. This is part of the worship a person has to perform to bring the mind under control. Though the goal is Self-knowledge, a person must first control the mind by doing some *upāsanā* (spiritual practices). The Īśa Upaniṣad (verse 11) also gives this advice. It asks a person to combine *vidyā* (worship of gods and goddesses) and *avidyā* (performing sacrifices.). This is the path of gradual liberation.

Śaṅkara also recommends this for those who are not yet ready for the more difficult path of renunciation. In his commentary on the Chāndogya Upaniṣad, he advises that they practise the udgītha, the recitation of Om. A sure way of controlling the mind is to recite Om whenever you do or say anything. To emphasize its importance, the Chāndogya Upaniṣad devotes its first five chapters to the udgītha. From then on it discusses nothing but Brahman.

The Chāndogya Upaniṣad was often quoted by Śaṅkara in his commentaries to establish his philosophy of non-dualism. In fact, there is hardly any issue in Vedānta which is not discussed in the Chāndogya. It is a complete manual on Vedānta.

CHAPTER ONE

Section One

ओमित्येतदक्षरमुद्गीथमुपासीत। ओमिति ह्युद्गायति तस्योपव्याख्यानम् ॥ १ ॥

Omityetadakṣaramudgīthamupāsīta; Omiti hyudgāyati tasyopavyākhyānam.

Om iti, this Om [is closest to Brahman]; *etat akṣaram udgītham upāsīta,* recite this syllable as part of your upāsanā [ritual]; *hi om iti udgāyati,* how you recite this Om; *tasya upavyākhyānam,* is being explained.

1. Om is the closest word to Brahman. Recite this Om as if you are worshipping Brahman. [That is, treat this Om as the symbol of Brahman and concentrate on the idea of their oneness.] How you recite this Om is being explained.

Om is as good as Brahman. To begin with, it is a symbol of Brahman. But it is not just a symbol; it is Brahman itself. The Upaniṣad says to recite Om as if you are worshipping Brahman. This recitation is called *udgītha,* and it is loud recitation. You recite Om aloud, but you do it with the feeling that you are worshipping Brahman. This worship then eventually purifies the mind.

The importance of Om is being explained in the following verses.

एषां भूतानां पृथिवी रसः पृथिव्या आपो रसः।
अपामोषधयो रस ओषधीनां पुरुषो रसः पुरुषस्य वाग्रसो
वाच ऋग्रस ऋचः साम रसः साम्न उद्गीथो रसः॥ २॥

Eṣāṁ bhūtānāṁ pṛthivī rasaḥ pṛthivyā āpo rasaḥ; Apāmoṣadhayo rasa oṣadhīnāṁ puruṣo rasaḥ puruṣasya vāgraso vāca ṛgrasa ṛcaḥ sāma rasaḥ sāmna udgītho rasaḥ.

Eṣām bhūtānām, of these beings; *pṛthivī rasaḥ,* the earth is the essence; *pṛthivyāḥ,* of the earth; *āpaḥ,* water; *rasaḥ,* is the essence; *apām oṣadhayaḥ rasaḥ,* plants are the essence of water; *oṣadhīnām puruṣaḥ rasaḥ,* human beings are the essence of plants; *puruṣasya vāk rasaḥ,* speech is the essence of human beings; *vācaḥ ṛg rasaḥ,* the Ṛg Veda is the essence of speech; *ṛcaḥ sāma rasaḥ,* the Sāma Veda is the essence of the Ṛg Veda; *sāmnaḥ udgīthaḥ rasaḥ,* the part known as udgītha is the essence of the Sāma Veda.

2. The earth is the essence of all things, living or non-living; water is the essence of the earth; plants are the essence of water; human beings are the essence of plants; speech is the essence of human beings; the Ṛg Veda is the essence of speech; the Sāma

Veda is the essence of the Ṛg Veda; and the udgītha is the essence of the Sāma Veda.

There are both living and non-living things on the earth. What sustains them? Obviously the earth. They all come out of the earth, are sustained by the earth, and finally dissolve into the earth. But what sustains the earth? Water. The earth is a mixture of water and earth, and there can be no earth without water.

Plants are said to be the essence of water, for they grow from water. Similarly, human beings are the essence of plants, because the human body is the outcome of the food eaten by human beings. Speech is the essence of human beings, for it is the best part of them. The best speech is the Ṛg Veda, and the essence of the Ṛg Veda is the Sāma Veda. Finally, udgītha—that is, Om—is the essence of the Sāma Veda.

स एष रसानां रसतमः परमः परार्ध्योऽष्टमो यदुद्गीथः ॥ ३ ॥

Sa eṣa rasānāṁ rasatamaḥ paramaḥ parārdhyo'ṣṭamo yadudgīthaḥ.

Saḥ, that; *eṣaḥ,* this; *rasānām,* of all the essences; *rasatamaḥ,* the best essence; *paramaḥ,* the best; *parārdhyaḥ,* ranking the highest; *aṣṭamaḥ,* the eighth [in the order of earth, water, plants, human beings;

speech, the Ṛg Veda, the Sāma Veda, and udgītha]; *yat,* that; *udgīthaḥ,* udgītha [Om].

3. This udgītha [Om] is the best of all essences. It is the best of all that exists. It is the eighth, and it has the highest status.

The best of all essences is the udgītha, which is Om. It is the highest and best because it is the same as Brahman.

कतमा कतमर्क्कतमत्कतमत्साम कतमः कतम उद्गीथ इति विमृष्टं भवति॥४॥

Katamā katamarkkatamatkatamatsāma katamaḥ katama udgītha iti vimṛṣṭaṁ bhavati.

Katamā, which; *katamā ṛk,* which are the Ṛks; *katamat katamat sāma,* which are the Sāmas; *katamaḥ katamaḥ udgīthaḥ,* which are the udgīthas; *iti vimṛṣṭam bhavati,* this is the question.

4. Which are the Ṛks? Which are the Sāmas? Which are the udgīthas? This is the question.

It has been stated that speech is the essence of the Ṛg Veda. The question now arises: Which ones are the Ṛk, which ones are the Sāma, and which ones are the udgītha? The word *katama,* 'which,' is repeated to emphasize the importance of the question.

But why is the word 'which' being used here? 'Which' is used when you have to pinpoint one thing out of many. The Ṛg Veda is taken as a single whole, so how is the use of 'which' justified here? The answer is that here 'which' refers to individual Ṛk mantras, and not to the whole body of the Ṛg Veda.

वागेवर्क्प्राणः सामोमित्येतदक्षरमुद्गीथः। तद्वा एतन्मिथुनं यद्वाक्च प्राणश्चर्क्च साम च॥५॥

Vāgevarkprāṇaḥ sāmomityetadakṣaramudgīthaḥ; Tadvā etanmithunaṁ yadvākca prāṇaścarkca sāma ca.

Vāk eva ṛk, speech is Ṛk [being the cause of the Ṛk]; *prāṇaḥ sāma,* prāṇa [breath, or the life force] is Sāma [for you can sing the Sāma if your prāṇa is strong]; *om iti etat akṣaram udgīthaḥ,* the syllable 'Om' is the udgītha [for you recite it out of love for the Sāma]; *tat etat vai mithunam,* it is like a couple; *yat vāk ca prāṇaḥ ca ṛk ca sāma ca,* which are speech and prāṇa, Ṛk and Sāma.

5. [In answer to the foregoing question:] Speech is the same as Ṛk; prāṇa [life] is the same as Sāma; and Om is nothing but udgītha [Brahman] itself. They are pairs: speech and life, Ṛk and Sāma.

The word 'couple,' or 'pair,' is being used to suggest a relationship of cause and effect. Cause and effect are, in fact, one and the same. Speech is the cause, and Ṛk is the effect. They are one because the cause becomes the effect. The same applies to prāṇa (the life force) and Sāma.

According to this Upaniṣad, the evolution of the gross world is in this order: earth, water, plants, human beings, speech, Ṛk, Sāma, and udgītha (Om). Udgītha is *rasatama,* the essence of all essences, the cause of all causes. It occupies the eighth position—that is, it is the ultimate in the evolution of things. It is the Paramātman, the Self of all selves.

तदेतन्मिथुनमोमित्येतस्मिन्नक्षरे संसृज्यते यदा वै मिथुनौ समागच्छत आपयतो वै तावन्योन्यस्य कामम्॥ ६॥

Tadetanmithunamomityetasminnakṣare saṁsṛjyate yadā vai mithunau samāgacchata āpayato vai tāvanyonyasya kāmam.

Tat, that; *etat,* this; *mithunam,* dual combination [i.e., speech and life]; *om iti etasmin akṣare saṁsṛjyate,* meet in this syllable Om; *yadā vai,* whenever; *mithunau samāgacchataḥ,* a couple [a male and a female] come together; *tau,* they; *anyonyasya kāmam āpayataḥ vai,* naturally satisfy each other's desires.

6. This dual combination of speech and life merge into each other and become one in this syllable Om. It is like a male and a female meeting and satisfying each other's desires.

Those two, speech and life, merge into each other in Om. They attain their fulfilment in this way. Om thus stands for the fulfilment of all things.

आपयिता ह वै कामानां भवति य एतदेवं विद्वानक्षरमुद्गीथमुपास्ते ॥ ७ ॥

Āpayitā ha vai kāmānāṁ bhavati ya etadevaṁ vidvānakṣaramudgīthamupāste.

Āpayitā, he receives; *ha vai kāmānām,* all he desires; *bhavati,* this happens; *yaḥ,* he who; *etat,* this; *evam,* this way [as the one who receives everything]; *vidvān,* knows; *akṣaram,* Om; *udgītham,* as udgītha [Brahman]; *upāste,* worships.

7. He who worships Om as the udgītha [Brahman], knowing it as the one who receives everything, himself [finally] receives everything he desires.

If you worship Om, you acquire the qualities of Om. If you worship Om as the one who receives everything, you also, like Om, receive everything you desire.

The śruti says: 'You become whatever or whomever your object of worship is.' (Maṇḍala Brāhmaṇa 20)

तद्वा एतदनुज्ञाक्षरं यद्धि किंचानुजानात्योमित्येव तदाहैषो एव समृद्धिर्यदनुज्ञा समर्धयिता ह वै कामानां भवति य एतदेवं विद्वानक्षरमुद्गीथमुपास्ते ॥ ८ ॥

Tadvā etadanujñākṣaraṁ yaddhi kiṁcānujānātyomit-yeva tadāhaiṣo eva samṛddhiryadanujñā samardhayitā ha vai kāmānāṁ bhavati ya etadevaṁ vidvānakṣaramud-gīthamupāste.

Tat, that; *vai etat,* this; *anujñā akṣaram,* syllable [Om] indicates assent; *yat,* when; *hi kim ca anujānāti,* assent is to be indicated; *om iti,* this Om; *eva tadā āha,* is then uttered; *eṣā u eva,* this; *samṛddhiḥ,* progress; *yat,* that; *anujñā,* assent; *samardhayitā,* makes it possible; *ha vai kāmānām bhavati,* one attains those desires; *yaḥ,* he who; *etat,* this; *evam,* this way; *vidvān,* having known; *akṣaram udgītham upāste,* worships the syllable Om as the udgītha [Brahman].

8. That akṣaram [Om] stands for assent. A person says Om whenever he wants to say yes. This Om is the key to progress. He who worships Om as the udgītha [Brahman], knowing it thus [as the fulfiller of all desires], has all his desires fulfilled.

The word Om means 'yes.' Once someone named Śākalya asked the sage Yājñavalkya, 'How many gods and goddesses are there?' Yājñavalkya replied, 'Thirty-three.' Then Śākalya indicated his agreement by saying 'Om.'

When you say Om it is also an indication of your faith in yourself. It is proof of your strength and vigour, and proof also of your prosperity.

Om is therefore a symbol of certain basic qualities. When you worship Om you acquire those qualities, and you begin to progress and also prosper.

तेनेयं त्रयी विद्या वर्तत ओमित्याश्रावयत्योमिति शंस-
त्योमित्युद्गायत्येतस्यैवाक्षरस्यापचित्यै महिम्ना रसेन ॥ ९ ॥

Teneyaṁ trayī vidyā vartata omityāśrāvayatyomiti śaṁsatyomityudgāyatyetasyaivākṣarasyāpacityai mahimnā rasena.

Tena, by this [Om]; *iyam,* this; *trayī vidyā vartate,* threefold Vedic ritual begins; *om iti,* with Om; *āśrāvayati,* the recitation begins; *om iti śaṁsati,* with Om begins the singing of the hymn; *om iti udgāyati,* with Om the udgān [the praise to Om] begins; *etasya akṣarasya,* to this akṣara [Brahman]; *eva apacityai,* to pay homage; *mahimnā,* for its greatness; *rasena,* with the essence [of Om].

9. With Om one begins the threefold Vedic ritual, and with Om one starts reciting the Vedas. With Om one starts singing the Vedic hymns, and again with Om one sings the udgān [from the Vedas, in praise of Om, or Brahman]. All this is a tribute to Om. Again, all this is possible by virtue of the

essence derived from Om [in the form of wheat and other food].

To create some interest in Om, it is being praised here.

Om is indispensable even if you are performing a Vedic ritual. You begin reciting a Vedic verse with Om, singing a Vedic hymn with Om, and closing your final udgān with Om. In short, the whole procedure is dedicated to Om. Not only that, those who participate in this ritualistic worship derive their strength and vigour from Om, for the butter or barley syrup they drink as a stimulant is from Om.

How? Om is the medium through which sacrifices are performed, and the effects of the sacrifices are carried to the sun. These then return to the earth as rain. From rain come life and food. Again, because of life and food, a person is able to perform sacrifices.

Thus, it is the essence of Om that makes ritualistic worship, such as sacrifices, possible. Ritualistic worship is therefore a testimony to the greatness of Om. Om is both the cause and the effect.

तेनोभौ कुरुतो यश्चैतदेवं वेद यश्च न वेद। नाना तु विद्या चाविद्या च यदेव विद्यया करोति श्रद्धयोपनिषदा तदेव वीर्यवत्तरं भवतीति खल्वेतस्यैवाक्षरस्योपव्याख्यानं भवति॥ १०॥ इति प्रथमः खण्डः॥ १॥

Tenobhau kuruto yaścaitadevaṁ veda yaśca na veda; Nānā tu vidyā cāvidyā ca yadeva vidyayā karoti śraddhayopaniṣadā tadeva vīryavattaraṁ bhavatīti khalvetasyaivākṣarasyopavyākhyānaṁ bhavati. Iti prathamaḥ khaṇḍaḥ.

Ubhau, both [kinds of persons]; *tena,* by the power of that [Om]; *kurutaḥ,* work; *yaḥ ca,* whoever; *evam,* as such; *veda,* knows; *etat,* this [i.e., about Om]; *yaḥ ca na veda,* he who does not know; *vidyā ca avidyā ca nānā tu,* knowledge and ignorance are entirely different things; *yat eva,* anything; *vidyayā karoti,* one does with knowledge [about Om]; *śraddhayā,* with respect for one's teachers and the scriptures; *upaniṣadā,* as taught by the Upaniṣads [i.e., according to yoga]; *tat eva,* that [work]; *vīryavattaram bhavati,* is more powerful [i.e., more fruitful]; *iti,* this; *khalu,* certainly; *etasya eva akṣarasya upavyākhyānam bhavati,* is the right tribute to this Om. *Iti prathamaḥ khaṇḍaḥ,* here ends the first section.

10. He who knows about Om and he who does not know about it both work with strength they derive from Om. But knowledge and ignorance produce different results. Anything done with knowledge [about Om], with faith in the teachers and in the scriptures, and according to the principles of the Upaniṣads [or of yoga] is more fruitful. This certainly is the right tribute to Om.

Two kinds of people work: one kind knowing what Om means and another kind knowing nothing about it. Both kinds of people, however, are able to work because of Om. What is the difference between the two? What special advantage does a person who knows about Om have? Someone may argue: Suppose a person takes a medicine knowing what medicine he is taking and why he is taking it, and another person takes it without any knowledge of what he is taking and why he is taking it. Will the medicine produce different results in them?

The answer is: The analogy does not apply here. Knowledge is always an advantage, especially knowledge about Om. If you work because you are told to work, and if you work because you want to use the work as a stepping-stone to the attainment of Om—there is a vast difference between the two approaches. In the first instance, you are content with whatever the work produces; in the second, you are content only if it paves the way to your attainment of Om.

Section Two

देवासुरा ह वै यत्र संयेतिर उभये प्राजापत्यास्तद्ध
देवा उद्गीथमाजह्रुरनेनैनानभिभविष्याम इति ॥ १ ॥

Devāsurā ha vai yatra saṁyetira ubhaye prājāpatyās-taddha devā udgīthamājahruranenainānabhibhaviṣyāma iti.

Devāsurāḥ, the gods and goddesses and the demons; *ha vai yatra saṁyetire,* fought among themselves; *ubhaye,* [though] both; *prājāpatyāḥ,* were Prajāpati's children; *tat,* at that time; *ha devāḥ,* the gods and goddesses then; *udgītham ājahruḥ,* adopted the path of the udgītha; *anena,* by this; *enān,* them [the demons]; *abhibhaviṣyāmaḥ,* will overcome; *iti,* thinking thus.

1. The gods and goddesses and the demons are both children of Prajāpati, yet they fought among themselves. The gods and goddesses then adopted the path of the udgītha, thinking they would thereby be able to overcome the demons.

The gods and goddesses are 'bright' by virtue of their self-control, while the demons are 'dark' because they have no control over themselves. Though they were offspring of the same Prajāpati, they often clashed with each other. The gods and goddesses represent virtue; the demons represent vice. This conflict between virtue and vice is eternal, but it is virtue that always prevails. Virtue is here said to be the udgītha—that is, reciting Om while performing sacrifices. The gods and goddesses choose the path prescribed by the scriptures, whereas the demons do just the opposite and defy the scriptures. No wonder then the demons lose.

The udgītha is supreme because it is Om. It is the Paramātman, the Cosmic Self.

ते ह नासिक्यं प्राणमुद्गीथमुपासाञ्चक्रिरे तं हासुराः पाप्मना विविधुस्तस्मात्तेनोभयं जिघ्रति सुरभि च दुर्गन्धि च पाप्मना ह्येष विद्धः ॥ २ ॥

Te ha nāsikyaṁ prāṇamudgīthamupāsāñcakrire taṁ hāsurāḥ pāpmanā vividhustasmāttenobhayaṁ jighrati surabhi ca durgandhi ca pāpmanā hyeṣa viddhaḥ.

Te, they [the gods and goddesses]; *ha nāsikyam prāṇam udgītham upāsāñcakrire,* worshipped as udgītha the prāṇa [life principle] presiding over the nostrils; *asurāḥ ha,* the asuras, however; *tam pāpmanā vividhuḥ,* pierced it with evil [i.e., misused it, as if it were meant only for sense pleasure such as enjoying fragrance]; *hi,* this is why; *eṣaḥ,* this [prāṇa presiding over the nostrils]; *pāpmanā viddhaḥ,* is tainted with evil; *tasmāt,* therefore; *tena,* by it [i.e., the nostrils]; *jighrati,* smells; *surabhi ca,* good odour; *durgandhi ca,* and also bad odour.

2. The gods and goddesses worshipped the prāṇa presiding over the nostrils as udgītha. The demons, however, misused it. [To them it was only an organ of smelling.] That is why [because of this misuse] people smell both good and bad odours through the nostrils.

Mark the contrast between the attitude of the gods and goddesses and of the demons. To the demons, the nostrils were only an organ for smelling. Being what they are, it is natural that they would think so. But to the gods and goddesses, the nostrils are the seat of prāṇa, the vital breath, and they worship prāṇa there. The nostrils are also holy to them for another reason: they use the nostrils in reciting the udgītha to prāṇa. The demons know nothing about prāṇa or udgītha. To them, prāṇa is merely that which carries good and bad odours.

अथ ह वाचमुद्गीथमुपासाञ्चक्रिरे तां हासुराः पाप्मना विविधुस्तस्मात्तयोभयं वदति सत्यं चानृतं च पाप्मना ह्येषा विद्धा ॥ ३ ॥

Atha ha vācamudgīthamupāsāñcakrire tāṁ hāsurāḥ pāpmanā vividhustasmāttayobhayaṁ vadati satyaṁ cānṛtaṁ ca pāpmanā hyeṣā viddhā.

Atha ha, next; *vācam,* speech; *udgītham upāsāñcakrire,* [the gods and goddesses] worshipped as udgītha; *tām ha asurāḥ pāpmanā vividhuḥ,* the asuras pierced it with evil [i.e., misused it]; *tasmāt,* that is why; *tayā,* by it [the organ of speech]; *vadati,* one speaks; *ubhayam satyam ca anṛtam ca,* both truth and untruth; *pāpmanā hi eṣā viddhā,* because this [speech] was pierced with evil [by the ignorant demons].

3. Next the gods and goddesses worshipped speech as udgītha [i.e., they used speech in praise of Om]. The demons, however, pierced it with evil [i.e., misused

it out of ignorance]. This is why people use the organ of speech to speak both truth and untruth. This happens because speech was pierced with evil.

अथ ह चक्षुरुद्गीथमुपासाञ्चक्रिरे तद्धासुराः पाप्मना विविधुस्तस्मात्तेनोभयं पश्यति दर्शनीयं चादर्शनीयं च पाप्मना ह्येतद्विद्धम् ॥ ४ ॥

Atha ha cakṣurudgīthamupāsāñcakrire taddhāsurāḥ pāpmanā vividhustasmāttenobhayaṁ paśyati darśanīyaṁ cādarśanīyaṁ ca pāpmanā hyetadviddham.

Atha ha, next; *cakṣuḥ udgītham upāsāñcakrire,* [the gods and goddesses] worshipped the eye as udgītha [in praise of Om]; *asurāḥ ha,* the demons, however; *tat,* that [eye]; *pāpmanā vividhuḥ,* pierced with evil [misused it from ignorance]; *tasmāt,* this is why; *tena,* by this [eye]; *paśyati,* one sees; *ubhayam darśanīyam ca adarśanīyam ca,* both good and bad sights; *hi,* because; *etat,* this [eye]; *pāpmanā viddham,* was pierced by evil.

4. Next the gods and goddesses worshipped the eye as udgītha [as a praise to Om]. The demons, however, pierced it with evil [i.e., misused it out of ignorance]. This is why people see both good and bad things with the eyes. They see both because of ignorance.

अथ ह श्रोत्रमुद्गीथमुपासाञ्चक्रिरे तद्धासुराः पाप्मना विविधुस्तस्मात्तेनोभयं शृणोति श्रवणीयं चाश्रवणीयं च पाप्मना ह्येतद्विद्धम् ॥ ५ ॥

Atha ha śrotramudgīthamupāsāñcakrire taddhāsurāḥ pāpmanā vividhustasmāttenobhayaṁ śṛṇoti śravaṇīyaṁ cāśravaṇīyaṁ ca pāpmanā hyetadviddham.

Atha ha, next; *śrotram udgītham upāsāñcakrire,* [the gods and goddesses] worshipped the faculty of hearing as their udgītha [praise to Om]; *asurāḥ ha,* the asuras, however; *tat,* that faculty; *pāpmanā vividhuḥ,* pierced with evil [misused from ignorance]; *tasmāt,* that is why; *tena,* by it [the organ of hearing]; *ubhayam śṛṇoti śravaṇīyam ca aśravaṇīyam ca,* one hears both pleasant and unpleasant things; *hi,* because; *etat,* this [faculty]; *pāpmanā viddham,* was pierced by evil [i.e., was misused by the ignorant].

5. Next the gods and goddesses worshipped the faculty of hearing as udgītha [in order to praise Om]. The demons, however, pierced it with evil [i.e., misused it out of ignorance]. As a result, people hear both pleasant and unpleasant things with the ears. This happens because of ignorance.

अथ ह मन उद्गीथमुपासाञ्चक्रिरे तद्धासुराः पाप्मना विविधुस्तस्मात्तेनोभयं सङ्कल्पयते सङ्कल्पनीयं चासङ्कल्पनीयं च पाप्मना ह्येतद्विद्धम् ॥ ६ ॥

Atha ha mana udgīthamupāsāñcakrire taddhāsurāḥ pāpmanā vividhustasmāttenobhayaṁ saṅkalpayate saṅkalpanīyaṁ cāsaṅkalpanīyaṁ ca pāpmanā hyetad-viddham.

Atha ha, next; *manaḥ udgītham upāsāñcakrire,* [the gods and goddesses] worshipped the mind for its role in chanting the udgītha; *asurāḥ ha,* the asuras, however; *tat,* that [mind]; *pāpmanā vividhuḥ,* poisoned it with bad thoughts; *tasmāt,* for that reason; *tena,* in the mind; *ubhayam saṅkalpanīyam ca asaṅkalpanīyam ca saṅkalpayate,* one thinks both good and bad thoughts; *pāpmanā hi etat viddham,* because the mind is vitiated by evil [ignorance].

6. Next, the gods and goddesses worshipped the mind, because the mind makes it possible for them to chant the udgītha [the praise to Om]. But the demons even vitiated the mind. As a result, the mind has both good and bad thoughts. This happens because of ignorance.

Prāṇa is another name for Brahman. Prāṇa is pure, but when it is associated with the sense organs it is not pure. Similarly, Brahman as Brahman is pure, but with adjuncts it is not pure. It is not pure in the sense that it is subject to change.

Here, these adjuncts are referred to as *pāpma,* impure or evil, because they are limitations imposed on Brahman. These limitations are not real, however, but only apparent.

When the Upaniṣad speaks of the organs, it means the organs with their presiding deities. Both are described as *pāpma.* In these verses, some of the organs are mentioned, but it is to be understood that what is stated here about some organs applies to all the organs and their presiding deities.

अथ ह य एवायं मुख्यः प्राणस्तमुद्गीथमुपासाञ्चक्रिरे तं हासुरा ऋत्वा विदध्वंसुर्यथाश्मानमाखणमृत्वा विध्वंसेत ॥ ७ ॥

Atha ha ya evāyaṁ mukhyaḥ prāṇastamudgītha-mupāsāñcakrire taṁ hāsurā ṛtvā vidadhvaṁsuryathāś-mānamākhaṇamṛtvā vidhvaṁseta.

Atha ha, next; *yaḥ eva mukhyaḥ prāṇaḥ,* the chief prāṇa [the vital force, inclusive of its five aspects—*prāṇa, apāna, vyāna, udāna,* and *samāna*]; *tam ud-gītham upāsāñcakrire,* [the gods and goddesses] worshipped him as udgītha; *yathā,* just as; *ākhaṇam,* unbreakable; *aśmānam,* stone; *ṛtvā,* hit against; *vidhvaṁseta,* broken into pieces [and are destroyed]; [in the same way] *asurāḥ ca,* the demons also; *tam ha ṛtvā vidadhvaṁsuḥ,* hit against it [prāṇa] and were destroyed.

7. Next, the gods and goddesses worshipped the chief prāṇa as udgītha. As regards the demons, they all met their end in prāṇa, just as [chunks of earth]

break into pieces when they hit an unbreakable stone.

The gods and goddesses worshipped pure prāṇa—that is, prāṇa without the organs—as udgītha. As before, the demons tried to hurt prāṇa, but they failed. In fact, they got lost in prāṇa. They met the same fate as chunks of earth thrown against granite. When the chunks hit the granite, they break into pieces and are destroyed. Similarly, it is beyond the power of the demons to do any harm to prāṇa.

एवं यथाश्मानमाखणमृत्वा विध्वंसत एवं हैव स विध्वंसते य एवंविदि पापं कामयते यश्चैनमभिदासति स एषोऽश्माखणः ॥ ८ ॥

Evaṁ yathāśmānamākhaṇamṛtvā vidhvaṁsata evaṁ haiva sa vidhvaṁsate ya evaṁvidi pāpaṁ kāmayate yaścainamabhidāsati sa eṣo'śmākhaṇaḥ.

Evam yathā, just as [chunks of earth]; *ākhaṇam,* unbreakable; *aśmānam,* stone; *ṛtvā,* having hit; *vidhvaṁsate,* are smashed; *evam ha eva,* in the same way; *saḥ vidhvaṁsate,* a person gets totally destroyed; *yaḥ pāpam kāmayate,* who wishes ill; *evamvidi,* of a person who knows thus [the true nature of prāṇa]; *yaḥ ca enam abhidāsati,* or who causes an injury to such a person; *saḥ eṣaḥ,* he [who knows] this [prāṇa]; *aśmā ākhaṇaḥ,* [is like] a stone that can never be broken.

8. Just as when chunks of earth are thrown against an unbreakable stone they are themselves reduced to dust, similarly, if anyone wishes ill or causes an injury to a person who knows prāṇa, he invites his own destruction thereby. The person who knows prāṇa is immune to injury like a piece of unbreakable stone.

What is the difference between *mukhya prāṇa* (the chief prāṇa) and the prāṇa that is associated with our breathing, or smelling? Mukhya prāṇa is supreme prāṇa—that is, it is Brahman. It is pure, all-pervasive, and self-sufficient. But our breathing is associated with the organ of smelling and is not independent. It is also not pure. It has limitations and is susceptible to *pāpma,* impurities—that is, it is sometimes good and sometimes bad. Mukhya prāṇa, however, is always pure, always the same.

One who knows the true nature of prāṇa is immune to injury. And anyone trying to hurt him will end up hurting himself.

नैवैतेन सुरभि न दुर्गन्धि विजानात्यपहतपाप्मा ह्येष तेन यदश्नाति यत्पिबति तेनेतरान्प्राणानवति। एतमु एवान्ततोऽवित्त्वोत्क्रामति व्याददात्येवान्तत इति॥ ९॥

Naivaitena surabhi na durgandhi vijānātyapahatapāpmā hyeṣa tena yadaśnāti yatpibati tenetarānprāṇānavati; Etamu evāntato'vittvotkrāmati vyādadātyevāntata iti.

Etena eva, by this [chief prāṇa]; *na surabhi,* no sweet odour; *na durgandhi,* no bad odour; *vijānāti,* is known; *hi,* because; *eṣaḥ,* this [prāṇa]; *apahata-pāpmā,* is pure [untouched by evil]; *tena,* by that [prāṇa]; *yat aśnāti,* whatever a person eats; *yat pibati,* whatever a person drinks; *tena,* by this [eating and drinking]; *itarān prāṇān,* the sense organs; *avati,* sustains; *u antataḥ,* at the time of death; *etam,* this [chief prāṇa]; *avittvā eva,* without receiving any food and drink; *utkrāmati,* goes out of the body; [this is why] *antataḥ,* at the time of death; *vyādadāti eva,* a person has the mouth open.

9. So far as the chief prāṇa is concerned, there is no good or bad odour for it. This is because it is pure [i.e., it is never touched by anything evil born of egotism]. If this prāṇa eats and drinks anything, it does so only to sustain the sense organs [such as the eyes, the ears, and so on]. When death occurs, the chief prāṇa does not eat or drink anything [and as a result, the sense organs collapse]. They seem to have left the body. [They still want to eat and drink, however, so that they may live, and] this is indicated by the fact that a person dies with the mouth open.

For the chief prāṇa, there is no good or bad odour because it is pure. Egotism is the source of impurity, and the chief prāṇa is free from egotism. And being free from egotism, the chief prāṇa is selfless. People eat and drink because of the chief prāṇa. But the chief prāṇa does not eat or drink for itself. It enables people to eat and drink to help sustain the sense organs. It thus sustains everything.

But how do we know that the food and drink the chief prāṇa consumes goes to sustain the organs? When death occurs the chief prāṇa stops eating and drinking. As a result, the sense organs stop functioning, as if they have left the body. It is seen, however, that when a person dies his mouth is open. This is indicative of the desire of the chief prāṇa to eat and drink.

तं हाङ्गिरा उद्गीथमुपासाञ्चक्र एतमु एवाङ्गिरसं मन्यन्तेऽङ्गानां यद्रसः ॥ १० ॥

Taṁ hāṅgirā udgīthamupāsāñcakra etamu evāṅgirasaṁ manyante'ṅgānāṁ yadrasaḥ.

Tam, that [the chief prāṇa]; *ha aṅgirāḥ,* the sage Aṅgirā; *udgītham,* as udgītha [the Supreme]; *upāsāñcakre,* worshipped; *etam,* this [Supreme Being, the chief prāṇa]; *u eva āṅgirasam,* as Āṅgirasa; *manyante,* [people] regard; *aṅgānām yat rasaḥ,* for it is the essence [support] of all the aṅgas [the organs].

10. The sage Aṅgirā worshipped the chief prāṇa as udgītha [i.e., Brahman, to whom the udgītha is addressed]. The chief prāṇa is referred to as *āṅgirasa,* for it is the *rasa* [i.e., the essence, or support] of all the *aṅgas* [organs].

The word *āṅgirasa* is derived from *aṅga* + *rasa.* That is, āṅgirasa is the *rasa* (essence) of the *aṅgas* (organs). It is the support of the organs. It is the same as prāṇa. When the sage Aṅgirā worships prāṇa, he is worshipping himself.

तेन तं ह बृहस्पतिरुद्गीथमुपासाञ्चक्र एतमु एव
बृहस्पतिं मन्यन्ते वाग्घि बृहती तस्या एष पतिः ॥ ११ ॥

Tena taṁ ha bṛhaspatirudgīthamupāsāñcakra etamu eva bṛhaspatiṁ manyante vāgghi bṛhatī tasyā eṣa patiḥ.

Tena, for that reason; *bṛhaspatiḥ,* Bṛhaspati; *ha tam,* that [prāṇa]; *udgītham upāsāñcakre,* worshipped prāṇa as udgītha [as Brahman, to whom Om is sung]; *etam u eva bṛhaspatim manyante,* they regard this [prāṇa] as Bṛhaspati; *hi,* for; *vāk,* speech; *bṛhatī,* is powerful; *tasyāḥ eṣaḥ patiḥ,* prāṇa is its lord.

11. This is why Bṛhaspati worshipped prāṇa as udgītha. Prāṇa is regarded as Bṛhaspati, for vāk [speech] is great [*bṛhatī*] and prāṇa is its lord [*pati*].

तेन तं हायास्य उद्गीथमुपासाञ्चक्र एतमु एवायास्यं
मन्यन्त आस्याद्यदयते ॥ १२ ॥

Tena taṁ hāyāsya udgīthamupāsāñcakra etamu evāyāsyaṁ manyanta āsyādyadayate.

Tena, for that reason; *tam,* that [i.e., the chief prāṇa]; *ha āyāsya,* the sage Āyāsya [or, that which comes out of the mouth]; *udgītham,* as udgītha; *upāsāñcakre,* worshipped; *etam u eva āyāsyam manyante,* they regarded this as Āyāsya; *yat āsyāt ayate,* that which comes out of the mouth.

12. This is why Āyāsya worshipped prāṇa as udgītha. They regarded this as Āyāsya for it is that which comes [*ayate*] out of the mouth [*āsyāt*].

Prāṇa is also Bṛhaspati because it is the lord of all speech. *Āyāsya* means 'that which comes out of the mouth.' It is prāṇa, but it is also the name of a sage.

Aṅgirā, Bṛhaspati, and Āyāsya—these sages worshipped prāṇa as udgītha. They, in fact, worshipped themselves.

तेन तं ह बको दाल्भ्यो विदाञ्चकार। स ह नैमिषीयानामुद्गाता बभूव स ह स्मैभ्यः कामाना-गायति॥ १३ ॥

Tena taṁ ha bako dālbhyo vidāñcakāra; Sa ha naimiṣīyānāmudgātā babhūva sa ha smaibhyaḥ kāmānāgāyati.

Dālbhyaḥ, the son of Dalbha; *bakaḥ,* the sage Baka; *ha tam,* that [prāṇa]; *tena,* with the qualities as stated; *vidāñcakāra,* came to know; *saḥ,* he [Baka]; *ha naimiṣīyānām,* of the sages of Naimiṣa forest; *udgātā,* the singer of the udgītha; *babhūva,* became; *ha ebhyaḥ kāmān,* according to the wishes [of the forest dwellers]; *saḥ āgāyati sma,* he sang [the udgītha].

13. The sage Baka, son of Dalbha, came to know prāṇa as it was. That is why the sages of Naimiṣa forest selected him as the singer of their udgītha. He, in his turn, fulfilled their wishes.

Not only did Aṅgirā and other sages worship prāṇa, but Baka, son of Dalbha, also did the same. That is, he recognized the power of prāṇa. The sages of Naimiṣa forest were pleased with him, and appointed him to sing the udgītha for them. He thus sang the udgītha in praise of prāṇa and pleased the sages by his performance.

आगाता ह वै कामानां भवति य एतदेवं विद्वानक्षरमुद्गीथमुपास्त इत्यध्यात्मम् ॥ १४ ॥ इति द्वितीयः खण्डः ॥ २ ॥

Āgātā ha vai kāmānāṁ bhavati ya etadevaṁ vidvānakṣaramudgīthamupāsta ityadhyātmam. Iti dvitīyaḥ khaṇḍaḥ.

Yaḥ, he who; *evam,* as such; *vidvān,* knows; *etat,* this [prāṇa]; *udgītham akṣaram,* as udgītha akṣara [*akṣara* means both 'syllable' and 'the undecaying,' which is a name of Brahman]; *upāste,* worships [or meditates on]; *vai kāmānām āgātā ha bhavati,* he thereby becomes the udgātā [singer] of all that he desires; *iti adhyātmam,* this is so far as the udgītha relating to the body is concerned. *Iti dvitīyaḥ khaṇḍaḥ,* here ends the second section.

14. If a person knows the real meaning of prāṇa and worships it as udgītha akṣara [i.e., as Akṣara Brahman] he himself becomes Akṣara Brahman. He then worships everyone he wants to worship [i.e., in singing for prāṇa he sings for all], and he attains all he desires. This is the attainment on the level of the body [*adhyātma*]. [The inner attainment is that he becomes one with prāṇa—that is, Akṣara Brahman.]

Singing for prāṇa is the same as singing for all, for prāṇa is all. You may even achieve all you desire through it.

This is so far as the individual is concerned. Praising Om has a threefold reward: relating to the body (*adhyātma*), relating to animals (*adhibhūta*), and relating to the elements (*adhidaiva*).

Section Three

अथाधिदैवतं य एवासौ तपति तमुद्गीथमुपासीतोद्यन्वा
एष प्रजाभ्य उद्गायति। उद्यंस्तमो भयमपहन्त्यपहन्ता
ह वै भयस्य तमसो भवति य एवं वेद॥ १॥

Athādhidaivataṁ ya evāsau tapati tamudgīthamupāsītodyanvā eṣa prajābhya udgāyati; Udyaṁstamo bhayamapahantyapahantā ha vai bhayasya tamaso bhavati ya evaṁ veda.

Atha, next; *adhidaivatam,* relating to the elements [such as rain, lightning, and other forces of nature]; *yaḥ eva asau,* that [i.e., the sun] over there which; *tapati,* gives us heat; *tam,* to that; *udgītham upāsīta,* worship as udgītha; *udyan,* as it rises; *vai eṣaḥ,* this [sun]; *prajābhyaḥ,* for all living beings; *udgāyati,* [as if] it prays for their well-being; *udyan,* as [the sun] rises; *tamaḥ bhayam apahanti,* it removes the fear of darkness; *yaḥ,* one who; *evam veda,* knows this; *vai bhayasya,* the fear [of birth and death]; *tamasaḥ,* ignorance; *apahantā bhavati,* overcomes.

1. Next, how you worship from the standpoint of the forces of nature: There is the sun rising to give us heat. Worship it as udgītha. The sun rises to pray, as it were, for the welfare of all living beings. As it rises, it dispels the fear of darkness. One who knows this overcomes the fear of ignorance about birth and death.

There are many ways of using udgītha as worship. This verse gives an example of how you use it in worshipping the forces of nature (*adhidaivata*). There is the sun above giving us heat. The Upaniṣad says to worship udgītha as the sun. But if udgītha is Om, how can it stand for the sun? The sun helps the plants, such as paddy, to grow. Without the sun, life on this planet would be impossible. It is as if the sun sings the udgītha for us to sustain us. This is why the sun is referred to as the udgītha. As udgītha, the sun also dispels our fear of darkness.

One who knows this is no longer afraid of birth and death. That is, he knows he is immortal.

समान उ एवायं चासौ चोष्णोऽयमुष्णोऽसौ स्वर इतीममाचक्षते स्वर इति प्रत्यास्वर इत्यमुं तस्माद्वा एतमिमममुं चोद्गीथमुपासीत ॥ २ ॥

Samāna u evāyaṁ cāsau coṣṇo'yamuṣṇo'sau svara itīmamācakṣate svara iti pratyāsvara ityamuṁ tasmādvā etamimamamuṁ codgīthamupāsīta.

Ayam, this [prāṇa]; *ca asau,* and that [sun]; *samānaḥ eva,* are equivalent; *u ayam,* this [prāṇa]; *uṣṇaḥ,* is warm; *ca asau,* and that [sun]; *uṣṇaḥ,* is warm; *imam,* this [prāṇa]; *svaraḥ iti ācakṣate,* [sages] call it svara ['outgoing,' at the time of death]; *amum,* that [sun]; *svaraḥ iti,* has set; *pratyāsvaraḥ iti,* [and] has returned [this is what people say]; *tasmāt vai,* for that reason; *etam,* this [going out]; *imam,* this [prāṇa]; *ca amum,* and that [sun]; *udgītham upāsīta,* worship as udgītha.

2. This prāṇa and that sun are alike. Prāṇa is warm, and the sun is also warm. Prāṇa is called *svara* [when it is 'going out' at the time of death]. The sun is also described as *svara* [when it 'sets'] and

pratyāsvara [when it 'comes back']. Therefore, worship both prāṇa and the sun as udgītha.

Prāṇa and āditya (the sun) are similar. Both are warm. Sages call both *svara,* which means 'going out.' The difference is that while prāṇa goes out (at the time of death), the sun goes out (when it sets) and also returns (*pratyāsvara,* when it rises). Thus, prāṇa and āditya are similar in name and quality.

It is therefore appropriate to worship both as udgītha. Both are Om.

अथ खलु व्यानमेवोद्गीथमुपासीत यद्वै प्राणिति स प्राणो यदपानिति सोऽपानः। अथ यः प्राणापानयोः सन्धिः स व्यानो यो व्यानः सा वाक्। तस्मादप्राण-न्ननपानन्वाचमभिव्याहरति॥ ३ ॥

Atha khalu vyānamevodgīthamupāsīta yadvai prāṇiti sa prāṇo yadapāniti so'pānaḥ; Atha yaḥ prāṇāpānayoḥ sandhiḥ sa vyāno yo vyānaḥ sā vāk; Tasmādaprāṇanna-napānanvācamabhivyāharati.

Atha, indirectly; *khalu vyānam eva udgītham upāsīta,* one should worship vyāna [the bridge between prāṇa (breathing in) and apāna (breathing out)] as udgītha; *yat vai prāṇiti,* that which is breathed in; *saḥ prāṇaḥ,* that is prāṇa; *yat apāniti,* that which is breathed out; *saḥ apānaḥ,* that is apāna; *atha yat prāṇa-apānayoḥ sandhiḥ,* then the bridge between prāṇa and apāna;

saḥ vyānaḥ, that is vyāna; *yaḥ vyānaḥ sā vāk,* that which is vyāna is speech; *tasmāt,* therefore; *aprāṇan,* without inhaling; *anapānan,* without exhaling; *vācam abhivyāharati,* a person speaks.

3. Worship vyāna [the breath held between prāṇa and apāna that enables you to speak] as udgītha. Prāṇa is the breath drawn in and apāna is the breath drawn out. Vyāna is the breath held between prāṇa and apāna. This vyāna is also called *vāk* [speech], for in speaking a person has to hold the breath.

Here vyāna is being presented for worship as udgītha, for vyāna is only a form of prāṇa. What is vyāna? Vyāna is the bridge between prāṇa and apāna, between breathing in and breathing out. Vyāna is the state in which you hold your breath. Vyāna is also called *vāk,* speech, for when you speak you have to hold your breath.

Śaṅkara says prāṇa is breathing out and apāna is breathing in. According to Monier-Williams, it is the other way around—prāṇa is breathing in and apāna is breathing out. Macdowell is of the same opinion. Both meanings are correct, depending on the context in which the word is used.

या वाक्सर्क्तस्मादप्राणन्ननपानन्नृचमभिव्याहरति यर्क्त-
त्साम तस्मादप्राणन्ननपानन्साम गायति यत्साम स
उद्गीथस्तस्मादप्राणन्ननपानन्नुद्गायति ॥ ४ ॥

Yā vāksarktasmādaprāṇannanapānannṛcamabhivyāharati yarktatsāma tasmādaprāṇannanapānansāma gāyati yatsāma sa udgīthastasmādaprāṇannanapānannudgāyati.

Yā vāk sā ṛk, that which is speech is Ṛk; *tasmāt,* because [they are one]; *aprāṇan anapānan,* breathing in and out are suspended; *ṛcam,* the Ṛg Veda; *abhivyāharati,* one recites; *yā ṛk tat sāma,* that which is the Ṛk is also the Sāma; *tasmāt,* because [they are one and the same]; *aprāṇan anapānan sāma gāyati,* one suspends breathing in and out when singing the Sāma; *yat sāma saḥ udgīthaḥ,* that which is the Sāma is the udgītha; *tasmāt aprāṇan anapānan udgāyati,* because one sings the udgītha by suspending both breathing in and breathing out.

4. Whatever is vāk [speech] is also the Ṛk [part of the Ṛg Veda]. This is why a person stops breathing in and breathing out when reciting the Ṛk mantras. Whatever is the Ṛk is also the Sāma. This is why one recites the Sāma without breathing in or breathing out. That which is the Sāma is also the udgītha. This is why when one sings the udgītha one stops both breathing in and breathing out.

The Ṛk is a collection of words, and the Sāma is based on the Ṛk. Again, the Sāma and the udgītha are the same. To recite any of these, or even to speak, you have to resort to vyāna—that is, you must hold your breath.

अतो यान्यन्यानि वीर्यवन्ति कर्माणि यथाग्नेर्मन्थनमाजेः सरणं दृढस्य धनुष आयमनमप्राणन्ननपानंस्तानि करोत्येतस्य हेतोर्व्यानमेवोद्गीथमुपासीत ॥ ५ ॥

Ato yānyanyāni vīryavanti karmāṇi yathāgnermanthanamājeḥ saraṇaṁ dṛḍhasya dhanuṣa āyamanamaprāṇannanapānaṁstāni karotyetasya hetorvyānamevodgīthamupāsīta.

Ataḥ, this is why; *yāni,* those; *anyāni,* other; *vīryavanti,* demanding great strength; *karmāṇi,* feats; *yathā,* such as; *agneḥ manthanam,* igniting a fire by rubbing one piece of wood against another; *ājeḥ,* a target; *saraṇam,* running up to; *dṛḍhasya dhanuṣaḥ āyamanam,* bending a stiff bow; *aprāṇan anapānan,* without breathing in or breathing out; *tāni,* all those [feats]; *karoti,* one accomplishes; *etasya hetoḥ,* for this reason; *vyānam eva,* vyāna; *udgītham,* as udgītha [Om]; *upāsīta,* one should worship.

5. This is why, while doing feats demanding great strength—such as producing a fire by rubbing one stick of wood against another, running up to a target, or bending a stiff bow—a person does not breathe in or breathe out. For this reason, one should worship this holding of breath, called *vyāna,* as udgītha [Om].

Whenever you do something that demands much application of strength, you must resort to vyāna. Take, for instance, deeds such as producing fire by grinding one piece of wood against another, or running up to a target, or bending a stiff bow. In doing each of these feats, you have to hold your breath. Even when you speak, you hold your breath. This distinguishes vyāna from other forms of breathing. Vyāna, therefore, deserves special worship, for vyāna is in a class by itself. It gives you strength.

अथ खलूद्गीथाक्षराण्युपासीतोद्गीथ इति प्राण एवोत्प्राणेन ह्युत्तिष्ठति वाग्गीर्वाचो ह गिर इत्याचक्षतेऽन्नं थमन्ने हीदं सर्वं स्थितम् ॥ ६ ॥

Atha khalūdgīthākṣarāṇyupāsītodgītha iti prāṇa evotprāṇena hyuttiṣṭhati vāggīrvāco ha gira ityācakṣate'nnaṁ thamanne hīdaṁ sarvaṁ sthitam.

Atha, now; *khalu udgīthākṣarāṇi 'ut-gī-tha' iti upāsīta,* worship the syllables *ut, gī,* and *tha* separately in the word *udgītha*; *prāṇaḥ eva ut,* prāṇa is this *ut*; *prāṇena hi,* because by prāṇa; *uttiṣṭhati,* arises [everything]; *vāk gīḥ,* vāk [speech] is *gī*; *vācaḥ ha giraḥ iti ācakṣate,* because words are called *'gira'*; *annam tham,* food is *tha*; *hi idam sarvam,* for all this [i.e., this world]; *anne sthitam,* is supported by food.

6. Now, one should worship the syllables *ut, gī,* and *tha* separately in the word *udgītha.* Prāṇa is represented by *ut,* for prāṇa is responsible for the

growth of all beings. Speech is *gī,* for scholars mean 'words' by the term *gira.* Food is *tha,* for the world is sustained by food.

The word *udgītha* is comprised of the syllables *ut, gī,* and *tha.* It is worthwhile meditating on these syllables, for each one is significant. For instance, *ut,* in brief, is *uttham,* rising. It stands for prāṇa, because out of prāṇa everything comes into being. From prāṇa everything 'rises'; otherwise it goes down.

The syllable *gī* stands for speech, because scholars prefer to use the word *gira* to mean speech. Similarly, the syllable *tha* stands for food, for *tha* means 'that which supports.' It is well known that food supports everything.

Thus the syllables *ut, gī,* and *tha* stand for the whole word *udgītha.* It is like thinking of the name 'Ram Misra.' As you think of the name, you also think of the person who bears that name.

Try to think of each syllable in the word *udgītha* as above.

द्यौरेवोदन्तरिक्षं गीः पृथिवी थमादित्य एवोद्वायुर्गीर-ग्निस्थं सामवेद एवोद्यजुर्वेदो गीर्ऋग्वेदस्थं दुग्धेऽस्मै वाग्दोहं यो वाचो दोहोऽन्नवानन्नादो भवति य एतान्येवं विद्वानुद्गी-थाक्षराण्युपास्त उद्गीथ इति॥ ७॥

Dyaurevodantarikṣaṁ gīḥ pṛthivī thamāditya evod-

vāyurgīragnisthaṁ sāmaveda evodyajurvedo gīrṛgvedasthaṁ dugdhe'smai vāgdohaṁ yo vāco doho'nnavānannādo bhavati ya etānyevaṁ vidvānudgīthākṣarāṇyupāsta udgītha iti.

Dyauḥ, heaven; *eva ut,* is *ut*; *antarikṣam gīḥ,* the space between heaven and earth is *gī*; *pṛthivī tham,* the earth is *tha*; *ādityaḥ eva ut,* the sun is *ut*; *vāyuḥ gīḥ,* air is *gī*; *agniḥ tham,* fire is *tha*; *sāma vedaḥ eva ut,* the Sāma Veda is *ut*; *yajur vedaḥ gīḥ,* the Yajur Veda is *gī*; *ṛg vedaḥ tham,* the Ṛg Veda is *tha*; *vāk,* the Ṛg Veda and other scriptures; *asmai,* to him [the spiritual seeker]; *doham,* the goal [he is seeking]; *dugdhe,* gives him of itself; *yaḥ vācaḥ dohaḥ,* the goal is the knowledge of the scriptures; *yaḥ evam vidvān,* the seeker who knows this; *etāni udgīthākṣarāṇi ut + gī + tha iti upāste,* [and] worships these syllables of udgītha; *annavān,* he has plenty of food; *annādaḥ bhavati,* [and] he enjoys eating that food [i.e., he becomes illumined].

7. Heaven is *ut,* the space between heaven and the earth is *gī,* and the earth is *tha.* The sun is *ut,* air is *gī,* and fire is *tha.* The Sāma Veda is *ut,* the Yajur Veda is *gī,* and the Ṛg Veda is *tha.* The scriptures reveal their meaning to the seeker if he knows all this. One who worships *ut-gī-tha* as above gets plenty of food and also eats plenty of food. [Such a person also gets enlightenment.]

Heaven is said to be *ut* because it is high above. Space is *gī* because it envelops the whole world.

And the earth is *tha* because it is the support of all beings. Āditya, the sun, is *ut* because it is far above everything. Vāyu, air, is *gī* because it envelops everything. Agni, fire, is *tha* because it is the common element in every sacrificial rite. The Sāma Veda is said to be *ut* because it is known even in heaven. The Yajur Veda is *gī* because the butter used in performing the Yajur Vedic rites is eaten by the gods and goddesses. The Ṛg Veda is *tha* because it supports the Sāma Veda.

What do you gain by worshipping *ut-gī-tha*? You gradually understand the meaning of the Ṛg Veda and other Vedas. You also have plenty to eat, and you become like 'a blazing fire'—that is, you become an illumined person.

अथ खल्वाशीः समृद्धिरुपसरणानीत्युपासीत येन साम्ना स्तोष्यन्स्यात्तत्सामोपधावेत् ॥ ८ ॥

Atha khalvāśīḥ samṛddhirupasaraṇānītyupāsīta yena sāmnā stoṣyansyāttatsāmopadhāvet.

Atha khalu, now; *āśīḥ samṛddhiḥ,* instructions about how desired objectives can be obtained; *upasaraṇāni,* the things desired; *iti,* in this way; *upāsīta,* one should meditate upon; *yena sāmnā,* by that Sāma; *stoṣyan syāt,* one sings; *tat sāma upadhāvet,* one should meditate upon that Sāma.

8. Now here are instructions about how one attains one's desired objectives: Keep meditating on the objectives. Also, pray for the objectives by singing the appropriate Sāma, and remember that the Sāma is the source of the things you are asking for.

You sing a particular Sāma for a particular thing you wish to get. Sing it always, and remember that it is the source of what you are wishing for.

यस्यामृचि तामृचं यदार्षेयं तमृषिं यां देवता-
मभिष्टोष्यन्स्यात्तां देवतामुपधावेत् ॥ ९ ॥

Yasyāmṛci tāmṛcaṁ yadārṣeyaṁ tamṛṣiṁ yāṁ devatāmabhiṣṭoṣyansyāttāṁ devatāmupadhāvet.

Tām ṛcam, that Ṛk; *yasyām ṛci,* on which Ṛk [the Sāma is based]; *tam ṛṣim yat ārṣeyam,* that sage who conceived of it; *yām devatām abhiṣṭoṣyan syāt,* the deity to whom the prayer is addressed; *tām devatām,* that deity; *upadhāvet,* one should meditate on.

9. The Ṛk from which this Sāma is derived, the sage who conceived of this Sāma prayer, and the deity to whom the prayer is addressed—meditate on all of them.

When you recite a Sāma mantra, you should remember the Ṛk mantra from which it is derived, the sage who first used it, and also the deity in whose honour it is used. The verse suggests that due respect should be shown to all of them.

येन च्छन्दसा स्तोष्यन्स्यात्तच्छन्द उपधावेद्येन स्तोमेन स्तोष्यमाणः स्यात्तं स्तोममुपधावेत्॥ १०॥

Yena cchandasā stoṣyansyāttacchanda upadhāvedyena stomena stoṣyamāṇaḥ syāttaṁ stomamupadhāvet.

Yena chandasā, by the Gāyatrī or whatever other hymn; *stoṣyan syāt,* one is going to pray; *tat chandaḥ upadhāvet,* one should meditate on that hymn; *yena stomena stoṣyamāṇaḥ syāt,* the group of Sāmas by which a person is going to pray; *tam stomam upadhāvet,* one should meditate on those Sāmas [along with the deities to whom they are addressed].

10. One may use the Gāyatrī or some other hymn when praying, but one should meditate on it. Again, one may use a number of Sāma mantras while praying, but one must meditate on them [along with the deities to whom they are addressed].

Whether you use the Gāyatrī or some other hymn while praying, you should not forget to meditate on that hymn. In fact, whatever mantras you use, you should meditate on them as well as on the deities to whom they are directed.

यां दिशमभिष्टोष्यन्स्यात्तां दिशमुपधावेत्॥ ११ ॥

Yāṁ diśamabhiṣṭoṣyansyāttāṁ diśamupadhāvet.

Yām diśam abhiṣṭoṣyan syāt, whatever direction a person may face while praying; *tām diśam upadhāvet,* one should worship that direction [and also the deities presiding over that direction].

11. No matter what direction one may face while praying, one should meditate on that direction [along with the presiding deities of that direction].

आत्मानमन्तत उपसृत्य स्तुवीत कामं ध्यायन्नप्रमत्तो-
ऽभ्याशो ह यदस्मै स कामः समृध्येत यत्कामः स्तुवीतेति
यत्कामः स्तुवीतेति॥ १२॥ इति तृतीयः खण्डः॥ ३॥

Ātmānamantata upasṛtya stuvīta kāmaṁ dhyāyanna-pramatto'bhyāśo ha yadasmai sa kāmaḥ samṛdhyeta yatkāmaḥ stuvīteti yatkāmaḥ stuvīteti. Iti tṛtīyaḥ khaṇḍaḥ.

Antataḥ, as one ends one's prayer; *kāmam dhyāyan apramattaḥ,* one should think of whatever one desires, making sure that the pronunciation of words is correct; *ātmānam,* oneself; *upasṛtya,* thinking of [one's name, lineage, and caste]; *stuvīta,* praise; *yat kāmaḥ,* whatever desire one has; *stuvīta,* while praying; *kāmaḥ,* that desire; *abhyāsaḥ,* promptly; *ha,* surely; *asmai,* to the person concerned; *samṛdhyeta,* prosperity goes. [The repetition is for emphasis.] *Iti tṛtīyaḥ khaṇḍaḥ,* here ends the third section.

12. Finally, as a person ends his prayer, he should ask for whatever he desires, making sure, however, that his pronunciation is correct. He should also think of himself [including his name, lineage, and caste]. Then whatever desire he has while praying is promptly and surely fulfilled.

Here the udgātā (the singer) is told how he should pray. He should first repeat the Sāma songs, and then he should pray for whatever he desires. His prayer should be correct in every detail. And while praying, he should mention his own name, his lineage, and his caste. If these conditions are fulfilled, his prayer will be promptly granted. That this will happen is indicated by the repetition of the statement.

Section Four

ओमित्येतदक्षरमुद्गीथमुपासीतोमिति ह्युद्गायति तस्यो-
पव्याख्यानम् ॥ १ ॥

Omityetadakṣaramudgīthamupāsītomiti hyudgāyati tasyopavyākhyānam.

Om iti, this Om [is closest to Brahman]; *etat akṣaram udgītham upāsīta,* recite this syllable as part of your upāsanā [ritual]; *hi om iti udgāyati,* how you recite this Om; *tasya upavyākhyānam,* is being explained.

1. Om is the closest word to Brahman. Recite this Om as if you are worshipping Brahman. [That is, treat this Om as the symbol of Brahman and concentrate on the idea of their oneness.] How you recite this Om is being explained.

This akśara is Brahman, and Om is that Brahman. Akṣara, Brahman, and Om are interchangeable words. As Brahman is *abhaya,* without fear, and *amṛta,* immortal, so Om and akṣara are also without fear and immortal.

देवा वै मृत्योर्बिभ्यतस्त्रयीं विद्यां प्राविशंस्ते छन्दोभिर-
च्छादयन्यदेभिरच्छादयंस्तच्छन्दसां छन्दस्त्वम् ॥ २ ॥

Devā vai mṛtyorbibhyatastrayīṁ vidyāṁ prāviśaṁste chandobhiracchādayanyadebhiracchādayaṁstacchandasāṁ chandastvam.

Devāḥ, the gods and goddesses; *vai mṛtyoḥ bibhyataḥ,* are afraid of death; *trayīm vidyām prāviśan,* they took refuge in the three Vedas [i.e., they decided to perform Vedic rites and rituals in order to escape death]; *te,* they; *chandobhiḥ acchādayan,* covered themselves with the mantras; *yat,* because; *ebhiḥ,* with these [mantras, or chandas]; *acchādayan,* they covered themselves; *tat,* that is why; *chandasām chandastvam,* the mantras have the name *chandas.*

2. The gods and goddesses were afraid of death, so they took refuge in the rites and rituals of the three Vedas. They covered themselves, as it were, with mantras. Because they covered themselves with mantras, the mantras came to be known as *chandas.*

In ancient times the gods and goddesses decided to perform the sacrifices mentioned in the three Vedas to save themselves from death. It was as if they took 'cover' behind the Vedic mantras. It is from this word 'cover' (*acchādan*) that the mantras have come to be known as *chandas.*

तानु तत्र मृत्युर्यथा मत्स्यमुदके परिपश्येदेवं पर्यपश्यदृचि साम्नि यजुषि। ते नु विदित्वोर्ध्वा ऋचः साम्नो यजुषः स्वरमेव प्राविशन्॥ ३॥

Tānu tatra mṛtyuryathā matsyamudake paripaśye-devaṁ paryapaśyadṛci sāmni yajuṣi; Te nu viditvordhvā ṛcaḥ sāmno yajuṣaḥ ṣvarameva prāviśan.

Yathā, just as; *udake,* in shallow water; *matsyam,* a fish [swimming]; *paripaśyet,* a person can see; *evam,* in the same way; *tatra,* in those [Vedic rites and rituals]; *ṛci sāmni yajuṣi,* in the Ṛg, Sāma, and Yajur

Vedas; *tān,* those gods and goddesses; *mṛtyuḥ,* Death; *paryapaśyat,* saw [i.e., they could not escape death through Vedic rituals]; *te,* they [the gods and goddesses]; *nu viditvā,* having realized [that they were still susceptible to death]; *ṛcaḥ sāmnaḥ yajuṣaḥ ūrdhvāḥ,* turned away from Ṛk, Sāma, and Yajur rituals; *svaram eva prāviśan,* took to [reciting] Om.

3. Just as a person can see a fish swimming in shallow water [i.e., the fish is exposed to the risk of being caught], in the same way, Death could see the gods and goddesses when they depended on Vedic rituals [i.e., they were in easy reach of Death]. Realizing this, the gods and goddesses switched over to the recitation of Om.

Fish in shallow water are never safe, for people can easily catch them. Similarly, those who depend on karma (i.e., Vedic rituals) are always liable to being caught by death. When people realize this, they stop performing the rites and rituals and concentrate on reciting Om. They know that Om is a symbol of immortality and fearlessness.

यदा वा ऋचमाप्नोत्योमित्येवातिस्वरत्येवं सामैवं यजुरेष उ स्वरो यदेतदक्षरमेतदमृतमभयं तत्प्रविश्य देवा अमृता अभया अभवन् ॥ ४ ॥

Yadā vā ṛcamāpnotyomityevātisvaratyevaṁ sāmaivaṁ

yajureṣa u svaro yadetadakṣarametadamṛtamabhayaṁ tatpraviśya devā amṛtā abhayā abhavan.

Yadā vai, whenever; *ṛcam āpnoti,* a person recites Ṛk mantras; *om iti eva atisvarati,* that person recites Om with great enthusiasm; *evam sāma evam yajuḥ,* so also the Yajus and Sāma mantras; *eṣaḥ u svaraḥ yat etat akṣaram,* this akṣara [Om] is svara; *etat amṛtam abhayam,* this is immortal and fearless; *tat praviśya,* having taken shelter in it; *devāḥ amṛtāḥ abhayāḥ abhavan,* the gods and goddesses became immortal and fearless.

4. When people recite the Ṛk, they start with Om, reciting it with great enthusiasm. They do the same when they recite the Sāma and Yajus. This Om is akṣara and also svara. It is a symbol of immortality and fearlessness. When the gods and goddesses took refuge in it, they attained immortality and fearlessness.

Akṣara, Om, and svara are the same. When people recite Vedic mantras, they always start with the akṣara Om. By taking refuge in Om, one attains immortality and fearlessness.

स य एतदेवं विद्वानक्षरं प्रणौत्येतदेवाक्षरं स्वरममृतमभयं प्रविशति तत्प्रविश्य यदमृता देवास्तदमृतो भवति॥५॥

इति चतुर्थः खण्डः॥४॥

Sa ya etadevaṁ vidvānakṣaraṁ praṇautyetadevākṣaraṁ svaramamṛtamabhayaṁ praviśati tatpraviśya yadamṛtā devāstadamṛto bhavati. Iti caturthaḥ khaṇḍaḥ.

Saḥ yaḥ, one who; *evam etat akṣaram vidvān praṇauti,* knows this akṣara and respects it as such; *etat eva svaram,* that known as svara; *amṛtam abhayam akṣaram praviśati,* becomes one with the immortal and fearless akṣara [Om]; *tat,* that [akṣara]; *praviśya,* having become one with [akṣara]; *devāḥ yat amṛtāḥ,* by which the gods and goddesses became immortal; *tat amṛtaḥ bhavati,* that person also becomes immortal. *Iti caturthaḥ khaṇḍaḥ,* here ends the fourth section.

5. Even now anyone who knows this Om and worships it thus can attain the fearlessness and immortality of Om, which is akṣara, or svara. By becoming one with Om, a person can attain immortality, just as the gods and goddesses did.

By worshipping svara (Om), the gods and goddesses entered into svara, which means they became one with it. And by becoming one with it, they became fearless and immortal. The same thing may happen to anyone who follows in their footsteps—that is, anyone who worships svara. The transformation is the same as in the case of the gods and goddesses—no more, no less.

Section Five

अथ खलु य उद्गीथः स प्रणवो यः प्रणवः स उद्गीथ इत्यसौ वा आदित्य उद्गीथ एष प्रणव ओमिति ह्येष स्वरन्नेति॥ १॥

Atha khalu ya udgīthaḥ sa praṇavo yaḥ praṇavaḥ sa udgītha ityasau vā āditya udgītha eṣa praṇava omiti hyeṣa svaranneti.

Atha, next; *yaḥ khalu udgīthaḥ,* that which is udgītha; *saḥ praṇavaḥ,* is praṇava [Om]; *yaḥ praṇavaḥ saḥ udgīthaḥ,* that which is praṇava is also udgītha; *asau vai ādityaḥ udgīthaḥ,* that sun is udgītha; *eṣaḥ praṇavaḥ,* it is also praṇava; *hi,* for; *eṣaḥ,* the sun; *om iti svaran eti,* appears with the word Om in its mind.

1. That which is udgītha is also praṇava [Om]. So also, that which is praṇava is udgītha. That sun is udgītha, and it is also praṇava, because it seems to say Om [or, has the word Om in its mind] when it appears.

This is how udgītha is to be worshipped: According to many scholars of the Ṛg Veda, udgītha is the same as praṇava (Om). What is praṇava to them is udgītha according to the Chāndogya.

Similarly, according to many scholars, the sun is udgītha and also praṇava. How can the sun be referred to as *udgītha*? When the sun appears, it looks as if it is saying Om, or it has Om in its thoughts.

According to Śaṅkara, the word *svaran* may also mean 'uttering.'

एतमु एवाहमभ्यगासिषं तस्मान्मम त्वमेकोऽसीति ह कौषीतकिः पुत्रमुवाच रश्मींस्त्वं पर्यावर्तयाद्बहवो वै ते भविष्यन्तीत्यधिदैवतम् ॥ २ ॥

Etamu evāhamabhyagāsiṣaṁ tasmānmama tvameko'sīti ha kauṣītakiḥ putramuvāca raśmīṁstvaṁ paryāvartayādbahavo vai te bhaviṣyantītyadhidaivatam.

Kauṣītakiḥ putram uvāca, the sage Kauṣītaki said to his son; *etam,* this [sun with its rays]; *eva,* as one; *aham abhyagāsiṣam,* I greeted [welcomed]; *tasmāt,* because [of my worshipping it as one]; *tvam mama ekaḥ asi,* you are my only son; *tvam raśmīn paryāvartayāt,* if you worship the sun and its rays separately; *te bahavaḥ vai bhaviṣyanti,* you will have many children; *iti adhidaivatam,* this is the worship of the forces of nature.

2. The sage Kauṣītaki said to his son: 'I worshipped the sun and its rays as one. That is why I had only one son, which is you. If you worship the sun and its rays separately, you will then have many children.' This is the worship of the forces of nature.

अथाध्यात्मं य एवायं मुख्यः प्राणस्तमुद्गीथमुपासीतो-
मिति ह्येष स्वरन्नेति॥ ३ ॥

Athādhyātmaṁ ya evāyaṁ mukhyaḥ prāṇastamud-gīthamupāsītomiti hyeṣa svaranneti.

Atha, now; *adhyātmaṁ,* concerning one's own body; *yaḥ eva ayam mukhyaḥ prāṇaḥ,* that which is the chief prāṇa [which divides itself into five functions: prāṇa, apāna, vyāna, udāna, and samāna]; *tam udgītham upāsīta,* one should worship as udgītha; *hi,* for; *eṣaḥ,* this [prāṇa]; *om iti svaran,* uttering Om; *eti,* activates [all the organs—of speech, vision, etc.].

3. Next, this is how worship concerning the physical body is performed: One should worship the chief prāṇa as udgītha, for it seems to say Om as it makes the organs [of perception and action] function.

As far as the physical body is concerned, the Upaniṣad says to treat the chief prāna as Om. The chief prāṇa is responsible for what the organs of perception (the eyes, ears, nose, etc.) and the organs of action (the hands, feet, speech, etc.) do. It makes them active. Just as some people say Om before they do or say anything, so prāṇa seems to say Om as it makes the organs function. Not that it really says Om, but because the organs cannot act without its support, it is suggested that the chief prāṇa has to give the signal (that is, by saying Om) and then only do the organs start operating.

एतमु एवाहमभ्यगासिषं तस्मान्मम त्वमेकोऽसीति ह कौषीतकिः पुत्रमुवाच प्राणांस्त्वं भूमानमभिगायताद्बहवो वै मे भविष्यन्तीति॥४॥

Etamu evāhamabhyagāsiṣaṁ tasmānmama tvameko-'sīti ha kauṣītakiḥ putramuvāca prāṇāṁstvaṁ bhūmāna-mabhigāyatādbahavo vai me bhaviṣyantīti.

Kauṣītakiḥ ha putram uvāca, Kauṣītaki said to his son; *aham u etam eva abhyagāsiṣam,* I worshipped this [prāṇa] as one; *tasmāt,* that is why; *tvam mama ekaḥ,* you are my only son; *tvam prāṇān bhūmānam abhigāyatāt,* you should worship prāṇa as many [i.e., with manifold qualities and forms]; *me bahavaḥ vai bhaviṣyanti iti,* thinking, 'May my children be many.'

4. The sage Kauṣītaki said to his son: 'I worshipped prāṇa as just one entity, and therefore I had only one son. I suggest that you worship prāṇa as one with manifold qualities and with many forms while thinking, "May my children be many."'

The sun and its rays are not separate, but if a person wants more than one child, he or she will have to worship the sun and its rays as separate entities. The same applies to the worship of the chief prāṇa and its subsidiaries (vyāna, udāna, etc.).

अथ खलु य उद्गीथः स प्रणवो यः प्रणवः
स उद्गीथ इति होतृषदनाद्धैवापि दुरुद्गीतमनुसमाहरती-
त्यनुसमाहरतीति ॥ ५ ॥ इति पञ्चमः खण्डः ॥ ५ ॥

Atha khalu ya udgīthaḥ sa praṇavo yaḥ praṇavaḥ sa udgītha iti hotṛṣadanāddhaivāpi durudgītamanusamā-haratītyanusamāharatīti. Iti pañcamaḥ khaṇḍaḥ.

Atha khalu, for certain; *yaḥ udgīthaḥ saḥ praṇavaḥ,* that which is udgītha is praṇava; *yaḥ praṇava saḥ udgīthaḥ,* that which is praṇava is also udgītha; *hotṛṣadanāt api eva ha durudgītam,* it is not unlikely that the person performing a sacrifice will err in pronunciation; *anusamāharati iti,* that can be rectified [the statement is repeated to emphasize its importance]. *Iti pañcamaḥ khaṇḍaḥ,* here ends the fifth section.

5. For certain, that which is udgītha is praṇava, and that which is praṇava is also udgītha. Should the person performing a sacrifice make mistakes in pronunciation, that can be rectified [when he has the knowledge that udgītha and praṇava are the same].

It has already been stressed that praṇava and udgītha should be regarded as one. Where the consciousness of this sameness prevails, any mistakes made while reciting the mantras may easily be rectified.

The statement is intended to illustrate how it helps to have the knowledge of the sameness of udgītha and praṇava.

Section Six

इयमेवर्गग्निः साम तदेतदेतस्यामृच्यध्यूढं साम तस्मा-
दृच्यध्यूढं साम गीयत इयमेव साग्निरमस्तत्साम ॥ १ ॥

Iyamevargagniḥ sāma tadetadetasyāmṛcyadhyūḍhaṁ sāma tasmādṛcyadhyūḍhaṁ sāma gīyata iyameva sāgniramastatsāma.

Iyam, this [earth]; *eva ṛk,* is like the Ṛg Veda; *agniḥ sāma,* fire is like the Sāma Veda; *tat etat sāma etasyām ṛci adhyūḍham,* the Sāma Veda is based on the Ṛg Veda; *tasmāt,* therefore; *ṛci aḍhyūḍham sāma gīyate,* the Sāma Veda is sung based on the Ṛg Veda; *iyam eva sā,* this [earth] is the *sā* [of Sāma]; *agniḥ amaḥ,* fire is *ama* [of Sāma]; *tat sāma,* that [if joined together] is Sāma [i.e., sā + ama].

1. This earth is like the Ṛg Veda, and fire is like the Sāma Veda. The Sāma is based on the Ṛg Veda, and this is why the Sāma is sung based on the Ṛg Veda. The earth is *sā* and fire is *ama.* This *sā* and *ama* together make *Sāma.*

The Upaniṣad says to treat the earth as the Ṛg Veda and fire as the Sāma Veda. But how are they so related? The Sāma is based on the Ṛg Veda, and fire is based on the earth. Because of this relationship between them, they are thought of as identical.

अन्तरिक्षमेवर्ग्वायुः साम तदेतदेतस्यामृच्यध्यूढं साम तस्मादृच्यध्यूढं साम गीयतेऽन्तरिक्षमेव सा वायुरमस्तत्साम ॥ २ ॥

Antarikṣamevargvāyuḥ sāma tadetadetasyāmṛcyadhyūḍhaṁ sāma tasmādṛcyadhyūḍhaṁ sāma gīyate'ntarikṣameva sā vāyuramastatsāma.

Antarikṣam, the space between heaven and earth; *eva ṛk,* is nothing but the Ṛk; *vāyuḥ sāma,* air is the Sāma; *tat etat sāma,* this Sāma [called air]; *etasyām ṛci adhyūḍham,* is based on the Ṛk [called the antarikṣa]; *tasmāt,* this is why; *ṛci adhyūḍham sāma gīyate,* the Sāma is sung as based on the Ṛk; *antarikṣam eva sā,* the space between heaven and earth is sā; *vāyuḥ amaḥ,* air is ama; *tat sāma,* that [if joined together] is Sāma.

2. The space between heaven and earth is the Ṛk, and air is the Sāma. This Sāma [called air] is based on the Ṛk [called the space between heaven and earth]. This is why the Sāma is sung based on the Ṛk. The space between heaven and earth is *sā,* and earth is *ama.* Together they are Sāma.

द्यौरेवर्गादित्यः साम तदेतदेतस्यामृच्यध्यूढं साम तस्मादृच्यध्यूढं साम गीयते द्यौरेव सादित्योऽमस्तत्साम ॥ ३ ॥

Dyaurevargādityaḥ sāma tadetadetasyāmṛcyadhyūḍhaṁ sāma tasmādṛcyadhyūḍhaṁ sāma gīyate dyaureva sādityo'mastatsāma.

Dyauḥ, the heaven; *eva ṛk,* is Ṛk; *ādityaḥ sāma,* the sun is Sāma; *tat etat sāma,* that Sāma [which is known as the sun]; *etasyām ṛci adhyūḍham,* is based on the Ṛk [heaven]; *tasmāt,* that is why; *ṛci adhyūḍham sāma* [*sāmagaiḥ*] *gīyate,* the Sāma scholars sing the Sāma based on the Ṛk; *dyauḥ eva sā,* heaven is nothing but sā; *ādityaḥ amaḥ,* the sun is ama; *tat sāma,* that [if joined together] is Sāma.

3. Heaven is the Ṛk, and the sun is the Sāma. This Sāma [called the sun] is based on the Ṛk [called heaven]. This is why Sāma scholars sing songs based on the Ṛk. Heaven is *sā,* and the sun is *ama.* Together they are Sāma.

नक्षत्राण्येवर्क्चन्द्रमाः साम तदेतदेतस्यामृच्यध्यूढं साम तस्मादृच्यध्यूढं साम गीयते नक्षत्राण्येव सा चन्द्रमा अम तत्साम॥ ४॥

Nakṣatrāṇyevarkcandramāḥ sāma tadetadetasyāmṛcyadhyūḍhaṁ sāma tasmādṛcyadhyūḍhaṁ sāma gīyate nakṣatrāṇyeva sā candramā ama tatsāma.

Nakṣatrāṇi eva ṛk, the stars together constitute the Ṛk; *candramāḥ sāma,* the moon is the Sāma; *tat etat sāma,* that Sāma; *etasyām ṛci adhyūḍham,* is based on the Ṛk; *tasmāt,* that is why; *ṛci adhyūḍham sāma gīyate,* the Sāma scholars sing the Sāma based on the Ṛk; *nakṣatrāṇi eva sā,* the stars are the sā; *candramāḥ amaḥ,* the moon is the ama; *tat sāma,* that [if joined together] is Sāma.

4. The stars are the Ṛk, and the moon is the Sāma. This Sāma [called the moon] is based on the Ṛk [called the stars]. This is why Sāma scholars sing songs based on the Ṛk. The stars are the *sā,* and the moon is *ama.* Together they are Sāma.

The moon is the lord of the stars. This is why it is given the status of the Sāma Veda.

अथ यदेतदादित्यस्य शुक्लं भाः सैवर्गथ यन्नीलं परः कृष्णं तत्साम तदेतदेतस्यामृच्यध्यूढं साम तस्मा-दृच्यध्यूढं साम गीयते॥ ५॥

Atha yadetadādityasya śuklaṁ bhāḥ saivargatha yannīlaṁ paraḥ kṛṣṇaṁ tatsāma tadetadetasyāmṛcya-dhyūḍhaṁ sāma tasmādṛcyadhyūḍhaṁ sāma gīyate.

Atha, next; *yat etat,* that which is this; *ādityasya śuklam,* whiteness of the sun; *bhāḥ,* the glow; *sā eva ṛk,* that is the Ṛk; *atha,* next; *yat nīlam,* that which is blue; *paraḥ,* deep; *kṛṣṇam,* black; *tat sāma,* that is the Sāma; *tat etat sāma,* this Sāma; *etasyām ṛci adhyūḍham,* is based on the Ṛk; *tasmāt,* that is why; *ṛci adhyūḍham sāma gīyate,* the Sāma is sung based on the Ṛk.

5. The white glow of the sun is the Ṛk, and its deep blue glow is the Sāma. The black glow called the Sāma is based on the white glow called the Ṛk. That is why the Sāma is sung based on the Ṛk.

The Upaniṣad gives another way of worshipping the udgītha: The white glow of the sun is compared to the Ṛk. But the sun also has a deep blue or black glow, which the Upaniṣad compares to the Sāma. This deep blue glow is not seen by many people. Only a few persons who have studied the scriptures and have acquired an enlightened mind can see it.

अथ यदेवैतदादित्यस्य शुक्लं भाः सैव साथ यन्नीलं परः कृष्णं तदम तत्सामाथ य एषोऽन्तरादित्ये हिरण्मयः पुरुषो दृश्यते हिरण्यश्मश्रुर्हिरण्यकेश आप्रणखात्सर्व एव सुवर्णः ॥ ६ ॥

Atha yadevaitadādityasya śuklaṁ bhāḥ saiva sātha yannīlaṁ paraḥ kṛṣṇaṁ tadama tatsāmātha ya eṣo-'ntaraditye hiraṇmayaḥ puruṣo dṛśyate hiraṇyaśmaśrur-hiraṇyakeśa āpraṇakhātsarva eva suvarṇaḥ.

Atha, then; *yat eva etat ādityasya śuklam bhāḥ,* that which is this white glow of the sun; *sā eva sā,* that is the 'sā' [of Sāma]; *atha yat nīlam paraḥ kṛṣṇam,* and that which is the deep black glow; *tat amaḥ,* that is 'ama'; *tat sāma,* [when they are put together] that is Sāma; *atha antarāditye,* again inside the orb of the sun; *yaḥ eṣaḥ hiraṇmayaḥ,* there is a bright figure; *hiraṇyaśmaśruḥ,* bright gold beard; *hiraṇyakeśaḥ puruṣaḥ dṛśyate,* the person with bright gold hair seen [by the yogīs]; *āpraṇakhāt sarva eva suvarṇaḥ,* bright gold all over the body, including even his nails.

6. Then, [worship of the effulgent being in the sun]: The white glow of the sun is *sā,* and the dark bluish-black glow is *ama.* These two together make up the word *Sāma.* There is a deity within the orb of the sun, who is seen by yogīs. His whole body glitters like gold, even to his toe-nails. He has a bright golden beard and bright golden hair.

The sun is partly white and partly dark. These colours together make up 'Sāma.'

The Upaniṣad does not mean to say that the sun is made of gold, and neither is the person in the orb of the sun. This is not to be taken literally. What is meant here is that the person in the sun is brilliant—brilliant in terms of moral and spiritual qualities. The word *gold* refers to his character and not to the colour of his skin.

The word *puruṣa* means 'one who covers the whole

world.' A puruṣa is a person who has full control of himself, who has withdrawn himself totally from the world and has gone through the strictest austerities.

तस्य यथा कप्यासं पुण्डरीकमेवमक्षिणी तस्योदिति नाम स एष सर्वेभ्यः पाप्मभ्य उदित उदेति ह वै सर्वेभ्यः पाप्मभ्यो य एवं वेद॥७॥

Tasya yathā kapyāsaṁ puṇḍarīkamevamakṣiṇī tasyoditi nāma sa eṣa sarvebhyaḥ pāpmabhya udita udeti ha vai sarvebhyaḥ pāpmabhyo ya evaṁ veda.

Tasya, his; *yathā,* like; *kapyāsam* [*kapi,* which means 'he who drinks water' (i.e, the sun) + *āsa,* which means blossomed], blossomed by the sun; *puṇḍarīkam evam,* like the lotus; *akṣiṇī,* the eyes; *tasya ut iti nāma,* his name is 'ut'; *saḥ eṣaḥ sarvebhyaḥ pāpmabhyaḥ uditaḥ,* he is above all weakness; *udeti,* he rises; *ha vai sarvebhyaḥ pāpmabhyaḥ,* above all weakness; *yaḥ,* who; *evam veda,* knows thus.

7. His eyes are like lotuses blossomed by the sun. He is called *ut* because he is above all weakness. He who knows this truth is also above all weakness.

It has been said that fire rests on the earth, space rests on air, the moon on the stars, and the dark glow of the sun on its white glow. But the Being in the orbit of the sun does not rest on anything

He is above all that is evil, above everything. To signify this he is given the name *ut* (that which is above everything). This 'ut' suggests supremacy. It is the kind of supremacy which Vedānta attributes to Brahman. This 'ut' and Brahman are the same.

Here, Rāmānuja's interpretation has been followed for the word *kapyāsam.* Śaṅkara gives another interpretation.

तस्यर्क्च साम च गेष्णौ तस्मादुद्गीथस्तस्मात्त्वे-
वोद्गातैतस्य हि गाता स एष ये चामुष्मात्पराञ्चो
लोकास्तेषां चेष्टे देवकामानां चेत्यधिदैवतम् ॥ ८ ॥ इति
षष्ठः खण्डः ॥ ६ ॥

Tasyarkca sāma ca geṣṇau tasmādudgīthastasmāttve-vodgātaitasya hi gātā sa eṣa ye cāmuṣmātparāñco lokāsteṣāṁ ceṣṭe devakāmānāṁ cetyadhidaivatam. Iti ṣaṣṭhaḥ khaṇḍaḥ.

Tasya, his; *ṛk ca sāma ca geṣṇau,* the Ṛk and the Sāma are two singers [who sing his praise]; *tasmāt,* this is why; *udgīthaḥ,* he is [called] udgītha [the great God in whose praise songs are sung]; *tasmāt,* this is why; *etasya hi gātā,* the singers of it; *tu eva udgātā,* are called udgātā, the musicians; *saḥ eṣaḥ,* he; *ye ca,* who; *amuṣmāt parāñcaḥ,* high above that [solar region]; *teṣām lokāḥ,* those worlds; *ca iṣṭe,* governs [decides]; *devakāmānām ca,* the desires of the gods and goddesses; *iti adhidaivatam,* this is so from the standpoint of the gods and goddesses. *Iti ṣaṣṭhaḥ khaṇḍaḥ,* here ends the sixth section.

8. The Ṛk and the Sāma are his two singers who sing in praise of this god. This is why he is called *udgītha,* and this is why a singer of the udgītha is called an *udgātā.* There are worlds above the solar region, but the god in the solar region rules over them [and also supports them]. He also decides the wishes of the gods and goddesses. This is from the standpoint of the gods and goddesses.

The word *ut* suggests supremacy. It is applied to that being who is the overlord of everything and also the source of everything—the earth, the air, and fire; the Ṛk and Sāma; the gods and goddesses; and even the worlds above the sun. This 'ut' rules everything and is therefore identical with Brahman.

Section Seven

अथाध्यात्मं वागेवर्क्प्राणः साम तदेतदेतस्यामृच्यध्यूढं साम तस्मादृच्यध्यूढं साम गीयते। वागेव सा प्राणोऽमस्तत्साम॥ १॥

Athādhyātmaṁ vāgevarkprāṇaḥ sāma tadetadetasyāmṛcyadhyūḍhaṁ sāma tasmādṛcyadhyūḍhaṁ sāma gīyate; Vāgeva sā prāṇo'mastatsāma.

Atha adhyātmam, now what relates to the body; *vāk eva ṛk,* speech is Ṛk; *prāṇaḥ sāma,* prāṇa is Sāma; *tat etat sāma,* this Sāma [called prāṇa]; *etasyām ṛci adhyūḍham,* is based on Ṛk [speech]; *tasmāt,* this is why; *ṛci adhyūḍham sāma gīyate,* the Sāma is sung as based on the Ṛk; *vāk eva sā,* speech is sā; *prāṇaḥ amaḥ,* prāṇa is ama; *tat sāma,* that [if joined together] is Sāma.

1. Now an explanation with reference to the body: Speech is Ṛk, and prāṇa is Sāma. This Sāma [called prāṇa] is based on the Ṛk [called speech]. This is why Sāma scholars sing songs based on the Ṛk. Speech is *sā,* and prāṇa is *ama.* Together they are Sāma.

The word *prāṇa* means both the vital breath and the organ by which we smell. Physically, the organ of speech is below the organ of smell. Similarly, Sāma is known to be based on the Rk. In view of their respective positions, Ṛk is equated with speech, and Sāma is equated with prāṇa.

चक्षुरेवर्गात्मा साम तदेतदेतस्यामृच्यध्यूढं साम तस्मा-
दृच्यध्यूढं साम गीयते। चक्षुरेव सात्मामस्तत्साम॥ २॥

Cakṣurevargātmā sāma tadetadetasyāmṛcyadhyūḍhaṁ sāma tasmādṛcyadhyūḍhaṁ sāma gīyate; Cakṣureva sātmāmastatsāma.

Cakṣuḥ eva ṛk, the eyes are like the Ṛg Veda; *ātmā sāma,* the self [as seen in the eyes] is the Sāma; *tat etat sāma,* this Sāma [called the ātmā]; *etasyām ṛci adhyūḍham,* is based on Ṛk [i.e., on the eyes]; *tasmāt,* this is why; *ṛci adhyūḍham sāma gīyate,* the Sāma is sung as based on the Ṛk; *cakṣuḥ eva sā,* the eyes are sā; *ātmā amaḥ,* the self [the form reflected in the eyes] is ama; *tat sāma,* that [if joined together] is Sāma.

2. The eyes are like the Ṛg Veda, and the self [i.e., the form seen in the eyes] is like the Sāma, which is based on the Ṛk. This is why the Sāma is sung based on the Ṛk. The eyes are the *sā,* and the self [the form in the eyes] is the *ama.* The two together are Sāma.

The ātmā, or self, here means the form which is reflected in the eyes. This is why the Upaniṣad says the eyes are the Ṛg Veda, and the self is the Sāma Veda.

श्रोत्रमेवर्ङ्मनः साम तदेतदेतस्यामृच्यध्यूढं साम तस्मादृच्यध्यूढं साम गीयते। श्रोत्रमेव सा मनोऽमस्तत्साम॥ ३॥

Śrotramevarṁmanaḥ sāma tadetadetasyāmṛcyadhyūḍhaṁ sāma tasmādṛcyadhyūḍhaṁ sāma gīyate; Śrotrameva sā mano'mastatsāma.

Śrotram eva ṛk, the organ of hearing is the Ṛg Veda; *manaḥ sāma,* the mind is the Sāma; *tat etat sāma,* this Sāma [called the mind]; *etasyām ṛci adhyūḍham,* is based on the Ṛk [the organ of hearing]; *tasmāt,* this is why; *ṛci adhyūḍham sāma gīyate,* the Sāma is sung as based on the Ṛk; *śrotram eva sā,* the organ of hearing is sā; *manaḥ amaḥ,* the mind is ama; *tat sāma,* that [if joined together] is Sāma.

3. The organ of hearing is the Ṛk, and the mind is Sāma. This Sāma [called the mind] is based on the Ṛk [called the organ of hearing]. This is why Sāma scholars sing songs based on the Ṛk. The organ of hearing is *sā,* and the mind is *ama.* Together they are Sāma.

The mind is said to be the Sāma because it controls the organ of hearing.

अथ यदेतदक्ष्णः शुक्लं भाः सैवर्गथ यन्नीलं परः कृष्णं तत्साम तदेतदेतस्यामृच्यध्यूढं साम तस्माद्दच्यध्यूढं साम गीयते। अथ यदेवैतदक्ष्णः शुक्लं भाः सैव साथ यन्नीलं परः कृष्णं तदमस्तत्साम॥ ४॥

Atha yadetadakṣṇaḥ śuklaṁ bhāḥ saivargatha yannīlaṁ paraḥ kṛṣṇaṁ tatsāma tadetadetasyāmṛcyadhyūḍhaṁ sāma tasmādṛcyadhyūḍhaṁ sāma gīyate; Atha yadevaitadakṣṇaḥ śuklaṁ bhāḥ saiva sātha yannīlaṁ paraḥ kṛṣṇaṁ tadamastatsāma.

Atha, then; *akṣṇaḥ yat etat śuklam bhāḥ,* that which is the white glow in the eyes; *saḥ eva ṛk,* that is the Ṛg Veda; *atha yat nīlam paraḥ kṛṣṇam,* then that which is blue and very dark; *tat sāma,* that is the Sāma; *tat etat sāma,* this Sāma; *etasyām ṛci adhyūḍham,* is based on the Ṛk; *tasmāt,* this is why; *ṛci adhyūḍham sāma gīyate,* the Sāma is sung as based on the Ṛk; *atha yat eva etat akṣṇaḥ śuklam bhāḥ,* then this white glow in the eye; *sā eva sā,* that is sā; *atha yat nīlam paraḥ kṛṣṇam,* and that which is blue and very dark; *tat amaḥ,* that is ama; *tat sāma,* that [if joined together] is Sāma.

4. Further, there is a white glow in the eyes, and this is compared with the Ṛg Veda. Then there is a similar glow which is a deep, dark blue. This is compared to the Sāma Veda. This dark glow is based on the white glow. This is why the Sāma is said to be based on the Ṛk. *Sā* of *Sāma* stands for the white glow in the eye, and *ama* stands for the deep blue glow. These two together are Sāma.

The sun is the support of the power of vision, because without the sun we cannot see. Similarly, the deep blue glow, which is identified with the Sāma, is supported by the white glow, which is the Ṛk.

अथ य एषोऽन्तरक्षिणि पुरुषो दृश्यते सैवर्क्तत्साम तदुक्थं तद्यजुस्तद्ब्रह्म तस्यैतस्य तदेव रूपं यदमुष्य रूपं यावमुष्य गेष्णौ तौ गेष्णौ यन्नाम तन्नाम॥ ५॥

Atha ya eṣo'ntarakṣiṇi puruṣo dṛśyate saivarktatsāma tadukthaṁ tadyajustadbrahma tasyaitasya tadeva rūpaṁ yadamuṣya rūpaṁ yāvamuṣya geṣṇau tau geṣṇau yannāma tannāma.

Atha, now; *yaḥ eṣaḥ puruṣaḥ,* that person who; *antarakṣiṇi,* inside the eye; *dṛśyate,* is seen; *saḥ,* that person; *eva ṛk,* is the Ṛk; *tat sāma,* he is the Sāma; *tat uktham,* he is the uktha [a part of the Sāma]; *tat yajuḥ,* he is the Yajus [i.e., mantras ending with svāhā, svadhā, and vaṣaṭ]; *tat brahma,* he is Brahman [i.e., the three Vedas]; *tasya etasya,* of this person [seen in the eye]; *tat eva rūpam,* that same form; *yat amuṣya rūpam,* of the form of that person [in the sun, having golden hair, etc.]; *amuṣya,* of that one [in the sun]; *yau geṣṇau,* two singers [i.e., the Ṛk and the Sāma sing in his praise]; *tau geṣṇau,* the same two singers [sing in praise of that one]; *yat nāma tat nāma,* the name of this is the same as the name of that.

5. The person seen in the eye is the Ṛk, the Sāma, the uktha [a part of the Sāma], and the Yajus. He is also the three Vedas. The person who is in the sun and the person who is in the eye are the same. The same two singers [i.e., the Ṛk and the Sāma] sing in praise of each of them, and they have the same names.

The Lord who rules the solar region is seen also in the eye. That Lord stands for the Ṛk. He controls the organ of speech and other organs of the body, as well as the earth and other planets. They are all parts of him. The three Vedas—Ṛk, Sāma, and Yajus—are often referred to as Brahman, so Brahman and the Vedas are the same. Brahman includes everything. It is in the sun, in the human body, and in the planets. It is here referred to as the Lord called *Hiraṇmaya,* the Lord with a golden body, because he is luminous. The words *uk* and *uktha,* and also *svāhā, svadhā,* and *vaṣat,* are all used in different Vedas in praise of the same Lord who is in the sun (*ādhidaivika*) as well as in the eye (*ādhyātmika*).

स एष ये चैतस्मादर्वाञ्चो लोकास्तेषां चेष्टे मनुष्यकामानां चेति तद्य इमे वीणायां गायन्त्येतं ते गायन्ति तस्मात्ते धनसनयः ॥ ६ ॥

Sa eṣa ye caitasmādarvāñco lokāsteṣāṁ ceṣṭe manuṣyakāmānāṁ ceti tadya ime vīṇāyāṁ gāyantyetaṁ te gāyanti tasmātte dhanasanayaḥ.

Saḥ eṣaḥ, the person [in the eye]; *etasmāt arvāñcaḥ ye ca lokāḥ,* those worlds below him; *teṣām ca iṣṭe,* rules over them; *manuṣya-kāmānām ca,* as well as all human desires; *iti,* this marks the limit; *tat,* therefore; *ye ime,* those people who; *vīṇāyām gāyanti,* sing with the vīṇā; *te etam gāyanti,* they in fact sing in his honour; *tasmāt,* therefore; *te,* they [the musicians]; *dhanasanayaḥ,* become wealthy.

6. The person in the eye rules the world below him and also rules the desires of the human mind. Those who sing accompanied by the vīṇā, are, in fact, singing in his honour. This is why such musicians become wealthy.

That person in the eye is the Lord of the world below and also of the minds of human beings. When people sing accompanied by the vīṇā, that music is dedicated to him. And because they sing in honour of him, they acquire much wealth.

अथ य एतदेवं विद्वान्साम गायत्युभौ स गायति सोऽमुनैव स एष ये चामुष्मात्पराञ्चो लोकास्तांश्चाप्नोति देवकामांश्च ॥ ७ ॥

Atha ya etadevaṁ vidvānsāma gāyatyubhau sa gāyati so'munaiva sa eṣa ye cāmuṣmātparāñco lokāstāṁścāp-noti devakāmāṁśca.

Atha yaḥ, now he who; *etat evam vidvān,* knows this in this way; *sāma gāyati,* sings the Sāma; *saḥ,* he [the musician]; *ubhau,* to both [to Āditya, the sun, and to the person in the eye]; *gāyati,* sings; *saḥ,* he [the musician]; *amunā eva,* as that [Āditya]; *ye ca amuṣmāt,* from that [Āditya]; *parāñcaḥ,* above; *lokāḥ,* the planes; *tām devakāmān,* the things the gods and goddesses wish for; *ca,* also; *saḥ eṣaḥ,* that musician; *āpnoti,* attains [i.e., he finds a place in the solar orb, and he becomes divine].

7. [This is what a worshipper achieves:] He who knows the Truth mentioned above [i.e., the Truth about Āditya, the sun], sings the Sāma in honour of both Āditya and the person in the eye. He then becomes one with Āditya. Not only that, he also attains mastery of the planes above Āditya and attains everything the gods and goddesses wish for. [In other words, such a person becomes divine.]

When a person knows the real identity of the deity to whom he is singing the Sāma—that is, when he knows he is singing the Sāma in praise of both Āditya, the sun, and the deity in the eye—what does he gain? He becomes one with Āditya and becomes the master of the worlds above Āditya. He is also entitled to the things that the gods and goddesses desire. He, in fact, becomes divine.

अथानेनैव ये चैतस्मादर्वाञ्चो लोकास्तांश्चाप्नोति मनुष्यकामांश्च तस्मादु हैवंविदुद्गाता ब्रूयात् ॥ ८ ॥

Athānenaiva ye caitasmādarvāñco lokāstāṁścāpnoti manuṣyakāmāṁśca tasmādu haivaṁvidudgātā brūyāt.

Atha, now; *anena eva,* by this [i.e., by the grace of the Lord in the eye]; *ye ca etasmāt arvāñcaḥ lokāḥ,* those planes which are below [him—i.e., the person in the eye]; *tām ca,* those [planes] also; *āpnoti manuṣyakāmān ca,* he also attains things desired by human beings; *tasmāt,* this is why; *u ha udgātā evamvit,* the singer who knows this; *brūyāt,* will say.

8. Now, [the same worshipper] also attains, by the grace of the Lord in the eye, all the worlds below that Lord. Again, he attains all that human beings may desire. This is why the singer will ask:

कं ते काममागायानीत्येष ह्येव कामागानस्येष्टे य एवं विद्वान्साम गायति साम गायति॥ ९ ॥ इति सप्तमः खण्डः ॥ ७ ॥

Kaṁ te kāmamāgāyānītyeṣa hyeva kāmāgānasyeṣṭe ya evaṁ vidvānsāma gāyati sāma gāyati. Iti saptamaḥ khaṇḍaḥ.

Kam, what; *te,* for you; *kāmam,* desire; *āgāyāni iti,* shall I sing for; *eṣaḥ hi eva,* he is the person who; *kāmāgānasya iṣṭe,* influences the fulfilment of the desires as expressed through songs; *yaḥ,* the musician [udgātā]; *evam,* this; *vidvān,* having known; *sāma gāyati sāma gāyati,* he sings the Sāma, he sings the Sāma. *Iti saptamaḥ khaṇḍaḥ,* here ends the seventh section.

9. [A learned udgātā, who sings the Sāma, will ask the person for whose benefit he is singing:] 'What shall I ask for on your behalf through my songs?' He says this [because he knows the Lord in the

eye presides over the Sāma and is capable of granting whatever the person wants] and he sings the Sāma, he sings the Sāma.

The Lord in the eye controls everything—the earth and other worlds, those who live in them, and also the desires of those people. This is the purport of the verse.

Section Eight

त्रयो होद्‌गीथे कुशला बभूवुः शिलकः शालावत्य-
श्चैकितायनो दाल्भ्यः प्रवाहणो जैवलिरिति ते होचुरुद्‌गीथे
वै कुशलाः स्मो हन्तोद्‌गीथे कथां वदाम इति॥ १॥

Trayo hodgīthe kuśalā babhūvuḥ śilakaḥ śālāvatya-ścaikitāyano dālbhyaḥ pravāhaṇo jaivaliriti te hocurud-gīthe vai kuśalāḥ smo hantodgīthe kathāṁ vadāma iti.

Trayaḥ ha udgīthe kuśalāḥ babhūvuḥ, in early days there were three sages skilled in the udgītha; *śilakaḥ śālāvatyaḥ,* Śilaka, the son of Śalāvat; *caikitāyanaḥ dālbhyaḥ,* Caikitāyana, the son of Cikitāyana, of the Dalbha clan; *pravāhaṇaḥ jaivaliḥ,* Pravāhaṇa, the son of Jīvala; *iti te ha ūcuḥ,* they declared; *udgīthe vai kuśalāḥ smaḥ,* we have mastered the art of the udgītha; *hanta udgīthe kathām vadāmaḥ iti,* if you so wish we can discuss the udgītha.

1. In ancient times, these three—Śilaka, the son of Śalāvat, Caikitāyana, the son of Cikitāyana of the Dalbha clan, and Pravāhaṇa, the son of Jīvala—were skilled in the art of the udgītha. They said: 'We have mastered the art of the udgītha. If you so wish, we can discuss the udgītha.'

Śilaka, Caikitāyana Dālbhyaḥ, and Pravāhaṇa—these three scholars had studied the udgītha very well, and in an assembly of scholars, they offered to discuss the subject, if the others so desired. It was not that they were trying to show off their knowledge. They just wanted the others to know that they were prepared to speak on this subject if the other scholars present so wished.

तथेति ह समुपविविशुः स ह प्रवाहणो जैवलिरुवाच भगवन्तावग्रे वदतां ब्राह्मणयोर्वदतोर्वाचं श्रोष्यामीति ॥ २ ॥

Tatheti ha samupavivisuḥ sa ha pravāhaṇo jaivaliru-vāca bhagavantāvagre vadatāṁ brāhmaṇayorvadator-vācaṁ śroṣyāmīti.

Tathā iti, saying, 'Let it be so'; *samupaviviśuḥ,* they sat down; *saḥ pravāhaṇaḥ jaivaliḥ ha uvāca,* Pravāhaṇa, the son of Jīvala, said; *bhagavantau agre vadatām,* you two respected ones may kindly start the discussion; *vadatoḥ brāhmaṇayoḥ vācam śroṣyāmi iti,* I will listen to the debate of you two brāhmins.

2. They said, 'Let it be so,' and then sat down. Pravāhaṇa, the son of Jīvala, said: 'You two may please begin the debate. I would like to listen to the debate between you two brāhmins.'

The scholars agreed to the debate, and sat down. Lest this be construed as impertinence, Prince Pravāhaṇa said to the other two that he wanted to hear the two brāhmins debating. The fact that Pravāhaṇa addressed them as brāhmins, shows that he regarded himself as inferior, being a kṣatriya.

स ह शिलकः शालावत्यश्चैकितायनं दाल्भ्यमुवाच
हन्त त्वा पृच्छानीति पृच्छेति होवाच॥ ३॥

Sa ha śilakaḥ śālāvatyaścaikitāyanaṁ dālbhyamuvāca hanta tvā pṛcchānīti pṛccheti hovāca.

Saḥ śilakaḥ śālāvatyaḥ ha caikitāyanam dālbhyam uvāca, Śilaka, the son of Śalāvat, said to Caikitāyana Dālbhya; *hanta tvā pṛcchāni iti,* if you permit, I would like to ask you this question; *pṛccha iti ha uvāca,* yes, ask, [replied Dālbhya].

3. Śalāvat's son Śilaka said to the sage Caikitāyana Dālbhya, 'If you permit, I would like to ask you a question.' Dālbhya replied, 'Yes, ask.'

का साम्नो गतिरिति स्वर इति होवाच स्वरस्य का गतिरिति प्राण इति होवाच प्राणस्य का गतिरित्यन्नमिति होवाचान्नस्य का गतिरित्याप इति होवाच॥ ४॥

Kā sāmno gatiriti svara iti hovāca svarasya kā gatiriti prāṇa iti hovāca prāṇasya kā gatirityannamiti hovācānnasya kā gatirityāpa iti hovāca.

Sāmnaḥ kā gatiḥ iti, [Śilaka asked,] what is it that supports Sāma [i.e., the udgītha of the Sāma]; *svaraḥ iti ha uvāca,* [Dālbhya] replied, it is the voice; *svarasya kā gatiḥ iti,* what is the support of the voice; *prāṇaḥ iti ha uvāca,* [Dālbhya] said, prāṇa [the vital breath]; *prāṇasya kā gatiḥ iti,* what is the support of prāṇa [asked Śilaka]; *annam iti ha uvāca,* [Dālbhya] replied, it is food; *annasya kā gatiḥ iti,* what is the support of food; *āpaḥ iti ha uvāca,* [Dālbhya] replied, water.

4. Śilaka asked, 'What is the support of Sāma?' 'It is the voice,' replied Dālbhya. 'What is the support of the voice?' 'The vital breath,' answered Dālbhya. 'What is the support of the vital breath?' asked Śilaka. Dālbhya replied, 'Food.' Then Śilaka asked, 'What is the support of food?' Dālbhya said, 'Water.'

Sāma here means the udgītha, the chanting. Dālbhya was asked what supported the chanting, and he replied, 'The voice.' Just as a pot is supported by the material of which it is made, which is earth, similarly, the chanting is supported by the voice. But what supports the voice? The vital breath. And the vital breath is supported by food. Similarly, food is supported by water, because it is from water that food grows.

अपां का गतिरित्यसौ लोक इति होवाचामुष्य लोकस्य का गतिरिति न स्वर्गं लोकमतिनयेदिति होवाच स्वर्गं वयं लोकं सामाभिसंस्थापयामः स्वर्गसंस्तावं हि सामेति ॥ ५ ॥

Apāṁ kā gatirityasau loka iti hovācāmuṣya lokasya kā gatiriti na svargaṁ lokamatinayediti hovāca svargaṁ vayaṁ lokaṁ sāmābhisaṁsthāpayāmaḥ svargasaṁstāvaṁ hi sāmeti.

Apām kā gatiḥ iti, what is the support of water; *asau lokaḥ,* that world [i.e., heaven]; *iti ha uvāca,* said [Dālbhya]; *amuṣya lokasya kā gatiḥ iti,* what is the support of that heaven; *svargam lokam na atinayet iti ha uvāca,* one should not go beyond that heaven, replied [Dālbhya]; *svargam lokam,* in that heavenly world; *vayam sāma abhisaṁsthāpayāmaḥ,* we install Sāma; *svargasaṁstāvam hi sāma iti,* this Sāma is worshipped as heaven.

5. [Śilaka:] 'What is the support of water?' [Dālbhya:] 'That world, heaven.' [Śilaka:] 'What is the support of that world?' [Dālbhya:] 'Don't go beyond that heaven. We know Sāma is in heaven, and this is why Sāma is respected as heaven.'

The next question Śilaka asked was about the support of water. To this Dālbhya replied, 'That world—that is, heaven.' Rain is said to come from heaven, so that is why heaven is called the support. But what supports heaven? When Śilaka put this question, Dalbhya replied that the question was irrelevant. There is nothing beyond heaven. Heaven is the ultimate. It is the real resort of Sāma. And this is why we say that Sāma is in heaven and why the scriptures show the same respect to heaven as to Sāma.

तं ह शिलकः शालावत्यश्चैकितायनं दाल्भ्यमुवाचा-
प्रतिष्ठितं वै किल ते दाल्भ्य साम यस्त्वेतर्हि ब्रूयान्मूर्धा
ते विपतिष्यतीति मूर्धा ते विपतेदिति॥ ६॥

Taṁ ha śilakaḥ śālāvatyaścaikitāyanaṁ dālbhyamuvācāpratiṣṭhitaṁ vai kila te dālbhya sāma yastvetarhi brūyānmūrdhā te vipatiṣyatīti mūrdhā te vipateditī.

Tam ha śilakaḥ śālāvatyaḥ caikitāyanam dālbhyam uvāca, Śilaka Śālāvatya said to Caikitāyana Dālbhya; *vai kila te dālbhya sāma,* your Sāma is, O Dālbhya; *apratiṣṭhitam,* without a base; *yaḥ tu etarhi brūyāt,* if anyone says now; *te mūrdhā vipatiṣyati iti,* your head will fall [if your statement about Sāma is found to be wrong]; *te mūrdhā vipatet iti,* your head will surely fall.

6. Śilaka Śālāvatya said to Caikitāyana Dālbhya: 'O Dālbhya, your Sāma is then without a base. If someone

knowledgeable about Sāma would now say [that your statement is wrong, and if he curses you saying,] "Your head will fall [if what you say turns out to be wrong]," your head will really fall.'

Śilaka said to Dālbhya that Sāma cannot have heaven as its support. He then quotes scriptures that what he says is true. He also adds that Dālbhya might be careful not to give the impression that he has any doubt about this. If he does, he will then risk being cursed by people who know the Sāma very well. They may curse him saying that his head will fall.

Whether Dālbhya's head will fall or not is a different matter. If you commit a mistake, you surely have to pay for it. The measure of your punishment, however, is decided by many factors.

हन्ताहमेतद्भगवतो वेदानीति विद्धीति होवाचामुष्य लोकस्य का गतिरित्ययं लोक इति होवाचास्य लोकस्य का गतिरिति न प्रतिष्ठां लोकमतिनयेदिति होवाच प्रतिष्ठां वयं लोकंसामाभिसंस्थापयामः प्रतिष्ठासंस्तावं हि सामेति ॥ ७ ॥

Hantāhametadbhagavato vedānīti viddhīti hovācāmuṣya lokasya kā gatirityayaṁ loka iti hovācāsya lokasya kā gatiriti na pratiṣṭhāṁ lokamatinayediti hovāca pratiṣṭhāṁ vayaṁ lokaṁsāmābhisaṁsthāpayāmaḥ pratiṣṭhāsaṁstāvaṁ hi sāmeti.

Hanta, if you permit; *aham etat bhagavataḥ vedāni iti,* I would like to learn this from you, revered sir [said Dālbhya]; *viddhi iti ha uvāca,* yes, learn from me, said [Śilaka]; *amuṣya lokasya kā gatiḥ iti,* what is the support of that world [Dālbhya asked]; *ayam lokaḥ iti ha uvāca,* this earth, said [Śilaka]; *asya lokasya kā gatiḥ iti,* what is the support of this earth [Dālbhya asked]; *pratiṣṭhām lokam na atinayet iti ha uvāca,* [in order to find the support of Sāma] don't go beyond the earth, replied [Śilaka]; *pratiṣṭhām lokam vayam sāma abhisaṁsthāpayāmaḥ,* 'we see Sāma based on this earth; *pratiṣṭhāsaṁstāvam hi sāma iti,* Sāma is respected because it is based on this earth.

7. Dālbhya said, 'Sir, if you permit, I would like to ask you about this.' Śilaka replied, 'Yes, ask.' Dālbhya then asked, 'What is the support of that heaven?' Śilaka said, 'This earth.' 'What supports this earth?' asked Dālbhya. Śilaka replied: 'Don't think Sāma's base is beyond this earth. We think Sāma is based on this earth, and we respect it as so.'

Heaven is supported by the various Vedic rites performed on the earth, and this is why the earth is said here to be the support of heaven. To be more precise, however, the gods and goddesses in heaven depend upon what men and women on earth offer them through their Vedic rites. In this sense, the earth is the support of heaven. The earth is the support of everything, and it is also the base of the Sāma. This is why the earth is described as a kind of chariot (*rathantara*) in the Sāma Veda.

तं ह प्रवाहणो जैवलिरुवाचान्तवद्वै किल ते शालावत्य साम यस्त्वेतर्हि ब्रूयान्मूर्धा ते विपतिष्यतीति मूर्धा ते विपतेदिति हन्ताहमेतद्भगवतो वेदानीति विद्धीति होवाच ॥ ८ ॥ इत्यष्टमः खण्डः ॥ ८ ॥

Taṁ ha pravāhaṇo jaivaliruvācāntavadvai kila te śālāvatya sāma yastvetarhi brūyānmūrdhā te vipatiṣyatīti mūrdhā te vipatediti hantāhametadbhagavato vedānīti viddhīti hovāca. Ityaṣṭamaḥ khaṇḍaḥ.

Tam ha pravāhaṇaḥ jaivaliḥ uvāca, Pravāhaṇa Jaivali said to him; *antavat vai kila te sāma śālāvatya,* O Śālāvatya [Śilaka], your Sāma is not without an end; *yaḥ tu,* if anyone; *etarhi,* now; *brūyāt,* says; *mūrdhā te vipatiṣyati iti,* your head will fall; *mūrdhā te vipatet,* your head will fall off; *hanta aham bhagavataḥ vadāni iti,* [Śilaka said,] if you please, O Lord, I would like to learn from you; *viddhi iti ha uvāca,* yes, learn [from me, Pravāhaṇa replied]. *Iti aṣṭamaḥ khaṇḍaḥ,* here ends the eighth section.

8. Pravāhaṇa Jaivali said: 'O Śālāvatya, your Sāma is not endless. If someone should now say that your head will fall off, it will fall off.' Śilaka Śālāvatya then said, 'O Lord, I want to learn from you [the truth about the Sāma].' Jaivali replied, 'Yes, learn from me.'

Section Nine

अस्य लोकस्य का गतिरित्याकाश इति होवाच
सर्वाणि ह वा इमानि भूतान्याकाशादेव समुत्पद्यन्त
आकाशं प्रत्यस्तं यन्त्याकाशो ह्येवैभ्यो ज्यायानाकाशः
परायणम् ॥ १ ॥

Asya lokasya kā gatirityākāśa iti hovāca sarvāṇi ha vā imāni bhūtānyākāśādeva samutpadyanta ākāśaṁ pratyastaṁ yantyākāśo hyevaibhyo jyāyānākāśaḥ parāyaṇam.

Asya lokasya kā gatiḥ iti, [Śilaka Śālāvatya asked,] what is the end of this earth; *ākāśaḥ iti ha uvāca,* [Pravāhaṇa] replied, space; *sarvāṇi ha vai imāni bhūtāni,* all these beings; *ākāśāt eva samutpadyante,* issue from space; *ākāśam prati astam yanti,* they disappear into space; *ākāśaḥ hi eva ebhyaḥ jyāyān,* space is superior to these; *ākāśaḥ parāyaṇam,* space is the highest goal.

1. Śilaka Śālāvatya asked Pravāhaṇa, 'What is the end of this earth?' Pravāhaṇa said: 'Space, for everything that exists arises from space and also goes back into space. Space is superior to everything. Space is the highest goal.'

Space is described here as the source of everything. It is the source as well as the end of everything. In short, it is Paramātman, the Cosmic Self. Because space is the biggest thing visible, it can rightly claim to be the symbol of the Paramātman. All the other elements (air, fire, water, and earth) come from space and go back to space. But the scriptures also say that the Cosmic Self is the source and the end of the elements—indeed, of everything.

स एष परोवरीयानुद्गीथः स एषोऽनन्तः परोवरीयो हास्य भवति परोवरीयसो ह लोकाञ्जयति य एतदेवं विद्वान् परोवरीयांसमुद्गीथमुपास्ते ॥ २ ॥

Sa eṣa parovarīyānudgīthaḥ sa eṣo'nantaḥ parovarīyo hāsya bhavati parovarīyaso ha lokāñjayati ya etadevaṁ vidvān parovarīyāṁsamudgīthamupāste.

Saḥ udgīthaḥ, that udgītha; *parovarīyān* [*paraḥ* + *varīyān*], the best; *eṣaḥ,* the Paramātman [i.e., the Supreme Self, earlier referred to as endless]; *saḥ eṣaḥ,* the udgītha [which is also the Cosmic Self]; *anantaḥ,* [is] endless; *yaḥ,* the worshipper; *evam,* as mentioned earlier; *vidvān,* having known; *etat,* this; *parovarīyāṁsam udgītham upāste,* worships this udgītha knowing it as the best; *parovarīyasaḥ lokān jayati,* he attains increasingly higher and higher worlds; *asya,* the life of that worshipper; *parovarīyaḥ ha bhavati,* also becomes higher and higher.

2. Earlier, mention was made of the udgītha being the best as also endless. He who is aware of this

and worships the udgītha as such keeps attaining higher and higher worlds, and he becomes increasingly a better individual.

It is important to realize that the udgītha is the Paramātman itself. When we know this we attain the highest—both materially and spiritually.

तं हैतमतिधन्वा शौनक उदरशाण्डिल्यायोक्त्वोवाच यावत्त एनं प्रजायामुद्गीथं वेदिष्यन्ते परोवरीयो हैभ्यस्ता-वदस्मिँल्लोके जीवनं भविष्यति॥ ३ ॥

Taṁ haitamatidhanvā śaunaka udaraśāṇḍilyāyoktvovāca yāvatta enaṁ prajāyāmudgīthaṁ vediṣyante parovarīyo haibhyastāvadasmiṁlloke jīvanaṁ bhaviṣyati.

Śaunakaḥ, the son of Śunaka; *atidhanvā,* Atidhanvā [the sage having that name]; *tam,* of that kind; *etam,* this [udgītha]; *udaraśāṇḍilyāya,* to Udaraśāṇḍilya [the disciple having that name]; *uktvā,* having taught; *uvāca,* he said; *ha yāvat,* as long as; *te prajāyām,* your progeny; *enam udgītham vediṣyante,* will know this udgītha; *tāvat,* so long; [*tāsām prajān,* the life of those progeny]; *asmin loke,* in this world; *jīvanam ebhyaḥ parovarīyaḥ ha bhaviṣyati,* will grow better and better in quality judged by the standard of ordinary people.

3. [In ancient times there was a sage named Atidhanvā, who was the son of Śunaka and who knew the science

of udgītha very well.] Once when he was teaching this to his disciple Udaraśāṇḍilya, he declared: 'So long as you and your family preserve this knowledge, the quality of life in the world of your family will be higher than that of average people.'

This udgītha is an invaluable asset which can uplift people both materially and spiritually for generations.

तथामुष्मिँल्लोके लोक इति स य एतदेवं विद्वानुपास्ते परोवरीय एव हास्यास्मिँल्लोके जीवनं भवति तथामुष्मिँल्लोके लोक इति लोके लोक इति ॥ ४ ॥ इति नवमः खण्डः ॥ ९ ॥

Tathāmuṣmiṁlloke loka iti sa ya etadevaṁ vidvānupāste parovarīya eva hāsyāsmiṁlloke jīvanaṁ bhavati tathāmuṣmiṁlloke loka iti loke loka iti. Iti navamaḥ khaṇḍaḥ.

Tathā, in the same way; *amuṣmin loke,* in that other world; *lokaḥ iti,* the place; *saḥ yaḥ,* he who; *etat evam vidvān upāste,* knows this and worships [the udgītha] accordingly; *parovarīyaḥ eva ha asya asmin loke jīvanam bhavati,* his life in this world is the best possible; *tathā amuṣmin loke lokaḥ iti loke lokaḥ iti,* his life in the other world [i.e., his life after death] is likewise the best, his life in the other world is likewise. *Iti navamaḥ khaṇḍaḥ,* here ends the ninth section.

4. As in this world, so also in the other world. He who knows the place of the udgītha and worships it accordingly enjoys the best in life in this world, and he enjoys the best in life in the other world also [after death].

The sage Atidhanvā told his disciple Udaraśāṇḍilya about the benefits of worshipping udgītha. He said that the benefits were not only material, but also spiritual. The worshipper is benefitted in this life as well as in his life after death.

But the question may be raised, is this still valid today? What was true in earlier times may not be true now. Śaṅkara dispels this doubt. He says that even now people are enjoying the same benefits of worshipping the udgītha (that is, of chanting the Sāma Veda)—especially that part which is addressed to the Supreme Being.

Section Ten

मटचीहतेषु कुरुष्वाटिक्या सह जाययोषस्तिर्ह चाक्रायण इभ्यग्रामे प्रद्राणक उवास॥ १ ॥

Maṭacīhateṣu kuruṣvāṭikyā saha jāyayoṣastirha cākrāyaṇa ibhyagrāme pradrāṇaka uvāsa.

Maṭacīhateṣu, destroyed [*hateṣu*] by a thunderstorm [*maṭacin*]; *kuruṣu,* in the land of the Kurus; *āṭikyā jāyayā saha,* with his child-wife; *uṣastiḥ,* Uṣasti [a young man by that name]; *cākrāyaṇaḥ,* the son of Cakra; *pradrāṇakaḥ,* in great misery; *ibhyagrāme* [*ibhyaḥ,* prosperous (i.e., where people owned elephants) + *grāme,* in a village], in a prosperous village; *uvāsa,* lived.

1. Once the land of the Kurus was hit by a bad thunderstorm, and a young man living there named Uṣasti, the son of Cakra, was in great distress. He left home accompanied by his child-wife and moved to a prosperous village.

So far, much praise has been given to the udgītha, the purpose being to show the importance of the Sāma Veda. Now, *prastāva* and *pratihāra* are being introduced with the same object in view—that is, worship of the Sāma Veda. In order to introduce the subject, however, and to make it easy to understand, a story is given:

At one time the land of the Kurus was hit by a very bad storm, which destroyed all the crops, and the country was in the grip of a famine. The son of Cakra, named Uṣasti, was starving and on the verge of death. He then moved with his child-wife to a prosperous village (that is, it was prosperous because people there owned elephants—*ibha*).

According to Śaṅkara, the word *maṭacī* means 'fire from thunder.' According to the *Śabdakalpadruma,* it refers to a species of small red birds, and according to Ānandagiri it means 'locusts.' Another meaning is 'hail.'

स हेभ्यं कुल्माषान्खादन्तं बिभिक्षे तं होवाच।
नेतोऽन्ये विद्यन्ते यच्च ये म इम उपनिहिता इति॥ २॥

Sa hebhyaṁ kulmāṣānkhādantaṁ bibhikṣe taṁ hovāca; Neto'nye vidyante yacca ye ma ima upanihitā iti.

Saḥ, he [Uṣasti]; *kulmāṣān,* bad food grains; *khādantam,* eating; *ibhyam,* an elephant[-driver]; *bibhikṣe,* begged; *ha tam uvāca,* that [elephant-driver] said to him; *itaḥ,* besides these [pulses]; *na anye vidyante,* nothing further exists; *yat ye ca ime,* that which [the pulses]; *me,* my; *upanihitāḥ,* thrown [into my eating bowl]; [*kim karomi,* what should I do].

2. Uṣasti saw an elephant-driver eating some pulses of poor quality, and he begged for a share of his food. The elephant-driver replied: 'This food in my bowl is all I have to eat. Besides this, I have nothing. [What should I do?]'

The food itself was bad, and besides that, it was hardly enough for the elephant-driver, but there was nothing else he could give Uṣasti. By implication, he regretted his inability to help.

एतेषां मे देहीति होवाच तानस्मै प्रददौ हन्तानुपान-
मित्युच्छिष्टं वै मे पीतं स्यादिति होवाच॥ ३॥

Eteṣāṁ me dehīti hovāca tānasmai pradadau hantā-nupānamityucchiṣṭaṁ vai me pītaṁ syāditi hovāca.

Ha uvāca, [Uṣasti] said; *eteṣām,* out of this; *me dehi iti,* give me [some]; *tān,* those [pulses]; *asmai,* to him [i.e., to Uṣasti]; *pradadau,* gave away; *hanta,* [the elephant-driver said] here is; *anupānam iti,* drinking water; *iti ha uvāca,* [Uṣasti] said; *me ucchiṣṭam vai pītam syāt,* [if I drink the water you are offering] I would be drinking unclean water [because someone else has drunk from it].

3. Uṣasti said to the elephant-driver, 'Please give me some [of the pulses].' The driver then gave away the pulses and said, 'Here is some water.' [But Uṣasti declined it, saying,] 'That will amount to my drinking unclean water.'

Uṣasti must have been very hungry. Although the elephant-driver said he had no other food than what was in his bowl, Uṣasti begged for that anyway. The driver kindly obliged and then also offered him some water to drink. This, however, Uṣasti declined. He said he would then be drinking unclean (*ucchiṣṭa*) water—that is, water that someone else had already drunk from. But the driver raised the question: If Uṣasti could take the unclean (according to him) food, why could he not take the unclean water also?

न स्विदेतेऽप्युच्छिष्टा इति न वा अजीविष्यमिमानखाद-
न्निति होवाच कामो म उदपानमिति॥ ४ ॥

*Na svidete'pyucchiṣṭā iti na vā ajīviṣyamimāna-
khādanniti hovāca kāmo ma udapānamiti.*

Svit ete api na ucchiṣṭāḥ iti, [the driver said, by the same token] aren't these [pulses] also unclean; *ha uvāca,* [Uṣasti] replied; *imān,* these [pulses]; *akhādan,* [if I] do not eat; *na vai ajīviṣyam iti,* I will not survive; *udapānam,* drinking water [on the other hand]; *me kāmaḥ iti,* is left to me.

4. The elephant-driver asked, 'Aren't the pulses also unclean?' Uṣasti replied: 'I would die if I did not have these grains to eat. As regards drinking water, [it is not that important]. I can get it when I like.'

Normally a person should not eat or drink anything unclean (*ucchiṣṭa*)—that is, something which someone else has already eaten or drunk a part of. But when it is a question of survival, the scriptures condone such eating or drinking. Uṣasti was aware of the injunctions of the scriptures in this respect, and he knew they would permit his eating the unclean pulses, but not his drinking the unclean water. Clean water was easily available, so he would not have died if he refrained from drinking it.

The scriptures take much pains to point out when eating or drinking unclean things is permissible. In this connection, the reader's attention is drawn to sūtra 3.4.28 of the Brahma Sūtras.

स ह खादित्वातिशेषाञ्जायाया आजहार साग्र एव सुभिक्षा बभूव तान्प्रतिगृह्य निदधौ॥ ५॥

Sa ha khāditvātiśeṣāñjāyāyā ājahāra sāgra eva subhikṣā babhūva tānpratigṛhya nidadhau.

Ha khāditvā, having eaten; *atiśeṣān,* whatever was left over; *saḥ jāyāyai ājahāra,* he [Uṣasti] brought for his wife; *sā,* she; *agre eva subhikṣā babhūva,* had already obtained good alms; *tān,* them [the pulses]; *pratigṛhya,* she accepted; *nidadhau,* [and] put them aside.

5. After eating some of the food, he [Uṣasti] brought back what was left for his wife. The wife, however, had meanwhile obtained good alms. She accepted the food [from her husband] and put it aside [for future use].

स ह प्रातः सञ्जिहान उवाच यद्बतान्नस्य लभेमहि लभेमहि धनमात्रांराजासौ यक्ष्यते स मा सर्वैरार्त्विज्यैर्वृणीतेति॥ ६॥

Sa ha prātaḥ sañjihāna uvāca yadbatānnasya labhemahi labhemahi dhanamātrāṁrājāsau yakṣyate sa mā sarvairārtvijyairvṛṇīteti.

Saḥ, he [Uṣasti]; *prātaḥ,* in the morning; *sañjihānaḥ,* while getting up from bed; *ha uvāca,* said [to his wife]; *yat bata,* oh, if only; *annasya labhemahi,* I could get some food; *labhemahi dhanamātrām,* I could earn a little money; *asau,* over there; *rājā,* the king; *yakṣyate,* is performing a sacrifice; *saḥ,* he [the king]; *mā,* me; *sarvaiḥ ārtvijyaiḥ,* all the work of a ṛtvik [a priest who sings hymns or otherwise helps with the performance of a sacrifice]; *vṛṇīta iti,* would have appointed.

6. While leaving bed the next morning, Uṣasti said to his wife: 'Oh, if only I could get something to eat, I could then earn some money. The king over there is going to perform a sacrifice, and very likely he would have entrusted to me all the work of a ṛtvik [a priest at a sacrifice].'

Uṣasti was a highly qualified ṛtvik, and he hoped the king would appoint him to assist at the sacrifice he was going to perform. If that hope of his materialized, he would then be able to earn some money. The snag was, however, that he was too weak from hunger to do anything. If he could only get something to eat!

तं जायोवाच हन्त पत इम एव कुल्माषा इति तान्खादित्वामुं यज्ञं वितितमेयाय॥ ७॥

Taṁ jāyovāca hanta pata ima eva kulmāṣā iti tānkhāditvāmuṁ yajñaṁ vitatameyāya.

Jāyā tam uvāca, the wife said to him; *hanta pate,* O dear husband; *ime eva kulmāṣāḥ iti,* here are those pulses [you gave me]; *tān,* them [the pulses]; *khāditvā,* having eaten; *amum vitatam yajñam,* that ensuing sacrifice; *eyāya,* he went.

7. The wife said to him, 'O dear husband, here are those pulses you gave me.' Having eaten the pulses, Uṣasti left for the place where the sacrifice was being held [other priests having already started it].

तत्रोद्गातॄनास्तावे स्तोष्यमाणानुपोपविवेश स ह प्रस्तोतारमुवाच॥ ८॥

Tatrodgātṛnāstāve stoṣyamāṇānupopaviveśa sa ha prastotāramuvāca.

Tatra, there [at the site of the sacrifice]; *āstāve,* at the place where hymns were being sung; *udgātṛn stoṣyamāṇān,* those who were singing the hymns; *upa,* near; *upaviveśa,* he sat; *prastotāram,* to him who was reciting the prastāva; *saḥ ha uvāca,* he said.

8. There at the sacrifice, he found those [the udgātṛs] who were singing the [Sāma] hymns and took a seat among them. Turning to the one who was singing the prastāva, he asked:

Prastāva, pratihāra, and udgītha—these are some of the Sāma mantras recited during a sacrifice. One who recites the prastāva is called the *prastotā,* one who recites the pratihāra is called the *pratihartā,* and one who recites the udgītha is called the *udgātā.*

प्रस्तोतर्या देवता प्रस्तावमन्वायत्ता तां चेदविद्वान्प्रस्तो-
ष्यसि मूर्धा ते विपतिष्यतीति॥ ९॥

Prastotaryā devatā prastāvamanvāyattā tāṁ cedavidvānprastoṣyasi mūrdhā te vipatiṣyatīti.

Prastotaḥ, O Prastotā; *yā devatā,* that god who; *prastāvam anvāyattā,* underlies this prastāva hymn; *tām avidvān,* without knowing anything about him; *cet,* if; *prastoṣyasi,* you recite the prastāva; *te,* your; *mūrdhā,* head; *vipatiṣyati iti,* will fall.

9. 'O Prastotā, if you recite the prastāva without knowing anything about the god to whom this hymn relates, your head will fall.'

Here the question arises whether or not an ignorant person is permitted to recite the scriptures. According to Śaṅkara, he is permitted, but if he commits errors, he will be liable to punishment. It may not cost him his head, but he may go after death to the world of his ancestors, rather than to the world of the gods. But perhaps he would have gone there anyway because of his other errors. As to the falling of the head, the curse need not be taken literally.

एवमेवोद्गातारमुवाचोद्गातर्या देवतोद्गीथमन्वायत्ता तां चेदविद्वानुद्गास्यसि मूर्धा ते विपतिष्यतीति॥ १०॥

Evamevodgātāramuvācodgātaryā devatodgīthamanvāyattā tāṁ cedavidvānudgāsyasi mūrdhā te vipatiṣyatīti.

Evam eva udgātāram uvāca, he then said the same thing to the udgātā [who sings the udgītha]; *udgātaḥ,* O Udgātā; *yā devatā udgītham anvāyattā,* the god who is related to the udgītha; *tām avidvān,* without knowing anything about him; *cet udgāsyasi,* if you sing about him; *te mūrdhā vipatiṣyati iti,* your head will fall.

10. Next Uṣasti said the same thing to the person singing the udgītha: 'O Udgātā, if you do not know anything about the god related to the udgītha and yet you sing the udgītha, your head will fall.'

एवमेव प्रतिहर्तारमुवाच प्रतिहर्तर्या देवता प्रतिहार-
मन्वायत्ता तां चेदविद्वान्प्रतिहरिष्यसि मूर्धा ते विपतिष्यतीति
ते ह समारतास्तूष्णीमासाञ्चक्रिरे ॥ ११ ॥ इति दशमः
खण्डः ॥ १० ॥

Evameva pratihartāramuvāca pratihartaryā devatā pratihāramanvāyattā tāṁ cedavidvānpratihariṣyasi mūrdhā te vipatiṣyatīti te ha samāratāstūṣṇīmāsāñcakrire. Iti daśamaḥ khaṇḍaḥ.

Evam eva pratihartāram uvāca, he said the same thing to the person who was singing the pratihāra; *pratihartaḥ,* O Pratihartā; *yā devatā pratihāram anvāyattā,* that god to whom your pratihāra relates; *tām avidvān,* without knowing anything about him; *cet pratihariṣyasi,* if you sing the pratihāra; *te mūrdhā vipatiṣyati iti,* your head will fall; *te,* they [the singers]; *ha samāratāḥ,* stopped; *āsāñcakrire tūṣṇīm,* [and] remained silent. *Iti daśamaḥ khaṇḍaḥ,* here ends the tenth section.

11. He again said the same thing to the person singing the pratihāra: 'O Pratihartā, if you sing the pratihāra without knowing anything about the deity relating to it, your head will fall.' At this, they stopped their respective hymns and remained silent.

When Uṣasti spoke thus to the singers, they all stopped their hymns. They were afraid they would lose their heads because they did not know about the deities relating to the hymns. They also wanted to know this from Uṣasti.

Section Eleven

अथ हैनं यजमान उवाच भगवन्तं वा अहं विविदिषाणीत्युषस्तिरस्मि चाक्रायण इति होवाच॥ १॥

Atha hainaṁ yajamāna uvāca bhagavantaṁ vā ahaṁ vividiṣāṇītyuṣastirasmi cākrāyaṇa iti hovāca.

Atha, then; *yajamānaḥ,* the person performing the sacrifice [the prince]; *ha enam uvāca,* said to him [to Uṣasti]; *bhagavantam vai aham vividiṣāṇi iti,* Sir, I want to know who you are; *iti ha uvāca,* [Uṣasti] replied; *uṣastiḥ cākrāyaṇaḥ asmi,* I am Uṣasti, the son of Cakra.

1. Then the prince performing the sacrifice said, 'Sir, I would like to know who you are.' He [Uṣasti] replied, 'I am Uṣasti, the son of Cakra.'

Uṣasti's reply suggests that he assumes the prince already knows him by name.

स होवाच भगवन्तं वा अहमेभिः सर्वैरार्त्विज्यैः पर्यैषिषं भगवतो वा अहमवित्त्यान्यानवृषि॥ २॥

Sa hovāca bhagavantaṁ vā ahamebhiḥ sarvairārtvijyaiḥ paryaiṣiṣaṁ bhagavato vā ahamavittyānyānavṛṣi.

Saḥ ha uvāca, he [the prince] said; *aham,* I; *bhagavantam,* you, revered sir; *vai ebhiḥ sarvaiḥ ārtvijyaiḥ,* for all the work of the priests; *paryaiṣiṣam,* looked for; *bhagavataḥ,* you, sir; *avittyā,* not being able to locate; *aham vai anyān avṛṣi,* I chose others.

2. He [the prince] said: 'I looked for you, revered sir, to give you all the work of the priests. As I could not find you, I entrusted the work to other [brāhmins].'

The prince had obviously heard of Uṣasti's reputation as a versatile scholar, and had wanted to give the responsibility of the sacrifice to him. As he could not find him, however, he had no option but to entrust the work to other brāhmins.

भगवांस्त्वेव मे सर्वैरार्त्विज्यैरिति तथेत्यथ तर्ह्येत एव समतिसृष्टाः स्तुवतां यावत्त्वेभ्यो धनं दद्यास्तावन्मम दद्या इति तथेति ह यजमान उवाच॥ ३ ॥

Bhagavāṁstveva me sarvairārtvijyairiti tathetyatha tarhyeta eva samatisṛṣṭāḥ stuvatāṁ yāvattvebhyo dhanaṁ dadyāstāvanmama dadyā iti tatheti ha yajamāna uvāca.

Bhagavān, O Lord; *eva tu,* for certain; *sarvaiḥ ārtvijyaiḥ me iti,* [take on] all the work of the ṛtvik for me; *tathā iti,* [Uṣasti said] let it be so; *atha tarhi,* now therefore; *ete eva,* these [priests already engaged by you]; *samatisṛṣṭāḥ,* as instructed [by me]; *stuvatām,* may recite; *tu ebhyaḥ yāvat dhanam dadyāḥ,* but as much money as you are giving these [priests]; *tāvat,* that much [money]; *mama dadyāḥ iti,* you have to give me [also]; *yajamānaḥ,* the performer of the sacrifice [the prince]; *iti ha uvāca,* said; *tathā,* it will be so.

3. [The prince said,] 'O Lord, please do for me all the work of the priest.' [Uṣasti replied:] 'Let it be so. Now let the priests already engaged by you recite as I instruct. But you will have to pay me as much as you promised to pay these priests.' 'It will be so,' said [the prince].

Uṣasti did not want the priests who had already been engaged to be dismissed. He only wanted them to follow his instructions about their recitations.

अथ हैनं प्रस्तोतोपससाद प्रस्तोतर्या देवता प्रस्ताव-
मन्वायत्ता तां चेदविद्वान्प्रस्तोष्यसि मूर्धा ते विपतिष्यतीति
मा भगवानवोचत्कतमा सा देवतेति ॥ ४ ॥

Atha hainaṁ prastotopasasāda prastotaryā devatā prastāvamanvāyattā tāṁ cedavidvānprastoṣyasi mūrdhā te vipatiṣyatīti mā bhagavānavocatkatamā sā devateti.

Atha, then; *prastotā,* the person reciting the prastāva; *ha enam upasasāda,* came to him [i.e., to Uṣasti, and said]; *prastotaḥ yā devatā prastāvam anvāyattā,* O Prastotā, that deity to whom the prastāva is related; *tām avidvān,* without knowing anything about him; *cet prastoṣyasi,* if you sing [about him]; *te mūrdhā vipatiṣyati iti,* your head will fall; *bhagavān mā avocat,* revered sir, you said to me; *katamā sā devatā iti,* what is that deity?

4. Then the Prastotā came to [Uṣasti and said:] 'Revered sir, you told me, "O Prastotā, if you sing the prastāva without knowing anything about the deity to whom the hymn is addressed, your head will fall." Please tell me who that deity is.'

प्राण इति होवाच सर्वाणि ह वा इमानि भूतानि प्राणमेवाभिसंविशन्ति प्राणमभ्युज्जिहते सैषा देवता प्रस्तावमन्वायत्ता तां चेदविद्वान्प्रस्तोष्यो मूर्धा ते व्यपतिष्यत्तथोक्तस्य मयेति॥ ५॥

Prāṇa iti hovāca sarvāṇi ha vā imāni bhūtāni prāṇamevābhisaṁviśanti prāṇamabhyujjihate saiṣā devatā prastāvamanvāyattā tāṁ cedavidvānprastoṣyo mūrdhā te vyapatiṣyattathoktasya mayeti.

Prāṇa iti ha uvāca, [Uṣasti] said, it is prāṇa [the vital force]; *ha vai,* for; *imāni sarvāṇi bhūtāni,* all these beings [moving or unmoving]; *prāṇam eva,* in prāṇa; *abhi,* totally; *saṁviśanti,* disappear [at the time of destruction]; *prāṇam abhi ujjihate,* [and] out of prāṇa they appear [when they come into existence]; *sā eṣā devatā,* that [prāṇa] is the deity; *prastāvam anvāyattā,* the prastāva is addressed to; *cet,* if; *tām,* that [deity]; *avidvān,* from ignorance; *prastoṣyaḥ,* you had praised; [then] *tathā,* like that; *mayā uktasya,* in spite of being warned by me; *te mūrdhā vyapatiṣyat iti,* your head would surely have fallen.

5. Uṣasti said: 'It is prāṇa [the vital force]. In prāṇa all things that we see around us [moving or unmoving], disappear [at the time of their destruction. And at the time of their appearance,] they appear from prāṇa. Prāṇa is that deity to whom the prastāva is addressed. If you had sung the hymn not knowing the deity to whom it is addressed, in spite of being warned by me, your head would surely have fallen.'

The prastotā had immediately stopped singing and then had approached Uṣasti in a humble manner. This pleased Uṣasti, and he gladly proceeded to teach the brāhmin.

अथ हैनमुद्गातोपससादोद्गातर्या देवतोद्गीथमन्वायत्ता तां चेदविद्वानुद्गास्यसि मूर्धा ते विपतिष्यतीति मा भगवानवोचत्कतमा सा देवतेति ॥ ६ ॥

Atha hainamudgātopasasādodgātaryā devatodgītha-

manvāyattā tāṁ cedavidvānudgāsyasi mūrdhā te vipatiṣyatīti mā bhagavānavocatkatamā sā devateti.

Atha, then; *udgātā,* the person reciting the udgītha; *ha enam upasasāda,* came to him [i.e., to Uṣasti, and said]; *bhagavān mā avocat,* revered sir, you said to me; *udgātaḥ yā devatā udgītham anvāyattā,* O Udgātā, that deity to whom the udgītha is related; *tām avidvān,* without knowing anything about him; *cet udgāsyasi,* if you sing [about him]; *te mūrdhā vipatiṣyati iti,* your head will fall; *katamā sā devatā iti,* what is that deity?

6. Then the udgātā came to [Uṣasti and said:] 'Revered sir, you told me, "O Udgātā, if you sing the udgītha without knowing anything about the deity to whom the hymn is addressed, your head will fall." Please tell me who that deity is.'

आदित्य इति होवाच सर्वाणि ह वा इमानि भूतान्यादित्यमुच्चैः सन्तं गायन्ति सैषा देवतोद्गीथमन्वायत्ता तां चेदविद्वानुदगास्यो मूर्धा ते व्यपतिष्यत्तथोक्तस्य मयेति ॥ ७ ॥

Āditya iti hovāca sarvāṇi ha vā imāni bhūtānyādityamuccaiḥ santaṁ gāyanti saiṣā devatodgīthamanvāyattā tāṁ cedavidvānudgāsyo mūrdhā te vyapatiṣyattathoktasya mayeti.

Ādityaḥ iti ha uvāca, [Uṣasti] said, it is āditya [the sun]; *ha vai,* for; *imāni sarvāṇi bhūtāni,* all these beings [moving and unmoving]; *uccaiḥ santaṁ ādityam gāyanti,* sing in praise of āditya, who is high above; *sā eṣā devatā,* that [āditya] is the deity; *udgītham anvāyattā,* the udgītha is addressed to; *cet,* if; *tām,* that [deity]; *avidvān,* from ignorance; *udgāsyaḥ,* you had sung the udgītha; [then] *tathā,* like that; *mayā uktasya,* in spite of being warned by me; *te mūrdhā vyapatiṣyat iti,* your head would surely have fallen.

7. Uṣasti said: 'It is āditya [the sun], for all these beings pay homage to the sun, which is high above. Āditya is that deity to whom the udgītha is addressed. If you had sung the udgītha not knowing the deity to whom it is addressed, your head would surely have fallen, as I had told you.'

Earlier, prāṇa was described as the deity of the prastāva. The word *prāṇa* begins with *pra,* and *prastāva* also begins with *pra.* It is surmised that this is why prāṇa is the deity of the prastāva.

By the same token, the udgītha is addressed to āditya, the sun, for āditya is *urdhatva,* which is *ut* (high), and *udgītha* is also *ut.* Therefore it is reasonable that the deity of the udgītha should be āditya.

अथ हैनं प्रतिहर्तोपससाद प्रतिहर्तर्या देवता प्रतिहार-
मन्वायत्ता तां चेदविद्वान्प्रतिहरिष्यसि मूर्धा ते विपतिष्यतीति
मा भगवानवोचत्कतमा सा देवतेति॥ ८॥

Atha hainaṁ pratihartopasasāda pratihartaryā devatā pratihāramanvāyattā tāṁ cedavidvānpratihariṣyasi mūrdhā te vipatiṣyatīti mā bhagavānavocatkatamā sā devateti.

Atha, next; *pratihartā,* the person reciting the pratihāra; *ha enam upasasāda,* came to him [i.e., to Uṣasti, and said]; *bhagavān mā avocat,* revered sir, you said to me; *pratihartaḥ yā devatā pratihāram anvāyattā,* O Pratihartā, that deity to whom the pratihāra is related; *tām avidvān,* without knowing anything about him; *cet pratihariṣyasi,* if you sing the pratihāra; *te mūrdhā vipatiṣyati iti,* your head will fall; *katamā sā devatā iti,* what is that deity?

8. Next, the pratihartā came to [Uṣasti and said:] 'Revered sir, you told me, "O Pratihartā, if you sing the pratihāra without knowing anything about the deity to whom the hymn is addressed, your head will fall." Please tell me who that deity is.'

अन्नमिति होवाच सर्वाणि ह वा इमानि भूतान्यन्नमेव प्रतिहरमाणानि जीवन्ति सैषा देवता प्रतिहारमन्वायत्ता तां चेदविद्वान्प्रत्यहरिष्यो मूर्धा ते व्यपतिष्यत्तथोक्तस्य मयेति तथोक्तस्य मयेति ॥ ९ ॥ इत्येकादशः खण्डः ॥ ११ ॥

Annamiti hovāca sarvāṇi ha vā imāni bhūtānyannameva pratiharamāṇāni jīvanti saiṣā devatā pratihāramanvāyattā tāṁ cedavidvānpratyahariṣyo mūrdhā te vyapatiṣyattathoktasya mayeti tathoktasya mayeti. Ityekādaśaḥ khaṇḍaḥ.

Annam iti ha uvāca, [Uṣasti] said, it is anna [food]; *ha vai,* for; *imāni sarvāṇi bhūtāni,* all these beings; *annam eva pratiharamāṇāni jīvanti,* support themselves by collecting food; *sā eṣā devatā,* that [food] is the deity; *pratihāram anvāyattā,* the pratihāra is addressed to; *cet,* if; *tām,* that [deity]; *avidvān,* from ignorance; *pratyahariṣyaḥ,* you had sung the pratihāra; [then] *tathā,* like that; *mayā uktasya,* in spite of being warned by me; *te mūrdhā vyapatiṣyat iti,* your head would surely have fallen [the repetition is for the sake of emphasis]. *Iti ekādaśaḥ khaṇḍaḥ,* here ends the eleventh section.

9. Uṣasti said: 'It is anna [food], for all these beings support themselves by eating food. Anna is that deity to whom the pratihāra is addressed. If you had sung the pratihāra not knowing the deity to whom it is addressed, your head would surely have fallen, as I had told you.'

Every living being has to support itself by collecting food. It involves much effort, but each one has to make that effort. *Prati* means 'each and every.' The deity is *pratihāra* because each and every being has to 'collect' (*āharam*) food for himself.

In short, you worship prāṇa (the vital force) through the prastāva, āditya (the sun) through the udgītha, and anna (food) through the pratihāra. What is the result of this? The result is progress in every way.

Section Twelve

अथातः शौव उद्गीथस्तद्ध बको दाल्भ्यो ग्लावो वा मैत्रेयः स्वाध्यायमुद्वव्राज ॥ १ ॥

Athātaḥ śauva udgīthastaddha bako dālbhyo glāvo vā maitreyaḥ svādhyāyamudvavrāja.

Atha ataḥ, since then; *tat ha,* in this connection; *śauvaḥ udgīthaḥ,* an udgītha [to food] sung by dogs [i.e., sages in the form of dogs]; *bakaḥ dālbhyaḥ,* Baka, the son of Dalbha; *glāvaḥ maitreyaḥ vā,* or Glāva, the son of Mitrā; *svādhyāyam udvavrāja,* went to a quiet place to study the scriptures [i.e., the udgītha].

1. Now, an udgītha [to food] sung by dogs. The story is: Baka Dālbhya, who was also known as Glāva Maitreya, went one day to a quiet place to study the scriptures [the udgītha].

Sometimes people are driven by hunger to eat 'unclean' food. The story of Uṣasti is an example. Here, in this section, a story is told of how some dogs avoid such a situation: There was a sage who was known as Baka on his father's side and Glāva on his mother's side. Wanting to learn an udgītha that would bring him food, he went to a quiet place to study the scriptures.

तस्मै श्वा श्वेतः प्रादुर्बभूव तमन्ये श्वान उपसमेत्योचुरन्नं
नो भगवानागायत्वशनायाम वा इति ॥ २ ॥

Tasmai śvā śvetaḥ prādurbabhūva tamanye śvāna upasametyocurannaṁ no bhagavānāgāyatvaśanāyāma vā iti.

Tasmai, [as a favour] to him; *śvā,* a dog; *śvetaḥ,* white; *prādurbabhūva,* appeared; *tam,* to him [i.e., to the white dog]; *anye śvānaḥ,* other dogs; *upasametya,* came; *ūcuḥ,* [and] said; *annam,* food; *naḥ,* for us; *bhagavān,* O Lord; *āgāyatu,* please sing; *aśanāyāma vai iti,* we are hungry [and want to eat].

2. A white dog appeared before him, as if he wanted to do the sage a favour. Then several other smaller dogs came to the white dog and said: 'O Lord, please sing for us. We are hungry and we want some food.'

It would seem that some god or sage was pleased with Baka's Vedic studies and as a favour, appeared before him as a white dog. Then, as if by coincidence, some other smaller dogs approached the white dog and told him they were very hungry and needed food. They asked the white dog to sing the appropriate Sāma so that they could get some food immediately. Very likely, these small dogs were also sages in disguise.

Another explanation is also possible: The white dog represents prāṇa, and the smaller dogs are the sense organs controlled by prāṇa. Prāṇa is pleased when someone studies the scriptures. And if prāṇa is pleased, the sense organs are able to perceive their respective sense objects well. Like dogs, the sense organs are 'hungry' and enjoy perceiving. In order to express their appreciation of the scholar's efforts, they appear before him as dogs.

तान्होवाचेहैव मा प्रातरुपसमीयातेति तद्ध बको दाल्भ्यो ग्लावो वा मैत्रेयः प्रतिपालयाञ्चकार॥ ३ ॥

Tānhovācehaiva mā prātarupasamīyāteti taddha bako dālbhyo glāvo vā maitreyaḥ pratipālayāñcakāra.

Tān, to them [the other dogs]; *ha uvāca,* [the white dog] said; *iha eva,* here; *prātaḥ,* tomorrow morning; *mā upasamīyāta iti,* all of you come to me; *bakaḥ dālbhyaḥ glāvaḥ maitreyaḥ vā,* Baka, the son of Dalbha, who was also known as Glāva, the son of Mitrā; *pratipālayāñcakāra,* waited [for the white dog]; *tat ha,* there.

3. [The white dog] replied, 'All of you meet me here tomorrow morning.' Baka Dālbhya, who was also known as Glāva Maitreya, waited there too [for the white dog].

The smaller dogs were obviously very hungry, so why didn't the white dog sing immediately? He asked them to come back in the morning because the morning is the best time to sing the udgītha. In the afternoon the sun turns away from us. He is the one who gives us food, and if he has already begun to turn away, it is too late to ask him to give us anything. Morning is the time when we are face to face with him, and that is why morning is the best time to make a request of him.

The sage Baka came early the next morning also and waited for the white dog.

ते ह यथैवेदं बहिष्पवमानेन स्तोष्यमाणाः संरब्धाः सर्पन्तीत्येवमाससृपुस्ते ह समुपविश्य हिं चक्रुः ॥ ४ ॥

Te ha yathaivedaṁ bahiṣpavamānena stoṣyamāṇāḥ saṁrabdhāḥ sarpantītyevamāsasṛpuste ha samupaviśya hiṁ cakruḥ.

Te ha, they; *yathā eva,* just as; *idam,* this; *bahiṣpavamānena,* by the hymn called bahiṣpavamāna; *stoṣyamāṇāḥ,* while reciting; *saṁrabdhāḥ,* touching each other; *sarpanti,* proceed; *iti evam āsasṛpuḥ,* went about this way; *te ha,* they; *samupaviśya,* sitting down; *hiṁ,* the word 'hiṁ'; *cakruḥ,* uttered.

4. Just as those who recite the hymn called *bahiṣpavamāna* move forward while touching each other, so the dogs also did the same. Then, sitting down, they said *hiṁ.*

When sages sing the hymn *bahiṣpavamāna,* they join their hands together, or otherwise touch each other, and then they move forward. The dogs did likewise. Each took the tail of the one in front in its mouth and started moving. Finally they sat down and uttered the sound *hiṁ.*

ओ३मदा३मों३ पिबा३मों३ देवो वरुणः प्रजापतिः सविता२न्नमिहा२हरदन्नपते३ऽन्नमिहा२हरा२हरो३मिति ॥ ५ ॥
इति द्वादशः खण्डः ॥ १२ ॥

O3madā3mo3ṁ pibā3mo3ṁ devo varuṇaḥ prajāpatiḥ savitā2nnamihā2haradannapate3'nnamihā2harā2haro3-miti. Iti dvādaśaḥ khaṇḍaḥ.

Om adāma, Om, we will eat; *om pibāma,* Om, we will drink; *om devaḥ varuṇaḥ prajāpatiḥ savitā,* Om Deva [the shining one], Varuṇa, Prajāpati, Savitā; *annam iha āharat,* bring food here; *annapate annam iha āhara āhara om,* O Lord of food, bring food here, bring [food here], Om. *Iti dvādaśaḥ khaṇḍaḥ,* here ends the twelfth section.

5. 'Om, we will eat. Om, we will drink. Om, Deva [the sun], Varuṇa, Prajāpati, Savitā, bring us food here. O Lord of food [the sun], bring us food here. Bring us food here. Om.'

This verse is also known as the *hiṁkāra.*

The sun is the only thing that shines, so he is called here *deva* (that which shines). Varuṇa is the deity who gives rain, and Prajāpati protects all beings. Because Āditya, the sun, gives birth to all, he is known as Savitā.

It is, in fact, Āditya who at one point gives us light, and at another gives us rain. It is because of him that there is food. This is why we ask him to bring us food (*anna*). As a mark of special respect, and also urgency, the request is repeated.

Section Thirteen

अयं वाव लोको हाउकारो वायुर्हाइकारश्चन्द्रमा अथकारः। आत्मेहकारोऽग्निरीकारः ॥१॥

Ayaṁ vāva loko hāukāro vāyurhāikāraścandramā athakāraḥ; Ātmehakāro'gnirīkāraḥ.

Ayam vāva lokaḥ hāukāraḥ, this earth [is known by] the syllable 'hāu'; *vāyuḥ hāikāraḥ,* air by the syllable 'hāi'; *candramā athakāraḥ,* the moon by the syllable 'atha'; *ātmā ihakāraḥ,* the individual self by the syllable 'iha'; *agniḥ īkāraḥ,* fire by the syllable 'ī'.

1. This planet, the earth, is represented by the syllable *hāu,* air is represented by the syllable *hāi,* the moon

by *atha,* the individual self [the jīvātmā] by *iha,* and fire by *ī.*

So long the Upaniṣad has shown how Sāma can be worshipped through the udgītha. Now another way of worshipping Sāma is being shown—through *stobhas.* Stobhas are syllables such as *hiṁ, hāu, hāi,* and so forth, and they are all from the Sāma Veda. By themselves these syllables have no meaning. They are symbols representing objects, or they are used to fill in gaps in sentences. The idea here is that stobhas like *hāu* should be applied to the earth, fire, etc.

A symbol has to have something in common with the object it represents. The Sāma Veda says, 'This earth is also called *rathantara.'* And in the Sāma, the stobha *hāu* stands for rathantara. Thus, it is reasonable to say that *hāu* stands for the earth.

The stobha *hāi* occurs in the Sāma called *Vāmadevya.* The Vāmadevya Sāma is about the relationship of air with water. This is why vāyu (air) is represented by the symbol *hāi.* Why is the moon represented by *atha*? This world is sustained by food (*anna*), and the moon and food are identical. *A* stands for anna, and *tha* stands for *stha* in *sthita,* which means 'sustained.' *A* plus *tha* is *atha.* Thus, *atha* can rightly be said to represent the moon.

Then the self is said to be *iha,* which means 'here' or 'this,' for the self is obvious to everyone. And the stobha *ī* represents fire, because wherever fire is referred to in the Sāma, the words end with *ī.*

The syllable *ī* then is rightly used as a symbol of fire, and to meditate on this symbol is to meditate on fire.

आदित्य ऊकारो निहव एकारो विश्वेदेवा औहोयि-कारः प्रजापतिर्हिङ्कारः प्राणः स्वरोऽन्नं या वाग्विराट्॥ २॥

Āditya ūkāro nihava ekāro viśvedevā auhoyi-kāraḥ prajāpatirhiṁkāraḥ prāṇaḥ svaro'nnaṁ yā vāgvirāṭ.

Ādityaḥ, Āditya, the sun; *ūkāraḥ,* [is represented by] the stobha 'ū'; *nihavaḥ,* the welcoming address; *ekāraḥ,* [is represented by] the stobha 'e'; *viśvedevāḥ,* the Viśvadevas [i.e., a class of gods]; *auhoyi-kāraḥ,* [are represented by] the stobha 'auhoyi'; *prajāpatiḥ,* Prajāpati [the Lord of all beings]; *hiṁkāraḥ,* [is represented by] the stobha 'hiṁ'; *prāṇaḥ,* prāṇa [the presiding deity of life]; *svaraḥ,* [is represented by] the stobha 'svara'; *annam,* food; *yā,* [is represented by] the stobha 'yā'; *virāṭ,* Virāṭ; *vāk,* [is represented by] the stobha 'vāk'.

2. Āditya, the sun, is represented by the stobha *ū*; nihava, the welcoming hymn, by the stobha *e*; the Viśvadeva gods by the stobha *auhoyi*; Prajāpati by the stobha *hiṁ*; prāṇa by the stobha *svara*; food by the stobha *yā*; and Virāṭ by the stobha *vāk*.

Āditya, the sun, is far above in the sky. The letter *ū* suggests *urdhvam,* which means 'above.' So in order to meditate on the sun, one may meditate on its symbol *ū.*

The word *nihava* means 'welcome,' which in Sanskrit is *ehi.* For this reason *e* stands for the nihava, the welcoming hymn. The stobha *auhoyi* stands for the Viśvadevas, the gods, for it occurs in the Sāma in honour of the Viśvadevas.

The stobha *hiṁ* represents Prajāpati. No one knows the meaning of the word *hiṁ*; similarly, no one knows what Prajāpati, the Lord of all beings, is like.

Prāṇa is represented by *svara,* because *svara,* the musical scale, is derived from prāṇa (the Lord of life, or the vital breath). *Yā* represents anna, food, for *yāti* (going) is possible because of food.

The stobha *vāk* occurs in the Sāma called Vairāja or Virāṭa. Thus *vāk* stands for Virāṭ.

अनिरुक्तस्त्रयोदशः स्तोभः सञ्चरो हुङ्कारः ॥ ३ ॥

Aniruktastrayodaśaḥ stobhaḥ sañcaro huṅkāraḥ.

Sañcaraḥ, variously interpreted; *aniruktaḥ,* not clearly defined; *trayodaśaḥ stobhaḥ,* the thirteenth stobha; *huṅkāraḥ,* the syllable 'huṁ'.

3. The thirteenth stobha *huṁ* is not clearly defined. Various scholars have defined it in various ways. [Thus, it is up to people to meditate on it as they like.]

Earlier, twelve stobhas were explained along with how they could be used for meditation. Those stobhas are: *hāu, hāi, atha, iha, ī, ū, e, auhoyi, hiṁ, svara, yā,* and *vāk.* Now the thirteenth stobha, *huṁ,* is being discussed. The Upaniṣad says here, however, that no one knows for certain what *huṁ* means, so people are free to meditate on it as they please.

दुग्धेऽस्मै वाग्दोहं यो वाचो दोहोऽन्नवानन्नादो भवति य एतामेवं साम्नामुपनिषदं वेदोपनिषदं वेदेति ॥ ४ ॥ इति त्रयोदशः खण्डः ॥ १३ ॥ इति छान्दोग्योपनिषदि प्रथमोऽध्यायः ॥ १ ॥

Dugdhe'smai vāgdohaṁ yo vāco doho'nnavānannādo bhavati ya etāmevaṁ sāmnāmupaniṣadaṁ vedopaniṣadaṁ vedeti. Iti trayodaśaḥ khaṇḍaḥ. Iti chāndogyopaniṣadi prathamo'dhyāyaḥ.

Yaḥ, that person who; *etām evam,* this as stated earlier; *sāmnām,* the Sāma with its stobhas; *upaniṣadam,* the science of it; *veda,* knows; *vācaḥ,* of the organ of speech; *yaḥ dohaḥ,* the essence; *doham,* [that] essence; *vāk,* the organ of speech; *asmai,* to him [who knows]; *dugdhe,* gives; [*saḥ,* he]; *annavān,* rich with food; *annādaḥ,* a great eater of food; *bhavati,* becomes. *Iti trayodaśaḥ khaṇḍaḥ,* here ends the thirteenth section. *Iti chāndogya upaniṣadi prathamaḥ adhyāyaḥ,* here ends the first chapter of the Chāndogya Upaniṣad.

4. To a person who knows the Sāma with its stobhas, as mentioned earlier, the organ of speech gives of its best. Such a person gets plenty of food to eat and can also eat much food.

In the previous verses, mention was made of the stobhas. Now the benefit of meditating on them is being described. A person who knows the real import of those stobhas receives the best that the organ of speech has to offer.

CHAPTER TWO

Section One

ॐ। समस्तस्य खलु साम्न उपासनं साधु यत्खलु साधु तत्सामेत्याचक्षते यदसाधु तदसामेति॥ १॥

Om. Samastasya khalu sāmna upāsanaṁ sādhu yatkhalu sādhu tatsāmetyācakṣate yadasādhu tadasāmeti.

Samastasya khalu sāmnaḥ upāsanam, the worship of the Sāma as a whole [inclusive of all its parts]; *sādhu,* [is] good; *yat khalu sādhu,* whatever is good; *tat sāma iti ācakṣate,* that is called sāma; *yat asādhu,* whatever is bad; *tat asāma iti,* that is asāma.

1. It is good to worship the Sāma with all its parts. All that is good, according to scholars, is called *sāma.* Similarly, all that is bad is *asāma.*

Much has been said already about the Sāma and the udgītha. And it has also been said that much good follows from their worship. Similarly, the Upaniṣad has discussed the stobhas and shown their importance. So long, the Sāma has been discussed in parts. Now it will be discussed as a whole.

The point of this verse is to emphasize how beautiful it is to worship the Sāma. The Sāma is beautiful and to worship the Sāma is beautiful. The qualifying word used is *sādhu.* Sādhu means 'good,' 'beautiful,' 'chaste,' 'elegant,' and so on. It also means 'honest,' 'morally sound,' 'beneficial,' 'perfect,' and 'above reproach.' Anything opposed to sādhu is *asāma.*

तदुताप्याहुः साम्नैनमुपागादिति साधुनैनमुपागादित्येव तदाहुरसाम्नैनमुपागादित्यसाधुनैनमुपागादित्येव तदाहुः ॥ २ ॥

Tadutāpyāhuḥ sāmnainamupāgāditi sādhunainamupāgādityeva tadāhurasāmnainamupāgādityasādhunainamupāgādityeva tadāhuḥ.

Tat uta āhuḥ api, this is why people say; *sāmnā,* by virtue of sāma; *enam,* a [high-placed] person; *upāgāt iti,* someone got access to; *sādhunā,* [they mean] by good conduct; *enam upāgāt iti eva,* he got access to him; *tat āhuḥ,* [similarly] this is what people say; *asāmnā,* by virtue of asāma; *enam upāgāt iti,* he got access to him; *asādhunā,* [when they mean] by bad conduct; *enam upāgāt iti eva,* he got access to him; *tat āhuḥ,* this is what people say.

2. This is why people say, 'He has succeeded in getting access to that distinguished person by virtue of sāma,' when they mean he has gone to that distinguished person by honest and legitimate means. Similarly, they say, 'By virtue of asāma he went to that distinguished person,' when they mean he got to that person by unethical means.

The question is: What is good and what is bad? Suppose you have to meet a very distinguished person who is far above you in status. It is very difficult to meet that person, but without doing anything wrong you are, somehow or other, able to meet him. This is called *sādhu*—fair, honest, good, beautiful, decent, elegant. The opposite of this is *asādhu*—bad, ugly, dishonest, condemnable.

अथोताप्याहुः साम नो बतेति यत्साधु भवति साधु बतेत्येव तदाहुरसाम नो बतेति यदसाधु भवत्यसाधु बतेत्येव तदाहुः ॥ ३ ॥

Athotāpyāhuḥ sāma no bateti yatsādhu bhavati sādhu batetyeva tadāhurasāma no bateti yadasādhu bhavatya-sādhu batetyeva tadāhuḥ.

Atha uta api, then also; *āhuḥ,* [people] say; *naḥ bata sāma iti,* it is sāma for us; *yat sādhu bhavati,* that which is good; *sādhu bata iti eva tat āhuḥ,* the words mean that what is good has happened; *naḥ bata asāma iti,* [similarly, people say] it is asāma for us; *yat asādhu bhavati,* that which is bad; *asādhu bata iti eva tat āhuḥ,* they mean to say that what is bad has happened.

3. Then when something good happens, people say, 'It is sāma for us,' when they mean that it is good for them. But when something bad happens, people

say, 'It is asāma for us,' when they mean that it is bad for them.

The words *sādhu* and *sāma* are synonymous. When people say, 'We have had something sāma happen,' they mean that they have had something sādhu happen. Both the words mean the same thing: good, beautiful, fair, and so on.

स य एतदेवं विद्वान्साधु सामेत्युपास्तेऽभ्याशो ह यदेनं साधवो धर्मा आ च गच्छेयुरुप च नमेयुः॥४॥ इति प्रथमः खण्डः॥१॥

Sa ya etadevaṁ vidvānsādhu sāmetyupāste'bhyāśo ha yadenaṁ sādhavo dharmā ā ca gaccheyurupa ca nameyuḥ. Iti prathamaḥ khaṇḍaḥ.

Saḥ yaḥ, whoever; *etat,* this [Sāma]; *evam vidvān,* knows in this way; *sādhu sāma iti upāste,* [and] worships Sāma as 'sādhu'; *enam,* to this worshipper; *sādhavaḥ dharmāḥ,* the good qualities that are associated with a perfect [sādhu] person; *abhyāśaḥ ha,* quickly; *yat āgaccheyuḥ ca,* come; *upa ca nameyuḥ,* and are a source of satisfaction. *Iti prathamaḥ khaṇḍaḥ,* here ends the first section.

4. If a person knows the Sāma as such and worships it with the awareness of the great qualities it possesses, those qualities very soon manifest themselves in him and become a source of happiness.

First and foremost, a person should know the good qualities of the Sāma. But that is not enough. He should also worship the Sāma along with those good qualities. Then those qualities will soon manifest themselves in him, and they will eventually become a great source of satisfaction too.

Section Two

लोकेषु पञ्चविधं सामोपासीत पृथिवी हिङ्कारः। अग्निः प्रस्तावोऽन्तरिक्षमुद्गीथ आदित्यः प्रतिहारो द्यौर्निधन-मित्यूर्ध्वेषु ॥ १ ॥

Lokeṣu pañcavidhaṁ sāmopāsīta pṛthivī hiṁkāraḥ; Agniḥ prastāvo'ntarikṣamudgītha ādityaḥ pratihāro dyaurnidhanamityūrdhveṣu.

Pañcavidham sāma upāsīta, one should worship the Sāma in a fivefold manner; *lokeṣu,* as the worlds [such as the earth]; *hiṁkāraḥ,* [for instance, thinking of] the syllable hiṁ; *pṛthivī,* [as] the earth; *prastāvaḥ agniḥ,* the prastāva as fire; *udgīthaḥ antarikṣam,* the udgītha as the sky; *pratihāraḥ ādityaḥ,* the pratihāra as the sun; *nidhanam dyauḥ,* the nidhana as heaven; *ūrdhveṣu iti,* which is up above.

1. One should worship the Sāma in a fivefold manner, treating the different parts as symbols of the worlds.

For instance, treat the syllable *hiṁ* as the earth, prastāva as fire, udgītha as the sky, pratihāra as the sun, and nidhana as heaven, which is up above.

What is the meaning of *sādhu*? It may mean either dharma or Brahman. Both, however, mean the same thing, more or less. Those who worship Sāma should know that they are worshipping either of these two, and that they are worshipping something uplifting, something propitious (sādhu). When a person worships thus, he becomes what he is worshipping. He becomes a new person altogether. He is totally transformed.

But where is a person to find the Sāma? This Sāma is everywhere, in everything—in the earth, in fire, in the sky, in the sun, and in heaven. But since you cannot approach all of these, you can worship them through their symbols. In this verse, five symbols have been mentioned, which can be used for worship: hiṁkāra, prastāva, udgītha, pratihāra, and nidhana. This fivefold worship of Sāma is being recommended here for everyone.

अथावृत्तेषु द्यौर्हिङ्कार आदित्यः प्रस्तावोऽन्तरिक्ष-
मुद्गीथोऽग्निः प्रतिहारः पृथिवी निधनम् ॥ २ ॥

Athāvṛtteṣu dyaurhiṁkāra ādityaḥ prastāvo'ntarikṣa-mudgītho'gniḥ pratihāraḥ pṛthivī nidhanam.

Atha, next; *āvṛtteṣu,* from the highest [world] to the lowest; *dyauḥ hiṁkāraḥ,* the heaven is the syllable hiṁ; *ādityaḥ prastāvaḥ,* the sun is the prastāva; *antarikṣam udgīthaḥ,* the sky is the udgītha; *agniḥ pratihāraḥ,* fire is the pratihāra; *pṛthivī nidhanam,* the earth is nidhana.

2. Now, the fivefold worship from the highest world to the lowest: heaven is hiṁkāra, the sun is prastāva, the sky is udgītha, fire is pratihāra, and the earth is nidhana.

As Sāma is everywhere, it is also in the five worlds most familiar to us. Starting from the top, these five worlds are dyauḥ (heaven), āditya (the sun), antarikṣa (the sky), agni (fire), and pṛthivī (the earth). To meditate on Sāma in these worlds, then, we can use the five symbols, which are respectively: hiṁkāra, prastāva, udgītha, pratihāra, and nidhana.

When we use the term *symbol,* we understand that there is always a connection between the symbol and the thing symbolized. In this case, hiṁkāra is the first among the symbols, and heaven is the highest among the worlds. This is why hiṁkāra stands for heaven. Prastāva stands for the sun, for when the sun rises everyone gets ready to work. The word *prastāva* means 'getting ready.' The sky is *gagana.* It begins with *ga,* and the word *udgītha* also contains *ga.* So udgītha stands for *gagana,* the sky. Pratihāra stands for fire, because fire makes people 'scatter' (*pratiharim*). The earth is nidhana (extinction), for all things fall from above and finally disappear on the earth.

कल्पन्ते हास्मै लोका ऊर्ध्वाश्चावृत्ताश्च य एतदेवं विद्वाँल्लोकेषु पञ्चविधं सामोपास्ते ॥ ३ ॥ इति द्वितीयः खण्डः ॥ २ ॥

Kalpante hāsmai lokā ūrdhvāścāvṛttāśca ya etadevaṁ vidvāṁllokeṣu pañcavidhaṁ sāmopāste. Iti dvitīyaḥ khaṇḍaḥ.

Yaḥ, he who; *etat,* this [Sāma]; *evam,* as such [i.e., as good]; *vidvān,* having known; *lokeṣu,* the worlds [the earth, etc.]; *pañcavidham,* fivefold [i.e., using *hiṁ* and the other four symbols]; *sāma upāste,* worships the Sāma; *ūrdhvāḥ ca,* going upwards; *āvṛttāḥ ca,* and coming downwards; *lokāḥ ha asmai kalpante,* the worlds are there for him to enjoy. *Iti dvitīyaḥ khaṇḍaḥ,* here ends the second section.

3. He who worships Sāma with the above knowledge, and worships it in the fivefold manner as described, has all these worlds, from the lowest to the highest and from the highest to the lowest, for his enjoyment.

What benefit do you derive from worshipping Sāma in the worlds? The benefit is that you have all the five worlds—from the lowest to the highest and from the highest to the lowest—for your enjoyment. This is because you know Sāma is the essence of everything in these worlds.

Section Three

वृष्टौ पञ्चविधं सामोपासीत पुरोवातो हिङ्कारो मेघो जायते स प्रस्तावो वर्षति स उद्गीथो विद्योतते स्तनयति स प्रतिहारः ॥ १ ॥

Vṛṣṭau pañcavidhaṁ sāmopāsīta purovāto hiṁkāro megho jāyate sa prastāvo varṣati sa udgītho vidyotate stanayati sa pratihāraḥ.

Vṛṣṭau, in the rain; *pañcavidham sāma upāsīta,* one can perform the fivefold Sāma worship; *purovātaḥ,* the wind that starts before the rainfall; *hiṁkāraḥ,* is hiṁkāra; *meghaḥ jāyate,* the clouds that gather; *saḥ prastāvaḥ,* that is the prastāva; *varṣati saḥ udgīthaḥ,* [when] the rain falls that is the udgītha; *vidyotate,* [when] the lightning flashes; *stanayati,* [and] roars; *saḥ pratihāra,* that is the pratihāra.

1. One can perform the fivefold Sāma worship during the rain. Think of the wind that comes before the rain as hiṁkāra. The clouds that gather are the prastāva, and the rain that follows is the udgītha. Then, when the lightning flashes and the thunder roars, that is pratihāra.

The syllable *hiṁ* indicates the beginning of something. When the wind starts blowing hard, we know that it will soon rain, so that is hiṁkāra. Then, when the clouds start gathering, that is the prastāva, for it means that rain is just about to start. Soon the rain follows. That is the udgītha, for the udgītha is always welcome. It is a blessing. The clouds produce lightning, and lightning is accompanied by thunder. That is the pratihāra, for the pratihāra is that which 'scatters,' or 'spreads out,' or is 'extensive.'

उद्गृह्णाति तन्निधनं वर्षति हास्मै वर्षयति ह य एतदेवं विद्वान्वृष्टौ पञ्चविधं सामोपास्ते॥ २ ॥ इति तृतीयः खण्डः॥ ३ ॥

Udgṛhṇāti tannidhanaṁ varṣati hāsmai varṣayati ha ya etadevaṁ vidvānvṛṣṭau pañcavidhaṁ sāmopāste. Iti tṛtīyaḥ khaṇḍaḥ.

Udgṛhṇāti tat nidhanam, the end of the rainfall is the nidhana [literally, 'the end']; *varṣati,* it pours; *ha asmai,* for him [i.e., for the worshipper]; *varṣayati,* he causes rain to fall; *ha yaḥ etat evam vidvān,* he who, knowing all this as such; *vṛṣṭau,* in the rain; *pañcavidham sāma upāste,* performs the fivefold Sāma worship. *Iti tṛtīyaḥ khaṇḍaḥ,* here ends the third section.

2. When the rain stops, that is the nidhana. If a person performs the fivefold Sāma worship, keeping all this in mind, clouds favour him with rain as

he likes when the rain is due, and they may do him this favour even when rain is not due.

Section Four

सर्वास्वप्सु पञ्चविधं सामोपासीत मेघो यत्संप्लवते स हिङ्कारो यद्वर्षति स प्रस्तावो याः प्राच्यः स्यन्दन्ते स उद्गीथो याः प्रतीच्यः स प्रतिहारः समुद्रो निधनम् ॥ १ ॥

Sarvāsvapsu pañcavidhaṁ sāmopāsīta megho yatsaṁplavate sa hiṁkāro yadvarṣati sa prastāvo yāḥ prācyaḥ syandante sa udgītho yāḥ pratīcyaḥ sa pratihāraḥ samudro nidhanam.

Sarvāsu apsu, in all kinds of water; *pañcavidham sāma upāsīta,* a person should perform the fivefold Sāma worship; *meghaḥ yat saṁplavate,* the clouds which join together and consolidate; *saḥ hiṁkāraḥ,* that is hiṁkāra; *yat varṣati,* that which pours rain; *saḥ prastāvaḥ,* that is the prastāva; *yāḥ prācyaḥ syandante,* that [water, or river] which goes eastward; *saḥ udgīthaḥ,* that is the udgītha; *yāḥ pratīcyaḥ,* that which goes westward; *saḥ pratihāraḥ,* that is the pratihāra; *samudraḥ nidhanam,* the sea is the nidhana.

1. One can perform the fivefold Sāma worship in all kinds of water. The coming together of scattered clouds is hiṁkāra. That which pours forth rain is

the prastāva. The udgītha is that [river] running eastward, and that which runs westward is the pratihāra. The sea is the nidhana.

The fivefold Sāma worship can be performed in all forms of water. For instance, when clouds come together to produce rain, that can be thought of as hiṁkāra, because the syllable *hiṁ* marks the beginning. And when rain starts falling, that is thought of as the prastāva, because the rain is 'ready' to scatter in all directions. (This 'readiness' is prastāva.) The water, or river, that flows eastward (the Ganges, for instance) is called the udgītha, because both represent excellence. The water flowing westward (pratīcya) is the pratihāra, because of the prefix *prati* being common to both. The sea is the nidhana, because when the water flows into the sea it loses its separate identity, which is 'death' (nidhana).

न हाप्सु प्रैत्यप्सुमान्भवति य एतदेवं विद्वान्सर्वास्वप्सु पञ्चविधं सामोपास्ते ॥ २ ॥ इति चतुर्थः खण्डः ॥ ४ ॥

Na hāpsu praityapsumānbhavati ya etadevaṁ vidvān-sarvāsvapsu pañcavidhaṁ sāmopāste. Iti caturthaḥ khaṇḍaḥ.

Yaḥ, he who; *evam,* as mentioned; *etat,* this [Sāma]; *vidvān,* having known; *sarvāsu apsu,* in all forms of water; *pañcavidham sāma upāste,* performs the fivefold worship of Sāma; [*sah,* that worshipper]; *apsu,* in water; *na ha praiti,* does not die [unless he wants to]; *apsumān bhavati,* he has much water at his disposal. *Iti caturthaḥ khaṇḍaḥ,* here ends the fourth section.

2. He who performs the fivefold Sāma worship in all forms of water, knowing it thus, will never be drowned in water unless he wishes to be, and he will have as much water as he wants.

A person who performs this Sāma worship, taking water as the object of worship, will never be drowned unless he himself seeks his death that way. Also, he may be so lucky about water that he will even get it in a desert.

Section Five

ऋतुषु पञ्चविधं सामोपासीत वसन्तो हिङ्कारो ग्रीष्मः प्रस्तावो वर्षा उद्गीथः शरत्प्रतिहारो हेमन्तो निधनम् ॥ १ ॥

Ṛtuṣu pañcavidhaṁ sāmopāsīta vasanto hiṁkāro grīṣmaḥ prastāvo varṣā udgīthaḥ śaratpratihāro hemanto nidhanam.

Ṛtuṣu, in the seasons [spring, etc.]; *pañcavidham sāma upāsīta,* one should perform the fivefold Sāma worship; *vasantaḥ hiṁkāraḥ,* spring is hiṁkāra; *grīṣmaḥ prastāvaḥ,* summer is the prastāva; *varṣāḥ udgīthaḥ,* the rainy season is the udgītha; *śarat pratihāraḥ,* autumn is the pratihāra; *hemantah nidhanam,* winter is the nidhana.

1. One can apply the same fivefold Sāma worship formula to the seasons. Treat spring as hiṁkāra, summer as the prastāva, the rainy season as the udgītha, autumn as the pratihāra, and winter as the nidhana.

Spring is the first among the seasons, just as hiṁkāra is the first among the Sāma stobhas. Summer is the prastāva, because in summer people 'get ready' to harvest. Then, the rainy season is very important for crops, just as the udgītha is important. Autumn is thought of as pratihāra, for that is the time when the old and the sick start being 'taken away.' Finally, winter is the nidhana, for that is the time when many people die.

कल्पन्ते हास्मा ऋतव ऋतुमान्भवति य एतदेवं विद्वानृतुषु पञ्चविधं सामोपास्ते॥ २॥ इति पञ्चमः खण्डः॥ ५॥

Kalpante hāsmā ṛtava ṛtumānbhavati ya etadevaṁ vidvānṛtuṣu pañcavidhaṁ sāmopāste. Iti pañcamaḥ khaṇḍaḥ.

Yaḥ, he who; *etat evam vidvān,* having known this [Sāma] as above; *ṛtuṣu,* in the seasons; *pañcavi-*

dham sāma upāste, performs this fivefold Sāma worship; *asmai,* to him; *ṛtavaḥ kalpante,* the seasons come for his enjoyment; *ha ṛtumān bhavati,* and he also gets the pleasant things of those seasons for his enjoyment. *Iti pañcamaḥ khaṇḍaḥ,* here ends the fifth section.

2. To the person who knows this principle of the fivefold Sāma worship and applies it to the seasons thus, the seasons become a source of enjoyment, and the best things that each of them has to offer present themselves to him.

The change of seasons does not bother such a worshipper. Each of them is pleasant to him, and the best things that each of them has are easily available to him.

Section Six

पशुषु पञ्चविधं सामोपासीताजा हिङ्कारोऽवयः प्रस्तावो गाव उद्गीथोऽश्वाः प्रतिहारः पुरुषो निधनम् ॥ १ ॥

Paśuṣu pañcavidhaṁ sāmopāsītājā hiṁkāro'vayaḥ prastāvo gāva udgītho'śvāḥ pratihāraḥ puruṣo nidhanam.

Paśuṣu, in animals; *pañcavidham sāma upāsīta,* one can perform the fivefold Sāma worship; *ajāḥ,* goats; *hiṁkāraḥ,* are the syllable hiṁ; *avayaḥ prastāvaḥ,* sheep are the prastāva; *gāvaḥ udgīthaḥ,* cows are the udgītha; *aśvāḥ pratihāraḥ,* horses are the pratihāra; *puruṣaḥ nidhanam,* a human being is the nidhana.

1. This is how a person can perform the fivefold Sāma worship in animals. Think of goats as himkāra, sheep as the prastāva, cows as the udgītha, horses as the pratihāra, and human beings as the nidhana.

Goats are the most common of these animals, and they are also the most widely used in sacrifices. This is why they are given the first place as himkāra. *Ajā,* goats, and *avi,* sheep, are often seen together, and they are very similar. So also, himkāra and the prastāva are often together. This is why *avi,* sheep, are said to be the prastāva. Cows are the udgītha because they are superior to other animals, as the udgītha is superior. Then horses 'carry' (*pratiharaṇa*) people, so they are the pratihāra. And as animals 'depend' entirely upon human beings, so human beings are their nidhana (here, nidhana means 'support').

भवन्ति हास्य पशवः पशुमान्भवति य एतदेवं विद्वान्पशुषु पञ्चविधं सामोपास्ते ॥ २ ॥ इति षष्ठः खण्डः ॥ ६ ॥

Bhavanti hāsya paśavaḥ paśumānbhavati ya etadevaṁ vidvānpaśuṣu pañcavidhaṁ sāmopāste. Iti ṣaṣṭhaḥ khaṇḍaḥ.

Yaḥ, he who; *etat evam vidvān,* having known this [Sāma] in this way; *paśuṣu pañcavidham sāma upāste,* performs the fivefold Sāma worship in animals; *asya paśavaḥ bhavanti ha,* he has many animals [for his enjoyment]; *paśumān bhavati,* he acquires a large number of animals [for his personal wealth]. *Iti ṣaṣṭhaḥ khaṇḍaḥ,* here ends the sixth section.

2. He who performs the fivefold Sāma worship in animals, knowing it in this way, gets many animals for his enjoyment, and he also has a large number of animals as his personal wealth.

Section Seven

प्राणेषु पञ्चविधं परोवरीयः सामोपासीत प्राणो हिङ्कारो वाक्प्रस्तावश्चक्षुरुद्गीथः श्रोत्रं प्रतिहारो मनो निधनं परोवरीयांसि वा एतानि॥ १॥

Prāṇeṣu pañcavidhaṁ parovarīyaḥ sāmopāsīta prāṇo hiṁkāro vākprastāvaścakṣurudgīthaḥ śrotraṁ pratihāro mano nidhanaṁ parovarīyāṁsi vā etāni.

Prāṇeṣu pañcavidham sāma upāsīta, one should perform the fivefold worship of Sāma in all forms of prāṇa, the vital breath [or, the organs]; *parovarīyaḥ,* in an increasingly better way; *prāṇaḥ hiṁkāraḥ,* prāṇa [or, the organ of smell] is hiṁkāra; *vāk prastāvaḥ,* the organ of speech is the prastāva; *cakṣuḥ udgīthaḥ,* the eyes are the udgītha; *śrotram pratihāraḥ,* the ears are the pratihāra; *manaḥ nidhanam,* the mind is the nidhana; *etāni parovarīyāṁsi vai,* all these should be worshipped, each more than the one before.

1. One should perform the fivefold worship of Sāma in the organs in an increasingly higher way. The organ of smell is hiṁkāra, the organ of speech is the prastāva, the eyes are the udgītha, the ears are the pratihāra, and the mind is the nidhana. These organs should be worshipped, each with greater respect than the previous one.

The first prāṇa is the organ of smelling. This may be regarded as hiṁkāra. Then the organ of speech may be regarded as the prastāva, for through speech we propose (*prastāva*) to do something. The organ of speech is superior to the organ of smelling because we express our thoughts through speech.

The eyes are better than the organ of speech, because through the eyes we can express even more than what we can through speech, so the eyes are the udgītha. The ears are the pratihāra, and they are superior to the eyes because the ears can hear more than the eyes can see.

The mind is the nidhana, and it is superior to all other organs. Whatever the other organs collect is all stored in the mind. Also the mind can grasp things that no other organ can perceive.

परोवरीयो हास्य भवति परोवरीयसो ह लोकाञ्जयति य एतदेवं विद्वान् प्राणेषु पञ्चविधं परोवरीयः सामोपास्त इति तु पञ्चविधस्य॥ २॥ इति सप्तमः खण्डः॥ ७॥

Parovarīyo hāsya bhavati parovarīyaso ha lokāñjayati ya etadevaṁ vidvān prāṇeṣu pañcavidhaṁ parovarīyaḥ sāmopāsta iti tu pañcavidhasya. Iti saptamaḥ khaṇḍaḥ.

Yaḥ, he who; *etat evam vidvān,* having known this thus; *prāṇeṣu,* in the organs; *pañcavidham sāma upāste,* performs the fivefold Sāma worship; *parovarīyaḥ,* in an increasingly higher order; *asya,* his [life]; *parovarīyaḥ ha bhavati,* becomes increasingly more excellent; *parovarīyasaḥ ha lokān jayati,* he also attains increasingly higher worlds; *iti tu pañcavidhasya,* this is the benefit of the fivefold [Sāma worship]. *Iti saptamaḥ khaṇḍaḥ,* here ends the seventh section.

2. When a person knows the fivefold Sāma worship and performs it in the organs, paying to each of the organs more respect than to the last, his life becomes more and more excellent, and he also attains better and better worlds.

Here much attention has been given to the fivefold Sāma worship. This is only to prepare the worshipper for the next step, in which he will be asked to perform the sevenfold Sāma worship. It would be quite all right, however, if he bypasses the fivefold worship and goes straight to the sevenfold worship.

Section Eight

अथ सप्तविधस्य वाचि सप्तविधं सामोपासीत यत्किंच वाचो हुमिति स हिङ्कारो यत्प्रेति स प्रस्तावो यदेति स आदिः ॥ १ ॥

Atha saptavidhasya vāci saptavidhaṁ sāmopāsīta yatkiṁca vāco humiti sa hiṁkāro yatpreti sa prastāvo yadeti sa ādiḥ.

Atha, next; *saptavidhasya,* [a discussion] on the sevenfold [Sāma worship]; *saptavidham sāma upāsīta,* one should perform the sevenfold worship of Sāma; *vāci,* in speech; *yat kiṁca vācaḥ huṁ iti,* in whatever speech occurs the syllable 'huṁ'; *saḥ hiṁkāraḥ,* that is the syllable 'hiṁ'; *yat pra iti,* where the syllable 'pra' occurs; *saḥ prastāvaḥ,* that is the prasṭāva; *yat ā iti,* where 'ā' occurs; *saḥ ādiḥ,* that is to be taken for ādi [the beginning].

1. Now begins a discussion on the sevenfold Sāma worship. One can perform this sevenfold Sāma worship in speech. Wherever the syllable *huṁ* occurs in speech, that is hiṁkāra. Similarly, wherever the syllable *pra* occurs, that is to be taken for the prastāva. And wherever *ā* occurs, that is *ādi* [the beginning].

The fivefold Sāma worship has been discussed. Now

a more comprehensive Sāma worship is being taken up—the sevenfold worship.

The first meditation is on speech. Sometimes you may come across the sound *huṁ* in speech. This sound is to be thought of as hiṁkāra, because the letter *h* is common in both. Then, when you come across the sound *pra,* that is to be thought of as the prastāva.

The sound *ā* in speech is to be thought of as *ādi.* But what is *ādi*? *Ādi* is that with which you begin something. It is Om, for everything in the Vedas starts with Om.

यदुदिति स उद्गीथो यत्प्रतीति स प्रतिहारो यदुपेति स उपद्रवो यन्नीति तन्निधनम्॥ २॥

Yaduditi sa udgītho yatpratīti sa pratihāro yadupeti sa upadravo yannīti tannidhanam.

Yat ut iti, where there is the sound 'ut'; *saḥ udgīthaḥ,* that is the udgītha; *yat prati iti,* where there is the sound 'prati'; *saḥ pratihāraḥ,* that is the pratihāra; *yat upa iti,* where there is the sound 'upa'; *saḥ upadravaḥ,* that is the upadrava [upadrava is anything in praise of the Sāma]; *yat ni iti,* where there is the syllable 'ni'; *tat nidhanam,* that is the nidhana.

2. Wherever the syllable *ut* occurs, that is the udgītha. Where there is *prati,* that is the pratihāra. Where you find *upa,* that is the upadrava. And where you find *ni,* that is the nidhana.

दुग्धेऽस्मै वाग्दोहं यो वाचो दोहोऽन्नवानन्नादो भवति य एतदेवं विद्वान्वाचि सप्तविधं सामोपास्ते॥ ३ ॥ इत्यष्टमः खण्डः ॥ ८ ॥

Dugdhe'smai vāgdohaṁ yo vāco doho'nnavānannādo bhavati ya etadevaṁ vidvānvāci saptavidhaṁ sāmopāste. Ityaṣṭamaḥ khaṇḍaḥ.

Yaḥ, the person who; *etat evam vidvān,* having known this [about the Sāma]; *vāci,* in speech; *saptavidham sāma upāste,* performs the sevenfold Sāma worship; *asmai,* to him [i.e., to the worshipper]; *vāk,* speech; *doham,* milk [i.e., a good, precious gift]; *yaḥ vācaḥ dohaḥ,* which is the essence of the words; *dugdhe,* presents; *annavān annādaḥ bhavati,* he has plenty of food and he eats it [thereby becoming radiant]. *Iti aṣṭamaḥ khaṇḍaḥ,* here ends the eighth section.

3. He who knows Sāma in this way, and performs the sevenfold Sāma worship in speech, gets from speech whatever good things it has to offer. He also gets plenty of food to eat, and he eats that food [and thereby looks radiant in health].

Section Nine

अथ खल्वमुमादित्यं सप्तविधं सामोपासीत सर्वदा समस्तेन साम मां प्रति मां प्रतीति सर्वेण समस्तेन साम ॥ १ ॥

Atha khalvamumādityaṁ saptavidhaṁ sāmopāsīta sarvadā samastena sāma māṁ prati māṁ pratīti sarveṇa samastena sāma.

Atha, next; *khalu,* for certain; *amum ādityam,* the sun over there; *saptavidham sāma upāsīta,* worship as the sevenfold Sāma; *sarvadā samaḥ,* [the sun is] always the same; *tena,* therefore; *sāma,* [the sun is] Sāma; *mām prati mām prati,* [for instance, 'It is looking] at me, [it is looking] at me'; *iti,* in this way [it makes everyone think]; *sarveṇa samaḥ,* it is the same to all; *tena,* for this reason; *sāma,* [the sun is called] Sāma.

1. Next, without fail, worship the sevenfold Sāma in the sun. The sun is the Sāma because it is always the same. Again, the sun makes each of us think, 'It is looking at me. It is looking at me.' Because it is the same to all, it is called *Sāma.*

The question is, how can the sun be identified with the Sāma? The sun is always the same [i.e., *sama*], for it never changes. This is where the sun and the Sāma are the same. Again, when we look at the sun, we all think it is turned towards us. Similarly, the Sāma is also the same for everyone.

तस्मिन्निमानि सर्वाणि भूतान्यन्वायत्तानीति विद्यात्तस्य यत्पुरोदयात्स हिङ्कारस्तदस्य पशवोऽन्वायत्तास्तस्मात्ते हिं कुर्वन्ति हिङ्कारभाजिनो ह्येतस्य साम्नः ॥ २ ॥

Tasminnimāni sarvāṇi bhūtānyanvāyattānīti vidyāttasya yatpurodayātsa hiṁkārastadasya paśavo'nvāyattāstasmātte hiṁ kurvanti hiṁkārabhājino hyetasya sāmnaḥ.

Tasmin, on that [i.e., the sun]; *imāni sarvāṇi bhūtāni,* all these beings; *anvāyattāni,* are dependent; *iti vidyāt,* one should know this; *tasya,* of that [sun]; *yat,* the way [it looks then]; *purodayāt,* before it rises; *saḥ,* that [form]; *hiṁkāraḥ,* is hiṁkāra; *paśavaḥ,* the animals; *tat asya anvāyattāḥ,* are dependent on that [form] of it [i.e., of the sun as Sāma]; *tasmāt,* this is why; *te,* they; *hiṁ kurvanti,* make the sound hiṁ; *hiṁkārabhājinaḥ hi etasya sāmnaḥ,* they share in the hiṁkāra of the Sāma.

2. One should know that all beings that exist are dependent on the sun. The sun has a distinctive look before it rises, and that look is its hiṁkāra. The animals, who are dependent on the sun, also have their share in this hiṁkāra. That is why they make the sound *hiṁ.*

Animals are all dependent on the sun. Without the sun, their life would be impossible.

As the sun rises, it has a very pleasant and favourable look. This is called hiṁkāra. It is an expression of love and adoration for the Sāma. The animals are devoted to this hiṁkāra, for they also make the sound *hiṁ* as the sun rises. This is how they pay their tribute to the hiṁkāra of the Sāma.

अथ यत्प्रथमोदिते स प्रस्तावस्तदस्य मनुष्या अन्वायत्तास्तस्मात्ते प्रस्तुतिकामाः प्रशंसाकामाः प्रस्ताव-भाजिनो ह्येतस्य साम्नः॥ ३ ॥

Atha yatprathamodite sa prastāvastadasya manuṣyā anvāyattāstasmātte prastutikāmāḥ praśaṁsākāmāḥ prastāvabhājino hyetasya sāmnaḥ.

Atha, next; *yat prathamodite* [i.e., *prathama* + *udite*], that [form] which [the sun has] when it first rises; *saḥ prastāvaḥ,* that is the prastāva; *manuṣyāḥ,* all human beings; *tat asya anvāyattāḥ,* are charmed by that [form] of it [i.e:, of the sun, which is the Sāma]; *tasmāt,* this is why; *te,* they; *prastutikāmāḥ,* wanting praise; *praśaṁsākāmāḥ,* wanting adoration; *prastāvabhājinaḥ hi etasya sāmnaḥ,* they join in the prastāva of the Sāma.

3. Next, the form that the sun has shortly after it rises is the prastāva. Human beings are charmed

by that form. Because they join in the praise and adoration of the prastāva, they seek adoration and praise for themselves.

The beauty that the sun has as it rises in the morning is the Sāma prastāva addressed to the sun god (Āditya). Human beings are under the spell of this beauty. And as they have the habit of praising and adoring the prastāva of the Sāma, they also desire praise and adoration for themselves. Praise means the good words you say about a person in his presence, and adoration means the good thoughts you cherish in your mind about that person.

अथ यत्सङ्गववेलायां स आदिस्तदस्य वयांस्य-
न्वायत्तानि तस्मात्तान्यन्तरिक्षेऽनारम्बणान्यादायात्मानं परि-
पतन्त्यादिभाजीनि ह्येतस्य साम्नः ॥ ४ ॥

Atha yatsaṅgavavelāyāṁ sa ādistadasya vayāṁsyanvā-
yattāni tasmāttānyantarikṣe'nārambaṇānyādāyātmānaṁ
paripatantyādibhājīni hyetasya sāmnaḥ.

Atha, next; *yat,* that; *saṅgavavelāyām,* in the morning [i.e., after sunrise, when the sunlight has spread far and wide]; *saḥ ādiḥ,* that is the ādi [of the Sāma worship]; *vayāṁsi,* birds; *tat asya,* that form of the sun [at that time]; *anvāyattāni,* makes them feel secure; *tasmāt,* this is why; *tāni,* they [the birds]; *anārambaṇāni,* without any support; *ātmānam,* their own bodies; *ādāya,* carry; *antarikṣe,* in the sky; *paripatanti,* travel around; *hi,* for this reason; *etasya sāmnaḥ ādibhājīni,* they join in singing the ādi of the Sāma.

4. Next, when the sunrays spread all over a short while after sunrise, that form of the sun is the ādi of the Sāma. This form is connected with the birds. They somehow or other feel they have a safe shelter then, and that is why they are able to fly freely about in the sky without any support. They also behave as if they are joining in the ādi offered to the Sāma.

The sight of the sun after sunrise fascinates the birds. The form of the sun at this time is the ādi (or Om) of the Sāma, and the birds feel they are a part of this ādi. They feel secure. Though they have no support, they are able to fly about in the sky freely. It is as if they are joining in the ādi hymn offered to the Sāma.

As the birds fly, they depend on their own 'self' (ātman). Because the words *ātman* and *ādi* have the common *ā,* the birds feel drawn towards the ādi.

अथ यत्सम्प्रति मध्यन्दिने स उद्गीथस्तदस्य देवा अन्वायत्तास्तस्मात्ते सत्तमाः प्राजापत्यानामुद्गीथभाजिनो ह्येतस्य साम्नः ॥ ५ ॥

Atha yatsamprati madhyandine sa udgīthastadasya

devā anvāyattāstasmātte sattamāḥ prājāpatyānāmud-gīthabhājino hyetasya sāmnaḥ.

Atha, next; *yat,* that; *samprati madhyandine,* precisely at noon; *saḥ udgīthaḥ,* that [form of the sun] is the udgītha; *devāḥ,* the gods and goddesses; *tat asya,* that form of the sun [at that time]; *anvāyattāni,* are part of; *tasmāt,* therefore; *prājāpatyānām,* among all of Prajāpati's children; *te,* they [the gods and goddesses]; *sattamāḥ,* are deemed the best; *hi,* because; *etasya sāmnaḥ udgīthabhājinaḥ,* they join in the udgītha of the Sāma.

5. Next, that form of the sun which it has exactly at noon is the udgītha. That form is connected with the gods and goddesses. Therefore, among all of Prajāpati's children, the gods and goddesses are considered to be the best, because they take part in singing the udgītha of the Sāma.

At midday the sun is at its brightest, and its form suggests that it is offering an udgītha. The gods and goddesses are devoted to the sun at this time, so they join in the offering of the udgītha. This is why they are the dearest to Prajāpati of all his children.

अथ यदूर्ध्वं मध्यन्दिनात्प्रागपराह्णात्स प्रतिहारस्तदस्य गर्भा अन्वायत्तास्तस्मात्ते प्रतिहृता नावपद्यन्ते प्रतिहार-भाजिनो ह्येतस्य साम्नः॥ ६ ॥

Atha yadūrdhvaṁ madhyandinātprāgaparāhṇātsa pratihārastadasya garbhā anvāyattāstasmātte pratihṛtā nāvapadyante pratihārabhājino hyetasya sāmnaḥ.

Atha, next; *yat,* that; *ūrdhvam madhyandināt,* after midday; *prāk aparāhṇāt,* before afternoon; *saḥ pratihāra,* that is the pratihāra; *garbhāḥ,* the foetuses in the womb; *tat asya,* that [form] of [the sun]; *anvāyattāḥ,* are attached to; *tasmāt,* that is why; *te,* those [foetuses]; *pratihṛtāḥ,* are held up; *na avapadyante,* [and] do not drop down; *hi,* for that reason; *etasya sāmnaḥ pratihārabhājinaḥ,* they are entitled to share in the pratihāra of the Sāma.

6. Next, between the noon and the afternoon, the sight the sun presents is that of the pratihāra. The foetuses in the wombs are attached to this pratihāra. This is why they are held up and do not drop down, and why they are entitled to take part in the pratihāra addressed to the Sāma.

अथ यदूर्ध्वमपराह्णात्प्रागस्तमयात्स उपद्रवस्तदस्यारण्या अन्वायत्तास्तस्मात्ते पुरुषं दृष्ट्वा कक्षंश्वभ्रमित्युपद्रवन्ति उपद्रवभाजिनो ह्येतस्य साम्नः ॥ ७ ॥

Atha yadūrdhvamaparāhṇātprāgastamayātsa upadravastadasyāraṇyā anvāyattāstasmātte puruṣaṁ dṛṣṭvā kakṣaṁśvabhramityupadravanti upadravabhājino hyetasya sāmnaḥ.

Atha, next; *yat,* that; *ūrdhvam aparāhṇāt,* as the afternoon begins; *prāk astamayāt,* before sunset; *saḥ upadravaḥ,* that is the upadrava; *āraṇyāḥ,* wild animals; *tat asya,* that [form] of [the sun]; *anvāyattāḥ,* are attached to; *tasmāt,* that is why; *te,* those [wild animals]; *puruṣam,* a human being; *dṛṣṭvā,* seeing; *kakṣam,* into their lair [or, the forest]; *śvabhram,* a hole; *upadravanti,* quickly run to; *hi,* for this reason; *etasya sāmnaḥ upadravabhājinaḥ,* they join in the upadrava offered to the Sāma.

7. Next, the form that the sun has between the afternoon and sunset is called the upadrava. Wild animals are fond of this form, for when the sun is in that position, the wild animals are able to scurry away into the forest or into their holes if they see a human being. These animals are also able to take part in the upadrava to the Sāma.

In the later part of the afternoon, the animals are able to find food to sustain themselves, and they can also watch out for human beings. If they see one, they hurry back to the forest or to any place where they feel safe. Their going away in haste (*upadruta*) suggests that they worship the upadrava (i.e., 'going back') of the Sāma.

अथ यत्प्रथमास्तमिते तन्निधनं तदस्य पितरोऽन्वायत्ता-
स्तस्मात्तान्निदधति निधनभाजिनो ह्येतस्य साम्न एवं

खल्वमुमादित्यं सप्तविधं सामोपास्ते ॥ ८ ॥ इति नवमः खण्डः ॥ ९ ॥

Atha yatprathamāstamite tannidhanaṁ tadasya pitaro-'nvāyattāstasmāttānnidadhati nidhanabhājino hyetasya sāmna evaṁ khalvamumādityaṁ saptavidhaṁ sāmo-pāste. Iti navamaḥ khaṇḍaḥ.

Atha, next; *yat,* that; *prathamāstamite* [i.e., *prathama + astamite*], just as the sun sets; *tat nidhanam,* that is the nidhana; *pitaraḥ,* the ancestors; *tat asya,* that [form] of [the sun]; *anvāyattāḥ,* are attached to; *tasmāt,* therefore; *tān,* them; *nidadhati,* one places on straws [or, one places offerings to the ancestors on straws while performing special rites in their honour]; *hi,* for this reason; *etasya sāmnaḥ nidhanabhājinaḥ,* they participate in the nidhana in honour of the Sāma; *khalu amum ādityam saptavidham sāma upāste,* this is how the sun is offered the sevenfold Sāma worship. *Iti navamaḥ khaṇḍaḥ,* here ends the ninth section.

8. Next, the nidhana is the form of the sun as it sets. The ancestors love this form of the sun, and this is why, as the sun sets, offerings are made to them [or, are placed on straws in honour of them at the time the *śrāddha* rites are performed]. For this reason, the ancestors participate in the nidhana in honour of the Sāma. This is how the sun is offered the sevenfold Sāma worship.

Because the ancestors love the form of the sun as it sets, people honour them at that time of the day by placing offerings to them on straw. And while doing so, they sing the nidhana hymn of the Sāma.

If a person performs the sevenfold Sāma worship with the feeling that he is worshipping the sun this way, he becomes one with the sun.

Section Ten

अथ खल्वात्मसम्मितमतिमृत्यु सप्तविधं सामोपासीत हिङ्कार इति त्र्यक्षरं प्रस्ताव इति त्र्यक्षरं तत्समम् ॥ १ ॥

Atha khalvātmasammitamatimṛtyu saptavidhaṁ sāmopāsīta hiṁkāra iti tryakṣaraṁ prastāva iti tryakṣaraṁ tatsamam.

Atha, next [i.e., after worshipping the sun as the Sāma]; *khalu,* for certain; *ātma-sammitam,* with an equal number of parts [i.e., syllables]; *atimṛtyu,* that which overcomes death; *saptavidham sāma upāsīta,* one should perform the sevenfold Sāma worship; *hiṁkāraḥ,* the word hiṁkāra; *iti tryakṣaram,* is three-syllabled; *prastāvaḥ,* the word prastāva; *iti tryakṣaram,* is [also] three-syllabled; *tat samam,* therefore they [hiṁkāra and prastāva] are equal.

1. After worshipping the Sāma as the sun, one should perform the sevenfold Sāma worship by using words of the same number of syllables. By this one overcomes death. The word *hiṁkāra* has three syllables; so also,

the word *prastāva* has three syllables. The two words are therefore the same.

Śaṅkara says that the sun divides time into units. It therefore distinguishes between life and death, and it is death itself. Is there any way of overcoming death? Yes, it can be overcome by worshipping the Sāma, and that is why these instructions are being given here.

आदिरिति द्व्यक्षरं प्रतिहार इति चतुरक्षरं तत इहैकं तत्समम् ॥ २ ॥

Ādiriti dvyakṣaraṁ pratihāra iti caturakṣaraṁ tata ihaikaṁ tatsamam.

Ādiḥ iti dvi-akṣaram, the word ādi is two-syllabled; *pratihāraḥ iti catuḥ-akṣaram,* the word pratihāra is four-syllabled; *tataḥ,* from that [i.e., from the word pratihāra]; *ekam,* [take away] one [syllable]; *iha,* [and add] here [to the word ādi]; *tat samam,* that makes them equal [both three-syllabled].

2. The word *ādi* is two-syllabled, and the word *pratihāra* is four-syllabled. If you take away one syllable from *pratihāra* and add it to *ādi,* then they will have the same number of syllables.

Om is the ādi of the sevenfold Sāma. It is ādi (the beginning) because a person begins singing the Sāma with Om.

उद्गीथ इति त्र्यक्षरमुपद्रव इति चतुरक्षरं त्रिभिस्त्रिभिः समं भवत्यक्षरमतिशिष्यते त्र्यक्षरं तत्समम्॥ ३ ॥

Udgītha iti tryakṣaramupadrava iti caturakṣaraṁ tribhistribhiḥ samaṁ bhavatyakṣaramatiśiṣyate tryakṣaraṁ tatsamam.

Udgīthaḥ iti tri-akṣaram, the word udgītha is three-syllabled; *upadravaḥ iti catuḥ-akṣaram,* the word upadrava is four-syllabled; *tribhiḥ tribhiḥ samam bhavati,* if they are taken as three-syllabled they become the same; *akṣaram atiśiṣyate,* one syllable becomes superfluous; *tri-akṣaram tat samam,* taken as three-syllabled they become identical.

3. The word *udgītha* has three syllables. The word *upadrava* has four syllables. If they are taken as three-syllabled they are equal. In that case, the syllable *va* in *upadrava* becomes superfluous. They are equal so far as their three syllables are concerned.

The syllable *va,* if taken away, makes no difference when a person recites the hymn.

निधनमिति त्र्यक्षरं तत्सममेव भवति तानि ह वा एतानि द्वाविंशतिरक्षराणि॥ ४ ॥

Nidhanamiti tryakṣaraṁ tatsamameva bhavati tāni ha vā etāni dvāviṁśatirakṣarāṇi.

Nidhanam iti tri-akṣaram, the word nidhana is three-syllabled; *tat samam eva bhavati,* that makes it the same [as the other three-syllabled words forming parts of the Sāma]; *tāni ha vai etāni,* all these together constitute; *dvāviṁśatiḥ akṣarāṇi,* twenty-two syllables.

4. The word *nidhana* has three syllables. All words, having three syllables each, are the same [when used in praise of the Sāma]. All these together have twenty-two syllables.

There are seven ways of worshipping the Sāma: through hiṁkāra, prastāva, ādi, pratihāra, udgītha, upadrava, and nidhana. Taken together these words have twenty-two syllables. Taken separately each of them may be treated as three-syllabled and recited accordingly. They are therefore all equal for purposes of the Sāma worship.

एकविंशत्यादित्यमाप्नोत्येकविंशो वा इतोऽसावा-
दित्यो द्वाविंशेन परमादित्याज्जयति तन्नाकं तद्वि-
शोकम् ॥ ५ ॥

Ekaviṁśatyādityamāpnotyekaviṁśo vā ito'sāvādityo dvāviṁśena paramādityājjayati tannākaṁ tadviśokam.

Ekaviṁśatyā, by twenty-one [syllables]; *ādityam āpnoti,* one attains union with the sun [because the sun marks the end of everything, and it is therefore death]; *ekaviṁśaḥ vai,* [the sun is] the twenty-first [after the twelve months, the five seasons, and the three worlds]; *itaḥ,* from this [world]; *asau ādityaḥ,* the sun over there; *dvāviṁśena,* by [knowing] the twenty-second [syllable]; *ādityāt param jayati,* one attains the next higher world from the sun; *tat nākam,* that [place is] joyful; *tat viśokam,* that [place is] free from all suffering.

5. With the help of those twenty-one syllables, one can attain the status of the sun [which is also Death]. The sun occupies the twenty-first place after the things that come between the earth and the sun [those things being the twelve months, the five seasons, and the three worlds]. One can then go beyond the sun if one knows the twenty-second syllable. That world is full of joy and free from all sorrows.

The Upaniṣad says that if you worship Sāma with these twenty-one syllables, you attain the sun, which is the same as death. But how is the number significant? It is significant because the sun occupies the twenty-first position after the things that intervene between the earth and the sun. According to the Vedas those things are the twelve months, the five seasons, and the three worlds. But if you worship the Sāma with twenty-two syllables, you then go beyond the sun. Where? To a place called *Nāka,* where there is only happiness and no suffering.

आप्नोति हादित्यस्य जयं परो हास्यादित्यजयाज्जयो भवति य एतदेवं विद्वानात्मसम्मितमतिमृत्यु सप्तविधं सामोपास्ते सामोपास्ते॥ ६॥ इति दशमः खण्डः॥ १०॥

Āpnoti hādityasya jayaṁ paro hāsyādityajayājjayo bhavati ya etadevaṁ vidvānātmasammitamatimṛtyu saptavidhaṁ sāmopāste sāmopāste. Iti daśamaḥ khaṇḍaḥ.

Āpnoti ha ādityasya jayam, one wins the state of the sun; *paraḥ ha ādityajayāt asya jayaḥ bhavati,* one wins a world even higher than the sun; *yaḥ,* one who; *etat evam vidvān,* knows this [Sāma] thus; *ātmasammitam,* as oneself; *atimṛtyu saptavidham sāma upāste sāma upāste,* performs the deathless sevenfold Sāma worship [the repetition marks the end of the section]. *Iti daśamaḥ khaṇḍaḥ,* here ends the tenth section.

6. If a person knows all about the Sāma, and performs the sevenfold Sāma worship, treating the Sāma as himself and as something beyond death, he wins the state of the sun and then wins a place even higher than the sun.

Section Eleven

मनो हिङ्कारो वाक्प्रस्तावश्चक्षुरुद्गीथः श्रोत्रं प्रतिहारः प्राणो निधनमेतद्गायत्रं प्राणेषु प्रोतम्॥ १॥

Mano hiṁkāro vākprastāvaścakṣurudgīthaḥ śrotraṁ pratihāraḥ prāṇo nidhanametadgāyatraṁ prāṇeṣu protam.

Manaḥ hiṁkāraḥ, the mind is the hiṁkāra; *vāk prastāvaḥ,* the organ of speech is the prastāva; *cakṣuḥ udgīthaḥ,* the eyes are the udgītha; *śrotram pratihāraḥ,* the ears are the pratihāra; *prāṇaḥ nidhanam,* the vital breath is the nidhana; *etat gāyatram,* this Gāyatrī prayer; *prāṇeṣu protam,* is rooted in the vital breath.

1. The mind is hiṁkāra, the organ of speech is the prastāva, the eyes are the udgītha, the ears are the pratihāra, and the vital breath [in its fine forms] is the nidhana. The Gāyatrī prayer is controlled by the vital breath.

So long the fivefold and the sevenfold Sāma worships have been discussed, but the names of those worships have not been mentioned. *Gāyatra* is the first among them. Corresponding to the Gāyatra is the hiṁkāra, with which the worship begins. Similarly, in any act of worship, the mind may be regarded as the hiṁkāra, for it is the mind that must act first before all the other organs.

Next to the mind is the organ of speech. A person first thinks and then speaks out his intentions. The organ of speech is therefore the prastāva. The eyes are the udgītha because of their importance. The ears are the pratihāra, for you can 'turn away from' things you don't want to hear.

Prāṇa, the vital breath, is the nidhana, for when you have *suṣupti,* dreamless sleep, all the organs merge into the vital breath. The Gāyatrī is worshipped as the vital breath. This is why the Sāma called *Gāyatra* is said to be rooted in the vital breath.

स य एवमेतद्गायत्रं प्राणेषु प्रोतं वेद प्राणी भवति सर्वमायुरेति ज्योग्जीवति महान्प्रजया पशुभिर्भवति महान्कीर्त्या महामनाः स्यात्तद्व्रतम् ॥ २ ॥ इत्येकादशः खण्डः ॥ ११ ॥

Sa ya evametadgāyatraṁ prāṇeṣu protaṁ veda prāṇī bhavati sarvamāyureti jyogjīvati mahānprajayā paśubhirbhavati mahānkīrtyā mahāmanāḥ syāttadvratam. Ityekādaśaḥ khaṇḍaḥ.

Saḥ yaḥ, he who; *evam,* this way; *etat gāyatram,* this Gāyatra Sāma; *prāṇeṣu protam,* rooted in the prāṇas; *veda,* knows; *prāṇī,* with life; *bhavati,* is endowed; *sarvam āyuḥ,* the full span of life; *eti,* attains; *jyok jīvati,* a bright [life]; *mahān prajayā,* great in progeny; *paśubhiḥ,* [and] animals; *bhavati,* becomes [rich with]; *mahān kīrtyā,* with a good reputation; *mahāmanāḥ syāt,* is noble in character; *tat vratam,* that is the aim of his life. *Iti ekādaśaḥ khaṇḍaḥ,* here ends the eleventh section.

2. This Gāyatra Sāma is rooted in the prāṇas. He who knows this becomes full of vitality, has a long

life, and his life is brilliant. Also, he is fortunate in his children, and he has many domestic animals. He is one of the most famous people. To be noble-minded is the aim of his life.

Whoever knows that the Sāma named Gāyatra is based on the prāṇas is truly alive—that is, all his organs are strong and healthy and he is never physically handicapped. The full span of a person's life is said to be a hundred years. A person who worships the Sāma lives that long. And he lives a wonderful life, able to influence many people. He is respected as one of the greatest people in the world. He has many children and many domestic animals, but his sole aim in life is to have a large heart, without a trace of meanness in his mind.

Section Twelve

अभिमन्थति स हिङ्कारो धूमो जायते स प्रस्तावो ज्वलति स उद्गीथोऽङ्गारा भवन्ति स प्रतिहार उपशाम्यति तन्निधनं संशाम्यति तन्निधनमेतद्रथन्तरमग्नौ प्रोतम् ॥ १ ॥

Abhimanthati sa hiṁkāro dhūmo jāyate sa prastāvo jvalati sa udgītho'ṅgārā bhavanti sa pratihāra upaśāmyati tannidhanaṁ saṁśāmyati tannidhanametadrathantara-magnau protam.

Abhimanthati, rubbing [one piece of wood against another to produce fire]; *saḥ hiṁkāraḥ,* that is the hiṁkāra; *dhūmaḥ jāyate,* the smoke it produces; *saḥ prastāvaḥ,* that is the prastāva; *jvalati,* the flames that appear; *saḥ udgīthaḥ,* that is the udgītha; *aṅgārāḥ bhavanti,* the charcoals that result; *saḥ pratihāraḥ,* that is the pratihāra; *upaśāmyati,* when the fire begins to go out; *tat nidhanam,* that is the nidhana; *saṁśāmyati,* when the fire is completely extinguished; *tat nidhanam,* that [also] is the nidhana; *etat rathantaram,* this [Sāma] called Rathantara; *agnau protam,* is rooted in fire.

1. When one rubs two pieces of wood against each other to light a fire, that is the hiṁkāra. When it produces smoke, that is the prastāva. Then when the flame appears, that is the udgītha. The charcoals that result are the pratihāra, and when the fire begins to go out, that is the nidhana. When the flame is completely extinguished, that also is the nidhana. This Sāma called *Rathantara* is rooted in fire.

The rubbing of two pieces of wood together to produce fire is the hiṁkāra, for that is the beginning of the fire. And the smoke that results is the prastāva, for both are likely to continue. When the fire bursts into flame, that is the udgītha, because when there are flames the oblations are offered into them for the gods and goddesses. This is why this part is superior and why the flames are called the udgītha. The charcoals that are formed are called the pratihāra, for the charcoals are collected for future use. *Upaśām* means the process of subsiding—that is, the fire begins to subside but does not quite go out. Then the word *saṁśām* means 'completely extinguished.' The fire is then dead, so it is like the nidhana (death).

The Rathantara Sāma is said to be based on fire, for when fire is being produced by rubbing the two sticks, the Rathantara Sāma is recited.

स य एवमेतद्रथन्तरमग्नौ प्रोतं वेद ब्रह्मवर्चस्यन्नादो भवति सर्वमायुरेति ज्योग्जीवति महान्प्रजया पशुभिर्भवति महान्कीर्त्या न प्रत्यङ्ङग्निमाचामेन्न निष्ठीवेत्तद्व्रतम् ॥ २ ॥
इति द्वादशः खण्डः ॥ १२ ॥

Sa ya evametadrathantaramagnau protaṁ veda brahmavarcasyannādo bhavati sarvamāyureti jyogjīvati mahānprajayā paśubhirbhavati mahānkīrtyā na pratyaṅ-ṅagnimācāmenna niṣṭhīvettadvratam. Iti dvādaśaḥ khaṇ-ḍaḥ.

Saḥ yaḥ evam etat rathantaram agnau protam veda, he who knows that this Rathantara Sāma is rooted in fire; *brahmavarcasī,* acquires the glow that Vedic knowledge gives; *annādaḥ bhavati,* he enjoys eating food; *sarvam āyuḥ eti,* he lives the full span of his life; *jyok jīvati,* he lives a bright life; *mahān prajayā paśubhiḥ bhavati,* he distinguishes himself by his children and by the animal wealth he acquires; *mahān kīrtyā,* his reputation spreads far and wide; *tat vratam,* his principle is; *na pratyak agnim ācāmet,* never to eat facing fire; *na niṣṭhīvet,* [and] never to spit. *Iti dvādaśaḥ khaṇḍaḥ,* here ends the twelfth section.

2. He who knows that this Rathantara Sāma is rooted in fire, acquires the kind of glow that Vedic scholarship produces. He also enjoys eating. He lives the full span of his life, and his life is brilliant. He is well known for his children and for his animal wealth, and he commands great respect in society. His vow is that he will never eat with fire in front of him and he will never spit.

By his moral character and his scholarship in the Vedas, he acquires a radiance about him.

Section Thirteen

उपमन्त्रयते स हिङ्कारो ज्ञपयते स प्रस्तावः स्त्रिया सह शेते स उद्गीथः प्रति स्त्रीं सह शेते स प्रतिहारः कालं गच्छति तन्निधनं पारं गच्छति तन्निधनमेतद्वामदेव्यं मिथुने प्रोतम् ॥ १ ॥

स य एवमेतद्वामदेव्यं मिथुने प्रोतं वेद मिथुनीभवति मिथुनान्मिथुनात्प्रजायते सर्वमायुरेति ज्योग्जीवति महान्प्रजया पशुभिर्भवति महान्कीर्त्या न काञ्चन परिहरेत्तद्व्रतम् ॥ २ ॥ इति त्रयोदशः खण्डः ॥ १३ ॥

Upamantrayate sa hiṁkāro jñapayate sa prastāvaḥ striyā saha śete sa udgīthaḥ prati strīṁ saha śete sa pratihāraḥ kālaṁ gacchati tannidhanaṁ pāraṁ gacchati tannidhanametadvāmadevyaṁ mithune protam.

Sa ya evametadvāmadevyaṁ mithune protaṁ veda mithunībhavati mithunānmithunātprajāyate sarvamāyureti jyogjīvati mahānprajayā paśubhirbhavati mahānkīrtyā na kāñcana pariharettadvratam. Iti trayodaśaḥ khaṇḍaḥ.

[The underlying thought in these two mantras is that everything a person does is spiritual. This includes even physical experiences.]

Section Fourteen

उद्यन्हिङ्कार उदितः प्रस्तावो मध्यन्दिन उद्गीथोऽपराह्णः
प्रतिहारोऽस्तं यन्निधनमेतद्बृहदादित्ये प्रोतम् ॥ १ ॥

Udyanhiṁkāra uditaḥ prastāvo madhyandina udgītho-'parāhṇaḥ pratihāro'staṁ yannidhanametadbṛhadāditye protam.

Udyan, the rising sun; *hiṁkāraḥ,* [is] the hiṁkāra; *uditaḥ,* the sun that has already risen; *prastāvaḥ,* [is] the prastāva; *madhyandina,* the midday sun; *udgīthaḥ,* [is] the udgītha; *aparāhṇaḥ,* the afternoon sun; *pratihāraḥ,* [is] the pratihāra; *yat astam,* that which is setting; *nidhanam,* [is] the nidhana; *etat bṛhat,* this [Sāma known as] Bṛhat; *ādityе protam,* is based on the Sun.

1. The rising sun is the hiṁkāra, the sun that has already risen is the prastāva, the midday sun is the udgītha, the afternoon sun is the pratihāra, and the setting sun is the nidhana. This Sāma called *Bṛhat* is based on the sun.

The rising sun is the hiṁkāra, for that is the time when we first see the sun. When the sun has risen it is the prastāva, for that is when people start performing their daily religious rites and rituals. The midday sun is the udgītha, because that is the best time of the day. Then the afternoon sun is the pratihāra, because that is the time when cattle are driven back home. And the setting sun is the nidhana, for at night domestic animals are kept confined in their pens. This Bṛhat Sāma is based on the sun, because the sun is its presiding deity.

स य एवमेतद्बृहदादित्ये प्रोतं वेद तेजस्व्यन्नादो भवति सर्वमायुरेति ज्योग्जीवति महान्प्रजया पशुभिर्भवति महान्कीर्त्या तपन्तं न निन्देत्तद्व्रतम् ॥ २ ॥ इति चतुर्दशः खण्डः ॥ १४ ॥

Sa ya evametadbṛhadāditye protaṁ veda tejasvyannādo bhavati sarvamāyureti jyogjīvati mahānprajayā paśubhirbhavati mahānkīrtyā tapantaṁ na nindettadvratam. Iti caturdaśaḥ khaṇḍaḥ.

Saḥ yaḥ evam etat bṛhat āditye protam veda, he who knows that the Sāma called Bṛhat is rooted in the sun; *tejasvi,* is spirited; *annādaḥ bhavati,* has a great appetite; *sarvam āyuḥ eti,* lives the full span of his life; *jyok jīvati,* has a brilliant life; *mahān prajayā paśubhiḥ bhavati,* becomes famous for his children and for his animal wealth; *mahān kīrtyā,* is highly respected; *tapantam na nindet,* he never uses a bad word against the hot sun; *tat vratam,* that is his vow. *Iti caturdaśaḥ khaṇḍaḥ,* here ends the fourteenth section.

2. He who knows that the Sāma called *Bṛhat* is rooted in the sun is spirited and has a great appetite. He lives the full span of his life, has a brilliant career, and is renowned for his children and for his animal wealth. His success in life brings him much fame. The vow he observes is that he will never utter a word against the sun, which gives us heat.

Section Fifteen

अभ्राणि संप्लवन्ते स हिङ्कारो मेघो जायते स प्रस्तावो वर्षति स उद्गीथो विद्योतते स्तनयति स प्रतिहार उद्गृह्णाति तन्निधनमेतद्वैरूपं पर्जन्ये प्रोतम् ॥ १ ॥

Abhrāṇi saṁplavante sa hiṁkāro megho jāyate sa prastāvo varṣati sa udgītho vidyotate stanayati sa pratihāra udgṛhṇāti tannidhanametadvairūpaṁ parjanye protam.

Abhrāṇi, light clouds [bearing water]; *saṁplavante,* when they consolidate; *saḥ hiṁkāraḥ,* that is the hiṁkāra; *meghaḥ jāyate,* when clouds likely to pour rain appear; *saḥ prastāvaḥ,* that is the prastāva; *varṣati saḥ udgīthaḥ,* when it starts raining that is the udgītha; *vidyotate,* when lightning flashes; *stanayati,* [and] thunder roars; *saḥ pratihāraḥ,* that is the pratihāra; *ut gṛhṇāti,* when everything is over; *tat nidhanam,* that is the nidhana; *etat vairūpam,* this [Sāma called] Vairūpa; *parjanye protam,* is rooted in the clouds.

1. When light clouds consolidate, that is the hiṁkāra. When clouds likely to pour rain collect, that is the prastāva. When the rain begins, that is the udgītha. Then there are flashes of lightning and the roar of thunder. This is the pratihāra. When it all stops, that is the nidhana. This Sāma called *Vairūpa* is rooted in the clouds.

The word *abhra* means a cloud which bears *ap,* water. A cloud that pours rain is called *megha.* The English word 'cloud' is actually in Sanskrit *parjanya. Abhra, megha, parjanya*—these different names all mean cloud, but indicate the cloud in a different state. This is why the cloud is described here as *vairūpa,* with different forms.

It is the sun that produces the cloud, and this is why the Sāma is first worshipped as the sun and then as the cloud.

स य एवमेतद्वैरूपं पर्जन्ये प्रोतं वेद विरूपांश्च सुरूपांश्च पशूनवरुन्धे सर्वमायुरेति ज्योग्जीवति महान्प्रजया पशुभिर्भवति महान्कीर्त्या वर्षन्तं न निन्देत्तद्व्रतम्॥ २॥
इति पञ्चदशः खण्डः॥ १५॥

Sa ya evametadvairūpaṁ parjanye protaṁ veda virūpāṁśca surūpāṁśca paśūnavarundhe sarvamāyureti jyogjīvati mahānprajayā paśubhirbhavati mahānkīrtyā varṣantaṁ na nindettadvratam. Iti pañcadaśaḥ khaṇḍaḥ.

Saḥ yaḥ evam etat vairūpam parjanye protam veda, he who knows that this [Sāma called] Vairūpa is rooted in the clouds; *virūpān ca surūpān ca paśūn avarundhe,* he comes to possess a large variety of animals and beautiful animals also; *sarvam āyuḥ eti,* he lives the full span of his life; *jyok jīvati,* he has a brilliant life; *mahān prajayā paśubhiḥ bhavati,* he becomes famous for his children and for his animal wealth; *mahān kīrtyā,* he is renowned for his achievements; *varṣantam na nindet tat vratam,* his vow is not to criticize the clouds that pour rain. *Iti pañcadaśaḥ khaṇḍaḥ,* here ends the fifteenth section.

2. He who knows that this Sāma called *Vairūpa* has its source in the clouds comes to acquire a large variety of animals, and all beautiful animals too. He has a long and brilliant life, and his children and animals are such that he becomes famous for them. His achievements also mark him as a great person.

His vow is that he will never criticize the clouds that pour rain.

It is a characteristic of those who worship the Sāma that they never find fault with others. This is why they do not say anything bad about even the clouds that give rain.

Section Sixteen

वसन्तो हिङ्कारो ग्रीष्मः प्रस्तावो वर्षा उद्गीथः शरत्प्रतिहारो हेमन्तो निधनमेतद्वैराजमृतुषु प्रोतम् ॥ १ ॥

Vasanto hiṁkāro grīṣmaḥ prastāvo varṣā udgīthaḥ śaratpratihāro hemanto nidhanametadvairājamṛtuṣu protam.

Vasantaḥ hiṁkāraḥ, spring is the hiṁkāra; *grīṣmaḥ prastāvaḥ,* summer is the prastāva; *varṣāḥ udgīthaḥ,* the rainy season is the udgītha; *śarat pratihāraḥ,* autumn is the pratihāra; *hemantaḥ nidhanam,* winter is the nidhana; *etat vairājam,* this [Sāma called] Vairāja; *ṛtuṣu protam,* is rooted in the seasons.

1. Spring is the hiṁkāra, summer the prastāva, the rainy season the udgītha, autumn the pratihāra, and winter the nidhana. This Sāma known as *Vairāja* is rooted in the seasons.

The clouds determine the seasons. This is why the Sāma is first worshipped as the clouds and after that as the seasons.

स य एवमेतद्वैराजमृतुषु प्रोतं वेद विराजति प्रजया पशुभिर्ब्रह्मवर्चसेन सर्वमायुरेति ज्योग्जीवति महान्प्रजया पशुभिर्भवति महान्कीर्त्यर्तून्न निन्देत्तद्व्रतम् ॥ २ ॥ इति षोडशः खण्डः ॥ १६ ॥

Sa ya evametadvairājamṛtuṣu protaṁ veda virājati prajayā paśubhirbrahmavarcasena sarvamāyureti jyog-jīvati mahānprajayā paśubhirbhavati mahānkīrtyartūnna nindettadvratam. Iti ṣoḍaśaḥ khaṇḍaḥ.

Saḥ yaḥ evam etat vairājam ṛtuṣu protam veda, he who knows that this [Sāma called] Vairāja is rooted in the seasons; *virājati,* he lives; *prajayā paśubhiḥ,* surrounded by his children and animals; *brahmavarcasena,* he has the kind of radiance that is born of Vedic scholarship; *sarvam āyuḥ eti,* he lives the full span of his life; *jyok jīvati,* he lives a brilliant life; *mahān prajayā paśubhiḥ bhavati,* he is known to be great for his children and animals; *mahān kīrtyā,* he is famous for his deeds; *ṛtūn na nindet tat vratam,* his vow is that he will never criticize the seasons. *Iti ṣoḍaśaḥ khaṇḍaḥ,* here ends the sixteenth section.

2. He who knows that the Sāma called *Vairāja* is rooted in the seasons is surrounded by his children and animals and has a radiance about him which is born of Vedic scholarship. He lives a long and brilliant life, and he is considered great for his children and for his animals. He is also highly respected for his great deeds. He follows the vow of never criticizing the seasons.

The person who knows that the Vairāja Sāma is rooted in the seasons becomes like the seasons himself. Each season has a beauty of its own. Similarly, this person has within him the beauty and grandeur of the good things he possesses, such as his wealth, good children, scholarship, and character.

The rules of the Sāma forbid him from saying anything bad about the seasons, and he follows this.

Section Seventeen

पृथिवी हिङ्कारोऽन्तरिक्षं प्रस्तावो द्यौरुद्गीथो दिशः प्रतिहारः समुद्रो निधनमेताः शक्वर्यो लोकेषु प्रोताः ॥ १ ॥

Pṛthivī himkāro'ntarikṣam prastāvo dyaurudgītho diśaḥ pratihāraḥ samudro nidhanametāḥ śakvaryo lokeṣu protāḥ.

Pṛthivī himkāraḥ, the earth is the himkāra; *antarikṣam prastāvaḥ,* the space between the earth and heaven is the prastāva; *dyauḥ udgīthaḥ,* heaven is the udgītha; *diśaḥ pratihāraḥ,* the quarters are the pratihāra; *samudraḥ nidhanam,* the ocean is the nidhana; *etāḥ śakvaryaḥ lokeṣu protāḥ,* these [the Sāma called] Śakvarī are rooted in the earth and other worlds.

1. The earth is the hiṁkāra, the space between the earth and heaven is the prastāva, heaven is the udgītha, the quarters are the pratihāra, and the ocean is the nidhana. The Sāma known as *Śakvarī* is rooted in the earth and other worlds.

If the seasons come and go, as they ought to, then things on the earth and the other worlds remain in balance. This is why the Sāma is first worshipped as the seasons and then as the worlds.

But the question is: Sāma is singular. Why then has a plural word, *śakvarī,* been used here for the Sāma? Doesn't it imply that there are many Sāmas? No, the Sāma is always one and the same. There are not many Sāmas. The word *śakvarī* has a plural form, but it stands for the singular Sāma. Śaṅkara gives the example of the word *revatī,* which is similarly always used in the plural.

स य एवमेताः शक्वर्यो लोकेषु प्रोता वेद लोकी भवति सर्वमायुरेति ज्योग्जीवति महान्प्रजया पशुभिर्भवति महान्कीर्त्या लोकान्न निन्देत्तद्व्रतम् ॥ २ ॥ इति सप्तदशः खण्डः ॥ १७ ॥

Sa ya evametāḥ śakvaryo lokeṣu protā veda lokī bhavati sarvamāyureti jyogjīvati mahānprajayā paśubhirbhavati mahānkīrtyā lokānna nindettadvratam. Iti saptadaśaḥ khaṇḍaḥ.

Saḥ yaḥ evam etāḥ śakvaryaḥ lokeṣu protāḥ veda, he who knows that these [i.e., the Sāma] known as Śakvarī are rooted in the worlds; *lokī bhavati,* goes to the best world; *sarvam āyuḥ eti,* lives the full span of his life; *jyok jīvati,* has a brilliant life; *mahān prajayā paśubhiḥ bhavati,* is well known for his children and for his animal wealth; *mahān kīrtyā,* is well known for his great deeds; *lokān na nindet tat vratam,* his vow is that he will never criticize the worlds. *Iti saptadaśaḥ khaṇḍaḥ,* here ends the seventeenth section.

2. He who knows that the Sāma known as *Śakvarī* is located in the worlds goes to the best world. He also has a long and brilliant life and is well known for his children and for his animal wealth. He is considered to be a great person because of his great deeds. He takes a vow that he will never criticize the worlds.

Section Eighteen

अजा हिङ्कारोऽवयः प्रस्तावो गाव उद्गीथोऽश्वाः प्रतिहारः पुरुषो निधनमेता रेवत्यः पशुषु प्रोताः ॥ १ ॥

Ajā hiṁkāro'vayaḥ prastāvo gāva udgītho'śvāḥ pratihāraḥ puruṣo nidhanametā revatyaḥ paśuṣu protāḥ.

Ajāḥ hiṁkāraḥ, goats are the hiṁkāra; *avayaḥ prastāvaḥ,* sheep are the prastāva; *gāvaḥ udgītha,* cows are the udgītha; *aśvāḥ pratihāraḥ,* horses are the pratihāra; *puruṣaḥ nidhanam,* a human being is the nidhana; *etāḥ revatyaḥ paśuṣu protāḥ,* these [i.e., the Sāma known as] Revatī are established in animals.

1. Goats are the hiṁkāra, sheep are the prastāva, cows represent the udgītha, horses are the pratihāra, and a human being is the nidhana. The Sāma called *Revatī* is established in animals.

Animals are useful to all the worlds. That is why, after worshipping the Sāma as the worlds, the worship as animals is suggested.

As in the previous section in which the word *śakvarī* is always used in the plural (as *śakvaryaḥ*), here also, the word *revatī* is always used in the plural (*revatyaḥ*).

स य एवमेता रेवत्यः पशुषु प्रोता वेद पशुमान्भवति सर्वमायुरेति ज्योग्जीवति महान्प्रजया पशुभिर्भवति महान्कीर्त्या पशून्न निन्देत्तद्व्रतम् ॥ २ ॥ इत्यष्टादशः खण्डः ॥ १८ ॥

Sa ya evametā revatyaḥ paśuṣu protā veda paśumānbhavati sarvamāyureti jyogjīvati mahānprajayā paśubhirbhavati mahānkīrtyā paśūnna nindettadvratam. Ityaṣṭādaśaḥ khaṇḍaḥ.

Saḥ yaḥ evam etāḥ revatyaḥ protāḥ veda, he who knows that these [i.e., the Sāma] called Revatī are rooted in animals; *paśumān bhavati,* comes to possess many animals; *sarvam āyuḥ eti,* lives the full span of his life; *jyok jīvati,* has a brilliant life; *mahān prajayā paśubhiḥ bhavati,* becomes a highly respected person because of his children and also his animal wealth; *mahān kīrtyā,* becomes a truly great person for his great deeds; *paśūn na nindet tat vratam,* he observes the vow of never saying anything bad about animals. *Iti aṣṭādaśaḥ khaṇḍaḥ,* here ends the eighteenth section.

2. He who knows that the Sāma called *Revatī* is rooted in animals acquires many animals. He has a long and brilliant life and becomes well known for his children and for his animal wealth. He also becomes a truly great person for his great deeds. His vow is that he will never say anything bad about animals.

Section Nineteen

लोम हिङ्कारस्त्वक्प्रस्तावो मांसमुद्गीथोऽस्थि प्रतिहारो मज्जा निधनमेतद्यज्ञायज्ञीयमङ्गेषु प्रोतम् ॥ १ ॥

Loma hiṁkārastvakprastāvo māṁsamudgītho'sthi pratihāro majjā nidhanametadyajñāyajñīyamaṅgeṣu protam.

Loma hiṁkāraḥ, hair is the hiṁkāra; *tvak prastāvaḥ,* skin is the prastāva; *māṁsam udgīthaḥ,* flesh is the udgītha; *asthi pratihāraḥ,* bone is the pratihāra; *majjā nidhanam,* marrow is the nidhana; *etat yajñāyajñīyam,* this [Sāma called] Yajñāyajñīya; *aṅgeṣu protam,* is spread all over the limbs of the body.

1. Hair is the hiṁkāra, skin is the prastāva, flesh is the udgītha, bone is the pratihāra, and marrow is the nidhana. The Sāma called *Yajñāyajñīya* is spread all over the limbs of the body.

We get much nourishment from animals to sustain our bodies. That is why, in the previous section, the Sāma has been worshipped in the animals, and now it is being worshipped in the various parts of the body.

Hair is on top of the body, so it is given first place—the place given to the hiṁkāra when the Sāma is recited. Next to the hair is the skin. Similarly, next to the hiṁkāra is the prastāva. The flesh is the udgītha, for both are the most important part. Then the bones are the pratihāra, because after a body is cremated there will still be pieces of bone left, and these are 'collected' by the relatives. The marrow is the nidhana, for that is the end of everything.

स य एवमेतद्यज्ञायज्ञीयमङ्गेषु प्रोतं वेदाङ्गी भवति नाङ्गेन विहूर्छति सर्वमायुरेति ज्योग्जीवति महान्प्रजया पशुभिर्भवति महान्कीर्त्या संवत्सरं मज्ज्ञो नाश्नीयात्तद्-व्रतं मज्ज्ञो नाश्नीयादिति वा ॥ २ ॥ इत्येकोनविंशः खण्डः ॥ १९ ॥

Sa ya evametadyajñāyajñīyamaṅgeṣu protaṁ vedāṅgī bhavati nāṅgena vihūrchati sarvamāyureti jyogjīvati mahānprajayā paśubhirbhavati mahānkīrtyā saṁvatsaraṁ majjño nāśnīyāttadvrataṁ majjño nāśnīyāditi vā. Ityekonaviṁśaḥ khaṇḍaḥ.

Saḥ yaḥ evam etat yajñāyajñīyam aṅgeṣu protam veda, he who knows that this Sāma called Yajñāyajñīya is located in the different parts of the body; *aṅgī bhavati,* has a firm body; *na aṅgena vihūrchati,* has no defect in his limbs or organs; *sarvam āyuḥ eti,* he lives the full span of his life; *jyok jīvati,* he has a brilliant life; *mahān prajayā paśubhiḥ bhavati,* he becomes great in respect of his children and his animal wealth; *mahān kīrtyā,* he becomes great because of his great deeds; *saṁvatsaram,* for one whole year; *majjñaḥ,* meat; *na aśnīyāt,* will not eat; *majjñaḥ na aśnīyāt iti vā,* or will not eat meat at all; *tat vratam,* this is his vow. *Iti ekonaviṁśaḥ khaṇḍaḥ,* here ends the nineteenth section.

2. He who knows that the Sāma known as *Yajñāyajñīya* is located in different parts of the body becomes

possessed of a firm body and none of his organs has any defect. He has a long and brilliant life; and he becomes great because of his children and his animal wealth. He also becomes famous for his great deeds. His vow is that he will not eat meat for one whole year, or he will not eat it at all.

'A firm body' means a good, sound body with none of its organs or limbs defective. Even his nails and his hair will be normal.

The word *majjña,* meat, is in the plural here. This implies that both fish and meat should be avoided.

Section Twenty

अग्निर्हिङ्कारो वायुः प्रस्ताव आदित्य उद्गीथो नक्षत्राणि प्रतिहारश्चन्द्रमा निधनमेतद्राजनं देवतासु प्रोतम् ॥ १ ॥

Agnirhiṁkāro vāyuḥ prastāva āditya udgītho nakṣatrāṇi pratihāraścandramā nidhanametadrājanaṁ devatāsu protam.

Agniḥ hiṁkāraḥ, fire is the hiṁkāra; *vāyuḥ prastāvaḥ,* air is the prastāva; *ādityaḥ udgīthaḥ,* the sun is the udgītha; *nakṣatrāṇi pratihāraḥ,* the stars are the pratihāra; *candramāḥ nidhanam,* the moon is the nidhana; *etat rājanam,* this [Sāma called] Rājana; *devatāsu protam,* is rooted in the gods and goddesses.

1. Fire is the himkāra, air is the prastāva, the sun is the udgītha, the stars are the pratihāra, and the moon is the nidhana. This Sāma known as *Rājana* is rooted in the gods and goddesses.

In the previous section the Sāma was worshipped in the parts of the body. Now it is being worshipped in the deities—that is, in the forces of nature.

Fire is the first among the forces of nature, so it is the himkāra. Next to the himkāra is the prastāva. Air is called the prastāva because it comes next after fire, and it is also infinite. The sun is the udgītha, for just as the udgītha is the best among the Sāma songs, so also the sun is the best among the forces of nature. The stars lie scattered, and as we locate them it seems that we are 'collecting' (*pratihāra*) them. That is why the stars are said to be the pratihāra. The moon is said to be the nidhana, because active people go to Candraloka, the world of the moon, after death.

The Sāma called *Rājana* is rooted in the gods and goddesses, for the deities are by nature luminous (*rājana*).

स य एवमेतद्राजनं देवतासु प्रोतं वेदैतासामेव देवतानां सलोकतां सार्ष्टितां सायुज्यं गच्छति सर्वमायुरेति ज्योग्जीवति महान्प्रजया पशुभिर्भवति महान्कीर्त्या ब्राह्मणान्न निन्देत्तद्व्रतम् ॥ २ ॥ इति विंशः खण्डः ॥ २० ॥

Sa ya evametadrājanaṁ devatāsu protaṁ vedaitāsāmeva devatānāṁ salokatāṁ sārṣṭitāṁ sāyujyaṁ gacchati sarvamāyureti jyogjīvati mahānprajayā paśubhirbhavati mahānkīrtyā brāhmaṇānna nindettadvratam. Iti viṁśaḥ khaṇḍaḥ.

Saḥ yaḥ evam etat rājanam devatāsu protam veda, he who knows that this Sāma known as Rājana is established in the gods and goddesses [such as Agni (fire), Vāyu (air), etc.]; *etāsām eva devatānām salokatām gacchati,* he shares with those gods and goddesses the same worlds; *sārṣṭitām,* the same rights and privileges; [*vā*] *sāyujyam,* [or] the same form; *sarvam āyuḥ eti,* he lives the full span of his life; *jyok jīvati,* he has a brilliant life; *mahān prajayā paśubhiḥ bhavati,* he becomes great by virtue of his children and also his animal wealth; *mahān kīrtyā,* he is great by his great deeds; *brāhmaṇān na nindet tat vratam,* it is his vow that he will not speak ill of the brāhmins. *Iti viṁśaḥ khaṇḍaḥ,* here ends the twentieth section.

2. He who knows that the Sāma known as *Rājana* is established in the gods and goddesses shares the same worlds with these gods and goddesses, has the same rights and privileges with them, or has the same form. He also has a long and brilliant life. And he becomes great by virtue of his children and his animal wealth, and also by virtue of his great deeds. His vow is that he will never speak ill of the brāhmins.

What does a person gain from worshipping the Sāma in such a way? He gets the right to live with the gods and goddesses in the same world, or to share the same rights and privileges with them, or to have the same form. It is not that he would get all these things. He would get any one of them.

The scriptures say that the brāhmins themselves are the gods and goddesses. Obviously then one should not say anything derogatory about the brāhmins.

Section Twenty-One

त्रयी विद्या हिङ्कारस्त्रय इमे लोकाः स प्रस्तावो-
ऽग्निर्वायुरादित्यः स उद्गीथो नक्षत्राणि वयांसि मरीचयः
स प्रतिहारः सर्पा गन्धर्वाः पितरस्तन्निधनमेतत्साम
सर्वस्मिन्प्रोतम् ॥ १ ॥

Trayī vidyā hiṁkārastraya ime lokāḥ sa prastāvo'gnir-vāyurādityaḥ sa udgītho nakṣatrāṇi vayāṁsi marīcayaḥ sa pratihāraḥ sarpā gandharvāḥ pitarastannidhanametat-sāma sarvasminprotam.

Trayī vidyā hiṁkāraḥ, the three Vedas [the Ṛk, the Yajuḥ, and the Sāma] are the hiṁkāra; *trayaḥ ime lokāḥ,* these three worlds [bhūḥ, bhuvaḥ, svaḥ]; *saḥ prastāvaḥ,* [together] that is the prastāva; *agniḥ vāyuḥ ādityaḥ,* fire, air, and the sun; *saḥ udgīthaḥ,* [together] that is the udgītha; *nakṣatrāṇi vayāṁsi marīcayaḥ,* the stars, the birds, and the rays; *saḥ pratihāraḥ,* [together] that is the pratihāra; *sarpāḥ gandharvāḥ pitaraḥ,* serpents, gandharvas [celestial musicians], and the ancestors; *tat nidhanam,* [together] that is the nidhana; *etat sāma sarvasmin protam,* this Sāma rests in everything.

1. The three *vidyās* [the Ṛk, the Yajuḥ, and the Sāma] are together the hiṁkāra; these three worlds [the earth, the space between the earth and heaven, and heaven] are together the prastāva; fire, air, and the sun are together the udgītha; the stars, the birds, and the rays are together the pratihāra; serpents, gandharvas, and the ancestors are together the nidhana. This Sāma resides in everything.

According to the scriptures the Ṛg Veda comes from fire, the Yajur Veda comes from air, and the Sāma Veda comes from the sun. In the previous section the worship of the Sāma as fire, air, etc., was discussed. Now the worship of the Sāma as the three Vedas is taken up.

Knowledge of the three Vedas may be regarded as the hiṁkāra, for you have to use the hiṁkāra before you start doing any worship. After the hiṁkāra comes the prastāva. Similarly, after the three Vedas come the three worlds, so they are said to be the prastāva. Fire, air, and the sun are like the udgītha, for among all things they are of a higher order. The stars, the birds, and the rays come and go, so they are like the pratihāra. The serpents, the gandharvas, and the ancestors are the nidhana, for there is some semblance between them and the letter *dha.*

The word *Sāma* does not refer to any specific Sāma. It refers to anything bearing that name. The word is meant according to the context, just as oblations are offered according to the deities for whom they are meant.

स य एवमेतत्साम सर्वस्मिन्प्रोतं वेद सर्वं ह भवति॥ २॥

Sa ya evametatsāma sarvasminprotaṁ veda sarvaṁ ha bhavati.

Saḥ yaḥ evam etat sāma sarvasmin protam veda, he who knows that this Sāma resides in everything; *sarvam ha bhavati,* he becomes everything.

2. He who knows that this Sāma is in everything becomes one with everything [or, becomes the Lord of everything].

This is an example of how far the benefit of the knowledge of the Sāma can extend: If you know that the Sāma is everywhere and in everything, you become the supreme Lord of everything.

तदेष श्लोको यानि पञ्चधा त्रीणि त्रीणि तेभ्यो
न ज्यायः परमन्यदस्ति ॥ ३ ॥

Tadeṣa śloko yāni pañcadhā trīṇi trīṇi tebhyo na jyāyaḥ paramanyadasti.

Tat eṣaḥ ślokaḥ, here is a verse on the subject; *yāni pañcadhā,* that [Sāma] which is divided into five parts [hiṁkāra, prastāva, udgītha, pratihāra, and nidhana]; *trīṇi trīṇi,* each again divided into three parts [such as hiṁkāra representing the three Vedas]; *tebhyaḥ jyāyaḥ param anyat na asti,* there is nothing higher than these.

3. Here is a verse in this connection: There are five parts of Sāma, and each of these is divided into three parts. There is nothing higher than these [fifteen forms of Sāma].

So long we have discussed the five forms of the Sāma: hiṁkāra, prastāva, udgītha, pratihāra, and nidhana. In the present verse the Upaniṣad says that each of these five can be divided further into three: hiṁkāra as the Ṛk, the Yajuḥ, and the Sāma; prastāva as the earth, the intermediate space (between the earth and heaven), and heaven; udgītha as fire, air, and the sun; pratihāra as the stars, the birds, and the rays; and nidhana as the snakes, the celestial musicians, and the ancestors.

It is Sāma which is manifest in all of these fifteen

forms. These forms include everything. They represent the highest and best of all things, because Sāma is the highest and best of all things.

यस्तद्वेद स वेद सर्वं सर्वा दिशो बलिमस्मै हरन्ति सर्वमस्मीत्युपासीत तद्व्रतं तद्व्रतम् ॥ ४ ॥ इत्येकविंशः खण्डः ॥ २१ ॥

Yastadveda sa veda sarvaṁ sarvā diśo balimasmai haranti sarvamasmītyupāsīta tadvrataṁ tadvratam. Ityekaviṁśaḥ khaṇḍaḥ.

Yaḥ tat veda, he who knows that [Sāma]; *saḥ veda sarvam,* he knows all; *sarvāḥ diśaḥ,* all the quarters; *balim,* gifts; *asmai,* for him; *haranti,* bring; *sarvam asmi,* I am all; *iti upāsīta,* this is how he will meditate; *tat vratam tat vratam,* this is his vow, this is his vow. *Iti ekaviṁśaḥ khaṇḍaḥ,* here ends the twenty-first section.

4. He who knows Sāma knows everything, and gifts come to him from all quarters. His vow will be to constantly say to himself, 'I am one with all.'

Sāma is the inmost being of all, and he who knows it as such becomes like Sāma—that is, he becomes the inmost being of all, and he knows everything. People come from everywhere with gifts to show him their respect.

'I am Sāma, the inmost being of all'—this is how Sāma is to be worshipped. One should constantly repeat this to oneself. In fact, it should be treated as a vow.

Section Twenty-Two

विनर्दि साम्नो वृणे पशव्यमित्यग्नेरुद्गीथोऽनिरुक्तः प्रजापतेर्निरुक्तः सोमस्य मृदु श्लक्ष्णं वायोः श्लक्ष्णं बलवदिन्द्रस्य क्रौञ्चं बृहस्पतेरपध्वान्तं वरुणस्य तान्सर्वानेवोपसेवेत वारुणं त्वेव वर्जयेत् ॥ १ ॥

Vinardi sāmno vṛṇe paśavyamityagnerudgītho'niruktaḥ prajāpaterniruktaḥ somasya mṛdu ślakṣṇaṁ vāyoḥ ślakṣṇaṁ balavadindrasya krauñcaṁ bṛhaspaterapadhvāntaṁ varuṇasya tānsarvānevopaseveta vāruṇaṁ tveva varjayet.

Vinardi, the voice called vinardi, which is deep, like that of a bull; *sāmnaḥ,* for [singing] the Sāma; *vṛṇe iti,* I pray for; *paśavyam,* good for animals; *agneḥ,* of the god of fire; *udgītha aniruktaḥ,* the udgītha sung in the anirukta voice, which is not very distinct; *prajāpateḥ,* of Prajāpati, the Lord of all; *niruktaḥ,* the voice called nirukta, which is clear; *somasya,* of the god Soma; *mṛdu ślakṣṇam,* the voice called ślakṣṇa that is soft and soothing; *vāyoḥ,* of the god Vāyu, air; *ślakṣṇam balavat,* the voice called ślakṣṇa that is soothing yet powerful; *indrasya,* of

Indra; *krauñcam,* the voice called krauñca, which is like that of the krauñca bird; *bṛhaspateḥ,* of Bṛhaspati; *apadhvāntam,* the voice called apadhvānta, which sounds like a broken metal pot; *varuṇasya,* of the god Varuṇa; *tān sarvān eva upaseveta,* practise on all of them; *tu eva vāruṇam,* except that of Varuṇa; *varjayet,* one should avoid.

1. The *vinardi* voice for singing the Sāma is good for animals, and Agni, the god of fire, is its presiding deity. I bear this in mind and pray that I may have this voice. The god Prajāpati presides over the udgītha sung in the *anirukta* [unclear] voice. The one having Soma as its presiding deity is *nirukta* [clear]. That of Vāyu, the god of air, is soft and pleasant, and Indra's is strong. That which has Bṛhaspati as its presiding deity is like the voice of the krauñca bird, and that of Varuṇa is like the sound of a broken metal pot. Cultivate all of these, but avoid the one of Varuṇa.

When you sing the udgītha, be careful that you sing it in the right voice. The voice is important because it determines the benefit you derive from your singing. For instance, there is a type of voice that sounds like that of a bull. Agni, fire, is the presiding deity of this voice. If you sing the udgītha in this type of voice, it means you are singing for the good of the animals and you are also praying that you may have that kind of voice.

Similarly, there is a type of voice called *anirukta,* which has Prajāpati as its presiding deity. Prajāpati, the Lord of all beings, has no form of his own. Similarly, he does not have a distinct voice. This is why it is called *anirukta,* indistinct. The voice of Soma, the moon, is *nirukta,* clear; that of Indra is powerful; and that of Bṛhaspati sounds like a krauñca, a bird similar to a crane. Varuṇa's voice is the worst. It is like the sound of a broken brass vessel. All these voices can be used except that of Varuṇa.

अमृतत्वं देवेभ्य आगायानीत्यागायेत्स्वधां पितृभ्य आशां मनुष्येभ्यस्तृणोदकं पशुभ्यः स्वर्गं लोकं यजमाना-यान्नमात्मन आगायानीत्येतानि मनसा ध्यायन्नप्रमत्तः स्तुवीत॥ २॥

Amṛtatvaṁ devebhya āgāyānītyāgāyetsvadhāṁ pitṛbhya āśāṁ manuṣyebhyastṛṇodakaṁ paśubhyaḥ svargaṁ lokaṁ yajamānāyānnamātmana āgāyānītyetāni manasā dhyāyannapramattaḥ stuvīta.

Āgāyet, one should sing [with the resolve]; *amṛtatvam devebhyaḥ āgāyāni iti,* I will get immortality for the gods and goddesses by singing; *svadhām,* offerings; *pitṛbhyaḥ,* for the ancestors; *āśām manuṣyebhyaḥ,* hope for humanity; *tṛṇodakam paśubhyaḥ,* food and water for the animals; *svargam lokam,* heavenly worlds; *yajamānāya,* for those who perform sacrifices; *annam ātmane,* food for myself; *āgāyāni iti,* I shall win by singing thus; *etāni,* all these; *manasā dhyāyan,* thinking mentally; *apramattaḥ,* without raising the voice too much; *stuvīta,* one should sing.

2. One should sing with the resolve: 'By singing I will get immortality for the gods and goddesses, food offerings for the ancestors, hope for humanity, food and water for the animals, heaven for those who perform sacrifices, and food for myself. All this I will get by singing.' Thinking thus, one should sing without raising the voice too much [or, without being too excited].

When you sing the Sāma, you should keep in mind the things you are singing for—such as immortality for the gods and goddesses, etc. But you must also take care that when you sing, your pronunciation and accents are correct, and that you do not miss any syllables.

सर्वे स्वरा इन्द्रस्यात्मानः सर्व ऊष्माणः प्रजापतेरात्मानः सर्वे स्पर्शा मृत्योरात्मानस्तं यदि स्वरेषूपालभेतेन्द्रं शरणं प्रपन्नोऽभूवं स त्वा प्रति वक्ष्यतीत्येनं ब्रूयात्॥ ३॥

Sarve svarā indrasyātmānaḥ sarva ūṣmāṇaḥ prajāpaterātmānaḥ sarve sparśā mṛtyorātmānastaṁ yadi svareṣūpālabhetendraṁ śaraṇaṁ prapanno'bhūvaṁ sa tvā prati vakṣyatītyenaṁ brūyāt.

Sarve svarāḥ, all the vowels; *indrasya ātmānaḥ,* are like the body [with its limbs] of Indra; *sarve ūṣmāṇaḥ,* all the sibilants; *prajāpateḥ ātmānaḥ,* are like the body [with its limbs] of Prajāpati; *sarve sparśāḥ,* all the consonants, starting with *ka*; *mṛtyoḥ ātmānaḥ,* are like the body [with all its limbs] of Death; *yadi upālabheta,* if anyone criticizes; *tam,* him [the udgātā, who is singing the Sāma]; *svareṣu,* regarding his pronunciation of the vowels; *indram śaraṇam prapannaḥ abhūvam,* [the udgātā will then say:] I took refuge in Indra [when I started singing the vowels]; *saḥ,* he [Indra]; *tvā prativakṣyati iti,* will give you the right reply; *enam brūyāt,* say to him.

3. All the vowels are like Indra's body with its various parts. The sibilants [*śa, ṣa,* etc.] are like Prajāpati's body with its various parts. The consonants, starting with *ka,* are the body and limbs of Death. If someone finds fault with the way the udgātā pronounces the vowels, he may say to that person: 'As I began singing, I took refuge in Indra [i.e., I sought Indra's blessings]. Ask him and he will give you the right answer [to your criticism].'

The vowels are said to be Indra's body, for when you start doing something, including even a recitation, you have to feel strong enough to do the job fully and correctly. And in order that you may feel that you have the requisite strength, you pray for Indra's blessings, and you feel that he is transmitting his strength to you. You feel that the vowels you are using are his body, the sibilants are the body of Prajāpati, and the consonants are the body of Death. Then if anyone criticizes your pronunciation of the vowels, you can tell him to ask Indra for the reason why you pronounced them that way, for Indra guided you in your recitation.

अथ यद्येनमूष्मसूपालभेत प्रजापतिं शरणं प्रपन्नोऽभूवं स त्वा प्रति पेक्ष्यतीत्येनं ब्रूयादथ यद्येनं स्पर्शेषूपालभेत मृत्युं शरणं प्रपन्नोऽभूवं स त्वा प्रति धक्ष्यतीत्येनं ब्रूयात् ॥ ४ ॥

Atha yadyenamūṣmasūpālabheta prajāpatiṁ śaraṇaṁ prapanno'bhūvaṁ sa tvā prati pekṣatītyenaṁ brūyādatha yadyenaṁ sparśeṣūpālabheta mṛtyuṁ śaraṇaṁ prapanno'bhūvaṁ sa tvā prati dhakṣyatītyenaṁ brūyāt.

Atha, then; *yadi enam ūṣmasu upālabheta,* if a person criticizes him for his pronunciation of the sibilants; *prajāpatim śaraṇam prapannaḥ abhūvam,* I took refuge in Prajāpati [when I started singing]; *saḥ,* he [Prajāpati]; *tvā pratipekṣati iti,* will crush you; *enam brūyāt,* he will say to him; *atha,* then; *yadi enam sparśeṣu upālabheta,* if someone criticizes him for his pronunciation of the consonants; *mṛtyum śaraṇam prapannaḥ abhūvam,* I took refuge in Death [when I started singing]; *saḥ,* he [Death]; *tvā pratidhakṣyati iti,* will burn you to ashes; *enam brūyāt,* he will say to him.

4. Then, if someone finds fault with his pronunciation of the sibilants, the singer will say to him: 'When I started singing I sought Prajāpati's blessings. He

will therefore crush you.' Then, if someone finds fault with his pronunciation of the consonants, the singer will say to him: 'I sought Death's protection while singing. He will therefore burn you to ashes.'

If you are reciting a hymn, seek Prajāpati's protection concerning the sibilants. Then, even if you err, he will protect you. Similarly, you should seek Death's protection concerning the consonants. He will protect you from harm for any mistakes you might make. In fact, those who find fault with you will themselves be punished, for by criticizing your singing, they are insulting Prajāpati or Death.

सर्वे स्वरा घोषवन्तो बलवन्तो वक्तव्या इन्द्रे बलं ददानीति सर्व ऊष्माणोऽग्रस्ता अनिरस्ता विवृता वक्तव्याः प्रजापतेरात्मानं परिददानीति सर्वे स्पर्शा लेशेनानभिनिहिता वक्तव्या मृत्योरात्मानं परिहराणीति॥ ५॥ इति द्वाविंशः खण्डः॥ २२॥

Sarve svarā ghoṣavanto balavanto vaktavyā indre balaṁ dadānīti sarva ūṣmāṇo'grastā anirastā vivṛtā vaktavyāḥ prajāpaterātmānaṁ paridadānīti sarve sparśā leśenānabhinihitā vaktavyā mṛtyorātmānaṁ parihara-rāṇīti. Iti dvāviṁśaḥ khaṇḍaḥ.

Sarve svarāḥ, all the vowels; *ghoṣavantaḥ balavantaḥ,* clearly and powerfully; *vaktavyāḥ,* articulated; *indre balam dadāni iti,* [say to yourself] I have to give strength to Indra [as if you are stronger than Indra and can afford to give him some of your strength]; *sarve ūṣmāṇah,* all the sibilants; *agrastāḥ,* clearly uttered [i.e., no part of the letter left within the mouth, as if you are swallowing it]; *anirastāḥ,* not uttering the letter as if you are throwing it out of your mouth; *vivṛtāḥ vaktavyāḥ,* clearly expressed; *prajāpateḥ ātmānam paridadāni iti,* I surrender myself to Prajāpati; *sarve sparśāḥ leśena anabhinihitāḥ vaktavyāḥ,* each of the consonants should be uttered separately and distinctly; *mṛtyoḥ ātmānam pariharāṇi iti,* [while thinking] I save myself from Death. *Iti dvāviṁśaḥ khaṇḍaḥ,* here ends the twenty-second section.

5. Each vowel should be articulated clearly and powerfully, [and while doing so, you should think,] 'I will give some of my strength to Indra.' The sibilants also should be uttered fully and distinctly, without sounding as if you are swallowing part of them or spitting them out. [While uttering them, you should think,] 'I surrender myself to Prajāpati.' Then each of the consonants also should be uttered separately and clearly, [and while doing so, you should think,] 'I will save myself from death.'

It is important that when we recite a hymn, we recite the vowels, consonants, and the sibilants clearly and loudly. Care has to be taken that no two letters get mixed up, or that any part of a letter remains inside the mouth or seems to be spat out.

Here it is said that the vowels are to be pronounced powerfully and that you should pray to Indra while singing, offering him some of your strength. This suggests that you feel very strong, as if you are stronger than Indra. You should also try to surrender yourself to Prajāpati while singing. You will then attain immortality.

Section Twenty-Three

त्रयो धर्मस्कन्धा यज्ञोऽध्ययनं दानमिति प्रथमस्तप एव द्वितीयो ब्रह्मचार्याचार्यकुलवासी तृतीयोऽत्यन्तमात्मानमाचार्यकुलेऽवसादयन्सर्व एते पुण्यलोका भवन्ति ब्रह्मसंस्थोऽमृतत्वमेति ॥ १ ॥

Trayo dharmaskandhā yajño'dhyayanaṁ dānamiti prathamastapa eva dvitīyo brahmacāryācāryakulavāsī tṛtīyo'tyantamātmānamācāryakule'vasādayansarva ete puṇyalokā bhavanti brahmasaṁstho'mṛtatvameti.

Trayaḥ dharmaskandhāḥ, three divisions of religion; *yajñaḥ adhyayanam dānam iti prathamaḥ,* the first [division comprises] sacrifices, study, and charity; *tapaḥ eva dvitīyaḥ,* the second is austerities; *tṛtīyaḥ,* the third; *brahmacārī ācāryakulavāsī atyantam ātmānam ācāryakule avasādayan,* the life of celibacy and living with the teacher in his house till death; *sarve ete,* all these; *puṇyalokāḥ bhavanti,* attain heavenly worlds; *brahmasaṁsthaḥ,* [but] one devoted to Brahman; *amṛtatvam eti,* attains immortality.

1. There are three divisions of religion: The first comprises sacrifices, study, and charity; the second consists of austerities, such as fasting; and the third is the life of celibacy and living with the teacher in his house till death. People devoted to these three divisions of religion go to heaven after death. But one who is devoted to Brahman attains immortality.

You may practise religion in three ways: First, by performing sacrifices, studying the scriptures, and giving in charity; second, by performing austerities; and third, by observing celibacy and living with the teacher till death. All these are good, but they only lead to heaven. If you want immortality (that is, liberation), you have to devote yourself to realizing Brahman.

There are certain words in our language that clearly distinguish one thing from another. For instance, barley is a particular type of grain. If you see the word 'grain,' it could mean wheat or rice or barley. But if you see the word 'barley,' you know exactly what is referred to. Similarly, the words *brahmaniṣṭhā,* or *brahmasaṁstha,* refer to a certain type of person whose only concern in life is to realize Brahman. This type of person may be of any age, any class, any caste, or any station of life. What distinguishes this type of person from any other is his or her total commitment to Brahman.

प्रजापतिर्लोकानभ्यतपत्तेभ्योऽभितप्तेभ्यस्त्रयी विद्या सम्प्रास्रवत्तामभ्यतपत्तस्या अभितप्ताया एतान्यक्षराणि सम्प्रास्रवन्त भूर्भुवः स्वरिति ॥ २ ॥

Prajāpatirlokānabhyatapattebhyo'bhitaptebhyastrayī vidyā samprāsravattāmabhyatapattasyā abhitaptāyā etānyakṣarāṇi samprāsravanta bhūrbhuvaḥ svariti.

Prajāpatiḥ lokān abhyatapat, Prajāpati meditated on the worlds; *tebhyaḥ abhitaptebhyaḥ,* from [the worlds] which he meditated on; *trayī vidyā samprāsravat,* emerged the three Vedas; *tām abhyatapat,* [Prajāpati] meditated on them [the three Vedas]; *tasyāḥ abhitaptāyāḥ,* out of [the Vedas] which he meditated upon; *etāni akṣarāṇi,* these akṣaras [syllables]; *samprāsravanta,* emerged; *bhūḥ bhuvaḥ svaḥ,* bhūḥ, bhuvaḥ, and svaḥ; *iti,* that is all.

2. Prajāpati [i.e., Virāṭ] thought about the worlds [he would have]. Out of his thinking, the three Vedas took shape. He then began to think about the Vedas. As a result of this thinking, the Vedas gave birth to the three vyāhṛtis: *bhūḥ, bhuvaḥ,* and *svaḥ.*

How can you attain liberation? You can attain it when you surrender everything for its sake. To make this clear, the story of how the world came into being is narrated:

God (or Virāṭ, or Kaśyapa) created this world by practising austerities. What kind of austerities? He simply planned the creation in his mind. This planning, this mental exercise, is enough austerity for him. And as thinking is doing for him, whatever he thinks immediately comes into being. The worlds emerge from within him. The first to manifest, however, were the three Vedas: Ṛk, Yajuḥ, and Sāma. When these emerged, the Creator thought about them, and from the Vedas came the three vyāhṛtis (lit., utterances): *bhūḥ, bhuvaḥ,* and *svaḥ.*

Then from these came Om, the symbol of Brahman. If we concentrate on Om, we attain Brahman. But we have to surrender everything for the sake of Brahman. This is the conclusion to be drawn from this story. Even the Creator has to concentrate on what he is going to create, and he has to surrender everything else.

तान्यभ्यतपत्तेभ्योऽभितप्तेभ्य ओंकारः सम्प्रास्रवत्तद्यथा शङ्कुना सर्वाणि पर्णानि संतृण्णान्येवमोङ्कारेण सर्वा वाक्संतृण्णोङ्कार एवेदं सर्वमोङ्कार एवेदं सर्वम् ॥ ३ ॥ इति त्रयोविंशः खण्डः ॥ २३ ॥

Tānyabhyatapattebhyo'bhitaptebhya oṁkāraḥ samprāsravattadyathā śaṅkunā sarvāṇi parṇāni saṁtṛṇṇānyevamoṁkāreṇa sarvā vāksaṁtṛṇṇoṁkāra evedaṁ sarvamoṁkāra evedaṁ sarvam. Iti trayoviṁśaḥ khaṇḍaḥ.

Tāni abhyatapat, he thought about those [vyāhṛtis]; *tebhyaḥ abhitaptebhyaḥ,* out of those which he thought about; *oṁkāra samprāsravat,* the syllable Om emerged; *tat yathā,* just as; *śaṅkunā,* by the ribs [of a leaf]; *sarvāṇi parṇāni saṁtṛṇṇāni,* all parts of the leaf are held together; *evam,* similarly; *oṁkāreṇa sarvā vāk saṁtṛṇṇā,* Oṁkāra permeates every form of speech; *oṁkāraḥ eva idam sarvam oṁkāraḥ eva idam sarvam,* all this is Oṁkāra, all this is Oṁkāra [the repetition is for emphasis]. *Iti trayoviṁśaḥ khaṇḍaḥ,* here ends the twenty-third section.

3. [Prajāpati then] meditated on those three vyāhṛtis [bhūḥ, bhuvaḥ, and svaḥ]. Out of the vyāhṛtis, which he thought about, emerged Oṁkāra. Just as a network of ribs is spread all over a leaf, similarly, Oṁkāra permeates every form of speech [or, everything]. All this is Oṁkāra. All this is Oṁkāra.

Om is the essence of everything. Because Prajāpati meditated to create the three worlds, Om manifested itself. Om, in fact, is the support of everything.

Section Twenty-Four

ब्रह्मवादिनो वदन्ति यद्वसूनां प्रातःसवनं रुद्राणां माध्यंदिनं सवनमादित्यानां च विश्वेषां च देवानां तृतीयसवनम्॥ १॥

Brahmavādino vadanti yadvasūnāṁ prātaḥsavanaṁ

rudrāṇāṁ mādhyandinaṁ savanamādityānāṁ ca viśve-ṣāṁ ca devānāṁ tṛtīyasavanam.

Brahmavādinaḥ, those who believe in Brahman; *vadanti,* say; *yat vasūnām prātaḥsavanam,* the morning savana [i.e., the time when the soma juice is extracted from the soma creeper for the sacrifice] is meant for the eight Vasus; *mādhyandinam savanam rudrāṇām,* the noon savana is meant for the eleven Rudras; *tṛtīya savanam,* the third [i.e., the evening] savana; *ādityānām ca viśveṣām devānām,* is meant for the twelve Ādityas and the Viśvadevas.

1. Those who believe in Brahman say: The morning savana is for the Vasus, the midday savana is for the Rudras, and the third, the evening savana, is for the Ādityas and the Viśvadevas [i.e., all the gods and goddesses].

'The morning savana belongs to the eight Vasus.' This means that the Vasus control the earth. In the same way, since the midday savana belongs to the eleven Rudras, they control the interspace—the space between the earth and heaven. And as the evening savana belongs to the twelve Ādityas and the Viśvadevas, that means they control heaven. It follows then that there is no world left for the performer of the sacrifice.

क्व तर्हि यजमानस्य लोक इति स यस्तं न विद्यात्कथं कुर्यादथ विद्वान्कुर्यात् ॥ २ ॥

Kva tarhi yajamānasya loka iti sa yastaṁ na vidyātkathaṁ kuryādatha vidvānkuryāt.

Kva tarhi yajamānasya lokaḥ iti, where then is the place for one who performs a sacrifice; *saḥ yaḥ,* he who; *tam,* that [place for the yajamāna]; *na vidyāt,* does not know; *katham,* how [can he]; *kuryāt,* perform [a sacrifice]; *atha vidvān kuryāt,* one who knows can [of course] perform [a sacrifice].

2. Where then is the place for the yajamāna [one who performs a sacrifice]? How can he who does not know that place perform a sacrifice? He who knows can perform a sacrifice.

When a person performs a sacrifice, he does so in order that he may attain a certain world for himself. But if the three worlds—bhūḥ, bhuvaḥ, and svaḥ—are already occupied by the Vasus and other gods, where is the place left for the sacrificer? In such a situation he would hardly have any inclination to perform a sacrifice, or even to sing attendant hymns such as the Sāma, or to engage in rituals connected with a sacrifice.

Ignorance on the part of a person is no bar to his performing a sacrifice. Rather, this verse is intended to praise knowledge. If a person knows how to recite the Sāma, that is a great help. It should be clearly understood, however, that though the Sāma or Oṁkāra is recited while a sacrifice is being performed, the

Sāma may be part of the sacrifice but Oṁkāra is not. Om is as good as Brahman. It is to be meditated upon; it does not involve any action.

पुरा प्रातरनुवाकस्योपाकरणाज्जघनेन गार्हपत्यस्यो-
दङ्मुख उपविश्य स वासवं सामाभिगायति॥ ३ ॥

Purā prātaranuvākasyopākaraṇājjaghanena gārhapatyasyodaṅmukha upaviśya sa vāsavaṁ sāmābhigāyati.

Prātaḥ anuvākasya upākaraṇāt purā, before beginning the morning chant; *jaghanena,* behind; *gārhapatyasya,* the Gārhapatya fire; *udaṅmukhaḥ,* facing north; *upaviśya,* sits; *saḥ,* he [the sacrificer]; *vāsavam,* about the Vasus; *sāma abhigāyati,* sings the Sāma.

3. Before starting the morning chant, the sacrificer sits behind the Gārhapatya fire facing north and sings the Sāma about the Vasus.

लो३कद्वारमपावा३र्णू३३ पश्येम त्वा वयंरा३३३३३
हु३म् आ३३ ज्या३यो३आ३२१११ इति॥ ४ ॥

Lo3kadvāramapāvā3rṇū33 paśyema tvā vayaṁrā33333 hu3m ā33 jyā3yo3ā32111 iti.

Lokadvāram apāvṛṇu, [O Fire,] please open the door of the world [i.e., make the path clear]; *vayam rājyāya,* so we may gain control of the earth; *tvā paśyema,* [and for that purpose] may see you.

4. O Fire, please open the door for us—that is, make the path clear—so that we may see you for obtaining full control of the earth.

The additional syllables in the verse have no special meaning. They merely serve to make the Sāma complete.

अथ जुहोति नमोऽग्नये पृथिवीक्षिते लोकक्षिते लोकं मे यजमानाय विन्दैष वै यजमानस्य लोक एतास्मि ॥ ५ ॥

Atha juhoti namo'gnaye pṛthivīkṣite lokakṣite lokaṁ me yajamānāya vindaiṣa vai yajamānasya loka etāsmi.

Atha juhoti, now the sacrificer begins the offerings; *pṛthivīkṣite,* living on the earth; *lokakṣite,* living in the loka [world]; *agnaye namaḥ,* salutations to fire; *yajamānāya me,* for me, the sacrificer; *lokam vinda,* acquire the right world; *eṣaḥ vai yajamānasya lokaḥ etā asmi,* I am going to this world fit for a sacrificer.

5. Then the sacrificer begins the offerings [with this mantra]: 'O Agni, you are in this world. I salute you. Please acquire the right world for me, who am performing a sacrifice. I am ready to go to a world appropriate for one who performs sacrifices.'

अत्र यजमानः परस्तादायुषः स्वाहापजहि परिघ-
मित्युक्त्वोत्तिष्ठति तस्मै वसवः प्रातःसवनं सम्प्रय-
च्छन्ति ॥ ६ ॥

Atra yajamānaḥ parastādāyuṣaḥ svāhāpajahi parighamityuktvottiṣṭhati tasmai vasavaḥ prātaḥsavanaṁ samprayacchanti.

Atra, here [in this world]; *yajamānaḥ parastāt āyuṣaḥ,* I, the sacrificer, have lived the full course of life; *svāhā,* [with these words, he will say] svāhā; *parigham,* the bolt [of the gateway to the world]; *apajahi,* remove; *iti uktvā,* saying this; *uttiṣṭhati,* he rises; *vasavaḥ,* the Vasus [to whom the morning savana is offered]; *tasmai,* to him [the sacrificer]; *prātaḥsavanam samprayacchanti,* give away the morning savana [i.e., give away this earth].

6. 'I, the yajamāna, have run the full course of my life in this world.' With these words, he will say, 'Svāhā,' [and offer his oblation]. Then he will rise, saying, 'Please unbolt the door to the world for which I am destined.' The Vasus then give him the ownership of the earth, which is the result of the savana performed in the morning.

The yajamāna (the sacrificer) keeps performing his sacrifices till he feels that it is time for him to die. He then offers his last oblation, saying, 'Svāhā.' Getting up, he says he is going to the world for which he is destined and demands that the door to that world be unbolted. The Vasus own the earth by virtue of the morning savana (that is, extracting the soma juice and having a morning wash with it). They are pleased with the yajamāna for his performance of the rituals, so they surrender the ownership of the earth to him.

पुरा माध्यन्दिनस्य सवनस्योपाकरणाज्जघनेनाग्नीध्रीय-
स्योदङ्मुख उपविश्य स रौद्रं सामाभिगायति॥ ७॥

Purā mādhyandinasya savanasyopākaraṇājjaghane-nāgnīdhrīyasyodaṅmukha upaviśya sa raudraṁ sāmābhi-gāyati.

Saḥ, he [the yajamāna]; *upākaraṇāt purā,* before beginning; *mādhyandinasya savanasya,* the midday savana; *āgnīdhrīyasya jaghanena,* behind the Dakṣiṇāgni fire; *udaṅmukhaḥ,* facing north; *upaviśya,* sitting; *raudram sāma abhigāyati,* sings the Sāma to the Rudras.

7. Before starting the midday savana, the yajamāna sits behind the Dakṣiṇāgni fire, facing north. He then sings the Sāma addressed to the Rudras.

Earlier, the way the yajamāna conquers the earth was shown. Now how the mid-region can be won is described. After sitting behind the Dakṣiṇāgni fire, facing north, he starts singing the Sāma addressed to the Rudras. He continues doing this with the idea of attaining union with Virāṭ.

लो३कद्वारमपावा३र्णू३३ पश्येम त्वा वयं वैरा३३३३३
हु३म् आ३३ ज्या३यो३आ३२१११ इति॥८॥

Lo3kadvāramapāvā3rṇū33 paśyema tvā vayaṁ vairā33333 hu3m ā33 jyā3yo3ā32111 iti.

Lokadvāram apāvṛṇu, [O Fire,] please open the door of the world [i.e., make the path clear]; *vayam vairājyāya,* so we may gain control of the world of Virāṭ; *tvā paśyema,* [and for that purpose] may see you.

8. O Fire, please open the door for us—that is, make the path clear—so that we may see you for obtaining full control of the world of Virāṭ.

अथ जुहोति नमो वायवेऽन्तरिक्षक्षिते लोकक्षिते लोकं
मे यजमानाय विन्दैष वै यजमानस्य लोक एतास्मि॥९॥

Atha juhoti namo vāyave'ntarikṣakṣite lokakṣite lokaṁ me yajamānāya vindaiṣa vai yajamānasya loka etāsmi.

Atha juhoti, now the sacrificer begins the offerings; *antarikṣakṣite,* living in the mid-region; *lokakṣite,* living in the loka [world]; *vāyave namaḥ,* salutations to Vāyu [air]; *yajamānāya me,* for me, the sacrificer; *lokam vinda,* acquire the right world; *eṣaḥ vai yajamānasya lokaḥ etā asmi,* I am going to the world fit for a sacrificer.

9. Then the sacrificer begins the offerings [with this mantra]: 'O Vāyu, you are in the mid-region. I salute you. Please acquire the right world for me, who am performing a sacrifice. I am ready to go to a world appropriate for one who performs sacrifices.'

अत्र यजमानः परस्तादायुषः स्वाहापजहि परिघमित्युक्त्वोत्तिष्ठति तस्मै रुद्रा माध्यन्दिनं सवनं सम्प्रयच्छन्ति ॥ १० ॥

Atra yajamānaḥ parastādāyuṣaḥ svāhāpajahi parighamityuktvottiṣṭhati tasmai rudrā mādhyandinaṁ savanaṁ samprayacchanti.

Atra, here [in this world]; *yajamānaḥ parastāt āyuṣaḥ,* I, the sacrificer, have lived the full course of life; *svāhā,* [with these words, he will say] svāhā; *parigham,* the bolt [of the gateway to the world]; *apajahi,* remove; *iti uktvā,* saying this; *uttiṣṭhati,* he rises; *rudrāḥ,* the Rudras [to whom the midday savana is offered]; *tasmai,* to him [the sacrificer]; *mādhyandinam savanam samprayacchanti,* give away the midday savana [i.e., give away the mid-region].

10. 'I, the yajamāna, have run the full course of my life in this world.' With these words, he will

say, 'Svāhā,' [and offer his oblation]. Then he will rise, saying, 'Please unbolt the door to the world for which I am destined.' The Rudras then give him the ownership of the mid-region, which is the result of the savana performed at midday.

पुरा तृतीयसवनस्योपाकरणाज्जघनेनाहवनीयस्योदङ्मुख उपविश्य स आदित्यं स वैश्वदेवं सामाभिगायति॥ ११ ॥

Purā tṛtīyasavanasyopākaraṇājjaghanenāhavanīyasyodaṅmukha upaviśya sa ādityaṁ sa vaiśvadevaṁ sāmābhigāyati.

Saḥ, he [the yajamāna]; *upākaraṇāt purā,* before beginning; *tṛtīyasavanasya,* the third savana; *āhavanīyasya jaghanena,* behind the Āhavanīya fire; *udaṅmukhaḥ,* facing north; *upaviśya,* sitting; *saḥ ādityam vaiśvadevam sāma abhigāyati,* he sings the Sāma to the Ādityas and the Viśvadevas.

11. Before starting the third [i.e., the evening] savana, the yajamāna sits behind the Āhavanīya fire, facing the north. He then sings the Sāma addressed to the Ādityas and the Viśvadevas.

लो३कद्वारमपावा३र्णू३३ पश्येम त्वा वयं स्वारा३३-
३३३ हु३म् आ३३ ज्या३यो३आ३२१११ इति॥ १२॥

Lo3kadvāramapāvā3rṇū33 paśyema tvā vayaṁ svā-rā33333 hu3m ā33 jyā3yo3ā32111 iti.

Lokadvāram apāvṛṇu, [O Fire,] please open the door of the world [of heaven]; *vayam svārājyāya,* so we may attain sovereignty; *tvā paśyema,* [and for that purpose] may see you.

12. [Addressing the Ādityas:] 'O Fire, please open the door to the world [i.e., heaven] for us so that we may see you for attaining sovereignty.'

आदित्यमथ वैश्वदेवं लो३कद्वारमपावा३र्णू३३ पश्येम त्वा वयं साम्रा३३३३३ हु३म् आ३३ ज्या३यो३आ३२-१११ इति॥१३॥

Ādityamatha vaiśvadevaṁ lo3kadvāramapāvā3rṇū33 paśyema tvā vayaṁ sāmrā33333 hu3m ā33 jyā3-yo3ā32111 iti.

Ādityam, that was addressed to the Ādityas; *atha,* next; *vaiśvadevam,* to the Viśvadevas; *lokadvāram apāvṛṇu,* [O Fire,] please open the door of the world [of heaven]; *vayam sāmrājyāya,* so we may attain sovereignty; *tvā paśyema,* [and for that purpose] may see you.

13. The earlier verse was addressed to the Ādityas. Now, addressing the Viśvadevas, [the yajamāna says,]

'O Fire, please open the door to the world [i.e., heaven] for us so that we may see you for attaining sovereignty.'

अथ जुहोति नम आदित्येभ्यश्च विश्वेभ्यश्च देवेभ्यो दिविक्षिद्भ्यो लोकक्षिद्भ्यो लोकं मे यजमानाय विन्दत ॥ १४ ॥

Atha juhoti nama ādityebhyaśca viśvebhyaśca devebhyo divikṣidbhyo lokakṣidbhyo lokaṁ me yajamānāya vindata.

Atha juhoti, then the sacrificer begins the offerings; *namaḥ ādityebhyaḥ ca viśvebhyaḥ ca devebhyaḥ,* salutations to the Ādityas and the Viśvadevas; *divikṣidbhyaḥ,* to those living in heaven; *lokakṣidbhyaḥ,* to those living in the worlds; *lokam me yajamānāya vindata,* help me, the yajamāna, acquire the right world.

14. Then the sacrificer begins the offerings [with this mantra]: 'Salutations to those who are in heaven and other worlds, to the Ādityas and the Viśvadevas. May I acquire the yajamāna's world.'

एष वै यजमानस्य लोक एतास्म्यत्र यजमानः परस्तादायुषः स्वाहापहत परिघमित्युक्त्वोत्तिष्ठति ॥ १५ ॥

Eṣa vai yajamānasya loka etāsmyatra yajamānaḥ parastādāyuṣaḥ svāhāpahata parighamityuktvottiṣṭhati.

Eṣaḥ vai yajamānasya loke etā asmi, I am ready to go to a world appropriate for one who performs sacrifices; *atra yajamānaḥ parastāt āyuṣaḥ,* I, the yajamāna, will live here after my death; *svāhā,* [saying] Svāhā [he completes the sacrifice]; *uttiṣṭhati,* he rises; *iti uktvā,* saying this; *apahata parigham,* may the bolt be removed.

15. 'I am ready to go to a world appropriate for one who performs sacrifices. I will live in this world after my death.' Saying 'Svāhā,' he completes the sacrifice. Then he rises, praying, 'May the bolt be removed.'

तस्मा आदित्याश्च विश्वे च देवास्तृतीयसवनं सम्प्रयच्छन्त्येष ह वै यज्ञस्य मात्रां वेद य एवं वेद य एवं वेद॥१६॥ इति चतुर्विंशः खण्डः॥२४॥ इति छान्दोग्योपनिषदि द्वितीयोऽध्यायः॥२॥

Tasmā ādityāśca viśve ca devāstṛtīyasavanaṁ samprayacchantyeṣa ha vai yajñasya mātrāṁ veda ya evaṁ veda ya evaṁ veda. Iti caturviṁśaḥ khaṇḍaḥ. Iti chāndogyopaniṣadi dvitīyo'dhyāyaḥ.

Tasmai, to him; *ādityāḥ ca viśve devāḥ ca,* the Ādityas and the Viśvadevas; *tṛtīya savanam sampra-*

yacchanti, present the result of the third savana; *yaḥ evam veda,* he who knows this; *eṣaḥ ha vai yajñasya mātrām veda,* he knows the true purport of the sacrifice. *Iti caturviṁśaḥ khaṇḍaḥ,* here ends the twenty-fourth section. *Iti chāndogyopaniṣadi dvitīyaḥ adhyāyaḥ,* here ends the second chapter of the Chāndogya Upaniṣad.

16. The Ādityas and the Viśvadevas then present to him, the sacrificer, the result of the third savana. He who knows this knows the true purport of the sacrifice.

CHAPTER THREE

Section One

ॐ। असौ वा आदित्यो देवमधु तस्य द्यौरेव तिरश्चीनवंशोऽन्तरिक्षमपूपो मरीचयः पुत्राः॥ १॥

Om. Asau vā ādityo devamadhu tasya dyaureva tiraścīnavaṁśo'ntarikṣamapūpo marīcayaḥ putrāḥ.

Asau vai ādityaḥ devamadhu, the sun over there is the honey of the gods; *tasya dyauḥ eva tiraścina-vaṁśaḥ,* heaven is its crossbeam [that supports it]; *antarikṣam apūpaḥ,* the mid-region is the beehive; *marīcayaḥ putrāḥ,* the rays are the eggs.

1. The sun over there is honey to the gods. Heaven is the crossbeam, the mid-region is the beehive, and the rays are the eggs.

This section begins the praise of the sun. The sun represents the sum total of the good work done by human beings. This is why the sun is like honey to the gods and why they love it. Heaven is said to be the crossbeam. It supports the mid-region, which is the beehive. The sun-rays attract water from the earth, and the water-drops in these rays are like the eggs of the bees.

तस्य ये प्राञ्चो रश्मयस्ता एवास्य प्राच्यो मधुनाड्यः। ऋच एव मधुकृत ऋग्वेद एव पुष्पं ता अमृता आपस्ता वा एता ऋचः॥ २॥

Tasya ye prāñco raśmayastā evāsya prācyo madhunāḍyaḥ; Ṛca eva madhukṛta ṛgveda eva puṣpaṁ tā amṛtā āpastā vā etā ṛcaḥ.

Tasya, of that [sun]; *ye,* those which are; *prāñcaḥ raśmayaḥ,* the rays in the east; *tāḥ eva,* they all; *asya prācyaḥ madhunāḍyaḥ,* are its eastern honey-cells; *ṛcaḥ eva madhukṛtaḥ,* the Ṛk mantras are the bees; *ṛgvedaḥ eva puṣpam,* the Ṛg Veda is the flower; *tāḥ āpaḥ amṛtāḥ,* the water [of the soma and other things offered as oblations] is the nectar; *tāḥ vai etāḥ ṛcaḥ,* these Ṛks—

2. The rays of the sun in the east are the eastern honey-cells [of the beehive]. The Ṛk mantras are the bees, and the Ṛg Veda is the flower. The water [from the sacrifice, such as the soma juice and other things] is the nectar [of the flower]. These Ṛk mantras—

The first rays of the sun seen in the east are like the honey cells of a beehive. In these cells are the bees, which are compared to the Ṛk mantras. The sun in the morning is red, like honey. The Ṛk mantras are called bees because bees produce honey, and the Ṛg Veda is called the flower because that is where the bees get the nectar to make the honey.

Here, the term *Ṛg Veda* does not mean words. It means work—that is, the rituals prescribed in the Veda. It is the result of the rituals that is described as honey. Just as the bees collect the juice from the flowers and change it into honey, so the Ṛks seem to collect from the sacrificial fire the liquid, consisting of the soma juice, butter, etc., from the oblations. This is called nectar because after the ingredients have been in the fire, they are transformed into the sweetest and purest thing possible. The result of the sacrificial ritual is the nectar (amṛta), because it leads to immortality. The word *amṛta* means both 'nectar' and 'immortality.'

एतमृग्वेदमभ्यतपंस्तस्याभितप्तस्य यशस्तेज इन्द्रियं वीर्यमन्नाद्यं रसोऽजायत॥ ३ ॥

Etamṛgvedamabhyatapaṁstasyābhitaptasya yaśasteja indriyaṁ vīryamannādyaṁ raso'jāyata.

Etam ṛgvedam, this Ṛg Veda; *abhyatapan,* stimulated; *tasya abhitaptasya,* from that [Ṛg Veda] so stimulated; *yaśaḥ,* fame; *tejaḥ,* vitality; *indriyam,* the power of the organs; *vīryam,* energy; *annādyam rasaḥ,* the essence of food; *ajāyata,* grew.

3. —stimulated this Ṛg Veda. Out of that Ṛg Veda so stimulated came fame, vitality, the power of the organs, energy, and the essence of food.

Earlier the Ṛk mantras were described as the bees and the Ṛg Veda as the flower, and so on. What then is produced from all this? Fame in the worlds, the beauty that comes from strength, the power of the organs, the strength and vigour which give the gods and goddesses supremacy, and so on.

The essence of all this comes from the sacrifices performed according to the Ṛg Veda.

तद्व्यक्षरत्तदादित्यमभितोऽश्रयत्तद्वा एतद्यदेतदादित्यस्य रोहितं रूपम्॥४॥ इति प्रथमः खण्डः॥१॥

Tadvyakṣarattadādityamabhito'śrayattadvā etadyade-tadādityasya rohitaṁ rūpam. Iti prathamaḥ khaṇḍaḥ.

Tat, that [fame, etc.]; *vyakṣarat,* spread out; *tat,* it; *ādityam abhitaḥ,* towards [in] the sun; *aśrayat,* took shelter; *tat vai etat,* it is this; *yat etat,* which is that; *rohitam rūpam,* red look; *ādityasya,* of the sun. *Iti prathamaḥ khaṇḍaḥ,* here ends the first section.

4. All this [fame, etc.] spread out to the sun and took shelter there. It is this that accounts for the red look of the sun.

The idea here is to praise good work done according to the scriptures. Such work gives people name and fame, strength, vigour, good health, and so on. And with these qualities a person can attain supremacy in the world. These qualities all collect around the sun in the morning, and this is why the sun looks red at that time. Name and fame, strength, etc., are there waiting for those who do virtuous work. This verse is to encourage people to do such work.

Section Two

अथ येऽस्य दक्षिणा रश्मयस्ता एवास्य दक्षिणा मधुनाड्यो यजूंष्येव मधुकृतो यजुर्वेद एव पुष्पं ता अमृता आपः ॥ १ ॥

Atha ye'sya dakṣiṇā raśmayastā evāsya dakṣiṇā madhunāḍyo yajūṁṣyeva madhukṛto yajurveda eva puṣpaṁ tā amṛtā āpaḥ.

Atha, then; *ye,* that which; *asya,* of it [the sun]; *dakṣiṇāḥ raśmayaḥ,* the rays in the south; *tāḥ eva,* they all; *asya dakṣiṇāḥ madhunāḍyaḥ,* are its southern honey-cells; *yajūṁṣi eva madhukṛtaḥ,* the Yajuḥ mantras are the bees; *yajurvedaḥ eva puṣpam,* the Yajur Veda is the flower; *tāḥ āpaḥ amṛtāḥ,* the water [of the soma and other things offered as oblations] is the nectar.

1. Then the rays of the sun in the south are the southern honey-cells [of the beehive]. The Yajuḥ mantras are the bees, and the Yajur Veda is the

flower. The water [from the sacrifice, such as the soma juice and other things] is the nectar [of the flower].

तानि वा एतानि यजूंष्येतं यजुर्वेदमभ्यतपंस्तस्याभितप्तस्य यशस्तेज इन्द्रियं वीर्यमन्नाद्यं रसोऽजायत ॥ २ ॥

Tāni vā etāni yajūṁṣyetaṁ yajurvedamabhyatapaṁstasyābhitaptasya yaśasteja indriyaṁ vīryamannādyaṁ raso'jāyata.

Tāni vai etāni, all these; *yajūṁṣi,* Yajuḥ mantras; *etam yajurvedam,* this Yajur Veda; *abhyatapan,* stimulated; *tasya abhitaptasya,* from that [Yajur Veda] so stimulated; *yaśaḥ,* fame; *tejaḥ,* vitality; *indriyam,* the power of the organs; *vīryam,* energy; *annādyam rasaḥ,* the essence of food; *ajāyata,* grew.

2. Those Yajuḥ mantras stimulated the Yajur Veda. Out of that Yajur Veda so stimulated came fame, vitality, the power of the organs, energy, and the essence of food.

तद्व्यक्षरत्तदादित्यमभितोऽश्रयत्तद्वा एतद्यदेतदादित्यस्य शुक्लं रूपम् ॥ ३ ॥ इति द्वितीयः खण्डः ॥ २ ॥

Tadvyakṣarattadādityamabhito'śrayattadvā etadyadetadādityasya śuklaṁ rūpam. Iti dvitīyaḥ khaṇḍaḥ.

Tat, that [fame, etc.]; *vyakṣarat,* spread out; *tat,* it; *ādityam abhitaḥ,* towards [in] the sun; *aśrayat,* took shelter; *tat vai etat,* it is this; *yat etat,* which is that; *śuklam rūpam,* white look; *ādityasya,* of the sun. *Iti dvitīyaḥ khaṇḍaḥ,* here ends the second section.

3. All this [fame, etc.] spread out to the sun and took shelter there. It is this that accounts for the white look of the sun.

Section Three

अथ येऽस्य प्रत्यञ्चो रश्मयस्ता एवास्य प्रतीच्यो मधुनाड्यः सामान्येव मधुकृतः सामवेद एव पुष्पं ता अमृता आपः ॥ १ ॥

Atha ye'sya pratyañco raśmayastā evāsya pratīcyo madhunāḍyaḥ sāmānyeva madhukṛtaḥ sāmaveda eva puṣpaṁ tā amṛtā āpaḥ.

Atha, then; *ye,* that which; *asya,* of it [the sun]; *pratyañcaḥ raśmayaḥ,* the rays in the west; *tāḥ eva,* they all; *asya pratīcyaḥ madhunāḍyaḥ,* are its western honey-cells; *sāmāni eva madhukṛtaḥ,* the Sāma mantras are the bees; *sāmavedaḥ eva puṣpam,* the Sāma Veda is the flower; *tāḥ āpaḥ amṛtāḥ,* the water [of the soma and other things offered as oblations] is the nectar.

1. Then the rays of the sun in the west are the western honey-cells [of the beehive]. The Sāma mantras are the bees, and the Sāma Veda is the flower. The water [from the sacrifice, such as the soma juice and other things] is the nectar [of the flower].

तानि वा एतानि सामान्येतं सामवेदमभ्यतपं-स्तस्याभितप्तस्य यशस्तेज इन्द्रियं वीर्यमन्नाद्यं रसो-ऽजायत ॥ २ ॥

Tāni vā etāni sāmānyetaṁ sāmavedamabhyatapaṁ-stasyābhitaptasya yaśasteja indriyaṁ vīryamannādyaṁ raso'jāyata.

Tāni vai etāni, these very; *sāmāni,* Sāma mantras; *etam sāmavedam,* this Sāma Veda; *abhyatapan,* stimulated; *tasya abhitaptasya,* from that [Sāma Veda] so stimulated; *yaśaḥ,* fame; *tejaḥ,* vitality; *indriyam,* the power of the organs; *vīryam,* energy; *annādyam rasaḥ,* the essence of food; *ajāyata,* grew.

2. Those Sāma mantras stimulated the Sāma Veda. Out of that Sāma Veda so stimulated came fame, vitality, the power of the organs, energy, and the essence of food.

तद्व्यक्षरत्तदादित्यमभितोऽश्रयत्तद्वा एतद्यदेतदादित्यस्य कृष्णं रूपम् ॥ ३ ॥ इति तृतीयः खण्डः ॥ ३ ॥

Tadvyakṣarattadādityamabhito'śrayattadvā etadyade-tadādityasya kṛṣṇaṁ rūpam. Iti tṛtīyaḥ khaṇḍaḥ.

Tat, that [fame, etc.]; *vyakṣarat,* spread out; *tat,* it; *ādityam abhitaḥ,* towards [in] the sun; *aśrayat,* took shelter; *tat vai etat,* it is this; *yat etat,* which is that; *kṛṣṇam rūpam,* black look; *ādityasya,* of the sun. *Iti tṛtīyaḥ khaṇḍaḥ,* here ends the third section.

3. All this [fame, etc.] spread out to the sun and took shelter there. It is this that gives rise to the black spots in the sun.

Section Four

अथ येऽस्योदञ्चो रश्मयस्ता एवास्योदीच्यो मधु-नाड्योऽथर्वाङ्गिरस एव मधुकृत इतिहासपुराणं पुष्पं ता अमृता आपः ॥ १ ॥

Atha ye'syodañco raśmayastā evāsyodīcyo madhu-nāḍyo'tharvāṅgirasa eva madhukṛta itihāsapurāṇaṁ puṣpaṁ tā amṛtā āpaḥ.

Atha, then; *ye,* that which; *asya,* of it [the sun]; *udañcaḥ raśmayaḥ,* the rays in the north; *tāḥ eva,* they all; *asya udīcyaḥ madhunāḍyaḥ,* are its northern honey-cells; *atharvāṅgirasaḥ eva madhukṛtaḥ,* the mantras envisioned by Atharvā and Aṅgirā are the bees; *itihāsapurāṇam eva puṣpam,* history and legends are the flower; *tāḥ āpaḥ amṛtāḥ,* the water [of the soma and other things offered as oblations] is the nectar.

1. Then the northern rays of the sun are the northern honey-cells [of the beehive]. The mantras envisioned by the sages Atharvā and Aṅgirā are the bees, and the Itihāsas and Purāṇas [i.e., history and legends] are the flower. The water [from the sacrifice, such as the soma juice and other things] is the nectar [of the flower].

ते वा एतेऽथर्वाङ्गिरस एतदितिहासपुराणमभ्य-
तपंस्तस्याभितप्तस्य यशस्तेज इन्द्रियं वीर्यमन्नाद्यं रसो-
ऽजायत ॥ २ ॥

*Te vā ete'tharvāṅgirasa etaditihāsapurāṇamabhya-
tapaṁstasyābhitaptasya yaśasteja indriyaṁ vīryamannādyaṁ raso'jāyata.*

Te vai ete, these very; *atharvāṅgirasaḥ,* mantras of Atharvā and Aṅgirā; *etat itihāsapurāṇam,* the Itihāsas and Purāṇas; *abhyatapan,* stimulated; *tasya abhitap-*

tasya, from that so stimulated; *yaśaḥ,* fame; *tejaḥ,* vitality; *indriyam,* the power of the organs; *vīryam,* energy; *annādyam rasaḥ,* the essence of food; *ajāyata,* grew.

2. Those Atharvā-Aṅgirasā mantras stimulated the Itihāsas and Purāṇas [i.e., the history and the legends]. Out of that so stimulated emerged fame, vitality, the power of the organs, energy, and the essence of food.

तद्व्यक्षरत्तदादित्यमभितोऽश्रयत्तद्वा एतद्यदेतदादित्यस्य परं कृष्णं रूपम्॥ ३॥ इति चतुर्थः खण्डः॥ ४॥

Tadvyakṣarattadādityamabhito'śrayattadvā etadyadetadādityasya paraṁ kṛṣṇaṁ rūpam. Iti caturthaḥ khaṇḍaḥ.

Tat, that [fame, etc.]; *vyakṣarat,* spread out; *tat,* it; *ādityam abhitaḥ,* towards [in] the sun; *aśrayat,* took shelter; *tat vai etat,* it is this; *yat etat,* which is that; *param kṛṣṇam rūpam,* deep black look; *ādityasya,* of the sun. *Iti caturthaḥ khaṇḍaḥ,* here ends the fourth section.

3. All this [fame, etc.] spread out to the sun and took shelter there. It is this that gives rise to the deep black spots in the sun.

Section Five

अथ येऽस्योर्ध्वा रश्मयस्ता एवास्योर्ध्वा मधुनाड्यो गुह्या एवादेशा मधुकृतो ब्रह्मैव पुष्पं ता अमृता आपः ॥ १ ॥

Atha ye'syordhvā raśmayastā evāsyordhvā madhunāḍyo guhyā evādeśā madhukṛto brahmaiva puṣpaṁ tā amṛtā āpaḥ.

Atha, next; *asya ye urdhvāḥ raśmayaḥ,* those rays [of the sun] which are in the higher region; *tāḥ eva asya urdhvāḥ madhunāḍyaḥ,* they are its honeycomb in the higher region; *guhyāḥ ādeśāḥ eva madhukṛtaḥ,* all secret directions are the bees; *brahma eva puṣpam,* Brahman [i.e., praṇava, Om] is the flower; *tāḥ āpaḥ amṛtāḥ,* the water [used in this connection] is the nectar.

1. Next, the rays of the sun which are in the higher region are also its honey-cells in the higher region. The secret instructions are the bees, and Brahman [praṇava] is the flower. The water [from the sacrifice] is the nectar.

The ṃantras used in the sacrifices are both secret and mystical. So also are the directions for a successful performance of a sacrifice. The mantras and the directions together constitute the bees in the illustration given here. The word *brahman* is used here in the sense of 'word,' so it means here *praṇava,* or Om. It is the flower.

ते वा एते गुह्या आदेशा एतद्ब्रह्माभ्यतपंस्तस्याभितप्तस्य यशस्तेज इन्द्रियं वीर्यमन्नाद्यं रसोऽजायत॥ २॥

Te vā ete guhyā ādeśā etadbrahmābhyatapaṁstasyābhitaptasya yaśasteja indriyaṁ vīryamannādyaṁ raso'jāyata.

Te vai ete, these very; *guhyāḥ ādeśāḥ,* secret directions; *etat brahma,* this Brahman [as praṇava]; *abhyatapan,* stimulated; *tasya abhitaptasya,* from that so stimulated; *yaśaḥ,* fame; *tejaḥ,* vitality; *indriyam,* the power of the organs; *vīryam,* energy; *annādyam rasaḥ,* the essence of food; *ajāyata,* grew.

2. These very secret directions stimulated Brahman [in the form of praṇava]. Out of that so stimulated emerged fame, vitality, the power of the organs, energy, and the essence of food.

तद्व्यक्षरत्तदादित्यमभितोऽश्रयत्तद्वा एतद्यदेतदादित्यस्य मध्ये क्षोभत इव॥ ३॥

Tadvyakṣarattadādityamabhito'śrayattadvā etadyadetadādityasya madhye kṣobhata iva.

Tat, that [fame, etc.]; *vyakṣarat,* spread out; *tat,* it; *ādityam abhitaḥ,* towards [in] the sun; *aśrayat,* took shelter; *tat vai etat,* it is this; *yat etat,* which is that; *kṣobhate iva,* seems to be vibrating; *ādityasya madhye,* within the sun.

3. All this [fame, etc.] spread out to the sun and took shelter there. It is this that seems to be vibrating within the sun.

ते वा एते रसानां रसा वेदा हि रसास्तेषामेते रसास्तानि वा एतान्यमृतानाममृतानि वेदा ह्यमृतास्तेषामे-तान्यमृतानि ॥ ४ ॥ इति पञ्चमः खण्डः ॥ ५ ॥

Te vā ete rasānāṁ rasā vedā hi rasāsteṣāmete rasāstāni vā etānyamṛtānāmamṛtāni vedā hyamṛtās-teṣāmetānyamṛtāni. Iti pañcamaḥ khaṇḍaḥ.

Te ete, these [the red and other colours]; *vai rasānām rasāḥ,* are the essence of the essences; *vedāḥ hi rasāḥ,* since the Vedas are the essence; *teṣām ete rasāḥ,* these [colours] are the essence of them [the Vedas]; *tāni etāni vai amṛtānāṁ amṛtāni,* these [colours] are the nectar of the nectar [the Vedas]; *hi vedāḥ amṛtāḥ,* as the Vedas are the nectar [or, eternal]; *etāni,* these [colours]; *teṣām amṛtāni,* are the nectar of them [the Vedas]. *Iti pañcamaḥ khaṇḍaḥ,* here ends the fifth section.

4. These colours [red, etc.] are the essence of all essences. The Vedas are the essence, and the colours are the essence of the Vedas. These colours are the nectar of the nectar [the Vedas]. The Vedas are the nectar [and therefore eternal], but the colours are the nectar of the Vedas.

Honey has been shown to be in different directions. This is just to stimulate our interest in seeking the essence of everything. The essence of everything is the Vedas, because through the Vedas we attain immortality. The term *Vedas* here means the Vedic ceremonies. Through these ceremonies we attain only relative immortality—that is, a long life, but a life that must end sooner or later. The expression 'essence of the essences' means that results which follow from the ceremonies are better than the ceremonies themselves. They are better, but they are short-lived. The implication is that we must not stop there.

Section Six

तद्यत्प्रथमममृतं तद्वसव उपजीवन्त्यग्निना मुखेन न वै देवा अश्नन्ति न पिबन्त्येतदेवामृतं दृष्ट्वा तृप्यन्ति॥ १॥

Tadyatprathamamamṛtaṁ tadvasava upajīvantyagninā mukhena na vai devā aśnanti na pibantyetadevāmṛtaṁ dṛṣṭvā tṛpyanti.

Tat yat, that which; *prathamam amṛtam,* the first nectar [i.e., the red colour of the sun]; *tat,* that; *vasavaḥ,* the Vasus; *upajīvanti,* enjoy; *agninā mukhena,* led by fire; *vai,* as a matter of fact; *devāḥ,* the gods and goddesses; *na aśnanti na pibanti,* neither eat nor drink; *etat amṛtam,* this nectar; *eva dṛṣṭvā tṛpyanti,* they are pleased by only seeing.

1. Led by fire, the Vasus enjoy the first nectar [which is the red colour]. As a matter of fact, the gods and goddesses neither eat nor drink. They are pleased merely by seeing the nectar.

Earlier it was described what the nectar is and how it may be meditated upon. The gods and goddesses enjoy this nectar. How these gods and goddesses may be meditated upon is now being stated.

Early in the morning the sun is red, and this red colour is the first nectar, which is enjoyed by the Vasus led by fire. They enjoy it by seeing, not by eating and drinking. They, in fact, enjoy it by using all their organs.

The body is a source of bad odour and bad secretions, but because the gods are all under the protection of the sun, they are therefore exempt from them.

त एतदेव रूपमभिसंविशन्त्येतस्माद्रूपादुद्यन्ति ॥ २ ॥

Ta etadeva rūpamabhisaṁviśantyetasmādrūpādud-yanti.

Te, they [the gods and goddesses]; *etat eva rūpam,* this [red] colour; *abhisaṁviśanti,* enter into [i.e., they keep looking at it and make no further attempt to enjoy it]; *etasmāt rūpāt,* from this colour [i.e., attracted by this colour]; *udyanti,* they come out [i.e., they try to reach it].

2. They enter into this [red] colour [of the sun], and they also come out of this colour. [i.e., They look at this red colour and are satisfied. They make no effort to get it. Nevertheless, they are at times attracted to it and try to reach it.]

The gods and goddesses look at the red colour and keep quiet. Why do they keep quiet? Why do they not try to reach it? Because they feel that the time is not yet ripe for them to get it. When they feel it is the right time, then they start trying. They are fully aware that they must try, and try hard, to attain the things they desire.

स य एतदेवममृतं वेद वसूनामेवैको भूत्वाग्निनैव मुखेनैतदेवामृतं दृष्ट्वा तृप्यति स एतदेव रूपमभिसंविश-त्येतस्माद्रूपादुदेति ॥ ३ ॥

Sa ya etadevamamṛtaṁ veda vasūnāmevaiko bhūtvāgninaiva mukhenaitadevāmṛtaṁ dṛṣṭvā tṛpyati sa etadeva rūpamabhisaṁviśatyetasmādrūpādudeti.

Saḥ yaḥ, he who; *evam,* thus; *etat amṛtam veda,* knows this nectar; *vasūnām eva ekaḥ bhūtvā,* having become one of the Vasus; *agninā eva mukhena,* led by fire; *etat eva amṛtam dṛṣṭvā tṛpyati,* enjoys by seeing the nectar; *saḥ etat eva rūpam abhisaṁviśati,* he enters into this [red] colour; *etasmāt rūpāt udeti,* he also comes out of this colour.

3. He who knows this nectar thus, becomes one of the Vasus [because only the Vasus know the meaning of this nectar]. Led by fire, he then enjoys looking at the nectar and is happy. He goes into this colour and again comes out of it.

Anyone can perform the ceremonies mentioned in the Ṛg Veda and thus attain the results mentioned earlier. These ceremonies are like flowers, and by reciting the Ṛk mantras, you can collect the honey in the form of fame, strength, etc. Not only that, when you attain these things, you are also able to preserve them by the grace of the sun.

Further, the beauty and grandeur of the sun in the early morning is like a special gift meant just for you. You are then one of the gods known as the Vasus. You can enjoy this state at will, and if you wish, can enjoy whatever the sun has to give. If you do not want to enjoy anything, you can merely look at it and that is enough enjoyment for you.

स यावदादित्यः पुरस्तादुदेता पश्चादस्तमेता वसूना-
मेव तावदाधिपत्यं स्वाराज्यं पर्येता॥४॥ इति षष्ठः
खण्डः॥६॥

Sa yāvadādityaḥ purastādudetā paścādastametā vasūnāmeva tāvadādhipatyaṁ svārājyaṁ paryetā. Iti ṣaṣṭhaḥ khaṇḍaḥ.

Yāvat, so long as; *ādityaḥ,* the sun; *purastāt udetā,* rises in the east; *paścāt astam-etā,* sets in the west; *eva tāvat,* that long; *saḥ,* he; *vasūnām,* of the Vasus; *ādhipatyam,* sovereignty; *svārājyam,* freedom; *pari-etā,* will enjoy. *Iti ṣaṣṭhaḥ khaṇḍaḥ,* here ends the sixth section.

4. As long as the sun rises in the east and sets in the west, so long will that person enjoy the sovereignty and freedom of the Vasus.

There is a difference between those who merely perform sacrifices and those who perform sacrifices but are, at the same time, deeply concerned with their spiritual development. The former may attain heaven, but only for a short while. The latter attain a status like the Vasus and become sovereigns. They attain liberation as and when they like.

Section Seven

अथ यद्द्वितीयममृतं तद्रुद्रा उपजीवन्तीन्द्रेण मुखेन
न वै देवा अश्नन्ति न पिबन्त्येतदेवामृतं दृष्ट्वा तृप्यन्ति ॥ १ ॥

Atha yaddvitīyamamṛtaṁ tadrudrā upajīvantīndreṇa mukhena na vai devā aśnanti na pibantyetadevāmṛtaṁ dṛṣṭvā tṛpyanti.

Atha, next; *yat,* that which; *dvitīyam amṛtam,* the second nectar [i.e., the white colour of the sun]; *tat,* that; *rudrāḥ,* the Rudras; *upajīvanti,* enjoy; *indreṇa mukhena,* led by Indra; *vai,* as a matter of fact; *devāḥ,* the gods and goddesses; *na aśnanti na pibanti,* neither eat nor drink; *etat amṛtam,* this nectar; *eva dṛṣṭvā tṛpyanti,* they are pleased by only seeing.

1. With Indra as their leader, the Rudras enjoy the second nectar [which is the white colour of the sun]. As a matter of fact, the gods and goddesses neither eat nor drink. They are pleased merely by seeing the nectar.

त एतदेव रूपमभिसंविशन्त्येतस्माद्रूपादुद्यन्ति ॥ २ ॥

Ta etadeva rūpamabhisaṁviśantyetasmādrūpādud-yanti.

Te, they [the Rudras]; *etat eva rūpam,* this [white] colour; *abhisaṁviśanti,* enter into [i.e., they keep looking at it and make no further attempt to enjoy it]; *etasmāt rūpāt,* from this colour [i.e., attracted by this colour]; *udyanti,* they come out [i.e., they try to reach it].

2. They enter into this [white] colour of the sun, and they also come out of this colour.

स य एतदेवममृतं वेद रुद्राणामेवैको भूत्वेन्द्रेणैव मुखेनैतदेवामृतं दृष्ट्वा तृप्यति स एतदेव रूपमभिसंविश- त्येतस्माद्रूपादुदेति ॥ ३ ॥

Sa ya etadevamamṛtaṁ veda rudrāṇāmevaiko bhūtvendreṇaiva mukhenaitadevāmṛtaṁ dṛṣṭvā tṛpyati sa etadeva rūpamabhisaṁviśatyetasmādrūpādudeti.

Saḥ yaḥ, he who; *evam,* thus; *etat amṛtam veda,* knows this nectar; *rudrāṇām eva ekaḥ bhūtvā,* becomes one of the Rudras; *indreṇa eva mukhena,* led by Indra; *etat eva amṛtam dṛṣṭvā tṛpyati,* enjoys by seeing the nectar; *saḥ etat eva rūpam abhisaṁviśati,* he enters into this [white] colour; *etasmāt rūpāt udeti,* he also comes out of this colour.

3. He who knows this nectar thus, becomes a Rudra himself. With Indra as the leader, he looks at the

nectar and is happy. He goes into this colour and again comes out of it.

स यावदादित्यः पुरस्तादुदेता पश्चादस्तमेता द्विस्तावद्दक्षिणत उदेतोत्तरतोऽस्तमेता रुद्राणामेव तावदाधिपत्यं स्वाराज्यं पर्येता॥ ४॥ इति सप्तमः खण्डः॥ ७॥

Sa yāvadādityaḥ purastādudetā paścādastametā dvistāvaddakṣiṇata udetottarato'stametā rudrāṇāmeva tāvadādhipatyaṁ svārājyaṁ paryetā. Iti saptamaḥ khaṇḍaḥ.

Yāvat, so long as; *ādityaḥ,* the sun; *purastāt udetā,* rises in the east; *paścāt astam-etā,* sets in the west; *saḥ,* he [who knows this]; *dviḥ-tāvat,* twice that long; *dakṣiṇataḥ udetā,* will rise in the south; *uttarataḥ astam-etā,* [and] set in the north; *eva tāvat,* that long; *rudrāṇām,* of the Rudras; *ādhipatyam,* sovereignty; *svārājyam,* freedom; *pari-etā,* will attain. *Iti saptamaḥ khaṇḍaḥ,* here ends the seventh section.

4. As long as the sun rises in the east and sets in the west, twice that long will he [who knows this] rise in the south and set in the north. That person will also attain sovereignty and freedom like the Rudras.

Section Eight

अथ यत्तृतीयममृतं तदादित्या उपजीवन्ति वरुणेन मुखेन न वै देवा अश्नन्ति न पिबन्त्येतदेवामृतं दृष्ट्वा तृप्यन्ति ॥ १ ॥

Atha yattṛtīyamamṛtaṁ tadādityā upajīvanti varuṇena mukhena na vai devā aśnanti na pibantyetadevāmṛtaṁ dṛṣṭvā tṛpyanti.

Atha, next; *yat,* that which; *tṛtīyam amṛtam,* the third nectar [i.e., the dark colour of the sun]; *tat,* that; *ādityāḥ,* the Ādityas; *upajīvanti,* sustain themselves with; *varuṇena mukhena,* led by Varuṇa; *vai,* as a matter of fact; *devāḥ,* the gods and goddesses; *na aśnanti na pibanti,* neither eat nor drink; *etat amṛtam,* this nectar; *eva dṛṣṭvā tṛpyanti,* they become happy by only seeing.

1. With Varuṇa as their leader, the Ādityas enjoy the third nectar [which is dark in colour]. As a matter of fact, the gods and goddesses neither eat nor drink. They are pleased merely by seeing the nectar.

त एतदेव रूपमभिसंविशन्त्येतस्माद्रूपादुद्यन्ति ॥ २ ॥

Ta etadeva rūpamabhisaṁviśantyetasmādrūpādud-yanti.

Te, they [the Ādityas]; *etat eva rūpam,* this [dark] colour; *abhisaṁviśanti,* enter into [i.e., they keep looking at it and make no further attempt to enjoy it]; *etasmāt rūpāt,* from this colour [i.e., attracted by this colour]; *udyanti,* they come out [i.e., they try to reach it].

2. They enter into this [dark] colour of the sun, and they also come out of this colour.

स य एतदेवममृतं वेदादित्यानामेवैको भूत्वा वरुणेनैव मुखेनैतदेवामृतं दृष्ट्वा तृप्यति स एतदेव रूपमभिसंविशत्येतस्माद्रूपादुदेति ॥ ३ ॥

Sa ya etadevamamṛtaṁ vedādityānāmevaiko bhūtvā varuṇenaiva mukhenaitadevāmṛtaṁ dṛṣṭvā tṛpyati sa etadeva rūpamabhisaṁviśatyetasmādrūpādudeti.

Saḥ yaḥ, he who; *evam,* thus; *etat amṛtam veda,* knows this nectar; *ādityānām eva ekaḥ bhūtvā,* becomes one of the Ādityas; *varuṇena eva mukhena,* led by Varuṇa; *etat eva amṛtam dṛṣṭvā tṛpyati,* enjoys by seeing the nectar; *saḥ etat eva rūpam abhisaṁviśati,* he enters into this [dark] colour; *etasmāt rūpāt udeti,* he also comes out of this colour.

3. He who knows this nectar thus, becomes one of the Ādityas. With Varuṇa as the leader, he enjoys

the nectar by looking at it. He goes into this colour and again comes out of it.

स यावदादित्यो दक्षिणत उदेतोत्तरतोऽस्तमेता द्विस्तावत्पश्चादुदेता पुरस्तादस्तमेतादित्यानामेव तावदाधिपत्यं स्वाराज्यं पर्येता ॥ ४ ॥ इत्यष्टमः खण्डः ॥ ८ ॥

Sa yāvadādityo dakṣiṇata udetottarato'stametā dvistāvatpaścādudetā purastādastametādityānāmeva tāvadādhipatyaṁ svārājyaṁ paryetā. Ityaṣṭamaḥ khaṇḍaḥ.

Yāvat, so long as; *ādityaḥ,* the sun; *dakṣiṇataḥ udetā,* rises in the south; *uttarataḥ astam-etā,* [and] sets in the north; *saḥ,* he [who knows this]; *dviḥ-tāvat,* twice that long; *paścāt udetā,* will rise in the west; *purastāt astam-etā,* [and] set in the east; *eva tāvat,* that long; *ādityānām,* of the Ādityas; *ādhipatyam,* sovereignty; *svārājyam,* freedom; *pari-etā,* will attain. *Iti aṣṭamaḥ khaṇḍaḥ,* here ends the eighth section.

4. As long as the sun rises in the south and sets in the north, twice that long will he [who knows this] rise in the west and set in the east. That person will also attain sovereignty and freedom like the Ādityas.

The sun neither rises nor sets; it is always stationary. It merely gives the impression of rising and setting.

Section Nine

अथ यच्चतुर्थममृतं तन्मरुत उपजीवन्ति सोमेन मुखेन
न वै देवा अश्नन्ति न पिबन्त्येतदेवामृतं दृष्ट्वा तृप्यन्ति ॥ १ ॥

Atha yaccaturthamamṛtaṁ tanmaruta upajīvanti somena mukhena na vai devā aśnanti na pibantyetadevāmṛtaṁ dṛṣṭvā tṛpyanti.

Atha, next; *yat,* that which; *caturtham amṛtam,* the fourth nectar [i.e., the deep black colour of the sun]; *tat,* that; *marutaḥ,* the Maruts; *upajīvanti,* enjoy; *somena mukhena,* led by Soma; *vai,* as a matter of fact; *devāḥ,* the gods and goddesses; *na aśnanti na pibanti,* neither eat nor drink; *etat amṛtam,* this nectar; *eva dṛṣṭvā tṛpyanti,* they become happy by only seeing.

1. With Soma as their leader, the Maruts enjoy the fourth nectar [which is deep black in colour]. As a matter of fact, the gods and goddesses neither eat nor drink. They enjoy merely by seeing the nectar.

त एतदेव रूपमभिसंविशन्त्येतस्माद्रूपादुद्यन्ति ॥ २ ॥

Ta etadeva rūpamabhisaṁviśantyetasmādrūpādudyanti.

Te, they [the Maruts]; *etat eva rūpam,* this [deep black] colour; *abhisaṁviśanti,* enter into [i.e., they keep looking at it and make no further attempt to enjoy it]; *etasmāt rūpāt,* from this colour [i.e., attracted by this colour]; *udyanti,* they come out [i.e., they try to reach it].

2. They enter into this [deep black] colour of the sun, and they also come out of this colour.

स य एतदेवममृतं वेद मरुतामेवैको भूत्वा सोमेनैव मुखेनैतदेवामृतं दृष्ट्वा तृप्यति स एतदेव रूपमभिसंविश-त्येतस्माद्रूपादुदेति ॥ ३ ॥

Sa ya etadevamamṛtaṁ veda marutāmevaiko bhūtvā somenaiva mukhenaitadevāmṛtaṁ dṛṣṭvā tṛpyati sa etadeva rūpamabhisaṁviśatyetasmādrūpādudeti.

Saḥ yaḥ, he who; *evam,* thus; *etat amṛtam veda,* knows this nectar; *marutām eva ekaḥ bhūtvā,* becomes one of the Maruts; *somena eva mukhena,* led by Soma; *etat eva amṛtam dṛṣṭvā tṛpyati,* he enjoys by seeing the nectar; *saḥ etat eva rūpam abhisaṁviśati,* he enters into this [deep black] colour; *etasmāt rūpāt udeti,* he also comes out of this colour.

3. He who knows this nectar thus, becomes one of the Maruts. With Soma as the leader, he enjoys

the nectar by looking at it. He goes into this colour and again comes out of it.

स यावदादित्यः पश्चादुदेता पुरस्तादस्तमेता द्विस्तावदुत्तरत उदेता दक्षिणतोऽस्तमेता मरुतामेव तावदाधिपत्यं स्वाराज्यं पर्येता ॥ ४ ॥ इति नवमः खण्डः ॥ ९ ॥

Sa yāvadādityaḥ paścādudetā purastādastametā dvistāvaduttarata udetā dakṣiṇato'stametā marutāmeva tāvadādhipatyaṁ svārājyaṁ paryetā. Iti navamaḥ khaṇḍaḥ.

Yāvat, so long as; *ādityaḥ,* the sun; *paścāt udetā,* rises in the west; *purastāt astam-etā,* [and] sets in the east; *saḥ,* he [who knows this]; *dviḥ-tāvat,* twice that long; *uttarataḥ udetā,* will rise in the north; *dakṣiṇataḥ astam-etā,* [and] set in the south; *eva tāvat,* that long; *marutām,* of the Maruts; *ādhipatyam,* sovereignty; *svārājyam,* freedom; *pari-etā,* will attain. *Iti navamaḥ khaṇḍaḥ,* here ends the ninth section.

4. As long as the sun rises in the west and sets in the east, twice that long will he [who knows this] rise in the north and set in the south. That person will also attain sovereignty and freedom like the Maruts.

Section Ten

अथ यत्पञ्चमममृतं तत्साध्या उपजीवन्ति ब्रह्मणा मुखेन न वै देवा अश्नन्ति न पिबन्त्येतदेवामृतं दृष्ट्वा तृप्यन्ति ॥ १ ॥

Atha yatpañcamamamṛtaṁ tatsādhyā upajīvanti brahmaṇā mukhena na vai devā aśnanti na pibantyetadevāmṛtaṁ dṛṣṭvā tṛpyanti.

Atha, next; *yat,* that which; *pañcamam amṛtam,* the fifth nectar [i.e., what appears to be vibrating within the sun]; *tat,* that; *sādhyāḥ,* the Sādhyas; *upajīvanti,* enjoy; *brahmaṇā mukhena,* led by Brahman [i.e., praṇava]; *vai,* as a matter of fact; *devāḥ,* the gods and goddesses; *na aśnanti na pibanti,* neither eat nor drink; *etat amṛtam,* this nectar; *eva dṛṣṭvā tṛpyanti,* they become happy by only seeing.

1. With Brahman [in the form of praṇava, Om] as their leader, the Sādhyas enjoy the fifth nectar [that which seems to be trembling within the sun]. As a matter of fact, the gods and goddesses neither eat nor drink. They enjoy merely by seeing the nectar.

त एतदेव रूपमभिसंविशन्त्येतस्माद्रूपादुद्यन्ति ॥ २ ॥

Ta etadeva rūpamabhisaṁviśantyetasmādrūpādud-yanti.

Te, they [the Sādhyas]; *etat eva rūpam,* this form [of the sun which seems to be vibrating]; *abhisaṁvi-śanti,* enter into [i.e., they keep looking at it and make no further attempt to enjoy it]; *etasmāt rūpāt,* from this form [i.e., attracted by this form]; *udyanti,* they come out [i.e., they try to reach it].

2. They enter into this form of the sun [which seems to be vibrating], and they also come out of this form.

स य एतदेवममृतं वेद साध्यानामेवैको भूत्वा ब्रह्मणैव मुखेनैतदेवामृतं दृष्ट्वा तृप्यति स एतदेव रूपमभिसंविश-त्येतस्माद्रूपादुदेति ॥ ३ ॥

Sa ya etadevamamṛtaṁ veda sādhyānāmevaiko bhūtvā brahmaṇaiva mukhenaitadevāmṛtaṁ dṛṣṭvā tṛpyati sa etadeva rūpamabhisaṁviśatyetasmādrūpādu-deti.

Saḥ yaḥ, he who; *evam,* thus; *etat amṛtam veda,* knows this nectar; *sādhyānām eva ekaḥ bhūtvā,* becomes one of the Sādhyas; *brahmaṇā eva mukhena,* led by Brahman [as praṇava]; *etat eva amṛtam dṛṣṭvā tṛpyati,* he enjoys by seeing the nectar; *saḥ etat eva rūpam abhisaṁviśati,* he enters into this form [of the sun]; *etasmāt rūpāt udeti,* he also comes out of this form.

3. He who knows this nectar thus, becomes one of the Sādhyas. With Brahman [in the form of praṇava] as the leader, he enjoys the nectar by looking at it. He goes into this form [of the sun] and again comes out of it.

स यावदादित्य उत्तरत उदेता दक्षिणतोऽस्तमेता द्विस्तावदूर्ध्व उदेतार्वाङस्तमेता साध्यानामेव तावदाधिपत्यं स्वाराज्यं पर्येता॥ ४॥ इति दशमः खण्डः॥ १०॥

Sa yāvadāditya uttarata udetā dakṣiṇato'stametā dvistāvadūrdhva udetārvāṅastametā sādhyānāmeva tāvadādhipatyaṁ svārājyaṁ paryetā. Iti daśamaḥ khaṇḍaḥ.

Yāvat, so long as; *ādityaḥ,* the sun; *uttarataḥ udetā,* rises in the north; *dakṣiṇataḥ astam-etā,* [and] sets in the south; *saḥ,* he [who knows this]; *dviḥ-tāvat,* twice that long; *ūrdhvaḥ udetā,* will rise above; *arvāk astam-etā,* [and] set down below; *eva tāvat,* that long; *sādhyānām,* of the Sādhyas; *ādhipatyam,* sovereignty; *svārājyam,* freedom; *pari-etā,* will attain. *Iti daśamaḥ khaṇḍaḥ,* here ends the tenth section.

4. As long as the sun rises in the north and sets in the south, twice that long will he [who knows

this] rise above and set below. That person will also attain sovereignty and freedom like the Sādhyas [i.e., he can move up and down as he likes].

The sun is stationary. It neither rises nor sets. If it appears to rise or set, it is because of how we perceive it. Similarly, the sun may seem to rise in a different direction, depending on where we are when we see it.

The Vasus, Rudras, Ādityas, etc., are minor gods and goddesses. They have not yet attained the status of Brahman, but they are on their way to doing so. However, anyone can attain the status of a minor god or godddess—that is, he can be like a Rudra, for instance. By performing sacrifices mentioned in the scriptures a person can share with those minor gods and goddesses the special worlds reserved for them. Such a person may even enjoy many powers and privileges, but he is still far away from the status of Brahman.

Section Eleven

अथ तत ऊर्ध्व उदेत्य नैवोदेता नास्तमेतैकल एव मध्ये स्थाता तदेष श्लोकः॥ १॥

Atha tata ūrdhva udetya naivodetā nāstametaikala eva madhye sthātā tadeṣa ślokaḥ.

Atha, next; *tataḥ,* after that [i.e., after giving the living beings the fruits of their work]; *ūrdhvaḥ udetya,* [and] having risen above [such tasks]; *na eva udetā,* it [the sun] will not rise again; *na astam-etā,* nor will it set; *ekalaḥ,* alone; *eva madhye sthātā,* it will stay midway; *tat eṣaḥ ślokaḥ,* here is a verse on the subject.

1. Next, after giving to all living beings the fruits of their work, the sun will be above such obligations. It will no longer rise nor set, and will stay by itself midway. Here is a verse on the subject:

न वै तत्र न निम्लोच नोदियाय कदाचन।
देवास्तेनाहं सत्येन मा विराधिषि ब्रह्मणा॥ इति॥ २॥

Na vai tatra na nimloca nodiyāya kadācana;
Devāstenāhaṁ satyena mā virādhiṣi brahmaṇā. Iti.

[You ask about the sunrise and sunset in Brahmaloka]—*na vai,* no indeed; *tatra,* there [in Brahmaloka]; *kadācana na nimloca,* [the sun] never set; *na udiyāya,* nor did it rise; *devāḥ,* O gods [listen to me]; *tena satyena,* by this which is true; *aham brahmaṇā mā virādhiṣi,* may I not have any hindrance to my realization of Brahman.

2. [In answer to a question]—No, indeed, in Brahmaloka the sun never rose, nor did it ever set. O gods, [listen and bear witness to me]. What I am saying

is true, and by it may I have no hindrance to my realization of Brahman.

This is an assertion that there is no day or night in Brahmaloka. When a person makes a statement like this, he invokes the gods to bear witness to what he is saying. He is confident that what he is saying is true and that it will be no bar to his being one with Brahman.

न ह वा अस्मा उदेति न निम्लोचति सकृद्दिवा हैवास्मै भवति य एतामेवं ब्रह्मोपनिषदं वेद॥ ३॥

Na ha vā asmā udeti na nimlocati sakṛddivā haivāsmai bhavati ya etāmevaṁ brahmopaniṣadaṁ veda.

Na, not; *ha vai asmai,* so far as he is concerned; *udeti,* does [the sun] rise; *na nimlocati,* nor does it set; *asmai,* for him; *sakṛt divā ha eva bhavati,* there is always day [i.e., light]; *yaḥ,* he who; *etām,* this; *evam,* in this way; *brahmopaniṣadam,* the secret teachings about Brahman; *veda,* knows.

3. For him who knows the secret teachings of Brahman there is no sunrise or sunset [or day or night]. For him there is always day [i.e., light].

Earlier it was described how Brahman manifests itself in various forms—as a crossbeam, a honeycomb, etc., or as various gods enjoying various nectars. If you understand the underlying meaning of such manifestations, you then attain the knowledge of Brahman. To you then there is no day or night. You are like the sun—self-luminous. You are, in fact, one with Brahman—always the same, eternal, infinite.

तद्धैतद्ब्रह्मा प्रजापतय उवाच प्रजापतिर्मनवे मनुः प्रजाभ्यस्तद्धैतदुद्दालकायारुणये ज्येष्ठाय पुत्राय पिता ब्रह्म प्रोवाच ॥ ४ ॥

Taddhaitadbrahmā prajāpataya uvāca prajāpatir-manave manuḥ prajābhyastaddhaitaduddālakāyāruṇaye jyeṣṭhāya putrāya pitā brahma provāca.

Tat ha etat, that [i.e., the teaching on honey]; *brahmā prajāpataya uvāca,* Brahmā [first] taught to Prajāpati; *prajāpatiḥ manave,* Prajāpati [taught it] to Manu; *manuḥ prajābhyaḥ,* Manu [taught it] to his children; *tat ha etat,* that; *brahma,* [knowledge of] Brahman; *pitā provāca,* the father [Aruṇa] taught; *jyeṣṭhāya putrāya uddālakāya āruṇaye,* to his eldest son Uddālaka Āruṇi.

4. First, Brahmā taught this instruction on honey to Prajāpati. Then Prajāpati taught it to Manu, and Manu taught it to his children. The father Aruṇa then taught this knowledge of Brahman to his eldest son Uddālaka Āruṇi.

Starting from Brahmā, this knowledge has passed from generation to generation. The mention of this is only to emphasize its importance. This instruction on honey is nothing but Brahma-vidyā, the knowledge of Brahman. It is the secret of how to attain Brahman.

इदं वाव तज्ज्येष्ठाय पुत्राय पिता ब्रह्म प्रब्रूयात्प्रणाय्याय वान्तेवासिने ॥ ५ ॥

Idaṁ vāva tajjyeṣṭhāya putrāya pitā brahma prabrūyātpraṇāyyāya vāntevāsine.

Tat vāva idam brahma, this knowledge of Brahman [previously mentioned as passing from teacher to student]; *pitā jyeṣṭhāya putrāya,* the father to his eldest son; *vā,* or; *praṇāyyāya,* a fit; *antevāsine,* resident student; *prabrūyāt,* will teach [or, pass on].

5. This knowledge of Brahman a father will pass on to his eldest son or to a competent resident student.

The knowledge of Brahman is the highest gift a person can confer on another. A father who has this knowledge can give it to his eldest son, or a competent teacher can pass it on to a competent student living with him.

नान्यस्मै कस्मैचन यद्यप्यस्मा इमामद्भिः परिगृहीतां धनस्य पूर्णां दद्यादेतदेव ततो भूय इत्येतदेव ततो भूय इति॥ ६॥ इत्येकादशः खण्डः॥ ११॥

Nānyasmai kasmaicana yadyapyasmā imāmadbhiḥ parigṛhītāṁ dhanasya pūrṇāṁ dadyādetadeva tato bhūya ityetadeva tato bhūya iti. Ityekādaśaḥ khaṇḍaḥ.

Na anyasmai kasmaicana, to nobody else; *yadi api asmai,* even if to him [to the teacher]; *imām,* this [world]; *adbhiḥ parigṛhītām,* surrounded by water; *dhanasya pūrṇām,* full of gold; *dadyāt,* gives; *etat,* this [instruction on honey]; *eva tataḥ bhūyaḥ iti,* is more precious than that [the repetition is for emphasis]. *Iti ekādaśaḥ khaṇḍaḥ,* here ends the eleventh section.

6. This should never be taught to anyone else, even if one is tempted with the whole world full of riches and surrounded by water. For this knowledge is more precious than that. This knowledge is surely more precious than that.

Section Twelve

गायत्री वा इदं सर्वं भूतं यदिदं किञ्च वाग्वै गायत्री वाग्वा इदं सर्वं भूतं गायति च त्रायते च॥ १॥

Gāyatrī vā idaṁ sarvaṁ bhūtaṁ yadidaṁ kiñca vāgvai gāyatrī vāgvā idaṁ sarvaṁ bhūtaṁ gāyati ca trāyate ca.

Gāyatrī vai idam sarvam bhūtam, all these beings are gāyatrī; *yat idam kiñca,* whatever is there; *vāk vai gāyatrī,* the word is gāyatrī; *vāk vai idam sarvam bhūtam gāyati ca,* it is vāk that gives names [or sings] to all things; *trāyate ca,* and also gives protection.

1. All that exists in this world, whatever there is, is gāyatrī. It is the word that is gāyatrī, for the word gives names to all things and it also tells them not to fear.

Here the importance of the gāyatrī is being emphasized. True, the gāyatrī is poetry, but it is that poetry which leads to Brahman. This gāyatrī is also called *vāk,* word, because it is vāk which identifies everything that exists. Vāk gives everything a name and thereby gives it a status.

The word *gāyatrī* means *gāyati ca trāyate ca*—that which gives names (or sings) to things and also gives them protection. It also means *gāyantam trāyate*—that is, he who repeats the gāyatrī is saved. (*Ga* means singing, and *tra* means saving or protecting.)

या वै सा गायत्रीयं वाव सा येयं पृथिव्यस्यां हीदं सर्वं भूतं प्रतिष्ठितमेतामेव नातिशीयते ॥ २ ॥

Yā vai sā gāyatrīyaṁ vāva sā yeyaṁ pṛthivyasyāṁ hīdaṁ sarvaṁ bhūtaṁ pratiṣṭhitametāmeva nātiśīyate.

Yā vai sā gāyatrī, that which is this gāyatrī; *iyam vāva sā,* it is that; *yā iyam pṛthivī,* which is this earth; *hi,* for; *asyām,* to this [earth]; *sarvam bhūtam,* all things [moving or unmoving]; *pratiṣṭhitam,* are attached; *etām eva na atiśīyate,* cannot get away from it.

2. That which is this gāyatrī is that which is this earth. For all things [moving or unmoving] are attached to this earth and cannot get away from it.

या वै सा पृथिवीयं वाव सा यदिदमस्मिन्पुरुषे शरीरमस्मिन्हीमे प्राणाः प्रतिष्ठिता एतदेव नातिशीयन्ते ॥ ३ ॥

Yā vai sā pṛthivīyaṁ vāva sā yadidamasminpuruṣe śarīramasminhīme prāṇāḥ pratiṣṭhitā etadeva nātiśīyante.

Yā vai sā pṛthivī, that which [has earlier been referred to as] this earth; *iyam vāva sā,* it is that; *yat idam asmin puruṣe śarīram,* the body which is associated with a human being; *hi,* because; *asmin,* on this [body]; *ime prāṇāḥ,* these prāṇas [i.e., prāṇa, apāna, etc., and also the five elements—ākāśa, vāyu, etc.]; *pratiṣṭhitāḥ,* are based; *etat eva na atiśīyante,* they cannot go beyond this [body—i.e., they cannot exist independent of this body].

3. That which is this earth is this human body, because all the prāṇas are based in this body and cannot exist independent of it.

The earth is the gāyatrī and this gāyatrī is also the human body because the human body is born of the earth. How is the human body born of the earth? This body is made up of the same elements (space, air, fire, etc.) that the earth is. The five prāṇas (prāṇa, apāna, vyāna, udāna, and samāna) are also known as elements, and they rest on this body. The body is therefore the gāyatrī like the earth. It is the gāyatrī because the prāṇas cannot exist without the body.

यद्वै तत्पुरुषे शरीरमिदं वाव तद्यदिदमस्मिन्नन्तः पुरुषे हृदयमस्मिन्हीमे प्राणाः प्रतिष्ठिता एतदेव नातिशीयन्ते ॥ ४ ॥

Yadvai tatpuruṣe śarīramidaṁ vāva tadyadidamasminnantaḥ puruṣe hṛdayamasminhīme prāṇāḥ pratiṣṭhitā etadeva nātiśīyante.

Yat vai tat puruṣe śarīram, that which is in this human body; *idam vāva tat,* it is that; *yat idam asmin antaḥ puruṣe hṛdayam,* which is in this human heart; *hi,* because; *asmin,* in this [heart]; *ime prāṇāḥ,* these prāṇas [the vital forces]; *pratiṣṭhitāḥ,* are based; *etat eva na atiśīyante,* they cannot go beyond this [heart—i.e., they cannot exist independent of this heart].

4. That which is in this human body is in this human heart, for all these prāṇas are based in this heart and cannot exist independent of it.

The human body has been described as the gāyatrī. But where is that gāyatrī? It is in the heart. In fact, the heart is the gāyatrī. In what sense can the heart be called the gāyatrī? In the sense that all the prāṇas are in the heart and cannot exist separate from it. And since the body is the gāyatrī, the heart is also the gāyatrī.

सैषा चतुष्पदा षड्विधा गायत्री तदेतदृचाभ्यनूक्तम् ॥ ५ ॥

Saiṣā catuṣpadā ṣaḍvidhā gāyatrī tadetadṛcābhyanūktam.

Sā eṣā gāyatrī catuṣpadā, this gāyatrī has four feet [i.e., quarters]; *ṣaḍvidhā,* each of them sixfold; *tat etat ṛcā abhyanūktam,* this is what is stated in a Ṛk mantra [Ṛg Veda 10.10.3].

5. The gāyatrī has four quarters, each being sixfold. This is what is stated in a Ṛk mantra:

The gāyatrī is also known as Brahma-gāyatrī. It is one with everything.

The Upaniṣad says here that the gāyatrī has four quarters and each quarter has six parts (that is, it has six syllables). These six are: vāk (speech), sarva bhūta (all beings), pṛthivī (the earth), śarīra (the body), hṛdaya (the heart), and prāṇa (the vital force).

तावानस्य महिमा ततो ज्यायांश्च पुरुषः।
पादोऽस्य सर्वा भूतानि त्रिपादस्यामृतं दिवि॥ इति॥ ६॥

Tāvānasya mahimā tato jyāyāṁśca puruṣaḥ;
Pādo'sya sarvā bhūtāni tripādasyāmṛtaṁ divi. Iti.

Tāvān, like this; *asya mahimā,* its glory; *tataḥ jyāyān ca puruṣaḥ,* that [i.e., the glory] of the puruṣa [i.e., Brahman, who fills the whole world] is still greater; *pādaḥ asya sarvā* [i.e., *sarvāṇi*] *bhūtāni,* all things constitute one foot [or, quarter] of him; *tripād asya,* [the remaining] three feet [or, quarters] of him; *amṛtam divi,* are like nectar in heaven.

6. Its glory is like this. But the glory of the puruṣa [i.e., Brahman, who fills the whole world] is still greater. All creatures constitute one quarter of him. The remaining three quarters are nectar in heaven.

Brahman has been described as the gāyatrī, having four feet (or, quarters) and being sixfold. This is just figurative, however. Brahman is Brahman and there is no way of describing it. In reality, it is without name and form, beyond thought and speech. It is the Absolute.

Brahman can be conceived as both the cause and the effect. As the cause (*karaṇa*) nothing can be predicated about it; it is *nirupādhika,* without attributes. As the effect (*kārya*) it is *sopādhika,* with attributes. Similarly, the gāyatrī is said here to have four quarters and six parts. These are attributes used to help a disciple understand. As the *Pañcadaśi* says (verse II.58), *'Niraṁśe api aṁśam āropya . . . .'* (that is, parts are superimposed on that which has no parts in order to explain what cannot be described).

यद्वै तदब्रह्मेतीदं वाव तद्योऽयं बहिर्धा पुरुषादाकाशो यो वै स बहिर्धा पुरुषादाकाशः॥ ७॥

अयं वाव स योऽयमन्तः पुरुष आकाशो यो वै सोऽन्तः पुरुष आकाशः॥ ८॥

अयं वाव स योऽयमन्तर्हृदय आकाशस्तदेतत्पूर्णमप्रवर्ति पूर्णामप्रवर्तिनीं श्रियं लभते य एवं वेद॥ ९॥ इति द्वादशः खण्डः॥ १२॥

Yadvai tadbrahmetīdaṁ vāva tadyo'yaṁ bahirdhā puruṣādākāśo yo vai sa bahirdhā puruṣādākāśaḥ.

Ayaṁ vāva sa yo'yamantaḥ puruṣa ākāśo yo vai so'ntaḥ puruṣa ākāśaḥ.

Ayaṁ vāva sa yo'yamantarhṛdaya ākāśastadetat-pūrṇamapravarti pūrṇāmapravartinīṁ śriyaṁ labhate ya evaṁ veda. Iti dvādaśaḥ khaṇḍaḥ.

Yat vai tat brahma iti, that which is Brahman; *idam vāva tat,* it is that; *yaḥ,* which; *ayam,* is this; *ākāśaḥ,* space; *bahirdhā puruṣāt,* outside the human body; *yaḥ vai saḥ ākāśaḥ,* that which is the space; *bahirdhā puruṣāt,* outside the human body; *ayam vāva saḥ,* it is that; *yaḥ ayam ākāśaḥ,* which is this space; *antaḥ puruṣe,* inside the human body; *yaḥ vai saḥ antaḥ puruṣe ākāśaḥ,* that which is the space inside the human body; *ayam vāva saḥ,* it is that; *yaḥ ayam ākāśaḥ,* which is this space; *antaḥ hṛdaye,* inside the heart; *tat etat,* it is that; *pūrṇam,* full; *apravarti,* unchanging; *śriyam,* treasure; *yaḥ evam veda,* he who knows this; *pūrṇām apravartinīm labhate,* becomes full and is not subject to change. *Iti dvādaśaḥ khaṇḍaḥ,* here ends the twelfth section.

7-9. That which is Brahman is also the space outside the body. That which is the space outside the body is also the space inside the body. And that which is the space inside the body is also the space within the heart. That treasure within the heart is full and unchanging. He who knows this is always full and not subject to change.

Earlier Brahman was described as the gāyatrī with four quarters and also as amṛta, nectar. Here it is described as space. It is the same space which is inside as well as outside the human body, and also within the heart. The Upaniṣad says that this ākāśa in the heart is full and never changes. That is to say, it is free from desire and because of that it is never subject to change. Anyone who knows that ākāśa in the heart as such is himself always full and free from desire.

Section Thirteen

तस्य ह वा एतस्य हृदयस्य पञ्च देवसुषयः स योऽस्य प्राङ्सुषिः स प्राणस्तच्चक्षुः स आदित्यस्तदेतत्तेजोऽन्नाद्यमित्युपासीत तेजस्व्यन्नादो भवति य एवं वेद ॥ १ ॥

Tasya ha vā etasya hṛdayasya pañca devasuṣayaḥ sa yo'sya prāṅsuṣiḥ sa prāṇastaccakṣuḥ sa ādityastadetattejo'nnādyamityupāsīta tejasvyannādo bhavati ya evaṁ veda.

Tasya ha vai etasya hṛdayasya, of this heart; *pañca devasuṣayaḥ,* five passages guarded by the gods; *saḥ yaḥ,* that which; *asya prāṅsuṣiḥ,* is its eastern passage; *saḥ prāṇaḥ,* that is prāṇa; *tat cakṣuḥ,* that is [also] the eye; *saḥ ādityaḥ,* [and] that is Āditya [the sun]; *tat etat,* it is that; *tejaḥ annādyam iti upāsīta,* meditate on as the source of brightness and food; *yaḥ evam veda,* he who knows this; *tejasvī annādaḥ bhavati,* becomes bright and an eater of food.

1. In the heart there are five doors guarded by the gods. The door in the east is prāṇa. It is also the eyes, and it is Āditya. Worship this as the source of brightness and food. He who knows this becomes bright and enjoys food.

If you want to enter a house, you must please those who are at the gates. Similarly, if you want to enter heaven, you must worship Brahman as prāṇa. As you do so, you should attribute to prāṇa the qualities of Āditya and annāda—that is, of brightness and strength. If prāṇa is pleased with you, you have no difficulty attaining heaven.

अथ योऽस्य दक्षिणः सुषिः स व्यानस्तच्छ्रोत्रं स चन्द्रमास्तदेतच्छ्रीश्च यशश्चेत्युपासीत श्रीमान्यशस्वी भवति य एवं वेद॥ २॥

Atha yo'sya dakṣiṇaḥ suṣiḥ sa vyānastacchrotraṁ sa candramāstadetacchrīśca yaśaścetyupāsīta śrīmānya-śasvī bhavati ya evaṁ veda.

Atha, next; *yaḥ asya dakṣiṇaḥ suṣiḥ,* that which is its southern passage; *saḥ vyānaḥ,* that is vyāna; *tat śrotram,* that is [also] the ear; *saḥ candramāḥ,* [and] that is the moon; *tat etat,* it is that; *śrīḥ ca yaśaḥ iti upāsīta,* meditate on as prosperity and fame; *yaḥ evam veda,* he who knows this; *śrīmān yaśasvī bhavati,* becomes fortunate and famous.

2. Next, the southern door of the heart is vyāna. It is also the ears, and it is the moon. Worship it as the source of prosperity and fame. He who knows this becomes prosperous and famous.

Vyāna is the air that is spread all over the body. It is also the breath you need when you are doing some hard work. Vyāna is the door, or passage, in the southern part of the heart, and it is connected with hearing and the moon.

A person learns by hearing, so the ear is said to be the source of knowledge. The moon is the source of food, which gives a person strength, and from strength and knowledge a person acquires prosperity and fame. By worshipping vyāna as Brahman a person can attain heaven, which is his primary concern, and secondarily he attains prosperity and fame.

अथ योऽस्य प्रत्यङ्सुषिः सोऽपानः सा वाक्सो-
ऽग्निस्तदेतद्ब्रह्मवर्चसमन्नाद्यमित्युपासीत ब्रह्मवर्चस्यन्नादो
भवति य एवं वेद॥ ३॥

Atha yo'sya pratyaṅsuṣiḥ so'pānaḥ sā vākso'gnistadetadbrahmavarcasamannādyamityupāsīta brahmavarcasyannādo bhavati ya evaṁ veda.

Atha, next; *yaḥ asya pratyaṅsuṣiḥ,* that which is its western passage; *saḥ apānaḥ,* that is apāna; *sā vāk,* that is [also] vāk [word]; *saḥ agniḥ,* [and] that is fire; *tat etat,* it is that [Brahman as apāna]; *brahmavarcasam ca annādyam iti upāsīta,* meditate on as the radiance of Brahman [that comes from living a disciplined life and from scholarship] and as food; *yaḥ evam veda,* he who knows this;

brahmavarcasi annādaḥ bhavati, becomes radiant with the light of Brahman and a great eater of food.

3. Next, the western door of the heart is apāna. It is also vāk, and it is fire. Worship this [Brahman in the form of apāna] as the radiance of Brahman and as food. He who knows this becomes radiant with the light of Brahman and a great eater of food.

Apāna's function is to remove all waste from the body. It is connected with speech and fire. *Brahmavarcasa* is the radiance a person acquires when he has much scholarship and has led a disciplined life. One who meditates on apāna as Brahman acquires this radiance and also food.

अथ योऽस्योदङ्सुषिः स समानस्तन्मनः स पर्जन्यस्तदेतत्कीर्तिश्च व्युष्टिश्चेत्युपासीत कीर्तिमान्व्युष्टिमान्भवति य एवं वेद॥४॥

Atha yo'syodaṅsuṣiḥ sa samānastanmanaḥ sa parjanyastadetatkīrtiśca vyuṣṭiścetyupāsīta kīrtimānvyuṣṭimānbhavati ya evaṁ veda.

Atha, next; *yaḥ asya udaṅsuṣiḥ,* that which is its northern passage; *saḥ samānaḥ,* that is samāna; *tat manaḥ,* that is [also] the mind; *saḥ parjanyaḥ,* [and] that is the god of rain; *tat etat,* it is that [Brahman as samāna]; *kīrtiḥ ca vyuṣṭiḥ ca iti upāsīta,* meditate on as fame and beauty; *yaḥ evam veda,* he who knows this; *kīrtimān vyuṣṭimān bhavati,* becomes famous and beautiful.

4. Next, the northern door of the heart is samāna. It is also the mind, and it is the god of rain. Worship this [Brahman in the form of samāna] as fame and beauty. He who knows this becomes famous and beautiful.

Samāna is so called because it digests all food and drink and makes them equal (*sama*). The mind and rain are connnected with samāna, and since fame is connected with the mind, it is attributed to samāna. Like fame, physical beauty is also the result of samāna.

अथ योऽस्योर्ध्वः सुषिः स उदानः स वायुः स आकाशस्तदेतदोजश्च महश्चेत्युपासीतौजस्वी महस्वान्भवति य एवं वेद॥५॥

Atha yo'syordhvaḥ suṣiḥ sa udānaḥ sa vāyuḥ sa ākāśastadetadojaśca mahaścetyupāsītaujasvī mahasvān-bhavati ya evaṁ veda.

Atha, next; *yaḥ asya ūrdhvaḥ suṣiḥ,* that which is its passage at the top [of the heart]; *saḥ udānaḥ,* that is udāna; *saḥ vāyuḥ,* that is [also] vāyu [air]; *saḥ ākāśaḥ,* [and] that is ākāśa [space]; *tat etat,* it is that [Brahman as udāna]; *ojaḥ ca mahaḥ ca iti upāsīta,* meditate on as strength and as greatness; *yaḥ evam veda,* he who knows this; *ojasvī mahasvān bhavati,* becomes strong and great.

5. Next, the door at the top of the heart is udāna. It is also vāyu [air], and it is ākāśa [space]. Worship this [Brahman in the form of udāna] as strength and greatness. He who knows this becomes strong and great.

There is an aperture at the upper part of the heart, and this is known as udāna. Air passes through this aperture from the feet to the head to help maintain the necessary operations of the body. The air that passes thus is also called udāna. Ākāśa (space) is the support of this udāna. Because udāna is one of the gateways to Brahman, it is meditated on as Brahman. If you do this, you become strong and famous. But, more important, you also attain heaven.

ते वा एते पञ्च ब्रह्मपुरुषाः स्वर्गस्य लोकस्य द्वारपाः स य एतानेवं पञ्च ब्रह्मपुरुषान्स्वर्गस्य लोकस्य द्वारपान्वेदास्य कुले वीरो जायते प्रतिपद्यते स्वर्गं लोकं य एतानेवं पञ्च ब्रह्मपुरुषान्स्वर्गस्य लोकस्य द्वारपान्वेद ॥ ६ ॥

Te vā ete pañca brahmapuruṣāḥ svargasya lokasya dvārapāḥ sa ya etānevaṁ pañca brahmapuruṣānsvar-

gasya lokasya dvārapānvedāsya kule vīro jāyate pratipadyate svargaṁ lokaṁ ya etānevaṁ pañca brahmapuruṣānsvargasya lokasya dvārapānveda.

Te vai ete pañca brahma-puruṣāḥ, these five [prāṇas] are the employees of Brahman; *svargasya lokasya dvārapāḥ,* the gatekeepers of the heavenly world; *saḥ yaḥ veda,* he who knows; *etān pañca brahma-puruṣān,* these five Brahma-puruṣas; *svargasya lokasya dvārapān,* as gatekeepers of the heavenly world; *evam,* thus; *asya kule vīraḥ jāyate,* a heroic child is born in his family; *yaḥ etān pañca brahma-puruṣān evam svargasya lokasya dvārapān veda,* he who knows these five Brahma-puruṣas thus as the gatekeepers of the heavenly world; *svargam lokam pratipadyate,* attains the heavenly world.

6. These five prāṇas are themselves like Brahman, and they are the gatekeepers of heaven. Anyone who regards these prāṇas as Brahman and as the gatekeepers to heaven has a heroic child born in his family. Knowing these prāṇas as Brahman and as the gatekeepers of heaven, a person attains heaven himself.

Here the advice is to regard everything as Brahman. If you practise thinking that everything is Brahman, you acquire self-restraint, which is the *sine qua non* of Self-realization. The advice here is to treat the five prāṇas with great respect, so that they may allow you to enter straight into heaven.

अथ यदतः परो दिवो ज्योतिर्दीप्यते विश्वतः पृष्ठेषु सर्वतः पृष्ठेष्वनुत्तमेषूत्तमेषु लोकेष्विदं वाव तद्यदिद-मस्मिन्नन्तः पुरुषे ज्योतिः ॥ ७ ॥

Atha yadataḥ paro divo jyotirdīpyate viśvataḥ pṛṣṭheṣu sarvataḥ pṛṣṭheṣvanuttameṣūttameṣu lokeṣvidaṁ vāva tadyadidamasminnantaḥ puruṣe jyotiḥ.

Atha, next; *ataḥ paraḥ divaḥ,* higher than this heaven; *yat jyotiḥ dīpyate,* the light which shines; *viśvataḥ pṛṣṭheṣu,* above the world; *sarvataḥ pṛṣṭheṣu,* above everything; *anuttameṣu uttameṣu lokeṣu,* in the highest worlds not excelled by any other world [known as satyaloka]; *idam vāva tat,* it is that; *jyotiḥ,* light; *yat idam asmin antaḥ puruṣe,* which is the same as in a human being.

7. Then, higher than this heaven, above the world, higher than everything, in the highest world, higher than which nothing exists—the light that shines there is the same light that is in a human being.

Brahman is said to be above everything else. It is the highest and the best. It shines in the highest world and it also shines in the heart of a human being.

तस्यैषा दृष्टिर्यत्रैतदस्मिञ्छरीरे संस्पर्शेनोष्णिमानं विजानाति तस्यैषा श्रुतिर्यत्रैतत्कर्णावपिगृह्य निनदमिव नदथुरिवाग्नेरिव ज्वलत उपशृणोति तदेतद्दृष्टं च श्रुतं चेत्युपासीत चक्षुष्यः श्रुतो भवति य एवं वेद य एवं वेद॥ ८॥ इति त्रयोदशः खण्डः॥ १३॥

Tasyaiṣā dṛṣṭiryatraitadasmiñcharīre saṁsparśenoṣṇimānaṁ vijānāti tasyaiṣā śrutiryatraitatkarṇāvapigṛhya ninadamiva nadathurivāgneriva jvalata upaśṛṇoti tadetaddṛṣṭaṁ ca śrutaṁ cetyupāsīta cakṣuṣyaḥ śruto bhavati ya evaṁ veda ya evaṁ veda. Iti trayodaśaḥ khaṇḍaḥ.

Tasya, its [i.e., of the Self in the bodies]; *eṣā dṛṣṭiḥ,* this visible [proof]; *yatra,* when; *etat asmin śarīre,* in this body; *saṁsparśena,* by touch; *uṣṇimānam,* warmth; *vijānāti,* one can feel; *tasya eṣā śrutiḥ,* this audible [proof] of it; *yatra etat karṇau apigṛhya,* when one covers the ears; *ninadam iva,* like the sound of a moving chariot; *nadathuḥ iva,* like the bellowing of a bullock; *agneḥ iva jvalataḥ,* like the sound of a burning fire; *upaśṛṇoti,* one can hear; *tat etat,* that [light]; *iti upāsīta,* one should meditate on; *dṛṣṭam ca śrutam ca,* as seen and as heard; *yaḥ evam veda,* he who knows this; *cakṣuṣyaḥ śrutaḥ bhavati,* becomes worth seeing and famous. *Iti trayodaśaḥ khaṇḍaḥ,* here ends the thirteenth section.

8. Here is proof of it: When you touch the body you can feel heat in it. There is also an audible

proof of it: When you cover your ears you can hear a sound like a moving chariot, or like the bellowing of a bullock, or like a burning fire. A person should meditate on that light in the body as something that is seen and heard. He who knows this becomes a distinguished person—people want to see him and he is widely known.

What proof is there that there is any light in the heart? One proof is the warmth of the body. This warmth comes from the light within. But there is yet another proof: If you cover your ears you will hear all manner of sounds. The sounds and the feeling of warmth both prove that Brahman is within.

Section Fourteen

सर्वं खल्विदं ब्रह्म तज्जलानिति शान्त उपासीत।
अथ खलु क्रतुमयः पुरुषो यथाक्रतुरस्मिँल्लोके पुरुषो
भवति तथेतः प्रेत्य भवति स क्रतुं कुर्वीत॥ १ ॥

Sarvaṁ khalvidaṁ brahma tajjalāniti śānta upāsīta; Atha khalu kratumayaḥ puruṣo yathākraturasmiṁlloke puruṣo bhavati tathetaḥ pretya bhavati sa kratuṁ kurvīta.

Sarvam idam, all this; *khalu,* no doubt; *brahma,* is Brahman; *tajjalān,* from this everything comes, into this everything disappears, and on this everything is sustained; *iti śāntaḥ upāsīta,* meditate on this fact quietly; *atha khalu kratumayaḥ puruṣaḥ,* because each person has a mind of his own; *asmin loke,* [therefore] in his present life; *yathā kratuḥ puruṣaḥ bhavati,* just as a person wills; *itaḥ pretya tathā bhavati,* he becomes that when he leaves this world; *saḥ kratum kurvīta,* [therefore] he should be careful about what he wants.

1. All this is Brahman. Everything comes from Brahman, everything goes back to Brahman, and everything is sustained by Brahman. One should therefore quietly meditate on Brahman. Each person has a mind of his own. What a person wills in his present life, he becomes when he leaves this world. One should bear this in mind and meditate accordingly.

The word *brahman* means 'the oldest,' 'the biggest.' *Tejas* (fire), *jala* (water), and *pṛthivī* (earth) emerged from Brahman in that order, so they are called *tajja.* Then they disappear in Brahman in the reverse order, so they are called *talla.* In the past, in the present, and in the future—they are sustained in Brahman. They are, therefore, one with Brahman. The Upaniṣad says here to think over this with *kratu*—that is, with great effort, and with deep concentration.

Kratu also means will, or will power. It is your will that decides your destiny. Śrī Kṛṣṇa said to Arjuna (Bhagavad Gītā 8.6): 'O son of Kunti, at the time of death when a person leaves the body, he attains whatever object he thinks of, as he has been [previously] constantly absorbed in its thought.' This shows the importance of your *kratu.*

मनोमयः प्राणशरीरो भारूपः सत्यसङ्कल्प आकाशात्मा सर्वकर्मा सर्वकामः सर्वगन्धः सर्वरसः सर्वमिद-मभ्यात्तोऽवाक्यनादरः ॥ २ ॥

Manomayaḥ prāṇaśarīro bhārūpaḥ satyasaṅkalpa ākāśātmā sarvakarmā sarvakāmaḥ sarvagandhaḥ sarva-rasaḥ sarvamidamabhyātto'vākyanādaraḥ.

Manomayaḥ, dominated by the mind; *prāṇaśarīraḥ,* with a subtle body; *bhārūpaḥ,* whose body is luminous; *satyasaṅkalpaḥ,* whose thoughts always prove true; *ākāśātmā,* spotless like the sky; *sarvakarmā,* whose creation is this world; *sarvakāmaḥ,* whose desires are always pure; *sarvagandhaḥ,* who possesses good odours; *sarvarasaḥ,* whose tastes are all pure; *idam sarvam abhyāttaḥ,* this is all-pervasive; *avākī anādaraḥ,* has no sense organs and no desires.

2. He is controlled by the mind [i.e., his mind decides what he should and should not do]. He has a subtle body, and he is luminous. If he wants something, he never fails to get it. His Self is spotless like the sky. The whole world is his creation. [Desires are many, and] all those desires are his desires. All odours are his; similarly, all tastes are his. He is everywhere in the world. He has no sense organs, and he is free from desires.

This is how you meditate on your Self. You have a mind, and with the help of that mind you can decide what you will or will not do. You have a subtle body consisting of the five organs of action (*pañca karmendriyas*), the five organs of perception (*pañca jñānendriyas*), the vital breath in its five forms (*prāṇa, apāna, vyāna, udāna,* and *samāna*), plus the mind and the intellect. You are luminous. Whatever you wish for, you acquire. You are spotless, like the sky, and all-pervasive. You are the sole doer of things. You are the source of all desires, and all your desires are pure. You are also the source of all odours and tastes. You have no organs, and you are everywhere. There is nothing you have not already achieved.

एष म आत्मान्तर्हृदयेऽणीयान्व्रीहेर्वा यवाद्वा सर्षपाद्वा श्यामाकाद्वा श्यामाकतण्डुलाद्वैष म आत्मान्तर्हृदये ज्यायान्पृथिव्या ज्यायानन्तरिक्षाज्ज्यायान्दिवो ज्यायानेभ्यो लोकेभ्यः ॥ ३ ॥

Eṣa ma ātmāntarhṛdaye'ṇīyānvrīhervā yavādvā sarṣapādvā śyāmākādvā śyāmākataṇḍulādvaiṣa ma ātmāntarhṛdaye jyāyānpṛthivyā jyāyānantarikṣājjyāyāndivo jyāyānebhyo lokebhyaḥ.

Eṣaḥ me ātmā, this my Self; *antaḥ hṛdaye,* inside the heart; *aṇīyān,* smaller than; *vrīheḥ vā,* a grain of rice; *yavāt vā,* or a grain of barley; *sarṣapāt vā,* or a mustard seed; *śyāmākāt vā,* or a grain of millet; *śyāmākataṇḍulāt vā,* or the kernel of a grain of millet;

eṣaḥ me ātmā antaḥ hṛdaye, this Self within my heart; *jyāyān pṛthivyā,* is larger than the earth; *jyāyān antarikṣāt,* larger than the mid-region; *jyāyān divaḥ,* larger than heaven; *jyāyān ebhyaḥ lokebhyaḥ,* larger than all these worlds.

3. My Self within my heart is smaller than a grain of rice, smaller than a grain of barley, smaller than a mustard seed, smaller than a grain of millet, smaller even than the kernel of a grain of millet. The Self in my heart is larger than the earth, larger than the mid-region, larger than heaven, and larger even than all these worlds.

The underlying idea in the verse is that the Self is everything and everywhere. It is therefore smaller than the smallest and bigger than the biggest.

सर्वकर्मा सर्वकामः सर्वगन्धः सर्वरसः सर्वमिद-
मभ्यात्तोऽवाक्यनादर एष म आत्मान्तर्हृदय एतद्ब्रह्मैतमितः
प्रेत्याभिसम्भवितास्मीति यस्य स्यादद्धा न विचिकि-
त्सास्तीति ह स्माह शाण्डिल्यः शाण्डिल्यः ॥ ४ ॥ इति
चतुर्दशः खण्डः ॥ १४ ॥

Sarvakarmā sarvakāmaḥ sarvagandhaḥ sarvarasaḥ sarvamidamabhyātto'vākyanādara eṣa ma ātmāntarhṛdaya etadbrahmaitamitaḥ pretyābhisambhavitāsmīti yasya syādaddhā na vicikitsāstīti ha smāha śāṇḍilyaḥ śāṇḍilyaḥ. Iti caturdaśaḥ khaṇḍaḥ.

Yaḥ, he who; *sarvakarmā,* is the sole creator of everything; *sarvakāmaḥ,* whose desires are the desires of all; *sarvagandhaḥ,* whose odours are the odours of all; *sarvarasaḥ,* whose tastes are the tastes of all; *sarvam idam abhyāttaḥ,* who is in all this; *avākī,* who is without any organs; *anādaraḥ,* who is not interested in anything; *eṣaḥ me ātmā antaḥ hṛdaye,* this Self of mine is within my heart; *etat brahma,* this is Brahman; *itaḥ pretya,* upon leaving this body; *etam abhisambhavitāsmi iti,* I shall attain him; *yasya syāt addhā,* one who has this kind of belief; *na vicikitsā asti,* has no doubt in his mind; *iti ha sma āha śāṇḍilyaḥ,* this is what Śāṇḍilya said; *śāṇḍilyaḥ,* [this is what] Śāṇḍilya [said]. *Iti caturdaśaḥ khaṇḍaḥ,* here ends the fourteenth section.

4. He who is the sole creator, whose desires are the desires of all, whose odours are the odours of all, whose tastes are the tastes of all, who is everywhere, who has no sense organs, and who is free from desires—he is my Self and is in my heart. He is no other than Brahman. When I leave this body, I shall attain him. He who firmly believes this has no doubt in his mind. [He will surely attain Brahman.] This is what Śāṇḍilya has said.

The word *Self* here means the Cosmic Self (Paramātman). If you believe that you are the Cosmic Self, and that you will be free as soon as your *prārabdha karma* (the results of your past actions that are now bearing fruit) is exhausted and your body falls—according to Śāṇḍilya, you will indeed be free.

Section Fifteen

अन्तरिक्षोदरः कोशो भूमिबुध्नो न जीर्यति।
दिशो ह्यस्य स्रक्तयो द्यौरस्योत्तरं बिलम्।
स एष कोशो वसुधानस्तस्मिन्विश्वमिदं श्रितम्॥ १ ॥

Antarikṣodaraḥ kośo bhūmibudhno na jīryati;
Diśo hyasya sraktayo dyaurasyottaraṁ bilam;
Sa eṣa kośo vasudhānastasminviśvamidaṁ śritam.

Kośaḥ, the chest; *antarikṣa-udaraḥ,* with the mid-region as its inside; *bhūmi-budhnaḥ,* the earth as its bottom; *na jīryati,* never decays; *diśaḥ,* the quarters; *hi asya sraktayaḥ,* are its sides; *dyauḥ,* the heaven; *asya uttaram bilam,* is its opening above; *saḥ eṣaḥ kośaḥ,* this chest; *vasudhānaḥ,* [is] the container of treasures; *tasmin,* in it; *viśvam idam śritam,* rests this universe.

1. There is a chest which has the mid-region as its inside and the earth as its bottom. It never decays. The quarters are its sides and the heaven its opening above. This chest is the container of treasures, for in it rests the whole universe.

The universe is here compared to a chest. Whatever you put inside a chest is safe there. Similarly, whatever is in the universe is safe and sound. It may change its form, but it does not totally disappear.

तस्य प्राची दिग्जुहूर्नाम सहमानां नाम दक्षिणा राज्ञी नाम प्रतीची सुभूता नामोदीची तासां वायुर्वत्सः स य एतमेवं वायुं दिशां वत्सं वेद न पुत्ररोदं रोदिति सोऽहमेतमेवं वायुं दिशां वत्सं वेद मा पुत्ररोदं रुदम् ॥ २ ॥

Tasya prācī digjuhūrnāma sahamānāṁ nāma dakṣiṇā rājñī nāma pratīcī subhūtā nāmodīcī tāsāṁ vāyurvatsaḥ sa ya etamevaṁ vāyuṁ diśāṁ vatsaṁ veda na putrarodaṁ roditi so'hametamevaṁ vāyuṁ diśāṁ vatsaṁ veda mā putrarodaṁ rudam.

Prācī dik, the eastern quarter; *tasya,* of it [i.e., of the chest]; *juhūḥ nāma,* is called juhū [after the vessel used for offering oblations facing the east]; *dakṣiṇā,* the southern [quarter]; *sahamānām nāma,* is named sahamānā; *pratīcī,* the western [quarter]; *rājñī nāma,* is named rājñī [because the western sky is red in the evening]; *udīcī,* the northern [quarter]; *subhūtā nāma,* is named subhūtā [because those who are rich dominate this quarter]; *vāyuḥ,* air; *tāsām,* their [i.e., the quarters']; *vatsaḥ,* son; *saḥ yaḥ etam veda,* he who knows this; *vāyum diśām vatsam,* that Vāyu is the child of the quarters; *putrarodam na roditi,* does not have to weep over the loss of his child; *saḥ aham etam evam veda,* I know this thus; *vāyum diśām vatsam,* that Vāyu is the son of the quarters; *mā putrarodam rudam,* may I not have to weep over the loss of my child.

2. The eastern quarter of the chest is called *juhū,* the southern quarter is called *sahamānā,* the western quarter is called *rājñī,* and the northern quarter is called *subhūtā.* Vāyu [air] is the son of these quarters. He who knows this, that Vāyu is the child of the quarters, does not have to weep over the loss of his child. 'I know that Vāyu is the child of the quarters. May I never have to weep over the loss of my child.'

The eastern quarter is called *juhū* because you face that direction when you offer that oblation in the sacrifice. The southern side is *sahamānā* because sinners go to that quarter to suffer the consequences of the sins they commit. The western side is called *rājñī* because when the sun sets in that direction, the sky becomes red.

Subhūtā is the name of the northern side, because it is dominated by Śiva, Kubera, and other deities of good fortune. Vāyu (air) is considered the child of the quarters because it arises from the quarters. If you believe that Vāyu is immortal and is the child of the quarters, you will then never suffer the loss of your child.

अरिष्टं कोशं प्रपद्येऽमुनामुनामुना प्राणं प्रपद्येऽमुनामुना-
मुना भूः प्रपद्येऽमुनामुनामुना भुवः प्रपद्येऽमुनामुनामुना
स्वः प्रपद्येऽमुनामुनामुना ॥ ३ ॥

Ariṣṭaṁ kośaṁ prapadye'munāmunāmunā prāṇaṁ prapadye'munāmunāmunā bhūḥ prapadye'munāmunāmunā bhuvaḥ prapadye'munāmunāmunā svaḥ prapadye'munāmunāmunā.

Amunā amunā amunā, for the sake of that [child's life], for the sake of that [child's life], for the sake of that [child's life]; *ariṣṭam kośam,* in the immortal chest; *prapadye,* I take refuge; *amunā amunā amunā,* for the sake of that [child's life—etc.]; *prāṇam prapadye,* I take refuge in prāṇa; *amunā amunā amunā,* for the sake of that [child's life—etc.]; *bhūḥ prapadye,* I take refuge in bhūḥ [the earth]; *amunā amunā amunā,* for the sake of that [child's life—etc.]; *bhuvaḥ prapadye,* I take refuge in bhuvaḥ [the mid-region]; *amunā amunā amunā,* for the sake of that [child's life—etc.]; *svaḥ prapadye,* I take refuge in svaḥ [heaven].

3. For the sake of my child's life, I take refuge in that immortal kośa [i.e., the chest, representing the universe]. For the sake of my child's life, I take refuge in prāṇa [the vital breath]. For the sake of my child's life, I take refuge in bhūḥ [the earth]. For the sake of my child's life, I take refuge in

bhuvaḥ [the mid-region]. For the sake of my child's life, I take refuge in svaḥ [heaven].

For the welfare of your child, surrender to every power on earth, in the mid-region, and in heaven. Repeat this three times, each time saying the name of the child thrice. Here the word *amunā* has been used instead of the name of the child.

स यदवोचं प्राणं प्रपद्य इति प्राणो वा इदं सर्वं भूतं यदिदं किञ्च तमेव तत्प्रापत्सि॥ ४॥

Sa yadavocaṁ prāṇaṁ prapadya iti prāṇo vā idaṁ sarvaṁ bhūtaṁ yadidaṁ kiñca tameva tatprāpatsi.

Saḥ yat avocam, when I said; *prāṇam prapadye iti,* I take refuge in prāṇa; *prāṇaḥ vai idam sarvam bhūtam,* I meant prāṇa is everything; *yat idaṃ kiñca,* whatever is here [visible]; *tat,* therefore; *tam eva prāpatsi,* I am under the care of that [prāṇa].

4. When I said, 'I take refuge in prāṇa,' I meant that prāṇa is everything visible, whatever there is, and therefore I have taken refuge in everything.

अथ यदवोचं भूः प्रपद्य इति पृथिवीं प्रपद्येऽन्तरिक्षं प्रपद्ये दिवं प्रपद्य इत्येव तदवोचम्॥ ५॥

Atha yadavocaṁ bhūḥ prapadya iti pṛthivīṁ prapadye'ntarikṣaṁ prapadye divaṁ prapadya ityeva tadavocam.

Atha, next; *yat avocam,* when I said; *bhūḥ prapadye iti,* I take refuge in bhūḥ [the earth]; *iti eva tat avocam,* it is this that I meant; *pṛthivīm prapadye,* I take refuge in the earth; *antarikṣam prapadye,* I take refuge in the mid-region; *divam prapadye,* I take refuge in heaven.

5. Then, when I said, 'I take refuge in bhūḥ,' what I meant was that I take refuge in the earth, I take refuge in the mid-region, and I take refuge in heaven.

That is to say, I meant that I had taken refuge in all the three worlds.

अथ यदवोचं भुवः प्रपद्य इत्यग्निं प्रपद्ये वायुं प्रपद्य आदित्यं प्रपद्य इत्येव तदवोचम्॥ ६॥

Atha yadavocaṁ bhuvaḥ prapadya ityagniṁ prapadye vāyuṁ prapadya ādityaṁ prapadya ityeva tadavocam.

Atha, next; *yat avocam,* when I said; *bhuvaḥ prapadye iti,* I take refuge in bhuvaḥ [the mid-region]; *iti eva tat avocam,* it is this that I meant; *agnim prapadye,* I take refuge in fire; *vāyum prapadye,* I take refuge in air; *ādityam prapadye,* I take refuge in the sun.

6. Then, when I said, 'I take refuge in bhuvaḥ,' what I meant was that I take refuge in fire, I take refuge in air, and I take refuge in the sun.

अथ यदवोचं स्वः प्रपद्य इत्यृग्वेदं प्रपद्ये यजुर्वेदं प्रपद्ये सामवेदं प्रपद्य इत्येव तदवोचं तदवोचम्॥ ७॥
इति पञ्चदशः खण्डः॥ १५॥

Atha yadavocaṁ svaḥ prapadya ityṛgvedaṁ prapadye yajurvedaṁ prapadye sāmavedaṁ prapadya ityeva tadavocaṁ tadavocam. Iti pañcadaśaḥ khaṇḍaḥ

Atha, next; *yat avocam,* when I said; *svaḥ prapadye iti,* I take refuge in svaḥ [heaven]; *iti eva tat avocam,* it is this that I meant; *ṛg vedam prapadye,* I take refuge in the Ṛg Veda; *yajur vedam prapadye,* I take refuge in the Yajur Veda; *sāma vedam prapadye,* I take refuge in the Sāma Veda; *tat avocam tat avocam,* it is this that I meant, this that I meant. *Iti pañcadaśaḥ khaṇḍaḥ,* here ends the fifteenth section.

7. Then, when I said, 'I take refuge in svaḥ,' what I meant was that I take refuge in the Ṛg Veda, I take refuge in the Yajur Veda, and I take refuge in the Sāma Veda. It is this that I meant.

One should first meditate on the immortal chest, and then repeat the mantras following the meditation. To emphasize the importance of the worship, the mantras are repeated again and again.

Section Sixteen

पुरुषो वाव यज्ञस्तस्य यानि चतुर्विंशतिवर्षाणि तत्प्रातःसवनं चतुर्विंशत्यक्षरा गायत्री गायत्रं प्रातःसवनं तदस्य वसवोऽन्वायत्ताः प्राणा वाव वसव एते हीदं सर्वं वासयन्ति ॥ १ ॥

Puruṣo vāva yajñastasya yāni caturviṁśativarṣāṇi tatprātaḥsavanaṁ caturviṁśatyakṣarā gāyatrī gāyatraṁ prātaḥsavanaṁ tadasya vasavo'nvāyattāḥ prāṇā vāva vasava ete hīdaṁ sarvaṁ vāsayanti.

Puruṣaḥ vāva yajñaḥ, the human body is like a sacrifice; *tasya yāni caturviṁśati varṣāṇi,* its first twenty-four years; *tat,* that; *prātaḥ savanam,* is the morning libation; *gāyatrī caturviṁśati akṣarā,* the gāyatrī is constituted of twenty-four syllables; *gāyatram prātaḥ savanam,* the morning libation is accompanied by the gāyatrī; *asya,* of this [i.e., this sacrifice of the human body]; *tat,* it [the morning libation covering the first twenty-four years]; *vasavaḥ,* the deities called Vasus; *anvāyattāḥ,* are connected; *prāṇāḥ vāva vasavaḥ,* the prāṇas [together with the sense organs] are the Vasus; *hi,* for; *ete,* these [Vasus]; *idam sarvam,* everything in this [world]; *vāsayanti,* cause to live [and they themselves also live (vasu)].

1. The human body is like a sacrifice, and the first twenty-four years are like the morning libation. The

gāyatrī has twenty-four syllables, and the morning libation is accompanied by the gāyatrī. The Vasus reside in this morning libation. The Vasus are the vital breaths and the sense organs, for the word *vasu* means those who make others live and who live themselves.

In the previous section, meditation and repetition of certain mantras was recommended for the long life of one's children. The same thing is being recommended now for one's own life. Here the meditation is that one's life is a sacrifice, and that the first twenty-four years are the morning offering. This offering is connected with the gāyatrī, which has twenty-four syllables. The Vasus are also connected with this offering, and they are thought of as the organs, which abide (*vasu*) and which also make others abide.

तं चेदेतस्मिन्वयसि किञ्चिदुपतपेत्स ब्रूयात्प्राणा वसव इदं मे प्रातःसवनं माध्यन्दिनं सवनमनुसन्तनुतेति माहं प्राणानां वसूनां मध्ये यज्ञो विलोप्सीयेत्युद्धैव तत एत्यगदो ह भवति॥ २॥

Taṁ cedetasminvayasi kiñcidupatapetsa brūyātprāṇā vasava idaṁ me prātaḥsavanaṁ mādhyandinaṁ savana-manusantanuteti māhaṁ prāṇānāṁ vasūnāṁ madhye yajño vilopsīyetyuddhaiva tata etyagado ha bhavati.

Cet, if; *etasmin vayasi,* within these [twenty-four] years of his life; *tam kiñcit upatapet,* something troubles him; *saḥ brūyāt,* he will say; *prāṇāḥ,* O Prāṇas; *vasavaḥ,* O Vasus; *idam me prātaḥ savanam,* this, my morning libation; *mādhyandinam savanam,* to the midday libation; *anusantanuta iti,* extend; *mā aham,* may I not; *yajñaḥ,* as the sacrifice; *madhye prāṇānām vasūnām,* in the midst of the prāṇas, who are the Vasus; *vilopsīya iti,* disappear; *tataḥ ha eva ut-eti,* he gets rid of that [ailment]; *agadaḥ ha bhavati,* [and] becomes well.

2. If, within these first twenty-four years of his life, he has some ailment, he should then say: 'O Prāṇas, O Vasus, please extend this first libation to the midday libation. As the sacrifice, may I not disappear among the Vasus, who are my prāṇas [i.e., who are like my life].' [If he prays like this,] he gets rid of his ailment and becomes fully well.

अथ यानि चतुश्चत्वारिंशद्वर्षाणि तन्माध्यन्दिनं सवनं चतुश्चत्वारिंशदक्षरा त्रिष्टुप्त्रैष्टुभं माध्यन्दिनं सवनं तदस्य रुद्रा अन्वायत्ताः प्राणा वाव रुद्रा एते हीदं सर्वं रोदयन्ति ॥ ३ ॥

Atha yāni catuścatvāriṁśadvarṣāṇi tanmādhyandinaṁ savanaṁ catuścatvāriṁśadakṣarā triṣṭuptraiṣṭubhaṁ mādhyandinaṁ savanaṁ tadasya rudrā anvāyattāḥ prāṇā vāva rudrā ete hīdaṁ sarvaṁ rodayanti.

Atha, then; *yāni catuścatvāriṁśat varṣāṇi,* that which is the next forty-four years; *tat,* that; *mādhyandinam savanam,* is the midday libation; *triṣṭup catuścatvāriṁśat akṣarā,* the triṣṭubh metre is constituted of forty-four syllables; *traiṣṭubham mādhyandinam savanam,* the midday libation is accompanied by a hymn in the triṣṭubh metre; *asya,* of this [i.e., this sacrifice of the human body]; *tat,* it [the midday libation covering the next forty-four years]; *rudrāḥ,* the deities called Rudras; *anvāyattāḥ,* are connected; *prāṇāḥ vāva rudrāḥ,* the prāṇas [together with the sense organs] are the Rudras; *hi,* for; *ete,* these [Rudras]; *idam sarvam rodayanti,* make everyone in this world weep.

3. Then the next forty-four years are like the midday libation. The triṣṭubh metre has forty-four syllables, and the midday libation is accompanied by a hymn which is in the triṣṭubh metre. The Rudras are connected with this midday libation. The prāṇas are called Rudras because they [are cruel and] make everyone in this world weep.

The sense organs become very powerful when a person has reached middle age, and they may make him do things he will regret and for which he will have to 'weep.' In this sacrifice, these next forty-four years correspond to the midday worship. The libation offered at this worship is accompanied by a hymn in the triṣṭubh metre, which has forty-four syllables. In this way, one can easily meditate on a human being as a ritualistic sacrifice.

तं चेदेतस्मिन्वयसि किञ्चिदुपतपेत्स ब्रूयात्प्राणा रुद्रा इदं मे माध्यन्दिनं सवनं तृतीयसवनमनुसन्तनुतेति माहं प्राणानां रुद्राणां मध्ये यज्ञो विलोप्सीयेत्युद्धैव तत एत्यगदो ह भवति॥ ४॥

Taṁ cedetasminvayasi kiñcidupatapetsa brūyātprāṇā rudrā idaṁ me mādhyandinaṁ savanaṁ tṛtīyasavana-manusantanuteti māhaṁ prāṇānāṁ rudrāṇāṁ madhye yajño vilopsīyetyuddhaiva tata etyagado ha bhavati.

Cet, if; *etasmin vayasi,* within these [forty-four] years of his life; *tam kiñcit upatapet,* something troubles him; *saḥ brūyāt,* he will say; *prāṇāḥ,* O Prāṇas; *rudrāḥ,* O Rudras; *idam me mādhyandinam savanam,* this, my midday libation; *tṛtīya savanam,* to the third libation; *anusantanuta iti,* extend; *mā aham,* may I not; *yajñaḥ,* as the sacrifice; *prāṇānām rudrāṇām madhye;* in the midst of the prāṇas, who are the Rudras; *vilopsīya iti,* disappear; *tataḥ ha eva ut-eti,* he gets rid of that [ailment]; *agadaḥ ha bhavati,* [and] becomes well.

4. If, within these next forty-four years of his life, he has some ailment, he should then say: 'O Prāṇas, O Rudras, please extend my midday libation and join it to the third libation. As the sacrifice, may I not disappear among the Rudras, who are my prāṇas [i.e., who are like my life].' [If he prays like this,] he gets rid of his ailment and becomes fully well.

The idea behind this prayer is: 'O Rudras, you are like my life. I am the sacrifice, and now the midday libation is going on. Will you please extend this libation so that I may do the third libation without a break [that is, may I live long enough to do the evening libation]? I am the sacrifice, and I don't want the sacrifice to be stopped before it reaches the end. And I don't want to be separated from the Rudras, who are like my life.'

If the afflicted person (who is the sacrifice) keeps praying like this, he will then get well and be fully fit again.

अथ यान्यष्टाचत्वारिंशद्वर्षाणि तत्तृतीयसवनमष्टाच-
त्वारिंशदक्षरा जगती जागतं तृतीयसवनं तदस्यादित्या
अन्वायत्ताः प्राणा वावादित्या एते हीदं सर्वमाददते॥ ५॥

Atha yānyaṣṭācatvāriṁśadvarṣāṇi tattṛtīyasavana-maṣṭācatvāriṁśadakṣarā jagatī jāgataṁ tṛtīyasavanaṁ tadasyādityā anvāyattāḥ prāṇā vāvādityā ete hīdaṁ sarvamādadate.

Atha, next; *yāni aṣṭācatvāriṁśat varṣāṇi,* that which is the next forty-eight years; *tat,* that; *tṛtīya savanam,* is the third libation; *jagatī aṣṭācatvāriṁśat akṣarā,* the jagatī metre is constituted of forty-eight syllables; *jāgatam tṛtīya savanam,* the third libation is accompanied by a hymn in the jagatī metre; *asya,* of this [i.e., this sacrifice of the human body]; *tat,* it [the third libation covering the next forty-eight years];

ādityāḥ, the deities called Āditya; *anvāyattāḥ,* are connected; *prāṇāḥ vāva ādityāḥ,* the prāṇas are the Ādityas; *hi,* for; *ete,* these [Ādityas]; *idam sarvam ādadate,* accept [*ādā*] all objects.

5. Then the next forty-eight years are the third libation. The jagatī metre has forty-eight syllables, and the third libation is accompanied by a hymn which is in the jagatī metre. The Ādityas are connected with this third libation. The prāṇas are called Ādityas because they accept [*ādā*] all things.

A human being is supposed to live a total of a hundred and sixteen years, which has three phases: the first twenty-four years, the next forty-four years, and the last forty-eight years. When this life is thought of as a sacrifice, the first twenty-four years would be the morning offering, the next forty-four years would be the midday offering, and the last forty-eight years would be the evening offering.

Just as the morning libation is connected with the Vasus, so the first twenty-four years of one's life are also connected with the Vasus. The gāyatrī is sung during the morning offering, and it has twenty-four syllables. The offering made at midday is connected with the Rudras, and it is accompanied by a hymn in the triṣṭubh metre, having forty-four syllables. Then the evening offering is connected with the Ādityas, and it is sung in the jagatī metre, having forty-eight syllables. The concept of a human life as a sacrifice arises from the similarity to the components of a ritualistic sacrifice.

तं चेदेतस्मिन्वयसि किञ्चिदुपतपेत्स ब्रूयात्प्राणा आदित्या इदं मे तृतीयसवनमायुरनुसन्तनुतेति माहं प्राणानामादित्यानां मध्ये यज्ञो विलोप्सीयेत्युद्धैव तत एत्यगदो हैव भवति॥ ६॥

Taṁ cedetasminvayasi kiñcidupatapetsa brūyātprāṇā ādityā idaṁ me tṛtīyasavanamāyuranusantanuteti māhaṁ prāṇānāmādityānāṁ madhye yajño vilopsīyetyuddhaiva tata etyagado haiva bhavati.

Cet, if; *etasmin vayasi,* within these [forty-eight] years of his life; *tam kiñcit upatapet,* something troubles him; *saḥ brūyāt,* he should say; *prāṇāḥ,* O Prāṇas; *ādityāḥ,* O Ādityas; *idam me tṛtīya savanam,* this, my evening libation; *āyuḥ,* to the full length; *anusantanuta iti,* extend; *mā aham,* may I not; *yajñaḥ,* as the sacrifice; *prāṇānām ādityānām madhye,* in the midst of the prāṇas, who are the Ādityas; *vilopsīya iti,* disappear; *tataḥ ha eva ut-eti,* he gets rid of that [ailment]; *agadaḥ ha eva bhavati,* [and] becomes well.

6. If, within the next forty-eight years of his life, he has some ailment, he should then say: 'O Prāṇas, O Ādityas, please extend my evening libation to the end of my life. As the sacrifice, may I not disappear among the Ādityas, who are my prāṇas [i.e., who are like my life].' [If he prays like this,] he gets rid of his ailment and becomes well.

एतद्ध स्म वै तद्विद्वानाह महिदास ऐतरेयः स किं म एतदुपतपसि योऽहमनेन न प्रेष्यामीति स ह षोडशं वर्षशतमजीवत्प्र ह षोडशं वर्षशतं जीवति य एवं वेद॥ ७॥ इति षोडशः खण्डः॥ १६॥

Etaddha sma vai tadvidvānāha mahidāsa aitareyaḥ sa kiṁ ma etadupatapasi yo'hamanena na preṣyāmīti sa ha ṣoḍaśaṁ varṣaśatamajīvatpra ha ṣoḍaśaṁ varṣaśatam jīvati ya evaṁ veda. Iti ṣoḍaśaḥ khaṇḍaḥ.

Etat ha vai vidvān, having known this; *mahidāsaḥ aitareyaḥ,* Mahidāsa Aitareya, the son of Itarā; *āha sma,* said; *saḥ* [i.e., *tvam*] *kim me etat upatapasi,* O disease, why are you troubling me; *yaḥ aham anena na preṣyāmi iti,* who for certain will not die of this; *saḥ,* he [Mahidāsa Aitareya]; *ha ṣoḍaśam varṣaśatam,* one hundred and sixteen years; *ajīvat,* lived; *yaḥ evam veda,* he who knows thus; *ha ṣoḍaśam varṣaśatam prajīvati,* also lives one hundred and sixteen years. *Iti ṣoḍaśaḥ khaṇḍaḥ,* here ends the sixteenth section.

7. Having known this, Itarā's son Mahidāsa said: 'O disease, why are you troubling me so? Rest assured, I am not going to die [of this disease].' He lived for one hundred and sixteen years. A person who knows this also lives that long.

Mahidāsa is an example of one who conquered death by his knowledge and strong will.

Section Seventeen

स यदशिशिषति यत्पिपासति यन्न रमते ता अस्य दीक्षाः ॥ १ ॥

Sa yadaśiśiṣati yatpipāsati yanna ramate tā asya dīkṣāḥ.

Saḥ, he [the person who is performing the puruṣa sacrifice just mentioned]; *yat aśiśiṣati,* that he wants to eat; *yat pipāsati,* that he wants to drink; *yat na ramate,* that he has no desire to indulge in sense pleasure; *tāḥ,* all these; *asya dīkṣāḥ,* are the initiation rites [to perform the sacrifice].

1. That he has the desire to eat, the desire to drink, and no desire to indulge in sense pleasures—this is his initiation [i.e., this is how he has to begin practising self-restraint].

अथ यदश्नाति यत्पिबति यद्रमते तदुपसदैरेति ॥ २ ॥

Atha yadaśnāti yatpibati yadramate tadupasadaireti.

Atha, after this; *yat aśnāti,* what he eats; *yat pibati,* what he drinks; *yat ramate,* the pleasure he enjoys; *tat upasadaiḥ eti,* that is his upasad [when one fasts by only taking milk or water].

2. After this he will eat, he will drink, or he will enjoy pleasure, as if he is observing *upasad* [when he can only take milk or water].

अथ यद्धसति यज्जक्षति यन्मैथुनं चरति स्तुतशस्त्रैरेव तदेति ॥ ३ ॥

Atha yaddhasati yajjakṣati yanmaithunaṁ carati stutaśastraireva tadeti.

Atha, next; *yat hasati,* he laughs; *yat jakṣati,* he eats; *yat maithunam carati,* he indulges in sense pleasure; *stuta-śastraiḥ eva tat eti,* they are like [the sounds of] the stutas and śastras [certain hymns and mantras recited during the sacrifice].

3. After this, he laughs, he eats, and he even enjoys some sense pleasure—these represent the sounds coming from the *stutas* and *śastras.*

अथ यत्तपो दानमार्जवमहिंसा सत्यवचनमिति ता अस्य दक्षिणाः ॥ ४ ॥

Atha yattapo dānamārjavamahiṁsā satyavacanamiti tā asya dakṣiṇāḥ.

Atha, next; *yat tapaḥ,* the austerity; *dānam,* charity; *ārjavam,* straightforwardness; *ahiṁsā,* non-violence;

satyavacanam, truthfulness; *iti tāḥ,* all these [good qualities]; *asya,* of him [the person who regards his life as a sacrifice]; *dakṣiṇāḥ,* are the special fee paid after the sacrifice.

4. Next, austerity, charity, straightforwardness, non-violence, and truthfulness—these are his *dakṣiṇā.*

These qualities of austerity, charity, etc., are an additional gain, besides what you get by living a life as if it is a sacrifice. These moral qualities and the life you live both contribute much to the growth of your religious life.

तस्मादाहुः सोष्यत्यसोष्टेति पुनरुत्पादनमेवास्य तन्मरणमेवावभृथः ॥ ५ ॥

Tasmādāhuḥ soṣyatyasoṣṭeti punarutpādaname-vāsya tanmaraṇamevāvabhṛthaḥ.

Tasmāt, therefore; *āhuḥ,* it is said; *soṣyati,* will give birth to; *asoṣṭa iti,* has given birth to; *punaḥ utpādanam eva,* [because] it is a rebirth; *tat maraṇam eva asya,* the death of the person; *avabhṛthaḥ,* is the conclusion of the sacrifice.

5. Therefore people say, 'He will give birth,' or 'He has given birth.' In either case, it is a rebirth [in the sense that when he starts living his life

as a sacrifice, that is his rebirth]. When death overtakes him, that is the conclusion of the sacrifice.

Life is a kind of sacrifice, but when a person dedicates his life as such, he is said to be reborn. The words *soṣyati* and *asoṣṭa* are used when a mother is about to give birth, or has given birth, to a child. But they are also used at the time when someone is about to begin performing a sacrifice (*soṣyati*), or has already begun performing it (*asoṣṭa*), because it is his rebirth.

When death comes to the person who treats his life as a sacrifice, it is the end of the sacrifice, just as it is the end of his life. Just as at the end of a sacrifice, a person bathes and puts on new clothes, so also, when a person dies, his body is bathed and new clothes are put on it. The treatment is the same, whether the sacrifice is that person's life or it is the usual sacrificial ritual. And the words used on both occasions are the same. This makes the similarity between the ritualistc sacrifice and life as a sacrifice more meaningful.

तद्धैतद्घोर आङ्गिरसः कृष्णाय देवकीपुत्रायोक्त्वो-
वाचापिपास एव स बभूव सोऽन्तवेलायामेतत्त्रयं
प्रतिपद्येताक्षितमस्यच्युतमसि प्राणसंशितमसीति तत्रैते द्वे
ऋचौ भवतः ॥ ६ ॥

Taddhaitadghora āṅgirasaḥ kṛṣṇāya devakīputrā-yoktvovācāpipāsa eva sa babhūva so'ntavelāyāmetat-trayaṁ pratipadyetākṣitamasyacyutamasi prāṇasaṁ-śitamasīti tatraite dve ṛcau bhavataḥ.

Tat ha etat, this [truth]; *ghoraḥ āṅgirasaḥ,* the sage Ghora, of the family of Aṅgirasa; *kṛṣṇāya devakīputrāya uktvā,* having taught to Kṛṣṇa, the son of Devakī; *apipāsaḥ,* free from desire; *eva saḥ babhūva,* he [Kṛṣṇa] became; *uvāca,* [Ghora] said; *saḥ,* a person; *antavelā-yām,* at the time of death; *etat trayam,* these three [mantras]; *pratipadyeta,* should take refuge in; *akṣitam asi,* you never decay; *acyutam asi,* you never change; *prāṇasaṁśitam asi iti,* you are the essence of life; *tatra,* in this connection; *ete dve ṛcau bhavataḥ,* there are these two Ṛk mantras.

6. The sage Ghora, of the family of Aṅgirasa, taught this truth to Kṛṣṇa, the son of Devakī. As a result, Kṛṣṇa became free from all desires. Then Ghora said: 'At the time of death a person should repeat these three mantras: "You never decay, you never change, and you are the essence of life."' Here are two Ṛk mantras in this connection:

आदित्प्रत्नस्य रेतसः ज्योतिः पश्यन्ति वासरम्। परो यदिध्यते दिवि॥ ७॥

उद्वयं तमसस्परि ज्योतिः पश्यन्त उत्तरंस्वः पश्यन्त उत्तरं देवं देवत्रा सूर्यमगन्म ज्योतिरुत्तममिति ज्योतिरुत्तममिति ॥ ८ ॥ इति सप्तदशः खण्डः ॥ १७ ॥

Āditpratnaṣya retasaḥ jyotiḥ paśyanti vāsaram; Paro yadidhyate divi.

Udvayaṁ tamasaspari jyotiḥ paśyanta uttaraṁsvaḥ paśyanta uttaraṁ devaṁ devatrā sūryamaganma jyotiruttamamiti jyotiruttamamiti. Iti saptadaśaḥ khaṇḍaḥ.

Ādit, [has no meaning except that it introduces a new line of thought]; *pratnasya,* ancient; *retasaḥ,* seed [of the world]; *jyotiḥ,* light [manifestation]; *paśyanti,* they see [everywhere]; *vāsaram,* daylight [i.e., as all-pervasive]; *paraḥ,* the best; *yat,* that which; *idhyate,* shines; *divi,* in heaven [i.e., in Para-Brahman].

Tamasaḥ, darkness [i.e., ignorance]; *pari,* beyond [dispels]; *uttaram,* the best; *jyotiḥ,* light; *paśyantaḥ,* having seen; *svaḥ,* in oneself [i.e., in one's own heart]; *devam,* bright; *devatrā,* among all the gods; *sūryam,* the sun; *vayam ut-aganma,* we have attained; *jyotiḥ uttamam iti jyotiḥ uttamam iti,* the best light, the best light. *Iti saptadaśaḥ khaṇḍaḥ,* here ends the seventeenth section.

7-8. [Those who know Brahman] see that the light shining in Para-Brahman is the seed of the world. This light is all-pervasive like daylight. It is eternal. It is that great light which is the cause of the world.

The greatest light is that which dispels the darkness of ignorance. Having seen this light within our own hearts, we have attained that shining god who is the Supreme Light of all.

There is an eternal light which is the cause of this universe. This light is the source of the light we see in the luminous bodies such as the sun, the moon, and the stars. This light is everywhere. Everything in this phenomenal universe moves and works the way it does because of this light.

Those who have lived a life of self-discipline, with their minds on the highest thoughts, and have thereby acquired a pure heart, can see this light. They see it within themselves and they also see it outside. They know this light as their own Self and as the Self of all. They know this light as Para Brahman.

Section Eighteen

मनो ब्रह्मेत्युपासीतेत्यध्यात्ममथाधिदैवतमाकाशो ब्रह्मे-
त्युभयमादिष्टं भवत्यध्यात्मं चाधिदैवतं च ॥ १ ॥

Mano brahmetyupāsītetyadhyātmamathādhidaivata-mākāśo brahmetyubhayamādiṣṭaṁ bhavatyadhyātmaṁ cādhidaivataṁ ca.

Manaḥ brahma iti upāsīta, meditate on the mind as Brahman; *iti adhyātmam,* this is so far as the body and mind is concerned; *atha adhidaivatam,* next is [the meditation] on the elements and the worlds; *ākāśaḥ brahma iti,* space is Brahman; *ubhayam ādiṣṭam bhavati,* two ways [of meditation] are advised; *adhyātmam ca adhidaivatam ca,* adhyātma and adhidaivata.

1. The mind is Brahman—this worship is called *adhyātma.* Next is that called *adhidaivata*: Space is Brahman. [That is, meditate on space as Brahman.] These two ways of meditation are advised: adhyātma and adhidaivata.

Brahman is extremely subtle. Similarly, the mind is also subtle. And it is in the mind that Brahman can be realized. This is why it is comparatively easy to think that the mind is Brahman.

In the same way, ākāśa (space) is also close to Brahman. Like Brahman, it is vast, invisible, all-pervasive, and without any attributes whatsoever. It is therefore appropriate to meditate on ākāśa as Brahman.

तदेतच्चतुष्पाद्ब्रह्म वाक्पादः प्राणः पादश्चक्षुः पादः श्रोत्रं पाद इत्यध्यात्ममथाधिदैवतमग्निः पादो वायुः पाद आदित्यः पादो दिशः पाद इत्युभयमेवादिष्टं भवत्यध्यात्मं चैवाधिदैवतं च॥ २॥

Tadetaccatuṣpādbrahma vākpādaḥ prāṇaḥ pādaś-cakṣuḥ pādaḥ śrotraṁ pāda ityadhyātmamathādhidaiva-

tamagniḥ pādo vāyuḥ pāda ādityaḥ pādo diśaḥ pāda ityubhayamevādiṣṭaṁ bhavatyadhyātmaṁ caivādhidaivataṁ ca.

Tat etat catuṣpāt brahma, this Brahman [as the mind] is fourfold; *vāk pādaḥ,* speech is a foot; *prāṇaḥ pādaḥ,* prāṇa [the vital force] is a foot; *cakṣuḥ pādaḥ,* the eyes are a foot; *śrotram pādaḥ,* the ears are a foot; *iti adhyātmam,* this is the adhyātma [meditation —i.e., on the body and mind]; *atha adhidaivatam,* next, the meditation relating to the elements and worlds; *agniḥ pādaḥ,* fire is a foot; *vāyuḥ pādaḥ,* air is a foot; *ādityaḥ pādaḥ,* the sun is a foot; *diśaḥ pādaḥ,* the quarters are a foot; *ubhayam ādiṣṭam bhavati,* two ways [of meditation] are advised; *adhyātmam ca adhidaivatam ca,* adhyātma and adhidaivata.

2. Brahman as the mind has four feet [or, quarters]. The organ of speech is one foot; prāṇa is the next foot; the eyes are the third foot; and the ears are the fourth foot. This is the adhyātma [the physical and mental] aspect of Brahman. Next is the adhidaivata aspect. Fire is one foot; air is another foot; the sun is the next foot; and the quarters are the fourth foot. These two ways of meditation are advised: adhyātma and adhidaivata.

The word *pāda* is not to be taken literally, for Brahman has no feet. Brahman is infinite, but here it is conceived as having four feet—as if it is covering the whole universe with them. *Pāda* also means a quarter, or a part.

First let us imagine our mind and body together as Brahman. This is a meditation on the adhyātma level. Then let us imagine that this Brahman has four feet. What are the four feet? They are the organ of speech, the vital breath, the eyes, and the ears.

We can also do this meditation on the adhidaivata level—that is, as the worlds and the elements. First, let us imagine Brahman as ākāśa, space. Brahman's four feet would then be fire (agni), air (vāyu), the sun (āditya), and the quarters (diśa).

A cow has four feet to take it where it wants to go. Similarly, a human being is guided to where he wants to go by his organ of speech, his organ of smelling, his eyes, and his ears.

Again, just as the four legs and feet of a cow come out of her body, in the same way, fire, air, the sun, and the quarters seem to come out of space.

वागेव ब्रह्मणश्चतुर्थः पादः सोऽग्निना ज्योतिषा भाति च तपति च भाति च तपति च कीर्त्या यशसा ब्रह्मवर्चसेन य एवं वेद॥ ३ ॥

Vāgeva brahmaṇaścaturthaḥ pādaḥ so'gninā jyotiṣā bhāti ca tapati ca bhāti ca tapati ca kīrtyā yaśasā brahmavarcasena ya evaṁ veda.

Vāk eva brahmaṇaḥ caturthaḥ pādaḥ, speech is the fourth foot of [manomaya] Brahman; *agninā jyotiṣā,* by the light it gets from fire; *saḥ bhāti ca tapati ca,* it shines and gives heat; *yaḥ evam veda,* he who knows thus; *bhāti ca tapati ca,* shines and radiates warmth; *kīrtyā,* through good work; *yaśasā,* through fame; *brahmavarcasena,* through the radiance that comes from a scholarly and disciplined life.

3. Vāk is one of the four feet of Brahman [as the mind]. It shines in the light of fire and also radiates heat. He who knows this shines and radiates warmth with his good work, with his fame, and with the radiance he acquires from leading a scholarly and disciplined life.

Animals move where they want by their feet. Similarly, people find their way to Brahman by hearing someone speak about it. This is why the organ of speech is called one of the four feet of Brahman.

Fire gives both light and heat. And because fire is the presiding deity of speech, speech also is said to give light and heat. A person who can speak well acquires fame and popularity. It is as if he has done much good work, or has given away much money in charity, or is a great scholar and has lived a disciplined life. Such a person has a shining personality and radiates heat (i.e., energy).

प्राण एव ब्रह्मणश्चतुर्थः पादः स वायुना ज्योतिषा भाति च तपति च भाति च तपति च कीर्त्या यशसा ब्रह्मवर्चसेन य एवं वेद॥४॥

Prāṇa eva brahmaṇaścaturthaḥ pādaḥ sa vāyunā jyotiṣā bhāti ca tapati ca bhāti ca tapati ca kīrtyā yaśasā brahmavarcasena ya evaṁ veda.

Prāṇaḥ eva brahmaṇaḥ caturthaḥ pādaḥ, prāṇa [the organ of smelling] is the fourth foot of [manomaya] Brahman; *vāyunā jyotiṣā,* by the light it gets from air [its presiding deity]; *saḥ bhāti ca tapati ca,* it shines and gives heat; *yaḥ evam veda,* he who knows thus; *bhāti ca tapati ca,* shines and radiates warmth; *kīrtyā,* through good work; *yaśasā,* through fame; *brahmavarcasena,* through the radiance that comes from a scholarly and disciplined life.

4. Prāṇa [the organ of smelling] is one of the four feet of Brahman [as the mind]. It shines by the light of vāyu [air] and also radiates heat. He who knows this shines and radiates warmth with his good work, with his fame, and with the radiance he acquires from leading a scholarly and disciplined life.

Vāyu, air, is the presiding deity of the organ of smell, because vāyu carries odours and reveals them.

चक्षुरेव ब्रह्मणश्चतुर्थः पादः स आदित्येन ज्योतिषा भाति च तपति च भाति च तपति च कीर्त्या यशसा ब्रह्मवर्चसेन य एवं वेद॥५॥

Cakṣureva brahmaṇaścaturthaḥ pādaḥ sa ādityena jyotiṣā bhāti ca tapati ca bhāti ca tapati ca kīrtyā yaśasā brahmavarcasena ya evam veda.

Cakṣuḥ eva brahmaṇaḥ caturthaḥ pādaḥ, the organ of vision is the fourth foot of [manomaya] Brahman; *ādityena jyotiṣā,* by the light it gets from the sun [its presiding deity]; *saḥ bhāti ca tapati ca,* it shines and gives heat; *yaḥ evam veda,* he who knows thus; *bhāti ca tapati ca,* shines and radiates warmth; *kīrtyā,* through good work; *yaśasā,* through fame; *brahmavarcasena,* through the radiance that comes from a scholarly and disciplined life.

5. The organ of vision is one of the four feet of Brahman [as the mind]. It shines by the light of the sun and also radiates heat. He who knows this shines and radiates warmth with his good work, with his fame, and with the radiance he acquires from leading a scholarly and disciplined life.

The eyes can distinguish colours because of the light they get from the sun. Just as cows can feel their way with their feet, similarly, human beings can recognize things through their eyes.

When a person knows how the eyes serve as feet,

he acquires fame, glory, and the brightness of Brahman, for he can then make good use of his eyes. He can read and learn the best things possible, things that transform him into a realized soul.

श्रोत्रमेव ब्रह्मणश्चतुर्थः पादः स दिग्भिर्ज्योतिषा भाति च तपति च भाति च तपति च कीर्त्या यशसा ब्रह्मवर्चसेन य एवं वेद य एवं वेद॥ ६॥ इत्यष्टादशः खण्डः ॥ १८ ॥

Śrotrameva brahmaṇaścaturthaḥ pādaḥ sa digbhir-jyotiṣā bhāti ca tapati ca bhāti ca tapati ca kīrtyā yaśasā brahmavarcasena ya evaṁ veda ya evaṁ veda. Ityaṣṭādaśaḥ khaṇḍaḥ.

Śrotram eva brahmaṇaḥ caturthaḥ pādaḥ, the organ of hearing is the fourth foot of [manomaya] Brahman; *digbhiḥ jyotiṣā,* by the light it gets from [its presiding deity,] the quarters; *saḥ bhāti ca tapati ca,* it shines and gives heat; *yaḥ evam veda yaḥ evam veda,* he who knows thus, he who knows thus; *bhāti ca tapati ca,* shines and radiates warmth; *kīrtyā,* through good work; *yaśasā,* through fame; *brahmavarcasena,* through the radiance that comes from a scholarly and disciplined life. *Iti aṣṭādaśaḥ khaṇḍaḥ,* here ends the eighteenth section.

6. The organ of hearing is one of the four feet of Brahman [as the mind]. It shines by the light

of the quarters and also radiates heat. He who knows this shines and radiates warmth with his good work, with his fame, and with the radiance he acquires from leading a scholarly and disciplined life.

The organ of hearing derives its power from the quarters, and through this organ we get knowledge. The results of that knowledge may be direct or indirect. True knowledge, however, is knowledge of Brahman. To emphasize this, 'he who knows' is repeated. This emphasis suggests that it is the knowledge of Brahman.

The organ of hearing is our 'foot' because it is the means by which we can know Brahman. Those who know the importance of the organ of hearing and use it in the right way, acquire name, fame, and become radiant like Brahman. They will also eventually realize Brahman.

Section Nineteen

आदित्यो ब्रह्मेत्यादेशस्तस्योपव्याख्यानमसदेवेदमग्र आसीत्। तत्सदासीत्तत्समभवत्तदाण्डं निरवर्तत तत्संवत्सरस्य मात्रामशयत तन्निरभिद्यत ते आण्डकपाले रजतं च सुवर्णं चाभवताम्॥ १॥

Ādityo brahmetyādeśastasyopavyākhyānamasadevedamagra āsīt; Tatsadāsīttatsamabhavattadāṇḍaṁ nira-

vartata tatsaṁvatsarasya mātrāmaśayata tannirabhidyata te āṇḍakapāle rajataṁ ca suvarṇaṁ cābhavatām.

Ādityaḥ brahma, Āditya [the sun] is Brahman; *iti ādeśaḥ,* so it is said; *tasya upavyākhyānam,* [here is] an explanation of that [statement]; *idam,* this [universe of name and form]; *agre asat eva āsīt,* was at first unmanifested [i.e., it was without its names and forms]; [lest the word *asat* give the impression that the universe was like 'a flower in the sky,' it is said,] *tat,* this [universe with its names and forms in a subtle state]; *sat āsīt,* became manifest; *tat,* that [subtle universe]; *samabhavat,* first emerged as a seed; *tat āṇḍam niravartata,* that developed into an egg; *tat,* it [i.e., the egg]; *saṁvatsarasya mātrām aśayata,* lay still for a period of a year; *tat,* it [the egg]; *nirabhidyata,* split open; *te āṇḍakapāle,* those two parts of the egg; *rajatam ca suvarṇam ca abhavatām,* turned silver and gold respectively.

1. It has been said, 'Āditya is Brahman.' Now this is being explained: This universe was at first non-existent, being without names and forms. [It was not visible, but it existed in a subtle form.] Slowly it manifested itself, as a shoot comes out of a seed. Next it developed into an egg and remained for a whole year like that. It then split in two, one half becoming silver and the other half becoming gold.

Earlier Āditya, the sun, was described as a foot of Brahman. Now this is being explained.

Many people think that the universe was created.

But Vedānta says that something cannot be created out of nothing. The universe has always existed, though sometimes it exists like a seed—invisible and without any names and forms.

But why is the sun being called Brahman? Because without the sun there is only darkness, and we are then not conscious of this universe with its names and forms. The universe is non-existent then. And in the absence of the universe, there is no way of knowing that Brahman exists, for it is this universe with its names and forms that makes us aware that Brahman is behind everything. Brahman manifests itself as this universe.

तद्यद्रजतं सेयं पृथिवी यत्सुवर्णं सा द्यौर्यज्जरायु ते पर्वता यदुल्बं समेघो नीहारो या धमनयस्ता नद्यो यद्वास्तेयमुदकं स समुद्रः ॥ २ ॥

Tadyadrajataṁ seyaṁ pṛthivī yatsuvarṇaṁ sā dyaur-yajjarāyu te parvatā yadulbaṁ samegho nīhāro yā dhamanayastā nadyo yadvāsteyamudakaṁ sa samudraḥ.

Tat yat rajatam, that [half] which is silver; *sā iyam pṛthivī,* that is this earth; *yat suvarṇam,* that [half] which is gold; *sā dyauḥ,* that is heaven; *yat jarāyu,* that which is the thick membrane; *te parvatāḥ,* they are the mountains; *yat ulbam,* that which is the thin membrane; *sameghaḥ nīhāraḥ,* are the clouds and mist; *yāḥ dhamanayaḥ,* that which are the veins;

tāḥ nadyaḥ, they are the rivers; *yat vāsteyam udakam,* that which is the fluid in the bladder; *saḥ samudraḥ,* that is the ocean.

2. Of these two parts of the egg, the one that is silver is this earth, and the one that is gold is heaven. The thick membranes are the mountains. The thin membranes are the clouds and mist. The veins are the rivers, and the fluid in the bladder is the ocean.

It has already been stated that at a certain point in time the cosmos takes the shape of an egg, and after remaining in that state for a while, the egg splits in two. The lower part iṣ silver and represents the earth. The upper half is gold and represents heaven.

The thick outer membrane around the baby represents the mountains, and the thin inner membrane represents the clouds and mist. The veins of the infant are likened to rivers, and the fluid inside the bladder to the ocean.

It is to be noted that these diverse things have all come from one source.

अथ यत्तदजायत सोऽसावादित्यस्तं जायमानं घोषा उलूलवोऽनूदतिष्ठन्सर्वाणि च भूतानि सर्वे च कामास्त-स्मात्तस्योदयं प्रति प्रत्यायनं प्रति घोषा उलूलवो-ऽनूत्तिष्ठन्ति सर्वाणि च भूतानि सर्वे च कामाः ॥ ३ ॥

Atha yattadajāyata so'sāvādityastaṁ jāyamānaṁ ghoṣā ulūlavo'nūdatiṣṭhansarvāṇi ca bhūtāni sarve ca kāmāstasmāttasyodayaṁ prati pratyāyanaṁ prati ghoṣā ulūlavo'nūttiṣṭhanti sarvāṇi ca bhūtāni sarve ca kāmāḥ.

Atha, next; *yat tat ajāyata,* that which was born; *saḥ asau ādityaḥ,* it is that sun; *tam jāyamānam anu,* after it was born; *ulūlavaḥ ghoṣāḥ,* the sounds of 'ulu'; *sarvāṇi ca bhūtāni,* from all beings; *sarve ca kāmāḥ,* and all desirable things; *udatiṣṭhan,* came forth; *tasmāt,* therefore; *udayam prati,* at the rising; *pratyāyanam prati,* at the setting; *tasya,* of that [sun]; *ulūlavaḥ ghoṣāḥ,* the sounds of 'ulu'; *sarvāṇi ca bhūtāni,* from all beings; *sarve ca kāmāḥ,* and all desirable things; *anūttiṣṭhanti,* appear.

3. Then that which was born was the sun. Its appearance was greeted by joyous sounds from all beings, and many desirable things appeared. Since then, the sunrise and the sunset are both marked by joyous sounds from all beings, and many enjoyable things also appear at that time.

Here it is said that the sun was born from the egg. When a child is born, there is much jubilation in the house, and also in the neighbourhood. Even today, people in India sometimes make the sound of 'ulu' on such occasions. Not only that, many precious gifts are also exchanged.

स य एतमेवं विद्वानादित्यं ब्रह्मेत्युपास्तेऽभ्याशो ह यदेनं साधवो घोषा आ च गच्छेयुरुप च निम्रेडेरन्निम्रेडेरन् ॥ ४ ॥ इत्येकोनविंशः खण्डः ॥ १९ ॥ इति छान्दोग्योपनिषदि तृतीयोऽध्यायः ॥ ३ ॥

Sa ya etamevaṁ vidvānādityaṁ brahmetyupāste-'bhyāśo ha yadenaṁ sādhavo ghoṣā ā ca gaccheyurupa ca nimreḍerannimreḍeran. Ityekonaviṁśaḥ khaṇḍaḥ. Iti chāndogyopaniṣadi tṛtīyo'dhyāyaḥ.

Saḥ yaḥ etam evam vidvān, he who knows this as such; *ādityam brahma iti upāste,* [and] worships the sun as Brahman; *abhyāśaḥ,* soon; *ha,* surely; *yat enam āgaccheyuḥ,* to him come; *sādhavaḥ ghoṣāḥ,* pleasant sounds; *ca upa-nimreḍeran ca nimreḍeran* and also good things to enjoy, good things to enjoy. [The repetition marks the end of the chapter.] *Iti ekonaviṁśaḥ khaṇḍaḥ,* here ends the nineteenth section. *Iti chāndogyopaniṣadi tṛtīyaḥ adhyāyaḥ,* here ends the third chapter of the Chāndogya Upaniṣad.

4. One who knows the sun as Brahman and worships it as such very soon hears sounds pleasing to the ears and also has many good things to enjoy.

CHAPTER FOUR

Section One

ॐ जानश्रुतिर्ह पौत्रायणः श्रद्धादेयो बहुदायी बहुपाक्य आस स ह सर्वत आवसथान्मापयाञ्चक्रे सर्वत एव मेऽन्नमत्स्यन्तीति ॥ १ ॥

Om. Jānaśrutirha pautrāyaṇaḥ śraddhādeyo bahudāyī bahupākya āsa sa ha sarvata āvasathānmāpayāñcakre sarvata eva me'nnamatsyantīti.

Pautrāyaṇaḥ, the grandson; *jānaśrutiḥ,* the son of Janaśruta; *śraddhādeyaḥ,* gave away in charity with due respect; *bahudāyī,* gave many gifts; *bahupākyaḥ,* cooked large quantities of food for free distribution; *āsa ha,* it happened like this; *saḥ,* he [Jānaśruti]; *sarvataḥ,* from all quarters; *me annam,* my food; *atsyanti,* [people] will eat; *iti,* this [i.e., with this thought in mind]; *sarvataḥ eva,* in all directions; *āvasathān,* rest-houses; *māpayāñcakre,* built.

1. In ancient times there was a king who was the great-grandson of Janaśruta. He was a highly charitable person, who gave many gifts in charity, and always with due respect. He also had large quantities of food cooked for people. With the thought in mind, 'People all over will eat my food,' he had many rest-houses built in different places.

There was once a king named Jānaśruti, who was the great-grandson of Janaśruta. He was a highly charitable person. He not only made large donations, but whatever he gave he gave with love and respect. Every day large quantities of food were cooked and he fed many people. He also had rest-houses built all over the country. He wanted people to come, stay in those rest-houses, and enjoy his food.

अथ ह हंसा निशायामतिपेतुस्तद्धैवं हंसो हंसमभ्युवाद हो होऽयि भल्लाक्ष भल्लाक्ष जानश्रुतेः पौत्रायणस्य समं दिवा ज्योतिराततं तन्मा प्रसाङ्क्षीस्तत्त्वा मा प्रधाक्षीरिति ॥ २ ॥

Atha ha haṁsā niśāyāmatipetustaddhaivaṁ haṁso haṁsamabhyuvāda ho ho'yi bhallākṣa bhallākṣa jānaśruteḥ pautrāyaṇasya samaṁ divā jyotirātataṁ tanmā prasāṅkṣīstattvā mā pradhākṣīriti.

Atha ha, once; *haṁsāḥ,* swans [i.e., some sages who had taken the form of swans]; *niśāyām,* at night; *atipetuḥ,* were flying; *tat,* then; *haṁsaḥ,* one of the swans; *evam ha abhyuvāda,* loudly said; *haṁsam,* to the other swan; *ho ho ayi bhallākṣa bhallākṣa,* hey, you short-sided one [don't you see?]; *jānaśruteḥ pautrāyaṇasya jyotiḥ,* the light [emanating] from Jānaśruti; *divā,* in the sky; *samam ātatam,* has spread like daylight; *tat,* that [light]; *mā prasāṅkṣīḥ,* don't touch; *tat tvā mā pradhākṣī iti,* don't let it burn you.

2. Once he saw some swans flying overhead at night. The swan flying behind called out to the one ahead: 'Hey, you short-sided one! Don't you see that the brightness of Jānaśruti has spread all over the sky like daylight? Beware you don't touch it. See that it doesn't burn you.'

One evening the king was resting on the roof of his palace and he noticed a couple of swans flying above him in the sky. These swans were actually sages or gods in disguise. Just then the swan flying behind joked with the one ahead about the king, within the king's hearing.

तमु ह परः प्रत्युवाच कम्वर एनमेतत्सन्तं सयुग्वानमिव रैक्वमात्थेति यो नु कथं सयुग्वा रैक्व इति॥ ३ ॥

Tamu ha paraḥ pratyuvāca kamvara enametatsantaṁ sayugvānamiva raikvamāttheti yo nu kathaṁ sayugvā raikva iti.

Paraḥ, the other [i.e., the swan in front]; *pratyuvāca,* replied; *are kam u enam etat santam,* [feigning contempt and a mood to debate] say, who is this one; *sayugvānam raikvam iva āttha iti,* you are talking as if he were Raikva with the cart; *yaḥ nu katham sayugvā raikvaḥ iti,* [the other swan asked] who is this Raikva with the cart that you are referring to?

3. The swan in front replied: 'Say, who is this person? From the way you are talking one would think he was Raikva with the cart.' Then the other swan asked, 'And who is this Raikva with the cart you are referring to?'

What the swan in front meant was: 'This prince is a worthless fellow. He by no means deserves the honour you are paying him. You are talking of him as if he had attained Self-knowledge—as if he were a great person like Sayugvā Raikva (that is, Raikva who rides the small cart).' But the other swan did not know who this Sayugvā Raikva was.

यथा कृतायविजितायाधरेयाः संयन्त्येवमेनं सर्वं तदभिसमैति यत्किञ्च प्रजाः साधु कुर्वन्ति यस्तद्वेद यत्स वेद स मयैतदुक्त इति॥ ४॥

Yathā kṛtāyavijitāyādhareyāḥ saṁyantyevamenaṁ sarvaṁ tadabhisamaiti yatkiñca prajāḥ sādhu kurvanti yastadveda yatsa veda sa mayaitadukta iti.

Yathā, just as; *kṛtāya-vijitāya,* if a person wins the toss of dice called kṛta; *adhareyāḥ,* all lower tosses [i.e., *tretā,* three; *dvāpara,* two; and *kali,* one]; *samyanti,* are included [i.e., are also won]; *evam,* in the same way; *yat kiñca prajāḥ sādhu kurvanti,* whatever good work people do; *enam sarvam tat abhisamaiti,* all that comes under that one [i.e., it goes to the credit of Raikva]; *yaḥ tat veda,* he who knows that; *yat saḥ veda,* whatever he [Raikva] knows; *saḥ mayā etat uktaḥ iti,* this is said of him by me.

4. 'Just as in a game of dice, when a person wins the toss called *kṛta* he automatically wins the lower tosses also, in the same way, whatever good work people do goes to the credit of Raikva. If anyone knows what Raikva knows, he becomes like Raikva. This is how I would describe Raikva.'

Kṛta is the highest number possible in a toss of dice, so it is said to include all the lower numbers within it. The swan says that Raikva is a person like kṛta, because he includes within himself all the good things that other people do. He is the sum total of all that is good in the world. If anyone has the knowledge that Raikva has, then he becomes the same as Raikva.

तदु ह जानश्रुतिः पौत्रायण उपशुश्राव स ह सञ्जिहान एव क्षत्तारमुवाचाङ्गारे ह सयुग्वानमिव रैक्वमात्थेति यो नु कथं सयुग्वा रैक्व इति॥ ५॥

यथा कृतायविजितायाधरेयाः संयन्त्येवमेनं सर्वं तदभिसमैति यत्किञ्च प्रजाः साधु कुर्वन्ति यस्तद्वेद यत्स वेद स मयैतदुक्त इति॥ ६॥

Tadu ha jānaśrutiḥ pautrāyaṇa upaśuśrāva sa ha sañjihāna eva kṣattāramuvācāṅgāre ha sayugvānamiva raikvamāttheti yo nu kathaṁ sayugvā raikva iti.

Yathā kṛtāyavijitāyādhareyāḥ saṁyantyevamenaṁ sarvaṁ tadabhisamaiti yatkiñca prajāḥ sādhu kurvanti yastadveda yatsa veda sa mayaitadukta iti.

U tat, that [what the swan said]; *jānaśrutiḥ pautrāyaṇa upaśuśrāva,* the great-grandson of Janaśruta overheard; *saḥ ha sañjihānaḥ,* he got up from his bed; *eva kṣattāram uvāca,* and immediately said to his charioteer; *aṅga are,* O my child; *sayugvānam iva raikvam āttha ha iti,* do you compare me with Raikva with the cart; *yaḥ sayugvā raikva iti,* who is this Raikva with the cart; *nu katham,* what sort of person is he?

Yathā, just as; *kṛtāya-vijitāya,* if a person wins the toss of dice called kṛta; *adhareyāḥ,* all lower tosses [i.e., *tretā,* three; *dvāpara,* two; and *kali,* one]; *samyanti,* are included [i.e., are also won]; *evam,* in the same way; *yat kiñca prajāḥ sādhu kurvanti,* whatever good work people do; *enam sarvam tat abhisamaiti,* all that comes under that one [i.e., it goes to the credit of Raikva]; *yaḥ tat veda,* he who knows that; *yat saḥ veda,* whatever he [Raikva] knows; *saḥ mayā etat uktaḥ iti,* this is said of him by me.

5-6. Jānaśruti Pautrāyaṇa overheard what the swan said. He got up from his bed and the first thing he did was to ask his attendant [who was standing nearby]: 'O my child, can I be compared to Raikva with the cart? Who is this Raikva with the cart? What sort of person is he?' [Then he quoted what the swan had said:] 'Just as in a game of dice, if a person wins the toss called *kṛta,* he automatically wins the lower tosses also, in the same way, whatever good work people do goes to the credit of Raikva. If anyone knows what Raikva knows, he becomes like Raikva. This is how I would describe Raikva.'

Jānaśruti was disturbed by what the swans had said about him. Maybe he could not be compared with Raikva, but in what way did Raikva excel over him? Who was this Raikva with a cart?

Jānaśruti had a sleepless night. The next morning when he got up, the first thing he did was to question his attendant about this Raikva. He wanted to somehow find out in what respect Raikva was superior to him.

स ह क्षत्तान्विष्य नाविदमिति प्रत्येयाय तं होवाच यत्रारे ब्राह्मणस्यान्वेषणा तदेनमर्छेति ॥ ७ ॥

Sa ha kṣattānviṣya nāvidamiti pratyeyāya taṁ hovāca yatrāre brāhmaṇasyānveṣaṇā tadenamarcheti.

Saḥ ha kṣattā, that attendant; *anviṣya,* having looked [for Raikva]; *na avidam iti,* thought 'I have not found him'; *pratyeyāya,* came back; *tam ha uvāca,* [then Jānaśruti] said to him; *are yatra brāhmaṇasya anveṣaṇā,* well, wherever brāhmins are to be found [i.e., in forests or solitary places]; *tat,* there [in such places]; *enam archeti,* look for him.

7. [Jānaśruti asked his attendant to go and look for Raikva.] Having looked for him, the attendant thought, 'I can't find him,' and returned to his master. Jānaśruti then said to him: 'Well, why don't you go to places where brāhmins are to be found—in forests and solitary places? Look for him there.'

Jānaśruti's attendant looked for Raikva in many places, but obviously they were unlikely places. Raikva could be found only in a quiet place, such as a forest or by the side of a river. It would be there that such a person would prefer to stay. So Jānaśruti asked the attendant to search in those places.

सोऽधस्ताच्छकटस्य पामानं कषमाणमुपोपविवेश तं हाभ्युवाद त्वं नु भगवः सयुग्वा रैक्व इत्यहं ह्यरा३ इति ह प्रतिजज्ञे स ह क्षत्ताविदमिति प्रत्येयाय॥ ८॥ इति प्रथमः खण्डः॥ १॥

So'dhastācchakaṭasya pāmānaṁ kaṣamāṇamupopaviveśa taṁ hābhyuvāda tvaṁ nu bhagavaḥ sayugvā raikva ityahaṁ hyarā3 iti ha pratijajñe sa ha kṣattāvidamiti pratyeyāya. Iti prathamaḥ khaṇḍaḥ.

Saḥ, he [the attendant]; *śakaṭasya adhastāt,* [noticed a man sitting] under a cart; *pāmānam,* with a rash on his skin; *kaṣamāṇam,* scratching; *upa upaviveśa,* he sat close to him; *tam ha abhyuvāda,* he said to him; *tvam nu bhagavaḥ sayugvā raikva iti,* Sir, are you Raikva with the cart; *aham hi arā iti,* well, yes, I am the same; *pratijajñe,* he admitted [rather contemptuously]; *saḥ ha kṣattā,* that attendant; *avidam iti,* thought 'I have found him'; *pratyeyāya,* came back. *Iti prathamaḥ khaṇḍaḥ,* here ends the first section.

8. The attendant noticed a man sitting under a cart, scratching a rash on his body. Sitting down close to him, the attendant asked, 'Sir, are you Raikva with the cart?' The man answered, 'Well, yes, I am.' The attendant thought, 'I have found him,' and returned.

Section Two

तदु ह जानश्रुतिः पौत्रायणः षट् शतानि गवां निष्कमश्वतरीरथं तदादाय प्रतिचक्रमे तं हाभ्युवाद॥ १ ॥

Tadu ha jānaśrutiḥ pautrāyaṇaḥ ṣaṭ śatāni gavāṁ niṣkamaśvatarīrathaṁ tadādāya praticakrame taṁ hābhyuvāda.

Tat u ha, next; *jānaśrutiḥ pautrāyaṇaḥ,* the great-grandson of Janaśruta; *ṣaṭ śatāni gavām,* six hundred cows; *niṣkam,* a gold necklace; *aśvatarīratham,* a chariot drawn by mules; *tat ādāya,* that with him; *praticakrame,* went [there]; *tam ha abhyuvāda,* he said to him.

1. Then Jānaśruti Pautrāyaṇa went to that place, taking with him six hundred cows, a gold necklace, and a chariot drawn by mules. He said to him [Raikva]:

Hearing the report from his attendant, and thinking that Raikva might be poor and in need of money, Jānaśruti went with some gifts to offer Raikva, so that Raikva would teach him.

रैक्वेमानि षट् शतानि गवामयं निष्कोऽयमश्वतरीरथोऽनु
म एतां भगवो देवतां शाधि यां देवतामुपास्स इति ॥ २ ॥

Raikvemāni ṣaṭ śatāni gavāmayaṁ niṣko'yamaśvatarī-ratho'nu ma etāṁ bhagavo devatāṁ śādhi yāṁ devatāmupāssa iti.

Raikva, O Raikva; *imāni,* all these; *ṣaṭ śatāni gavām,* six hundred cows; *ayam niṣkaḥ,* this gold necklace; *ayam aśvatarīrathaḥ,* this chariot drawn by mules; *bhagavaḥ,* sir; *anuśādhi me,* please teach me; *etām devatām,* about the god; *yām devatām upāsse iti,* that god which you worship.

2. 'O Raikva, all these—six hundred cows, a gold necklace, and a chariot drawn by mules—are for you. Please tell me about the god you worship.'

तमु ह परः प्रत्युवाचाह हारेत्वा शूद्र तवैव सह गोभिरस्त्विति तदु ह पुनरेव जानश्रुतिः पौत्रायणः सहस्रं गवां निष्कमश्वतरीरथं दुहितरं तदादाय प्रतिचक्रमे ॥ ३ ॥

Tamu ha paraḥ pratyuvācāha hāretvā śūdra tavaiva saha gobhirastviti tadu ha punareva jānaśrutiḥ pautrāyaṇaḥ sahasraṁ gavāṁ niṣkamaśvatarīrathaṁ duhitaraṁ tadādāya praticakrame.

Tam u, to him [Jānaśruti]; *ha paraḥ,* the other [i.e., Raikva]; *pratyuvāca,* replied; *aha śūdra,* O you śūdra; *hāra-itvā,* the necklace and chariot; *saha gobhiḥ,* along with the cows; *tava eva astu iti,* they may be with you; *tat u ha jānaśrutiḥ pautrāyaṇaḥ,* then Jānaśruti Pautrāyaṇa; *punaḥ eva,* again; *sahasram gavām,* one thousand cows; *niṣkam,* a gold necklace; *aśvatarīratham,* a chariot drawn by mules; *duhitaram,* his own daughter; *tat ādāya,* taking that with him; *praticakrame,* he went back.

3. Raikva said to him, 'You śūdra, the necklace and chariot along with the cows—let all these be yours.' Jānaśruti left and then again came back—this time with one thousand cows, a gold necklace, a chariot drawn by mules, and his own daughter.

Jānaśruti was a kṣatriya. Why then did Raikva address him as a śūdra? Because Jānaśruti thought he could tempt Raikva to teach him *Brahmavidyā,* the knowledge of Brahman, through wealth. He did not understand that a teacher does not care for money. A teacher becomes pleased when a student renders him proper service.

तं हाभ्युवाद रैक्केदं सहस्रं गवामयं निष्कोऽयमश्वतरीरथ इयं जायायं ग्रामो यस्मिन्नास्सेऽन्वेव मा भगवः शाधीति ॥ ४ ॥

Taṁ hābhyuvāda raikvedaṁ sahasraṁ gavāmayaṁ niṣko'yamaśvatarīratha iyaṁ jāyāyaṁ grāmo yasmin-nāsse'nveva mā bhagavaḥ śādhīṭi.

Tam, to him [Raikva]; *ha abhyuvāda,* [Jānaśruta] said; *raikva,* O Raikva; *idam sahasram gavām,* these thousand cows; *ayam niṣkaḥ,* this gold necklace; *ayam aśvatarīrathaḥ,* this chariot drawn by mules; *iyam jāyā,* this wife [my daughter]; *ayam grāmaḥ,* this village; *yasmin āsse,* where you live; [I am presenting all these to you]; *bhagavaḥ,* sir; *eva anuśādhi iti,* now please teach me.

4. He said to Raikva: 'I am giving you these thousand cows, this gold necklace, this chariot drawn by mules, this daughter of mine to be your wife, and also this village in which you live. Now, sir, please teach me.'

Jānaśruti offered Raikva many things, but most important, he offered his daughter in marriage and also the village where Raikva was living. The only thing he wanted in return was that Raikva accept him as a disciple.

तस्या ह मुखमुपोद्गृह्णन्नुवाचाजहारेमाः शूद्रानेनैव मुखेनालापयिष्यथा इति ते हैते रैक्वपर्णा नाम महावृषेषु यत्रास्मा उवास तस्मै होवाच ॥ ५ ॥ इति द्वितीयः खण्डः ॥ २ ॥

Tasyā ha mukhamupodgṛhṇannuvācājahāremāḥ śūdrānenaiva mukhenālāpayiṣyathā iti te haite raikvaparṇā nāma mahāvṛṣeṣu yatrāsmā uvāsa tasmai hovāca. Iti dvitīyaḥ khaṇḍaḥ.

Tasyāḥ ha mukham upodgṛhṇan, lifting her face; *uvāca,* [Raikva] said; *śūdra,* O śūdra; *ajahāra,* you have brought; *imāḥ,* all these; *anena eva mukhena,* by this face [or, mouth]; *ālāpayiṣyathā iti,* you will make me speak; *te ha ete raikvaparṇāḥ nāma,* these [villages] known as Raikvaparṇā; *mahāvṛṣeṣu,* in the province of Mahāvṛṣa; *yatra,* where; *uvāsa,* [Raikva] lived; *asmai,* [and where Raikva taught] him [i.e., Jānaśruti]; *tasmai ha uvāca,* he said to him. *Iti dvitīyaḥ khaṇḍaḥ,* here ends the second section.

5. Lifting the face of the princess, Raikva said: 'You have brought me many things [but they are not making me speak]. It is this face that is making me speak.' The villages in the Mahāvṛṣa province, where Raikva

lived, were known thenceforth as Raikvaparṇā. It was here Raikva taught Jānaśruti. Raikva said to him:

Raikva was a brahmacārin. He had no home, and he lived an austere life. He had, however, attained Self-knowledge. When Jānaśruti approached him for spiritual instructions, he was unwilling. He did not like Jānaśruti's offering him wealth. This is why he called him a śūdra. But when Jānaśruti offered him his daughter in marriage, Raikva was impressed by his keenness. He then agreed to teach him.

Section Three

वायुर्वाव सम्वर्गो यदा वा अग्निरुद्वायति वायुमेवाप्येति यदा सूर्योऽस्तमेति वायुमेवाप्येति यदा चन्द्रोऽस्तमेति वायुमेवाप्येति ॥ १ ॥

Vāyurvāva samvargo yadā vā agnirudvāyati vāyumevāpyeti yadā sūryo'stameti vāyumevāpyeti yadā candro'stameti vāyumevāpyeti.

Vāyuḥ vāva samvargaḥ, the air swallows everything; *yadā vai agniḥ udvāyati,* when fire is extinguished; *vāyum eva apyeti,* it disappears into the air; *yadā sūryaḥ astam eti,* when the sun sets; *vāyum eva apyeti,* it disappears into the air; *yadā candraḥ astam eti,* when the moon sets; *vāyum eva apyeti,* it disappears into the air.

1. The air swallows everything. When fire is extinguished, it disappears into the air. When the sun sets, it disappears into the air. And when the moon sets, it disappears into the air.

Earlier, the question of imparting spiritual instructions has been discussed. Here, how the instruction is given is being shown. The instruction begins with the forces of nature (*adhidaivata*)—by stressing the importance of air. Air can overcome everything, including even the sun, the moon, and fire.

यदाप उच्छुष्यन्ति वायुमेवापियन्ति वायुर्ह्येवैतान्स-
र्वान्संवृङ्क्त इत्यधिदैवतम् ॥ २ ॥

Yadāpa ucchuṣyanti vāyumevāpiyanti vāyurhyevaitān-sarvānsaṁvṛṅkta ityadhidaivatam.

Yadā āpaḥ ucchuṣyanti, when water dries up; *vāyum eva apiyanti,* it goes into the air; *vāyuḥ hi etān sarvān saṁvṛṅkte,* the air swallows all these; *iti adhidaivatam,* this is the worship of the forces of nature.

2. When water dries up, it disappears into the air. The air swallows all these. This is the worship of the forces of nature (*adhidaivata*).

This is to show that air is supreme. It can even destroy such a powerful thing as fire.

अथाध्यात्मं प्राणो वाव सम्वर्गः स यदा स्वपिति प्राणमेव वागप्येति प्राणं चक्षुः प्राणं श्रोत्रं प्राणं मनः प्राणो ह्येवैतान्सर्वान्संवृङ्क्त इति॥ ३॥

Athādhyātmaṁ prāṇo vāva samvargaḥ sa yadā svapiti prāṇameva vāgapyeti prāṇaṁ cakṣuḥ prāṇaṁ śrotraṁ prāṇaṁ manaḥ prāṇo hyevaitānsarvānsaṁvṛṅkta iti.

Atha adhyātmam, now, that relating to the body; *prāṇaḥ vāva samvargaḥ,* prāṇa [the vital force] swallows everything; *saḥ yadā svapiti,* when a person is sleeping; *prāṇam eva vāk apyeti,* speech disappears into prāṇa; *prāṇam cakṣuḥ,* the eyes [disappear] into prāṇa; *prāṇam śrotram,* the ears [disappear] into prāṇa; *prāṇam manaḥ,* the mind [disappears] into prāṇa; *prāṇaḥ hi eva etān sarvān saṁvṛṇkte iti,* prāṇa swallows all these.

3. Next is the worship concerning the body. Prāṇa swallows everything. When a person sleeps, speech, the eyes, the ears, and the mind—all these go into prana. Prāṇa swallows all these.

When a person falls asleep, the sense organs stop working. They retire into prāṇa, as if they have been swallowed by it.

तौ वा एतौ द्वौ सम्वर्गौ वायुरेव देवेषु प्राणः प्राणेषु॥ ४॥

Tau vā etau dvau saṁvargau vāyureva deveṣu prāṇaḥ prāṇeṣu.

Tau vai etau dvau, these are those two; *saṁvargau,* all-swallowing; *vāyuḥ eva deveṣu,* the air among the gods; *prāṇaḥ prāṇeṣu,* prāṇa [the vital breath] among the organs.

4. These two swallow everything: air among the gods and prāṇa among the organs.

Briefly, vāyu, air, is the source of fire, the sun, the moon, and water. Therefore one should worship vāyu as outside, in nature (*adhidaivata*). Likewise, prāṇa, the vital breath, is the source of speech, the eyes, the ears, and the mind, and therefore one should worship this prāṇa as within oneself (*adhyātma*).

अथ ह शौनकं च कापेयमभिप्रतारिणं च काक्षसेनिं परिविष्यमाणौ ब्रह्मचारी बिभिक्षे तस्मा उ ह न ददतुः ॥ ५ ॥

Atha ha śaunakaṁ ca kāpeyamabhipratāriṇaṁ ca kākṣaseniṁ pariviṣyamāṇau brahmacārī bibhikṣe tasmā u ha na dadatuḥ.

Atha ha, once; *śaunakam kāpeyam ca abhipratāriṇam kākṣasenim ca pariviṣyamāṇau,* food was being served to Śaunaka, the son of Kapi, and Abhipratārin, the son of Kaksasena; *brahmacārī bibhikṣe,* a brahmacārin begged for some food; *tasmai u ha na dadatuḥ,* they, however, did not give him any.

5. Once Śaunaka, the son of Kapi, and Abhipratārin, the son of Kakṣasena, were being served their meals when a brahmacārin appeared and begged for some food. They, however, refused to give him any.

Śaunaka and Abhipratārin were having their meals, and the cook was serving. Just then a brahmacārin came to them for some food. He was one who had attained the knowledge of Brahman. Śaunaka and Abhipratārin, however, wanted to see if the brahmacārin's knowledge was genuine, so they did not give him anything.

स होवाच महात्मनश्चतुरो देव एकः कः स जगार भुवनस्य गोपास्तं कापेय नाभिपश्यन्ति मर्त्या अभिप्रतारिन्बहुधा वसन्तं यस्मै वा एतदन्नं तस्मा एतन्न दत्तमिति ॥ ६ ॥

Sa hovāca mahātmanaścaturo deva ekaḥ kaḥ sa jagāra bhuvanasya gopāstaṁ kāpeya nābhipaśyanti martyā abhipratārinbahudhā vasantaṁ yasmai vā etadannaṁ tasmā etanna dattamiti.

Saḥ ha uvāca, he [the brahmacārin] said; *ekaḥ devaḥ,* one god; *mahātmanaḥ caturaḥ,* four sages; *jagāra,* swallowed; *kaḥ saḥ,* who is that [god]; *bhuvanasya gopāḥ,* the guardian of the world; *kāpeya abhipratārin,* O Kāpeya, O Abhipratārin; *martyāḥ tam na abhipaśyanti,* human beings cannot see him; *bahudhā vasantam,* existing in many forms; *yasmai,* for whom; *vai etat annam,* this food; *tasmai,* to him; *etat na dattam iti,* did not give it.

6. The brahmacārin said: 'One god has swallowed four sages. Who is he who protects this world? O Kāpeya, O Abhipratārin, that god exists in many forms, but human beings cannot see him. The food is meant for him, but you are not giving it to him.'

Fire, the sun, the moon, and water—these are said to be four sages. Air controls all these, and air is called the god Prajāpati. Similarly, prāṇa is also the god Prajāpati, and the sages are speech, the eyes, the ears, and the mind.

Prajāpati is the protector of all, and he resides in diverse forms—sometimes within the human body (*ādhyātmika*), sometimes in the forces of nature (*ādhidaivika*), and sometimes within other living beings (*ādhibautika*). People are ignorant about him and do not recognize him. They prepare food for him but do not know it, and they refuse to give it to him.

तदु ह शौनकः कापेयः प्रतिमन्वानः प्रत्येयायात्मा देवानां जनिता प्रजानां हिरण्यदंष्ट्रो बभसोऽनसूरिर्महान्तमस्य महिमानमाहुरनद्यमानो यदनन्नमत्तीति वै वयं ब्रह्मचारिन्नेदमुपास्महे दत्तास्मै भिक्षामिति॥ ७॥

Tadu ha śaunakaḥ kāpeyaḥ pratimanvānaḥ pratyeyā-yātmā devānāṁ janitā prajānāṁ hiraṇyadaṁṣṭro babha-so'nasūrirmahāntamasya mahimānamāhuranadyamāno yadanannamattīti vai vayaṁ brahmacārinnedamupās-mahe dattāsmai bhikṣāmiti.

Tat u ha, that [statement]; *śaunaka kāpeyaḥ prati-manvānaḥ,* thought over; *pratyeyāya,* [and then] went to him; *ātmā devānām,* the self of all the gods and goddesses; *janitā,* the creator; *prajānām,* of all things [moving or unmoving]; *hiraṇyadaṁstraḥ,* with teeth made of gold; *babhasaḥ,* the eater; *anasūriḥ,* intelligent; *mahāntam,* great; *asya,* its; *mahimānam,* greatness; *āhuḥ,* is so described; *anadyamānaḥ,* uneatable; *yat,* that; *anannam,* no food; *atti,* eats; *brahmacārin,* O brahmacārin; *vayam,* we; *idam vai ā-upāsmahe iti,* worship this one; *datta asmai bhikṣām iti,* give alms to him.

7. After thinking this over, Śaunaka Kāpeya went to the brahmacārin and said, 'He who is the self of all the gods and goddesses, the creator of all things moveable and immoveable, who eats with his golden [i.e., firm] teeth, who is intelligent, whom others cannot eat, who eats things which are not food, whose greatness wise people think highly of—O brahmacārin, we worship him.' After this he said, 'Give this man alms.'

Śaunaka told the brahmacāriṇ: 'It is not correct that we do not know him. We do know him. He is Prajāpati. He creates and also destroys everything.

He is the self of all, and he is also the destroyer of all. He is supreme. All wise people worship him as such.' Śaunaka then told his servant to give the brahmacārin some food.

तस्मा उ ह ददुस्ते वा एते पञ्चान्ये पञ्चान्ये दश सन्तस्तत्कृतं तस्मात्सर्वासु दिक्ष्वन्नमेव दश कृतं सैषा विराडन्नादी तयेदं सर्वं दृष्टं सर्वमस्येदं दृष्टं भवत्यन्नादो भवति य एवं वेद य एवं वेद॥८॥ इति तृतीयः खण्डः॥३॥

Tasmā u ha daduste vā ete pañcānye pañcānye daśa santastatkṛtaṁ tasmātsarvāsu dikṣvannameva daśa kṛtaṁ saiṣā virāḍannādī tayedaṁ sarvaṁ dṛṣṭaṁ sarvamasyedaṁ dṛṣṭaṁ bhavatyannādo bhavati ya evaṁ veda ya evaṁ veda. Iti tṛtīyaḥ khaṇḍaḥ.

Tasmai, to him [the brahmacārin]; *u ha daduḥ,* they gave [alms]; *te vai ete,* all these; *pañca anye,* five other [i.e., air, plus the four others (fire, the sun, the moon, and water) constituting its food]; *pañca anye,* five other [i.e., prāṇa, plus the four others (speech, the eyes, the ears, and the mind) constituting its food]; *daśa santaḥ,* make ten; *tat kṛtam,* that is kṛta [the turn of the dice that swallows all others]; *tasmāt,* therefore; *sarvāsu dikṣu daśa,* these which are in the ten directions; *annam eva,* are the food; *kṛtam,* [and also] kṛta; *sā eṣā virāṭ,* that is

Virāṭ; *annādi,* that which swallows; *tayā,* by that [Virāṭ]; *sarvam idam dṛṣṭam,* all this is seen; *yaḥ evam veda,* he who knows thus; *asya sarvam idam dṛṣṭam bhavati,* all this to him becomes seen; *annādaḥ bhavati,* [and] he becomes an eater of food. *Iti tṛtīyaḥ khaṇḍaḥ,* here ends the third section.

8. Then they gave him alms. The first five [Vāyu, etc.] and the second five [prāṇa, etc.] together make ten. That is kṛta [the throw of dice of the highest denomination]. These ten are the ten directions, and they are the food. This kṛta is Virāṭ. As Virāṭ is all-pervasive, everything is its food. By that Virāṭ all this is seen. He who knows this Virāṭ becomes Virāṭ himself. He becomes all-pervasive and everything becomes his food.

Prāṇa (the vital force), speech, the eyes, the ears, and the mind—these five represent our physical (adhyātmika) self. Air, fire, the sun, the moon, and water—these five represent nature (adhidaivika), which surrounds us. These ten together are compared to the dice throw called *kṛta.* Being the highest number, kṛta 'swallows' the other throws of dice, adds their numbers to itself, and then becomes ten. (Kṛta is 4, so the other numbers are 3, 2, and 1; therefore 4+3+2+1=10.)

Then it is said that the adhyātmika and adhidaivika elements together are the ten quarters. They represent the whole world, so they are Virāṭ. This Virāṭ is both the eater and the food. The person who knows this then becomes Virāṭ.

Section Four

सत्यकामो ह जाबालो जबालां मातरमामन्त्रयाञ्चक्रे
ब्रह्मचर्यं भवति विवत्स्यामि किंगोत्रो न्वहमस्मीति ॥ १ ॥

Satyakāmo ha jābālo jabālāṁ mātaramāmantrayāñ-cakre brahmacaryaṁ bhavati vivatsyāmi kiṁgotro nvahamasmīti.

Satyakāmaḥ jābālaḥ ha, once Satyakāma Jābāla; *jabālām mātaram āmantrayāñcakre,* said to his mother Jabālā; *brahmacaryam bhavati vivatsyāmi,* O revered mother, I want to live as a brahmacārin [with a teacher]; *kim gotraḥ nu aham asmi iti,* what is my lineage?

1. Once Satyakāma Jābāla said to his mother Jabālā: 'Revered mother, I would like to live with a teacher as a celibate student. What is my lineage?'

To attain Self-realization, one has to practise austerities, study the scriptures, and live a life of self-discipline. The story of Satyakāma illustrates this.

सा हैनमुवाच नाहमेतद्वेद तात यद्गोत्रस्त्वमसि बह्वहं
चरन्ती परिचारिणी यौवने त्वामलभे साहमेतन्न वेद

यद्गोत्रस्त्वमसि जबाला तु नामाहमस्मि सत्यकामो नाम त्वमसि स सत्यकाम एव जाबालो ब्रुवीथा इति॥ २॥

Sā hainamuvāca nāhametadveda tāta yadgotrastvamasi bahvahaṁ carantī paricāriṇī yauvane tvāmalabhe sāhametanna veda yadgotrastvamasi jabālā tu nāmāhamasmi satyakāmo nāma tvamasi sa satyakāma eva jābālo bruvīthā iti.

Sā, she [Jabālā]; *ha enam uvāca,* said to him; *na aham etat veda,* I don't know this; *tāta,* my son; *yat gotraḥ tvam asi,* what your lineage is; *bahu aham carantī paricāriṇī,* I was busy serving many people; *yauvane tvām alabhe,* I had you when I was young; *sā etat,* for this reason; *aham yat gotraḥ tvam asi na veda,* I know nothing about what your lineage is; *jabālā tu nāma aham asmi,* but my name is Jabālā; *satyakāmaḥ nāma tvam asi,* your name is Satyakāma; *saḥ satyakāmaḥ eva jābālaḥ bruvīthāḥ iti,* [when asked about your lineage] say this that you are Satyakāma Jābāla.

2. Jabālā said to him: 'My son, I don't know what your lineage is. I was very busy serving many people when I was young, and I had you. As this was the situation, I know nothing about your lineage. My name is Jabālā, and your name is Satyakāma. When asked about your lineage, say, "I am Satyakāma Jābāla."'

स ह हारिद्रुमतं गौतममेत्योवाच ब्रह्मचर्यं भगवति वत्स्याम्युपेयां भगवन्तमिति ॥ ३ ॥

Sa ha hāridrumataṁ gautamametyovāca brahmacaryaṁ bhagavati vatsyāmyupeyāṁ bhagavantamiti.

Saḥ ha hāridrumatam gautamam etya, he went to Gautama, the son of Haridrumata; *uvāca,* [and] said; *brahmacaryam bhagavati vatsyāmi,* revered sir, I wish to live [with you] as a celibate student; *upeyām bhagavantam iti,* I have come to you, revered sir, [as a disciple].

3. Satyakāma went to Gautama, the son of Haridrumata, and said: 'Revered sir, I wish to live with you as a celibate. I have come, revered sir, to be your disciple.'

तं होवाच किंगोत्रो नु सोम्यासीति स होवाच नाहमेतद्वेद भो यद्गोत्रोऽहमस्म्यपृच्छं मातरं सा मा प्रत्यब्रवीद्बह्वहं चरन्ती परिचारिणी यौवने त्वामलभे साहमेतन्न वेद यद्गोत्रस्त्वमसि जबाला तु नामाहमस्मि सत्यकामो नाम त्वमसीति सोऽहं सत्यकामो जाबालोऽस्मि भो इति ॥ ४ ॥

Taṁ hovāca kiṁgotro nu somyāsīti sa hovāca nāhametadveda bho yadgotro'hamasmyapṛcchaṁ māta-

raṁ sā mā pratyabravīdbahvahaṁ carantī paricāriṇī yauvane tvāmalabhe sāhametanna veda yadgotrastvamasi jabālā tu nāmāhamasmi satyakāmo nāma tvamasīti so'haṁ satyakāmo jābālo'smi bho iti.

Tam ha uvāca, he [Gautama] said to him; *kim gotraḥ nu somya asi iti,* O Somya, what is your lineage; *saḥ ha uvāca,* he [Satyakāma] said; *na aham etat veda bhoḥ,* I do not know this, sir; *yat gotraḥ aham asmi,* of what lineage I am; *apṛccham mātaram,* I asked my mother; *sā mā pratyabravīt,* she said to me; *bahu aham carantī paricāriṇī,* I was busy serving many people; *yauvane tvām alabhe,* I had you when I was young; *sā etat,* for this reason; *aham yat gotraḥ tvam asi na veda,* I know nothing about what your lineage is; *jabālā tu nāma aham asmi,* but my name is Jabālā; *satyakāmaḥ nāma tvam asi,* your name is Satyakāma; *saḥ aham satyakāmaḥ jābālaḥ asmi bhoḥ iti,* so I am Satyakāma Jābāla, sir.

4. Gautama asked him, 'O Somya, what is your lineage?' Satyakāma said: 'Sir, I do not know what my lineage is. When I asked my mother, she said to me: "I was very busy serving many people when I was young, and I had you. As this was the situation, I know nothing about your lineage. My name is Jabālā, and your name is Satyakāma." So, sir, I am Satyakāma Jābāla.'

Jabālā told Satyakāma the truth and, should anyone ask him, she told him to tell the truth also—irrespective of the consequences. Satyakāma did just as his mother said. He never tried to hide the truth.

तं होवाच नैतदब्राह्मणो विवक्तुमर्हति समिधं सोम्याहरोप त्वा नेष्ये न सत्यादगा इति तमुपनीय कृशानामबलानां चतुःशता गा निराकृत्योवाचेमाः सोम्यानुसंव्रजेति ता अभिप्रस्थापयन्नुवाच नासहस्रेणावर्तेयेति स ह वर्षगणं प्रोवास ता यदा सहस्रं सम्पेदुः ॥ ५ ॥ इति चतुर्थः खण्डः ॥ ४ ॥

Taṁ hovāca naitadabrāhmaṇo vivaktumarhati samidhaṁ somyāharopa tvā neṣye na satyādagā iti tamupanīya kṛśānāmabalānāṁ catuḥśatā gā nirākṛtyovācemāḥ somyānusaṁvrajeti tā abhiprasthāpayannuvāca nāsahasreṇāvarteyeti sa ha varṣagaṇaṁ provāsa tā yadā sahasraṁ sampeduḥ. Iti caturthaḥ khaṇḍaḥ.

Tam ha uvāca, he [Gautama] said to him; *na etat abrāhmaṇaḥ vivaktum arhati,* no non-brāhmin could speak like this; *samidham āhara,* get some fuel; *somya,* O Somya; *tvā upaneṣye,* I shall initiate you; *na satyāt agāḥ iti,* you have not deviated from truth; *tam upanīya,* having initiated him; *kṛśānām abalānām catuḥśatāḥ gāḥ,* four hundred thin and famished cows; *nirākṛtya uvāca,* having chosen, he said; *somya,* O Somya; *anusaṁvraja iti,* take these away; *tāḥ abhiprasthāpayan,* as he was leaving with them; *uvāca,* he [Satyakāma] said; *na āvarteya asahasreṇa,* I will not come back until they are a thousand in number; *saḥ ha varṣagaṇam provāsa,* he lived away for a long time; *tāḥ yadā sahasram sampeduḥ,* until they were a thousand. *Iti caturthaḥ khaṇḍaḥ,* here ends the fourth section.

5. Gautama said to him: 'No non-brāhmin could speak like this. [Therefore, you must be a brāhmin.] O Somya, go and get me some fuel [for the sacrificial fire]. I will initiate you [as a brāhmin by presenting you with the sacred thread], as you have not deviated from truth.' After the initiation, he selected four hundred feeble and famished cows. Addressing Satyakāma, Gautama said, 'O Somya, take these cows away [and look after them].' As Satyakāma was taking them away, he said, 'I will not come back until there are a thousand of them.' He lived away for many years until they had become a thousand.

The point is, no matter what Satyakāma's birth was, he had the qualities of a brāhmin—love of truth and learning. Though he had to suffer much hardship living in the forest looking after the cows, he was more concerned with keeping his word than with seeking physical comforts.

Section Five

अथ हैनमृषभोऽभ्युवाद सत्यकाम३ इति भगव इति ह प्रतिशुश्राव प्राप्ताः सोम्य सहस्रं स्मः प्रापय न आचार्यकुलम् ॥ १ ॥

Atha hainamṛṣabho'bhyuvāda satyakāma3 iti bhagava iti ha pratiśuśrāva prāptāḥ somya sahasraṁ smaḥ prāpaya na ācāryakulam.

Atha, then; *ha enam ṛṣabhaḥ abhyuvāda iti,* a bull called to him [Satyakāma] saying; *satyakāma,* O Satyakāma; *bhagavaḥ iti ha pratiśuśrāva,* he replied, 'Yes, lord'; *prāptāḥ somya sahasram smaḥ,* we are now a thousand; *prāpaya naḥ ācāryakulam,* lead us to the teacher's house.

1. Then a bull called to Satyakāma, saying, 'O Satyakāma!' He replied, 'Yes, lord.' [The bull then said:] 'We are now a thousand. Take us to the teacher's house.'

Vāyu (air) is the presiding deity of the quarters (the directions). Being pleased with Satyakāma for the way he fulfilled his promise to his teacher, Vāyu entered the body of a bull and spoke to Satyakāma in a very heavy voice. Satyakāma recognized the deity, and so he addressed him as 'lord.'

ब्रह्मणश्च ते पादं ब्रवाणीति ब्रवीतु मे भगवानिति तस्मै होवाच प्राची दिक्कला प्रतीची दिक्कला दक्षिणा दिक्कलोदीची दिक्कलैष वै सोम्य चतुष्कलः पादो ब्रह्मणः प्रकाशवान्नाम ॥ २ ॥

Brahmaṇaśca te pādaṁ bravāṇīti bravītu me bhagavāniti tasmai hovāca prācī dikkalā pratīcī dikkalā dakṣiṇā dikkalodīcī dikkalaiṣa vai somya catuṣkalaḥ pādo brahmaṇaḥ prakāśavānnāma.

Brahmaṇaḥ ca te pādam bravāṇi iti, [the bull said,] let me also tell you about a foot [a quarter] of Brahman; *bravītu me bhagavān iti,* yes, lord, please tell me; *tasmai ha uvāca,* [the bull] said to him; *prācī dik kalā,* the east is one part [i.e., one sixteenth—a quarter of a quarter]; *pratīcī dik kalā,* the west is one part; *dakṣiṇā dik kalā,* the south is one part; *udīcī dik kalā,* the north is one part; *eṣaḥ vai somya catuṣkalaḥ pādaḥ brahmaṇaḥ,* O Somya, this is one foot of Brahman having four parts; *prakāśavān nāma,* it is called Prakāśavān [the shining].

2. The bull said, 'Let me also tell you about one foot of Brahman.' Satyakāma replied, 'Yes, lord, please tell me.' Then the bull said to him: 'The east is one part of Brahman, the west is another, the south is another, and the north is yet another. O Somya, this is one foot of Brahman, consisting of four parts. This foot is called Prakāśavān, the shining.'

स य एतमेवं विद्वांश्चतुष्कलं पादं ब्रह्मणः प्रकाशवानित्युपास्ते प्रकाशवानस्मिँल्लोके भवति प्रकाशवतो ह लोकाञ्जयति य एतमेवं विद्वांश्चतुष्कलं पादं ब्रह्मणः प्रकाशवानित्युपास्ते ॥ ३ ॥ इति पञ्चमः खण्डः ॥ ५ ॥

Sa ya etamevaṁ vidvāṁścatuṣkalaṁ pādaṁ brahma-

ṇaḥ prakāśavānityupāste prakāśavānasmiṁlloke bhavati prakāśavato ha lokāñjayati ya etamevaṁ vidvāṁścatuṣkalaṁ pādaṁ brahmaṇaḥ prakāśavānityupāste. Iti pañcamaḥ khaṇḍaḥ.

Saḥ yaḥ etam evam vidvān, he who knows this thus; *catuṣkalam pādam brahmaṇaḥ,* one foot [or quarter] of Brahman having four parts; *prakāśavān iti,* known as the shining; *upāste,* [and] meditates on it; *prakāśavān asmin loke bhavati,* becomes famous in this world; *yaḥ etam evam vidvān,* he who knows this thus; *catuṣkalam pādam brahmaṇaḥ,* one foot of Brahman having four parts; *prakāśavān iti,* known as the shining; *upāste,* [and] meditates on it; *prakāśavataḥ ha lokān jayati,* wins luminous worlds after death. *Iti pañcamaḥ khaṇḍaḥ,* here ends the fifth section.

3. 'He who knows this foot of Brahman, which has four parts and is called "the Shining," and worships it as such becomes famous in this world. He who knows this foot of Brahman, which has four parts and is called "the Shining," and worships it as such attains other worlds which are luminous.'

If you worship Brahman as luminous, you yourself become luminous—that is, you become famous. But not only that, after your death you go to those luminous worlds where gods and goddesses live.

Section Six

अग्निष्टे पादं वक्तेति स ह श्वोभूते गा अभिप्रस्था-
पयाञ्चकार ता यत्राभि सायं बभूवुस्तत्राग्निमुपसमाधाय
गा उपरुध्य समिधमाधाय पश्चादग्नेः प्राङुपोपविवेश ॥ १ ॥

Agniṣṭe pādaṁ vakteti sa ha śvobhūte gā abhiprasthāpayāñcakāra tā yatrābhi sāyaṁ babhūvustatrāgnimupasamādhāya gā uparudhya samidhamādhāya paścādagneḥ prāṅupopaviveśa.

Agniḥ te pādam vaktā iti, Agni [fire] will tell you about [another] foot; *saḥ ha śvaḥ-bhūte gāḥ abhiprasthāpayāñcakāra,* the next day he led the cows [towards his teacher's house]; *yatra sāyam,* when it was dusk; *tāḥ abhi-babhūvuḥ,* they arrived at a place; *tatra agnim upasamādhāya,* having made a fire there; *gāḥ uparudhya,* keeping the cows confined; *samidham ādhāya,* having collected fuel; *paścāt agneḥ,* behind the fire; *prāk upa-upaviveśa,* sat facing the east.

1. [Then the bull said,] 'Agni [fire] will tell you about another foot of Brahman.' The next day Satyakāma collected the cows and drove them towards his teacher's house. At dusk they arrived at a place [where they halted for the night]. Having confined the cows and collected some fuel, he lit a fire and sat down just behind it facing east.

The next day Satyakāma finished his morning rites and then started for the teacher's house with the cows. They halted for the night at a suitable spot, and after gathering the cows together, Satyakāma lit a fire and sat by it facing east. The bull had told him that Agni (fire) would teach him about another foot of Brahman. He began to wonder what Agni would say and when he would say it. He could not think of anything else.

तमग्निरभ्युवाद सत्यकाम३ इति भगव इति ह प्रतिशुश्राव ॥ २ ॥

Tamagnirabhyuvāda satyakāma3 iti bhagava iti ha pratiśuśrāva.

Agniḥ, fire; *tam abhyuvāda,* called to him; *satyakāma iti,* O Satyakāma; *bhagavaḥ iti ha pratiśuśrāva,* he replied, 'Yes, lord.'

2. Fire called to him, 'O Satyakāma.' He replied, 'Yes, lord.'

ब्रह्मणः सोम्य ते पादं ब्रवाणीति ब्रवीतु मे भगवानिति तस्मै होवाच पृथिवी कलान्तरिक्षं कला द्यौः कला समुद्रः कलैष वै सोम्य चतुष्कलः पादो ब्रह्मणोऽनन्त-वान्नाम ॥ ३ ॥

Brahmaṇaḥ somya te pādaṁ bravāṇīti bravītu me bhagavāniti tasmai hovāca pṛthivī kalāntarikṣaṁ kalā dyauḥ kalā samudraḥ kalaiṣa vai somya catuṣkalaḥ pādo brahmaṇo'nantavānnāma.

Somya, O Somya; *brahmaṇaḥ te pādam bravāṇi iti,* I will now tell you about a foot of Brahman; *bravītu me bhagavān iti,* yes, lord, please tell me; *tasmai ha uvāca,* [fire] said to him; *pṛthivī kalā,* the earth is one part; *antarikṣam kalā,* the space between heaven and earth is one part; *dyauḥ kalā,* heaven is one part; *samudraḥ kalā,* the ocean is one part; *eṣaḥ vai somya catuṣkalaḥ pādaḥ brahmaṇaḥ,* O Somya, these are the four parts that make up one foot of Brahman; *anantavān nāma,* named Anantavān, the Unlimited.

3. [Fire said,] 'O Somya, let me tell you about one foot of Brahman.' [Satyakāma replied,] 'Yes, lord, please tell me.' [Fire] said to him: 'The earth is one part, the mid-region is another part, heaven is a third part, and the ocean is a fourth part. O Somya, these are the four parts that make up a foot of Brahman. This foot is named Anantavān, the Unlimited.'

स य एतमेवं विद्वांश्चतुष्कलं पादं ब्रह्मणोऽनन्त-
वानित्युपास्तेऽनन्तवानस्मिँल्लोके भवत्यनन्तवतो ह लोका-

ञ्जयति य एतमेवं विद्वांश्चतुष्कलं पादं ब्रह्मणोऽनन्तवानित्युपास्ते॥४॥ इति षष्ठः खण्डः॥६॥

Sa ya etamevaṁ vidvāṁścatuṣkalaṁ pādaṁ brahmaṇo'nantavānityupāste'nantavānasmiṁlloke bhavatyanantavato ha lokāñjayati ya etamevaṁ vidvāṁścatuṣkalaṁ pādaṁ brahmaṇo'nantavānityupāste. Iti ṣaṣṭhaḥ khaṇḍaḥ.

Saḥ yaḥ etam evam vidvān, he who knows this thus; *catuṣkalam pādam brahmaṇaḥ,* one foot of Brahman having four parts; *anantavān iti,* known as the Unlimited; *upāste,* [and] meditates on it; *anantavān asmin loke bhavati,* becomes long-lived in this world; *yaḥ etam evam vidvān,* he who knows this thus; *catuṣkalam pādam brahmaṇaḥ,* one foot of Brahman having four parts; *anantavān iti,* known as the Unlimited; *upāste,* [and] meditates on it; *anantavataḥ ha lokān jayati,* wins long-lasting worlds after death. *Iti ṣaṣṭhaḥ khaṇḍaḥ,* here ends the sixth section.

4. 'He who knows this foot of Brahman, which has four parts and is known as "the Unlimited," and worships it as such becomes long-lived in this world. He who knows this foot of Brahman, which has four parts and is known as "the Unlimited," and worships it as such attains worlds which are long-lasting.'

Section Seven

हंसस्ते पादं वक्तेति स ह श्वोभूते गा अभिप्रस्थापयाञ्चकार ता यत्राभि सायं बभूवुस्तत्राग्निमुपसमाधाय गा उपरुध्य समिधमाधाय पश्चादग्नेः प्राङुपोपविवेश ॥ १ ॥

Haṁsaste pādaṁ vakteti sa ha śvobhūte gā abhiprasthāpayāñcakāra tā yatrābhi sāyaṁ babhūvustatrāgnimupasamādhāya gā uparudhya samidhamādhāya paścādagneḥ prāṅupopaviveśa.

Haṁsaḥ te pādam vaktā iti, the swan will tell you about [another] foot; *saḥ ha śvaḥ-bhūte gāḥ abhiprasthāpayāñcakāra,* the next day he led the cows [towards his teacher's house]; *yatra sāyam,* when it was dusk; *tāḥ abhi-babhūvuḥ,* they arrived at a place; *tatra agnim upasamādhāya,* having made a fire there; *gāḥ uparudhya,* keeping the cows confined; *samidham ādhāya,* having collected fuel; *paścāt agneḥ,* behind the fire; *prāk upa-upaviveśa,* sat facing the east.

1. [Then the fire said,] 'The swan will tell you about another foot of Brahman.' The next day Satyakāma collected the cows and drove them towards his teacher's house. At dusk they arrived at a place [where they halted for the night]. Having confined the cows and collected some fuel, he lit a fire and sat down just behind it facing east.

The word *haṁsa,* swan, means in this context the sun. Like the sun, the swan is white and it also flies very high.

तं हंस उपनिपत्याभ्युवाद सत्यकाम३ इति भगव इति ह प्रतिशुश्राव॥ २॥

Taṁ haṁsa upanipatyābhyuvāda satyakāma 3 iti bhagava iti ha pratiśuśrāva.

Haṁsaḥ upanipatya, the swan flew near; *tam abhyuvāda satyakāma iti,* [and] called to him, 'O Satyakāma'; *bhagavaḥ iti ha pratiśuśrāva,* he replied, 'Yes, lord.'

2. The swan came flying to him and said, 'O Satyakāma.' Satyakāma replied, 'Yes, lord.'

ब्रह्मणः सोम्य ते पादं ब्रवाणीति ब्रवीतु मे भगवानिति तस्मै होवाचाग्निः कला सूर्यः कला चन्द्रः कला विद्युत्कलैष वै सोम्य चतुष्कलः पादो ब्रह्मणो ज्योतिष्मान्नाम॥ ३॥

Brahmaṇaḥ somya te pādaṁ bravāṇīti bravītu me bhagavāniti tasmai hovācāgniḥ kalā sūryaḥ kalā candraḥ kalā vidyutkalaiṣa vai somya catuṣkalaḥ pādo brahmaṇo jyotiṣmānnāma.

Somya, O Somya; *brahmaṇaḥ te pādam bravāṇi iti,* I will now tell you about a foot [quarter] of Brahman; *bravītu me bhagavān iti,* yes, lord, please tell me; *tasmai ha uvāca,* [the swan] said to him; *agniḥ kalā,* fire is one part; *sūryaḥ kalā,* the sun is one part; *candraḥ kalā,* the moon is one part; *vidyut kalā,* lightning is one part; *eṣaḥ vai somya catuṣkalaḥ pādaḥ brahmaṇaḥ,* O Somya, these are the four parts that make up a foot of Brahman; *jyotiṣmān nāma,* named Jyotiṣmān, the Luminous.

3. [The swan said,] 'O Somya, let me tell you about one foot of Brahman.' [Satyakāma replied,] 'Yes, lord, please tell me.' [The swan] said to him: 'Fire is one part, the sun is another part, the moon is a third part, and lightning is a fourth part. O Somya, these are the four parts that make up a foot of Brahman. This foot is named Jyotiṣmān, the Luminous.'

The swan is speaking here of luminous things, such as fire, the sun, etc. Its partiality for luminous things gives rise to the suspicion that it is itself something luminous. It is, in fact, Āditya, the sun.

स य एतमेवं विद्वांश्चतुष्कलं पादं ब्रह्मणो ज्योति-
ष्मानित्युपास्ते ज्योतिष्मानस्मिँल्लोके भवति ज्योतिष्मतो
ह लोकाञ्जयति य एतमेवं विद्वांश्चतुष्कलं पादं ब्रह्मणो
ज्योतिष्मानित्युपास्ते॥ ४॥ इति सप्तमः खण्डः॥ ७॥

Sa ya etamevaṁ vidvāṁścatuṣkalaṁ pādaṁ brahmaṇo jyotiṣmānityupāste jyotiṣmānasmiṁlloke bhavati jyotiṣmato ha lokāñjayati ya etamevaṁ vidvāṁścatuṣkalaṁ pādaṁ brahmaṇo jyotiṣmānityupāste. Iti saptamaḥ khaṇḍaḥ.

Saḥ yaḥ etam evam vidvān, he who knows this thus; *catuṣkalam pādaṃ brahmaṇaḥ,* one foot [or quarter] of Brahman having four parts; *jyotiṣmān iti,* known as the Luminous; *upāste,* [and] meditates on it; *jyotiṣmān asmin loke bhavati,* becomes illustrious in this world; *yaḥ etam evam vidvān,* he who knows this thus; *catuṣkalam pādam brahmaṇaḥ,* one foot of Brahman having four parts; *jyotiṣmān iti,* known as the Luminous; *upāste,* [and] meditates on it; *jyotiṣmataḥ ha lokān jayati,* wins luminous worlds after death. *Iti saptamaḥ khaṇḍaḥ,* here ends the seventh section.

4. 'He who knows this foot of Brahman, which has four parts and is known as "the Luminous," and worships it as such becomes illustrious in this world. He who knows this foot of Brahman, which has four parts and is known as "the Luminous," and worships it as such attains worlds which are luminous.

If you know luminous things well, you yourself become luminous—that is to say, famous—in this world. Then after death you win a luminous world.

The idea is that you attain whatever you worship.

Section Eight

मद्गुष्टे पादं वक्तेति स ह श्वोभूते गा अभिप्रस्था-
पयाञ्चकार ता यत्राभि सायं बभूवुस्तत्राग्निमुपसमाधाय
गा उपरुध्य समिधमाधाय पश्चादग्नेः प्राङुपोपविवेश ॥ १ ॥

Madguṣṭe pādaṁ vakteti sa ha śvobhūte gā abhiprasthāpayāñcakāra tā yatrābhi sāyaṁ babhūvustatrāgnimupasamādhāya gā uparudhya samidhamādhāya paścādagneḥ prāṅupopaviveśa.

Madguḥ te pādam vaktā iti, the diver-bird will tell you about [another] foot; *saḥ ha śvaḥ-bhūte gāḥ abhiprasthāpayāñcakāra,* the next day he led the cows [towards his teacher's house]; *yatra sāyam,* when it was dusk; *tāḥ abhi-babhūvuḥ,* they arrived at a place; *tatra agnim upasamādhāya,* having made a fire there; *gāḥ uparudhya,* keeping the cows confined; *samidham ādhāya,* having collected fuel; *paścāt agneḥ,* behind the fire; *prāk upa-upaviveśa,* sat facing the east.

1. [Then the swan said,] 'The madgu will tell you about another foot of Brahman.' The next day Satyakāma collected the cows and drove them towards his teacher's house. At dusk they arrived at a place [where they halted for the night]. Having confined the cows and collected some fuel, he lit a fire and sat down just behind it facing east.

The madgu, or diver-bird, is most of the time in water. Because of its close connection with water, and because water sustains life, the diver-bird stands for life (prāṇa).

तं मद्गुरुपनिपत्याभ्युवाद सत्यकाम३ इति भगव इति ह प्रतिशुश्राव ॥ २ ॥

Taṁ madgurupanipatyābhyuvāda satyakāma 3 iti bhagava iti ha pratiśuśrāva.

Madguḥ upanipatya, the diver-bird flew down; *tam abhyuvāda satyakāma iti,* [and] called to him, 'O Satyakāma'; *bhagavaḥ iti ha pratiśuśrāva,* he replied, 'Yes, lord.'

2. The madgu came flying to him and said, 'O Satyakāma.' Satyakāma replied, 'Yes, lord.'

ब्रह्मणः सोम्य ते पादं ब्रवाणीति ब्रवीतु मे भगवानिति तस्मै होवाच प्राणः कला चक्षुः कला श्रोत्रं कला मनः कलैष वै सोम्य चतुष्कलः पादो ब्रह्मण आयतनवान्नाम ॥ ३ ॥

Brahmaṇaḥ somya te pādaṁ bravāṇīti bravītu me bhagavāniti tasmai hovāca prāṇaḥ kalā cakṣuḥ kalā śrotraṁ kalā manaḥ kalaiṣa vai somya catuṣkalaḥ pādo brahmaṇa āyatanavānnāma.

Somya, O Somya; *brahmaṇaḥ te pādam bravāṇi iti,* I will now tell you about a foot [or quarter] of Brahman; *bravītu me bhagavān iti,* yes, lord, please tell me; *tasmai ha uvāca,* [the madgu] said to him; *prāṇaḥ kalā,* prāṇaḥ [the vital force] is one part; *cakṣuḥ kalā,* the eyes are one part; *śrotram kalā,* the ears are one part; *manaḥ kalā,* the mind is one part; *eṣaḥ vai somya catuṣkalaḥ pādaḥ brahmaṇaḥ,* O Somya, these are the four parts that make up a foot of Brahman; *āyatanavān nāma,* named Āyatanavān, the Support.

3. [The madgu said,] 'O Somya, let me tell you about one foot of Brahman.' [Satyakāma replied,] 'Yes, lord, please tell me.' [The madgu] said to him: 'Prāṇa is one part, the eyes are another part, the ears are a third part, and the mind is a fourth part. O Somya, these are the four parts that make up a foot of Brahman. This foot is named Āyatanavān, the Support.'

This part of the story, about the madgu, is devoted to the teaching of prāṇa. In fact, the madgu represents prāṇa.

Here the role of the mind has to be understood. The mind is the fourth part of this foot of Brahman, and it is the repository of all that we experience through our diverse organs. This is why it is called *Āyatanavān,* the Support.

स य एतमेवं विद्वांश्चतुष्कलं पादं ब्रह्मण आयतनवानित्युपास्त आयतनवानस्मिँल्लोके भवत्यायतनवतो ह लोकाञ्जयति य एतमेवं विद्वांश्चतुष्कलं पादं ब्रह्मण आयतनवानित्युपास्ते ॥ ४ ॥ इत्यष्टमः खण्डः ॥ ८ ॥

Sa ya etamevaṁ vidvāṁścatuṣkalaṁ pādaṁ brahmaṇa āyatanavānityupāsta āyatanavānasmiṁlloke bhavatyāyatanavato ha lokāñjayati ya etamevaṁ vidvāṁścatuṣkalaṁ pādaṁ brahmaṇa āyatanavānityupāste. Ityaṣṭamaḥ khaṇḍaḥ.

Saḥ yaḥ etam evam vidvān, he who knows this thus; *catuṣkalam pādam brahmaṇaḥ,* one foot [or quarter] of Brahman having four parts; *āyatanavān iti,* known as the Support; *upāste,* [and] meditates on it; *āyatanavān asmin loke bhavati,* becomes āyatanavān [i.e., a support to others] in this world; *yaḥ etam evam vidvān,* he who knows this thus; *catuṣkalam pādam brahmaṇaḥ,* one foot of Brahman having four parts; *āyatanavān iti,* known as the Support [i.e., it is spacious and therefore able to support things]; *upāste,* [and] meditates on it; *āyatanavataḥ ha lokān jayati,* wins spacious worlds after death. *Iti aṣṭamaḥ khaṇḍaḥ,* here ends the eighth section.

4. 'He who knows this foot of Brahman, which has four parts and is known as "the Support," and worships it as such becomes a support [to others] in this world. He who knows this foot of Brahman, which

has four parts and is known as "the Support," and worships it as such attains worlds which are spacious.'

If a person worships this foot of Brahman as āyatanavān—that is, as spacious—he himself becomes spacious. Being spacious means that he can give shelter to many. He has this advantage as long as he is alive. Then when he dies he is able to attain many larger worlds.

Section Nine

प्राप हाचार्यकुलं तमाचार्योऽभ्युवाद सत्यकाम३ इति भगव इति ह प्रतिशुश्राव॥ १॥

Prāpa hācāryakulaṁ tamācāryo'bhyuvāda satyakāma 3 iti bhagava iti ha pratiśuśrāva.

Prāpa ha, he reached; *ācāryakulam,* the teacher's house; *tam ācāryaḥ abhyuvāda,* the teacher greeted him; *satyakāma iti,* O Satyakāma; *bhagavaḥ iti ha pratiśuśrāva,* [Satyakāma] replied, 'Yes, lord.'

1. [In due course, Satyakāma] reached his teacher's house. The teacher greeted him, saying, 'O Satyakāma.' He replied, 'Yes, lord.'

Satyakāma tended his teacher's cattle, but while doing so he lived an austere life and a life of deep meditation.

As a result of that, plus the instructions he received on his way back to his teacher's house, he had attained the knowledge of Brahman.

ब्रह्मविदिव वै सोम्य भासि को नु त्वानुशशासेत्यन्ये मनुष्येभ्य इति ह प्रतिजज्ञे भगवांस्त्वेव मे कामे ब्रूयात् ॥ २ ॥

Brahmavidiva vai somya bhāsi ko nu tvānuśaśāset-yanye manuṣyebhya iti ha pratijajñe bhagavāṁstveva me kāme brūyāt.

Brahmavit iva vai somya bhāsi, [the teacher, Gautama, said to Satyakāma,] Somya, you are shining like one who has known Brahman; *kaḥ nu tvā anuśaśāsa iti,* who taught you; *anye manuṣyebhyaḥ,* somebody other than a human being; *iti ha pratijajñe,* he assured him; *bhagavān tu eva me kāme bruyāt,* but, Lord, teach me now about Brahman, the subject closest to my heart.

2. The teacher said: 'Somya, you shine like one who has known Brahman. Who taught you?' Satyakāma assured him: 'Certainly no human being. But will you, O Lord, please teach me now about Brahman, the subject closest to my heart?'

The look on Satyakāma's face surprised his teacher. He looked like a knower of Brahman. He was shining.

What are the signs of a person who has known Brahman? According to Śaṅkara, that person is happy and cheerful, with a smile on his face all the time. His mind is always under control, as are his sense organs. He is also free from desires and therefore from worries.

Satyakāma had these signs. This is why his teacher asked him who had taught him. Satyakāma emphatically said that no human being had taught him. He meant thereby that so long as his teacher was there he needed no other human being to teach him. He also assured his teacher that he had now come to him to learn about Brahman, the subject dearest to him.

श्रुतं ह्येव मे भगवद्दृशेभ्य आचार्याद्धैव विद्या विदिता साधिष्ठं प्रापतीति तस्मै हैतदेवोवाचात्र ह न किञ्चन वीयायेति वीयायेति ॥ ३ ॥ इति नवमः खण्डः ॥ ९ ॥

Śrutaṁ hyeva me bhagavaddṛśebhya ācāryāddhaiva vidyā viditā sādhiṣṭhaṁ prāpatīti tasmai haitadevovācātra ha na kiñcana vīyāyeti vīyāyeti. Iti navamaḥ khaṇḍaḥ.

Śrutam hi eva me, I have heard; *bhagavat-dṛśebhyaḥ,* from revered ones like you; *ācāryāt ha eva vidyā viditā sādhiṣṭham prāpati iti,* knowledge learned from a competent teacher is the best; *tasmai,* to him

[Satyakāma]; *ha etat eva uvāca,* he taught all this [i.e., what Satyakāma had already learnt from the bull, fire, the swan, and the madgu]; *atra ha na kiñcana vīyāya iti vīyāya iti,* nothing was left out, nothing was left out. *Iti navamaḥ khaṇḍaḥ,* here ends the ninth section.

3. [Satyakāma said,] 'I have heard from revered ones like you that a person learns best when he learns from a competent teacher.' The teacher then taught Satyakāma everything. Nothing was left out.

You learn things best when you learn them from a good teacher. This is why Satyakāma asked Gautama to teach him. Gautama then taught him all sixteen kalās, or parts, about Brahman. That is to say, he taught him everything. Earlier, the bull, fire, the swan, and the madgu had taught him about Brahman. Gautama did not leave that out. He taught him everything.

The word *vīyāya* is repeated twice to emphasize that Gautama did not leave out anything.

Section Ten

उपकोसलो ह वै कामलायनः सत्यकामे जाबाले ब्रह्मचर्यमुवास तस्य ह द्वादश वर्षाण्यग्नीन्परिचचार स ह स्मान्यानन्तेवासिनः समावर्तयंस्तं ह स्मैव न समावर्तयति ॥ १ ॥

Upakosalo ha vai kāmalāyanaḥ satyakāme jābāle brahmacaryamuvāsa tasya ha dvādaśa varṣāṇyagnīnparicacāra sa ha smānyānantevāsinaḥ samāvartayaṁstaṁ ha smaiva na samāvartayati.

Upakosalaḥ kāmalāyanaḥ ha vai satyakāme jābāle brahmacaryam uvāsa, Upakosala Kāmalāyana lived with Satyakāma Jābāla as a celibate student; *tasya ha dvādaśa varṣāṇi agnīn paricacāra,* for twelve years he looked after his [teacher's] sacrificial fires; *saḥ,* he [Satyakāma]; *ha sma anyān antevāsinaḥ samāvartayan,* permitted the other disciples to return home [after the completion of their Vedic studies]; *tam ha eva na samāvartayati sma,* but did not let him [Upakosala] go home.

1. Upakosala Kāmalāyana lived twelve years with Satyakāma Jābāla as a celibate disciple, studying the scriptures and looking after his teacher's sacrificial fires. On the completion of that period, other students were permitted to go home. The only exception was Upakosala. He was detained.

तं जायोवाच तप्तो ब्रह्मचारी कुशलमग्नीन्परिचचारीन्मा त्वाग्नयः परिप्रवोचन्प्रब्रूह्यस्मा इति तस्मै हाप्रोच्यैव प्रवासाञ्चक्रे ॥ २ ॥

Taṁ jāyovāca tapto brahmacārī kuśalamagnīnparicacārīnmā tvāgnayaḥ paripravocanprabrūhyasmā iti tasmai hāprocyaiva pravāsāñcakre.

Tam, to him [Satyakāma]; *jāyā uvāca,* his wife said; *taptaḥ,* much reduced by austerities; *brahmacārī,* the brahmacārin; *kuśalam,* with great efficiency; *agnīn paricacārīt,* has tended the fires; *mā tvā agnayaḥ paripravocan,* may the fires not speak ill of you; *prabrūhi asmai iti,* please teach him; *tasmai ha aprocya eva,* he did not teach him; *pravāsāñcakre,* he left on a journey.

2. Satyakāma's wife said to him: 'The brahmacārin is much reduced by austerities and has looked after the fires with great care. Lest the fires blame you, I suggest you teach him.' But Satyakāma did not teach him. Instead, he left on a journey.

स ह व्याधिनानशितुं दध्रे तमाचार्यजायोवाच ब्रह्मचारिन्नशान किं नु नाश्नासीति स होवाच बहव इमेऽस्मिन्पुरुषे कामा नानात्यया व्याधिभिः प्रतिपूर्णोऽस्मि नाशिष्यामीति ॥ ३ ॥

Sa ha vyādhinānaśitum̐ dadhre tamācāryajāyovāca brahmacārinnaśāna kim̐ nu nāśnāsīti sa hovāca bahava ime'sminpuruṣe kāmā nānātyayā vyādhibhiḥ pratipūrṇo-'smi nāśiṣyāmīti.

Saḥ, he [Upakosala]; *ha vyādhinā,* due to mental affliction; *anaśitum dadhre,* started fasting; *tam ācārya-jāyā uvāca,* the teacher's wife said to him; *brahmacārin aśāna,* brahmacārin, start eating; *kim nu na āśnāsi iti,* why are you not eating; *saḥ ha uvāca,* he [Upakosala] said; *bahavaḥ ime asmin puruṣe kāmāḥ,* there are many desires in this person; *nānātyayāḥ,* they are pulling me in different directions; *vyādhibhiḥ pratipūrṇaḥ asmi,* I am full of ailments; *na aśiṣyāmi iti,* I will not eat anything.

3. Upakosala was upset and started fasting. His teacher's wife said to him: 'Brahmacārin, eat something. Why are you not eating?' Upakosala said: 'There are too many desires in me and they are pulling me in different directions. I am like one suffering from many ailments. I don't want to eat.'

अथ हाग्नयः समूदिरे तप्तो ब्रह्मचारी कुशलं नः पर्यचारीद्धन्तास्मै प्रब्रवामेति तस्मै होचुः प्राणो ब्रह्म कं ब्रह्म खं ब्रह्मेति ॥ ४ ॥

Atha hāgnayaḥ samūdire tapto brahmacārī kuśalaṁ naḥ paryacārīddhantāsmai prabravāmeti tasmai hocuḥ prāṇo brahma kaṁ brahma khaṁ brahmeti.

Atha ha agnayaḥ samūdire, then the fires [the Dakṣiṇāgni, the Gārhapatya, and the Āhavanīya] began to say; *taptaḥ brahmacārī,* the austere brahmacārin; *kuśalam,* with great care; *naḥ paryacārīt,* looked after us; *hanta asmai prabravāma iti,* so we will teach him; *tasmai ha ucuḥ,* they said to him; *prāṇaḥ brahma,* prāṇa is Brahman; *kam brahma,* happiness is Brahman; *kham brahma iti,* ākāśa [space] is Brahman.

4. Then the fires—the Dakṣiṇāgni, the Gārhapatya, and the Āhavanīya—began to say to each other: 'This brahmacārin has become thin from practising austerities. He has so long looked after us with great care. Let us teach him.' They said to Upakosala, 'Prāṇa is Brahman, *ka* [happiness] is Brahman, and *kha* [space] is Brahman.'

The three fires that had been so well taken care of by Upakosala were moved to see his condition. They also felt that a great injustice had been done to him by his teacher, Satyakāma. They then decided to take it upon themselves to teach him.

स होवाच विजानाम्यहं यत्प्राणो ब्रह्म कं च तु खं च न विजानामीति ते होचुर्यद्वाव कं तदेव खं यदेव खं तदेव कमिति प्राणं च हास्मै तदाकाशं चोचुः ॥ ५ ॥ इति दशमः खण्डः ॥ १० ॥

Sa hovāca vijānāmyahaṁ yatprāṇo brahma kaṁ ca tu khaṁ ca na vijānāmīti te hocuryadvāva kaṁ tadeva khaṁ yadeva khaṁ tadeva kamiti prāṇaṁ ca hāsmai tadākāśaṁ cocuḥ. Iti daśamaḥ khaṇḍaḥ.

Saḥ ha uvāca, he [Upakosala] said; *vijānāmi aham yat prāṇa brahma,* I know that prāṇa is Brahman; *kam ca tu kham ca na vijānāmi iti,* but I don't know that 'ka' and 'kha' are Brahman; *te ha ucuḥ,* they [the fires] said; *yat vāva kam tat eva kham,* that which is 'ka' is also 'kha'; *yat eva kham tat eva kam iti,* that which is 'kha' is also 'ka'; *prāṇam ca ha asmai tat ākāśam ca ucuḥ,* then they taught him about prāṇa and ākāśa [space]. *Iti daśamaḥ khaṇḍaḥ,* here ends the tenth section.

5. Upakosala said: 'I know that prāṇa is Brahman. But that *ka* and *kha* are Brahman I do not know.' The fires replied, 'That which is *ka* is also *kha,* and that which is *kha* is also *ka.'* Then the fires taught him that Brahman was both prāṇa and ākāśa [space].

Upakosala had no difficulty accepting that prāṇa was Brahman, for prāṇa is the vital breath and without the vital breath, life is impossible. In view of its importance it may be conceded that prāṇa is Brahman. But how can *ka* and *kha* be Brahman?

Upakosala thought to himself: '*Ka* is happiness, but what kind of happiness? It is happiness born of sense experience. It is therefore transitory. It cannot be the same as Brahman. Similarly, *kha* is also transitory, for it means ākāśa, space. Ākāśa is material and therefore transitory.'

The fires then said that *ka* and *kha* are used as both nouns and adjectives, and sometimes they qualify each other. *Kha* as an adjective may qualify *ka* when *ka* stands for Brahman. What does *ka* mean here? Here it means Brahman without any attributes. Similarly, when we say *kha,* we mean ākāśa. When we say *ka* is *kha,* we mean 'pleasure' is ākāśa. But this is not the material ākāśa. Here it means the ākāśa, space, inside the heart. The idea is that Brahman and joy (*ka*) are both in the space inside the heart (*kha*).

Section Eleven

अथ हैनं गार्हपत्योऽनुशशास पृथिव्यग्निरन्नमादित्य इति य एष आदित्ये पुरुषो दृश्यते सोऽहमस्मि स एवाहमस्मीति ॥ १ ॥

Atha hainaṁ gārhapatyo'nuśaśāsa pṛthivyagniranna-māditya iti ya eṣa āditye puruṣo dṛśyate so'hamasmi sa evāhamasmīti.

Atha ha enam gārhapatyaḥ anuśaśāsa, next the Gārhapatya fire gave him this instruction; *pṛthivī agniḥ annam ādityaḥ iti,* the earth, fire, food, and the sun [are all part of me—i.e., of Brahman]; *yaḥ eṣaḥ āditye puruṣaḥ dṛśyate,* the person seen in the sun; *saḥ aham asmi saḥ eva aham asmi iti,* I am he, I am he.

1. Then the Gārhapatya fire said to him [Upakosala]: 'The earth, fire, food, and the sun—these are all part of my [i.e., part of Brahman's] body. The person seen in the solar orb is me. I am that.'

First the fires taught Upakosala together. Now they are teaching him separately. The Gārhapatya fire begins.

He said: 'The earth, fire, food, and the sun—these constitute my body. I divide myself into these things. There in the solar region is a person. That is me. I am known as the Gārhapatya fire and I am also this person in the solar region. Earth and food are both objects of enjoyment and consumption, but fire and the sun are not in this category. They are similar to each other, however, just as food and the earth are similar to each other, being objects that people can enjoy.'

स य एतमेवं विद्वानुपास्तेऽपहते पापकृत्यां लोकी भवति सर्वमायुरेति ज्योग्जीवति नास्यावरपुरुषाः क्षीयन्त उप वयं तं भुञ्जामोऽस्मिंश्च लोकेऽमुष्मिंश्च य एतमेवं विद्वानुपास्ते ॥ २ ॥ इत्येकादशः खण्डः ॥ ११ ॥

Sa ya etamevaṁ vidvānupāste'pahate pāpakṛtyāṁ lokī bhavati sarvamāyureti jyogjīvati nāsyāvarapuruṣāḥ kṣīyanta upa vayaṁ taṁ bhuñjāmo'smiṁśca loke'muṣmiṁśca ya etamevaṁ vidvānupāste. Ityekādaśaḥ khaṇḍaḥ.

Saḥ yaḥ, he who; *etam evam vidvān,* knowing this in this way; *upāste,* [and] worships; *apahate pāpakṛtyām,* he destroys his sins; *lokī bhavati,* becomes a dweller in the world of the god of fire; *sarvam āyuḥ eti,* lives the full range of his life; *jyok jīvati,* he lives a bright life; *asya āvarapuruṣāḥ,* his descendants; *na kṣīyante,* do not perish [i.e., his line is never broken]; *asmin ca loke amuṣmin ca,* in this world and also in the other world; *vayam tam upabhuñjāmaḥ,* we will look after him; *yaḥ etam evam vidvān upāste,* he who knows this [fire] thus and worships it. *Iti ekādaśaḥ khaṇḍaḥ,* here ends the eleventh section.

2. 'He who knows this Gārhapatya fire and worships it thus has all his sins removed, and he attains the world of the Gārhapatya fire. He lives a long and bright life, and his descendants do not perish. In this world and the next, we look after that person who knows this fire and worships it thus.'

Here the benefit of worshipping the Gārhapatya fire in the right manner is being given. The first benefit is that all the worshipper's sins are burned away. He also attains the world reserved for the worshippers of this fire. When the fire says that the worshipper's descendants do not perish, he means that his line will not be broken.

Section Twelve

अथ हैनमन्वाहार्यपचनोऽनुशशासापो दिशो नक्षत्राणि चन्द्रमा इति य एष चन्द्रमसि पुरुषो दृश्यते सोऽहमस्मि स एवाहमस्मीति॥ १ ॥

Atha hainamanvāhāryapacano'nuśaśāsāpo diśo nakṣatrāṇi candramā iti ya eṣa candramasi puruṣo dṛśyate so'hamasmi sa evāhamasmīti.

Atha ha enam anvāhārya-pacanaḥ anuśaśāsa, next the Anvāhārya Pacana [the Dakṣiṇāgni, or Southern] fire gave him this instruction; *āpaḥ diśaḥ nakṣatrāṇi candramā iti,* water, the quarters, the stars, and the moon [are all part of me—i.e., of Brahman]; *yaḥ eṣaḥ candramasi puruṣaḥ dṛśyate,* the person seen in the moon; *saḥ aham asmi saḥ eva aham asmi iti,* I am he, I am he.

1. Next the Dakṣiṇāgni [Southern] fire said to Upakosala: 'Water, the quarters, the stars, and the moon—these are all part of my [i.e., part of Brahman's] body. The person seen in the moon is me. I am that.'

स य एतमेवं विद्वानुपास्तेऽपहते पापकृत्यां लोकी भवति सर्वमायुरेति ज्योग्जीवति नास्यावरपुरुषाः क्षीयन्त उप वयं तं भुञ्जामोऽस्मिंश्च लोकेऽमुष्मिंश्च य एतमेवं विद्वानुपास्ते ॥ २ ॥ इति द्वादशः खण्डः ॥ १२ ॥

Sa ya etamevaṁ vidvānupāste'pahate pāpakṛtyāṁ lokī bhavati sarvamāyureti jyogjīvati nāsyāvarapuruṣāḥ kṣīyanta upa vayaṁ taṁ bhuñjāmo'smiṁśca loke'muṣmiṁśca ya etamevaṁ vidvānupāste. Iti dvādaśaḥ khaṇḍaḥ.

Saḥ yaḥ, he who; *etam evam vidvān,* knowing this in this way; *upāste,* [and] worships; *apahate pāpakṛtyām,* he destroys his sins; *lokī bhavati,* becomes a dweller in the world of the god of fire; *sarvam āyuḥ eti,* lives the full range of his life; *jyok jīvati,* he lives a bright life; *asya āvarapuruṣāḥ,* his descendants; *na kṣīyante,* do not perish [i.e., his line is never broken]; *asmin ca loke amuṣmin ca,* in this world and also in the other world; *vayam tam upabhuñjāmaḥ,* we will look after him; *yaḥ etam evam vidvān upāste,* he who knows this [fire] thus and worships it. *Iti dvādaśaḥ khaṇḍaḥ,* here ends the twelfth section.

2. 'He who knows this Dakṣiṇāgni fire and worships it thus has all his sins removed, and he attains the world of the Dakṣiṇāgni fire. He lives a long and bright life, and his descendants do not perish. In this world and the next, we look after that person who knows this fire and worships it thus.'

Section Thirteen

अथ हैनमाहवनीयोऽनुशशास प्राण आकाशो द्यौर्विद्युदिति य एष विद्युति पुरुषो दृश्यते सोऽहमस्मि स एवाहमस्मीति ॥ १ ॥

Atha hainamāhavanīyo'nuśaśāsa prāṇa ākāśo dyaur-

vidyuditi ya eṣa vidyuti puruṣo dṛśyate so'hamasmi sa evāhamasmīti.

Atha ha enam āhavanīyaḥ ānuśaśāsa, next the Āhavanīya fire gave him this instruction; *prāṇaḥ ākāśaḥ dyauḥ vidyut iti,* prāṇa, space, heaven, and lightning [are all part of me—i.e., of Brahman]; *yaḥ eṣaḥ vidyuti puruṣaḥ dṛśyate,* the person seen in lightning; *saḥ aham asmi saḥ eva aham asmi iti,* I am he, I am he.

1. Next the Āhavanīya fire said to Upakosala: 'Prāṇa, space, heaven, and lightning—these are all part of my [i.e., part of Brahman's] body. The person seen in lightning is me. I am that.'

स य एतमेवं विद्वानुपास्तेऽपहते पापकृत्यां लोकी भवति सर्वमायुरेति ज्योग्जीवति नास्यावरपुरुषाः क्षीयन्त उप वयं तं भुञ्जामोऽस्मिंश्च लोकेऽमुष्मिंश्च य एतमेवं विद्वानुपास्ते॥ २॥ इति त्रयोदशः खण्डः॥ १३॥

Sa ya etamevaṁ vidvānupāste'pahate pāpakṛtyāṁ lokī bhavati sarvamāyureti jyogjīvati nāsyāvarapuruṣāḥ kṣīyanta upa vayaṁ taṁ bhuñjāmo'smiṁśca loke'muṣmiṁśca ya etamevaṁ vidvānupāste. Iti trayodaśaḥ khaṇḍaḥ.

Saḥ yaḥ, he who; *etam evam vidvān,* knowing this in this way; *upāste,* [and] worships; *apahate pāpa-*

kṛtyām, he destroys his sins; *lokī bhavati,* becomes a dweller in the world of the god of fire; *sarvam āyuḥ eti,* lives the full range of his life; *jyok jīvati,* he lives a bright life; *asya āvarapuruṣāḥ,* his descendants; *na kṣīyante,* do not perish [i.e., his line is never broken]; *asmin ca loke amuṣmin ca,* in this world and also in the other world; *vayam tam upabhuñjāmaḥ,* we will look after him; *yaḥ etam evam vidvān upāste,* he who knows this [fire] thus and worships it. *Iti trayodaśaḥ khaṇḍaḥ,* here ends the thirteenth section.

2. 'He who knows this Āhavanīya fire and worships it thus has all his sins removed, and he attains the world of the Āhavanīya fire. He lives a long and bright life, and his descendants do not perish. In this world and the next, we look after that person who knows this fire and worships it thus.'

Section Fourteen

ते होचुरुपकोसलैषा सोम्य तेऽस्मद्विद्यात्मविद्या चाचार्यस्तु ते गतिं वक्तेत्याजगाम हास्याचार्यस्तमाचार्यो-ऽभ्युवादोपकोसल३ इति ॥ १ ॥

Te hocurupakosalaiṣā somya te'smadvidyātmavidyā cācāryastu te gatiṁ vaktetyājagāma hāsyācāryastamācāryo'bhyuvādopakosala 3 iti.

Te ha ucuḥ, they [the fires] said; *upakosala somya,* O Somya Upakosala; *eṣā te asmat vidyā,* this knowledge about us [we have given] to you; *ca ātma-vidyā,* that is also Self-knowledge; *ācāryaḥ tu te gatim vakta iti,* but the teacher will tell you about the way [to the next world]; *asya ācāryaḥ,* his teacher; *ājagāma ha,* returned; *ācāryaḥ abhyuvāda tam upakosala iti,* the teacher called him, 'O Upakosala.'

1. The fires said: 'O Somya Upakosala, we have just told you the knowledge of fire. That is also Self-knowledge. Your teacher will tell you about the way to the next world.' In due course, his teacher returned, and he called him, saying, 'Upakosala.'

What the fire meant was that Upakosala's teacher would give him the final lesson. He would tell Upakosala what he should do to get the full benefit of what he had learned from the fires.

भगव इति ह प्रतिशुश्राव ब्रह्मविद इव सोम्य ते मुखं भाति को नु त्वानुशशासेति को नु मानुशिष्याद्भो इतीहापेव निह्नुत इमे नूनमीदृशा अन्यादृशा इतीहाग्नीनभ्यूदे किं नु सोम्य किल तेऽवोचन्निति॥ २॥

Bhagava iti ha pratiśuśrāva brahmavida iva somya te mukhaṁ bhāti ko nu tvānuśaśāseti ko nu mānuśiṣyād-bho itīhāpeva nihnuta ime nūnamīdṛśā anyādṛśā itīhāgnīnabhyūde kiṁ nu somya kila te'vocanniti.

Bhagavaḥ iti ha pratiśuśrāva, 'Yes, lord,' he replied; *brahmavidaḥ iva somya te mukham bhāti,* your face is shining like that of a knower of Brahman; *kaḥ nu tvā anuśaśāsa iti,* who has taught you; *kaḥ nu mā anuśiṣyāt bho iti,* who will teach me, sir; *iha iva apanihnute,* [he said this] as if he was trying to hide [the truth]; *ime,* these [pointing to the fires]; *nūnam īdṛśāḥ,* look like this [as if they are frightened]; *anyādṛśāḥ iti,* looked different before; *iha agnīn abhyūde,* in this way he spoke about the fires; *kim nu somya kila te avocan iti,* Somya, what did they teach you?

2. [Upakosala] replied, 'Yes, lord.' [His teacher said:] 'O Somya, your face is shining like that of a knower of Brahman. Who has taught you?' 'Sir, who will teach me?' He said this as if he was trying to hide the truth. Then, pointing to the fires, he said: 'Earlier they looked different. Now they look like this.' In this way, he indicated the fires. [The teacher asked,] 'Somya, what did the fires teach you?'

Upakosala knew the limitations of the fires, and that is why he did not want to tell his teacher what they had taught him, or that they had taught him anything at all. Further, he noticed that in the presence of his teacher the fires appeared to be frozen with fear. This is why he was vague and evasive in his reply.

इदमिति ह प्रतिजज्ञे लोकान्वाव किल सोम्य तेऽवोचन्नहं तु ते तद्वक्ष्यामि यथा पुष्करपलाश आपो न श्लिष्यन्त एवमेवंविदि पापं कर्म न श्लिष्यत इति ब्रवीतु मे भगवानिति तस्मै होवाच ॥ ३ ॥ इति चतुर्दशः खण्डः ॥ १४ ॥

Idamiti ha pratijajñe lokānvāva kila somya te'vocannahaṁ tu te tadvakṣyāmi yathā puṣkarapalāśa āpo na śliṣyanta evamevaṁvidi pāpaṁ karma na śliṣyata iti bravītu me bhagavāniti tasmai hovāca. Iti caturdaśaḥ khaṇḍaḥ.

Idam iti ha pratijajñe, 'This [is what they taught,]' he [Upakosala] replied; *lokān vāva kila somya te avocan,* they have only told you about the worlds, O Somya; *aham tu te tat vakṣyāmi,* but I will tell you about that [Brahman]; *yathā puṣkara-palāśe āpaḥ na śliṣyante,* as water does not stick to the lotus leaf; *evam,* in the same way; *vidi,* one who knows [Brahman]; *evam,* thus; *pāpam karma na śliṣyate iti,* is not tainted by sinful work; *bravītu me bhagavān iti,* sir, please teach me; *tasmai ha uvāca,* he said to him. *Iti caturdaśaḥ khaṇḍaḥ,* here ends the fourteenth section.

3. Upakosala replied, 'This is what they said.' [And he told his teacher all that the fires had taught him.] The teacher said: 'O Somya, they taught you only about the worlds, but I will teach you about Brahman.

Just as water never sticks to a lotus leaf, similarly, sin never sticks to one who knows Brahman thus.' Upakosala replied, 'Sir, please teach me about Brahman.' The teacher said—

A person who has known Brahman is always pure. Nothing can taint him. He is incapable of doing anything wrong.

Section Fifteen

य एषोऽक्षिणि पुरुषो दृश्यत एष आत्मेति होवाचैतदमृतमभयमेतद्ब्रह्मेति तद्यद्यप्यस्मिन्सर्पिर्वोदकं वा सिञ्चति वर्त्मनी एव गच्छति॥ १॥

Ya eṣo'kṣiṇi puruṣo dṛśyata eṣa ātmeti hovācaitada-mṛtamabhayametadbrahmeti tadyadyapyasminsarpirvo-dakaṁ vā siñcati vartmanī eva gacchati.

Yaḥ eṣaḥ akṣiṇi puruṣaḥ dṛśyate, this person who is seen in the eyes; *eṣaḥ ātmā,* this is the Self; *iti ha uvāca,* he [the teacher] said; *etat amṛtam abhayam,* this is immortal and fearless; *etat brahma iti,* this is Brahman; *tat,* this is why; *asmin,* into this [eye]; *yadi api sarpiḥ vā udakam vā siñcati,* if anyone puts clarified butter or water; *vartmanī eva gacchati,* it goes into the corners [of the eye].

1. The teacher said: 'The person seen in the eyes is the Self. It is immortal and fearless. It is Brahman. This is why, if anyone puts clarified butter or water in the eyes, it goes to the corners of the eyes.'

How do you know the Self? You have to have full self-control. You have to have a gentle nature, and you must withdraw your mind completely from the external world. Then you can see the Self in the eyes. That Self is immortal, fearless, and it is Brahman (literally, 'the biggest').

As water does not stick to a lotus leaf, so also, if water or something else is put in the eyes, it does not hurt them because the eyelids protect them. This is why the eyelids are called 'lotuses.' The eyes are the seat of the Self. What the Upaniṣad is saying is that if the seat of the Self is pure and not susceptible to any impurity, the Self is naturally the same.

एतं संयद्वाम इत्याचक्षत एतं हि सर्वाणि वामान्य-
भिसंयन्ति सर्वाण्येनं वामान्यभिसंयन्ति य एवं वेद॥ २॥

Etaṁ saṁyadvāma ityācakṣata etaṁ hi sarvāṇi vāmānyabhisaṁyanti sarvāṇyenaṁ vāmānyabhisaṁyanti ya evaṁ veda.

Etam saṁyadvāmaḥ iti ācakṣate, they call him Saṁyadvāma [i.e., one in whom everything that is good is concentrated]; *hi,* because; *etam sarvāṇi vāmāni abhisaṁyanti,* all good and beautiful things come to him; *yaḥ evam veda,* he who knows thus; *sarvāṇi enam vāmāni abhisaṁyanti,* all good and beautiful things come to him.

2. They call him *Saṁyadvāma,* for everything that is good and beautiful comes to him. One who knows this has everything that is good and beautiful come to him.

The word *vāma* means 'attractive,' 'beautiful,' or 'desirable.' The Self is *Saṁyadvāma* because all good things become concentrated in it. And one who knows the Self also becomes the receptacle of all good things.

एष उ एव वामनीरेष हि सर्वाणि वामानि नयति सर्वाणि वामानि नयति य एवं वेद॥ ३ ॥

Eṣa u eva vāmanīreṣa hi sarvāṇi vāmāni nayati sarvāṇi vāmāni nayati ya evaṁ veda.

Eṣah u eva vāmanīḥ, and this [person in the eyes] is Vāmanī [the source of all that is good and pure]; *hi,* for; *eṣaḥ,* this [person in the eyes]; *eva,* surely; *sarvāṇi vāmāni nayati,* grants all that is good and pure; *yaḥ evam veda,* he who knows thus; *sarvāṇi vāmāni nayati,* grants all that is good and pure.

3. This person in the eyes is *Vāmanī,* the source of all that is good and pure, for he inspires in people all that is good and pure. One who knows this grants all that is good and pure to others.

The word *vāmanī* means one who carries the fruits of good work to all beings according to what they deserve. He is the support of all that is good.

One who knows this conveys the fruits of good work to others.

एष उ एव भामनीरेष हि सर्वेषु लोकेषु भाति
सर्वेषु लोकेषु भाति य एवं वेद॥४॥

Eṣa u eva bhāmanīreṣa hi sarveṣu lokeṣu bhāti sarveṣu lokeṣu bhāti ya evaṁ veda.

Eṣaḥ u eva bhāmanīḥ, and this [person in the eyes] is Bhāmanī [shining]; *eṣaḥ hi sarveṣu lokeṣu bhāti,* for he shines in all the worlds [including the sun]; *yaḥ evam veda,* he who knows thus; *sarveṣu lokeṣu bhāti,* shines in all the worlds.

4. The person in the eyes is *Bhāmanī,* shining, for he shines in all the worlds [including the sun]. One who knows this shines in all the worlds.

This person in the eyes is the source of all light. The Kaṭha Upaniṣad [II.2.15] says, 'All this shines because he shines.'

अथ यदु चैवास्मिञ्छव्यं कुर्वन्ति यदि च नार्चिष-
मेवाभिसम्भवन्त्यर्चिषोऽहरह्न आपूर्यमाणपक्षमापूर्यमाण-
पक्षाद्यान्षडुदङ्ङेति मासांस्तान्मासेभ्यः संवत्सरं संव-
त्सरादादित्यमादित्याच्चन्द्रमसं चन्द्रमसो विद्युतं तत्पुरुषो-
ऽमानवः स एनान्ब्रह्म गमयत्येष देवपथो ब्रह्मपथ एतेन
प्रतिपद्यमाना इमं मानवमावर्तं नावर्तन्ते नावर्तन्ते ॥ ५ ॥
इति पञ्चदशः खण्डः ॥ १५ ॥

Atha yadu caivāsmiñchavyaṁ kurvanti yadi ca nārciṣamevābhisambhavantyarciṣo'harahna āpūryamāṇapakṣamāpūryamāṇapakṣādyānṣaḍudaṅṅeti māsāṁstānmāsebhyaḥ saṁvatsaraṁ saṁvatsarādādityamādityāccandramasaṁ candramaso vidyutaṁ tatpuruṣo'mānavaḥ sa enānbrahma gamayatyeṣa devapatho brahmapatha etena pratipadyamānā imaṁ mānavamāvartaṃ nāvartante nāvartante. Iti pañcadaśaḥ khaṇḍaḥ.

Atha, then; *yat,* if; *u ca eva asmin,* in this situation [i.e., for those who know the Self in the eyes]; *śavyam,* funeral rites; *kurvanti,* they perform; *yadi ca na,* or if not; *arciṣam,* to light; *eva abhisambhavanti,* they go; *arciṣaḥ,* from light; *ahaḥ,* to day; *ahnaḥ,* from day; *āpūryamāṇapakṣam,* to the bright fortnight; *āpūryamāṇapakṣāt,* from the bright fortnight; *ṣaṭ māsān,* to the six months; *yān udan eti,* [when the sun] moves to the north; *tān,* to that; *māsebhyaḥ,* from those months; *saṁvatsaram,* to the year; *saṁvatsarāt,* from the year; *ādityam,* to the sun; *ādityāt,* from the sun; *candramasam,* to the moon; *candramasaḥ,* from the moon; *vidyutam,* to lightning; *tat,* there; *puruṣaḥ,* a person [existing there]; *amānavaḥ,* not human; *enān,* those [human beings]; *saḥ gamayati,* he leads; *brahma,* to brahmaloka; *eṣaḥ devapathaḥ,* this is the path of the gods; *brahmapathaḥ,* the way to Brahman; *etena,* by this [path]; *pratipadyamānāḥ,* those who go; *imam mānavam āvartam,* to this world of human beings; *na āvartante,* do not return; *na āvartante,* do not return. *Iti pañcadaśaḥ khaṇḍaḥ,* here ends the fifteenth section.

5. Then, for those who know this, whether proper funeral rites are performed or not, they go after death to the world of light. From the world of light they go to the world of day; from the world of day to the world of the bright fortnight; from the world of the bright fortnight to the six months when the sun moves northward; from there they go to the year; from the year to the sun; from the sun to the moon; and from the moon to lightning. There someone, not human, receives them and leads them to brahmaloka. This is the way of the gods. This is also the way to Brahman. Those who go by this path never return to this mortal world. They never return.

Normally when a person dies, his funeral rites should be performed with great care. This, however, does not apply in the case of one who has known Brahman. If the funeral rites are performed for him, it is good. But if for one reason or another they are not, it makes no difference to him. Having known Brahman he becomes one with Brahman.

As regards those who worship the Self in the eyes by attributing to it qualities such as *saṁyadvāma, vāmanī,* or *bhāmanī,* or those who worship the fires as earth, water, prāṇa, etc., they go after death to the deity of light. From there they go to the deities of day, the bright fortnight, the six months of the northern solstice, and so on. Finally they reach a point where someone appears who is higher than a human being. He leads them to *satyaloka,* which is the realm of Brahmā. This is not, however, Para Brahman (Pure Consciousness). To attain liberation, one must realize one's identity with Para Brahman, where there is no going or coming from one realm to another.

Section Sixteen

एष ह वै यज्ञो योऽयं पवत एष ह यन्निदं सर्वं पुनाति यदेष यन्निदं सर्वं पुनाति तस्मादेष एव यज्ञस्तस्य मनश्च वाक्च वर्तनी॥ १ ॥

Eṣa ha vai yajño yo'yaṁ pavata eṣa ha yannidaṁ sarvaṁ punāti yadeṣa yannidaṁ sarvaṁ punāti tasmā-deṣa eva yajñastasya manaśca vākca vartanī.

Eṣaḥ ha vai yajñaḥ, he is a sacrifice; *yaḥ ayam pavate,* this one who blows [i.e., air]; *eṣaḥ ha,* he;

yan, while moving; *idam sarvam,* all this; *punāti,* purifies; *yat,* since; *eṣaḥ yan idam sarvam punāti,* he purifies all this while moving; *tasmāt,* therefore; *eṣaḥ eva yajñaḥ,* he is the sacrifice; *manaḥ ca vāk ca,* mind and speech; *tasya vartanī,* are his paths.

1. He who blows [i.e., air] is the sacrifice. While moving, he purifies all this. Since he purifies all this while moving, he is the sacrifice. The mind and speech are both his paths.

Anything that moves can clean or purify things, and this process of cleaning or purifying is a kind of sacrifice. Air is called here a sacrifice because it moves and by moving it purifies.

There are two ways by which the air purifies—by speech and by the mind. By speech we utter mantras, and by the mind we understand them. Speech and the mind both operate by the power derived from air.

तयोरन्यतरां मनसा संस्करोति ब्रह्मा वाचा होताध्वर्युरुद्गातान्यतरां स यत्रोपाकृते प्रातरनुवाके पुरा परिधानीयाया ब्रह्मा व्यववदति॥ २॥

अन्यतरामेव वर्तनीं संस्करोति हीयतेऽन्यतरा स यथैकपाद्व्रजन्रथो वैकेन चक्रेण वर्तमानो रिष्यत्येवमस्य

यज्ञो रिष्यति यज्ञं रिष्यन्तं यजमानोऽनुरिष्यति स इष्ट्वा पापीयान्भवति ॥ ३ ॥

Tayoranyatarāṁ manasā saṁskaroti brahmā vācā hotādhvaryurudgātānyatarāṁ sa yatropākṛte prātaranuvāke purā paridhānīyāyā brahmā vyavavadati.

Anyatarāmeva vartanīṁ saṁskaroti hīyate'nyatarā sa yathaikapādvrajanratho vaikena cakreṇa vartamāno riṣyatyevamasya yajño riṣyati yajñaṁ riṣyantaṁ yajamāno'nuriṣyati sa iṣṭvā pāpīyānbhavati.

Brahmā, the priest called brahmā [in a sacrifice]; *tayoḥ anyatarām,* one of these two; *manasā,* mentally; *saṁskaroti,* purifies; *vācā,* by speech; *hotā adhvaryuḥ udgātā anyatarām,* the hotā, the adhvaryu, and the udgātā priests [purify] the other; *yatra,* when; *prātaḥ anuvāke upākṛte,* the anuvāka which is read in the morning has begun; *purā paridhānīyāyāḥ,* before the Ṛk hymn called paridhānīya; *saḥ,* he [the brahmā priest]; *vyavavadati,* breaks his silence; *anyatarām eva vartanīm saṁskaroti,* only one path [i.e., the path of speech] he purifies; *anyatarā,* the other [the path of the mind]; *hīyate,* is spoiled; *yathā,* just as; *ekapāt,* a person with one leg; *vrajan,* walking; *vā,* or; *rathaḥ ekena cakreṇa vartamānaḥ,* a chariot moving on one wheel; *riṣyati,* is doomed; *evam,* likewise; *asya yajñaḥ riṣyati,* his sacrifice is ruined; *yajñam riṣyantam,* when the sacrifice is ruined; *yajamānaḥ anu-riṣyati,* the sacrificer is also ruined; *saḥ,* he [the sacrificer]; *iṣṭvā,* having performed the sacrifice in this way; *pāpīyān bhavati,* becomes a sinner.

2-3. The priest called brahmā in a sacrifice purifies one of these two paths [i.e., the path of the mind] by his [discriminating] mind. The hotā, the adhvaryu, and the udgātā priests purify the other [i.e., the path of speech] by [chaste and elegant] speech. If, however, the brahmā priest breaks his silence when the morning anuvāka has begun, before the paridhānīya Ṛk hymn has been read, then only one path [the path of speech] has been purified. The other is ruined. Just as a one-legged person trying to walk, or a one-wheeled chariot trying to move, is doomed, in the same way the sacrifice is ruined. And when the sacrifice is ruined, the sacrificer is also ruined. In fact, the sacrificer is even liable for having committed a sin by performing the sacrifice in that way.

In the previous verse, two paths were mentioned for the performance of a sacrifice—the path of speech (*vāk*) and the path of the mind (*manas*).

In a sacrifice, there are four types of priests: brahmā, hotā, adhvaryu, and udgātā. The brahmā priest is supposed to purify the path of the mind by his own purified mind, while observing silence. The other three priests take care of the path of speech, purifying it by their pure words.

But suppose the brahmā priest breaks his silence while the reading of the morning anuvāka is going on, before the paridhānīya Ṛk hymn has begun. He is supposed to remain silent then, with his mind on a high level. Through this he is to purify the path of the mind. But if he breaks his silence, his mind is no longer 'pure.' Then the sacrificer has to make do with only one path—the path of speech. His position is now like that of a one-legged man trying to walk, or like a one-wheeled chariot trying to move. Both the sacrificer and the sacrifice are doomed, and the sacrificer is to be regarded as having committed a sin.

अथ यत्रोपाकृते प्रातरनुवाके न पुरा परिधानीयाया ब्रह्मा व्यववदत्युभे एव वर्तनी संस्कुर्वन्ति न हीयते-ऽन्यतरा ॥ ४ ॥

Atha yatropākṛte prātaranuvāke na purā paridhānīyāyā brahmā vyavavadatyubhe eva vartanī saṁskurvanti na hīyate'nyatarā.

Atha yatra, in the case of that sacrifice; *upākṛte prātaḥ anuvāke,* in which the reading of the morning anuvāka has begun; *purā paridhānīyāyāḥ,* before the beginning of the paridhānīya Ṛk hymn; *brahmā na vyavavadati,* the brahmā priest does not speak; *ubhe eva vartanī,* both the paths; *saṁskurvanti,* they purify; *na hīyate anyatarā,* neither of them is destroyed.

4. But in the case of the sacrifice in which the reading of the morning anuvāka has already begun, and the brahmā priest does not break his silence before the paridhānīya has started, then both paths are purified. Neither of them becomes destroyed.

स यथोभयपाद्व्रजन्रथो वोभाभ्यां चक्राभ्यां वर्तमानः प्रतितिष्ठत्येवमस्य यज्ञः प्रतितिष्ठति यज्ञं प्रतितिष्ठन्तं यजमानोऽनुप्रतितिष्ठति स इष्ट्वा श्रेयान्भवति ॥ ५ ॥ इति षोडशः खण्डः ॥ १६ ॥

Sa yathobhayapādvrajanratho vobhābhyāṁ cakrābhyāṁ vartamānaḥ pratitiṣṭhatyevamasya yajñaḥ pratitiṣṭhati yajñaṁ pratitiṣṭhantaṁ yajamāno'nupratitiṣṭhati sa iṣṭvā śreyānbhavati. Iti ṣoḍaśaḥ khaṇḍaḥ.

Yathā, as; *ubhayapāt,* a person with both legs; *vrajam,* walking; *vā,* or; *rathaḥ ubhābhyām cakrābhyām,* a chariot with both wheels; *vartamānaḥ,* moving; *pratitiṣṭhati,* succeeds; *evam,* so also; *asya yajñaḥ pratitiṣṭhati,* his [the sacrificer's] sacrifice succeeds; *yajñam pratitiṣṭhantam yajamānaḥ anupratitiṣṭhati,* if the sacrifice succeeds, the sacrificer also succeeds; *saḥ,* he [the sacrificer]; *iṣṭvā śreyān bhavati,* becomes greater through his sacrifice. *Iti ṣoḍaśaḥ khaṇḍaḥ,* here ends the sixteenth section.

5. Just as a person with two legs can walk, or a chariot with two wheels can move, and attain the goal, so also his sacrifice succeeds. And if the sacrifice succeeds, the sacrificer also succeeds. He attains much greatness through his sacrifice.

Section Seventeen

प्रजापतिर्लोकानभ्यतपत्तेषां तप्यमानानां रसान्प्रावृहदग्निं पृथिव्या वायुमन्तरिक्षादादित्यं दिवः ॥ १ ॥

Prajāpatirlokānabhyatapatteṣāṁ tapyamānānāṁ rasānprāvṛhadagniṁ pṛthivyā vāyumantarikṣādādityaṁ divaḥ.

Prajāpatiḥ lokān abhyatapat, Prajāpati worshipped the worlds; *teṣām tapyamānānām,* from those which were worshipped; *rasān prāvṛhat,* he extracted the essence; *agnim pṛthivyāḥ,* fire from the earth; *vāyum antarikṣāt,* air from the space between the earth and heaven; *ādityam divaḥ,* and the sun from heaven.

1. Prajāpati worshipped the worlds, and from those which he worshipped he was able to extract their essence. From earth he took fire, from the interspace he took air, and from heaven he took the sun.

The brahmā priest must observe silence to maintain the sanctity of the sacrifice he is performing. If the sanctity is lost, then the purpose of the sacrifice will be defeated. So if, for some reason or other, the sanctity is lost, due amends have to be made.

One way to make amends is to seek the blessings of the *lokas,* the worlds. You pray to the worlds and then you are able to get their essence to support you. From earth you get fire, from the interspace you get air, and from heaven you get the sun.

Your worship of the worlds is the amends you make, and the extracts you get in return are the blessings that protect you.

स एतास्तिस्रो देवता अभ्यतपत्तासां तप्यमानानां रसान्प्रावृहदग्नेर्ऋचो वायोर्यजूंषि सामान्यादित्यात् ॥ २ ॥

Sa etāstisro devatā abhyatapattāsāṁ tapyamānānāṁ rasānprāvṛhadagnerṛco vāyoryajūṁṣi sāmānyādityāt.

Saḥ etāḥ tisraḥ devatāḥ abhyatapat, [then] he worshipped these three deities [fire, air, and the sun]; *tāsām tapyamānānām,* from those which he worshipped; *rasān prāvṛhat,* he extracted the essence; *agneḥ ṛcaḥ,* the Ṛk mantras from fire; *vāyoḥ yajūṁṣi,* the Yajuḥ mantras from air; *sāmāni ādityāt,* the Sāma mantras from the sun.

2. Then he worshipped these three deities. From those which he worshipped he extracted the essence. He got the Ṛk mantras from fire, the Yajuḥ mantras from air, and the Sāma mantras from the sun.

स एतां त्रयीं विद्यामभ्यतपत्तस्यास्तप्यमानाया रसान्प्रावृहद्भूरित्यृग्भ्यो भुवरिति यजुर्भ्यः स्वरिति सामभ्यः ॥ ३ ॥

Sa etāṁ trayīṁ vidyāmabhyatapattasyāstapyamānāyā rasānprāvṛhadbhūrityṛgbhyo bhuvariti yajurbhyaḥ svariti sāmabhyaḥ.

Saḥ etām trayīm vidyām abhyatapat, [then] he worshipped the knowledge from these three; *tasyāḥ tapyamānāyāḥ,* from these that he worshipped; *rasān prāvṛhat,* he extracted the essence; *bhūḥ iti ṛgbhyaḥ,* 'bhūḥ' from the Ṛg Veda; *bhuvaḥ iti yajurbhyaḥ,* 'bhuvaḥ' from the Yajur Veda; *svaḥ iti sāmabhyaḥ,* 'svaḥ' from the Sāma Veda.

3. Then Prajāpati worshipped these three Vedas. And from those Vedas that were worshipped he extracted the essence. From the Ṛg Veda he got 'bhūḥ,' from the Yajur Veda he got 'bhuvaḥ,' and from the Sāma Veda he got 'svaḥ.'

तद्यदृक्तो रिष्येद्भूः स्वाहेति गार्हपत्ये जुहुयादृचामेव तद्रसेनर्चां वीर्येणर्चां यज्ञस्य विरिष्टं सन्दधाति॥ ४॥

Tadyadṛkto riṣyedbhūḥ svāheti gārhapatye juhuyā-dṛcāmeva tadrasenarcāṁ vīryeṇarcāṁ yajñasya viriṣṭaṁ sandadhāti.

Tat, that is why; *yat ṛktaḥ riṣyet,* if there should be any harm done [to the sacrifice] because of [a mistake] in the Ṛk; *bhūḥ svāhā iti gārhapatye juhuyāt,* then he should offer oblations in the Gārhapatya fire saying, 'Bhūḥ svāhā'; *ṛcām eva taṭ rasena,* by that essence of the Ṛk; *ṛcām vīryeṇa,* by the strength of the Ṛk; *ṛcām yajñasya viriṣṭam,* the harm done to the sacrifice by the mistake in the Ṛk; *sandadhāti,* is averted.

4. This is why, if it seems likely that there will be any harm done to the sacrifice because of a mistake in the Ṛk, the priest should offer oblations in the Gārhapatya fire saying, 'Bhūḥ svāhā.' Then, by the essence and strength of the Ṛk, any likely harm done to the sacrifice from a mistake in the Ṛk will be averted.

अथ यदि यजुष्टो रिष्येद्भुवः स्वाहेति दक्षिणाग्नौ जुहुयाद्यजुषामेव तद्रसेन यजुषां वीर्येण यजुषां यज्ञस्य विरिष्टं सन्दधाति॥ ५॥

Atha yadi yajuṣṭo riṣyedbhuvaḥ svāheti dakṣiṇāgnau juhuyādyajuṣāmeva tadrasena yajuṣāṁ vīryeṇa yajuṣāṁ yajñasya viriṣṭaṁ sandadhāti.

Atha yadi yajuṣṭaḥ riṣyet, then if there should be any harm done [to the sacrifice] because of [a mistake] in the Yajuḥ; *bhuvaḥ svāhā iti dakṣiṇāgnau juhuyāt,* then he should offer oblations in the Dakṣiṇāgni fire saying, 'Bhuvaḥ svāhā'; *yajuṣām eva tat rasena,* by that essence of the Yajuḥ; *yajuṣām vīryeṇa,* by the strength of the Yajuḥ; *yajuṣām yajñasya viriṣṭam,* the harm done to the sacrifice by the mistake in the Yajuḥ; *sandadhāti,* is averted.

5. Then if it seems likely that there will be any harm done to the sacrifice because of a mistake in the Yajuḥ, the priest should offer oblations in the Dakṣiṇāgni fire saying, 'Bhuvaḥ svāhā.' Then, by the essence and strength of the Yajuḥ, any likely harm done to the sacrifice from a mistake in the Yajuḥ will be averted.

अथ यदि सामतो रिष्येत्स्वः स्वाहेत्याहवनीये जुहुयात्साम्नामेव तद्रसेन साम्नां वीर्येण साम्नां यज्ञस्य विरिष्टं सन्दधाति॥ ६॥

Atha yadi sāmato riṣyetsvaḥ svāhetyāhavanīye juhuyātsāmnāmeva tadrasena sāmnāṁ vīryeṇa sāmnāṁ yajñasya viriṣṭaṁ sandadhāti.

Atha yadi sāmataḥ riṣyet, then if there should be any harm done [to the sacrifice] because of [a mistake] in the Sāma; *svaḥ svāhā iti āhavanīye juhuyāt,* then he should offer oblations in the Āhavanīya fire saying, 'svaḥ svāhā'; *sāmnām eva tat rasena,* by that essence of the Sāma; *sāmnām vīryeṇa,* by the strength of the Sāṃa; *sāmnām yajñasya viriṣṭaṁ,* the harm done to the sacrifice by the mistake in the Sāma; *sandadhāti,* is averted.

6. Then if it seems likely that there will be any harm done to the sacrifice because of a mistake in the Sāma, the priest should offer oblations in

the Āhavanīya fire saying, 'svaḥ svāhā.' Then, by the essence and strength of the Sāma, any likely harm done to the sacrifice from a mistake in the Sāma will be averted.

तद्यथा लवणेन सुवर्णं सन्दध्यात्सुवर्णेन रजतं रजतेन त्रपु त्रपुणा सीसं सीसेन लोहं लोहेन दारु दारु चर्मणा ॥ ७ ॥

Tadyathā lavaṇena suvarṇaṁ sandadhyātsuvarṇena rajataṁ rajatena trapu trapuṇā sīsaṁ sīsena lohaṁ lohena dāru dāru carmaṇā.

Tat yathā, it is like; *lavaṇena,* with the help of borax; *suvarṇam sandadhyāt,* one joins gold; *suvarṇena rajatam,* silver with the help of gold; *rajatena trapu,* tin with the help of silver; *trapuṇā sīsam,* lead with the help of tin; *sīsena loham,* iron with the help of lead; *lohena dāru,* wood with the help of iron; *dāru carmaṇā,* [and] wood with the help of leather.

7. It is like joining gold with the help of borax, silver with the help of gold, tin with the help of silver, lead with the help of tin, iron with the help of lead, wood with the help of iron, and wood with the help of leather.

Two things can join together when the right combination of materials is used. In the same way, if there is any error in a sacrifice, it can be rectified by taking the help of the appropriate remedy.

एवमेषां लोकानामासां देवतानामस्यास्त्रय्या विद्याया वीर्येण यज्ञस्य विरिष्टं सन्दधाति भेषजकृतो ह वा एष यज्ञो यत्रैवंविद्ब्रह्मा भवति ॥ ८ ॥

Evameṣāṁ lokānāmāsāṁ devatānāmasyāstrayyā vidyāyā vīryeṇa yajñasya viriṣṭaṁ sandadhāti bheṣajakṛto ha vā eṣa yajño yatraivaṁvidbrahmā bhavati.

Evam, in this way; *vīryeṇa,* by the strength; *eṣām lokānām,* of these worlds; *āsām devatānām,* of these deities; *asyāḥ trayyāḥ vidyāyāḥ,* of these three holy scriptures; *yajñasya viriṣtam sandadhāti,* he [the brahmā priest] makes up for the flaws of a sacrifice; *yatra evamvit brahmā bhavati,* when there is a knowledgeable brahmā priest; *eṣaḥ yajñaḥ,* this sacrifice; *bheṣajakṛtaḥ ha vai,* gets the right medicine.

8. Similarly, by the power of these worlds, these deities, and these three holy scriptures, any flaws in the sacrifice are made up. Where there is a knowledgeable brahmā priest, that sacrifice gets the right medicine.

When a person is sick he must take the appropriate medicine. Similar is the case of a sacrifice that has gotten off to a bad start. If the priest is a knowledgeable one, he will take the right steps to rectify the errors. Like a good doctor, he will apply the right medicine—that is, the combined powers of the worlds, the deities, and the scriptures.

एष ह वा उदक्प्रवणो यज्ञो यत्रैवंविद्ब्रह्मा भवत्येवंविदं ह वा एषा ब्रह्माणमनुगाथा यतो यत आवर्तते तत्तद्गच्छति ॥ ९ ॥

Eṣa ha vā udakpravaṇo yajño yatraivaṁvidbrahmā bhavatyevaṁvidaṁ ha vā eṣā brahmāṇamanugāthā yato yata āvartate tattadgacchati.

Eṣaḥ ha vai yajñaḥ udakpravaṇaḥ, this sacrifice is the way to the uttarāyaṇa [the path of the gods]; *yatra evamvit brahmā bhavati,* where there is a knowledgeable brahmā priest; *evam vidam ha vai eṣaḥ brahmāṇam anu gāthā,* there is this praise for such a learned brahmā priest; *yataḥ yataḥ āvartate,* wherever there is a flaw [in the sacrifice]; *tat tat gacchati,* he [the brahmā priest] goes there [to make amends].

9. That sacrifice which is directed by a capable brahmā priest leads to the uttarāyaṇa [the path of the gods]. There is a verse in praise of such a learned priest: 'Wherever the sacrifice goes wrong, this priest goes there to set things right.'

Whenever a sacrifice is to be held, a competent priest should be placed in charge. This will ensure that nothing goes wrong. But should there inadvertently be a flaw, this priest can then save the situation by taking the necessary steps.

A capable priest is always in demand wherever a sacrifice is being held, because, first, he can avoid mistakes, and second, should there be any mistake, in spite of all the care taken, the priest knows how to correct it.

मानवो ब्रह्मैवैक ऋत्विक्कुरूनश्वाभिरक्षत्येवंविद्ध वै ब्रह्मा यज्ञं यजमानं सर्वांश्चर्त्विजोऽभिरक्षति तस्मादेवंविदमेव ब्रह्माणं कुर्वीत नानेवंविदं नानेवंविदम् ॥ १० ॥ इति सप्तदशः खण्डः ॥ १७ ॥ इति छान्दोग्योपनिषदि चतुर्थोऽध्यायः ॥ ४ ॥

Mānavo brahmaivaika ṛtvikkurūnaśvābhirakṣatyevaṁviddha vai brahmā yajñaṁ yajamānaṁ sarvāṁścartvijo'bhirakṣati tasmādevaṁvidameva brahmāṇaṁ kurvīta nānevaṁvidaṁ nānevaṁvidam. Iti saptadaśaḥ khaṇḍaḥ. Iti chāndogyopaniṣadi caturtho'dhyāyaḥ.

Mānavaḥ brahmā eva ekaḥ ṛtvik, a true brahmā priest is one who is thoughtful [or, is able to observe silence]; *kurūn aśvā abhirakṣati,* [just as] a horse protects the soldiers; *evamvit ha vai brahmā,* such a learned brahmā priest; *yajñam yajamānam sarvān ca ṛtvijaḥ abhirakṣati,* protects the sacrifice, **the** sacrificer, and all the other priests; *tasmāt,* therefore;

evam vidam eva brahmāṇam kurvīta, one should appoint only such a learned brahmā priest; *na anevam vidam,* not one who is otherwise; *na anevam vidam,* not one who is otherwise. *Iti saptadaśaḥ khaṇḍaḥ,* here ends the seventeenth section. *Iti chāndogyopaniṣadi caturthaḥ adhyāyaḥ,* here ends the fourth chapter of the Chāndogya Upaniṣad.

10. A good brahmā priest is one who is able to observe silence, or one who is thoughtful. Just as a horse protects the soldiers, a learned brahmā priest protects the sacrifice, the sacrificer, and all the other priests. Therefore, one should appoint only such a learned brahmā for one's sacrifice. One should not appoint anyone else.

When a priest is able to maintain silence and is by nature thoughtful, he may be appointed as the brahmā for a sacrifice. He is the chief priest by virtue of his scholarship and his character. The Upaniṣad compares him to a horse which protects his master when he is in trouble. A good brahmā priest can take care of the sacrifice, the sacrificer, and the subordinate priests. For this reason, only one who is qualified should be appointed. One who is not fit should not be given the honour.

CHAPTER FIVE

Section One

ॐ। यो ह वै ज्येष्ठं च श्रेष्ठं च वेद ज्येष्ठश्च ह वै श्रेष्ठश्च भवति प्राणो वाव ज्येष्ठश्च श्रेष्ठश्च॥ १ ॥

Om. Yo ha vai jyeṣṭhaṁ ca śreṣṭhaṁ ca veda jyeṣṭhaśca ha vai śreṣṭhaśca bhavati prāṇo vāva jyeṣṭhaśca śreṣṭhaśca.

Yaḥ ha vai, he who; *jyeṣṭham ca śreṣṭham ca veda,* knows the oldest and the best; *jyeṣṭhaḥ ca ha vai śreṣṭhaḥ ca bhavati,* himself becomes the oldest and the best; *prāṇaḥ vāva jyeṣṭhaḥ ca śreṣṭhaḥ ca,* prāṇa is indeed the oldest and the best.

1. Om. He who knows the oldest and the best himself becomes the oldest and the best. It is prāṇa which is the oldest and the best.

The importance of prāṇa has been mentioned earlier. True, it works in conjunction with the organs of speaking, hearing, seeing, etc., but it is the first and foremost of all of them. Prāṇa is in a child even when it is still in it's mother's womb. It is active before the various organs are active. Prāṇa therefore commands respect from all.

The reason why so much importance is given to

prāṇa is to teach us to show respect where respect is due. We should respect both age and merit. Then we also shall command respect from all because of our age and merit. Indirectly, this is a hint that we should respect knowledge.

यो ह वै वसिष्ठं वेद वसिष्ठो ह स्वानां भवति वाग्वाव वसिष्ठः ॥ २ ॥

Yo ha vai vasiṣṭhaṁ veda vasiṣṭho ha svānāṁ bhavati vāgvāva vasiṣṭhaḥ.

Yaḥ ha vai, he who; *vasiṣṭham veda,* knows that which is of high standing; *vasiṣṭhaḥ ha svānām bhavati,* becomes of high standing among his own relatives; *vāk vāva vasiṣṭhaḥ,* speech [i.e., eloquence] is surely of high standing [i.e., it is the secret of high standing].

2. He who knows that which is of high standing himself becomes of high standing among his own relatives. Eloquence gives one this high standing [in society].

If a person respects another for his power to influence others, he himself some day has the same power and commands respect from others.

It is, in fact, the power of eloquence which is behind this influence.

यो ह वै प्रतिष्ठां वेद प्रति ह तिष्ठत्यस्मिंश्च लोकेऽमुष्मिंश्च चक्षुर्वाव प्रतिष्ठा ॥ ३ ॥

Yo ha vai pratiṣṭhāṁ veda prati ha tiṣṭhatyasmiṁśca loke'muṣmiṁśca cakṣurvāva pratiṣṭhā.

Yaḥ ha vai, he who; *pratiṣṭhām veda,* knows the support; *asmin ca loke,* in this world; *amuṣmin ca,* and in the other [world]; *pratitiṣṭhati,* attains a support; *cakṣuḥ vāva pratiṣṭhā,* the eye is surely the support.

3. He who knows the support attains a support in this world and also in the other world [i.e., heaven]. The eye is indeed the support.

Good sight is necessary for success in life. A sharp eye is not merely a physical asset; it is also a mental asset. It means a good and sharp sense of judgement. One can easily avoid the pitfalls of life, physical as well as moral, with good sight. Given this quality, you are safe in this world as well as in the other.

यो ह वै सम्पदं वेद सं हास्मै कामाः पद्यन्ते दैवाश्च मानुषाश्च श्रोत्रं वाव सम्पत् ॥ ४ ॥

Yo ha vai sampadaṁ veda saṁ hāsmai kāmāḥ padyante daivāśca mānuṣāśca śrotraṁ vāva sampat.

Yaḥ ha vai, he who; *sampadam veda,* knows affluence; *asmai,* to him; *kāmāḥ,* desirable things; *sam-padyante,* come; *daivāḥ ca,* [things meant for] gods; *mānuṣāḥ ca,* and [things meant for] human beings; *śrotram vāva sampat,* the ears are surely affluence.

4. He who knows affluence has all things desired by human beings and gods come to him. Affluence is represented by the ears.

यो ह वा आयतनं वेदायतनं ह स्वानां भवति
मनो ह वा आयतनम्॥५॥

Yo ha vā āyatanaṁ vedāyatanaṁ ha svānāṁ bhavati mano ha vā āyatanam.

Yaḥ ha vai, he who; *āyatanam veda,* knows the abode; *āyatanam ha svānām bhavati,* becomes the abode [i.e., shelter] of his family; *manaḥ ha vai āyatanam,* the mind is surely the abode.

5. He who knows the abode becomes the shelter of his family. The mind is the abode.

There is something in the body-mind complex of human beings called *āyatana.* If a person knows this 'āyatana,' it is to be understood that he is a wise person. And such a person is able to serve as an āyatana to his own relatives. That is to say, he is able to give them support, as if he is giving shelter to them.

The mind is the āyatana of the body-mind complex. Why? Because the sense organs have their experiences, but all those experiences take shelter in the mind.

अथ ह प्राणा अहंश्रेयसि व्यूदिरेऽहं श्रेयानस्म्यहं श्रेयानस्मीति ॥ ६ ॥

Atha ha prāṇā ahaṁśreyasi vyūdire'haṁ śreyānasmyahaṁ śreyānasmīti.

Atha ha, once; *prāṇāḥ,* the sense organs; *vyūdire,* began to quarrel [among themselves]; *aham-śreyasi,* each thinking it was the best; *aham śreyān asmi aham śreyān asmi iti,* saying, 'I am the best, I am the best.'

6. Once the sense organs began to quarrel among themselves, each one claiming it was supreme. They each said, 'I am the best. I am the best.'

ते ह प्राणाः प्रजापतिं पितरमेत्योचुर्भगवन्को नः श्रेष्ठ इति तान्होवाच यस्मिन्व उत्क्रान्ते शरीरं पापिष्ठतरमिव दृश्येत स वः श्रेष्ठ इति ॥ ७ ॥

Te ha prāṇāḥ prajāpatiṁ pitarametyocurbhagavanko naḥ śreṣṭha iti tānhovāca yasminva utkrānte śarīraṁ pāpiṣṭhataramiva dṛśyeta sa vaḥ śreṣṭha iti.

Te ha prāṇāḥ, those organs; *pitaram prajāpatim etya,* coming to their father Prajāpati; *ucuḥ,* said; *bhagavan,* revered sir; *naḥ,* among us; *kaḥ śreṣṭhaḥ iti,* who is the best; *tān ha uvāca,* he said to them; *vaḥ,* among you; *yasmin utkrānte,* on whose leaving; *śarīram pāpiṣṭhataram iva dṛśyeta,* the body appears to be untouchable; *saḥ vaḥ śreṣṭhaḥ,* he is the best among you.

7. The organs then went to their father Prajāpati and said, 'Revered sir, who among us is the best?' He replied, 'He is the best among you on whose departure the body becomes totally untouchable.'

We all know what happens when life leaves the body. It is not the same body. It shrinks. It becomes ugly. And soon it starts decomposing. No one wants to touch it. Prajāpati indirectly declared in this way that prāṇa was the best among them.

When Prajāpati said this, he changed his voice lest he hurt the other organs. The way he changed his voice is called *kaku.*

सा ह वागुच्चक्राम सा संवत्सरं प्रोष्य पर्येत्योवाच कथमशकतर्ते मज्जीवितुमिति यथा कला अवदन्तः प्राणन्तः

प्राणेन पश्यन्तश्चक्षुषा शृण्वन्तः श्रोत्रेण ध्यायन्तो मनसैवमिति प्रविवेश ह वाक्॥८॥

Sā ha vāguccakrāma sā saṁvatsaraṁ proṣya paryetyovāca kathamaśakatarte majjīvitumiti yathā kalā avadantaḥ prāṇantaḥ prāṇena paśyantaścakṣuṣā śṛṇvantaḥ śrotreṇa dhyāyanto manasaivamiti praviveśa ha vāk.

Sā ha vāk, that speech; *ut-cakrāma,* left [the body]; *saṁvatsaram proṣya,* after staying away one year; *sā paretya uvāca,* he came back and said; *mat ṛte,* in my absence; *katham,* how; *jīvitum aśakata iti,* did you manage to survive; *yathā kalāḥ,* [the other organs said:] just as the mute; *avadantaḥ,* do not speak; *prāṇantaḥ prāṇena,* [but] are able to survive with the help of prāṇa, the vital force; *paśyantaḥ cakṣuṣā,* to see with the help of the eyes; *śṛṇvantaḥ śrotreṇa,* to hear with the help of the ears; *dhyāyantaḥ manasā,* to think with the help of the mind; *evam iti,* in the same way; *vāk praviveśa ha,* [hearing this] speech re-entered the body.

8. First speech left the body. After staying away one whole year, he came back and asked the other organs, 'How did you sustain yourselves in my absence?' The rest of the organs said: 'Just as mute people do without speaking, but they are able to survive by breathing, and see with the eyes, hear with the ears, and think with the mind. We did the same.' Hearing all this, speech re-entered the body.

चक्षुर्होच्चक्राम तत्संवत्सरं प्रोष्य पर्येत्योवाच कथमशकतर्ते मज्जीवितुमिति यथान्धा अपश्यन्तः प्राणन्तः प्राणेन वदन्तो वाचा शृण्वन्तः श्रोत्रेण ध्यायन्तो मनसैवमिति प्रविवेश ह चक्षुः ॥ ९ ॥

Cakṣurhoccakrāma tatsaṁvatsaraṁ proṣya paryetyovāca kathamaśakatarte majjīvitumiti yathāndhā apaśyantaḥ prāṇantaḥ prāṇena vadanto vācā śṛṇvantaḥ śrotreṇa dhyāyanto manasaivamiti praviveśa ha cakṣuḥ.

Cakṣuḥ ha, the organ of vision; *ut-cakrāma,* left [the body]; *saṁvatsaram proṣya,* after staying away one year; *tat paretya uvāca,* it came back and said; *mat ṛte,* in my absence; *katham,* how; *jīvitum aśakata iti,* did you manage to survive; *yathā andhāḥ,* [the other organs said:] just as the blind; *apaśyantaḥ,* do not see; *prāṇantaḥ prāṇena,* [but] are able to survive with the help of prāṇa, the vital force; *vadantaḥ vācā,* to speak with the help of the organ of speech; *śṛṇvantaḥ śrotreṇa,* to hear with the help of the ears; *dhyāyantaḥ manasā,* to think with the help of the mind; *evam iti,* in the same way; *cakṣuḥ praviveśa ha,* [hearing this] the organ of vision re-entered the body.

9. Next the organ of vision left the body. After staying away one whole year, it came back and asked the other organs, 'How did you sustain yourselves in my absence?' The rest of the organs said: 'Just as blind people do without seeing, but they are able

to survive by breathing, and speak with the organ of speech, hear with the ears, and think with the mind. We did the same.' Hearing all this, the organ of vision re-entered the body.

श्रोत्रं होच्चक्राम तत्संवत्सरं प्रोष्य पर्येत्योवाच कथमशकततें मज्जीवितुमिति यथा बधिरा अशृण्वन्तः प्राणन्तः प्राणेन वदन्तो वाचा पश्यन्तश्चक्षुषा ध्यायन्तो मनसैवमिति प्रविवेश ह श्रोत्रम् ॥ १० ॥

Śrotraṁ hoccakrāma tatsaṁvatsaraṁ proṣya paryetyovāca kathamaśakatarte majjīvitumiti yathā badhirā aśṛṇvantaḥ prāṇantaḥ prāṇena vadanto vācā paśyantaścakṣuṣā dhyāyanto manasaivamiti praviveśa ha śrotram.

Śrotram ha, the organ of hearing; *ut-cakrāma,* left [the body]; *saṁvatsaram proṣya,* after staying away one year; *tat paretya uvāca,* it came back and said; *mat ṛte,* in my absence; *katham,* how; *jīvitum aśakata iti,* did you manage to survive; *yathā badhirāḥ,* [the other organs said:] just as the deaf; *aśṛṇvantaḥ,* do not hear; *prāṇantaḥ prāṇena,* [but] are able to survive with the help of prāṇa, the vital force; *vadantaḥ vācā,* to speak with the help of the organ of speech; *paśyantaḥ cakṣuṣā,* to see with the help of the eyes; *dhyāyantaḥ manasā,* to think with the help of the mind; *evam iti,* in the same way; *śrotram praviveśa ha,* [hearing this] the organ of hearing re-entered the body.

10. Next the organ of hearing left the body. After staying away one whole year, it came back and asked the other organs, 'How did you sustain yourselves in my absence?' The rest of the organs said: 'Just as deaf people do without hearing, but they are able to survive by breathing, and speak with the organ of speech, see with the eyes, and think with the mind. We did the same.' Hearing all this, the organ of hearing re-entered the body.

मनो होच्चक्राम तत्संवत्सरं प्रोष्य पर्येत्योवाच कथमशकतर्ते मज्जीवितुमिति यथा बाला अमनसः प्राणन्तः प्राणेन वदन्तो वाचा पश्यन्तश्चक्षुषा शृण्वन्तः श्रोत्रेणैवमिति प्रविवेश ह मनः॥ ११ ॥

Mano hoccakrāma tatsaṁvatsaraṁ proṣya paryetyovāca kathamaśakatarte majjīvitumiti yathā bālā amanasaḥ prāṇantaḥ prāṇena vadanto vācā paśyantaścakṣuṣā śṛṇvantaḥ śrotreṇaivamiti praviveśa ha manaḥ.

Manaḥ ha, the mind; *ut-cakrāma,* left [the body]; *saṁvatsaram proṣya,* after staying away one year; *tat paretya uvāca,* he came back and said; *mat ṛte,* in my absence; *katham,* how; *jīvitum aśakata iti,* did you manage to survive; *yathā bālāḥ,* [the other organs said:] just as the children; *amanasaḥ,* do not receive much support from the mind; *prāṇantaḥ prāṇena,* [but] are able to survive with the help of prāṇa, the vital force; *vadantaḥ vācā,* to speak with the help of the organ of speech; *paśyantaḥ cakṣuṣā,* to see with the help of the eyes; *śṛṇvantaḥ śrotreṇa,* to hear with the help of the ears; *evam iti,* in the same way; *manaḥ praviveśa ha,* [hearing this] the mind re-entered the body.

11. Next the mind left the body. After staying away one whole year, he came back and asked the other organs, 'How did you sustain yourselves in my absence?' The rest of the organs said: 'Just as children do without thinking for themselves, but they are able to survive by breathing, and speak with the organ of speech, see with the eyes, and hear with the ears. We did the same.' Hearing all this, the mind re-entered the body.

अथ ह प्राण उच्चिक्रमिषन्स यथा सुहयः पड्वीश-
शङ्कून्संखिदेदेवमितरान्प्राणान्समखिदत्तं हाभिसमेत्योचु-
र्भगवन्नेधि त्वं नः श्रेष्ठोऽसि मोत्क्रमीरिति॥ १२॥

Atha ha prāṇa uccikramiṣansa yathā suhayaḥ paḍvīśaśaṅkūnsaṁkhidedevamitarānprāṇānsamakhidattaṁ hābhisametyocurbhagavannedhi tvaṁ naḥ śreṣṭho'si motkramīriti.

Atha ha saḥ prāṇaḥ, now that prāṇa, the vital force; *uccikramiṣan,* wishing to go out; *yathā,* just as; *suhayaḥ,* a good horse; *paḍvīśa-śaṅkūn,* the pegs to which his feet are tied; *saṁkhidet,* uproots; *evam,* in the same way; *itarān prāṇān,* the other organs; *samakhidat,* began to leave with him; *tam abhisametya,* coming to him [with great humility]; *ucuḥ ha,* [and] said; *bhagavan,* lord; *edhi,* be our leader; *naḥ tvam śreṣṭhaḥ asi,* you are the best among us; *mā utkramīḥ iti,* please do not leave us.

12. Now prāṇa, the vital force, decided to leave. Just as a good horse is able to uproot the pegs to which its feet are tied, similarly, the chief prāṇa was about to carry the other organs away with him. Those other organs then came to him and with great humility said: 'O lord, be our leader. You are the greatest among us. Please don't leave us.'

The organs, beginning with vāk (speech), left the body one after another. But that made little or no difference to the body or to the rest of the organs. Then prāṇa decided to leave. Just as he started to go, all the other organs felt that they were being forced to leave also. They realized then that they were not free; they were utterly dependent on the chief prāṇa. Coming to him, they showed him respect and said that they now recognized his superiority.

अथ हैनं वागुवाच यदहं वसिष्ठोऽस्मि त्वं तद्वसिष्ठोऽसीत्यथ हैनं चक्षुरुवाच यदहं प्रतिष्ठास्मि त्वं तत्प्रतिष्ठासीति ॥ १३ ॥

Atha hainaṁ vāguvāca yadahaṁ vasiṣṭho'smi tvaṁ tadvasiṣṭho'sītyatha hainaṁ cakṣuruvāca yadahaṁ pratiṣṭhāsmi tvaṁ tatpratiṣṭhāsīti.

Atha ha enam vāk uvāca, next vāk [speech] said to him [i.e., to prāṇa]; *yat aham vasiṣṭhaḥ asmi,* I am as much endowed with [the quality of] high standing; *tat tvam vasiṣṭhaḥ asi iti,* as you are endowed with [the quality of] high standing; *atha ha enam cakṣuḥ uvāca,* next the organ of vision said to him; *yat aham pratiṣṭhā asmi,* I am as much endowed with [the quality of] support; *tat tvam pratiṣṭhā asi iti,* as you are a support.

13. The organ of speech then said to the chief prāṇa, 'If I have the quality of high standing, it is because you have that quality.' Next the organ of vision said to him, 'True, I have the quality of supporting others, but I owe that quality to you.'

अथ हैनं श्रोत्रमुवाच यदहं सम्पदस्मि त्वं तत्सम्पदसीत्यथ हैनं मन उवाच यदहमायतनमस्मि त्वं तदायतनमसीति ॥ १४ ॥

Atha hainaṁ śrotramuvāca yadahaṁ sampadasmi tvaṁ tatsampadasītyatha hainaṁ mana uvāca yadahamāyatanamasmi tvaṁ tadāyatanamasīti.

Atha ha enam śrotram uvāca, next the organ of hearing said to him [i.e., to prāṇa]; *yat aham sampat asmi,* I am as much endowed with [the quality of] affluence; *tat tvam sampat asi iti,* as you are endowed with [the quality of] affluence; *atha ha enam manaḥ uvāca,* next the mind said to him; *yat aham āyatanam asmi,* I am as much endowed with [the quality of] a shelter; *tat tvam āyatanam asi iti,* as you are a shelter.

14. The organ of hearing then said to the chief prāṇa, 'If I have the quality of affluence, it is because you have that quality.' Next the mind said to him, 'True, I have the quality of being a shelter to many, but that quality is, in fact, yours.'

Tenants may go to their landlord and say many things to please him and exhibit their loyalty. Like that, the various sense organs which had earlier fought among themselves, each claiming superiority, are now, with great humility, declaring that they have nothing of their own—that whatever good qualities they have they owe to their master, the chief prāṇa.

न वै वाचो न चक्षूंषि न श्रोत्राणि न मनांसीत्याचक्षते प्राणा इत्येवाचक्षते प्राणो ह्येवैतानि सर्वाणि भवति॥ १५॥
इति प्रथमः खण्डः॥ १॥

Na vai vāco na cakṣūṁṣi na śrotrāṇi na manāṁsītyā-cakṣate prāṇā ityevācakṣate prāṇo hyevaitāni sarvāṇi bhavati. Iti prathamaḥ khaṇḍaḥ.

Na vai vācaḥ, not organs of speech; *na cakṣūṁṣi,* not eyes; *na śrotrāṇi,* not ears; *na manāṁsi,* not minds; *iti eva ācakṣate,* they say; *prāṇāḥ iti eva ācakṣate,* they say the prāṇas; *hi,* for; *prāṇaḥ bhavati,* prāṇa has become; *etāni sarvāṇi,* all these. *Iti prathamaḥ khaṇḍaḥ,* here ends the first section.

15. Scholars do not call them organs of speech, eyes, ears, or minds. They call them 'prāṇas,' for prāṇa has become all these organs.

The Self is the source of everything that exists, living or non-living. The Self manifests itself in many forms—as human beings, animals, plants, etc. And it is because of the Self that we live, speak, and act.

Human beings have two sets of organs—organs of perception and organs of action. We also have a mind. These organs are powerful, but the most powerful is the mind. Yet none of these organs is independent. Each one exists and functions only to serve the Self, the master.

The Self is within the body as well as without. Within the body it is the Ātman, which functions through prāṇa, the vital breath. As prāṇa, it animates the body and all the organs. Without prāṇa, the body with all its organs is dead, useless.

Section Two

स होवाच किं मेऽन्नं भविष्यतीति यत्किञ्चिदिदमा श्वभ्य आ शकुनिभ्य इति होचुस्तद्वा एतदनस्यान्नमनो ह वै नाम प्रत्यक्षं न ह वा एवंविदि किञ्चनानन्नं भवतीति॥ १ ॥

Sa hovāca kiṁ me'nnaṁ bhaviṣyatīti yatkiñcididamā śvabhya ā śakunibhya iti hocustadvā etadanasyānnamano ha vai nāma pratyakṣaṁ na ha vā evaṁvidi kiñcanānannaṁ bhavatīti.

Saḥ ha uvāca, he [prāṇa] asked; *kim me annam bhaviṣyati iti,* what will be my food; *iti ucuḥ ha,* [the other organs] replied; *ā-śvabhyaḥ ā-śakunibhyaḥ,* for dogs as well as birds; *yat idam kiñcit,* whatever there is; *tat vai,* all that; *etat anasya annam,* is this food for prāṇa; *anaḥ ha vai nāma pratyakṣam,* 'ana' is the name of prāṇa itself; *ha vai evam vidi,* for one who knows thus; *kiñcana na anannam bhavati iti,* nothing becomes uneatable [i.e., anything an animal can eat is food for him].

1. Prāṇa then asked, 'What will be my food?' The other organs said: 'Anything that even dogs, birds, and other animals can eat in this world is your food.' All that is food for *ana. Ana* is a name of prāṇa. For one who knows this nothing is uneatable. [That is, he can eat any food that an animal can eat.]

There is some difference between the words *prāṇa* and *ana*. *Prāṇa* has a limited meaning. It refers to something characterized by breathing. It breathes, and in order to keep breathing it needs food. It may be a specific kind of food. It may not eat every kind of food. *Ana*, however, is that which can eat any kind of food.

The Bṛhadāraṇyaka Upaniṣad (I.5.23) says, 'The sun rises and sets in prāṇa.' It also says that the person who knows the true nature of prāṇa is one from whom the sun rises and into whom it sets.

स होवाच किं मे वासो भविष्यतीत्याप इति होचुस्तस्माद्वा एतदशिष्यन्तः पुरस्ताच्चोपरिष्टाच्चाद्भिः परिदधति लम्भुको ह वासो भवत्यनग्नो ह भवति॥ २॥

Sa hovāca kiṁ me vāso bhaviṣyatītyāpa iti hocustasmādvā etadaśiṣyantaḥ purastāccopariṣṭāccādbhiḥ paridadhati lambhuko ha vāso bhavatyanagno ha bhavati.

Saḥ ha uvāca, he [prāṇa] said; *kim me vāsaḥ bhaviṣyati iti,* what will be my covering; *āpaḥ iti ha ucuḥ,* [the other organs] replied, 'Water'; *tasmāt,* that is why; *vai aśiṣyantaḥ purastāt ca,* people before eating; *upariṣṭāt ca,* and after [eating]; *etat adbhiḥ paridadhati,* cover him [prāṇa] with water [i.e., they sip water]; *lambhukaḥ ha vāsaḥ bhavati,* thereby he becomes covered with a cloth; *anagnaḥ ha bhavati,* he is no longer naked.

2. Prāṇa asked, 'What will be my covering?' The organs replied, 'Water.' This is why, before and after eating their meals, people cover him with water [i.e., they sip water]. He then becomes covered with a cloth and is no longer naked.

The water that is sipped before the meal is said to be the lower cloth, and that which is sipped afterwards is said to be the upper cloth.

तद्धैतत्सत्यकामो जाबालो गोश्रुतये वैयाघ्रपद्यायो-
क्त्वोवाच यद्यप्येतच्छुष्काय स्थाणवे ब्रूयाज्जायेरन्नेवा-
स्मिञ्छाखाः प्ररोहेयुः पलाशानीति ॥ ३ ॥

Taddhaitatsatyakāmo jābālo gośrutaye vaiyāghrapadyāyoktvovāca yadyapyetacchuṣkāya sthāṇave brūyājjāyerannevāsmiñchākhāḥ praroheyuḥ palāśānīti.

Tat ha etat, this [teaching]; *satyakāmaḥ jābālaḥ,* Satyakāma Jābāla; *gośrutaye vaiyāhrapadyāya uktva,* saying to Vyāghrapada's son Gośruti; *uvāca,* he said; *yadi api,* even if; *etat,* this [teaching]; *śuṣkāya athāṇave brūyāt,* a person gives to a dry stump; *śākhāḥ praroheyuḥ palāśān,* branches and leaves; *jāyeran eva asmin,* will grow off it.

3. Having told this to Vyāghrapada's son Gośruti, Satyakāma Jābāla said, 'If a person tells this even to a dry stump [of a tree], branches and leaves will grow off it.'

This verse is meant to praise the philosophy of prāṇa. Teaching this philosophy to Gośruti, the son of Vyāghrapada, Satyakāma said that this teaching is capable of restoring life to a dead tree. Even if there is only a dry stump of a tree, leaves and branches will begin to sprout from it on hearing this teaching. Imagine then what effect it will produce if it is taught to a living human being.

अथ यदि महज्जिगमिषेदमावास्यायां दीक्षित्वा पौर्णमास्यां रात्रौ सर्वौषधस्य मन्थं दधिमधुनोरुपमथ्य ज्येष्ठाय श्रेष्ठाय स्वाहेत्यग्नावाज्यस्य हुत्वा मन्थे सम्पातमवनयेत् ॥ ४ ॥

Atha yadi mahajjigamiṣedamāvāsyāyāṁ dīkṣitvā paurṇamāsyāṁ rātrau sarvauṣadhasya manthaṁ dadhi-madhunorupamathya jyeṣṭhāya śreṣṭhāya svāhetyagnā-vājyasya hutvā manthe sampātamavanayet.

Atha yadi, then if; *mahat jigamiṣet,* a person wants to attain greatness; *amāvāsyāyām dīkṣitvā,* having been initiated on the day of a new moon; *paurṇamāsyām rātrau,* on the night of the full moon; *sarvauṣadhyasya mantham,* a paste of various herbs; *dadhi-madhunoḥ upamathya,* [and] mixing with curd and honey; *jyeṣṭhāya śreṣṭhāya svāhā iti,* say 'Svāhā to the oldest and the best'; *agnau ājyasya hutvā,* offer this as oblations to the fire; *manthe sampātam avanayet,* put the residue from the offering spoon in the pot.

4. Then if anyone wishes to attain greatness, he should first become initiated on a new moon day, and after that, on the night of a full moon, he should prepare a paste of various herbs and mix them together with curd and honey. He should then offer this oblation to the fire saying, 'Jyeṣṭhāya śreṣṭhāya svāhā,' [i.e., Svāhā to the oldest and to the best]. Whatever is left over in the offering spoon he should put into the homa pot.

If a person wants to attain greatness, it should not be for worldly gain, but for his spiritual benefit. Here, some instructions are given concerning the sacrifices he should perform. Prior to those sacrifices, however, he should practise strict self-control for some time. This whole discipline is intended to take him to a higher world after death, but the over-all result is that he becomes a better person spiritually.

वसिष्ठाय स्वाहेत्यग्नावाज्यस्य हुत्वा मन्थे सम्पातमवनयेत्प्रतिष्ठायै स्वाहेत्यग्नावाज्यस्य हुत्वा मन्थे सम्पातमवनयेत्सम्पदे स्वाहेत्यग्नावाज्यस्य हुत्वा मन्थे सम्पातमवनयेदायतनाय स्वाहेत्यग्नावाज्यस्य हुत्वा मन्थे सम्पातमवनयेत् ॥ ५ ॥

Vasiṣṭhāya svāhetyagnāvājyasya hutvā manthe sampātamavanayetpratiṣṭhāyai svāhetyagnāvājyasya hutvā manthe sampātamavanayetsampade svāhetyagnāvājyas-

ya hutvā manthe sampātamavanayedāyatanāya svāhetyagnāvājyasya hutvā manthe sampātamavanayet.

Vasiṣṭhāya svāhā iti, saying 'Vasiṣṭhāya svāhā' [i.e., Svāhā to high standing]; *agnau ājyasya hutvā,* one should offer the oblation to the fire; *manthe sampātam avanayet,* and put whatever is left over in the offering spoon into the homa pot; *pratiṣṭhāyai svāhā iti,* saying 'Pratiṣṭhāyai svāhā' [i.e., Svāhā to the support]; *agnau ājyasya hutvā,* one should offer the oblation to the fire; *manthe sampātam avanayet,* and put whatever is left over in the offering spoon into the homa pot; *sampade svāhā iti,* saying 'Sampade svāhā' [i.e., Svāhā to affluence]; *agnau ājyasya hutvā,* one should offer the oblation to the fire; *manthe sampātam avanayet,* and put whatever is left over in the offering spoon into the homa pot; *āyatanāya svāhā iti,* saying 'Āyatanāya svāhā' [i.e., Svāhā to the abode]; *agnau ājyasya hutvā,* one should offer the oblation to the fire; *manthe sampātam avanayet,* and put whatever is left over in the offering spoon into the homa pot.

5. Saying, 'Vasiṣṭhāya svāhā' [i.e., svāhā to high standing], one should offer the oblation to the fire and then put whatever is left over in the offering spoon into the homa pot. Saying, 'Pratiṣṭhāyai svāhā' [i.e., svāhā to the support], one should offer the oblation to the fire and then put whatever is left over in the offering spoon into the homa pot. Saying, 'Sampade svāhā' [i.e., svāhā to affluence], one should offer the oblation to the fire and then put whatever

is left over in the offering spoon into the homa pot. Saying, 'Āyatanāya svāhā' [i.e., svāhā to the abode], one should offer the oblation to the fire and then put whatever is left over in the offering spoon into the homa pot.

अथ प्रतिसृप्याञ्जलौ मन्थमाधाय जपत्यमो नामास्यमा हि ते सर्वमिदं स हि ज्येष्ठः श्रेष्ठो राजाधिपतिः स मा ज्यैष्ठ्यं श्रैष्ठ्यं राज्यमाधिपत्यं गमयत्वहमेवेदं सर्वमसानीति ॥ ६ ॥

Atha pratisṛpyāñjalau manthamādhāya japatyamo nāmāsyamā hi te sarvamidaṁ sa hi jyeṣṭhaḥ śreṣṭho rājādhipatiḥ sa mā jyaiṣṭhyaṁ śraiṣṭhyaṁ rājyamādhi-patyaṁ gamayatvahamevedaṁ sarvamasānīti.

Atha, then; *pratisṛpya,* moving away [from the fire]; *añjalau mantham ādhāya,* holding the homa pot in his hands; *japati,* he keeps repeating; *amaḥ nāma asi,* you are named 'ama'; *amā hi te,* because on you [as prāṇa]; *sarvam idam,* all this [rests]; *saḥ hi jyeṣṭhaḥ śreṣṭhaḥ,* he [i.e., prāṇa, called here 'ama'] is the oldest and the best; *rājā,* princely; *adhipatiḥ,* supreme; *saḥ,* that [prāṇa]; *mā gamayatu,* make me; *jyaiṣṭhyam śraiṣṭhyam rājyam ādhipatyam,* the first, the best, outstanding, and supreme; *aham eva idam sarvam asāni iti,* may I be all this.

6. Then, moving some distance from the fire and holding the homa pot in his hands, he keeps repeating the mantra: 'You are named *ama,* because all this rests on you. You are the first, the best, outstanding, and supreme. May I also be the first, the best, outstanding, and supreme. May I be all all this.'

According to Śaṅkara, *ama* is another name for prāṇa.

The whole world rests on prāṇa. This is why prāṇa is also called *ama* (all). Prāṇa is the best and the highest. Prāṇa is this world.

अथ खल्वेतयर्चा पच्छ आचामति। तत्सवितुर्वृणीमह इत्याचामति। वयं देवस्य भोजनमित्याचामति। श्रेष्ठं सर्वधातममित्याचामति। तुरं भगस्य धीमहीति सर्वं पिबति। निर्णिज्य कंसं चमसं वा पश्चादग्नेः संविशति चर्मणि वा स्थण्डिले वा वाचंयमोऽप्रसाहः। स यदि स्त्रियं पश्येत्समृद्धं कर्मेति विद्यात्॥ ७॥

Atha khalvetayarcā paccha ācāmati; Tatsaviturvṛṇīmaha ityācāmati; Vayaṁ devasya bhojanamityācāmati; Śreṣṭhaṁ sarvadhātamamityācāmati; Turaṁ bhagasya dhīmahīti sarvaṁ pibati; Nirṇijya kaṁsaṁ camasaṁ vā paścādagneḥ saṁviśati carmaṇi vā sthaṇḍile vā vācaṁyamo'prasāhaḥ; Sa yadi striyaṁ paśyetsamṛddhaṁ karmeti vidyāt.

Atha khalu etayā ṛcā, then while [saying] this Ṛk mantra; *pacchaḥ* foot by foot; *ācāmati,* he eats a little [of what is in the homa pot]; *tat savituḥ vṛṇīmahe,* we pray for that [food] of the shining deity; *iti ācāmati,* saying this he eats a little [of what is in the homa pot]; *vayam devasya bhojanam,* we eat the food of the deity; *iti ācāmati,* saying this he eats a little [of what is in the homa pot]; *śreṣṭham sarvadhātamam,* it is the best and the support of all; *iti ācāmati,* saying this he eats a little [of what is in the homa pot]; *turam,* quickly; *bhagasya dhīmahi,* we meditate on Bhaga; *iti sarvam pibati,* saying this he drinks the rest; *nirṇijya kaṁsam,* [and] washing the vessel [i.e., the homa pot]; *vā camasam,* or spoon; *aprasāhaḥ,* with his mind under control; *vācaṁyamaḥ,* [and] his speech under control; *agneḥ paścāt,* behind the fire; *carmaṇi vā sthaṇḍile vā,* on the skin of an animal or directly on the sacrificial ground; *saṁviśati,* he sleeps; *saḥ yadi,* if he; *striyam paśyet,* sees a woman [in his dream]; *karma samṛddham,* the sacrificial rite is successful; *iti vidyāt,* he knows that.

7. Then, while saying this Ṛk mantra foot by foot, he eats some of what is in the homa pot. He says, 'We pray for that food of the shining deity,' and then eats a little of what is in the homa pot. Saying, 'We eat the food of that deity,' he eats a little of what is in the homa pot. Saying, 'It is the best and the support of all,' he eats a little of what is in the homa pot. Saying, 'We quickly meditate on Bhaga,' he eats the rest and washes the vessel or spoon. Then, with his speech and mind under

control, he lies down behind the fire, either on the skin of an animal or directly on the sacrificial ground. If he sees a woman in his dream, he knows that the rite has been successful [and that he will succeed in whatever he does].

While eating, the sacrificer should repeat the appropriate mantra. That is, he should eat a little and then repeat one foot of the Ṛk mantra; then eat a little more and repeat another foot, and so on. What is this mantra? It is a prayer to Savitā, the sun god. If you repeat this prayer with the appropriate rite, you will become as bright and pure as the sun.

तदेष श्लोको यदा कर्मसु काम्येषु स्त्रियं स्वप्नेषु पश्यति समृद्धिं तत्र जानीयात्तस्मिन्स्वप्ननिदर्शने तस्मिन्स्वप्ननिदर्शने ॥ ८ ॥ इति द्वितीयः खण्डः ॥ २ ॥

Tadeṣa śloko yadā karmasu kāmyeṣu striyaṁ svapneṣu paśyati samṛddhiṁ tatra jānīyāttasminsvapnanidarśane tasminsvapnanidarśane. Iti dvitīyaḥ khaṇḍaḥ.

Tat eṣaḥ ślokaḥ, here is a verse on the subject; *yadā,* when; *karmasu kāmyeṣu,* in a rite for fulfilling a desire; *striyam svapneṣu paśyati,* one sees a woman in a dream; *samṛddhim tatra,* there is success; *jānīyāt tasmin svapnanidarśane tasmin svapnanidarśane,* one knows from seeing this in a dream, from seeing this in a dream. *Iti dvitīyaḥ khaṇḍaḥ,* here ends the second section.

8. Here is a verse in this connection: When one sees a woman in a dream while performing a rite for the fulfillment of a desire, that means it is successful. One can know this from the dream.

Section Three

श्वेतकेतुर्हारुणेयः पञ्चालानां समितिमेयाय तं ह प्रवाहणो जैवलिरुवाच कुमारानु त्वाशिषत्पितेत्यनु हि भगव इति॥ १ ॥

Śvetaketurhāruṇeyaḥ pañcālānāṁ samitimeyāya taṁ ha pravāhaṇo jaivaliruvāca kumārānu tvāśiṣatpitetyanu hi bhagava iti.

Śvetaketuḥ āruṇeyaḥ ha, once Śvetaketu, the grandson of Aruṇa; *pañcālānām samitim eyāya,* went to the court of the Pañcālas; *tam ha,* to him; *pravāhaṇaḥ jaivaliḥ uvāca,* Pravāhaṇa, the son of Jīvala, said; *kumāra,* young man; *tvā pitā anu-aśiṣat iti,* did your father teach you; *bhagavaḥ anu hi iti,* yes, revered sir, he did.

1. Once Śvetaketu, the grandson of Aruṇa, went to the court of the Pañcālas. Pravāhaṇa, the son of Jīvala, asked him, 'Young man, did your father teach you?' [Śvetaketu replied:] 'Yes, revered sir, he did.'

Those who want liberation should have a strong spirit of renunciation, and they should know the nature of everything, from Brahmā to a blade of grass. Earlier there was a discussion on prāṇa. Now a discussion on agni, fire, begins. The story of Śvetaketu and his father is being introduced here for that purpose.

वेत्थ यदितोऽधि प्रजाः प्रयन्तीति न भगव इति। वेत्थ यथा पुनरावर्तन्त३ इति न भगव इति। वेत्थ पथोर्देवयानस्य पितृयाणस्य च व्यावर्तना३ इति न भगव इति॥ २॥

Vettha yadito'dhi prajāḥ prayantīti na bhagava iti; Vettha yathā punarāvartanta 3 iti na bhagava iti; Vettha pathordevayānasya pitṛyāṇasya ca vyāvartanā 3 iti na bhagava iti.

Vettha, do you know; *yat,* where; *itaḥ,* from this place; *adhi,* high up; *prajāḥ,* living beings; *prayanti iti,* go; *na bhagavaḥ iti,* no, revered sir, I don't; *vettha,* do you know; *yathā,* the way; *punaḥ āvartante iti,* they come back; *na bhagavaḥ iti,* no, revered sir, I don't; *vettha,* do you know; *pathoḥ,* of the two paths; *devayānasya,* the path of the gods; *pitṛyāṇasya ca,* and the path of the ancestors; *vyāvartanā iti,* where they part; *na bhagavaḥ iti,* no, revered sir, I don't.

2. [Pravāhaṇa asked,] 'Do you have any idea where, from this world, human beings go in heaven?' 'No, sir, I have no idea,' [replied Śvetaketu]. 'Do you know how they come back?' 'No, sir, I don't.' 'Have you any idea where the two paths—the path of the gods and the path of the ancestors—part?' 'No, sir, I don't know.'

The path of the gods and the path of the manes both go the same way for some distance. They separate only towards the end. Śvetaketu did not know at what point they separate, nor did he know what path those who are reborn take while coming back to the earth.

वेत्थ यथासौ लोको न सम्पूर्यत३ इति न भगव इति। वेत्थ यथा पञ्चम्यामाहुतावापः पुरुषवचसो भवन्तीति नैव भगव इति॥ ३॥

Vettha yathāsau loko na sampūryata 3 iti na bhagava iti; Vettha yathā pañcamyāmāhutāvāpaḥ puruṣavacaso bhavantīti naiva bhagava iti.

Vettha yathā, do you know why; *asau lokaḥ,* that world [i.e., the world of the moon]; *na sampūryate iti,* is not filled up; *na bhagavaḥ iti,* no, revered sir; *vettha yathā,* do you know why; *pañcamyām āhutau,* after the fifth oblation; *āpaḥ puruṣavacasaḥ bhavanti iti,* water becomes known as 'man'; *na eva bhagavaḥ iti,* no, revered sir, I don't.

3. [Pravāhaṇa asked,] 'Do you know why the other world [the world of the moon] is not filled with people?' [Śvetaketu replied,] 'No, revered sir, I don't know.' 'Do you know why after the fifth oblation water comes to be called "puruṣa" [man]?' 'No, sir, I don't know.'

अथानु किमनुशिष्टोऽवोचथा यो हीमानि न विद्यात्कथं सोऽनुशिष्टो ब्रुवीतेति। स हायस्तः पितुरर्धमेयाय तं होवाचाननुशिष्य वाव किल मा भगवानब्रवीदनु त्वाशिषमिति॥ ४॥

Athānu kimanuśiṣṭo'vocathā yo hīmāni na vidyātkathaṁ so'nuśiṣṭo bruvīteti; Sa hāyastaḥ piturardhameyāya taṁ hovācānanuśiṣya vāva kila mā bhagavānabravīdanu tvāśiṣamiti.

Atha kim anuśiṣṭaḥ anu avocathāḥ, then why did you say, 'I have been taught'; *yaḥ hi imāni na vidyāt,* for he who does not know these things; *katham saḥ anuśiṣṭaḥ bruvīta iti,* how can he say 'I have been taught'; *saḥ,* he [Śvetaketu]; *ha āyastaḥ,* was hurt; *pituḥ ardham eyāya,* went back to his father's place; *tam ha uvāca,* he said to him [i.e., to his father]; *mā ananuśiṣya vāva kila,* without really teaching me; *bhagavān,* revered sir; *abravīt tvā anu aśiṣam iti,* you said, 'I have taught you.'

4. [Pravāhaṇa said:] 'Why did you say then, "I have been taught"? How can one who does not know these things say, "I have been taught"?' Śvetaketu was hurt. He went back to his father and said, 'You have not really taught me, yet you said, "I have taught you."'

पञ्च मा राजन्यबन्धुः प्रश्नानप्राक्षीत्तेषां नैकञ्चनाशकं विवक्तुमिति स होवाच यथा मा त्वं तदैतानवदो यथाहमेषां नैकञ्चन वेद यद्यहमिमानवेदिष्यं कथं ते नावक्ष्यमिति ॥ ५ ॥

Pañca mā rājanyabandhuḥ praśnānaprākṣītteṣāṁ naikañcanāśakaṁ vivaktumiti sa hovāca yathā mā tvaṁ tadaitānavado yathāhameṣāṁ naikañcana veda yadyaha-mimānavediṣyaṁ kathaṁ te nāvakṣyamiti.

Rājanyabandhuḥ, the friend of princes; *pañca praśnān mā aprākṣīt,* asked me five questions; *teṣām na ekañcana aśakam vivaktum iti,* I was not able to answer a single one of them; *saḥ ha uvāca,* he [his father] said; *yathā mā tvam tadā,* [on your return from the court] as you were then; *etān,* all these [questions]; *avadaḥ,* you told [me]; *yathā,* so; *aham eṣām na ekañcana veda,* I do not know even one of them; *yadi aham imān avediṣyam,* if I knew them; *katham te na avakṣyam iti,* why should I not have told you?

5. [Śvetaketu said:] 'That friend of the princes put five questions to me. I was not able to answer a single one of them.' [He then told his father the five questions. After pondering over them for some time, his father] said: 'Those questions you told me about on your return from the court—I am not able to answer even one of them. If I knew the answers, why should I have not told you?'

The word *rājanyabandhuḥ,* a friend of kings or princes, is not to be taken literally. Here the word is used sarcastically. Actually, the man is a rogue.

स ह गौतमो राज्ञोऽर्धमेयाय तस्मै ह प्राप्तायार्हाञ्चकार स ह प्रातः सभाग उदेयाय तं होवाच मानुषस्य भगवन्गौतम वित्तस्य वरं वृणीथा इति। स होवाच तवैव राजन्मानुषं वित्तं यामेव कुमारस्यान्ते वाचमभाषथास्तामेव मे ब्रूहीति स ह कृच्छ्री बभूव॥ ६॥

Sa ha gautamo rājño'rdhameyāya tasmai ha prāptā-yārhāñcakāra sa ha prātaḥ sabhāga udeyāya taṁ hovāca mānuṣasya bhagavangautama vittasya varaṁ vṛṇīthā iti; Sa hovāca tavaiva rājanmānuṣaṁ vittaṁ yāmeva kumārasyānte vācamabhāṣathāstāmeva me brūhīti sa ha kṛcchrī babhūva.

Saḥ ha gautamaḥ, then Gautama; *rājñaḥ ardham eyāya,* went to the king's palace; *prāptāya,* when he arrived; *tasmai ha arhām cakāra,* the king respectfully welcomed him; *saḥ,* he [Gautama]; *ha prātaḥ,* the next morning; *sabhāge udeyāya,* went to see the king in the court; *tam ha uvāca,* he [the king] said to him [Gautama]; *bhagavan gautama,* revered Gautama; *mānuṣasya vittasya varam vṛṇīthāḥ iti,* ask for any precious thing a person may wish for as a boon; *saḥ ha uvāca,* he [Gautama] said; *rājan,* O king; *tava eva mānuṣam vittam,* let the human wealth be yours; *yām eva kumārasya ante vācam abhāṣathāḥ,* that which you said to my son; *tām eva,* the same; *me brūhi iti,* tell me; *saḥ ha kṛcchrī babhūva,* he [the king] was very depressed.

6. Gautama then went to the king's palace. On his arrival, the king welcomed him respectfully. The next morning, when the king was in his court, Gautama went there to meet him. The king said to him, 'Revered Gautama, ask for a boon from me—anything a person might wish for.' Gautama replied: 'Let those things be with you. Please tell me whatever you said to my son.' Hearing this, the king turned pale.

It was against the custom for a kṣatriya, a king, to teach a brāhmin. This is why the king became depressed.

तं ह चिरं वसेत्याज्ञापयाञ्चकार तं होवाच यथा मा त्वं गौतमावदो यथेयं न प्राक्त्वत्तः पुरा विद्या

ब्राह्मणान्गच्छति तस्मादु सर्वेषु लोकेषु क्षत्रस्यैव प्रशासनमभूदिति तस्मै होवाच ॥ ७ ॥ इति तृतीयः खण्डः ॥ ३ ॥

Taṁ ha ciraṁ vasetyājñāpayāñcakāra taṁ hovāca yathā mā tvaṁ gautamāvado yatheyaṁ na prāktvattaḥ purā vidyā brāhmaṇāngacchati tasmādu sarveṣu lokeṣu kṣatrasyaiva praśāsanamabhūditi tasmai hovāca. Iti tṛtīyaḥ khaṇḍaḥ.

Tam, to him [to Gautama]; *ciram vasa ha iti,* stay for a long time; *ājñāpayāñcakāra,* he issued orders; *tam ha uvāca,* he said to him [to Gautama]; *gautama,* O Gautama; *yathā mā tvam āvadaḥ,* as you said to me; *yathā iyam vidyā,* because this knowledge; *prāk tvattaḥ,* before you; *brāhmaṇān na gacchati,* did not go to the brāhmins; *purā,* in the past; *tasmāt u,* that is why; *sarveṣu lokeṣu,* in all the worlds; *kṣatrasya eva praśāsanam abhūt iti,* only kṣatriyas had the right to teach it; *tasmai ha uvāca,* he said to him. *Iti tṛtīyaḥ khaṇḍaḥ,* here ends the third section.

7. The king then issued orders that Gautama should stay with him for a long time [as a brahmacari. Gautama did that. One day] the king said to him: 'O Gautama, regarding the matter which you asked about, no brāhmin before you had access to this knowledge. This is why in the past, in all the worlds, it was only the kṣatriyas who had the right to impart this knowledge.' Having said this, he proceeded to teach Gautama.

Section Four

असौ वाव लोको गौतमाग्निस्तस्यादित्य एव समिद्रश्मयो धूमोऽहरर्चिश्चन्द्रमा अङ्गारा नक्षत्राणि विस्फुलिङ्गाः ॥ १ ॥

Asau vāva loko gautamāgnistasyāditya eva samid-raśmayo dhūmo'hararciścandramā aṅgārā nakṣatrāṇi visphuliṅgāḥ.

Gautama, O Gautama; *asau vāva lokaḥ agniḥ,* that world there [i.e., heaven] is the fire; *ādityaḥ eva tasya samit,* the sun is its fuel; *raśmayaḥ dhūmaḥ,* the rays are the smoke; *ahaḥ arciḥ,* the day is the flame; *candramāḥ aṅgārāḥ,* the moon is the embers; *nakṣatrāṇi visphuliṅgāḥ,* the stars are the sparks.

1. O Gautama, heaven is the [sacrificial] fire; the sun is its fuel; the rays are the smoke; day is the flame; the moon is the embers; and the stars are the sparks.

तस्मिन्नेतस्मिन्नग्नौ देवाः श्रद्धां जुह्वति तस्या आहुतेः सोमो राजा सम्भवति ॥ २ ॥ इति चतुर्थः खण्डः ॥ ४ ॥

Tasminnetasminnagnau devāḥ śraddhāṁ juhvati tasyā āhuteḥ somo rājā sambhavati. Iti caturthaḥ khaṇḍaḥ.

Tasmin etasmin agnau, in that fire [which is also heaven]; *devāḥ,* the gods [i.e., the organs of the sacrificer]; *śraddhām juhvati,* offer faith [as water] as the oblation; *tasyāḥ āhuteḥ,* out of that oblation; *rājā somaḥ,* King Soma [i.e., the shining moon]; *sambhavati,* appears. *Iti caturthaḥ khaṇḍaḥ,* here ends the fourth section.

2. The gods [i.e., the organs of the sacrificer] offer water as a token of respect to the fire [heaven]. Out of that oblation appears King Soma [the shining moon].

Section Five

पर्जन्यो वाव गौतमाग्निस्तस्य वायुरेव समिदभ्रं धूमो विद्युदर्चिरशनिरङ्गारा ह्रादनयो विस्फुलिङ्गाः ॥ १ ॥

Parjanyo vāva gautamāgnistasya vāyureva samidabhraṁ dhūmo vidyudarciraśaniraṅgārā hrādanayo visphuliṅgāḥ.

Gautama, O Gautama; *parjanyaḥ vāva agniḥ,* the god of rain is the fire; *vāyuḥ eva tasya samit,* air is its fuel; *abhram dhūmaḥ,* the cloud is the smoke; *vidyut arciḥ,* lightning is the flame; *aśaniḥ aṅgārāḥ,* the thunderbolt is the embers; *hrādanayaḥ visphuliṅgāḥ,* thunder is the sparks.

1. O Gautama, the god of rain is the [sacrificial] fire; air is its fuel; the cloud is the smoke; lightning is the flame; the thunderbolt is the embers; and thunder is the sparks.

तस्मिन्नेतस्मिन्नग्नौ देवाः सोमं राजानं जुह्वति तस्या आहुतेर्वर्षं सम्भवति ॥ २ ॥ इति पञ्चमः खण्डः ॥ ५ ॥

Tasminnetasminnagnau devāḥ somaṁ rājānaṁ juhvati tasyā āhutervarṣaṁ sambhavati. Iti pañcamaḥ khaṇḍaḥ.

Tasmin etasmin agnau, in that fire; *devāḥ,* the gods; *somam rājānam juhvati,* offer King Soma [the shining moon] as the oblation; *tasyāḥ āhuteḥ,* out of that oblation; *varṣam,* rain; *sambhavati,* appears. *Iti pañcamaḥ khaṇḍaḥ,* here ends the fifth section.

2. The gods offer King Soma [the shining moon] as the oblation to the fire. Out of that oblation appears rain.

Section Six

पृथिवी वाव गौतमाग्निस्तस्याः संवत्सर एव समिदाकाशो धूमो रात्रिरर्चिर्दिशोऽङ्गारा अवान्तरदिशो विस्फुलिङ्गाः ॥ १ ॥

Pṛthivī vāva gautamāgnistasyāḥ saṁvatsara eva samidākāśo dhūmo rātrirarcirdiśo'ṅgārā avāntaradiśo visphuliṅgāḥ.

Gautama, O Gautama; *pṛthivī vāva agniḥ,* earth is the fire; *saṁvatsaraḥ eva tasyāḥ samit,* the year is its fuel; *ākāśaḥ dhūmaḥ,* the sky is the smoke; *rātriḥ arciḥ,* night is the flame; *diśaḥ aṅgārāḥ,* the quarters are the embers; *avāntaradiśaḥ visphuliṅgāḥ,* the intermediate directions are the sparks.

1. O Gautama, the earth is the [sacrificial] fire; the year is its fuel; the sky is the smoke; night is the flame; the quarters are the embers; and the intermediate directions are the sparks.

तस्मिन्नेतस्मिन्नग्नौ देवा वर्षं जुह्वति तस्या आहुतेरन्नं सम्भवति॥ २॥ इति षष्ठः खण्डः॥ ६॥

Tasminnetasminnagnau devā varṣaṁ juhvati tasyā āhuterannaṁ sambhavati. Iti ṣaṣṭhaḥ khaṇḍaḥ.

Tasmin etasmin agnau, in that fire; *devāḥ,* the gods; *varṣam juhvati,* offer rain as the oblation; *tasyāḥ āhuteḥ,* out of that oblation; *annam,* food; *sambhavati,* appears. *Iti ṣaṣṭhaḥ khaṇḍaḥ,* here ends the sixth section.

2. The gods offer rain as the oblation to the fire. Out of that oblation appears food.

Section Seven

पुरुषो वाव गौतमाग्निस्तस्य वागेव समित्प्राणो धूमो जिह्वार्चिश्चक्षुरङ्गाराः श्रोत्रं विस्फुलिङ्गाः ॥ १ ॥

Puruṣo vāva gautamāgnistasya vāgeva samitprāṇo dhūmo jihvārciścakṣuraṅgārāḥ śrotraṁ visphuliṅgāḥ.

Gautama, O Gautama; *puruṣaḥ vāva agniḥ,* man is the fire; *vāk eva tasya samit,* speech is his fuel; *prāṇaḥ dhūmaḥ,* prāṇa is the smoke; *jihvā arciḥ,* the tongue is the flame; *cakṣuḥ aṅgārāḥ,* the eyes are the embers; *śrotram visphuliṅgāḥ,* the ears are the sparks.

1. O Gautama, man is the [sacrificial] fire; speech is his fuel; prāṇa is the smoke; the tongue is the flame; the eyes are the embers; and the ears are the sparks.

Speech is said to be the fuel because it is the source of strength. A person who cannot speak is helpless. Prāṇa is the smoke because the breath comes out of the mouth just as smoke comes out of fire. The tongue is the flame because both are red. The eyes are the embers because both appear to be shining. And the ears are the sparks because both spread out and cover a large area.

तस्मिन्नेतस्मिन्नग्नौ देवा अन्नं जुह्वति तस्या आहुते रेतः सम्भवति॥ २॥ इति सप्तमः खण्डः॥ ७॥

Tasminnetasminnagnau devā annaṁ juhvati tasyā āhute retaḥ sambhavati. Iti saptamaḥ khaṇḍaḥ.

Tasmin etasmin agnau, in that fire; *devāḥ,* the gods; *annam juhvati,* offer food as the oblation; *tasyāḥ āhuteḥ,* out of that oblation; *retaḥ,* semen; *sambhavati,* appears. *Iti saptamaḥ khaṇḍaḥ,* here ends the seventh section.

2. The gods offer food as the oblation to the fire. Out of that oblation appears semen.

Section Eight

योषा वाव गौतमाग्निस्तस्या उपस्थ एव समिद्य-दुपमन्त्रयते स धूमो योनिरर्चिर्यदन्तःकरोति तेऽङ्गारा अभिनन्दा विस्फुलिङ्गाः॥ १॥

तस्मिन्नेतस्मिन्नग्नौ देवा रेतो जुह्वति तस्या आहुतेर्गर्भः सम्भवति॥ २॥ इत्यष्टमः खण्डः॥ ८॥

Yoṣā vāva gautamāgnistasyā upastha eva samidyadupamantrayate sa dhūmo yonirarciryadantaḥkaroti te-'ṅgārā abhinandā visphuliṅgāḥ

Tasminnetasminnagnau devā reto juhvati tasyā āhutergarbhaḥ sambhavati. Ityaṣṭamaḥ khaṇḍaḥ.

1-2. O Gautama, woman is the [sacrificial] fire. . . The gods offer semen as the oblation to the fire. Out of that oblation appears the foetus.

Section Nine

इति तु पञ्चम्यामाहुतावापः पुरुषवचसो भवन्तीति स उल्बावृतो गर्भो दश वा नव वा मासानन्तः शयित्वा यावद्वाथ जायते॥ १ ॥

Iti tu pañcamyāmāhutāvāpaḥ puruṣavacaso bhavantīti sa ulbāvṛto garbho daśa vā nava vā māsānantaḥ śayitvā yāvadvātha jāyate.

Iti tu, thus [the fifth question has been answered]; *pañcamyām āhutau,* after the fifth oblation; *āpaḥ,* water; *puruṣavacasaḥ bhavanti iti,* becomes known as 'man'; *ulbāvṛtaḥ,* covered with membrane; *saḥ garbhaḥ,* that foetus; *daśa vā nava vā māsān,* for nine or ten months; *yāvat vā,* or so; *antaḥ śayitvā,* lying inside [the mother's womb]; *atha jāyate,* is then born.

1. Thus, after the fifth oblation, water becomes known as 'man.' The foetus lies within the mother's womb, covered with membrane, for about nine or ten months, and then it is born.

If all five oblations have been offered, then the water of the first oblation becomes a puruṣa, a human being. It lies in its mother's womb for nine or ten months and is then born as a child. This is the answer to the last of the five questions that Pravāhaṇa asked Śvetaketu. By answering the last question first, he could answer the others more easily.

स जातो यावदायुषं जीवति तं प्रेतं दिष्टमितोऽग्नय एव हरन्ति यत एवेतो यतः सम्भूतो भवति ॥ २ ॥ इति नवमः खण्डः ॥ ९ ॥

Sa jāto yāvadāyuṣaṁ jīvati taṁ pretaṁ diṣṭamito'gna-ya eva haranti yata eveto yataḥ sambhūto bhavati. Iti navamaḥ khaṇḍaḥ.

Saḥ jātaḥ, [when] he is born; *yāvat-āyuṣam jīvati,* he lives as long as he is destined; *diṣṭaṁ pretam,* dying as ordained; *itaḥ,* from here [his home]; *tam agnaye eva haranti,* they take him to the fire; *yataḥ eva itaḥ,* from which he came here; *yataḥ sambhūtaḥ bhavati,* that from which he was born. *Iti navamaḥ khaṇḍaḥ,* here ends the ninth section.

2. When a person is born, he lives as long as he is destined to live. Then, when he dies as ordained, they [his sons or disciples] take him from his home to the fire from which he came. It is that same fire from which he was born [and to which he owes his birth].

From each oblation, something is born that is offered as the next oblation in the fire. The last thing born is a human being. This is why it is said that a human being is born of fire. In the end, when that person dies, his body also is offered in that same fire.

Section Ten

तद्य इत्थं विदुः। ये चेमेऽरण्ये श्रद्धा तप इत्युपासते तेऽर्चिषमभिसम्भवन्त्यर्चिषोऽहरह्न आपूर्यमाणपक्षमापूर्य-माणपक्षाद्यान्षड्उदङ्ङेति मासांस्तान्॥ १॥

मासेभ्यः संवत्सरं संवत्सरादादित्यमादित्याच्चन्द्रमसं चन्द्रमसो विद्युतं तत्पुरुषोऽमानवः स एनान्ब्रह्म गमयत्येष देवयानः पन्था इति॥ २॥

Tadya itthaṁ viduḥ; Ye ceme'raṇye śraddhā tapa ityupāsate te'rciṣamabhisambhavantyarciṣo'harahna āpūryamāṇapakṣamāpūryamāṇapakṣādyānṣaḍudaṅṅeti māsāṁstān.

Māsebhyaḥ saṁvatsaraṁ saṁvatsarādādityamādityāccandramasaṁ candramaso vidyutaṁ tatpuruṣo'mānavaḥ sa enānbrahma gamayatyeṣa devayānaḥ panthā iti.

Tat ye viduḥ, those who know this [i.e., about the five fires]; *ittham,* thus; *ye ca ime,* and these people who; *araṇye,* in the forest; *śraddhā tapaḥ iti upāsate,* practise austerities with faith; *te arciṣam abhisambhavanti,* they become [attain] light; *arciṣaḥ,* from light; *ahaḥ,* to the day; *ahnaḥ,* from the day; *āpūryamāṇapakṣam,* to the bright fortnight; *āpūryamāṇapakṣāt,* from the bright fortnight; *yān ṣaṭ māsān,* to the six months; *udan eti,* [when the sun] moves to the north; *tān,* to that; *māsebhyaḥ,* from those months; *saṁvatsaram,* to the year; *saṁvatsarāt,* from the year; *ādityam,* to the sun; *ādityāt,* from the sun; *candramasam,* to the moon; *candramasaḥ,* from the moon; *vidyutam,* to lightning; *tat,* there; *puruṣaḥ,* a person [existing there]; *amānavaḥ,* not human; *enān,* those [human beings]; *saḥ gamayati,* leads; *brahma,* to brahmaloka; *eṣaḥ devayānaḥ panthāḥ iti,* this is the path of the gods

1-2. Those who know this [about the five fires], and those who live in the forest practising austerities with faith—they go after death to the world of light. From the world of light they go to the world of day; from the world of day to the world of the bright fortnight; from the world of the bright fortnight to the six months when the sun moves northward; from there they go to the year; from the year to the sun; from the sun to the moon; and from the moon to lightning. There someone, not human, receives them and leads them to brahmaloka. This is the path of the gods.

अथ य इमे ग्राम इष्टापूर्ते दत्तमित्युपासते ते धूममभिसम्भवन्ति धूमाद्रात्रिं रात्रेरपरपक्षमपरपक्षाद्यान् षड्दक्षिणैति मासांस्तान्नैते संवत्सरमभिप्राप्नुवन्ति ॥ ३ ॥

Atha ya ime grāma iṣṭāpūrte dattamityupāsate te dhūmamabhisambhavanti dhūmādrātriṁ rātreraparapakṣamaparapakṣādyān ṣaḍdakṣiṇaiti māsāṁstānnaite saṁvatsaramabhiprāpnuvanti.

Atha, then; *ye ime,* these who; *grāme,* live in the village; *iṣṭāpūrte dattam iti upāsate,* perform works of public service and give in charity, and so on; *te,* they; *dhūmam abhisambhavanti,* go to the world of smoke; *dhūmāt rātrim,* from the world of smoke to the world of night; *rātreḥ aparapakṣam,* from the world of night to the world of the dark fortnight; *aparapakṣāt yān ṣaḍ māsān tān,* from the world of the dark fortnight to the world of the six months when; *dakṣiṇa eti,* [the sun] moves to the south; *ete,* they; *saṁvatsaram abhiprāpnuvanti,* never attain the world of the year.

3. On the other hand, those who live in the village and perform acts of public service, charity, and so on, attain the world of smoke. From there they go to the world of the night; from night they go to the world of the dark fortnight; and from the dark fortnight they go to the world of the six months when the sun moves to the south. This means that they never attain the world of the year.

Here, 'smoke,' 'night,' and so on mean the presiding deities of those realms. This is how ordinary human beings are raised to divine realms through good work.

मासेभ्यः पितृलोकं पितृलोकादाकाशमाकाशाच्चन्द्रम-
समेष सोमो राजा तद्देवानामन्नं तं देवा भक्षयन्ति॥ ४॥

Māsebhyaḥ pitṛlokaṁ pitṛlokādākāśamākāśāccandramasameṣa somo rājā taddevānāmannaṁ taṁ devā bhakṣayanti.

Māsebhyaḥ, from the months [of the southern solstice]; *pitṛlokam,* [they go] to the world of the ancestors; *pitṛlokāt ākāśam,* from the world of the ancestors to the sky; *ākāśāt candramasam,* from the sky to the world of the moon; *eṣaḥ somaḥ rājā,* this is King Soma [the shining moon]; *tat,* that; *devānām annam,* is the food of the gods [i.e., Indra and others]; *tam devāḥ bhakṣayanti,* the gods eat that [food].

4. From the six months of the southern solstice, they go to the world of the ancestors, and from there they go to the sky. Then from the sky they go to the moon. This is King Soma. This is the food of the gods. The gods enjoy eating this food.

तस्मिन्यावत्सम्पातमुषित्वाथैतमेवाध्वानं पुनर्निवर्तन्ते यथेतमाकाशमाकाशाद्वायुं वायुर्भूत्वा धूमो भवति धूमो भूत्वाभ्रं भवति॥ ५॥

Tasminyāvatsampātamuṣitvāthaitamevādhvānaṁ punarnivartante yathetamākāśamākāśādvāyuṁ vāyurbhūtvā dhūmo bhavati dhūmo bhūtvābhraṁ bhavati.

Tasmin, in that [world of the moon]; *yāvat sampātam,* until the fruits of their work are exhausted; *uṣitvā,* living; *atha,* thereafter; *etam eva punaḥ nivartante,* they return again to this [world]; *adhvānam,* along this path; *yathā itam,* as one came; *ākāśam,* to the sky; *ākāśāt vāyum,* from the sky to the air; *vāyuḥ bhūtvā dhūmaḥ bhavati,* having become air he becomes smoke; *dhūmaḥ bhūtvā,* having become smoke; *abhram bhavati,* he becomes mist.

5. Living in the world of the moon until the fruits of his work are exhausted, he then goes back to this world along the path he came. First going to the sky, he then goes to air. Having become air, he next becomes smoke. Having become smoke, he then becomes mist.

अभ्रं भूत्वा मेघो भवति मेघो भूत्वा प्रवर्षति त इह व्रीहियवा ओषधिवनस्पतयस्तिलमाषा इति

जायन्तेऽतो वै खलु दुर्निष्प्रपतरं यो यो ह्यन्नमत्ति यो रेतः सिञ्चति तद्भूय एव भवति ॥ ६ ॥

Abhraṁ bhūtvā megho bhavati megho bhūtvā pravarṣati ta iha vrīhiyavā oṣadhivanaspatayastilamāṣā iti jāyante'to vai khalu durniṣprapataraṁ yo yo hyannamatti yo retaḥ siñcati tadbhūya eva bhavati.

Abhram bhūtvā meghaḥ bhavati, having become mist, it becomes a cloud; *meghaḥ bhūtvā pravarṣati,* having become a cloud, it comes down as rain; *te,* they; *iha,* in this world; *vrīhi-yavāḥ,* paddy and barley; *oṣadhi-vanaspatayaḥ,* plants and trees; *tila-māṣaḥ iti,* sesame, beans, and so forth; *jāyante,* this is how they are born; *ataḥ,* from this [state]; *vai khalu,* for sure; *durniṣprapataram,* the way is difficult; *yaḥ yaḥ,* whoever [humans or animals]; *hi annam atti,* eats this food; *yaḥ retaḥ siñcati,* as it procreates; *tat bhūyaḥ eva bhavati,* he becomes like that [its parents].

6. Having become mist, it changes into clouds. Then from clouds, it becomes rain and falls to the earth. Finally it grows as paddy, barley, plants, trees, sesame, beans, and so forth. The change from this state is very difficult. Those who eat these things produce children just like themselves.

Here Śaṅkara explains that a person does not become the mist or cloud or paddy, etc. He merely becomes associated with these things as a person is associated with a vehicle he is riding on.

Śaṅkara also says that when a person ascends to the higher worlds, he does so in full consciousness. But when he descends, to return to this earth, he is like a person who falls from a tree and immedately becomes unconscious. His friends come and pick him up and carry him to his home without his ever being aware of it. Similarly, a person who descends from the lunar world is never aware of how he returns to the earth.

तद्य इह रमणीयचरणा अभ्याशो ह यत्ते रमणीयां योनिमापद्येरन्ब्राह्मणयोनिं वा क्षत्रिययोनिं वा वैश्ययोनिं वाथ य इह कपूयचरणा अभ्याशो ह यत्ते कपूयां योनिमापद्येरञ्श्वयोनिं वा सूकरयोनिं वा चण्डालयोनिं वा॥ ७॥

Tadya iha ramaṇīyacaraṇā abhyāśo ha yatte ramaṇīyāṁ yonimāpadyeranbrāhmaṇayoniṁ vā kṣatriyayoniṁ vā vaiśyayoniṁ vātha ya iha kapūyacaraṇā abhyāśo ha yatte kapūyāṁ yonimāpadyerañśvayoniṁ vā sūkarayoniṁ vā caṇḍālayoniṁ vā.

Tat, among them; *ye,* those who; *iha,* in this world; *ramaṇīyacaraṇāḥ,* did good work; *abhyāśaḥ ha yat,* like that; *te,* they; *ramaṇīyām yonim,* a good birth; *āpadyeran,* get; *brāhmaṇa yonim vā,* a birth as a brāhmin; *kṣatriya yonim vā,* or a birth as a kṣatriya; *vaiśya yonim vā,* or a birth as a vaiśya; *atha,* but;

ye iha kapūyacaraṇāḥ, those who did bad work here in this world; *abhyāśaḥ ha yat,* like that; *te,* they; *kapūyām yonim āpadyeran,* get a bad birth; *śva yonim vā,* a birth as a dog; *sūkara yonim vā,* or a birth as a pig; *caṇḍāla yonim vā,* or a birth as a casteless person.

7. Among them, those who did good work in this world [in their past life] attain a good birth accordingly. They are born as a brāhmin, a kṣatriya, or a vaiśya. But those who did bad work in this world [in their past life] attain a bad birth accordingly, being born as a dog, a pig, or as a casteless person.

अथैतयोः पथोर्न कतरेण च न तानीमानि क्षुद्राण्य-
सकृदावर्तीनि भूतानि भवन्ति जायस्व म्रियस्वेत्येतत्तृतीयं
स्थानं तेनासौ लोको न सम्पूर्यते तस्माज्जुगुप्सेत तदेष
श्लोकः ॥ ८ ॥

Athaitayoḥ pathorna katareṇa ca na tānīmāni kṣudrāṇyasakṛdāvartīni bhūtāni bhavanti jāyasva mriyasvetyetattṛtīyaṁ sthānaṁ tenāsau loko na sampūryate tasmājjugupseta tadeṣa ślokaḥ.

Atha, then; *etayoḥ pathoḥ,* of these two paths [the path of light (i.e., the path of the gods) or the path of smoke (i.e., the path of the ancestors)]; *na katareṇa ca na,* not by either; *tāni imāni,* all these; *kṣudrāṇi bhūtāni,* small beings [i.e., animals and insects, etc.]; *asakṛt āvartīni,* which are born again and again; *jāyasva mriyasva iti,* 'be born and die'; *etat tṛtīyaṁ sthānum,* this is the third position [which is neither of the two previous paths]; *tena,* this is why; *asau lokaḥ,* that world; *na sampūryate,* is not filled up [with people]; *tasmāt,* therefore; *jugupseta,* one should despise it; *tat eṣaḥ ślokaḥ,* here is a verse on the subject.

8. But those who do not follow either of these two paths are born among small animals and insects again and again. [This can be said about those who are born in] this third state: 'Be born and die.' This is why the other world does not get filled up. Therefore one should despise this state. Here is a verse on the subject—

Those born in this state are so short-lived that no sooner are they born than they die, as if life has no other purpose for them.

This completes the answers to the five questions.

स्तेनो हिरण्यस्य सुरां पिबंश्च गुरोस्तल्पमावसन्ब्रह्महा
चैते पतन्ति चत्वारः पञ्चमश्चाचरंस्तैरिति ॥ ९ ॥

Steno hiraṇyasya surāṁ pibaṁśca gurostalpamāvasanbrahmahā caite patanti catvāraḥ pañcamaścācaraṁstairiti.

Stenaḥ, a thief; *hiraṇyasya,* of gold; *surām piban ca,* and one who drinks liquor; *guroḥ talpam āvasan,* uses his teacher's bed [i.e., goes to bed with his teacher's wife]; *brahmahā ca,* and a murderer of a brāhmin; *ete,* these; *catvāraḥ,* four; *patanti,* are lost; *pañcamaḥ ca,* and the fifth; *ācaran taiḥ iti,* is one who mixes with them.

9. A person who steals gold, or drinks liquor, or goes to bed with his teacher's wife, or kills a brāhmin—these four are lost. Also lost is the fifth—one who keeps company with such people.

अथ ह य एतानेवं पञ्चाग्नीन्वेद न सह तैरप्याचरन्पाप्मना लिप्यते शुद्धः पूतः पुण्यलोको भवति य एवं वेद य एवं वेद॥ १०॥ इति दशमः खण्डः॥ १०॥

Atha ha ya etānevaṁ pañcāgnīnveda na saha tairapyācaranpāpmanā lipyate śuddhaḥ pūtaḥ puṇyaloko bhavati ya evaṁ veda ya evaṁ veda. Iti daśamaḥ khaṇḍaḥ.

Atha ha, but; *yaḥ,* he who; *evam,* thus; *etān pañcāgnīn veda,* knows these five fires; *pāpmanā na lipyate,* is not tainted with sin; *saha taiḥ api,* even with them [the previous five people]; *ācaran,* he mixes; *śuddhaḥ,* pure; *pūtaḥ,* innocent; *puṇyalokaḥ,* an inhabitant of a holy world; *bhavati,* he becomes; *yaḥ evam veda yaḥ evam veda,* he who knows thus, he who knows thus. *Iti daśamaḥ khaṇḍaḥ,* here ends the tenth section.

10. But he who knows the five fires remains pure even if he is in the company of these people. He who knows this is pure and innocent, and after death he goes to a holy world.

Section Eleven

प्राचीनशाल औपमन्यवः सत्ययज्ञः पौलुषिरिन्द्रद्युम्नो भाल्लवेयो जनः शार्कराक्ष्यो बुडिल आश्वतराश्विस्ते हैते महाशाला महाश्रोत्रियाः समेत्य मीमांसां चक्रुः को न आत्मा किं ब्रह्मेति॥ १ ॥

Prācīnaśāla aupamanyavaḥ satyayajñaḥ pauluṣirindradyumno bhāllaveyo janaḥ śārkarākṣyo buḍila āśvatarāśviste haite mahāśālā mahāśrotriyāḥ sametya mīmāṁsāṁ cakruḥ ko na ātmā kiṁ brahmeti.

Prācīnaśālaḥ aupamanyavaḥ, Upamanyu's son, Prācīnaśāla; *satyayajñaḥ pauluṣiḥ,* Puluṣa's son, Satyayajña; *indradyumnaḥ bhāllaveyaḥ,* Bhāllavi's son, Indradyumna; *janaḥ śārkarākṣyaḥ,* Śarkarākṣa's son, Jana; *buḍilaḥ āśvatarāśviḥ,* Aśvatarāśva's son, Buḍila; *te ha ete,* these; *mahāśālā,* eminent householders; *mahāśrotriyāḥ,* well read in the Vedas; *sametya,* got together; *mīmāṁsām cakruḥ,* to decide the issue; *kaḥ,* who; *naḥ ātmā,* is our Self; *kim brahma iti,* what is Brahman?

1. Upamanyu's son, Prācīnaśāla; Puluṣa's son, Satyayajña; Bhāllavi's son, Indradyumna; Śarkarākṣa's son, Jana; and Aśvatarāśva's son, Buḍila—these eminent householders, who were Vedic scholars, once met to decide the issue: Who is our Self? And what is Brahman?

ते ह सम्पादयाञ्चक्रुरुद्दालको वै भगवन्तोऽयमारुणिः सम्प्रतीममात्मानं वैश्वानरमध्येति तं हन्ताभ्यागच्छामेति तं हाभ्याजग्मुः ॥ २ ॥

Te ha sampādayāñcakruruddālako vai bhagavanto'yamāruṇiḥ sampratīmamātmānaṁ vaiśvānaramadhyeti taṁ hantābhyāgacchāmeti taṁ hābhyājagmuḥ.

Te ha, they; *sampādayān cakruḥ,* decided about the matter; *bhagavantaḥ,* [one of them said to the others:] revered sirs; *ayam,* this; *uddālakaḥ āruṇiḥ,* Uddālaka, the son of Aruṇa; *samprati,* at the moment; *imam ātmānam vaiśvānaram adhyeti,* knows about the Vaiśvānara Self; *tam,* to him; *hanta abhyāgacchāma iti,* then let us go; *tam ha abhyājagmuḥ,* they all went to him.

2. They talked among themselves and decided what to do. One of them said: 'Revered sirs, Uddālaka Āruṇi is the person who now knows about this Vaiśvānara Self. Let us go to him then.' So they all went to him.

The word *vaiśvānara* has three meanings: (a) he who is within all; (b) he who leads all; and (c) the friend of all.

स ह सम्पादयाञ्चकार प्रक्ष्यन्ति मामिमे महाशाला महाश्रोत्रियास्तेभ्यो न सर्वमिव प्रतिपत्स्ये हन्ताहमन्यमभ्यनुशासानीति ॥ ३ ॥

Sa ha sampādayāñcakāra prakṣyanti māmime mahāśālā mahāśrotriyāstebhyo na sarvamiva pratipatsye hantāhamanyamabhyanuśāsānīti.

Saḥ, he [Uddālaka]; *ha sampādayāñcakāra,* decided; *ime mahāśālāḥ,* these eminent householders; *mahāśrotriyāḥ,* and Vedic scholars; *mām prakṣyanti,* will ask me questions; *tebhyaḥ,* to them; *sarvam iva na pratipatsye,* I will not be able to answer everything; *hanta aham anyam abhyanuśāsāni iti,* therefore I will direct them to another [teacher].

3. [Uddālaka understood that they had come to ask him about the Vaiśvānara Ātman.] He decided: 'These eminent householders and Vedic scholars will ask me questions, and I may not be able to answer all of them. Therefore I will direct them to another teacher.'

तान्होवाचाश्वपतिर्वै भगवन्तोऽयं कैकेयः सम्प्रतीममात्मानं वैश्वानरमध्येति तं हन्ताभ्यागच्छामेति तं हाभ्याजग्मुः ॥ ४ ॥

Tānhovācāśvapatirvai bhagavanto'yaṁ kaikeyaḥ sampratīmamātmānaṁ vaiśvānaramadhyeti taṁ hantābhyāgacchāmeti taṁ hābhyājagmuḥ.

Tān, to them [the Vedic scholars]; *ha uvāca,* he said; *bhagavantaḥ,* O sirs; *samprati,* at the present time; *ayam kaikeyaḥ,* this son of Kekaya; *aśvapatiḥ,* Aśvapati; *imam,* this; *vaiśvānaram ātmānam,* Vaiśvānara Self [the Self that is in the heart of everyone]; *adhyeti,* knows; *tam hanta abhyāgacchāma iti,* if you permit, we will go to him; *tam ha abhyājagmuḥ,* they went to him.

4. Uddālaka told them: 'Sirs, at the present time King Aśvapati, the son of Kekaya, alone knows about the Vaiśvānara Ātman. With your permission, we will go to him.' They then left to see Aśvapati.

तेभ्यो ह प्राप्तेभ्यः पृथगर्हाणि कारयाञ्चकार स ह प्रातः सञ्जिहान उवाच न मे स्तेनो जनपदे न कदर्यो न मद्यपो नानाहिताग्निर्नाविद्वान्न स्वैरी स्वैरिणी कुतो यक्ष्यमाणो वै भगवन्तोऽहमस्मि यावदेकैकस्मा ऋत्विजे

धनं दास्यामि तावद्भगवद्भ्यो दास्यामि वसन्तु भगवन्त इति॥ ५ ॥

Tebhyo ha prāptebhyaḥ pṛthagarhāṇi kārayāñcakāra sa ha prātaḥ sañjihāna uvāca na me steno janapade na kadaryo na madyapo nānāhitāgnirnāvidvānna svairī svairiṇī kuto yakṣyamāṇo vai bhagavanto'hamasmi yāvadekaikasmā ṛtvije dhanaṁ dāsyāmi tāvadbhagavadbhyo dāsyāmi vasantu bhagavanta iti.

Tebhyaḥ ha prāptebhyaḥ, when they arrived; *pṛthak arjāṇikārayāñcakāra,* he had each one of them worshipped; *prātaḥ,* the next morning; *sañjihānaḥ,* getting up from bed; *saḥ ha uvāca,* he said; *na me stenaḥ janapade,* there is no thief in my kingdom; *na kadaryaḥ,* no miserly person; *na madyapaḥ,* no drunkard; *na anāhitāgniḥ,* no brāhmin who does not perform the agnihotra sacrifice; *na avidvān,* no one who is uneducated; *na svairī,* no adulterer; *kutaḥ svairiṇī,* how can there be an adulteress; *bhagavantaḥ,* O sirs; *aham yakṣyamāṇaḥ vai asmi,* I am performing a sacrifice; *yāvat dhanam,* as much wealth; *eka-ekasmai ṛtvije dāsyāmi,* I will give to each priest; *tāvat,* that same amount; *bhagavadbhyaḥ dāsyāmi,* I will give to each of you revered sirs; *vasantu bhagavantaḥ iti,* sirs, please stay here.

5. When they arrived, Aśvapati had each of his guests worshipped separately. The next morning, after getting up from bed, he said to them: 'There is no thief in my state, no miserly person, no drunkard, no brāhmin who does not perform the agnihotra sacrifice,

no one who is uneducated, no adulterer, and therefore no adulteress. Sirs, I am performing a sacrifice. The amount of money I will be giving to each priest in this sacrifice, I will give to each one of you. Revered sirs, please stay here.'

ते होचुर्येन हैवार्थेन पुरुषश्चरेत्तं हैव वदेदात्मानमेवेमं वैश्वानरं सम्प्रत्यध्येषि तमेव नो ब्रूहीति ॥ ६ ॥

Te hocuryena haivārthena puruṣaścarettaṁ haiva vadedātmānamevemaṁ vaiśvānaraṁ sampratyadhyeṣi tameva no brūhīti.

Te ha ūcuḥ, they said; *yena ha eva arthena,* the purpose for which; *puruṣaḥ caret,* a person visits [another]; *tam ha eva vadet,* he should state that [first]; *imam eva ātmānam vaiśvānaram,* this Vaiśvānara Ātman; *samprati,* now; *adhyeṣi,* you know; *tam eva naḥ brūhi iti,* please tell us about it.

6. They said: 'When a person visits someone, first and foremost, he states why he has come. At the present time, you are the one who knows about the Vaiśvānara Ātman. Please tell us about it.'

तान्होवाच प्रातर्वः प्रतिवक्तास्मीति ते ह समित्पाणयः पूर्वाह्णे प्रतिचक्रमिरे तान्हानुपनीयैवैतदुवाच ॥ ७ ॥ इत्येकादशः खण्डः ॥ ११ ॥

Tānhovāca prātarvaḥ prativaktāsmīti te ha samitpāṇayaḥ pūrvāhṇe praticakramire tānhānupanīyaivaitaduvāca. Ityekādaśaḥ khaṇḍaḥ.

Tān ha uvāca, he said to them; *prātaḥ,* in the morning; *vaḥ prativaktā asmi iti,* I will give you the answer; *te,* they; *ha samitpāṇayaḥ,* with fuel in their hands; *pūrvāhṇe praticakramire,* came again the next day in the forenoon; *tān ha anupanīya eva,* without initiating them; *etat uvāca,* he said this. *Iti ekādaśaḥ khaṇḍaḥ,* here ends the eleventh section.

7. He said to them, 'I will give you my answer tomorrow morning.' The next day they went back to him in the forenoon with some fuel in their hands. Without initiating them, he said this—

Section Twelve

औपमन्यव कं त्वमात्मानमुपास्स इति। दिवमेव भगवो राजन्निति होवाचैष वै सुतेजा आत्मा वैश्वानरो यं त्वमात्मानमुपास्से तस्मात्तव सुतं प्रसुतमासुतं कुले दृश्यते॥ १॥

Aupamanyava kaṁ tvamātmānamupāssa iti; Divameva bhagavo rājanniti hovācaiṣa vai sutejā ātmā vaiśvānaro yaṁ tvamātmānamupāsse tasmāttava sutaṁ prasutamāsutaṁ kule dṛśyate.

Aupamanyava, O son of Upamanyu; *kam,* whom; *tvam,* you; *ātmānam,* as your self; *upāsse iti,* worship; *bhagavaḥ rājan,* revered king; *divam eva iti,* [I worship] heaven; *ha uvāca,* he [the king] said; *yam tvam ātmānam upāsse,* the Self which you worship; *eṣaḥ,* this [heaven]; *vai,* for sure; *ātmā vaiśvānaraḥ,* is Vaiśvānara Ātman; *sutejāḥ,* as Suteja [i.e., beautiful and bright]; *tasmāt,* therefore; *tava kule,* in your family; *sutam,* soma juice [i.e., children]; *prasutam,* better soma juice; *āsutam,* and much better soma juice; *dṛśyate,* are seen [i.e., better, much better, and still better children are seen].

1. The king said, 'O son of Upamanyu, whom do you worship as the Vaiśvānara Self?' The son of Upamanyu replied, 'O King, I worship heaven.' The king said: 'The Self you worship is the Vaiśvānara Self which is Suteja—i.e., bright and beautiful. That is why whoever is born in your family is bright, brighter, and still brighter.'

अत्स्यन्नं पश्यसि प्रियमत्त्यन्नं पश्यति प्रियं भवत्यस्य ब्रह्मवर्चसं कुले य एतमेवमात्मानं वैश्वानरमुपास्ते मूर्धा त्वेष आत्मन इति होवाच मूर्धा ते व्यपतिष्यद्यन्मां नागमिष्य इति॥ २॥ इति द्वादशः खण्डः॥ १२॥

Atsyannaṁ paśyasi priyamattyannaṁ paśyati priyaṁ

bhavatyasya brahmavarcasaṁ kule ya etamevamātmānaṁ vaiśvānaramupāste mūrdhā tveṣa ātmana iti hovāca mūrdhā te vyapatiṣyadyanmāṁ nāgamiṣya iti. Iti dvādaśaḥ khaṇḍaḥ.

Annam atsi, [the king said:] you eat food; *priyam paśyasi,* you see everything pleasant [i.e., your children, grandchildren, etc.]; *yaḥ,* he who; *etam evam vaiśvānaram ātmānam upāste,* worships this Vaiśvānara Ātman thus; *annam atti,* eats food; *priyam paśyati,* [and] sees everything pleasant [or, sees his dear ones]; *asya kule,* in his family; *brahmavarcasam bhavati,* are born those who shine with the brightness of Brahman; *eṣaḥ tu ātmanaḥ mūrdhā iti,* but this [heaven] is like the head of the Self; *ha uvāca,* he [the king] said; *te mūrdhā vyapatiṣyat,* your head would have fallen; *yat māṁ na āgamiṣyaḥ iti,* if you had not come to me. *Iti dvādaśaḥ khaṇḍaḥ,* here ends the twelfth section.

2. 'You enjoy eating food and you see your dear ones and everything pleasant. He who worships the Vaiśvānara Self thus enjoys eating food and is able to see his dear ones. He also has children in his family who shine with the radiance of Brahman [i.e., they become well known for their good conduct and scholarship]. But heaven is like the head of the Self.' Then the king said, 'If you had not come to me your head would have fallen off.'

Section Thirteen

अथ होवाच सत्ययज्ञं पौलुषिं प्राचीनयोग्य कं त्वमात्मानमुपास्स इत्यादित्यमेव भगवो राजन्निति होवाचैष वै विश्वरूप आत्मा वैश्वानरो यं त्वमात्मानमुपास्से तस्मात्तव बहु विश्वरूपं कुले दृश्यते॥ १ ॥

Atha hovāca satyayajñaṁ pauluṣiṁ prācīnayogya kaṁ tvamātmānamupāssa ityādityameva bhagavo rājanniti hovācaiṣa vai viśvarūpa ātmā vaiśvānaro yaṁ tvamātmā-namupāsse tasmāttava bahu viśvarūpaṁ kule dṛśyate.

Atha, next; *ha uvāca,* he [the king] said; *satyayajñam pauluṣim,* to Satyayajña Pauluṣi; *prācīnayogya,* O Prācīnayogya; *kam,* whom; *tvam ātmānam upāsse iti,* do you worship as the Self; *bhagavaḥ rājan,* revered king; *ādityam eva iti,* [I worship] Āditya [the sun]; *ha uvāca,* [the king] said; *yam tvam ātmānam upāsse,* the Self which you worship; *eṣaḥ,* this [Āditya]; *vai,* for sure; *ātmā vaiśvānaraḥ,* is the Vaiśvānara Ātman; *viśvarūpaḥ,* as Viśvarūpa [having many forms]; *tasmāt,* therefore; *tava kule,* in your family; *bahu viśvarūpam,* wealth in many forms; *dṛśyate,* is seen.

1. The king then said to Satyayajña Pauluṣi, 'O Prācīnayogya, whom do you worship as the Self?' Satyayajña replied, 'I worship Āditya, the sun, revered king.' The king said: 'That which you worship as

the Vaiśvānara Ātmaṁ is named Viśvarūpa. This is why you have in your family wealth in many forms.'

Āditya, the sun, has many colours—white, blue, etc. For that reason Āditya is called Viśvarūpa, 'of many forms.' And this is why, by the favour of Āditya, one who worships him is able to have good fortune, both spiritual and material.

प्रवृत्तोऽश्वतरीरथो दासीनिष्कोऽत्स्यन्नं पश्यसि प्रियमत्त्यन्नं पश्यति प्रियं भवत्यस्य ब्रह्मवर्चसं कुले य एतमेवमात्मानं वैश्वानरमुपास्ते चक्षुष्ट्वेतदात्मन इति होवाचान्धोऽभविष्यो यन्मां नागमिष्य इति॥ २॥ इति त्रयोदशः खण्डः॥ १३॥

Pravṛtto'śvatarīratho dāsīniṣko'tsyannaṁ paśyasi priyamattyannaṁ paśyati priyaṁ bhavatyasya brahmavarcasaṁ kule ya etamevamātmānaṁ vaiśvānaramupāste cakṣuṣṭvetadātmana iti hovācāndho'bhaviṣyo yanmāṁ nāgamiṣya iti. Iti trayodaśaḥ khaṇḍaḥ.

Aśvatarīrathaḥ, a chariot drawn by mules; *dāsī-niṣkaḥ,* maidservants and a necklace; *pravṛttaḥ,* you have; *annam atsi,* you eat food; *priyam paśyasi,* you see everything pleasant [i.e., your children, grandchildren, etc.]; *yaḥ,* he who; *etam evam vaiśvānaram ātmānam upāste,* worships this Vaiśvānara Ātman thus; *annam atti,* eats food; *priyam paśyati,* [and] sees everything pleasant [or, sees his dear ones]; *asya kule,* in his family; *brahmavarcasam bhavati,* are born those who shine with the brightness of Brahman; *eṣaḥ tu ātmanaḥ cakṣuḥ iti,* but this [Āditya] is like the eye of the Self; *ha uvāca,* he [the king] said; *andhaḥ abhaviṣyaḥ,* you would have become blind; *yat mām na āgamiṣyaḥ iti,* if you had not come to me. *Iti trayodaśaḥ khaṇḍaḥ,* here ends the thirteenth section.

2. 'You now have chariots drawn by mules. You are served by maidservants, and you have a necklace. You enjoy eating food and you see your dear ones and everything pleasant. He who worships the Vaiśvānara Self thus enjoys eating food and is able to see his dear ones. He also has children in his family who shine with the radiance of Brahman [i.e., they become well known for their good conduct and scholarship]. But this Āditya is like the eye of the Self.' Then the king said, 'If you had not come to me you would have become blind.'

Āditya is like the eye of the Vaiśvānara Ātman, but it is not the whole of it. If one mistakes the part for the whole, that is a great blunder. He misses the truth and is like one who is blind. The king says to Satyayajña, 'Luckily you have come to me and have been saved from that misfortune.'

Section Fourteen

अथ होवाचेन्द्रद्युम्नं भाल्लवेयं वैयाघ्रपद्य कं त्वमात्मानमुपास्स इति वायुमेव भगवो राजन्निति होवाचैष

वै पृथग्वर्त्मात्मा वैश्वानरो यं त्वमात्मानमुपास्से तस्मात्त्वा पृथग्बलय आयन्ति पृथग्रथश्रेणयोऽनुयन्ति ॥ १ ॥

Atha hovācendradyumnaṁ bhāllaveyaṁ vaiyāghrapadya kaṁ tvamātmānamupāssa iti vāyumeva bhagavo rājanniti hovācaiṣa vai pṛthagvartmātmā vaiśvānaro yaṁ tvamātmānamupāsse tasmāttvāṁ pṛthagbalaya āyanti pṛthagrathaśreṇayo'nuyanti.

Atha, next; *ha uvāca,* he [the king] said; *indradyumnam bhāllaveyam,* to Indradyumna Bhāllaveya; *vaiyāghrapadya,* O Vaiyāghrapadya; *kam,* whom; *tvam ātmānam upāsse iti,* do you worship as the Self; *bhagavaḥ rājan,* revered king; *vāyum eva iti,* [I worship] Vāyu [air]; *ha uvāca,* [the king] said; *yam tvam ātmānam upāsse,* the Self which you worship; *eṣaḥ,* this [Vāyu]; *vai,* for sure; *ātmā vaiśvānaraḥ,* is the Vaiśvānara Ātman; *pṛthagvartmā,* as Pṛthagvartmā [going in many directions]; *tasmāt,* therefore; *pṛthak,* from different directions; *balayaḥ,* gifts; *tvām,* to you; *āyanti,* come; *pṛthak rathaśreṇayaḥ anuyanti,* different lines of chariots follow you [i.e., they are at your disposal].

1. The king then said to Indradyumna Bhāllaveya, 'O Vaiyāghrapadya, whom do you worship as the Self?' Indradyumna replied, 'I worship Vāyu [air], revered king.' The king said: 'That which you worship as the Vaiśvānara Ātman is named Pṛthagvartmā [one who changes direction]. This is why you receive gifts from all directions. And this is also why different kinds of chariots follow you in rows.'

Air is always the same, but it can change its direction and also serve different purposes. This is why one who worships it as the Self is rewarded with gifts coming from different directions.

अत्स्यन्नं पश्यसि प्रियमत्त्यन्नं पश्यति प्रियं भवत्यस्य ब्रह्मवर्चसं कुले य एतमेवमात्मानं वैश्वानरमुपास्ते प्राणस्त्वेष आत्मन इति होवाच प्राणस्त उदक्रमिष्यद्यन्मां नागमिष्य इति॥ २॥ इति चतुर्दशः खण्डः॥ १४॥

Atsyannaṁ paśyasi priyamattyannaṁ paśyati priyaṁ bhavatyasya brahmavarcasaṁ kule ya etamevamātmānaṁ vaiśvānaramupāste prāṇastveṣa ātmana iti hovāca prāṇasta udakramiṣyadyanmāṁ nāgamiṣya iti. Iti caturdaśaḥ khaṇḍaḥ.

Annam atsi, [the king said:] you eat food; *priyam paśyasi,* you see everything pleasant [i.e., your children, grandchildren, etc.]; *yaḥ,* he who; *etam evam vaiśvānaram ātmānam upāste,* worships this Vaiśvānara Ātman thus; *annam atti,* eats food; *priyam paśyati,* [and] sees everything pleasant [or, sees his dear ones]; *asya kule,* in his family; *brahmavarcasam bhavati,* are born those who shine with the brightness of Brahman; *eṣaḥ tu ātmanaḥ prāṇaḥ iti,* but this [Vāyu] is like the life of the Self; *ha uvāca,* he [the king] said; *te prāṇaḥ udakramiṣyat,* your life would have left the body; *yat mām na āgamiṣyaḥ iti,* if you had not come to me. *Iti caturdaśaḥ khaṇḍaḥ,* here ends the fourteenth section.

2. 'You enjoy eating food and you see your dear ones and everything pleasant. He who worships the Vaiśvānara Self thus enjoys eating food and is able to see his dear ones. He also has children in his family who shine with the radiance of Brahman [i.e., they become well known for their good conduct and scholarship]. But Vāyu [air] is like the life [i.e., the vital force] of the Self.' Then the king said, 'If you had not come to me your vital force would have left the body.'

Section Fifteen

अथ होवाच जनं शार्कराक्ष्य कं त्वमात्मानमुपास्स इत्याकाशमेव भगवो राजन्निति होवाचैष वै बहुल आत्मा वैश्वानरो यं त्वमात्मानमुपास्से तस्मात्त्वं बहुलोऽसि प्रजया च धनेन च॥ १॥

Atha hovāca janaṁ śārkarākṣya kaṁ tvamātmānamupāssa ityākāśameva bhagavo rājanniti hovācaiṣa vai bahula ātmā vaiśvānaro yaṁ tvamātmānamupāsse tasmāttvaṁ bahulo'si prajayā ca dhanena ca.

Atha, next; *ha uvāca,* he [the king] said; *janam,* to Jana; *śārkarākṣya,* O Śārkarākṣya; *kam,* whom;

tvam ātmānam upāsse iti, do you worship as the Self; *bhagavaḥ rājan,* revered king; *ākāśam eva iti,* [I worship] Ākāśa [space]; *ha uvāca,* [the king] said; *yam tvam ātmānam upāsse,* the Self which you worship; *eṣaḥ,* this [Ākāśa]; *vai,* for sure; *ātmā vaiśvānaraḥ,* is the Vaiśvānara Ātman; *bahulaḥ,* as Bahula [pervasive]; *tasmāt,* therefore; *tvam,* you; *bahulaḥ asi prajayā ca dhanena ca,* have a great number of children and much wealth.

1. The king then said to Jana, 'O Śārkarākṣya, whom do you worship as the Self?' Jana replied, 'I worship Ākāśa [space], revered king.' The king said: 'That which you worship as the Vaiśvānara Ātman is named Bahula [pervasive]. This is why you have so many children and so much wealth.'

The qualifying word *bahula* is applied to ākāśa (space) because it is vast and pervasive and it also has many other qualities. Those who worship space acquire some of those qualities.

अत्स्यन्नं पश्यसि प्रियमत्त्यन्नं पश्यति प्रियं भवत्यस्य ब्रह्मवर्चसं कुले य एतमेवमात्मानं वैश्वानरमुपास्ते सन्देहस्त्वेष आत्मन इति होवाच सन्देहस्ते व्यशीर्यद्यन्मां नागमिष्य इति॥ २॥ इति पञ्चदशः खण्डः॥ १५॥

Atsyannaṁ paśyasi priyamattyannaṁ paśyati priyaṁ bhavatyasya brahmavarcasaṁ kule ya etamevamātmā-

naṁ vaiśvānaramupāste sandehastveṣa ātmana iti hovāca sandehaste vyaśīryadyanmāṁ nāgamiṣya iti. Iti pañcadaśaḥ khaṇḍaḥ.

Annam atsi, [the king said:] you eat food; *priyam paśyasi,* you see everything pleasant [i.e., your children, grandchildren, etc.]; *yaḥ,* he who; *etam evam vaiśvānaram ātmānam upāste,* worships this Vaiśvānara Ātman thus; *annam atti,* eats food; *priyam paśyati,* [and] sees everything pleasant [or, sees his dear ones]; *asya kule,* in his family; *brahmavarcasam bhavati,* are born those who shine with the brightness of Brahman; *eṣaḥ tu ātmanaḥ sandehaḥ iti,* but this [Ākāśa] is like the mid part of the Self; *ha uvāca,* he [the king] said; *te sandehaḥ vyaśīryat,* the middle part of your body would have shrunk; *yat māṁ na āgamiṣyaḥ iti,* if you had not come to me. *Iti pañcadaśaḥ khaṇḍaḥ,* here ends the fifteenth section.

2. 'You enjoy eating food and you see your dear ones and everything pleasant. He who worships the Vaiśvānara Self thus enjoys eating food and is able to see his dear ones. He also has children in his family who shine with the radiance of Brahman [i.e., they become well known for their good conduct and scholarship]. But Ākāśa [space] is like the mid part of the Self.' Then the king said, 'If you had not come to me the middle part of your body would have shrunk.'

Space is only the middle part of the Vaiśvānara Ātman, and is not the whole of it. Anyone who makes the mistake of meditating on it as the Self will find his body shrinking. This happens because he does not give due importance to the Self.

Section Sixteen

अथ होवाच बुडिलमाश्वतराश्विं वैयाघ्रपद्य कं त्वमात्मानमुपास्स इत्यप एव भगवो राजन्निति होवाचैष वै रयिरात्मा वैश्वानरो यं त्वमात्मानमुपास्से तस्मात्त्वं रयिमान्पुष्टिमानसि ॥ १ ॥

Atha hovāca buḍilamāśvatarāśviṁ vaiyāghrapadya kaṁ tvamātmānamupāssa ityapa eva bhagavo rājanniti hovācaiṣa vai rayirātmā vaiśvānaro yaṁ tvamātmāna-mupāsse tasmāttvaṁ rayimānpuṣṭimānasi.

Atha, next; *ha uvāca,* he [the king] said; *buḍilam āśvatarāśvim,* to Buḍila Āśvatarāśvi; *Vaiyāghrapadya,* O Vaiyāghrapadya; *kam,* whom; *tvam ātmānam upāsse iti,* do you worship as the Self; *bhagavaḥ rājan,* revered king; *apaḥ eva iti,* [I worship] water; *ha uvāca,* [the king] said; *yam tvam ātmānam upāsse,* the Self which you worship; *eṣaḥ,* this [water]; *vai,* for sure; *ātmā vaiśvānaraḥ,* is the Vaiśvānara Ātman; *rayiḥ,* as Rayi [wealth]; *tasmāt,* therefore; *tvam,* you; *rayimān puṣṭimān asi,* are rich and have a strong, healthy body.

1. The king then said to Buḍila Āśvatarāśvi, 'O Vaiyāghrapadya, whom do you worship as the Self?' Buḍila replied, 'I worship water, revered king.' The king said: 'That which you worship as the Vaiśvānara Ātman is named Rayi [wealth]. This is why you are rich and healthy.'

Water is 'wealth' (rayi) because it is from water that we get food and all the good things we need.

अत्स्यन्नं पश्यसि प्रियमत्त्यन्नं पश्यति प्रियं भवत्यस्य ब्रह्मवर्चसं कुले य एतमेवमात्मानं वैश्वानरमुपास्ते बस्तिस्त्वेष आत्मन इति होवाच बस्तिस्ते व्यभेत्स्यद्यन्मां नागमिष्य इति ॥ २ ॥ इति षोडशः खण्डः ॥ १६ ॥

Atsyannaṁ paśyasi priyamattyannaṁ paśyati priyaṁ bhavatyasya brahmavarcasaṁ kule ya etamevamātmā-naṁ vaiśvānaramupāste bastistveṣa ātmana iti hovāca bastiste vyabhetsyadyanmāṁ nāgamiṣya iti. Iti ṣoḍaśaḥ khaṇḍaḥ.

Annam atsi, [the king said:] you eat food; *priyam paśyasi,* you see everything pleasant [i.e., your children, grandchildren, etc.]; *yaḥ,* he who; *etam evam vaiśvānaram ātmānam upāste,* worships this Vaiśvānara Ātman thus; *annam atti,* eats food; *priyam paśyati,* [and] sees everything pleasant [or, sees his dear ones]; *asya kule,* in his family; *brahmavarcasam bhavati,* are born those who shine with the brightness of

Brahman; *eṣaḥ tu ātmanaḥ bastiḥ iti,* but this [water] is like the bladder of the Self; *ha uvāca,* he [the king] said; *te bastiḥ vyabhetsyat,* your bladder would have burst; *yat mām na āgamiṣyaḥ iti,* if you had not come to me. *Iti ṣoḍaśaḥ khaṇḍaḥ,* here ends the sixteenth section.

2. 'You enjoy eating food and you see your dear ones and everything pleasant. He who worships the Vaiśvānara Self thus enjoys eating food and is able to see his dear ones. He also has children in his family who shine with the radiance of Brahman [i.e., they become well known for their good conduct and scholarship]. But water is like the bladder of the Self.' Then the king said, 'If you had not come to me your bladder would have burst.'

Section Seventeen

अथ होवाचोद्दालकमारुणिं गौतम कं त्वमात्मानमुपास्स इति पृथिवीमेव भगवो राजन्निति होवाचैष वै प्रतिष्ठात्मा वैश्वानरो यं त्वमात्मानमुपास्से तस्मात्त्वं प्रतिष्ठितोऽसि प्रजया च पशुभिश्च॥ १॥

Atha hovācoddālakamāruṇiṁ gautama kaṁ tvamātmānamupāssa iti pṛthivīmeva bhagavo rājanniti hovācaiṣa vai pratiṣṭhātmā vaiśvānaro yaṁ tvamātmānamupāsse tasmāttvaṁ pratiṣṭhito'si prajayā ca paśubhiśca.

Atha, next; *ha uvāca,* he [the king] said; *uddālakam āruṇim,* to Uddālaka Āruṇi; *gautama,* O Gautama; *kam,* whom; *tvam ātmānam upāsse iti,* do you worship as the Self; *bhagavaḥ rājan,* revered king; *pṛthivīm eva iti,* [I worship] the earth; *ha uvāca,* [the king] said; *yam tvam ātmānam upāsse,* the Self which you worship; *eṣaḥ,* this [earth]; *vai,* for sure; *ātmā vaiśvānaraḥ,* is the Vaiśvānara Ātman; *pratiṣṭhā,* as Pratiṣṭhā [the support]; *tasmāt,* therefore; *tvam,* you; *pratiṣṭhitaḥ prajayā ca paśubhiḥ ca asi,* are supported by children and animals.

1. The king then said to Uddālaka Āruṇi, 'O Gautama, whom do you worship as the Self?' Uddālaka replied, 'I worship the earth, revered king.' The king said: 'That which you worship as the Vaiśvānara Ātman is named Pratiṣṭhā [the support]. This is why you have so many children and animals to support you.'

The earth is like the feet of Vaiśvānara Ātman. This is why it is 'the support.'

अत्स्यन्नं पश्यसि प्रियमत्त्यन्नं पश्यति प्रियं भवत्यस्य ब्रह्मवर्चसं कुले य एतमेवमात्मानं वैश्वानरमुपास्ते पादौ त्वेतावात्मन इति होवाच पादौ ते व्यम्लास्येतां यन्मां नागमिष्य इति ॥ २ ॥ इति सप्तदशः खण्डः ॥ १७ ॥

Atsyannaṁ paśyasi priyamattyannaṁ paśyati priyaṁ bhavatyasya brahmavarcasaṁ kule ya etamevamātmā-

naṁ vaiśvānaramupāste pādau tvetāvātmana iti hovāca pādau te vyamlāsyetāṁ yanmāṁ nāgamiṣya iti. Iti saptadaśaḥ khaṇḍaḥ.

Annam atsi, [the king said:] you eat food; *priyam paśyasi,* you see everything pleasant [i.e., your children, grandchildren, etc.]; *yaḥ,* he who; *etam evam vaiśvānaram ātmānam upāste,* worships this Vaiśvānara Ātman thus; *annam atti,* eats food; *priyam paśyati,* [and] sees everything pleasant [or, sees his dear ones]; *asya kule,* in his family; *brahmavarcasam bhavati,* are born those who shine with the brightness of Brahman; *eṣaḥ tu ātmanaḥ pādau iti,* but this [earth] is like the two feet of the Self; *ha uvāca,* he [the king] said; *te pādau vyamlāsyetām,* your feet would have become very weak; *yat mām na āgamiṣyaḥ iti,* if you had not come to me. *Iti saptadaśaḥ khaṇḍaḥ,* here ends the seventeenth section.

2. 'You enjoy eating food and you see your dear ones and everything pleasant. He who worships the Vaiśvānara Self thus enjoys eating food and is able to see his dear ones. He also has children in his family who shine with the radiance of Brahman [i.e., they become well known for their good conduct and scholarship]. But the earth is like the feet of the Self.' Then the king said, 'If you had not come to me your feet would have become extremely weak.'

Section Eighteen

तान्होवाचैते वै खलु यूयं पृथगिवेममात्मानं वैश्वानरं विद्वांसोऽन्नमत्थ यस्त्वेतमेवं प्रादेशमात्रमभिविमानमात्मानं वैश्वानरमुपास्ते स सर्वेषु लोकेषु सर्वेषु भूतेषु सर्वेष्वात्मस्वन्नमत्ति ॥ १ ॥

Tānhovācaite vai khalu yūyaṁ pṛthagivemamātmānaṁ vaiśvānaraṁ vidvāṁso'nnamattha yastvetamevaṁ prādeśamātramabhivimānamātmānaṁ vaiśvānaramupāste sa sarveṣu lokeṣu sarveṣu bhūteṣu sarveṣvātmasvannamatti.

Tān, to them [the brāhmins]; *ha uvāca,* [the king] said; *ete yūyam vai khalu,* those of you here; *imam vaiśvānaram ātmānam vidvāṁsaḥ,* have known this [undivided] Vaiśvānara Ātman; *pṛthak iva,* only in part [and as separate in each individual]; *annam attha,* [and that is why] you eat food [thinking you are eating separately; *yaḥ tu,* but he who; *etam evam vaiśvānaram ātmānam upāste,* worships this Vaiśvānara Ātman thus; *prādeśamātram,* as all-pervasive [i.e., as covering the various worlds]; *abhivimānam,* [and] infinite; *saḥ,* he; *sarveṣu lokeṣu,* in all the worlds; *sarveṣu bhūteṣu,* in all beings; *sarveṣu ātmasu,* in all selves; *annam atti,* eats food.

1. The king said to the brāhmins: 'Those of you who are here meditate on the Vaiśvānara Self only

in part. [That is why when you eat you think you are eating separately.] He who worships the Self as all-pervasive and infinite, enjoys eating through whoever eats in the worlds, through all beings, and through all selves.

Prādeśamātra means one who covers all the worlds, from heaven to the earth—including everything and every being. *Abhivimāna* means infinite, beyond measure.

Here the principle is that if you worship God as finite, you remain finite; if you worship him as infinite, you become infinite. Another principle suggested is that you are one with all. You are happy if all are happy. You cannot expect anything for yourself to the exclusion of others.

Yet another principle is to regard your body as the place of an Agnihotra sacrifice, and the food you eat as the oblation.

The six scholars mentioned here worshipped the Vaiśvānara Ātman in part—as either heaven, the sun, air, space, water, or the earth. Aśvapati told them their worship was not complete. They should include their own self also as the Vaiśvānara Ātman. In fact, they should realize that there is but one Self and that Self is in everything and in every being.

तस्य ह वा एतस्यात्मनो वैश्वानरस्य मूर्धैव
सुतेजाश्चक्षुर्विश्वरूपः प्राणः पृथग्वर्त्मात्मा सन्देहो बहुलो

बस्तिरेव रयिः पृथिव्येव पादावुर एव वेदिर्लोमानि बर्हिर्हृदयं गार्हपत्यो मनोऽन्वाहार्यपचन आस्यमाहवनीयः ॥ २ ॥

इत्यष्टादशः खण्डः ॥ १८ ॥

Tasya ha vā etasyātmano vaiśvānarasya mūrdhaiva sutejāścakṣurviśvarūpaḥ prāṇaḥ pṛthagvartmātmā sandeho bahulo bastireva rayiḥ pṛthivyeva pādāvura eva vedirlomāni barhirhṛdayaṁ gārhapatyo mano'nvāhāryapacana āsyamāhavanīyaḥ. Ityaṣṭādaśaḥ khaṇḍaḥ.

Tasya etasya ha vai vaiśvānarasya ātmanaḥ, of this Vaiśvānara Ātman; *sutejāḥ eva mūrdhā,* heaven is the head; *viśvarūpaḥ cakṣuḥ,* the sun is the eye; *pṛthakvartmātmā prāṇaḥ,* air is prāṇa; *bahulaḥ sandehaḥ,* the sky is the middle part of the body; *rayiḥ bastiḥ eva,* water is the bladder; *pṛthivī eva pādau,* the earth is the feet; *vediḥ,* the sacrificial altar; *ura eva,* is the chest; *barhiḥ lomāni,* the kuśa grass [used in the sacrifice] is the hair [on the chest]; *gārhapatyaḥ hṛdayam,* the Gārhapatya fire is the heart; *anvāhāryapacana manaḥ,* the Anvāhāryapacana fire [i.e., the Dakṣiṇāgni fire] is the mind; *āhavanīyaḥ āsyam,* the Āhavanīya fire is the mouth. *Iti aṣṭādaśaḥ khaṇḍaḥ,* here ends the eighteenth section.

2. Suteja [i.e., 'the bright and beautiful'—heaven] is the head of this Vaiśvānara Self; Viśvarūpa ['having many forms'—the sun] is the eye; Pṛthagvartmā ['one who changes direction'—air] is the prāṇa; Bahula ['pervasive'—space] is the middle part; Rayi ['wealth'—water] is the bladder; the earth [Pratiṣṭhā—'the

support'] is the feet; the sacrificial altar is the chest; the kuśa grass is the hair on the chest; the Gārhapatya fire is the heart; the Anvāhāryapacana [i.e., the Dakṣiṇāgni] fire is the mind; and the Āhavanīya fire is the mouth.

The implication is that none of these taken separately can be the Vaiśvānara Self. It is only a part of it.

Section Nineteen

तद्यद्भक्तं प्रथममागच्छेत्तद्धोमीयंस यां प्रथमामाहुतिं जुहुयात्तां जुहुयात्प्राणाय स्वाहेति प्राणस्तृप्यति॥ १॥

Tadyadbhaktaṁ prathamamāgacchettaddhomīyaṁsa yāṁ prathamāmāhutiṁ juhuyāttāṁ juhuyātprāṇāya svāheti prāṇastṛpyati.

Tat, therefore; *yat bhaktam,* that food which; *prathamam āgacchet,* comes first; *tat,* that; *homīyam,* is meant as an oblation; *saḥ,* he [who eats]; *yām prathamām āhutim,* that first oblation; *juhuyāt,* offers; *tām,* that; *juhuyāt,* offers; *prāṇāya svāhā iti,* [with the mantra] 'Prāṇāya svāhā'; *prāṇaḥ tṛpyati,* [then] prāṇa is pleased.

1. The first part of the food is like the first oblation. One who eats should offer it as an oblation to prāṇa,

saying, 'Prāṇāya svāhā' [i.e., I offer this as an oblation to prāṇa]. With this, your prāṇa becomes pleased.

Here eating is being compared to performing a sacrifice. Every time you put food into your mouth, it is as if you are offering an oblation. Prāṇa is the deity to whom you offer the first oblation. The word *prāṇa* in this context means that aspect of the vital force which is responsible for respiration.

प्राणे तृप्यति चक्षुस्तृप्यति चक्षुषि तृप्यत्यादित्यस्तृप्यत्यादित्ये तृप्यति द्यौस्तृप्यति दिवि तृप्यन्त्यां यत्किञ्च द्यौश्चादित्यश्चाधितिष्ठतस्तत्तृप्यति तस्यानु तृप्तिं तृप्यति प्रजया पशुभिरन्नाद्येन तेजसा ब्रह्मवर्चसेनेति ॥ २ ॥ इत्येकोनविंशः खण्डः ॥ १९ ॥

Prāṇe tṛpyati cakṣustṛpyati cakṣuṣi tṛpyatyādityastṛpyatyāditye tṛpyati dyaustṛpyati divi tṛpyantyāṁ yatkiñca dyauścādityaścādhitiṣṭhatastattṛpyati tasyānu tṛptiṁ tṛpyati prajayā paśubhirannādyena tejasā brahmavarcaseneti. Ityekonaviṁśaḥ khaṇḍaḥ.

Prāṇe tṛpyati, when prāṇa is pleased; *cakṣuḥ tṛpyati,* the eye is pleased; *cakṣuṣi tṛpyati,* when the eye is pleased; *ādityaḥ tṛpyati,* the sun is pleased; *āditye tṛpyati,* when the sun is pleased; *dyauḥ tṛpyati,* heaven is pleased; *divi tṛpyantyām,* when heaven is pleased; *yat kiñca,* whatever; *dyauḥ ca·ādityaḥ ca adhitiṣṭhataḥ,* is there ruled by heaven and the sun; *tat tṛpyati,* that is pleased; *tasya anu tṛptim,* with its being pleased; *tṛpyati,* he [the eater] is pleased; *prajayā,* by children; *paśubhiḥ,* by animals; *annādyena,* by food; *tejasā,* by vigour; *brahmavarcasena iti,* by the radiance of Brahman derived from good character and scholarship. *Iti ekonaviṁśaḥ khaṇḍaḥ,* here ends the nineteenth section.

2. When prāṇa is pleased, the eye is pleased; when the eye is pleased, the sun is pleased; when the sun is pleased, heaven is pleased; when heaven is pleased, whatever there is ruled by heaven and the sun is pleased. Then when that is pleased, the eater derives pleasure from his children, from his animals, from an abundance of food, from physical strength, and from his good life and scholarship.

Section Twenty

अथ यां द्वितीयां जुहुयात्तां जुहुयाद्व्यानाय स्वाहेति व्यानस्तृप्यति ॥ १ ॥

Atha yāṁ dvitīyāṁ juhuyāttāṁ juhuyādvyānāya svāheti vyānastṛpyati.

Atha, next; *yām dvitīyām juhuyāt,* when he offers the second [oblation]; *tām juhuyāt,* he offers that; *vyānāya svāhā iti,* [with the mantra] 'Vyānāya svāhā'; *vyānaḥ tṛpyati,* [then] vyāna is pleased.

1. When he [the eater] offers the second oblation, he offers it saying, 'Vyānāya svāhā' [I offer this as an oblation to vyāna]. With this, vyāna becomes pleased.

Vyāna is the aspect of the vital force responsible for our speech and for feats requiring great effort. It operates on the nerves.

व्याने तृप्यति श्रोत्रं तृप्यति श्रोत्रे तृप्यति चन्द्रमास्तृप्यति चन्द्रमसि तृप्यति दिशस्तृप्यन्ति दिक्षु तृप्यन्तीषु यत्किञ्च दिशश्च चन्द्रमाश्चाधितिष्ठन्ति तत्तृप्यति तस्यानु तृप्तिं तृप्यति प्रजया पशुभिरन्नाद्येन तेजसा ब्रह्मवर्चसेनेति ॥ २ ॥ इति विंशः खण्डः ॥ २० ॥

Vyāne tṛpyati śrotraṁ tṛpyati śrotre tṛpyati candramāstṛpyati candramasi tṛpyati diśastṛpyanti dikṣu tṛpyantīṣu yatkiñca diśaśca candramāścādhitiṣṭhanti tattṛpyati tasyānu tṛptiṁ tṛpyati prajayā paśubhirannādyena tejasā brahmavarcaseneti. Iti viṁśaḥ khaṇḍaḥ.

Vyāne tṛpyati, when vyāna is pleased; *śrotram tṛpyati,* the ear is pleased; *śrotre tṛpyati,* when the ear is pleased; *candramāḥ tṛpyati,* the moon is pleased; *candramasi tṛpyati,* when the moon is pleased; *diśaḥ tṛpyanti,* the quarters are pleased; *dikṣu tṛpyantīṣu,* if the quarters are pleased; *yat kiñca,* whatever; *diśaḥ ca candramāḥ ca adhitiṣṭhanti,* there is ruled by the quarters and the moon; *tat tṛpyati,* that is pleased; *tasya anu tṛptim,* with its being pleased; *tṛpyati,* he [the eater] is pleased; *prajayā,* by children; *paśubhiḥ,* by animals; *annādyena,* by food; *tejasā,* by vigour; *brahmavarcasena iti,* by the radiance of Brahman derived from good character and scholarship. *Iti viṁśaḥ khaṇḍaḥ,* here ends the twentieth section.

2. When vyāna is pleased, the ear is pleased; when the ear is pleased, the moon is pleased; when the moon is pleased, the quarters are pleased; with the quarters being pleased, whatever there is ruled by the quarters and the moon is pleased. Then when that is pleased, the eater derives pleasure from his children, from his animals, from an abundance of food, from physical strength, and from his good life and scholarship.

Section Twenty-One

अथ यां तृतीयां जुहुयात्तां जुहुयादपानाय स्वाहे-
त्यपानस्तृप्यति ॥ १ ॥

Atha yāṁ tṛtīyāṁ juhuyāttāṁ juhuyādapānāya svāhe-tyapānastṛpyati.

Atha, next; *yām tṛtīyām juhuyāt,* when he offers the third [oblation]; *tām juhuyāt,* he offers that; *apānāya svāhā iti,* [with the mantra] 'Apānāya svāhā'; *apānaḥ tṛpyati,* [then] apāna is pleased.

1. When he [the eater] offers the third oblation, he offers it saying, 'Apānāya svāhā' [I offer this as an oblation to apāna]. With this, apāna becomes pleased.

Apāna is the aspect of the vital force responsible for elimination of waste from the body.

अपाने तृप्यति वाक्तृप्यति वाचि तृप्यन्त्यामग्निस्तृप्यत्यग्नौ तृप्यति पृथिवी तृप्यति पृथिव्यां तृप्यन्त्यां यत्किञ्च पृथिवी चाग्निश्चाधितिष्ठतस्तत्तृप्यति तस्यानु तृप्तिं तृप्यति प्रजया पशुभिरन्नाद्येन तेजसा ब्रह्मवर्चसेनेति ॥ २ ॥
इत्येकविंशः खण्डः ॥ २१ ॥

Apāne tṛpyati vāktṛpyati vāci tṛpyantyāmagnistṛpyatyagnau tṛpyati pṛthivī tṛpyati pṛthivyāṁ tṛpyantyāṁ yatkiñca pṛthivī cāgniścādhitiṣṭhatastattṛpyati tasyānu tṛptiṁ tṛpyati prajayā paśubhirannādyena tejasā brahmavarcaseneti. Ityekaviṁśaḥ khaṇḍaḥ.

Apāne tṛpyati, when apāna is pleased; *vāk tṛpyati,* the organ of speech is pleased; *vāci tṛpyantyām,* the organ of speech being pleased; *agniḥ tṛpyati,* fire is pleased; *agnau tṛpyati,* when fire is pleased; *pṛthivī tṛpyati,* the earth is pleased; *pṛthivyām tṛpyantyām,* the earth being pleased; *yat kiñca,* whatever; *pṛthivī ca agniḥ ca adhitiṣṭhataḥ,* is under the control of the earth and fire; *tat tṛpyati,* that is pleased; *tasya anu tṛptim,* with its being pleased; *tṛpyati,* he [the eater] is pleased; *prajayā,* by children; *paśubhiḥ,* by animals; *annādyena,* by food; *tejasā,* by vigour; *brahmavarcasena iti,* by the radiance of Brahman derived from good character and scholarship. *Iti ekaviṁśaḥ khaṇḍaḥ,* here ends the twenty-first section.

2. When apāna is pleased, the organ of speech is pleased; the organ of speech being pleased, fire is pleased; when fire is pleased, the earth is pleased; the earth being pleased, whatever is under the control of the earth and fire is pleased. Then when that is pleased, the eater derives pleasure from his children, from his animals, from an abundance of food, from physical strength, and from his good life and scholarship.

Section Twenty-Two

अथ यां चतुर्थीं जुहुयात्तां जुहुयात्समानाय स्वाहेति समानस्तृप्यति ॥ १ ॥

Atha yāṁ caturthīṁ juhuyāttāṁ juhuyātsamānāya svāheti samānastṛpyati.

Atha, next; *yām caturthīm juhuyāt,* when he offers the fourth [oblation]; *tām juhuyāt,* he offers that; *samānāya svāhā iti,* [with the mantra] 'Samānāya svāhā'; *samānaḥ tṛpyati,* [then] samāna is pleased.

1. When he [the eater] offers the fourth oblation, he offers it saying, 'Samānāya svāhā' [I offer this as an oblation to samāna]. With this, samāna becomes pleased.

Samāna is the aspect of the vital force responsible for digestion and assimilation of food.

समाने तृप्यति मनस्तृप्यति मनसि तृप्यति पर्जन्यस्तृप्यति पर्जन्ये तृप्यति विद्युत्तृप्यति विद्युति तृप्यन्त्यां यत्किञ्च विद्युच्च पर्जन्यश्चाधितिष्ठतस्तत्तृप्यति तस्यानु तृप्तिं तृप्यति प्रजया पशुभिरन्नाद्येन तेजसा ब्रह्मवर्चसेनेति॥ २॥ इति द्वाविंशः खण्डः॥ २२॥

Samāne tṛpyati manastṛpyati manasi tṛpyati parjanyastṛpyati parjanye tṛpyati vidyuttṛpyati vidyuti tṛpyantyāṁ yatkiñca vidyucca parjanyaścādhitiṣṭhatastattṛpyati tasyānu tṛptiṁ tṛpyati prajayā paśubhirannādyena tejasā brahmavarcaseneti. Iti dvāviṁśaḥ khaṇḍaḥ.

Samāne tṛpyati, when samāna is pleased; *manaḥ tṛpyati,* the mind is pleased; *manasi tṛpyati,* when the mind is pleased; *parjanyaḥ tṛpyati,* the cloud is pleased; *parjanye tṛpyati,* when the cloud is pleased; *vidyut tṛpyati,* lightning is pleased; *vidyuti tṛpyantyām,* lightning being pleased; *yat kiñca,* whatever; *vidyut ca parjanyaḥ ca adhitiṣṭhataḥ,* is under the control of lightning and the cloud; *tat tṛpyati,* that is pleased;

tasya anu tṛptim, with its being pleased; *tṛpyati,* he [the eater] is pleased; *prajayā,* by children; *paśubhiḥ,* by animals; *annādyena,* by food; *tejasā,* by vigour; *brahmavarcasena iti,* by the radiance of Brahman derived from good character and scholarship. *Iti dvāviṁśaḥ khaṇḍaḥ,* here ends the twenty-second section.

2. When samāna is pleased, the mind is pleased; when the mind is pleased, the cloud is pleased; when the cloud is pleased, lightning is pleased; lightning being pleased, whatever is under the control of lightning and the cloud is pleased. Then when that is pleased, the eater derives pleasure from his children, from his animals, from an abundance of food, from physical strength, and from his good life and scholarship.

Section Twenty-Three

अथ यां पञ्चमीं जुहुयात्तां जुहुयादुदानाय स्वाहेत्यु-
दानस्तृप्यति ॥ १ ॥

Atha yāṁ pañcamīṁ juhuyāttāṁ juhuyādudānāya svāhetyudānastṛpyati.

Atha, next; *yām pañcamīm juhuyāt,* when he offers the fifth [oblation]; *tām juhuyāt,* he offers that; *udānāya svāhā iti,* [with the mantra] 'Udānāya svāhā'; *udānaḥ tṛpyati,* [then] udāna is pleased.

1. When he [the eater] offers the fifth oblation, he offers it saying, 'Udānāya svāhā' [I offer this as an oblation to udāna]. With this, udāna becomes pleased.

Udāna is the aspect of the vital force responsible for helping the individual self leave the body at the time of death.

उदाने तृप्यति त्वक्तृप्यति त्वचि तृप्यन्त्यां वायुस्तृप्यति वायौ तृप्यत्याकाशस्तृप्यत्याकाशे तृप्यति यत्किञ्च वायुश्चाकाशश्चाधितिष्ठतस्तत्तृप्यति तस्यानु तृप्तिं तृप्यति प्रजया पशुभिरन्नाद्येन तेजसा ब्रह्मवर्चसेनेति॥ २ ॥ इति त्रयोविंशः खण्डः॥ २३ ॥

Udāne tṛpyati tvaktṛpyati tvaci tṛpyantyāṁ vāyustṛpyati vāyau tṛpyatyākāśastṛpyatyākāśe tṛpyati yatkiñca vāyuścākāśaścādhitiṣṭhatastattṛpyati tasyānu tṛptiṁ tṛpyati prajayā paśubhirannādyena tejasā brahmavarcaseneti. Iti trayoviṁśaḥ khaṇḍaḥ.

Udāne tṛpyati, when udāna is pleased; *tvak tṛpyati,* the organ of touch [i.e., the skin] is pleased; *tvaci tṛpyantyām,* the organ of touch being pleased; *vāyuḥ tṛpyati,* air is pleased; *vāyau tṛpyati,* when air is pleased; *ākāśaḥ tṛpyati,* space is pleased; *ākāśe tṛpyati,* when space is pleased; *yat kiñca,* whatever; *vāyuḥ ca ākāśaḥ ca adhitiṣṭhataḥ,* is under the control of air and space; *tat tṛpyati,* that is pleased; *tasya anu tṛptim,* with its being pleased; *tṛpyati,* he [the eater] is pleased; *prajayā,* by children; *paśubhiḥ,* by animals; *annādyena,* by food; *tejasā,* by vigour; *brahmavarcasena iti,* by the radiance of Brahman derived from good character and scholarship. *Iti trayoviṁśaḥ khaṇḍaḥ,* here ends the twenty-third section.

2. When udāna is pleased, the organ of touch is pleased; the organ of touch being pleased, air is pleased; when air is pleased, space is pleased; when space is pleased, whatever is under the control of air and space is pleased. Then when that is pleased, the eater derives pleasure from his children, from his animals, from an abundance of food, from physical strength, and from his good life and scholarship.

Section Twenty-Four

स य इदमविद्वानग्निहोत्रं जुहोति यथाङ्गारानपोह्य भस्मनि जुहुयात्तादृक्तत्स्यात् ॥ १ ॥

Sa ya idamavidvānagnihotraṁ juhoti yathāṅgārānapohya bhasmani juhuyāttādṛktatsyāt.

Saḥ yaḥ, he who; *agnihotram juhoti,* performs the Agnihotra sacrifice; *idam avidvān,* without knowing this [i.e., about the Vaiśvānara Ātman]; *yathā,* just as; *aṅgārān,* embers; *apohya,* rejecting; *bhasmani juhuyāt,* offers [oblations] into ashes; *tat tādṛk syāt,* it is like that.

1. If a person performs the Agnihotra sacrifice without knowing anything about the Vaiśvānara Self, it will be like offering oblations into ashes instead of the fire.

अथ य एतदेवं विद्वानग्निहोत्रं जुहोति तस्य सर्वेषु लोकेषु सर्वेषु भूतेषु सर्वेष्वात्मसु हुतं भवति॥ २॥

Atha ya etadevaṁ vidvānagnihotraṁ juhoti tasya sarveṣu lokeṣu sarveṣu bhūteṣu sarveṣvātmasu hutaṁ bhavati.

Atha, but; *yaḥ,* he who; *agnihotram juhoti,* performs the Agnihotra sacrifice; *etat evam vidvān,* knowing it accordingly; *tasya,* his; *hutam bhavati,* oblation is offered; *sarveṣu lokeṣu,* to all the worlds; *sarveṣu bhūteṣu,* to all beings; *sarveṣu ātmasu,* to all selves.

2. But he who performs the Agnihotra sacrifice with full knowledge of the Vaiśvānara Self is deemed to have offered oblations to all the worlds, to all beings, and to all selves.

तद्यथेषीकातूलमग्नौ प्रोतं प्रदूयेतैवं हास्य सर्वे पाप्मानः
प्रदूयन्ते य एतदेवं विद्वानग्निहोत्रं जुहोति॥ ३॥

Tadyatheṣīkātūlamagnau protaṁ pradūyetaivaṁ hāsya sarve pāpmānaḥ pradūyante ya etadevaṁ vidvānagnihotraṁ juhoti.

Tat yathā, just as; *iṣīkā-tūlam,* the cotton-like fibre of the iṣīkā grass; *agnau,* into the fire; *protam,* on being thrown; *pradūyeta,* is totally consumed; *evam,* like this; *asya ha,* his; *sarve pāpmānaḥ,* all sins; *pradūyante,* are burnt up; *yaḥ,* he who; *etat evam vidvān,* having known this in this way; *agnihotram juhoti,* performs the Agnihotra sacrifice.

3. Just as the cotton fibres of the iṣīkā grass are totally consumed when thrown into the fire, similarly all sins are consumed of one who performs the Agnihotra sacrifice with the knowledge of the Vaiśvānara Self.

Iṣīkā is a kind of grass that grows very tall and has a cotton-like substance coming from it which is easily consumed when thrown into fire. Similarly, the knowledge that a person is one with all easily consumes the fruits of his *sañcita* (accumulated) karma and his *āgāmī* (future) karma. But a person may have to suffer from *prārabdha* karma, which is already in the process of bearing fruit. Prārabdha karma is like an arrow that has already been shot.

तस्मादु हैवंविद्यद्यपि चण्डालायोच्छिष्टं प्रयच्छेदात्मनि हैवास्य तद्वैश्वानरे हुतं स्यादिति तदेष श्लोकः ॥ ४ ॥

Tasmādu haivaṁvidyadyapi caṇḍālāyocchiṣṭaṁ prayacchedātmani haivāsya tadvaiśvānare hutaṁ syāditi tadeṣa ślokaḥ.

Tasmāt, therefore; *u ha evam vit,* one who knows [the Vaiśvānara Self]; yadi api, even if; *caṇḍālāya,* to a caṇḍāla [an outcaste]; *ucchiṣṭam,* part of the food left after eating; *prayacchet,* one gives; *tat,* that [leftover food]; *asya ha eva hutam syāt,* will be his oblation offered; *vaiśvānare ātmani iti,* to the Vaiśvānara Ātman; *tat eṣaḥ ślokaḥ,* here is a verse on the subject.

4. Therefore, even if a person who knows the Vaiśvānara Ātman gives the remnants of his food after eating to a person who has no caste, that will be like his oblation offered to his own Vaiśvānara Self. Here is a verse on the subject:

Normally food that is left over after eating should not be given to anyone. But suppose a person has realized his Vaiśvānara Self and he gives such food to an outcaste. That is not a breach of any rule. Rather, it will be like an oblation offered to his own Self, for it is the same Self who is giving and who is receiving.

यथेह क्षुधिता बाला मातरं पर्युपासत एवं सर्वाणि भूतान्यग्निहोत्रमुपासत इत्यग्निहोत्रमुपासत इति ॥ ५ ॥ इति चतुर्विंशः खण्डः ॥ २४ ॥ इति छान्दोग्योपनिषदि पञ्चमोऽध्यायः ॥ ५ ॥

Yatheha kṣudhitā bālā mātaraṁ paryupāsata evaṁ sarvāṇi bhūtanyagnihotramupāsata ityagnihotramupāsata iti. Iti caturviṁśaḥ khaṇḍaḥ. Iti chāndogyopaniṣadi pañcamo'dhyāyaḥ.

Yathā, just as; *iha,* in this world; *kṣudhitāḥ bālāḥ,* hungry children; *mātaram paryupāsate,* go to their mother [for food]; *evam,* in the same way; *sarvāṇi bhūtāni,* all living beings; *agnihotram upāsate iti,* wait for the Agnihotra sacrifice to begin; *agnihotram upāsate iti,* wait for the Agnihotra sacrifice to begin. *Iti caturviṁśaḥ khaṇḍaḥ,* here ends the twenty-fourth section. *Iti chāndogyopaniṣadi pañcamaḥ adhyāyaḥ,* here ends the fifth chapter of the Chāndogya Upaniṣad.

5. Just as here in this world, when children are hungry they go to their mother and beg for food, in the same way, all living beings beg that the Agnihotra sacrifice may be performed without any delay.

Here the reference is to a person who has attained Self-knowledge. When such a person performs his Agnihotra sacrifice as described before, by taking his meal, it is as if all living beings are eating. This happens because he is one with all.

CHAPTER SIX

Section One

ॐ। श्वेतकेतुर्हारुणेय आस तं ह पितोवाच श्वेतकेतो वस ब्रह्मचर्यं न वै सोम्यास्मत्कुलीनोऽननूच्य ब्रह्मबन्धुरिव भवतीति ॥ १ ॥

Om. Śvetaketurhāruṇeya āsa taṁ ha pitovāca śvetaketo vasa brahmacaryaṁ na vai somyāsmatkulīno-'nanūcya brahmabandhuriva bhavatīti.

Śvetaketuḥ ha Āruṇeyaḥ āsa, Āruṇi had a son named Śvetaketu; *tam ha pita uvāca,* his father said to him [to Śvetaketu]; *śvetaketo,* O Śvetaketu; *vasa brahma-caryam,* live as a brahmacārin [i.e., a celibate student]; *na vai somya asmat kulīnaḥ,* no one in our family, my child; *ananūcya,* has not studied the scriptures; *brahma-bandhuḥ iva bhavati iti,* and has not been a good brāhmin.

1. Āruṇi had a son named Śvetaketu. Once Āruṇi told him: 'Śvetaketu, you should now live as a brahmacārin. No one in our family has not studied the scriptures and has not been a good brāhmin.'

The word *brahma-bandhu* literally means a relative or friend of a brāhmin—in other words, one who is a brāhmin in name only.

The question arises here, why did Āruṇi himself not invest his son with the sacred thread, initiating him into the life of a brahmacārin? Why did he suggest that his son go to another brāhmin for his sacred thread and for his education and training? Śaṅkara says, it is likely that Āruṇi was about to start on a journey and would be away from home for some time, and that is why he decided to send his son to another brāhmin.

स ह द्वादशवर्ष उपेत्य चतुर्विंशतिवर्षः सर्वान्वेदानधीत्य महामना अनूचानमानी स्तब्ध एयाय तं ह पितोवाच श्वेतकेतो यन्नु सोम्येदं महामना अनूचानमानी स्तब्धोऽस्युत तमादेशमप्राक्ष्यः ॥ २ ॥

Sa ha dvādaśavarṣa upetya caturviṁśativarṣaḥ sarvān-vedānadhītya mahāmanā anūcānamānī stabdha eyāya taṁ ha pitovāca śvetaketo yannu somyedaṁ mahāmanā anūcānamānī stabdho'syuta tamādeśamaprākṣyaḥ.

Saḥ ha, he [Śvetaketu]; *dvādaśa-varṣaḥ,* at the age of twelve; *upetya,* having gone [to his teacher as directed by his father]; *caturviṁśati-varṣaḥ,* till he was twenty-four; *sarvān vedān adhītya,* having studied all the Vedas; *eyāya,* returned home; *mahāmanāḥ,* very serious; *anūcānamānī,* vain; *stabdhaḥ,* having a high opinion of his scholarship; *tam ha pita uvāca,* his father said to him; *śvetaketo,* O Śvetaketu; *yat nu idam somya,* now young man; *mahāmanāḥ asi,* you have become very serious; *anūcānamānī,* vain; *stabdhaḥ,* thinking yourself to be a great scholar; *tam ādeśam,* that teaching; *aprākṣyaḥ uta,* did you ask [your teacher].

2. Śvetaketu went to his teacher's house at the age of twelve. After studying all the Vedas, he returned home when he was twenty-four, having become very serious and vain, and thinking himself to be a great scholar. [Noticing this,] his father said to him: 'O Śvetaketu, you have now become very serious and vain, and you think you are a great scholar. But did you ask your teacher for that teaching [about Brahman]—

Āruṇi must have been disappointed to see Śvetaketu's manners when he returned home. In order to instil into Śvetaketu the spirit of humility, Āruṇi put a question to him. He wanted to remind his son that scholarship was not the same as Self-knowledge. He also wanted Śvetaketu to understand that unless he knew the secret of Self-knowledge, his education was pointless. This secret of Self-knowledge is *ādeśa.*

येनाश्रुतं श्रुतं भवत्यमतं मतमविज्ञातं विज्ञातमिति
कथं नु भगवः स आदेशो भवतीति॥ ३॥

Yenāśrutaṁ śrutaṁ bhavatyamataṁ matamavijñātaṁ vijñātamiti kathaṁ nu bhagavaḥ sa ādeśo bhavatīti.

Yena, [that teaching] by which; *aśrutam,* what is never heard; *śrutam bhavati,* becomes heard; *amatam matam,* what is never thought of [becomes] thought of; *avijñātam vijñātam iti,* what is never known [becomes] known; *bhagavaḥ,* O lord; *katham nu saḥ ādeśaḥ bhavati iti,* what is that teaching?

3. '—that teaching by which what is never heard becomes heard, what is never thought of becomes thought of, what is never known becomes known?' [Śvetaketu asked,] 'Sir, what is that teaching?'

How can there be such a thing by knowing which you know everything else? This is what is puzzling Śvetaketu. Is it possible that by knowing one thing you also know something else? Separate things are to be known separately. But the claim is being made here that unless you know the Self you know nothing. And if you know the Self you know everything. This sounds like an absurd proposition.

This *ādeśa,* or teaching, that Āruṇi is talking about is the secret that opens up one's eyes, that makes one conscious of the fact that until and unless one knows the Self, one knows nothing.

यथा सोम्यैकेन मृत्पिण्डेन सर्वं मृन्मयं विज्ञातं स्याद्वाचारम्भणं विकारो नामधेयं मृत्तिकेत्येव सत्यम् ॥ ४ ॥

Yathā somyaikena mṛtpiṇḍena sarvaṁ mṛnmayaṁ

vijñātaṁ syādvācārambhaṇaṁ vikāro nāmadheyaṁ mṛttiketyeva satyam.

Somya, young man; *yathā,* just as; *ekena mṛtpiṇḍena,* from one single lump of earth; *sarvam mṛnmayam vijñātam,* all objects made of earth are known; *vācārambhaṇam nāmadheyam vikāraḥ,* all changes are mere words, in name only; *mṛttika iti eva satyam,* the earth is the reality.

4. O Somya, it is like this: By knowing a single lump of earth you know all objects made of earth. All changes are mere words, in name only. But earth is the reality.

What is this *ādeśa* that Śvetaketu's father wanted him to learn from his teacher? It is that there is only one single reality in this world, and that reality appears to be many because of the different names and forms superimposed on it.

Here he is using earth as an example. If you know a single thing made of earth—for instance, a pot—then you know all things made of earth. How? The word 'pot' is merely a name; the real object is earth. Earth may assume different names and forms, but it remains the same earth.

यथा सोम्यैकेन लोहमणिना सर्वं लोहमयं विज्ञातं
स्याद्वाचारम्भणं विकारो नामधेयं लोहमित्येव सत्यम् ॥ ५ ॥

Yathā somyaikena lohamaṇinā sarvaṁ lohamayaṁ vijñātaṁ syādvācārambhaṇaṁ vikāro nāmadheyaṁ lohamityeva satyam.

Somya, young man; *yathā,* just as; *ekena lohamaṇinā,* from one single lump of gold; *sarvam lohamayam vijñātam,* all objects made of gold [bangles, crowns, necklaces, etc.] are known; *vācārambhaṇam nāmadheyam vikāraḥ,* all changes are mere words, in name only; *loham iti eva satyam,* the gold is the reality.

5. O Somya, it is like this: By knowing a single lump of gold you know all objects made of gold. All changes are mere words, in name only. But gold is the reality.

यथा सोम्यैकेन नखनिकृन्तनेन सर्वं कार्ष्णायसं विज्ञातं स्याद्वाचारम्भणं विकारो नामधेयं कृष्णायसमित्येव सत्यमेवं सोम्य स आदेशो भवतीति॥ ६ ॥

Yathā somyaikena nakhanikṛntanena sarvaṁ kārṣṇāyasaṁ vijñātaṁ syādvācārambhaṇaṁ vikāro nāmadheyaṁ kṛṣṇāyasamityeva satyamevaṁ somya sa ādeṣo bhavatīti.

Somya, young man; *yathā,* just as; *ekena nakhanikṛntanena,* from one single nail-cutter; *sarvam kārṣṇāyasam vijñātam,* all objects made of iron are known; *vācārambhaṇam nāmadheyam vikāraḥ,* all changes are mere words, in name only; *kṛṣṇāyasam iti eva satyam,* the iron is the reality; *somya,* O Somya; *evam saḥ ādeśaḥ bhavati iti,* this is that teaching [I told you of].

6. O Somya, it is like this: By knowing a single nail-cutter you know all objects made of iron. All changes are mere words, in name only. But iron is the reality. O Somya, this is the teaching I spoke of.

न वै नूनं भगवन्तस्त एतदवेदिषुर्यद्ध्येतदवेदिष्यन्कथं मे नावक्ष्यन्निति भगवांस्त्वेव मे तद्ब्रवीत्विति तथा सोम्येति होवाच ॥ ७ ॥ इति प्रथमः खण्डः ॥ १ ॥

Na vai nūnaṁ bhagavantasta etadavediṣuryaddhyetadavediṣyankathaṁ me nāvakṣyanniti bhagavāṁstveva me tadbravītviti tathā somyeti hovāca. Iti prathamaḥ khaṇḍaḥ.

Bhagavantaḥ te, those revered teachers; *na vai nūnam avediṣuḥ,* surely did not know; *etat,* this [fact that if you know one you know all]; *yat,* if; *hi,* for sure; *etat avediṣyan,* they knew this; *me,* to me [their favourite disciple]; *katham,* why; *na avakṣyan iti,* did they not impart it; *bhagavān,* sir; *tu eva me tat bravītu iti,* so please explain it to me; *tathā,* let it be so; *somya,* young man; *iti ha uvāca,* he [the father] said. *Iti prathamaḥ khaṇḍaḥ,* here ends the first section.

7. [Śvetaketu said:] 'Surely my revered teachers did not know this truth. If they knew it, why should they not have told me? So please explain it to me, sir.' His father said, 'Let it be so, my son.'

Section Two

सदेव सोम्येदमग्र आसीदेकमेवाद्वितीयम्। तद्धैक आहुरसदेवेदमग्र आसीदेकमेवाद्वितीयं तस्मादसतः सज्जायत॥ १ ॥

Sadeva somyedamagra āsīdekamevādvitīyam; Taddhaika āhurasadevedamagra āsīdekamevādvitīyaṁ tasmādasataḥ sajjāyata.

Somya, young man; *idam,* this [world as we see it, with its names and forms]; *agre,* before [its manifestation]; *sat eva,* was existence only; *ekam eva advitīyam,* one without a second; *āsīt,* existed; *tat,* about that; *eke,* some [Buddhists and others]; *āhuḥ,* say; *idam,* this [world]; *agre,* first [before its manifestation]; *asat eva,* nothingness only; *ekam eva advitīyam,* one without a second; *āsīt,* existed; *tasmāt,* from that; *asataḥ,* nothingness; *sat jāyata,* existence emerged.

1. Somya, before this world was manifest there was only existence, one without a second. On this subject,

some maintain that before this world was manifest there was only non-existence, one without a second. Out of that non-existence, existence emerged.

'Something out of nothing' is an absurd idea. If there is a tree, it must have come out of a seed, whether the seed was seen by anyone or not. Sometimes you see a tree sprouting from a crack on the roof of a building. Where did it come from? From a seed which the wind must have blown on to the roof. A tree can only grow from a seed. Similarly, existence can only come from existence. This is what the Upaniṣad is suggesting when it says that before the world was manifest there was existence, one without a second.

The word *sat* means 'existence.' The Vedānta scriptures describe this existence as a state of being. It is one without a second. It is pure, all-pervasive, beyond thought and speech, and formless. It is consciousness.

Some philosophers maintain, however, that before the world originated there was nothing, one without a second. They claim that the world emerged from this nothing.

Vedānta says, suppose you are passing by a potter's house and you see him with a huge lump of clay. Then you return that same way a few hours later, and you are surprised to see that the nameless and formless lump of clay is transformed into a number of pots, plates, bowls, cups, etc.—each distinct with a name and a form. Similarly, existence becomes manifest as this world, but it remains existence. It has merely assumed various names and forms. In reality it is all existence.

The Naiyāyikas, the Buddhists, and others think just the opposite—that existence has come out of non-existence. But how can they know anything about a past non-existence? And how can they know, in particular, that it is one only without a second?

In fact, the concept of non-existence is being introduced here only to make a stronger foundation for the concept of existence. In order to know what to avoid, one must be able to see it. Similarly, the concept of non-existence is added only to make it clear what is meant by existence.

कुतस्तु खलु सोम्यैवं स्यादिति होवाच कथमसतः सज्जायेतेति। सत्त्वेव सोम्येदमग्र आसीदेकमेवाद्वितीयम्॥ २॥

Kutastu khalu somyaivaṁ syāditi hovāca kathamasataḥ sajjāyeteti; Sattveva somyedamagra āsīdekamevādvitīyam.

Somya, O Somya; *kutaḥ tu,* but what [proof is there]; *khalu,* indeed; *evam syāt,* could this be so; *iti ha uvāca,* he [Āruṇi] said; *katham,* in what way; *asataḥ,* from non-existence; *sat,* existence; *jāyata iti,* will come; *tu,* on the other hand; *somya,* O Somya; *idam agre,* before this [world]; *sat eva āsīt,* there was existence only; *ekam eva advitīyam,* one without a second.

2. The father said: 'O Somya, what proof is there for this—that from nothing something has emerged? Rather, before this world came into being, O Somya, there was only existence, one without a second.'

Let us say the world was not here before, but it came into existence at a certain point of time. What does this mean? Does this mean that there was a void and out of that void the world as we now see it emerged?

As has been stated already, the idea of something coming out of nothing is absurd. Yet some Buddhist scholars, who believe that existence comes from non-existence, argue that unless a seed is destroyed, a tree cannot grow from it. So according to them something comes out of nothing. Śaṅkara argues that it is only the form of the seed that is destroyed. The material that makes up the seed goes on to produce the tree. There is no example anywhere of something coming from nothing.

A potter makes pots out of clay. Can he make a pot out of nothing? No. But then the Buddhists argue, can a pot produce another pot? Vedānta says, no, but a pot can change its form. It can become potsherds or it can go back to the form of clay.

Vedānta says, the world always existed, but it did not always exist in the form we see it now. A snake is always a snake, whether it is lying like a long rope or it is coiled up. The world is Sat (Existence), and it is nameless and formless. But how it does come to have names and forms? The answer is that Existence is the only reality, but if it seems to have different names and forms, they are merely superimpositions and are not real.

तदैक्षत बहु स्यां प्रजायेयेति तत्तेजोऽसृजत तत्तेज ऐक्षत बहु स्यां प्रजायेयेति तदपोऽसृजत तस्माद्यत्र क्वच शोचति स्वेदते वा पुरुषस्तेजस एव तदध्यापो जायन्ते ॥ ३ ॥

Tadaikṣata bahu syāṁ prajāyeyeti tattejo'sṛjata tatteja aikṣata bahu syāṁ prajāyeyeti tadapo'sṛjata tasmādyatra kvaca śocati svedate vā puruṣastejasa eva tadadhyāpo jāyante.

Tat, that [existence]; *aikṣata,* decided; *bahu syām,* I shall be many; *prajāyeya iti,* I shall be born; *tat,* that [existence]; *asṛjata,* created; *tejaḥ,* fire; *tat tejaḥ,* that [existence as] fire; *aikṣata,* decided; *bahu syām,* I shall be many; *prajāyeya iti,* I shall be born; *tat,* that [fire]; *apaḥ,* water; *asṛjata,* created; *tasmāt,* that is why; *yatra kva ca,* whenever and wherever; *puruṣaḥ,* a person; *śocati,* grieves; *svedate vā,* or perspires; *tat,* [it happens] that; *tejasaḥ eva,* from fire; *āpaḥ adhijāyante,* water comes.

3. That Existence decided: 'I shall be many. I shall be born.' He then created fire. That fire also decided: 'I shall be many. I shall be born.' Then fire produced water. That is why whenever or wherever a person mourns or perspires, he produces water.

The word *aikṣata* means 'saw,' 'thought,' or 'decided.' It can only apply to a conscious principle, because only a conscious principle can decide or think or see. And only a conscious being can say that he will be many.

The scriptures say that this Existence, or Brahman, is one without a second, always the same, unchanging, and unchangeable. So how can it at the same time be many? Vedānta says that it is like a lump of earth sometimes taking different forms of pots, cups, etc. Or it is like a rope which sometimes looks like a snake. The change is only in names and forms. It is not a real change.

Vedānta says, this applies to all that we see in this world. Underlying the seeming diversity there is unity. This unity—this One—supports the diversity. It is this One that has become many, but only in appearance. To go back to the example of the earth, the earth remains earth, though in appearance it may take the form of a lump or of some pots or of some other things.

An apt description of this is 'unity in diversity.' It is Brahman that has become everything—space, air, fire, water, earth.

Then the question arises, how can fire, which is

inanimate, think? The answer is that here fire stands for Brahman. Brahman as fire is making things happen. Brahman is the source of everything. It is the base, the reality. Just as earth can be in the form of a lump or a pot, similarly, Brahman can be in the form of fire, water, or something else.

It is not that Brahman undergoes any change. Brahman remains Brahman. It is Sat, eternal Existence. It is the Absolute. It is never conditioned by anything. When it says it will be 'many,' it means it will appear in many forms, just as earth or gold can be in many forms. But it must be borne in mind that this Existence is also pure consciousness.

ता आप ऐक्षन्त बह्व्यः स्याम प्रजायेमहीति ता अन्नमसृजन्त तस्माद्यत्र क्वच वर्षति तदेव भूयिष्ठमन्नं भवत्यद्भ्य एव तदध्यन्नाद्यं जायते॥ ४॥ इति द्वितीयः खण्डः॥ २॥

Tā āpa aikṣanta bahvyaḥ syāma prajāyemahīti tā annamasṛjanta tasmādyatra kvaca varṣati tadeva bhūyiṣṭhamannaṁ bhavatyadbhya eva tadadhyannādyaṁ jāyate. Iti dvitīyaḥ khaṇḍaḥ.

Tāḥ āpaḥ, that water; *aikṣanta,* decided; *bahvyaḥ syāma,* I shall be many; *prajāyemahi iti,* I shall be born; *tāḥ,* that [water]; *annam asṛjanta,* produced food; *tasmāt,* that is why; *yatra kva ca,* whenever and wherever; *varṣati,* it rains; *tat,* at once; *bhūyiṣṭham,* in great abundance; *annam bhavati,* food grows; *adbhyaḥ eva,* it is from water; *tat,* then; *annādyam adhijāyate,* food is produced. *Iti dvitīyaḥ khaṇḍaḥ,* here ends the second section.

4. That water decided: 'I shall be many. I shall be born.' That water then created food. This is why whenever and wherever there is rain, at once food grows in great abundance. It is from water that food is produced.

Here, food represents earth.

Section Three

तेषां खल्वेषां भूतानां त्रीण्येव बीजानि भवन्त्याण्डजं जीवजमुद्भिज्जमिति ॥ १ ॥

Teṣāṁ khalveṣāṁ bhūtānāṁ trīṇyeva bījāni bhavantyāṇḍajaṁ jīvajamudbhijjamiti.

Teṣām khalu eṣām bhūtānām, of these living beings; *trīṇi eva bījāni bhavanti,* there are three kinds of origin; *āṇḍajam,* birth from eggs; *jīvajam,* from parents; *udbhijjam iti,* from plants.

1. Living beings have their origin in three ways: from eggs, from parents, and from plants.

सेयं देवतैक्षत हन्ताहमिमास्तिस्रो देवता अनेन जीवेनात्मनानुप्रविश्य नामरूपे व्याकरवाणीति ॥ २ ॥

Seyaṁ devataikṣata hantāhamimāstisro devatā anena jīvenātmanānupraviśya nāmarūpe vyākaravāṇīti.

Sā iyam devatā, that deity [i.e., Sat, Existence]; *aikṣata,* decided; *hanta,* so; *aham,* I; *imāḥ tisraḥ devatāḥ,* these three gods [i.e., fire, water, and earth]; *anena jīvena ātmanā,* as the jīvātman [i.e., the individual self]; *anupraviśya,* having entered; *nāmarūpe,* as names and forms; *vyākaravāṇi iti,* I shall manifest.

2. That god [Existence] decided: 'Entering into these three deities [fire, water, and earth], as the individual self, I shall manifest myself in many names and forms.'

The Self (Sat) is within fire, water, and earth, but that is not to say that it is in any way affected by them. If you stand before a mirror, you see your reflection. The reflection may be good or it may not be good, but does that affect the mirror? The sun gives light to the eyes, but if there is anything wrong with the eyes, does that affect the sun?

Similarly, the Self is everywhere and in everything. But wherever it is, it is the same. Names and forms, apart from the Self, are false. But there is, in reality, nothing apart from the Self. Everything is the Self. In that sense, the names and forms are also the Self and therefore real.

तासां त्रिवृतं त्रिवृतमेकैकां करवाणीति सेयं देवतेमास्तिस्रो देवता अनेनैव जीवेनात्मनानुप्रविश्य नामरूपे व्याकरोत्॥ ३ ॥

Tāsāṁ trivṛtaṁ trivṛtamekaikāṁ karavāṇīti seyaṁ devatemāstisro devatā anenaiva jīvenātmanānupraviśya nāmarūpe vyākarot.

Tāsām, of these [three deities]; *trivṛtam trivṛtam,* dividing them threefold; *ekaikām,* each of them; *karavāṇi iti,* I shall make; *sā iyam devatā,* that deity [Existence]; *imāḥ tisraḥ devatā,* these three deities; *anena jīvena eva ātmanā,* as the individual self; *anupraviśya,* having entered; *nāmarūpe vyākarot,* manifested himself as names and forms.

3. Sat [Existence] thought, 'I shall divide each of these three deities threefold.' Then, having entered into these three deities as the individual self, he manifested himself as names and forms.

Trivṛtam is applied in the case of fire, water, and earth as follows:

gross fire = 1/2 subtle fire + 1/4 subtle water + 1/4 subtle earth
gross water = 1/2 subtle water + 1/4 subtle fire + 1/4 subtle earth
gross earth = 1/2 subtle earth + 1/4 subtle fire + 1/4 subtle water

This mixture turns the subtle elements into gross elements. It makes them separate and yet one. A similar process, called *pañcikaraṇa,* is applied in the case of the five elements—space, air, fire, water, and earth.

Sat, or Brahman, is present in all the elements as their Self. First he is manifest as their sum total, called *Virāṭ.* He then manifests himself as names and forms.

तासां त्रिवृतं त्रिवृतमेकैकामकरोद्यथा तु खलु सोम्येमास्तिस्रो देवतास्त्रिवृत्त्रिवृदेकैका भवति तन्मे विजानीहीति ॥ ४ ॥ इति तृतीयः खण्डः ॥ ३ ॥

Tāsāṁ trivṛtaṁ trivṛtamekaikāmakarodyathā tu khalu somyemāstisro devatāstrivṛttrivṛdekaikā bhavati tanme vijānīhīti. Iti tṛtīyaḥ khaṇḍaḥ.

Tāsām of those [three elements]; *ekaikām,* each one of them; *trivṛtam trivṛtam akarot,* he made threefold; *somya,* O Somya; *yathā tu khalu,* but as to how; *imāḥ tisraḥ devatā,* these three deities; *trivṛt trivṛt ekaikā bhavati,* each becomes threefold; *tat me vijānīhi iti,* learn this from me. *Iti tṛtīyaḥ khaṇḍaḥ,* here ends the third section.

4. [Having so decided,] he made each of these three elements threefold. But as to how each of these three deities becomes threefold, O Somya, learn this from me.

Section Four

यदग्ने रोहितं रूपं तेजसस्तद्रूपं यच्छुक्लं तदपां यत्कृष्णं तदन्नस्यापागादग्नेरग्नित्वं वाचारम्भणं विकारो नामधेयं त्रीणि रूपाणीत्येव सत्यम्॥ १॥

Yadagne rohitaṁ rūpaṁ tejasastadrūpaṁ yacchuklaṁ tadapāṁ yatkṛṣṇaṁ tadannasyāpāgādagneragnitvaṁ vācārambhaṇaṁ vikāro nāmadheyaṁ trīṇi rūpāṇītyeva satyam.

Yat agneḥ rohitam rūpam, that red colour of [gross] fire; *tat rūpam tejasaḥ,* that colour is from [subtle] fire; *yat śuklam,* that which is white; *tat apām,* that is from [subtle] water; *yat kṛṣṇam,* that which is dark; *tat annasya,* that is from [subtle] earth [lit., food]; *agneḥ agnitvam apāgāt,* [thus] the 'fire'-ness of fire is gone; *vācārambhaṇam nāmadheyam vikāraḥ,* all changes are mere words, in name only; *trīṇi rūpāṇi iti eva satyam,* only the three colours are the reality [i.e., outside of the three colours, there is no fire].

1. The red colour of gross fire is from subtle fire, the white colour is from subtle water, and the dark colour is from subtle earth. Thus that which constitutes the 'fire'-ness of fire is gone. All changes are mere words, in name only [i.e., fire is only a name indicating a certain condition]. The three colours are the reality.

When fire is gross it has a red colour which comes from its subtle aspect. But there is also a white colour in it which comes from the subtle water element. Similarly, sometimes it has a dark colour which comes from the subtle earth element. The Upaniṣad says, in reality, fire is nothing beyond these three colours —red, white, and black. This proves the falsity of the idea of gross fire.

यदादित्यस्य रोहितं रूपं तेजसस्तद्रूपं यच्छुक्लं तदपां यत्कृष्णं तदन्नस्यापागादादित्यादादित्यत्वं वाचारम्भणं विकारो नामधेयं त्रीणि रूपाणीत्येव सत्यम् ॥ २ ॥

Yadādityasya rohitaṁ rūpaṁ tejasastadrūpaṁ yac-chuklaṁ tadapāṁ yatkṛṣṇaṁ tadannasyāpāgādādityā-dādityatvaṁ vācārambhaṇaṁ vikāro nāmadheyaṁ trīṇi rūpāṇītyeva satyam.

Yat ādityasya rohitam rūpam, that red colour of the sun; *tat rūpam tejasaḥ,* that colour is from fire; *yat śuklam,* that which is white; *tat apām,* that is from water; *yat kṛṣṇam,* that which is dark; *tat annasya,* that is from earth [lit., food]; *ādityāt ādityatvam apāgāt,* [thus] the 'sun'-ness of the sun is gone; *vācārambhaṇam nāmadheyam vikāraḥ,* all changes are mere words, in name only; *trīṇi rūpāṇi iti eva satyam,* only the three colours are the reality [i.e., outside of the three colours, there is no sun].

2. The red colour of the sun is from fire, the white colour is from water, and the dark colour is from earth. Thus that which constitutes the 'sun'-ness of the sun is gone. All changes are mere words, in name only. The three colours are the reality.

यच्चन्द्रमसो रोहितं रूपं तेजसस्तद्रूपं यच्छुक्लं तदपां यत्कृष्णं तदन्नस्यापागाच्चन्द्राच्चन्द्रत्वं वाचारम्भणं विकारो नामधेयं त्रीणि रूपाणीत्येव सत्यम् ॥ ३ ॥

Yaccandramaso rohitaṁ rūpaṁ tejasastadrūpaṁ yacchuklaṁ tadapāṁ yatkṛṣṇaṁ tadannasyāpāgāccandrāccandratvaṁ vācārambhaṇaṁ vikāro nāmadheyaṁ trīṇi rūpāṇītyeva satyam.

Yat candramasaḥ rohitam rūpam, that red colour of the moon; *tat rūpam tejasaḥ,* that colour is from fire; *yat śuklam,* that which is white; *tat apām,* that is from water; *yat kṛṣṇam,* that which is dark; *tat annasya,* that is from earth [lit., food]; *candrāt candratvam apāgāt,* [thus] the 'moon'-ness of the moon is gone; *vācārambhaṇam nāmadheyam vikāraḥ,* all changes are mere words, in name only; *trīṇi rūpāṇi iti eva satyam,* only the three colours are the reality [i.e., outside of the three colours, there is no moon].

3. The red colour of the moon is from fire, the white colour is from water, and the dark colour is from earth. Thus that which constitutes the

'moon'-ness of the moon is gone. All changes are mere words, in name only. The three colours are the reality.

यद्विद्युतो रोहितं रूपं तेजसस्तद्रूपं यच्छुक्लं तदपां यत्कृष्णं तदन्नस्यापागाद्विद्युतो विद्युत्त्वं वाचारम्भणं विकारो नामधेयं त्रीणि रूपाणीत्येव सत्यम् ॥ ४ ॥

Yadvidyuto rohitaṁ rūpaṁ tejasastadrūpaṁ yacchuklaṁ tadapāṁ yatkṛṣṇaṁ tadannasyāpāgādvidyuto vidyuttvaṁ vācārambhaṇaṁ vikāro nāmadheyaṁ trīṇi rūpāṇītyeva satyam.

Yat vidyutaḥ rohitam rūpam, that red colour of lightning; *tat rūpam tejasaḥ,* that colour is from fire; *yat śuklam,* that which is white; *tat apām,* that is from water; *yat kṛṣṇam,* that which is dark; *tat annasya,* that is from earth [lit., food]; *vidyutaḥ vidyuttvam apāgāt,* [thus] the 'lightning'-ness of lightning is gone; *vācārambhaṇam nāmadheyam vikāraḥ,* all changes are mere words, in name only; *trīṇi rūpāṇi iti eva satyam,* only the three colours are the reality [i.e., outside of the three colours, there is no lightning].

4. The red colour of lightning is from fire, the white colour is from water, and the dark colour is from earth. Thus that which constitutes the 'lightning'-ness of lightning is gone. All changes are mere words, in name only. The three colours are the reality.

एतद्ध स्म वै तद्विद्वांस आहुः पूर्वे महाशाला महाश्रोत्रिया न नोऽद्य कश्चनाश्रुतममतमविज्ञात-मुदाहरिष्यतीति ह्येभ्यो विदाञ्चक्रुः ॥ ५ ॥

Etaddha sma vai tadvidvāṁsa āhuḥ pūrve mahāśālā mahāśrotriyā na no'dya kaścanāśrutamamatamavijñāta-mudāhariṣyatīti hyebhyo vidāñcakruḥ.

Tat etat vidvāṁsaḥ ha, having known this; *vai pūrve,* the earlier; *mahāśālāḥ,* great householders; *mahāśrotriyāḥ,* who were well read in the Vedas; *āhuḥ sma,* said; *adya,* now; *kaścana,* anyone [i.e., any scholar]; *naḥ,* to us; *aśrutam,* unheard of; *amatam,* unthought of; *avijñātam,* unknown; *udāhariṣyati iti,* can speak of; *hi,* since; *ebhyaḥ,* these three [colours]; *vidāñcakruḥ,* they came to know [that by knowing one, a person knows all].

5. The earlier great householders, who were well read in the Vedas, knew this. They said, 'There is nothing anyone can mention that is not heard of or thought of or already known to us.' This is because they came to know about the three colours.

यदु रोहितमिवाभूदिति तेजसस्तद्रूपमिति तद्विदाञ्चक्रुर्यदु शुक्लमिवाभूदित्यपां रूपमिति तद्विदाञ्चक्रुर्यदु कृष्ण-मिवाभूदित्यन्नस्य रूपमिति तद्विदाञ्चक्रुः ॥ ६ ॥

Yadu rohitamivābhūditi tejasastadrūpamiti tadvidāñcakruryadu śuklamivābhūdityapāṁ rūpamiti tadvidāñcakruryadu kṛṣṇamivābhūdityannasya rūpamiti tadvidāñcakruḥ.

Yat u rohitam iva abhūt iti, whatever else was seen as red; *tat rūpam tejasaḥ iti,* that is the colour of fire; *tat vidāñcakruḥ,* they knew that; *yat u śuklam iva abhūt iti,* whatever else was seen as white; *tat apām rūpam iti,* that is the colour of water; *vidāñcakruḥ,* they knew; *yat u kṛṣṇam iva abhūt iti,* whatever else was seen as dark; *tat annasya rūpam iti,* that is the colour of earth [lit., food]; *vidāñcakruḥ,* they knew.

6. They knew that whatever else was seen as red was the colour of fire; whatever else was seen as white was the colour of water; and whatever else was seen as dark was the colour of earth.

यद्वविज्ञातमिवाभूदित्येतासामेव देवतानां समास इति तद्विदाञ्चक्रुर्यथा खलु नु सोम्येमास्तिस्रो देवताः पुरुषं प्राप्य त्रिवृत्त्रिवृदेकैका भवति तन्मे विजानीहीति ॥ ७॥ इति चतुर्थः खण्डः ॥ ४ ॥

Yadvavijñātamivābhūdityetāsāmeva devatānāṁ samāsa iti tadvidāñcakruryathā khalu nu somyemāstisro devatāḥ puruṣaṁ prāpya trivṛttrivṛdekaikā bhavati tanme vijānīhīti. Iti caturthaḥ khaṇḍaḥ.

Yat u avijñātam iva abhūt iti, and whatever they saw that was not properly known; *samāsaḥ iti,* the combination; *etāsām eva devatānām,* of these deities [fire, water, and earth]; *tat vidāñcakruḥ,* that they knew; *somya,* my son; *yathā,* as to how; *imāḥ khalu nu,* these very; *tisraḥ devatāḥ,* three deities; *puruṣam,* a living being; *prāpya,* entering [as food]; *trivṛt trivṛt ekaikā bhavati,* each one becomes threefold; *tat me vijānīhi iti,* learn that from me. *Iti caturthaḥ khaṇḍaḥ,* here ends the fourth section.

7. And whatever else was not properly known they understood was the combination of those three deities [fire, water, and earth]. O Somya, now learn from me how these three deities enter into a person and become threefold.

Previously the scholars did not know these deities—the three elements—separately. They began to understand better when they saw the elements working in living beings.

Section Five

अन्नमशितं त्रेधा विधीयते तस्य यः स्थविष्ठो धातुस्तत्पुरीषं भवति यो मध्यमस्तन्मांसं योऽणिष्ठ-स्तन्मनः ॥ १ ॥

Annamaśitaṁ tredhā vidhīyate tasya yaḥ sthaviṣṭho dhātustatpurīṣaṁ bhavati yo madhyamastanmāṁsaṁ yo'ṇiṣṭhastanmanaḥ.

Annam aśitam, when food is eaten; *tredhā,* in three ways; *vidhīyate,* is divided; *tasya,* of it; *yaḥ sthaviṣṭhaḥ,* that which is the grossest; *dhātuḥ,* part; *tat purīṣam bhavati,* that becomes excreta; *yaḥ madhyamaḥ,* that which is less gross [lit., middle]; *tat māṁsam,* that [becomes] flesh; *yaḥ aṇiṣṭhaḥ,* that which is the subtlest; *tat manaḥ,* that [becomes] the mind.

1. When we eat food, it divides itself into three parts. The grossest part of it becomes excreta; that which is less gross becomes our flesh; and the finest part becomes our mind.

When we eat, the food nourishes the body in different ways. How? First, the grossest part of the food is rejected by the body. Then that which is less gross, a bit finer, becomes our flesh. And finally the finest part becomes the mind. According to Vedānta, the mind is material. It functions through the nervous system, which is called *hitā.*

How does this food get transformed into the mind? Śaṅkara says that the subtlest part of the food becomes blood and enters into the heart. From there it goes through the veins and nerves, nourishing the mind. The term *mind* refers here to the phenomena of our thinking, feeling, willing, etc., plus the aggregate of our sense organs—our seeing, hearing, and so forth.

Suppose you do not eat anything. What happens? Slowly you will feel that your mind is becoming more and more feeble. Your memory starts failing, and you cannot concentrate. The finest part of your system is affected. Then the body begins to shrink. You become thinner and thinner, and finally you die. Food nourishes all these. This is why Vedānta says that the mind is material.

आपः पीतास्त्रेधा विधीयन्ते तासां यः स्थविष्ठो धातुस्तन्मूत्रं भवति यो मध्यमस्तल्लोहितं योऽणिष्ठः स प्राणः ॥ २ ॥

Āpaḥ pītāstredhā vidhīyante tāsāṁ yaḥ sthaviṣṭho dhātustanmūtraṁ bhavati yo madhyamastallohitaṁ yo'ṇiṣṭhaḥ sa prāṇaḥ.

Āpaḥ, water; *pītāḥ,* when drunk; *tredhā,* in three ways; *vidhīyante,* is divided; *tāsām,* of it; *yaḥ sthaviṣṭaḥ dhātuḥ,* that which is the grossest part; *tat mūtram bhavati,* that becomes urine; *yaḥ madhyamaḥ,* that which is less gross; *tat lohitam,* that [becomes] blood; *yaḥ aṇiṣṭhaḥ,* that which is the finest part; *saḥ prāṇaḥ,* that is prāṇa.

2. When we drink water, it becomes divided in three parts. The grossest part of it becomes urine; that which is less gross becomes blood; and the finest part becomes prāṇa, the vital force.

Water also has a threefold function. When we drink water, the grossest part of it flushes our whole system and at last passes out of the body as urine. Then that which is less gross becomes blood. If I do not drink water, the blood would clot and there would be no more blood supply. Then the finest aspect becomes prāṇa, the vital force. Without water, we could not breathe or live.

तेजोऽशितं त्रेधा विधीयते तस्य यः स्थविष्ठो धातुस्तदस्थि भवति यो मध्यमः स मज्जा योऽणिष्ठः सा वाक्॥ ३ ॥

Tejo'śitaṁ tredhā vidhīyate tasya yaḥ sthaviṣṭho dhātustadasthi bhavati yo madhyamaḥ sa majjā yo'ṇiṣṭhaḥ sā vāk.

Tejaḥ aśitam, when fire [i.e., oil, butter, etc., which produce energy] is eaten; *tredhā,* in three ways; *vidhīyate,* is divided; *tasya,* of it; *yaḥ sthaviṣṭhaḥ,* that which is the grossest; *dhātuḥ,* part; *tat asthi bhavati,* that becomes bone; *yaḥ madhyamaḥ,* that which is midway; *saḥ majjā,* that [becomes] marrow; *yaḥ aṇiṣṭhaḥ,* that which is the subtlest; *sā vāk,* that is speech.

3. When we eat fire [i.e., butter, oil, etc.], it divides itself into three parts. The grossest part of it becomes bone; that which is less gross becomes marrow; and the subtlest part becomes speech.

Tejas literally means 'fire.' The idea here is that if you eat butter or fatty substances such as oil, it is like eating fire. Why? Because butter and oil are sources of tejas—that is, they provide us energy and vitality. These substances, when eaten, also become transformed into three different things. That which is gross becomes our bones; that which is between the gross and the subtle becomes our marrow; and that which is subtle becomes our speech. If our organ of speech is supported by the right kind of food, we are able to speak logically and articulately.

The Upaniṣad is showing us here how we depend on these elements—earth, water, and fire. We are able to think, speak, and move about all because of the support we get from them. But all these things depend on Brahman, pure Spirit. If you think of the way nature functions, and how the planets rotate in their orbits, and so forth, you are extremely impressed. Everything is so well organized. But we must remember, it is Brahman that is manifesting as nature, as the planets, as you and me and each individual—as even the tiny insects. The idea is that the One has become the many. Let us not be deluded by seeing the many.

अन्नमयं हि सोम्य मन आपोमयः प्राणस्तेजोमयी वागिति भूय एव मा भगवान्विज्ञापयत्विति तथा सोम्येति होवाच॥४॥ इति पञ्चमः खण्डः॥५॥

Annamayaṁ hi somya mana āpomayaḥ prāṇastejomayī vāgiti bhūya eva mā bhagavānvijñāpayatviti tathā somyeti hovāca. Iti pañcamaḥ khaṇḍaḥ.

Somya, O Somya; *manaḥ hi annamayam,* the mind is nourished by food; *prāṇaḥ āpomayaḥ,* the vital force is nourished by water; *vāk tejomayī iti,* speech is nourished by fire; *bhagavān,* sir; *bhūyaḥ eva,* again; *mā,* to me; *vijñāpayatu iti,* will you please explain; *tathā,* so be it; *somya iti,* O Somya; *ha uvāca,* he [the father] said. *Iti pañcamaḥ khaṇḍaḥ,* here ends the fifth section.

4. 'O Somya, the mind is nourished by food, prāṇa by water, and speech by fire.' [Śvetaketu then said,] 'Sir, will you please explain this to me again?' 'Yes, Somya, I will explain again,' replied his father.

In the Vedānta philosophy there are said to be five elements. The first two—ākāśa (space, or ether) and vāyu (air)—are not visible to us. The other three —pṛthivī (earth—here referred to as annam, food), āpa (water), and agni, or tejas (fire, or energy)—are visible, and this is why they have been discussed here. These three elements, however, are never to be found in their pure form. When we perceive them, they are always in a combined state. For instance, the water that we see always has some earth and other elements mixed with it. In reality, though, it is pure Spirit which we see as earth, water, or fire.

The father has been telling his son that the mind is the finest product of food, that prāṇa, the vital force, is the finest product of water, and that speech is the finest product of fire. Naturally the son is confused. It is not very clear. So he asks his father to explain it further.

Section Six

दध्नः सोम्य मथ्यमानस्य योऽणिमा स ऊर्ध्वः समुदीषति तत्सर्पिर्भवति ॥ १ ॥

Dadhnaḥ somya mathyamānasya yo'ṇimā sa ūrdhvaḥ samudīṣati tatsarpirbhavati.

Somya, O Somya; *dadhnaḥ mathyamānasya,* of curd when it is churned; *yaḥ aṇimā,* what is the finest part; *saḥ ūrdhvaḥ samudīṣati,* that rises to the surface; *tat sarpiḥ bhavati,* that becomes butter.

1. When curd is churned, the finest part of it rises to the surface. That becomes butter.

Even now, in many homes in India, people make their own butter by churning curd. When you churn the curd, cream starts appearing on the surface. Gradually that cream turns into butter. It was already in the curd. In fact, it was the finest part of the curd. Only the churning was needed to make it rise to the top.

एवमेव खलु सोम्यान्नस्याश्यमानस्य योऽणिमा स ऊर्ध्वः समुदीषति तन्मनो भवति॥ २॥

Evameva khalu somyānnasyāśyamānasya yo'ṇimā sa ūrdhvaḥ samudīṣati tanmano bhavati.

Evam eva khalu, in the same way; *somya,* O Somya; *annasya aśyamānasya,* of the food that is eaten; *yaḥ aṇimā,* that which is the finest part; *saḥ ūrdhvaḥ samudīṣati,* it rises to the surface; *tat manaḥ bhavati,* that becomes the mind.

2. O Somya, in the same way, the finest part of the food that is eaten rises to the surface and becomes the mind.

Anna means the food that you eat—any food. Wheat, rice, fish, meat, vegetables, milk, and so on—all this is *anna.* The Upaniṣad says, that which is the finest part of the food rises to the surface, like the butter in curd. It then becomes the mind. It is the subtlest part of the food, the essence. According to Vedānta, the mind is material. It is a by-product of food and is nourished by food.

अपां सोम्य पीयमानानां योऽणिमा स ऊर्ध्वः समुदीषति स प्राणो भवति॥ ३॥

Apāṁ somya pīyamānānāṁ yo'ṇimā sa ūrdhvaḥ samudīṣati sa prāṇo bhavati.

Somya, O Somya; *apām pīyamānānām,* of the water that is drunk; *yaḥ aṇimā,* that which is the finest part; *saḥ ūrdhvaḥ samudīṣati,* it rises to the surface; *saḥ prāṇaḥ bhavati,* that becomes prāṇa, the vital force.

3. O Somya, the finest part of water that is drunk rises to the surface and becomes our prāṇa.

Similarly, if you drink water, the finest part of that water becomes separated from the rest and rises to the surface to become prāṇa, the vital force. This is why in Sanskrit water and life (*jala* and *jīvana*) are synonymous. Without water, life cannot exist. In fact, science says that life first appeared in water.

तेजसः सोम्याश्यमानस्य योऽणिमा स ऊर्ध्वः समुदीषति सा वाग्भवति ॥ ४ ॥

Tejasaḥ somyāśyamānasya yo'ṇimā sa ūrdhvaḥ samudīṣati sā vāgbhavati.

Somya, O Somya; *tejasaḥ aśyamānasya,* of the fire [butter, etc.] that is eaten; *yaḥ aṇimā,* that which is the finest part; *saḥ ūrdhvaḥ samudīṣati,* it rises to the surface; *sā vāk bhavati,* that becomes speech.

4. O Somya, the finest part of fire [butter, etc.] that is eaten rises to the surface and becomes our speech.

अन्नमयं हि सोम्य मन आपोमयः प्राणस्तेजोमयी वागिति भूय एव मा भगवान्विज्ञापयत्विति तथा सोम्येति होवाच॥५॥ इति षष्ठः खण्डः॥६॥

Annamayaṁ hi somya mana āpomayaḥ prāṇastejo-mayī vāgiti bhūya eva mā bhagavānvijñāpayatviti tathā somyeti hovāca. Iti ṣaṣṭhaḥ khaṇḍaḥ.

Somya, O Somya; *manaḥ hi annamayam,* the mind is certainly nourished by food; *prāṇaḥ āpomayaḥ,* the vital force is nourished by water; *vāk tejomayī iti,* speech is nourished by fire; *bhagavān,* sir; *bhūyaḥ eva,* again; *mā,* to me; *vijñāpayatu iti,* will you please explain; *tathā,* so be it; *somya iti,* O Somya; *ha uvāca,* he [the father] said. *Iti ṣaṣṭhaḥ khaṇḍaḥ,* here ends the sixth section.

5. 'O Somya, the mind is certainly nourished by food, prāṇa by water, and speech by fire.' [Śvetaketu then said,] 'Sir, will you please explain this to me again?' 'Yes, I will explain again, O Somya,' replied his father.

Section Seven

षोडशकलः सोम्य पुरुषः पञ्चदशाहानि माशीः काममपः
पिबापोमयः प्राणो न पिबतो विच्छेत्स्यत इति ॥ १ ॥

Ṣoḍaśakalaḥ somya puruṣaḥ pañcadaśāhāni māśīḥ kāmamapaḥ pibāpomayaḥ prāṇo na pibato vicchetsyata iti.

Somya, O Somya; *puruṣaḥ,* a person; *ṣoḍaśakalaḥ,* has sixteen parts; *pañcadaśa ahāni,* for fifteen days; *mā aśīḥ,* do not eat; *apaḥ piba,* drink water; *kāmam,* as much as you like; *prāṇaḥ āpomayaḥ,* life is dependent on water; *na pibataḥ,* if you do not drink water; *vicchetsyate iti,* it will leave.

1. O Somya, a person has sixteen parts, [and all your sixteen parts are intact]. Do not eat anything for fifteen days, but drink as much water as you like. Life is dependent on water. If you do not drink water, you will lose your life.

Now the son says, 'I still can't understand.' So the father tries something else. A normal human being in good health is said, in Vedānta, to be made up of sixteen parts. If a person neither eats nor drinks water for fifteen days, he will die. But if he does not eat yet continues to drink water during that time he will remain alive. When Gandhiji used to fast, he would drink plenty of water and would put some lemon juice in it. That would keep him alive. But what happens to a person when he drinks water but does not eat? His mind fails. He cannot remember anything.

So, to convince his son, the father asks him to fast for fifteen days but to drink water.

स ह पञ्चदशाहानि नाशाथ हैनमुपससाद किं ब्रवीमि भो इत्यृचः सोम्य यजूंषि सामानीति स होवाच न वै मा प्रतिभान्ति भो इति॥ २॥

Sa ha pañcadaśāhāni nāśātha hainamupasasāda kiṁ bravīmi bho ityṛcaḥ somya yajūṁṣi sāmānīti sa hovāca na vai mā pratibhānti bho iti.

Saḥ, he [Śvetaketu]; *ha pañcadaśa ahāni,* for fifteen days; *na āśa,* did not eat anything; *atha,* then [on the sixteenth day]; *enam ha upasasāda,* he went to him [his father]; *bhoḥ,* O Father; *kim bravīmi iti,* what shall I recite; *somya,* O Somya; *ṛcaḥ yajūṁṣi sāmāni iti,* the Ṛk, the Yajuḥ, and the Sāmas; *saḥ ha uvāca,* [Śvetaketu] said; *bhoḥ,* O Father; *na vai mā pratibhānti iti,* they do not come to my mind.

2. Śvetaketu did not eat anything for fifteen days. After that he came to his father and said, 'O Father, what shall I recite?' His father said, 'Recite the Ṛk, Yajuḥ, and Sāma mantras.' Śvetaketu replied, 'I can't recall any of them, sir.'

Now the father says to his son, 'Will you please recite to me the Ṛk, Yajuḥ, and Sāma mantras?' But the son replies: 'They are completely gone. I do not remember them. They do not appear in my mind at all.' Having been without food for fifteen days, Śvetaketu's mind was almost gone. The mind is the finest part, the essence, of food—not of water, not of anything else. Therefore, the mind must be material.

तं होवाच यथा सोम्य महतोऽभ्याहितस्यैकोऽङ्गारः खद्योतमात्रः परिशिष्टः स्यात्तेन ततोऽपि न बहु दहेदेवं सोम्य ते षोडशानां कलानामेका कलातिशिष्टा स्यात्तयैतर्हि वेदान्नानुभवस्यशानाथ मे विज्ञास्यसीति ॥ ३ ॥

Taṁ hovāca yathā somya mahato'bhyāhitasyaiko-'ṅgāraḥ khadyotamātraḥ pariśiṣṭaḥ syāttena tato'pi na bahu dahedevaṁ somya te ṣoḍaśānāṁ kalānāmekā kalātiśiṣṭā syāttayaitarhi vedānnānubhavasyaśānātha me vijñāsyasīti.

Tam ha uvāca, he said to him [to Śvetaketu]; *somya,* O Somya; *yathā,* as; *mahataḥ abhyāhitasya,* of a big blazing fire; *ekaḥ aṅgāraḥ,* one ember; *khadyotamātraḥ,* the size of a firefly; *pariśiṣṭaḥ syāt,* that is left; *tena,* by that; *tataḥ api bahu,* anything larger than its size; *na dahet,* cannot burn; *evam,* like that; *somya,* my son; *ekā kalā,* only one part; *ṣoḍaśānām kalānām,* of [your] sixteen parts; *atiśiṣṭā syāt,* has remained; *etarhi,* now; *tayā,* by that [small part]; *vedān,* the Vedas; *na anubhavasi,* you do not remember; *aśāna,* eat; *atha,* then; *me,* my [words]; *vijñāsyasi iti,* you will grasp.

3. The father said to Śvetaketu: 'O Somya, from a blazing fire, if there is but a small piece of ember left, the size of a firefly, it cannot burn anything bigger than that. Similarly, O Somya, because only one small part of your sixteen parts remains, you cannot remember the Vedas. Eat something and then you will understand what I am saying.'

Suppose you have a big pile of wood, and you start a fire with it. After awhile practically the whole pile is consumed, and there is only a small spark left—a spark as small as a firefly. Very little can be burnt with such a tiny spark, yet even so, if you add some fuel to it you can again start a big fire.

'Similarly,' Uddālaka says to his son, 'your mind is like that tiny spark. It is not functioning now because you have not given it any fuel these last fifteen days. There is just a flicker of your mind working, and it cannot serve any useful purpose. If you eat something now, everything will come back to your mind.'

स हाशाथ हैनमुपससाद तं ह यत्किञ्च पप्रच्छ सर्वं ह प्रतिपेदे॥४॥

Sa hāśātha hainamupasasāda taṁ ha yatkiñca papraccha sarvaṁ ha pratipede.

Saḥ, he [Śvetaketu]; *ha āśa,* ate; *atha,* then; *enam,* to him [his father]; *ha upasasāda,* he went; *tam,* to him [to Śvetaketu]; *yat kiñca,* whatever; *papraccha,* he asked; *sarvam ha pratipede,* he was able to follow everything.

4. Śvetaketu ate something and then went to his father. Whatever his father asked him, he was able to follow.

After eating, Śvetaketu's mind was back to normal. He then approached his father, and everything his father said was clear to him.

तं होवाच यथा सोम्य महतोऽभ्याहितस्यैकमङ्गारं खद्योतमात्रं परिशिष्टं तं तृणैरुपसमाधाय प्राज्वलयेत्तेन ततोऽपि बहु दहेत् ॥ ५ ॥

Taṁ hovāca yathā somya mahato'bhyāhitasyaika-maṅgāraṁ khadyotamātraṁ pariśiṣṭaṁ taṁ tṛṇairupasa-mādhāya prājvalayettena tato'pi bahu dahet.

Tam ha uvāca, he said to him [to Śvetaketu]; *somya,* O Somya; *yathā,* just as; *mahataḥ abhyāhitasya,* of a big blazing fire; *ekam aṅgāram,* one ember; *khadyotamātram,* the size of a firefly; *pariśiṣṭam,* that is left; *tam,* that; *tṛṇaiḥ upasamādhāya,* with some grass; *prājvalayet,* becomes blazing; *tena,* by that [grass]; *tataḥ api bahu,* even more than before; *dahet,* burns.

5. The father said to him: 'O Somya, from a blazing fire, if there is but a small piece of ember left, the size of a firefly, the fire can again blaze up when you add some grass. The fire, in fact, can then blaze up even more than it did before.'

एवं सोम्य ते षोडशानां कलानामेका कलातिशिष्टा-भूत्सान्नेनोपसमाहिता प्राज्वाली तयैतर्हि वेदाननुभवस्यन्न-मयं हि सोम्य मन आपोमयः प्राणस्तेजोमयी वागिति तद्धास्य विजज्ञाविति विजज्ञाविति॥ ६ ॥ इति सप्तमः खण्डः॥ ७ ॥

Evaṁ somya te ṣoḍaśānāṁ kalānāmekā kalātiśiṣṭā-bhūtsānnenopasamāhitā prājvālī tayaitarhi vedānanu-bhavasyannamayaṁ hi somya mana āpomayaḥ prāṇas-tejomayī vāgiti taddhāsya vijajñāviti vijajñāviti. Iti saptamaḥ khaṇḍaḥ.

Evam, in the same way; *somya,* O Somya; *ekā kalā,* one part; *te ṣoḍaśānām kalānām,* of your sixteen parts; *atiśiṣṭā abhūt,* remained; *sā,* it; *upasamāhitā annena,* nourished by food; *prājvālī,* has revived; *etarhi,* now; *tayā,* by that [remaining part]; *vedān,* the Vedas; *anubhavasi,* you can understand; *somya,* O Somya;

hi, this is why [I said]; *manaḥ annamayam,* the mind is nourished by food; *prāṇaḥ āpomayaḥ,* prāṇa is nourished by water; *vāk tejomayī iti,* speech is nourished by fire; *asya,* of that [what his father had said]; *tat ha vijajñau iti,* he understood it; *vijajñau iti,* he understood. *Iti saptamaḥ khaṇḍaḥ,* here ends the seventh section.

6. 'In the same way, O Somya, of your sixteen parts, only one remained. But that, when nourished by food, has revived, and by that you are now able to follow the Vedas. O Somya, this is why I said that the mind was nourished by food, prāṇa was nourished by water, and speech was nourished by fire.' Śvetaketu now understood what his father was saying.

Just as a fire will go out if fuel is not added to it, so also the mind will cease to function if you do not eat. After fasting for fifteen days, Śvetaketu still had a small portion of his mind left working. It was reduced to a fragment, as it were. But after eating, his memory returned and his mind was again active and vigorous.

The idea is, this human body is a very powerful instrument. The mind is powerful; speech is powerful; life itself is powerful. But it is all dependent on food (i.e., earth), water, and energy (i.e., fire). Yet even these gross elements are not independent. As we have seen earlier, earth is a mixture of water and fire with earth. Water also is a mixture of earth and fire with water. Similarly, fire is a mixture of earth and water with fire. This process is called *trivṛta,* or triplication. It is the permutation and combination of the three elements. Vedānta says, we cannot see these elements in their pure form, because that pure form is Existence, *sat.*

What the Upaniṣad is saying is suggestive: That which we do not see in its pure form, but in a form which is a by-product of a combination of other things, really does not exist. This is the argument Buddhism also advances. They say: 'You talk about a chariot, but where is the chariot? Is it a reality? No, it can't be a reality, because a chariot is a combination of different things put together. Where is the chariot? Is it the wheels? The platform? The canopy? No. When you speak of an object which is not independent, which is dependent on factors combining together, then it is not real.'

Here is the same argument. All objects are dependent. What exists then? Vedānta says it is *sat,* Existence. That Existence is our own Self, the real Self, the essence, the real being, pure Spirit. When the Upaniṣad refers to our mind, our life force, and our speech, it is referring to this phenomenal world.

We have to look at these things from two levels: From the cosmic level there is one Reality, one Existence. From the individual level we owe our mind, life force, and speech to these elements. But in reality all these elements, all these manifestations of creation, are pure Spirit. One Reality, pure Spirit, has assumed diverse forms. The whole manifestation of this universe is dependent. Even the mind.

Where does the mind come from? Science has not yet been able to answer this question. According to Vedānta, the mind is nothing but matter; yet consciousness, which is pure Spirit, is the source. Vedānta does not make any distinction between matter and consciousness. We say it is one and the same. Consciousness is the source, and out of that one source, all that exists—call it matter, call it energy, call it mind—has come.

Science has its own terms. They may call the source of life DNA or something else. Vedānta says it is *tat,* That. Or it is *sat,* Existence. From Existence, everything has emerged. In essence there is one—the same thing appearing in different forms.

You may ask, how did the One became manifest as many? Why did it happen? The fact that we can ask this question shows that that One is conscious. Only a conscious being can think, plan, and wish. Because that one Reality is consciousness it can say, 'I will be many.' If it were inert, it could not wish to become many. So Vedānta says, that one Reality, pure Spirit, is consciousness.

Yet, that consciousness can also take the form of something inert. Matter and consciousness are not different. For instance, if you break a paperweight into atoms, and then smash even those atoms, you will find so much energy—so much motion. So, whether the manifestations of this creation are conscious or unconscious, intelligent or unintelligent, they all have their source in that one conscious Reality.

Section Eight

उद्दालको हारुणिः श्वेतकेतुं पुत्रमुवाच स्वप्नान्तं मे सोम्य विजानीहीति यत्रैतत्पुरुषः स्वपिति नाम सता सोम्य तदा सम्पन्नो भवति स्वमपीतो भवति तस्मादेनं स्वपितीत्याचक्षते स्वं ह्यपीतो भवति ॥ १ ॥

Uddālako hāruṇiḥ śvetaketuṁ putramuvāca svapnāntaṁ me somya vijānīhīti yatraitatpuruṣaḥ svapiti nāma satā somya tadā sampanno bhavati svamapīto bhavati tasmādenaṁ svapitītyācakṣate svaṁ hyapīto bhavati.

Uddālakaḥ āruṇiḥ, Uddālaka Āruṇi [the son of Aruṇa]; *śvetaketum putram,* to his son Śvetaketu; *ha uvāca,* said; *svapnāntam,* the concept of [deep] sleep; *me,* from me; *somya,* O Somya; *vijānīhi iti,* learn; *yatra,* when; *etat puruṣaḥ,* this person; *svapiti nāma,* is said to be in deep sleep; *somya,* O Somya; *tadā,* then; *sampannaḥ bhavati,* he is merged; *satā,* with Sat [Existence, Paramātmā]; *svam apītaḥ bhavati,* he attains his real Self; *tasmāt,* for this reason; *ācakṣate,* people say; *enam,* about him; *svapiti iti,* he is sleeping; *svam hi apītaḥ bhavati,* he attains his real Self.

1. Uddālaka Āruṇi said to his son Śvetaketu: 'O Somya, let me explain to you the concept of deep sleep. When a person is said to be sleeping, O Somya, he becomes one with Sat [Existence], and

he attains his real Self. That is why people say about him, "He is sleeping." He is then in his Self.'

In ancient India, all skills were passed from the father to the son. This is how the caste system eventually became so rigid. A father tended to be selfish and favour his son over his other students, especially if the father was a great scholar. Unless he had a student who was exceptionally good and intelligent, he would generally pass on the best things to his own son.

Why does Uddālaka call his son Śvetaketu by the name Somya? The name Somya means one who is quiet, humble, very good, and gentle. If you want to learn something, you must be quiet and modest. So the father is saying, *vijānīhi*—'learn from me, you who are so quiet and humble.'

The word *puruṣa* means *pure,* 'in the heart,' and *śayate,* 'residing.' That which resides in the heart—i.e., the Self. It is a living being. It could be a man, a woman, an animal, or an insect.

The word *svapnāntam* means the concept of deep sleep, or dreamless sleep. When we dream, our sleep is disturbed, and it does not give us any rest. But dreamless sleep is very restful. If we have that kind of sleep for even a few minutes, we become temporarily free from this world. When we wake up then, it takes us some time to realize where we are and what time of day it is. While we were sleeping, the whole world was wiped out for us.

When we say, 'This person is sleeping,' what does

that mean? What happens when we sleep? Where does the mind go? That is what is being discussed here. The Upaniṣad says, during deep sleep a person becomes united with the Self. The individual self—that is, the jīva who is ignorant—merges into the Cosmic Self.

The individual self has to have a body and a mind, and it is the mind that is closest to the Self. In fact, many people think the mind is the Self. The mind, however, is like a crystal. A crystal has no colour of its own, but suppose you put a red flower next to it. What happens? The crystal assumes the colour of the flower. Similarly, the mind has no consciousness of its own. But because it is close to the Paramātman, the Supreme Self, it gets the reflection of consciousness from the Self. Then, through the mind, all our organs function—the eyes, the ears, the hands, the feet, etc. The organs and the mind are all dependent on the Self.

When we are awake, the body and mind are both functioning. Then when we are dreaming, the body is not functioning but the mind is still functioning. But when we are in deep sleep, the mind also ceases to function. We then become one with our own Self. That is why deep sleep is so refreshing. Yet when we wake up we are the same individual that we were before we slept. The Self is there. We are always one with it. Yet sleep does not give us any knowledge of our Self. Why? Because our ignorance creates a barrier that keeps us from knowing our real nature.

But if we are one with the Self, how can we be separate from it? In reality, we are never separate from the Self, but when we are attached to our names and forms, we have desires. And when we have desires, ignorance has its full grip on us.

During dreamless sleep the barrier that keeps us from the Self is temporarily removed, but we are not conscious of it. That is why, when we wake up, we are exactly the same person we were before we slept. If I was a tiger before I went to sleep, I am a tiger again when I get up. A sleeping tiger cannot do any harm, but if it wakes up, beware! Similarly, if I was a bad person before, I am still a bad person when I wake up.

So, when I sleep, for the time being my ignorance is also sleeping, as it were. Only Self-knowledge can dispel my ignorance and give me true peace.

It is a common belief in India that if you bathe in the Ganga, you will get rid of all your sins. Sri Ramakrishna used to say, though, that the sins are very clever. As you go to the river the sins say to each other: 'Well, this person is going into the Ganga. Let's take shelter on that tree.' So they fly off and perch on a tree. Then, when you come out of the river, they all pounce back on you and once again you are in their grip.

Similarly, deep sleep can give us temporary rest, but it cannot remove our ignorance. Only if we have real knowledge, knowledge of the Self, can we remove the seeds of our karma. Knowledge is like a sword. With that sword we can cut off the roots of our ignorance and become free. Once we attain Self-knowledge we are totally transformed, because it goes to the root of our being. And when we wake up from our sleep of ignorance we are no longer the same individual.

स यथा शकुनिः सूत्रेण प्रबद्धो दिशं दिशं पतित्वान्यत्रायतनमलब्ध्वा बन्धनमेवोपश्रयत एवमेव खलु सोम्य तन्मनो दिशं दिशं पतित्वान्यत्रायतनमलब्ध्वा प्राणमेवोपश्रयते प्राणबन्धनं हि सोम्य मन इति॥२॥

Sa yathā śakuniḥ sūtreṇa prabaddho diśaṁ diśaṁ patitvānyatrāyatanamalabdhvā bandhanamevopaśrayata evameva khalu somya tanmano diśaṁ diśaṁ patitvānyatrāyatanamalabdhvā prāṇamevopaśrayate prāṇabandhanaṁ hi somya mana iti.

Saḥ yathā, it is like; *śakuniḥ,* a bird; *sūtreṇa prabaddhaḥ,* tied to a rope; *diśam diśam,* in all directions; *patitvā,* fluttering; *anyatra,* elsewhere; *āyatanam,* a shelter; *alabdhvā,* without getting; *bandhanam eva upaśrayate,* surrenders to its bondage; *evam eva khalu,* similarly; *somya,* O Somya; *tat manaḥ,* this mind; *diśam diśam,* in all directions; *patitvā,* running about; *anyatra,* elsewhere; *āyatanam,* a shelter; *alabdhvā,* without getting; *prāṇam eva upaśrayate,* surrenders to prāṇa; *somya,* O Somya; *prāṇa-bandhanam hi manaḥ iti,* the mind is tied to prāṇa.

2. Just as a bird tied to a rope flutters here and there, and when it cannot get any shelter anywere, it surrenders itself to its bondage; in the same way, O Somya, the mind runs in every direction, and when it fails to get a resting place anywhere, it surrenders itself to prāṇa, the vital force. The mind, O Somya, is tied to prāṇa.

When we are sound asleep, what happens to the mind? The mind withdraws; it retires and temporarily goes back to the Self. Is this the same as samādhi, the superconscious state? Vedānta says, no, there is a distinction between samādhi and this experience of sound sleep. Both experiences bring great joy and peace, but deep sleep is only temporary. It is just for a while. We are still held by the rope of ignorance, and we do not know our real Self. When we come back from deep sleep, we are just as tightly bound as we were before we slept.

The Upaniṣad gives the example here of a bird tied to a rope, struggling to get free. It starts flying in all directions, seeking a safe place—any place, anywhere else than where it is bound. At last it must give up and return to its place of bondage.

Sri Ramakrishna used to give an illustration very similar to this. A bird is sitting on the mast of a ship and soon falls asleep. It does not notice that the ship has set sail. Finally, when the ship has gone far out to sea, it wakes up and starts looking around for land. Flying to the east, it eventually gets tired, and, not finding any land, comes back to the ship.

In the same way, it flies out to the west, to the north, and to the south, but all it sees is water everywhere. At last the bird decides to take refuge on the mast of the ship.

Swami Vivekananda says that all of us are struggling to be free. Freedom is our birthright. You are trying to be free; a student is trying to be free; a teacher is trying to be free. All of us, irrespective of our situation in life, are trying in one way or another to attain freedom.

The Upaniṣad is saying that when we are awake, we are like the bird flying in different directions. We are constantly fluttering around, doing this and doing that. Sometimes we are attracted by something here, and then again by something there. Our minds are always roaming about. But finally we get tired and surrender our minds to prāṇa—that is, we lie down and go to sleep. And if we are lucky, we have good sound sleep. The word *prāṇa* here means the Self.

Meister Eckhart once said that the mind has two eyes. One eye is always looking outside, looking at the things around. But the other eye is looking inside, looking and searching, as it were, into one's own Being. Finally one discovers the 'Castle of Security.' What is this Castle of Security? It is the Self. When we enter into this castle we are at peace.

That is what the Upaniṣad also says here. When a person is able to retreat into his own Self, even temporarily, he attains a state of peace and joy. In deep sleep, we temporarily enter the castle. It is a kind of retreat. But very soon we come back to everything waiting outside, and we are again back in the pandemonium of this world.

अशनापिपासे मे सोम्य विजानीहीति यत्रैतत्पुरुषो-
ऽशिशिषति नामाप एव तदशितं नयन्ते तद्यथा
गोनायोऽश्वनायः पुरुषनाय इत्येवं तदप आचक्षतेऽशनायेति
तत्रैतच्छुङ्गमुत्पतितं सोम्य विजानीहि नेदममूलं
भविष्यतीति ॥ ३ ॥

Aśanāpipāse me somya vijānīhīti yatraitatpuruṣo'śiśiṣati nāmāpa eva tadaśitaṁ nayante tadyathā gonāyo'śvanāyaḥ puruṣanāya ityevaṁ tadapa ācakṣate'śanāyeti tatraitacchuṅgamutpatitaṁ somya vijānīhi nedamamūlaṁ bhaviṣyatīti.

Somya, O Somya; *me,* from me; *aśanā-pipāse,* about hunger and thirst; *vijānīhi iti,* learn; *yatra,* when; *puruṣaḥ,* a person; *aśiśiṣati etat nāma,* is said to be hungry; *tat,* then; *āpaḥ eva aśitam,* the water which has been drunk; *nayante,* has carried [the food that he ate] away; *tat yathā,* just as, for example; *go-nāyaḥ,* a leader of cows; *aśva-nāyaḥ,* a leader of horses; *puruṣa-nāyaḥ,* one who leads other people; *iti,* these terms people use; *evam,* similarly; *tat apaḥ,* that water; *ācakṣate,* people say; *aśanāya iti,* is the leader of food; *tatra,* so also; *vijānīhi,* know; *somya,* O Somya; *etat śuṅgam,* this sprout [i.e., the body];

utpatitam, is produced [by something]; *idam,* it; *amūlam na bhaviṣyati iti,* is not without a root.

3. O Somya, now learn from me about hunger and thirst. When a person is said to be hungry, it is to be understood that the food he ate has been carried away by water. Just as people refer to a leader of cows, or a leader of horses, or a leader of people, similarly, people say that water is the leader of food. So also, O Somya, know that this sprout [i.e., the body] is the product of something [i.e., of food and drink]. It cannot be without a root.

In this universe we always see two things—one is the cause, and the other is the effect. These two forces are always at work. The cause becomes the effect, and again the effect becomes the cause of something else. For instance, a duck is the effect of an egg, and again, that same duck is the cause of another egg.

Buddhism also emphasizes this point. Many people are under the impression that Buddhism is an entirely new religion. But really speaking, it is not a new religion, as Buddha himself pointed out. In Buddhism, the cause and effect theory is termed *pratītya-samutpāda,* 'dependent-arising'—that is, an effect arises dependent on its cause.

The Upaniṣad here takes the example of a sprout and its roots. When you see a sprout, you know at once that there must be roots, and out of those roots the sprout has come. Similarly, we see in this universe many things. They seem to have come from different sources, but in reality the ultimate source is one and the same. It is Sat, pure Existence, Brahman.

In this verse, the father begins by telling his son about hunger and thirst. What does it mean when a person says, 'I am hungry'? A few hours previously he ate something, but again he is hungry. What happened? It means that whatever he ate before has been carried away by water. Some of the water becomes blood and distributes the food to different parts of the body, and then the water carries away the waste part of the food and takes it out of the body. Then the person feels hungry again. This is why water is said to be the leader of food.

The Upaniṣad says it is like a herd of cows. Wherever there is a herd of cows, you will find that the herd chooses a particular cow as the leader. When the cows move from place to place, the leader is ahead and all the others follow behind. Similarly, water is the leader, and the food you eat is distributed and then taken away by the water. The idea is, this body comes from food, and water is what gives it life. They go together. Nothing is independent.

Just as this body has a source, this universe also has a source. The Upaniṣad says that when you see a sprout, you know it has its source in a root. Similarly, this universe and everything that makes up this universe—such as food and water—has a source, and that source is Sat, pure Existence.

तस्य क्व मूलं स्यादन्यत्रान्नादेवमेव खलु सोम्यान्नेन शुङ्गेनापो मूलमन्विच्छाद्भिः सोम्य शुङ्गेन तेजो मूलमन्विच्छ तेजसा सोम्य शुङ्गेन सन्मूलमन्विच्छ सन्मूलाः सोम्येमाः सर्वाः प्रजाः सदायतनाः सत्प्रतिष्ठाः ॥ ४ ॥

Tasya kva mūlaṁ syādanyatrānnādevameva khalu somyānnena śuṅgenāpo mūlamanvicchādbhiḥ somya śuṅgena tejo mūlamanviccha tejasā somya śuṅgena sanmūlamanviccha sanmūlāḥ somyemāḥ sarvāḥ prajāḥ sadāyatanāḥ satpratiṣṭhāḥ.

Tasya, of it [the body]; *annāt,* [besides] from food; *anyatra kva,* where else; *mūlam syāt,* can the root [of the body] be; *evam eva khalu,* in this way; *somya,* O Somya; *annena śuṅgena,* with food as the sprout; *apaḥ mūlam,* water as the root; *anviccha,* search for; *adbhiḥ śuṅgena,* water as the sprout; *somya,* O Somya; *tejaḥ mūlam,* fire as the root; *anviccha,* search for; *tejasā śuṅgena,* fire as the sprout; *somya,* O Somya; *sat mūlam,* Sat [Existence] as the root; *anviccha,* search for; *somya,* O Somya; *imāḥ sarvāḥ prajāḥ,* all these beings; *sat mūlam,* have Sat as the root; *sat āyatanāḥ,* Sat as the abode; *sat pratiṣṭhāḥ,* Sat as the support.

4. Where else, except in food, can the body have its root? In the same way, O Somya, when food is the sprout, search for water as the root; when water is the sprout, O Somya, search for fire as

the root; when fire is the sprout, O Somya, search for Ṣat [Existence] as the root. O Somya, Sat is the root, Sat is the abode, and Sat is the support of all these beings.

Where there is a sprout, you know there is a root. Similarly, where there is a body, you know there is a root—that is, a source, and that source is food. Then what is the root of food? It is water. Again, water has its root in fire, and fire has its root in Existence.

The Upaniṣad gives a number of links here. They follow one after another. But the ultimate root, the ultimate source, is Sat, Existence—pure Spirit. All beings—men, women, children, trees, animals, everything—are based on Sat. *Praja* means what is born. All that are born (*sarvā prajā*) are dependent on and resting on Sat.

अथ यत्रैतत्पुरुषः पिपासति नाम तेज एव तत्पीतं नयते तद्यथा गोनायोऽश्वनायः पुरुषनाय इत्येवं तत्तेज आचष्ट उदन्येति तत्रैतदेव शुङ्गमुत्पतितं सोम्य विजानीहि नेदममूलं भविष्यतीति॥ ५॥

Atha yatraitatpuruṣaḥ pipāsati nāma teja eva tatpītaṁ nayate tadyathā gonāyo'śvanāyaḥ puruṣanāya ityevaṁ tatteja ācaṣṭa udanyeti tatraitadeva śuṅgamutpatitaṁ somya vijānīhi nedamamūlaṁ bhaviṣyatīti.

Atha, next; *yatra,* when; *puruṣaḥ,* a person; *pipāsati etat nāma,* is said to be thirsty; *tat,* then; *tejaḥ eva pītam nayate,* fire has carried away [the water that he drank]; *tat yathā,* just as, for example; *go-nāyaḥ,* a leader of cows; *aśva-nāyaḥ,* a leader of horses; *puruṣa-nāyaḥ,* one who leads other people; *iti,* these terms people use; *evam,* similarly; *tat tejaḥ,* that fire; *ācaṣṭe,* is called; *udanyā iti,* the leader of water; *tatra,* so also; *vijānīhi,* know; *somya,* O Somya; *etat eva śuṅgam,* this sprout [i.e., the body]; *utpatitam,* is produced [by something]; *idam,* it; *amūlam na bhaviṣyati iti,* is not without a root.

5. Then when a person is said to be thirsty, it is to be understood that the water he drank has been carried away by fire. Just as people refer to a leader of cows, or a leader of horses, or a leader of people, similarly, people say that fire is the leader of water. So also, O Somya, know that this sprout [i.e., the body] is the product of something [i.e., of food and drink]. It cannot be without a root.

When does a person feel thirsty? When there is a shortage of water in his body. How does this shortage occur? It occurs when the heat in the body turns the water into blood and other things. As soon as the water is consumed in this way a person feels that he has to drink more water.

42

तस्य क्व मूलं स्यादन्यत्राद्भ्योऽद्भिः सोम्य शुङ्गेन तेजो मूलमन्विच्छ तेजसा सोम्य शुङ्गेन सन्मूलमन्विच्छ सन्मूलाः सोम्येमाः सर्वाः प्रजाः सदायतनाः सत्प्रतिष्ठा यथा नु खलु सोम्येमास्तिस्रो देवताः पुरुषं प्राप्य त्रिवृत्त्रिवृदेकैका भवति तदुक्तं पुरस्तादेव भवत्यस्य सोम्य पुरुषस्य प्रयतो वाङ्मनसि सम्पद्यते मनः प्राणे प्राणस्तेजसि तेजः परस्यां देवतायाम् ॥ ६ ॥

Tasya kva mūlaṁ syādanyatrādbhyo'dbhiḥ somya śuṅgena tejo mūlamanviccha tejasā somya śuṅgena sanmūlamanviccha sanmūlāḥ somyemāḥ sarvāḥ prajāḥ sadāyatanāḥ satpratiṣṭhā yathā nu khalu somyemāstisro devatāḥ puruṣaṁ prāpya trivṛttrivṛdekaikā bhavati taduktaṁ purastādeva bhavatyasya somya puruṣasya prayato vāṅmanasi sampadyate manaḥ prāṇe prāṇasteja-si tejaḥ parasyāṁ devatāyām.

Tasya, of it [the body]; *adbhyaḥ,* [besides] from water; *anyatra kva,* where else; *mūlam syāt,* can the root [of the body] be; *somya,* O Somya; *adbhiḥ śuṅgena,* with water as the sprout; *tejaḥ mūlam,* fire as the root; *anviccha,* search for; *tejasā śuṅgena,* fire as the sprout; *somya,* O Somya; *sat mūlam,* Sat [Existence] as the root; *anviccha,* search for; *somya,* O Somya; *imāḥ sarvāḥ prajāḥ,* all these beings; *sat mūlam,* have Sat as the root; *sat āyatanāḥ,* Sat as the abode; *sat pratiṣṭhāḥ,* Sat as the support; *yathā nu khalu,* as to how; *somya,* O Somya; *imāḥ tisraḥ devatāḥ,* these three deities [fire, water, and earth]; *puruṣam prāpya,* enter a person; *ekaikā bhavati,* each one becomes; *trivṛt trivṛt,* threefold; *tat uktam purastāt eva bhavati,* this has been explained already; *somya,* O Somya; *asya puruṣasya prayataḥ,* as this person is dying; *vāk,* the organ of speech; *manasi sampadyate,* merges into the mind; *manaḥ prāne,* the mind into prāṇa; *prāṇaḥ tejasi,* prāṇa into fire; *tejaḥ parasyām devatāyām,* fire into the Supreme Deity [Brahman].

6. Where else, except in water, can the body have its root? O Somya, when water is the sprout, search for fire as the root; when fire is the sprout, O Somya, search for Sat [Existence] as the root. O Somya, Sat is the root, Sat is the abode, and Sat is the support of all these beings. As to how, O Somya, these three deities [fire, water, and earth] enter a body and each becomes threefold, this has already been explained. O Somya, as this person is dying, his speech merges into the mind, his mind into prāṇa, his prāṇa into fire, and then fire merges into Brahman, the Supreme Deity.

What happens when a person dies? First, his speech merges into his mind. He cannot speak any more, but his mind is still active. Sometimes when a person has a stroke, he cannot speak but his mind is alert. Then the mind merges into prāṇa, his life force. The mind ceases to function, but he is still breathing. Then prāṇa merges into fire. Fire here means the heat in the body. If the body is still warm, you know the person is not dead. When heat goes, then everything merges into the Supreme Self, Sat.

स य एषोऽणिमैतदात्म्यमिदं सर्वं तत्सत्यं स आत्मा तत्त्वमसि श्वेतकेतो इति भूय एव मा भगवान्विज्ञापयत्विति तथा सोम्येति होवाच॥ ७॥ इत्यष्टमः खण्डः॥ ८॥

Sa ya eṣo'ṇimaitadātmyamidaṁ sarvaṁ tatsatyaṁ sa ātmā tattvamasi śvetaketo iti bhūya eva mā bhagavānvijñāpayatviti tathā somyeti hovāca. Ityaṣṭamaḥ khaṇḍaḥ.

Saḥ yaḥ, that which; *eṣaḥ,* this; *aṇimā,* the subtlest of all; *idam sarvam aitadātmyam,* the Self of all this; *tat satyam,* that is the Truth; *saḥ ātmā,* that is the Self; *tat,* that; *tvam,* you; *asi,* are; *śvetaketo iti,* O Śvetaketu; *bhagavān,* sir; *bhūyaḥ eva,* again; *mā,* to me; *vijñāpayatu iti,* will you please explain; *tathā,* so be it; *somya iti,* O Somya; *ha uvāca,* he [the father] said. *Iti aṣṭamaḥ khaṇḍaḥ,* here ends the eighth section.

7. 'That which is the subtlest of all is the Self of all this. It is the Truth. It is the Self. That thou art, O Śvetaketu.' [Śvetaketu then said,] 'Sir, please explain this to me again.' 'Yes, Somya, I will explain again,' replied his father.

That which is the finest of all things, the subtlest, has that Existence, Sat, as its Self. That is the Truth, the Reality. We see all these forms before us. They are constantly changing. But that which we cannot see, which is the essence of everything, does not change. And that is our real identity. 'That thou art'—this is the final message that Vedānta has to give. That Self, that essence, that pure Spirit, is your real identity.

The phenomena we see before us are nothing but names and forms—*nāma* and *rūpa*. They are attributes superimposed on that which is constant, unchanging, unchangeable. You may call a person by one name today, but tomorrow he may have another name. And as regards forms, these are always changing. We are never the same. Then again, after some time these forms are gone. Vedānta defines *satya*, real, as that which existed in the past, which exists now, and which will exist in the future. But the names and forms we see before us are ephemeral. One day they are here and the next they are gone, so they cannot be real.

Vedānta says, forget about your name and form. You are that eternal, unchanging Reality. Our form, our body, is the starting point of all our troubles. As soon as we identify ourselves with the body we feel we are separate and different from others. 'I am a brāhmin.' 'I am learned.' 'I am ignorant.' 'I come from such-and-such a place.' Then you go on adding and adding—'I am tall.' 'I am short.' 'I am fair.'

'I am dark.' Remove these. Go to the essence, to the root—*mūla.*

Sir P.C. Roy did not believe in the caste system. In fact, he had contempt for it. Sometimes he would get together with some students and argue with them. Among the students, some were brāhmins and some were non-brāhmins. He would say: 'Look, I am a chemist. I can prove that the blood of the brāhmin and the blood of the śūdra are both the same. They are composed of the same elements. But you say that this is a person of brāhmin blood and this is a person of śūdra blood. These distinctions are not real.'

Vedānta also says these differences are mere *upādhis,* attributes. They are superimpositions. What is real? Pure Spirit. In essence we are all one.

Section Nine

यथा सोम्य मधु मधुकृतो निस्तिष्ठन्ति नानात्ययानां वृक्षाणां रसान्समवहारमेकतां रसं गमयन्ति ॥ १ ॥

Yathā somya madhu madhukṛto nistiṣṭhanti nānātyayānāṁ vṛkṣāṇāṁ rasānsamavahāramekatāṁ rasaṁ gamayanti.

Yathā, as; *somya,* O Somya; *madhukṛtaḥ,* bees; *madhu nistiṣṭhanti,* produce honey; *nānātyayānām vṛkṣāṇām,* of various tree; *rasān samavahāram,* by collecting the juice; *ekatām rasam gamayanti,* [and] mixing them together to make one juice.

1. O Somya, as bees produce honey by collecting the juice from various trees and mixing them together to make one juice—

Śvetaketu was still having a hard time understanding, so his father gave another example: You see bees going around to different places. They collect pollen from many different trees and put it all together to make honey. Can you distinguish which flower a particular drop of honey came from? No, The pollen has become mixed together to make the honey.

ते यथा तत्र न विवेकं लभन्तेऽमुष्याहं वृक्षस्य रसोऽस्म्यमुष्याहं वृक्षस्य रसोऽस्मीत्येवमेव खलु सोम्येमाः सर्वाः प्रजाः सति सम्पद्य न विदुः सति सम्पद्यामह इति ॥ २ ॥

Te yathā tatra na vivekaṁ labhante'muṣyāhaṁ vṛkṣasya raso'smyamuṣyāhaṁ vṛkṣasya raso'smītyeva-meva khalu somyemāḥ sarvāḥ prajāḥ sati sampadya na viduḥ sati sampadyāmaha iti.

Te, those [juices which have mixed together]; *yathā tatra,* now as [honey]; *aham amuṣya vṛkṣasya rasaḥ asmi iti,* I am the juice of such-and-such tree; *aham amuṣya vṛkṣasya rasaḥ asmi iti,* I am the juice of such-and-such tree; *vivekam na labhante,* this kind of consciousness [i.e., discrimination] they do not have; *somya,* O Somya; *evam eva,* like this; *khalu,* surely; *imāḥ sarvāḥ prajāḥ,* all these beings; *sati,* in the Self [Brahman]; *sampadya,* having attained unity; *sati sampadyāmahe,* we are now all one with the Self; *na viduḥ iti,* are not conscious of this.

2. —O Somya, and just as those juices now are no longer conscious of their separate identities, thinking, 'I am the juice from such-and-such tree,' and 'I am the juice from such-and-such tree'; similarly, when all these beings attain unity in the Self, they are not conscious of it. They do not think, 'We [were once separate, but] now we are all one with the Self.'

Can a drop of honey say, 'I am from one tree, and you are from another tree'? No, there is no such discrimination there. The pollen from different flowers becomes one mass of honey. Similarly, we may seem to come from different sources, but in essence we are all one. When we merge into pure Being, we are free from all such discriminating ideas. There is no more diversity there.

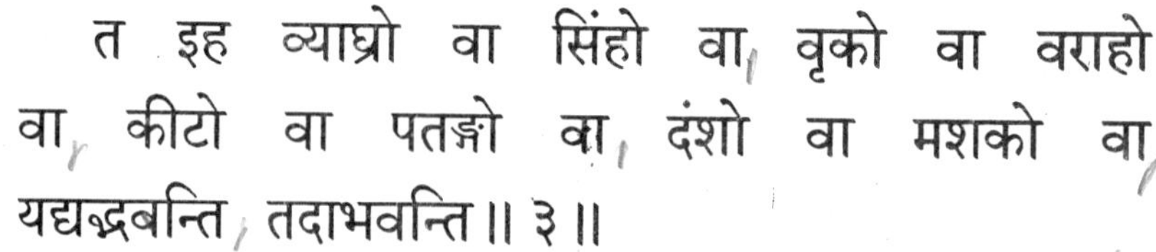
त इह व्याघ्रो वा सिंहो वा वृको वा वराहो
वा कीटो वा पतङ्गो वा दंशो वा मशको वा
यद्यद्भवन्ति तदाभवन्ति ॥ ३ ॥

Ta iha vyāghro vā siṁho vā vṛko vā varāho vā kīṭo vā pataṅgo vā daṁśo vā maśako vā yadyadbhavanti tadābhavanti.

Te, these; *iha,* here [in this world]; *vyāghraḥ vā,* a tiger; *siṁhaḥ vā,* or a lion; *vṛkaḥ vā,* or a leopard; *varāhaḥ vā,* or a boar; *kīṭaḥ vā,* or a bug; *pataṅgaḥ vā,* or an insect; *daṁśaḥ vā,* or a flea; *maśakaḥ vā,* or a mosquito; *yat yat,* whatever; *bhavanti,* they are [before]; *tat,* that; *ābhavanti,* they are after [because they do not yet know the Self].

3. Whatever they were before in this world—whether a tiger or lion or leopard or boar or bug or insect or flea or mosquito—they are born again. [They never know that they came from Sat.]

We are born again and again till we overcome our ignorance and attain Self-knowledge. Death, for an ignorant person, is not liberation. It is like going into deep sleep. And when you are reborn it is as if you are waking up. You die again and again, and again and again you are reborn. This goes on until you attain Self-knowledge. Once you know the Self, you are free—free from birth and death.

स य एषोऽणिमैतदात्म्यमिदं सर्वं तत्सत्यं स आत्मा तत्त्वमसि श्वेतकेतो इति भूय एव मा भगवान्विज्ञापयत्विति तथा सोम्येति होवाच॥४॥ इति नवमः खण्डः॥९॥

Sa ya eṣo'ṇimaitadātmyamidaṁ sarvaṁ tatsatyaṁ sa ātmā tattvamasi śvetaketo iti bhūya eva mā bhagavānvijñāpayatviti tathā somyeti hovāca. Iti navamaḥ khaṇḍaḥ.

Saḥ yaḥ, that which; *eṣaḥ,* this; *aṇimā,* the subtlest of all; *idam sarvam aitadātmyam,* the Self of all this; *tat satyam,* that is the Truth; *saḥ ātmā,* that is the Self; *tat,* that; *tvam,* you; *asi,* are; *śvetaketo iti,* O Śvetaketu; *bhagavān,* sir; *bhūyaḥ eva,* again; *mā,* to me; *vijñāpayatu iti,* will you please explain; *tathā,* so be it; *somya iti,* O Somya; *ha uvāca,* he [the father] said. *Iti navamaḥ khaṇḍaḥ,* here ends the ninth section.

4. 'That which is the subtlest of all is the Self of all this. It is the Truth. It is the Self. That thou art, O Śvetaketu.' [Śvetaketu then said,] 'Sir, please explain this to me again.' 'Yes, Somya, I will explain it again,' replied his father.

Tat tvam asi—thou art that. This is called the *mahāvākya,* the great saying. It is the magic formula. If your mind has been purified, as soon as the mahāvākya is uttered your eyes are opened and you realize your own Self. But this can happen only after a long process of preparation. It does not come by a fluke. After years of hard work and after shedding many tears, at last one day your mind becomes pure and free from ego. You have attained *cittaśuddhi,* purification of the mind. Your mind is then like a clean mirror. Now there is a layer of dust on the mirror. If you remove the dust, you can clearly see your reflection. Then you know who you are.

Once you know who you are you can never be deluded. Can there be darkness where there is light? If you are really enlightened there can be no room for ignorance in your mind. But without *cittaśuddhi,* even if the teacher tells you that you are the Self, you will not believe it. You will think: 'No, that is nonsense. I am this body.' The father is again telling Śvetaketu, 'You are That,' but still it is not clear to him.

How does it become clear? First we must study the Upaniṣads. Then we have to try and grasp the ideas intellectually. So long as the teacher is giving us instructions the idea fascinates us. That's fine, but it's not enough. We must realize it. We must feel it in the very depth of our being.

Spiritual knowledge does not come through an intellectual process. It's something more, something deeper, something that touches the very root of our being. It's an experience. When you have this experience you are totally transformed. You are not the same individual anymore.

Section Ten

इमाः सोम्य नद्यः पुरस्तात्प्राच्यः स्यन्दन्ते पश्चात्प्रती-
च्यस्ताः समुद्रात्समुद्रमेवापियन्ति स समुद्र एव भवति
ता यथा तत्र न विदुरियमहमस्मीयमहमस्मीति ॥ १ ॥

Imāḥ somya nadyaḥ purastātprācyaḥ syandante paścātpratīcyastāḥ samudrātsamudramevāpiyanti sa samudra eva bhavati tā yathā tatra na viduriyamahamasmīyamahamasmīti.

Imāḥ, these; *somya,* O Somya; *nadyaḥ,* rivers; *purastāt,* of the east; *prācyaḥ syandante,* flow to the east; *pratīcyaḥ,* of the west; *paścāt,* to the west; *tāḥ,* they; *samudrāt,* [rising] from the sea; *samudram eva apiyanti,* go to the sea; *saḥ samudraḥ eva bhavati,* become one with that sea; *yathā,* as; *tatra,* there; *tāḥ,* they; *na viduḥ,* do not know; *iyam aham asmi iyam aham asmi iti,* I am this [river], I am this [river].

1. O Somya, those rivers belonging to the east run to the east, and those belonging to the west run to the west. Rising from the sea, they go back to it and become one with it. Just as, when they reach the sea, they do not know their separate identities—'I am this river,' or 'I am that river'—

Uddālaka gives another illustration. There are so many rivers in this country, and each originates from a different area. Ultimately, however, they all flow into the sea. They then lose their separate identities and become one with the sea. When the Ganga flows into the sea, you can no longer identify it as such. Can a drop of water in the sea say, 'I am the Ganga,' or 'I am the Sindhu'? No. So also, when we die our sense of identity disappears temporarily.

Then again, where did these rivers come from? They

came from the sea. Sea water becomes vapour, rises, and forms into clouds. The clouds then go over the land and pour down rain, which eventually goes into the rivers and at last into the sea. The rivers come from the sea and go back to the sea. The sea is the source, but the rivers do not know this. This cycle is going on all the time.

So also we come from pure Spirit and go back to pure Spirit, but we are not aware of it. We are only conscious of our separate identities. In dreamless sleep, our separate identities are wiped out for the time being. We sleep so soundly we do not even know we exist. We are then part of the Cosmic Self. Then when we wake up, we resume our separate identities again.

Similarly, when we die, it is the body that dies. The individual self continues and is one with Existence. This does not mean liberation, however. We do not know that we have become one with Existence. It is as if we are in deep sleep. As the water rises from the sea and again falls down to become the Ganga or the Sindhu, so also, we again become some individual with a new body.

Why are we not liberated? Because ignorance is there. When we die our ignorance is suspended for some time, and we are temporarily not conscious of our separate existence. But when we are reborn we resume our life from the point where we left off. We then have a new body but we retain all the impressions that we had in our previous life.

These impressions manifest themselves again in our

new birth because they have become part of our being. This is why we often find so much difference between one brother and another. Two brothers may be close in age but poles apart in temperament. One may be very studious, with scholarly inclinations, and the other may be very outgoing, more interested in sports and other activities. Even in terms of physical appearance they may be quite different. They are two separate identities.

So, unless we attain Self-knowledge and become free, death is like going into deep sleep. It is a temporary pause in our life's struggle. But the struggle must go on because of our ignorance.

एवमेव खलु सोम्येमाः सर्वाः प्रजाः सत आगम्य न विदुः सत आगच्छामह इति त इह व्याघ्रो वा सिंहो वा वृको वा वराहो वा कीटो वा पतङ्गो वा दंशो वा मशको वा यद्यद्भवन्ति तदाभवन्ति ॥ २ ॥

Evameva khalu somyemāḥ sarvāḥ prajāḥ sata āgamya na viduḥ sata āgacchāmaha iti ta iha vyāghro vā siṁho vā vṛko vā varāho vā kīṭo vā pataṅgo vā daṁśo vā maśako vā yadyadbhavanti tadābhavanti.

Evam eva khalu, in the same way; *somya,* O Somya; *imāḥ sarvāḥ prajāḥ,* all these beings; *sataḥ,* from Sat [Brahman]; *āgamya,* having come; *sataḥ āgacchāmahe iti,* we have come from Sat; *na viduḥ,* do not know;

te, these [beings]; *iha,* here [in this world]; *vyāghraḥ vā,* a tiger; *siṁhaḥ vā,* or a lion; *vṛkaḥ vā,* or a leopard; *varāhaḥ vā,* or a boar; *kīṭaḥ vā,* or a bug; *pataṅgaḥ vā,* or an insect; *daṁśaḥ vā,* or a flea; *maśakaḥ vā,* or a mosquito; *yat yat,* whatever; *bhavanti,* they are [before]; *tat,* that; *ābhavanti,* they are after [because they do not yet know the Self].

2. —In the same way, O Somya, all these beings, having come from Sat [Brahman], never know this. They never think, 'We have come from Sat.' Whatever they were before in this world—whether a tiger or lion or leopard or boar or bug or insect or flea or mosquito—they are born again [according to their karma. They never know that they came from Sat.]

The Upaniṣad does not mean to imply in this example of the rivers that we are not divine now and we are trying to become divine. No, we are always divine. Whether we know it or not, we are never separate from pure Spirit. But it is our misfortune that we do not know it.

Here the Upaniṣad is giving us a warning. Our goal is Self-knowledge. Death or deep sleep is not our goal.

स य एषोऽणिमैतदात्म्यमिदं सर्वं तत्सत्यं स आत्मा तत्त्वमसि श्वेतकेतो इति भूय एव मा भगवान्विज्ञापयत्विति तथा सोम्येति होवाच॥ ३॥ इति दशमः खण्डः॥ १०॥

Sa ya eṣo'ṇimaitadātmyamidaṁ sarvaṁ tatsatyaṁ sa ātmā tattvamasi śvetaketo iti bhūya eva mā bhagavānvijñāpayatviti tathā somyeti hovāca. Iti daśamaḥ khaṇḍaḥ.

Saḥ yaḥ, that which; *eṣaḥ,* this; *aṇimā,* the subtlest of all; *idam sarvam aitaḍātmyam,* the Self of all this; *tat satyam,* that is the Truth; *saḥ ātmā,* that is the Self; *tat,* that; *tvam,* you; *asi,* are; *śvetaketo iti,* O Śvetaketu; *bhagavān,* sir; *bhūyaḥ eva,* again; *mā,* to me; *vijñāpayatu iti,* will you please explain; *tathā,* so be it; *somya iti,* O Somya; *ha uvāca,* he [the father] said. *Iti daśamaḥ khaṇḍaḥ,* here ends the tenth section.

3. 'That which is the subtlest of all is the Self of all this. It is the Truth. It is the Self. That thou art, O Śvetaketu.' [Śvetaketu then said,] 'Sir, please explain this to me again.' 'Yes, Somya, I will explain it again,' replied his father.

Section Eleven

अस्य सोम्य महतो वृक्षस्य यो मूलेऽभ्याहन्याज्जीवन्स्रवेद्यो मध्येऽभ्याहन्याज्जीवन्स्रवेद्योऽग्रेऽभ्याहन्याज्जीवन्स्रवेत्स एष जीवेनात्मनानुप्रभूतः पेपीयमानो मोदमानस्तिष्ठति ॥ १ ॥

अस्य यदेकां शाखां जीवो जहात्यथ सा शुष्यति द्वितीयां जहात्यथ सा शुष्यति तृतीयां जहात्यथ सा शुष्यति सर्वं जहाति सर्वः शुष्यति॥ २॥

Asya somya mahato vṛkṣasya yo mūle'bhyāhanyājjīvansravedyo madhye'bhyāhanyājjīvansravedyo'gre'bhyāhanyājjīvansravetsa eṣa jīvenātmanānuprabhūtaḥ pepīyamāno modamānastiṣṭhati.

Asya yadekāṁ śākhāṁ jīvo jahātyatha sā śuṣyati dvitīyāṁ jahātyatha sā śuṣyati tṛtīyāṁ jahātyatha sā śuṣyati sarvaṁ jahāti sarvaḥ śuṣyati.

Somya, O Somya; *asya mahataḥ vṛkṣasya,* of this big tree; *yaḥ mūle abhyāhanyāt,* [if] a person strikes at the root; *jīvan,* it [the tree] continues to live; *sravet,* [though] it exudes juice; *yaḥ madhye abhyāhanyāt,* [if] a person strikes in the middle; *jīvan,* it [the tree] continues to live; *sravet,* [though] it exudes juice; *yaḥ agre abhyāhanyāt,* [if] a person strikes at the top; *jīvan,* it [the tree] continues to live; *sravet,* [though] it exudes juice; *saḥ eṣaḥ,* this [tree]; *jīvena ātmanā anuprabhūtaḥ,* is pervaded by the living Self; *pepīyamānaḥ,* it continues drinking; *modamānaḥ tiṣṭhati,* [and] living happily.

Yat, if; *jīvaḥ,* the self [life]; *asya ekām śākhām,* one branch of it [the tree]; *jahāti,* abandons; *atha,* then; *sā śuṣyati,* it [the branch] withers away; *dvitīyām,* a second [branch]; *jahāti,* [if] it leaves; *atha sā śuṣyati,* then it [the branch] withers away; *tṛtīyām,* a third [branch]; *jahāti,* [if] it leaves; *atha sā śuṣyati,* then it [the branch] withers away; *sarvam jahāti,* [if] it leaves all [the whole tree]; *sarvaḥ śuṣyati,* the whole tree withers away.

1-2. O Somya, if someone strikes at the root of a big tree, it will continue to live, though it may exude some juice. If he strikes at the middle, it will still live, though it may exude some juice. If he strikes at the top of the tree, it will survive, though it may exude some juice. Pervaded by the self, the tree will keep drinking juice and living happily. But if the self leaves a branch of a tree, that branch withers away and dies. If it leaves a second branch, that branch too will die. If it leaves a third branch, that branch also will die. If the self withdraws from the whole tree, then the whole tree will die.

Suppose you strike at a tree. If the tree is not dead, water will come out of the wound, and eventually the wound will heal. According to Vedānta, a tree is a living individual, like a human being. It has life; it has a self. As my self permeates the whole of my body, similarly, the self of a tree permeates the whole body of the tree.

If one part of my body becomes paralyzed, it means that the self which previously permeated the whole of my body has withdrawn itself from that part. So also, if the self of a tree leaves a limb of the tree, that limb becomes dried up.

The Upaniṣad is trying to say here that death merely

means the withdrawal of the individual self from the whole body. Suppose you are living at a certain house. If you leave that house and move somewhere else, that house becomes vacant and useless. It's exactly like that. When the Self leaves the body, the body becomes empty and useless.

एवमेव खलु सोम्य विद्धीति होवाच जीवापेतं वाव किलेदं म्रियते न जीवो म्रियत इति स य एषोऽणिमैतदात्म्यमिदं सर्वं तत्सत्यं स आत्मा तत्त्वमसि श्वेतकेतो इति भूय एव मा भगवान्विज्ञापयत्विति तथा सोम्येति होवाच॥ ३॥ इत्येकादशः खण्डः॥ ११॥

Evameva khalu somya viddhīti hovāca jīvāpetaṁ vāva kiledaṁ mriyate na jīvo mriyata iti sa ya eṣo'ṇimaitadātmyamidaṁ sarvaṁ tatsatyaṁ sa ātmā tattvamasi śvetaketo iti bhūya eva mā bhagavānvijñāpayatviti tathā somyeti hovāca. Ityekādaśaḥ khaṇḍaḥ.

Evam eva khalu, like this; *somya,* O Somya; *viddhi,* know; *iti ha uvāca,* he said; *jīva-apetam,* deserted by the self; *idam,* this [body]; *vāva kila mriyate,* is truly dead; *jīvaḥ na mriyate,* the self never dies; *saḥ yaḥ,* that which; *eṣaḥ,* this; *aṇimā,* the subtlest of all; *idam sarvam aitadātmyam,* the Self of all this; *tat satyam,* that is the Truth; *saḥ ātmā,* that is the Self; *tat,* that; *tvam,* you; *asi,* are; *śvetaketo iti,* O Śvetaketu; *bhagavān,* sir; *bhūyaḥ eva,* again; *mā,* to me; *vijñāpayatu iti,* will you please explain; *tathā,* so be it; *somya iti,* O Somya; *ha uvāca,* he [the father] said. *Iti ekādaśaḥ khaṇḍaḥ,* here ends the eleventh section.

3. The father said: 'O Somya, know this: When the self leaves the body, the body surely dies. The self, however, never dies. That which is the subtlest of all is the Self of all this. It is the Truth. It is the Self. That thou art, O Śvetaketu.' [Śvetaketu then said,] 'Sir, please explain this to me again.' 'Yes, Somya, I will explain it again,' replied his father.

The self is immortal. It is the body that dies, and it dies when the self leaves it.

Suppose you go to sleep leaving some of your work incomplete. As soon as you wake up, you remember that it was not finished, and you immediately start doing the work from where you left off. Your sleep was like the death of your body, for it was inactive and you were totally unconscious of your body. But the self never dies, and that is why when you wake up you remember your work is unfinished. Whether you are awake or asleep, you are the same self. The self never changes.

You may have seen how a new-born kitten behaves. It knows where to get its mother's milk. No one teaches it, but how does it know? It knows from its past life.

Some of the scriptures say to perform sacrifices such as the Agnihotra. They say we will be duly rewarded for this. But we are asked to perform them to the last day of our life. If we perform them till we die, when are we going to get the reward? Obviously in our future life. The individual is born again and again to receive rewards and punishments, but the real Self remains the same.

Section Twelve

न्यग्रोधफलमत आहरेतीदं भगव इति भिन्द्धीति भिन्नं भगव इति किमत्र पश्यसीत्यण्व्य इवेमा धाना भगव इत्यासामङ्गैकां भिन्द्धीति भिन्ना भगव इति किमत्र पश्यसीति न किञ्चन भगव इति॥ १॥

Nyagrodhaphalamata āharetīdaṁ bhagava iti bhinddhīti bhinnaṁ bhagava iti kimatra paśyasītyaṇvya ivemā dhānā bhagava ityāsāmaṅgaikāṁ bhinddhīti bhinnā bhagava iti kimatra paśyasīti na kiñcana bhagava iti.

Nyagrodha-phalam ataḥ āhara iti, [Uddālaka said,] bring me a fruit from this banyan tree; *idam bhagavaḥ iti,* [Śvetaketu replied,] here it is, sir; *bhinddhi iti,* break it; *bhinnam bhagavaḥ iti,* I have broken it sir; *kim atra paśyasi iti,* what do you see in it; *aṇvyaḥ iva imāḥ dhānāḥ,* these tiny seeds; *bhagavaḥ iti,* sir; *āsām ekām bhinddhi,* break one of them; *aṅga iti,* my child; *bhinnā bhagavaḥ iti,* it is broken, sir; *kim atra paśyasi iti,* what do you see in it; *na kiñcana bhagavaḥ iti,* nothing, sir.

1. Uddālaka said, 'Bring me a fruit from this banyan tree.' Śvetaketu replied, 'I have brought it, sir.' Uddālaka: 'Break it.' Śvetaketu: 'I've broken it, sir.' Uddālaka: 'What do you see inside?' Śvetaketu: 'There are tiny seeds, sir.' Uddālaka: 'Break one of them, my son.' Śvetaketu: 'Sir, I've broken it.' Uddālaka: 'What do you see in it?' Śvetaketu: 'Nothing, sir.'

तं होवाच यं वै सोम्यैतमणिमानं न निभालयस एतस्य वै सोम्यैषोऽणिम्न एवं महान्यग्रोधस्तिष्ठति श्रद्धत्स्व सोम्येति॥ २॥

Taṁ hovāca yaṁ vai somyaitamaṇimānaṁ na nibhālayasa etasya vai somyaiṣo'ṇimna evaṁ mahānya-grodhastiṣṭhati śraddhatsva somyeti.

Tam, to him [his son]; *ha uvāca,* [Uddālaka] said; *somya,* O Somya; *etam vai aṇimānam,* that subtle part; *yam na nibhālayase,* which you do not see; *etasya vai,* of this very; *aṇimnaḥ,* subtle part; *somya,* O Somya; *eṣaḥ mahānyagrodhaḥ,* this big banyan tree; *tiṣṭhati,* exists; *śraddhatsva somya iti,* have faith [in what I say], O Somya.

2. Uddālaka said: 'O Somya, the finest part in that seed is not visible to you. But in that finest part lies hidden the huge banyan tree. Have faith in what I say, O Somya.'

A banyan tree is such a huge tree, but its seed is very tiny. If you split open the seed what do you see? Nothing. Yet the essence of that big tree is there in that tiny seed. How do you know? If you put the seed in the ground, very soon a sprout will appear. Then that sprout will grow and gradually become a big tree. Though there seems to be nothing inside the seed, the essence of the tree must be there; otherwise a tree could not grow from it.

Then the father says, 'Have *śraddhā,* faith—faith in what I am saying.' Śaṅkara says that faith makes the mind concentrated. If your mind is restless and always running after sense pleasures, you will never realize the Self. How can a mind that is outgoing and attached to gross external things, see that which is fine? It can't. In the Kaṭha Upaniṣad, Yama said to Naciketā that our senses are all outgoing. The eyes, the ears, the mind—they are all going to the sense objects. We must reverse the process—that is, we must turn the senses inward. But this is very difficult to do if you lack faith.

Sri Ramakrishna used to say that the mind was like a bag of mustard seeds. Suppose there is a leak in a bag of mustard seeds. The mustard seeds will fall out and be scattered all over the place, and it is then very difficult to gather them up again. Similarly, the leak in the bag is like our attachment to sense enjoyments. Once the mind is scattered on external things, it is difficult to bring it back and focus it on the Self.

But if you have faith—faith that the Self is the

Reality—then it becomes easy to concentrate the mind. Once you have control over the mind, you can grasp the subtleties of spiritual truths very quickly. In fact, it is said that the Truth reveals itself to you. This is quite rational. If you really want to know something, your mind will automatically be focussed on it. And if you are not interested, your mind will be elsewhere. You may be sitting in front of the teacher, but if your mind is on a cricket game you will not hear anything the teacher says.

स य एषोऽणिमैतदात्म्यमिदं सर्वं तत्सत्यं स आत्मा तत्त्वमसि श्वेतकेतो इति भूय एव मा भगवान्विज्ञापयत्विति तथा सोम्येति होवाच॥ ३॥ इति द्वादशः खण्डः॥ १२॥

Sa ya eṣo'ṇimaitadātmyamidaṁ sarvaṁ tatsatyaṁ sa ātmā tattvamasi śvetaketo iti bhūya eva mā bhagavānvijñāpayatviti tathā somyeti hovāca. Iti dvādaśaḥ khaṇḍaḥ.

Saḥ yaḥ, that which; *eṣaḥ,* this; *aṇimā,* the subtlest of all; *idam sarvam aitadātmyam,* the Self of all this; *tat satyam,* that is the Truth; *saḥ ātmā,* that is the Self; *tat,* that; *tvam,* you; *asi,* are; *śvetaketo iti,* O Śvetaketu; *bhagavān,* sir; *bhūyaḥ eva,* again; *mā,* to me; *vijñāpayatu iti,* will you please explain; *tathā,* so be it; *somya iti,* O Somya; *ha uvāca,* he [the father] said. *Iti dvādaśaḥ khaṇḍaḥ,* here ends the twelfth section.

3. 'That which is the subtlest of all is the Self of all this. It is the Truth. It is the Self. That thou art, O Śvetaketu.' [Śvetaketu then said,] 'Sir, please explain this to me again.' 'Yes, Somya, I will explain it again,' replied his father.

This idea is very difficult to grasp, but how much patience the father has. Now Śvetaketu has another doubt: You say that the Self exists, but it cannot be seen. You say it is *aṇimā,* extremely fine—finer than an atom. Yet everything has come from the Self. How then did the Self become so gross? How did it become this physical universe that we can see?

Here we must remember the principle of cause and effect. The cause becomes the effect. The cause is subtle, fine, but when it becomes the effect it becomes gross. The tiny seed becomes the vast banyan tree. The Self manifests itself as everything that exists.

The goal of life is to realize the Self. Life is useless otherwise. This is why Śvetaketu keeps bothering his father. Again and again he says, 'Father, please explain further.' Uddālaka is patient. The relationship between the Self and the world is quite a riddle. How the invisible Self becomes the visible world is difficult to comprehend. The example of the seed and the banyan tree helps, but it is still not clear, so Śvetaketu pesters his father for more explanation. His father then tells him to have faith. 'Faith' means faith in the teacher, in the scriptures, and even in oneself. Faith is what at last clears all doubts.

Section Thirteen

लवणमेतदुदकेऽवधायाथ मा प्रातरुपसीदथा इति स
ह तथा चकार तं होवाच यद्दोषा लवणमुदकेऽवाधा
अङ्ग तदाहरेति तद्धावमृश्य न विवेद॥ १॥

यथा विलीनमेवाङ्गास्यान्तादाचामेति कथमिति
लवणमिति मध्यादाचामेति कथमिति लवणमित्यन्तादा-
चामेति कथमिति लवणमित्यभिप्रास्यैतदथ मोपसीदथा
इति तद्ध तथा चकार तच्छश्वत्संवर्तते तं होवाचात्र
वाव किल सत्सोम्य न निभालयसेऽत्रैव किलेति॥ २॥

Lavaṇametadudake'vadhāyātha mā prātarupasīdathā iti sa ha tathā cakāra taṁ hovāca yaddoṣā lavaṇamudake'vādhā aṅga tadāhareti taddhāvamṛśya na viveda.

Yathā vilīnamevāṅgāsyāntādācāmeti kathamiti lavaṇamiti madhyādācāmeti kathamiti lavaṇamityantādācāmeti kathamiti lavaṇamityabhiprāsyaitadatha mopasīdathā iti taddha tathā cakāra tacchaśvatsaṁvartate taṁ hovācātra vāva kila satsomya na nibhālayase'traiva kileti.

Lavaṇam etat, this salt; *udake,* in water; *avadhāya,* put; *atha mā,* then to me; *prātaḥ,* in the morning; *upasīdathāḥ iti,* come; *saḥ,* he [Śvetaketu]; *tathā,* that way; *ha cakāra,* did; *tam ha uvāca,* he said to him [to Śvetaketu]; *yat lavaṇam,* that salt which; *doṣā,* at night; *udake avādhāḥ,* you put into water; *aṅga,* my son; *tat,* that; *āhara iti,* bring it back; *tat,* that; *ha avamṛśya,* having searched for; *na viveda,* he did not find.

Yathā, since; *vilīnam eva,* it had disappeared [in the water]; *aṅga,* my son; *asya antāt ācāma iti,* drink from its surface; *katham iti,* how is it; *lavaṇam iti,* saline; *madhyāt ācāma iti,* drink from the middle; *katham iti,* how is it; *lavaṇam iti,* saline; *antāt ācāma iti,* drink from the bottom; *katham iti,* how is it; *lavaṇam iti,* saline; *abhiprāya etat,* throw this away; *atha mā upasīdathāḥ iti,* then come to me; *tat ha tathā cakāra,* he did likewise; *tat,* that [salinity]; *śaśvat,* always; *saṁvartate,* prevails everywhere; *tam ha uvāca,* he said to him [to Śvetaketu]; *atra vāva kila,* here [in this body]; *somya,* O Somya; *sat,* the self [exists]; *na nibhālayase,* [but] you do not see it; *atra eva kila iti,* here [in the body].

1-2. [Uddālaka said,] 'Put this lump of salt into water and come to me in the morning.' Śvetaketu did as he was told. Uddālaka said to him, 'My son, bring me the salt that you put in the water.' Śvetaketu looked, but he could not find it, as the salt had dissolved in the water. [Uddālaka said,] 'My son, drink the water at the surface.' [Śvetaketu did that, and Uddālaka asked,] 'How does it taste?' [Śvetaketu replied,] 'It is saline.' [Uddālaka then said:] 'Drink it from the middle. How does it taste?' 'It is saline.' 'Drink it from the bottom. How does it taste?' 'It is saline.' 'Throw the water away and then come to me.' Śvetaketu did so. The father said to him:

'There is salt in every part of the water, yet you cannot see it. Similarly, O Somya, Sat [the Self] is here in this body, yet you cannot see it in the body.'

The question that is being examined is, why are we not able to perceive the Self, which is the essence of our being? It is because the Self is all-pervasive. The Self and I are one and the same. If the Self were something separate from me, then I could see it. Can I see myself? I can see myself if I have a mirror—something else. But there is nothing but the Self, so how can I see it? It's not possible.

Because you don't see something that doesn't mean it does not exist. The process of seeing involves separate entities: the seer and the seen—that is, the subject and the object. These two must be separate. Then only the process of seeing can take place. But if there is only one, who sees whom?

The Upaniṣad gives two examples of how things may exist that we do not perceive. One is of the banyan tree and the seed, and the other is of salt in water. Suppose you put a lump of salt in a glass of water. Soon the salt dissolves. You no longer see it, but that doesn't mean it is not there. If you taste the water you will find that it tastes salty throughout.

Similarly, just because we do not see the Self, that doesn't prove it does not exist. Reality is not something that is perceptible to our sense organs. It is *vākyamanātīta*—beyond speech and mind, beyond thought. Words fail to describe it and our mind cannot grasp it, because it is so fine, so subtle. The Self is not something on the relative plane that we can see or touch. Our sense organs are very limited. Our eyes can see things only up to a point and beyond that they cannot see any more. There are many things around us that our eyes cannot see. Similarly with our hearing and other organs. So, in order to perceive the Self we must go beyond the relative plane to the transcendental level.

Śaṅkara says that this body is a product of food (or, earth), water, and fire, and the Self is within this body. Though you cannot see the Self, it permeates the body—just as the salt permeates the water

स य एषोऽणिमैतदात्म्यमिदं सर्वं तत्सत्यं स आत्मा तत्त्वमसि श्वेतकेतो इति भूय एव मा भगवा-न्विज्ञापयत्विति तथा सोम्येति होवाच॥ ३ ॥ इति त्रयोदशः खण्डः ॥ १३ ॥

Sa ya eṣo'ṇimaitadātmyamidaṁ sarvaṁ tatsatyaṁ sa ātmā tattvamasi śvetaketo iti bhūya eva mā bhagavānvijñāpayatviti tathā somyeti hovāca. Iti trayo-daśaḥ khaṇḍaḥ.

Saḥ yaḥ, that which; *eṣaḥ,* this; *aṇimā,* the subtlest of all; *idam sarvam aitadātmyam,* the Self of all this; *tat satyam,* that is the Truth; *saḥ ātmā,* that is the the Self; *tat,* that; *tvam,* you; *asi,* are; *śvetaketo iti,* O

Śvetaketu; *bhagavān,* sir; *bhūyaḥ eva,* again; *mā,* to me; *vijñāpayatu iti,* will you please explain; *tathā,* so be it; *somya iti,* O Somya; *ha uvāca,* he [the father] said. *Iti trayodaśaḥ khaṇḍaḥ,* here ends the thirteenth section.

3. 'That which is the subtlest of all is the Self of all this. It is the Truth. It is the Self. That thou art, O Śvetaketu.' [Śvetaketu then said,] 'Sir, please explain this to me again.' 'Yes, Somya, I will explain it again,' replied his father.

Again, the same idea: Just as salt is everywhere in the glass of water, pervading all the particles of the water, so also, the Self is all-pervasive. It is the essence. That is the Reality, and you are that.

Section Fourteen

यथा सोम्य पुरुषं गन्धारेभ्योऽभिनद्धाक्षमानीय तं ततोऽतिजने विसृजेत्स यथा तत्र प्राङ्वोदङ्वाधराङ्वा प्रत्यङ्वा प्रध्मायीताभिनद्धाक्ष आनीतोऽभिनद्धाक्षो विसृष्टः ॥ १ ॥

Yathā somya puruṣaṁ gandhārebhyo'bhinaddhākṣa-māṇīya taṁ tato'tijane visṛjetsa yathā tatra prāṅvodaṅ-vādharāṅvā pratyaṅvā pradhmāyītābhinaddhākṣa ānīto-'bhinaddhākṣo visṛṣṭaḥ.

Yathā, just as; *somya,* O Somya; *puruṣam,* a person; *gandhārebhyaḥ,* from the Gandhāra region; *abhinaddha-akṣam-ānīya,* is brought blindfolded; *tataḥ,* from there; *tam visṛjet,* [and] leaves him; *atijane,* in a deserted place; *yathā,* as; *saḥ,* he; *tatra,* there; *prāṅ vā,* facing the east; *udaṅ vā,* or facing the north; *adharāṅ vā,* or facing the south; *pratyaṅ vā,* or facing the west; *pradhmāyīta,* shouts; *abhinaddhākṣaḥ ānītaḥ,* I have been brought blindfolded; *abhinaddhākṣaḥ visṛṣṭaḥ,* I have been left blindfolded.

1. O Somya, as when a person is brought blindfolded from the Gandhāra country and left in a deserted place, he turns sometimes to the east, sometimes to the north, sometimes to the south, and sometimes to the west, shouting: 'I have been brought here blindfolded! I have been left here blindfolded!'—

The Upaniṣad is trying to convey a very difficult idea, but fortunately it gives many illustrations. Here is another one: Suppose you have been seized by some robbers. They put a blindfold on your eyes and then take you away into the forest and leave you there. Perhaps the forest is infested with wild animals. Somehow or other you have to get out, but you don't know where you are and you can't see anything. What do you do? You run around in every direction, shouting: 'I am so-and-so. I belong to such-and-such village. I can't see anything. Please help me get out of here.' Then at last someone takes pity on you and leads you out of the forest. That someone is the teacher.

You are ignorant and don't know the way. You don't know how to reach God, how to attain the Truth. But someone has compassion on you—someone who knows the way. You say, 'I must go back home.' But what is this home? It is the Self. The small self wants to return to the Cosmic Self.

It is as if the self is alienated from itself—as if there is a barrier between one self and the other. The individual self and the Cosmic Self are the same, but there seems to be a barrier between them. We have to remove that barrier.

तस्य यथाभिनहनं प्रमुच्य प्रब्रूयादेतां दिशं गन्धारा एतां दिशं व्रजेति स ग्रामाद्ग्रामं पृच्छन्पण्डितो मेधावी गन्धारानेवोपसम्पद्येतैवमेवेहाचार्यवान्पुरुषो वेद तस्य तावदेव चिरं यावन्न विमोक्ष्येऽथ सम्पत्स्य इति॥ २ ॥

Tasya yathābhinahanaṁ pramucya prabrūyādetāṁ diśaṁ gandhārā etāṁ diśaṁ vrajeti sa grāmādgrāmaṁ pṛcchanpaṇḍito medhāvī gandhārānevopasampadyetai-vamevehācāryavānpuruṣo veda tasya tāvadeva ciraṁ yāvanna vimokṣye'tha sampatsya iti.

Yathā, as; *tasya,* his; *abhinahanam,* blindfold; *pramucya,* having removed; *prabrūyāt,* someone says; *etām diśam,* this way; *gandhārāḥ,* is the Gandhāra country; *etām diśam vraja iti,* go this way; *saḥ,* he; *grāmāt grāmam pṛcchan,* asking from village to village;

paṇḍitaḥ medhāvī, the enlightened person who gets knowledge [of what direction to go in]; *gandhārān eva upasampadyeta,* reaches Gandhāra itself; *evam eva,* in the same way; *iha,* in this world; *puruṣaḥ veda,* a person knows; *ācāryavān,* guided by a teacher; *tasya,* his; *tāvat eva,* that long; *ciram,* delay; *yāvat,* as long as; *na vimokṣye,* he is not free [from the body]; *atha sampatsye iti,* then he becomes merged in the Self.

2. —And as someone may remove that person's blindfold and say, 'Gandhāra is this way; go this way,' and the intelligent man goes from one village to another, asking his way and relying on the information people give, until he reaches Gandhāra; similarly, a person who gets a teacher attains knowledge. His delay is only as long as he is not free of his body. After that he becomes merged in the Self.

The question being considered here is, if I am ignorant how will my ignorance be removed? It can be removed through the instructions of a teacher. But he must be a competent teacher. Can a blind person lead another blind person? No. There is sure to be a disaster if they try.

In this verse the Upaniṣad gives an example of a person led blindfolded into a forest and left there. We are like that person. We are blind, ignorant, and we are unhappy and suffer because of our ignorance. This world of attachment is like a dense forest. Though it is self-created, we do not know the way out. We need someone to help us—someone who knows the way. We need a good teacher.

Śaṅkara says the word *medhāvī* means one who is capable of understanding. You may have a good teacher, and you may have been given instructions, but you have to use your intelligence also.

Now suppose you have a good teacher and you have attained Self-knowledge. According to Vedānta, when you attain Self-knowledge you automatically attain liberation. But the Upaniṣad says there is still one snag. What is that snag? Our *prārabdha karma.* Karma means the results of our actions. If I do something good, I will experience a good result; and if I do something bad, I must suffer. Vedānta says there are three kinds of karma. One kind is called *sañcita karma.* It is our karma that has been accumulated from one birth to another. We have done so many things, and all these actions are waiting to bear fruit.

Another kind of karma is called *āgāmī karma.* While we are experiencing the fruits of our past actions, we are also creating new karma now by our present actions. Some of these actions will bear fruit immediately, but others will take time.

The third kind of karma is called *prārabdha karma.* It is that which has already started bearing fruit in our present life.

According to Vedānta, if you have attained Self-knowledge, both your sañcita karma and your āgāmī karma are destroyed. Śaṅkara says they are burned in the fire of knowledge (*jñānāgni*). But your prārabdha karma will continue. It is the momentum. If you are to suffer from cancer or something else, you cannot escape it. You have to wait till your prārabdha karma exhausts itself.

There are two examples of prārabdha karma. One example is: Suppose you are sawing a tree down. You saw it through completely, but it keeps standing there. It does not immediately fall down. Then a little breeze comes and it falls over. Prārabdha is like the tree standing for a while before falling down.

Then there is the example of the arrow that has been shot. Once you shoot an arrow, you cannot call it back. The same is the case with prārabdha karma. It goes on till the force that has put it into motion is expended.

Now, if you have attained Self-knowledge, your actions will not be like those of an ordinary person. Whatever you do from then on is for the good of others. Śaṅkara says a liberated person does nothing out of desire. If you do something out of desire, that action binds you, even if it is something good. Very often a person does something good out of desire for fame, for power, or for some other selfish motive.

A liberated person, according to Śaṅkara, will do nothing that is against the spirit of the scriptures. His actions will always be right. And they will be only for the good of others (*lokahitārtham*), or for God (*Īśvarārtham*).

स य एषोऽणिमैतदात्म्यमिदं सर्वं तत्सत्यं स आत्मा तत्त्वमसि श्वेतकेतो इति भूय एव मा भगवा-न्विज्ञापयत्विति तथा सोम्येति होवाच ॥ ३ ॥ इति चतुर्दशः खण्डः ॥ १४ ॥

Sa ya eṣo'ṇimaitadātmyamidaṁ sarvaṁ tatsatyaṁ sa ātmā tattvamasi śvetaketo iti bhūya eva mā bhagavānvijñāpayatviti tathā somyeti hovāca. Iti caturdaśaḥ khaṇḍaḥ.

Saḥ yaḥ, that which; *eṣaḥ,* this; *aṇimā,* the subtlest of all; *idam sarvam aitadātmyam,* the Self of all this; *tat satyam,* that is the Truth; *saḥ ātmā,* that is the Self; *tat,* that; *tvam,* you; *asi,* are; *śvetaketo iti,* O Śvetaketu; *bhagavān,* sir; *bhūyaḥ eva,* again; *mā,* to me; *vijñāpayatu iti,* will you please explain; *tathā,* so be it; *somya iti,* O Somya; *ha uvāca,* he [the father] said. *Iti caturdaśaḥ khaṇḍaḥ,* here ends the fourteenth section.

3. 'That which is the subtlest of all is the Self of all this. It is the Truth. It is the Self. That thou art, O Śvetaketu.' [Śvetaketu then said,] 'Sir, please explain this to me again.' 'Yes, Somya, I will explain it again,' replied his father.

Section Fifteen

पुरुषं सोम्योतोपतापिनं ज्ञातयः पर्युपासते जानासि मां जानासि मामिति तस्य यावन्न वाङ्‌ मनसि सम्पद्यते मनः प्राणे प्राणस्तेजसि तेजः परस्यां देवतायां तावज्जानाति ॥ १ ॥

Puruṣaṁ somyotopatāpinaṁ jñātayaḥ paryupāsate jānāsi māṁ jānāsi māmiti tasya yāvanna vāṅ manasi sampadyate manaḥ prāṇe prāṇastejasi tejaḥ parasyāṁ devatāyāṁ tāvajjānāti.

Puruṣam, a person; *uta,* also; *somya,* O Somya; *upatāpinam,* who is sick; *jñātayaḥ,* relatives; *pari-upāsate,* sit around him; *jānāsi mām jānāsi mām iti,* saying 'Do you recognize me, do you recognize me?'; *yāvat,* so long as; *tasya,* his; *vāk,* speech; *manasi na sampadyate,* does not merge in his mind; *manaḥ prāṇe,* the mind into prāṇa; *prāṇaḥ tejasi,* prāṇa into heat; *tejaḥ parasyām devatāyām,* heat into the Supreme Deity; *tāvat jānāti,* that long he knows [them].

1. When a person is seriously ill, O Somya, his relatives sit around him and ask: 'Do you recognize me? Do you recognize me?' So long as his speech does not merge with his mind, his mind with his prāṇa, his prāṇa with the heat in his body, and the heat with the Supreme Self, he will be able to recognize them.

The Upaniṣad has previously said that from the Self comes heat, from heat comes prāṇa (the life force), from prāṇa comes the mind, and from the mind comes speech. Then at the time of death, these things go back in the reverse order—speech goes back into the mind, etc. The resting place is the Self, Pure Spirit. Everything goes back there, and everything comes from there.

When a person is dying, it is common for his relatives to gather round and ask the person, 'Do you recognize me?' How long does he recognize them? So long as heat has not left the body. Even though his breathing has stopped, as long as the body is warm, the person is still alive.

अथ यदास्य वाङ्मनसि सम्पद्यते मनः प्राणे प्राणस्तेजसि तेजः परस्यां देवतायामथ न जानाति॥ २॥

Atha yadāsya vāṅ manasi sampadyate manaḥ prāṇe prāṇastejasi tejaḥ parasyāṁ devatāyāmatha na jānāti.

Atha, then; *yadā,* when; *asya,* his; *vāk manasi sampadyate,* speech merges into the mind; *manaḥ prāṇe,* the mind into prāṇa; *prāṇaḥ tejasi,* prāṇa into heat; *tejaḥ parasyām devatāyām,* heat into the Supreme Self; *atha na jānāti,* then he does not know.

2. Then when his speech merges into his mind, his mind into prāṇa, his prāṇa into the heat in his body,

and the heat into the Supreme Self, he no longer knows them.

After heat leaves the body, a person can no longer recognize anyone. Heat merges in the Self. The Self is the final resting place.

Then what is the difference between the death of an ignorant person and the death of one who has attained Self-knowledge? Śaṅkara says a person who is ignorant merges in the Self only to re-emerge again and be reborn. But when a person who is enlightened dies, that is his mokṣa, his liberation.

Why are we born again and again? Because we have unfulfilled desires. Suppose we die now—what happens to those desires? They have to be fulfilled, so again we seek a body. Perhaps we want to be rich, or we want to rule over people, or we want to eat good food, or we want to be a great scholar. Unless we have a body, we cannot fulfil these desires. But our goal is desirelessness. Only when we become desireless can we attain Self-knowledge. Holy Mother, Sri Sarada Devi, used to say, 'If you have to pray for anything, pray for desirelessness.'

But some people say: 'What's the harm in being reborn? Life is fun.' The scriptures say: 'All right, go ahead. But how long will the fun last? At some point you will be tired of all this and realize what a bondage life is. Then you will seek liberation from this cycle of birth and death.'

On the other hand, there are a few people who, after becoming free themselves, want to help others become free. In Mahāyāna Buddhism, these people are called *bodhisattvas.* They have knowledge, but as long as others are suffering, they will not take the benefit of that knowledge to attain final release. They will return to this world for the good of others.

There is a very interesting story about Rāmānuja, the expounder of Viśiṣṭādvaita (qualified monism). When Rāmānuja was initiated, his guru said to him: 'You see, this is a very great mantra. You must keep it a secret and not tell it to others.' Then Rāmānuja asked, 'What would happen if others hear this mantra?' The teacher answered, 'They would all be liberated, but you would go to hell.' As soon as Rāmānuja left his teacher, he went to the top of a temple tower and called all the people to come. When everyone had gathered there, he repeated the mantra to them all. This is the ideal.

There is a theory called *sarvamuktivāda*—all shall be liberated together. That is to say, I do not want to be liberated until all are liberated. Sri Ramakrishna used to say that some people are very selfish. Even when they go to a public feast they enjoy it themselves and then quietly leave without telling others about it. But there are others who, as soon as they hear about it, gather everyone together to enjoy it with them.

One day Swami Vivekananda went to Sri Ramakrishna and begged him to let him remain absorbed in samādhi. But Sri Ramakrishna scolded him, saying: 'I thought you would be like a big banyan tree, giving shade and rest to many people who are scorched by the heat of the sun. But now I see you are merely seeking your own liberation. You are a fool. Don't you know there is a state higher than that?'

This is the ideal—to be like that tree, to make no distinction between a good person and a bad person, to be ready to give relief to everyone, whether friend or foe. That is a bodhisattva. When you have that ideal you do not care for your own liberation. That is true selflessness.

What we have to remember is that we are all one in the Self. Unless we are conscious of this, we are not liberated.

स य एषोऽणिमैतदात्म्यमिदं सर्वं तत्सत्यं स आत्मा तत्त्वमसि श्वेतकेतो इति भूय एव मा भगवान्विज्ञापयत्विति तथा सोम्येति होवाच॥ ३॥ इति पञ्चदशः खण्डः॥ १५॥

Sa ya eṣo'ṇimaitadātmyamidaṁ sarvaṁ tatsatyaṁ sa ātmā tattvamasi śvetaketo iti bhūya eva mā bhagavānvijñāpayatviti tathā somyeti hovāca. Iti pañcadaśaḥ khaṇḍaḥ.

Saḥ yaḥ, that which; *eṣaḥ,* this; *aṇimā,* the subtlest of all; *idam sarvam aitadātmyam,* the Self of all this; *tat satyam,* that is the Truth; *saḥ ātmā,* that is the Self; *tat,* that; *tvam,* you; *asi,* are; *śvetaketo iti,* O Śvetaketu; *bhagavān,* sir; *bhūyaḥ eva,* again; *mā,* to me; *vijñāpayatu iti,* will you please explain; *tathā,* so be it; *somya iti,* O Somya; *ha uvāca,* he [the father] said. *Iti pañcadaśaḥ khaṇḍaḥ,* here ends the fifteenth section.

3. 'That which is the subtlest of all is the Self of all this. It is the Truth. It is the Self. That thou art, O Śvetaketu.' [Śvetaketu then said,] 'Sir, please explain this to me again.' 'Yes, Somya, I will explain it again,' replied his father.

Section Sixteen

पुरुषं सोम्योत हस्तगृहीतमानयन्त्यपहार्षीत्स्तेयमकार्षीत्परशुमस्मै तपतेति स यदि तस्य कर्ता भवति तत एवानृतमात्मानं कुरुते सोऽनृताभिसन्धोऽनृतेनात्मानमन्तर्धाय परशुं तप्तं प्रतिगृह्णाति स दह्यतेऽथ हन्यते॥ १॥

Puruṣaṁ somyota hastagṛhītamānayantyapahārṣītsteyamakārṣītparaśumasmai tapateti sa yadi tasya kartā bhavati tata evānṛtamātmānaṁ kurute so'nṛtābhisandho'nṛtenātmānamantardhāya paraśuṁ taptaṁ pratigṛhṇāti sa dahyate'tha hanyate.

Somya, O Somya; *puruṣam,* a person; *hastagṛhītam,* with his hands tied; *ānayanti,* they bring; *apahārṣīt,* he has stolen something; *steyam akārṣīt,* he has committed robbery; *paraśum,* an axe; *asmai,* for him;

tapata iti, heat; *yadi,* if; *saḥ,* he; *kartā tasya bhavati,* is the one who has done it; *tataḥ,* then; *eva,* surely; *anṛtam,* false [a liar]; *ātmānam kurute,* proves himself; *anṛta-abhisandhaḥ,* having a dishonest character; *saḥ ātmānam,* he himself; *anṛtena,* by falsehood; *antardhāya,* under the cover [of falsehood]; *paraśum taptam,* the hot axe; *pratigṛhṇāti,* grasps; *saḥ dahyate,* he gets burned; *atha hanyate,* then he dies.

1. O Somya, suppose a man is brought with his hands tied, and they say: 'This man has stolen something. He has committed robbery. Heat up an axe for him.' If he has committed the offence, then surely he will prove himself to be a liar. Being dishonest and trying to hide under the cover of falsehood, he will be burned when he grasps the hot axe, and then he will be killed.

What is liberation? Liberation is the state in which I know I am the Self—I know that I am never born and will never die. When I know that I am free, then I am *aptakāma,* fully satisfied. There is nothing more to achieve, because nothing more exists outside of myself. If there is something outside myself, then I might think, 'Oh, let me have that.' But if I am everything, if everything exists within me, what is there to desire? *Sarvam khalu idam brahma*—all this is Brahman. And I am that Brahman. I am free, immortal. There is no more birth and death for me.

Now here the question arises, what is the test of whether you have Self-knowledge or not? The Upaniṣad gives another illustration: Suppose someone is brought to you and you are told he has committed a theft. You ask him if he has done it and he denies it. But all the evidence seems to point to him as the culprit. What do you do? In ancient days they had a test, a rather cruel test. They put the blade of an axe in fire, and when it was very hot they would put it against the hand of the suspect. If his hand was burnt he was considered guilty, because he was covered, as it were, by falsehood. And if his hand was not burnt he was considered innocent, because he was protected by truth.

Similarly, if we do not have Self-knowledge, we will continue to burn in this world. We will be born again and again. But if we have attained Self-knowledge, we will be liberated. Truth will set us free.

Self-knowledge is not something you can demonstrate or take out and show. The only proof of it is that we do not have to continue in this cycle of birth and death. Nevertheless, when a person attains Self-knowledge, he is not the same any more. His attitude towards others changes. For instance, he can never hurt anyone, because if he hurts someone he hurts himself. Then again, no one is a stranger to him. He accepts everyone. If someone is happy, he is happy. If someone is in pain, he is also in pain. If someone has done well, he feels proud of that person—as if it is his own success. He can never be jealous, because he feels one with everybody.

अथ यदि तस्याकर्ता भवति तत एव सत्यमात्मानं कुरुते स सत्याभिसन्धः सत्येनात्मानमन्तर्धाय परशुं तप्तं प्रतिगृह्णाति स न दह्यतेऽथ मुच्यते॥ २॥

Atha yadi tasyākartā bhavati tata eva satyamātmānaṁ kurute sa satyābhisandhaḥ satyenātmānamantardhāya paraśuṁ taptaṁ pratigṛhṇāti sa na dahyate'tha mucyate.

Atha, but; *yadi,* if; *akartā tasya bhavati,* he is not the one who has done it; *tataḥ,* then; *eva,* surely; *satyam,* truthful; *ātmānam kurute,* proves himself; *satya-abhisandhaḥ,* having an honest character; *saḥ ātmānam,* he himself; *satyena,* by truth; *antardhāya,* under the cover [of truth]; *paraśum taptam,* the hot axe; *pratigṛhṇāti,* grasps; *saḥ na dahyate,* he does not get burned; *atha mucyate,* then he is set free.

2. But if he has not committed the offence, then surely he will prove himself to be truthful. Being honest, he will be protected by the cover of truth and will not be burned when he grasps the hot axe. He will then be set free.

स यथा तत्र नादाह्येतैतदात्म्यमिदं सर्वं तत्सत्यं स आत्मा तत्त्वमसि श्वेतकेतो इति तद्धास्य विजज्ञाविति विजज्ञाविति॥ ३॥ इति षोडशः खण्डः॥ १६॥ इति छान्दोग्योपनिषदि षष्ठोऽध्यायः॥ ६॥

Sa yathā tatra nādāhyetaitadātmyamidaṁ sarvaṁ tatsatyaṁ sa ātmā tattvamasi śvetaketo iti taddhāsya vijajñāviti vijajñāviti. Iti ṣoḍaśaḥ khaṇḍaḥ. Iti chāndogyopaniṣadi ṣaṣṭho'dhyāyaḥ.

Yathā, as; *saḥ,* he; *tatra,* in such circumstances; *na adāhyet,* is not burned; *idam sarvam aitadātmyam,* the Self of all this; *tat satyam,* that is the Truth; *saḥ ātmā,* that is the Self; *tat,* that; *tvam,* you; *asi,* are; *śvetaketo iti,* O Śvetaketu; *asya,* from him [his father]; *tat ha,* that [Self]; *vijajñau iti,* he clearly learnt; *vijajñau iti,* he clearly learnt. *Iti ṣoḍaśaḥ khaṇḍaḥ,* here ends the sixteenth section. *Iti chāndogyopaniṣadi ṣaṣṭhaḥ adhyāyaḥ,* here ends the sixth chapter of the Chāndogya Upaniṣad.

3. 'That man, being honest, is not affected by the hot axe. That [Self] is the Self of all this. It is the Truth. It is the Self. That thou art, O Śvetaketu.' Śvetaketu learnt this well from his father.

Idam sarvam—all this. 'This' refers to this phenomenal world which we see, with which we are familiar. Please remember, even in this unreal phenomenal world that one unchangeable essence exists. *Tat satyam*—that is the Reality. Sri Ramakrishna used to give the example of pillows. Pillows may be different sizes, different shapes, and have different functions, but inside all of them is the same silk-cotton, the same essence. Similarly, within this phenomenal world there is one essence, one Reality. And that is our Self. *Tat tvam asi*—you are that.

Uddālaka had been repeating again and again, *'Tat tvam asi, Śvetaketu,'* but each time his son could not understand. Now at last he has understood.

This chapter stresses the idea that there is something —we call it pure Spirit—from which everything has emerged, on which everything rests, and into which everything finally merges. There is something common from which we have all come, on which we all rest, and into which we all go back. That something is always constant.

Think of the ocean, for example. Where do the waves come from? The ocean. What supports them? The ocean. Where do they finally go? Back to the ocean. This coming and going, back and forth—we see this happening all the time, with everything. We are born, we remain for a while, and then we die. Over and over again—we come from Brahman, we are sustained by Brahman, and we go back to Brahman. But all the time we are that Brahman. As the waves are nothing but the ocean, similarly, we are nothing but Brahman.

Sri Ramakrishna used to say that the relative and the Absolute are the same. The Absolute is compared to a snake coiled up, sleeping on the ground, and the relative is like a snake in motion, raising its hood.

But when everything disappears, when there is no phenomenal world, what remains? We do not know. There is a vast, infinite One. We cannot describe it, because it has no name and no form. How can you describe something that is nameless and formless?

Suppose you say 'white.' Can you understand 'white' without a white object? There must be a particularization. A white flower, or a white shirt, we can understand. Similarly, how can we understand pure Existence? This is why the Upaniṣad simply calls it *tat,* that.

Vedānta says that the One has become many, but this many does not make a real modification or change in the One. The One remains One. It only appears to be many.

CHAPTER SEVEN

Section One

ॐ। अधीहि भगव इति होपससाद सनत्कुमारं नारदस्तं होवाच यद्वेत्थ तेन मोपसीद ततस्त ऊर्ध्वं वक्ष्यामीति स होवाच॥ १॥

Om. Adhīhi bhagava iti hopasasāda sanatkumāraṁ nāradastaṁ hovāca yadvettha tena mopasīda tatasta ūrdhvaṁ vakṣyāmīti sa hovāca.

Bhagavaḥ, sir; *adhīhi iti,* please teach me; *sanatkumāram,* to Sanatkumāra; *nāradaḥ ha upasasāda,* Nārada went [and said]; *tam ha uvāca,* [Sanatkumāra] said to him; *yat vettha,* whatever you know; *tena mā upasīda,* tell me that; *tataḥ ūrdhvam,* from that point; *te vakṣyāmi iti,* I will teach you; *saḥ ha uvāca,* he [Nārada] said.

1. Nārada went [for spiritual instruction] to Sanatkumāra and said, 'Sir, please teach me.' Sanatkumāra said to him: 'First tell me what you know already. I'll teach you from that point.' Nārada said—

ऋग्वेदं भगवोऽध्येमि यजुर्वेदं सामवेदमाथर्वणं चतुर्थमितिहासपुराणं पञ्चमं वेदानां वेदं पित्र्यं राशिं

दैवं निधिं वाकोवाक्यमेकायनं देवविद्यां ब्रह्मविद्यां भूतविद्यां क्षत्त्रविद्यां नक्षत्रविद्यां सर्पदेवजनविद्यामेतद्भगवो-ऽध्येमि ॥ २ ॥

Ṛgvedaṁ bhagavo'dhyemi yajurvedaṁ sāmaveda-mātharvaṇaṁ caturthamitihāsapurāṇaṁ pañcamaṁ ve-dānāṁ vedaṁ pitryaṁ rāśiṁ daivaṁ nidhiṁ vākovākya-mekāyanaṁ devavidyāṁ brahmavidyāṁ bhūtavidyāṁ kṣattravidyāṁ nakṣatravidyāṁ sarpadevajanavidyāme-tadbhagavo'dhyemi.

Bhagavaḥ, sir; *adhyemi,* I know; *ṛg vedam yajur vedam sāma vedam ātharvaṇam caturtham,* the Ṛg Veda, the Yajur Veda, the Sāma Veda, and the fourth, the Atharva Veda; *itihāsa purāṇam pañcamam,* history and the Purāṇas, as the fifth; *vedānām vedam,* grammar [lit., the Veda of the Vedas]; *pitryam,* rites offered out of respect to the ancestors; *rāśim,* mathematics; *daivam,* the science of meteors and other natural phenomena [and omens]; *nidhim,* the science of underground resources; *vākovākyam,* logic; *ekāyanam,* moral science; *deva-vidyām,* astrology; *brahma-vidyām,* knowledge of the Vedas; *bhūta-vidyām,* geology; *kṣattra-vidyām,* archery; *nakṣatra-vidyām,* astronomy; *sarpa* [*-vidyām*], snake-charming; *devajana-vidyām,* fine arts; *bhagavaḥ,* sir; *etat adhyemi,* I know all this.

2. Sir, I have read the Ṛg Veda, the Yajur Veda, the Sāma Veda, and the fourth—the Atharva Veda;

then the fifth—history and the Purāṇas; also, grammar, funeral rites, mathematics, the science of omens, the science of underground resources, logic, moral science, astrology, Vedic knowledge, the science of the elements, archery, astronomy, the science relating to snakes, plus music, dance, and other fine arts. Sir, this is what I know.

सोऽहं भगवो मन्त्रविदेवास्मि नात्मविच्छ्रुतं ह्येव मे भगवद्दृशेभ्यस्तरति शोकमात्मविदिति सोऽहं भगवः शोचामि तं मा भगवाञ्छोकस्य पारं तारयत्विति तं होवाच यद्वै किञ्चैतदध्यगीष्ठा नामैवैतत् ॥ ३ ॥

So'haṁ bhagavo mantravidevāsmi nātmavicchrutaṁ hyeva me bhagavaddṛśebhyastarati śokamātmaviditi so'haṁ bhagavaḥ śocāmi taṁ mā bhagavāñchokasya pāraṁ tārayatviti taṁ hovāca yadvai kiñcaitadadhya-gīṣṭhā nāmaivaitat.

Bhagavaḥ, sir; *saḥ aham mantravit eva asmi,* [though I have studied much] I know only the word meaning; *na ātmavit,* I do not know the Self; *śrutam hi eva me,* I have also heard; *bhagavat dṛśebhyaḥ,* from people like you; *tarati śokam ātmavit iti,* one who knows the Self overcomes sorrow; *bhagavaḥ,* sir; *saḥ aham śocāmi,* I am suffering from sorrow; *tam mā bhagavān śokasya pāram tārayatu iti,* sir, please take me across [the ocean of] sorrow; *tam ha uvāca,* [Sanatkumāra] said to him; *yat vai kiñca etat,* whatever it is; *adhyagīṣṭhāḥ etat nāma eva,* you have learnt is only words.

3. 'True, I have learnt much, but I know only the word meaning. I do not know the Self. Sir, I have heard from great persons like you that only those who know the Self are able to overcome sorrow. I am suffering from sorrow. Please take me across the ocean of sorrow.' Sanatkumāra then said to Nārada, 'Everything you have learnt so far is just words.'

Nārada was a great scholar. But in spite of all his knowledge, he did not know the Self and was very unhappy. So, with great humility, he approached the sage Sanatkumāra and said, 'Sir, would you please teach me?' Sanatkumāra replied, 'Tell me what you already know.' The teacher must know what level the student is at so he can raise him from where he is.

Then Nārada began to list all the subjects he had studied: the Vedas, history and mythology, grammar, mathematics, astrology, and so forth. But Nārada felt that all this was pointless. It served no purpose, because if he did not know the Self he knew nothing. His knowledge was merely *aparā vidyā,* lower knowledge, and not *parā vidyā,* higher knowledge—that is, knowledge of the Self. Moreover, Nārada said: 'I know only the words. I do not know the Self.'

The finest, most subtle, knowledge is knowledge of the Self. You begin with the gross and go step by step until you reach the finest. First you are only a *mantra-vit*—that is, you know only the word meanings of the scriptures. But this is nothing. The scriptures are all about the Self. If you don't know the Self, your knowledge of the scriptures is useless.

Being a scholar without knowing the real meaning of the scriptures is like being a beast of burden. A donkey may carry a load of sandalwood. In fact, his back may almost be breaking with the weight of it. Yet he does not enjoy the fragrance. Similarly, being a scholar is not the same as having Self-knowledge.

Nārada has great yearning. He says: 'I have heard that saints like you have no more grief because you know the Self. Please take me across the ocean of sorrow. You alone can do that by giving me Self-knowledge. Life has a purpose. Please make me feel that I have achieved that purpose.'

Now Sanatkumāra says to Nārada: 'You have studied much, but you have studied only words. Each word has a meaning, and that meaning has to be grasped.' How do we grasp the meaning? Śaṅkara gives an example here: Suppose the king is coming by in a procession and you are very anxious to see him. But along with the king are thousands of other people, bands, vehicles, horses, elephants—so much pomp and grandeur. Where is the king?

Śaṅkara says this world is like that procession. The king is there, but he is hidden from you—hidden behind all the pomp and pageantry. Similarly, in this world we perceive only names and forms—words, not substance. Merely knowing the word *Brahman* does not give us the knowledge of Brahman. We have to become Brahman. We must be one with the Self.

Now the question may arise: Sanatkumāra says that this knowledge of the Vedas and other things is mere words. But perhaps you have studied all the scriptures and performed many sacrifices—is all this then futile? Śaṅkara says no, it's not futile. He gives the example: Suppose a child wants to know what the moon is. How do you show him the moon? First you say, 'Do you see that big tree over there?' When the child says yes, you say, 'Do you see the top of the tree?' Again, when the child says yes, you say: 'Do you see that big shining ball behind the branches? That is the moon.' You go step by step.

Can you teach an ignorant person the highest science? Will he be able to grasp it? You must start with something he can understand. Similarly, there is the world of sense experience before us, and it is very real to us. We don't see the Self, so we can't understand what it is. Self-knowledge is the highest knowledge. We cannot expect to attain it immediately. First we must know what this world is. First we must know what it is to have money, scholarship, fame, and other things.

After experiencing these things of the world and finding them to be hollow, only then can we become disillusioned with this world. And only then can we renounce this world of name and form and fix our minds on the Self. We may hear about the Self, but first we must know that this world we are so familiar with is a world of illusion—that everything here is transitory. This is why the teacher takes Nārada step by step.

नाम वा ऋग्वेदो यजुर्वेदः सामवेद आथर्वणश्चतुर्थ इतिहासपुराणः पञ्चमो वेदानां वेदः पित्र्यो राशिर्दैवो निधिर्वाकोवाक्यमेकायनं देवविद्या ब्रह्मविद्या भूतविद्या क्षत्त्रविद्या नक्षत्रविद्या सर्पदेवजनविद्या नामैवैतन्नामोपास्स्वेति ॥ ४ ॥

Nāma vā ṛgvedo yajurvedaḥ sāmaveda ātharvaṇaś-caturtha itihāsapurāṇaḥ pañcamo vedānāṁ vedaḥ pitryo rāśirdaivo nidhirvākovākyamekāyanaṁ devavidyā brah-mavidyā bhūtavidyā kṣattravidyā nakṣatravidyā sarpa-devajanavidyā nāmaivaitannāmopāssveti.

Nāma vai, name is; *ṛg vedaḥ yajur vedaḥ sāma vedaḥ ātharvaṇaḥ caturthaḥ,* the Ṛg Veda, the Yajur Veda, the Sāma Veda, and the fourth, the Atharva Veda; *itihāsa purāṇaḥ pañcamaḥ,* history and the Purāṇas, as the fifth; *vedānām vedaḥ,* grammar [lit., the Veda of the Vedas]; *pitryaḥ,* rites offered out of respect to the ancestors; *rāśiḥ,* mathematics; *daivaḥ,* the science of meteors and other natural phenomena [and omens]; *nidhiḥ,* the science of underground re-sources; *vākovākyam,* logic; *ekāyanam,* moral science; *deva-vidyā,* astrology; *brahma-vidyā,* knowledge of the Vedas; *bhūta-vidyā,* geology; *kṣattra-vidyā,* archery;

nakṣatra-vidyā, astronomy; *sarpa* [*-vidyā*], snake-charming; *devajana-vidyā,* fine arts; *nāma eva etat,* these are mere names; *nāma upāssva iti,* worship name.

4. Name is the Ṛg Veda, the Yajur Veda, the Sāma Veda, and the fourth—the Atharva Veda; then the fifth—history and the Purāṇas; also, grammar, funeral rites, mathematics, the science of omens, the science of underground resources, logic, moral science, astrology, Vedic knowledge, the science of the elements, archery, astronomy, the science relating to snakes, plus music, dance, and other fine arts. These are only names. Worship name.

स यो नाम ब्रह्मेत्युपास्ते यावन्नाम्नो गतं तत्रास्य यथाकामचारो भवति यो नाम ब्रह्मेत्युपास्तेऽस्ति भगवो नाम्नो भूय इति नाम्नो वाव भूयोऽस्तीति तन्मे भगवान्ब्रवीत्विति ॥ ५ ॥ इति प्रथमः खण्डः ॥ १ ॥

Sa yo nāma brahmetyupāste yāvannāmno gataṁ tatrāsya yathākāmacāro bhavati yo nāma brahmetyupās-te'sti bhagavo nāmno bhūya iti nāmno vāva bhūyo'stīti tanme bhagavānbravītviti. Iti prathamaḥ khaṇḍaḥ.

Saḥ yaḥ, he who; *nāma brahma iti upāste,* worships name as Brahman; *yāvat nāmnaḥ gatam,* as far as name can go; *tatra,* that far; *asya yathā-kāmacāraḥ bhavati,* as he wishes he can go; *yaḥ nāma brahma iti upāste,* he who worships name as Brahman; *bhagavaḥ,* sir; *nāmnaḥ bhūyaḥ asti iti,* is there anything higher than name; *nāmnaḥ vāva bhūyaḥ asti iti,* there is certainly something higher than name; *bhagavān,* sir; *tat me bravītu iti,* please explain it to me. *Iti prathamaḥ khaṇḍaḥ,* here ends the first section.

5. 'Anyone who worships name as Brahman can do what he pleases within the limits of the name.' Nārada asked, 'Sir, is there anything higher than name?' 'Of course there is something higher than name,' replied Sanatkumāra. Nārada then said, 'Sir, please explain that to me.'

If you worship name as Brahman then you can achieve anything you want within certain limits. But Brahman is the real purport. The names by themselves are not important.

Names have a limited use. When you call a flower a rose, you are obviously referring to a particular species of flower. Within the limits of that species, you have as much freedom as you like. You may be referring to a rose of any colour you like—white, red, yellow, etc. You are free within the limits of the colours and other characteristics of the rose.

But when you identify the rose as Brahman, you impose on Brahman the limitations that the name 'rose' has. As Brahman is nameless, you have no right to impose the limitations that name implies on it.

Section Two

वाग्वाव नाम्नो भूयसी वाग्वा ऋग्वेदं विज्ञापयति यजुर्वेदं सामवेदमाथर्वणं चतुर्थमितिहासपुराणं पञ्चमं वेदानां वेदं पित्र्यं राशिं दैवं निधिं वाकोवाक्यमेकायनं देवविद्यां ब्रह्मविद्यां भूतविद्यां क्षत्त्रविद्यां नक्षत्रविद्यां सर्पदेवजनविद्यां दिवं च पृथिवीं च वायुं चाकाशं चापश्च तेजश्च देवांश्च मनुष्यांश्च पशूंश्च वयांसि च तृणवनस्पतीञ्श्वापदान्याकीटपतङ्गपिपीलिकं धर्मं चाधर्मं च सत्यं चानृतं च साधु चासाधु च हृदयज्ञं चाहृदयज्ञं च यद्वै वाङ्नाभविष्यन्न धर्मो नाधर्मो व्यज्ञापयिष्यन्न सत्यं नानृतं न साधु नासाधु न हृदयज्ञो नाहृदयज्ञो वागेवैतत्सर्वं विज्ञापयति वाचमुपास्स्वेति॥ १ ॥

Vāgvāva nāmno bhūyasī vāgvā ṛgvedaṁ vijñāpayati yajurvedaṁ sāmavedamātharvaṇaṁ caturthamitihāsa-purāṇaṁ pañcamaṁ vedānāṁ vedaṁ pitryaṁ rāśiṁ daivaṁ nidhiṁ vākovākyamekāyanaṁ devavidyāṁ brahmavidyāṁ bhūtavidyāṁ kṣattravidyāṁ nakṣatravidyāṁ sarpadevajanavidyāṁ divaṁ ca pṛthivīṁ ca vāyuṁ cākāśaṁ cāpaśca tejaśca devāṁśca manuṣyāṁśca paśūṁśca vayāṁsi ca tṛṇavanaspatīñśvāpadānyākīṭapataṅgapipīlikaṁ dharmaṁ cādharmaṁ ca satyaṁ cānṛtaṁ ca sādhu cāsādhu ca hṛdayajñaṁ cāhṛdayajñaṁ ca yadvai vāṅnābhaviṣyanna dharmo nādharmo vyajñāpayiṣyanna satyaṁ nānṛtaṁ na sādhu nāsādhu na hṛdayajño nāhṛdayajño vāgevaitatsarvaṁ vijñāpayati vācamupāssveti.

Vāk vāva nāmnaḥ bhūyasī, speech is certainly superior to name; *vāk vai vijñāpayati,* speech makes known; *ṛg vedam yajur vedam sāma vedam ātharvaṇam caturtham,* the Ṛg Veda, the Yajur Veda, the Sāma Veda, and the fourth, the Atharva Veda; *itihāsa purāṇam pañcamam,* history and the Purāṇas, as the fifth; *vedānām vedam,* grammar [lit., the Veda of the Vedas]; *pitryam,* rites offered out of respect to the ancestors; *rāśim,* mathematics; *daivam,* the science of meteors and other natural phenomena [and omens]; *nidhim,* the science of underground resources; *vākovākyam,* logic; *ekāyanam,* moral science; *deva-vidyām,* astrology; *brahma-vidyām,* knowledge of the Vedas; *bhūta-vidyām,* geology; *kṣattra-vidyām,* archery; *nakṣatra-vidyām,* astronomy; *sarpa* [*-vidyām*], snake-charming; *devajana-vidyām,* fine arts; *divam ca,* heaven; *pṛthivīm ca,* and the earth; *vāyum ca,* and air; *ākāśam ca,* and space; *āpaḥ ca,* and water; *tejaḥ ca,* and fire; *devān ca,* and the gods; *manuṣyān ca,* and human beings; *paśūn ca,* and animals; *vayāṁsi ca,* and birds; *tṛṇa-vanaspatīn,* creepers and big trees; *śvāpadāni,* animals of prey; *ākīṭa-pataṅga-pipīlikam,* worms, fleas, and ants; *dharmam ca adharmam ca,* merit and demerit; *satyam ca anṛtam ca,* and truth and untruth; *sādhu ca asādhu ca,* and good and evil; *hṛdayajñam ca ahṛdayajñam ca,* pleasant and unpleasant; *yat vai vāk,* if speech; *na abhaviṣyat,* did not exist; *na dharmaḥ* *na adharmaḥ vyajñāpayiṣyat,* there would be no awareness of merit and demerit; *satyam na anṛtam,* nor of truth and untruth; *sādhu na asādhu na,* nor of good and evil; *hṛdayajñaḥ na ahṛdayajñaḥ,* nor of pleasant and unpleasant; *vāk eva etat sarvam vijñāpayati,* speech alone makes it possible to understand all this; *vāk upāssva iti,* worship speech.

1. Speech is certainly superior to name. Speech makes known the Ṛg Veda, the Yajur Veda, the Sāma Veda, and the fourth—the Atharva Veda; then the fifth—history and the Purāṇas; also, grammar, funeral rites, mathematics, the science of omens, the science of underground resources, logic, moral science, astrology, Vedic knowledge, the science of the elements, archery, astronomy, the science relating to snakes, plus music, dance, and other fine arts; also heaven and earth; air, space, water, and fire; the gods and human beings; cattle and birds; creepers and big trees; animals of prey as well as worms, fleas, and ants; merit and demerit; truth and untruth; good and evil; and the pleasant and the unpleasant. If speech did not exist there would be no awareness of merit and demerit, nor of truth and untruth, good and evil, the pleasant and the unpleasant. Speech alone makes it possible to understand all this. Worship speech.

Vāk is the organ of speech. It produces not only words, but words with deep meanings. For instance, we have access to the wisdom of the Vedas through these words. These words represent Brahman and should be worshipped as such.

स यो वाचं ब्रह्मेत्युपास्ते यावद्वाचो गतं तत्रास्य यथाकामचारो भवति यो वाचं ब्रह्मेत्युपास्तेऽस्ति भगवो वाचो भूय इति वाचो वाव भूयोऽस्तीति तन्मे भगवान्ब्रवीत्विति॥ २॥ इति द्वितीयः खण्डः॥ २॥

Sa yo vācaṁ brahmetyupāste yāvadvāco gataṁ tatrāsya yathākāmacāro bhavati yo vācaṁ brahmetyupāste'sti bhagavo vāco bhūya iti vāco vāva bhūyo'stīti tanme bhagavānbravītviti. Iti dvitīyaḥ khaṇḍaḥ.

Saḥ yaḥ, he who; *vācam brahma iti upāste,* worships speech as Brahman; *yāvat vācaḥ gatam,* as far as the power of speech goes; *tatra,* that far; *asya yathā-kāmacāraḥ bhavati,* as he wishes he can go; *yaḥ vācam brahma iti upāste,* he who worships speech as Brahman; *bhagavaḥ,* sir; *vācaḥ bhūyaḥ asti iti,* is there anything higher than speech; *vācaḥ vāva bhūyaḥ asti iti,* there is certainly something higher than speech; *bhagavān,* sir; *tat me bravītu iti,* please explain it to me. *Iti dvitīyaḥ khaṇḍaḥ,* here ends the second section.

2. 'Anyone who worships speech as Brahman can do what he pleases within the limits of speech.' Nārada asked, 'Sir, is there anything higher than speech?' 'Of course there is something higher than speech,' replied Sanatkumāra. Nārada then said, 'Sir, please explain that to me.'

If you worship speech as Brahman, you have whatever power speech has. But that marks the limit of your power.

Section Three

मनो वाव वाचो भूयो यथा वै द्वे वामलके द्वे वा कोले द्वौ वाक्षौ मुष्टिरनुभवत्येवं वाचं च नाम च मनोऽनुभवति स यदा मनसा मनस्यति मन्त्रानधीयीयेत्यथाधीते कर्माणि कुर्वीयेत्यथ कुरुते पुत्रांश्च पशूंश्चेच्छेयेत्यथेच्छत इमं च लोकममुं चेच्छेयेत्यथेच्छते मनो ह्यात्मा मनो हि लोको मनो हि ब्रह्म मन उपास्स्वेति ॥ १ ॥

Mano vāva vāco bhūyo yathā vai dve vāmalake dve vā kole dvau vākṣau muṣṭiranubhavatyevaṁ vācaṁ ca nāma ca mano'nubhavati sa yadā manasā manasyati mantrānadhīyīyetyathādhīte karmāṇi kurvīyetyatha kurute putrāṁśca paśūṁśceccheyetyathecchata imaṁ ca lokamamuṁ ceccheyetyathecchate mano hyātmā mano hi loko mano hi brahma mana upāssveti.

Manaḥ vāva vācaḥ bhūyaḥ, the mind is certainly superior to speech; *yathā vai,* just as; *dve vā āmalake,* two āmalaka fruits; *dve vā kole,* or two kolas [plums]; *dvau vā akṣau,* or two akṣa fruits; *muṣṭiḥ anubhavati,* the fist can hold; *evam,* in the same way; *manaḥ anubhavati,* the mind can hold; *vācam ca nāma ca,* speech and mind; *yadā,* when; *saḥ,* someone; *manasā,* in his mind; *manasyati,* thinks; *mantrān adhīyīya iti,* I will read the mantras; *atha,* then; *adhīte,* he reads; *karmāṇi kurvīya iti,* I will work; *atha,* then; *kurute,* he works; *putrān ca paśūn ca,* children and animals; *iccheya iti,* let me wish for; *atha icchate,* then he wishes; *imam ca lokam amum ca,* this world and the other world; *iccheya iti,* let me wish for; *atha icchate,* then he wishes; *manaḥ hi ātmā,* the mind is the self; *manaḥ hi lokaḥ,* the mind is the world; *manaḥ hi brahma,* the mind is Brahman; *manaḥ upāssva iti,* worship the mind.

1. The mind is superior to speech. Just as a person can hold in his fist two āmalaka fruits, or two kola fruits [plums], or two akṣa fruits, so also the mind can hold within it both speech and name. If a person thinks, 'I will read the mantras,' he reads them. If he thinks, 'I will do this,' he does it. If he decides, 'I will have children and animals,' he can try to have them. If he decides, 'I will conquer this world and the next,' he can try to do it. [This is the characteristic of the mind. If it says it will do something, it can do it.] The mind is the self. The mind is the world. The mind is Brahman. Worship the mind.

Speech and name are important, but they are not enough. They will not take you very far. Suppose you repeat the name of God, but your mind is elsewhere, thinking of something else. Will that serve any purpose? No.

The Upaniṣad says here, first you decide in your mind what you will do, and after that you act on the thought. Just as you hold fruits within your hand, similarly, you hold within your mind what you want—whether it is children, property, scholarship, or something else. So the mind is higher than speech.

स यो मनो ब्रह्मेत्युपास्ते यावन्मनसो गतं तत्रास्य यथाकामचारो भवति यो मनो ब्रह्मेत्युपास्तेऽस्ति भगवो मनसो भूय इति मनसो वाव भूयोऽस्तीति तन्मे भगवान्ब्रवीत्विति ॥ २ ॥ इति तृतीयः खण्डः ॥ ३ ॥

Sa yo mano brahmetyupāste yāvanmanaso gataṁ tatrāsya yathākāmacāro bhavati yo mano brahmetyupāste'sti bhagavo manaso bhūya iti manaso vāva bhūyo'stīti tanme bhagavānbravītviti. Iti tṛtīyaḥ khaṇḍaḥ.

Saḥ yaḥ, he who; *manaḥ brahma iti upāste,* worships the mind as Brahman; *yāvat manasaḥ gatam,* as far as the mind goes; *tatra,* that far; *asya yathā-kāmacāraḥ bhavati,* as he wishes he can go; *yaḥ manaḥ brahma iti upāste,* he who worships the mind as Brahman; *bhagavaḥ,* sir; *manasaḥ bhūyaḥ asti iti,* is there anything higher than the mind; *manasaḥ vāva bhūyaḥ asti iti,* there is certainly something higher than the mind; *bhagavān,* sir; *tat me bravītu iti,* please explain it to me. *Iti tṛtīyaḥ khaṇḍaḥ,* here ends the third section.

2. 'Anyone who worships the mind as Brahman can do what he pleases within the limits of the mind.' Nārada asked, 'Sir, is there anything higher than the mind?' 'Of course there is something higher than the mind,' replied Sanatkumāra. Nārada then said, 'Sir, please explain that to me.'

Section Four

सङ्कल्पो वाव मनसो भूयान्यदा वै सङ्कल्पयतेऽथ मनस्यत्यथ वाचमीरयति तामु नाम्नीरयति नाम्नि मन्त्रा एकं भवन्ति मन्त्रेषु कर्माणि॥ १ ॥

Saṅkalpo vāva manaso bhūyānyadā vai saṅkalpayate-'tha manasyatyatha vācamīrayati tāmu nāmnīrayati nāmni mantrā ekaṁ bhavanti mantreṣu karmāṇi.

Saṅkalpaḥ vāva manasaḥ bhūyān, the will is indeed superior to the mind; *yadā vai,* when; *saṅkalpayate,* a person decides; *atha,* then; *manasyati,* he thinks; *atha,* then; *vācam īrayati,* he directs the organ of speech; *tām u nāmni īrayati,* he makes speech utter the name; *nāmni,* in the names; *mantrāḥ,* all the mantras; *ekam bhavanti,* are united; *mantreṣu karmāṇi,* the actions [are united] in the mantras.

1. The will is certainly superior to the mind. When a person wills, he starts thinking. Then he directs

the organ of speech, and finally he makes the organ of speech utter the name. All the mantras merge in the names and all the actions merge in the mantras.

The mind is very important, but it needs to be guided by the will. Why? Because the mind is always wavering. It cannot decide. In the Bhagavad Gītā the mind is described as being *vāyoḥ iva,* like the wind. It is restless and difficult to control. Sometimes the mind is even compared to a mad elephant.

All of us have minds, no doubt, but not all have an equal degree of will power, or determination. For instance, anyone may utter some mantras, but unless they are recited with saṅkalpa, they do not mean anything. They are just words. When you add saṅkalpa to the mantras, then the words become active and powerful. This is why saṅkalpa is higher.

तानि ह वा एतानि सङ्कल्पैकायनानि सङ्कल्पात्मकानि
सङ्कल्पे प्रतिष्ठितानि समक्लृपतां द्यावापृथिवी समकल्पेतां
वायुश्चाकाशं च समकल्पन्तापश्च तेजश्च तेषां संक्लृप्त्यै
वर्षं सङ्कल्पते वर्षस्य संक्लृप्त्या अन्नं सङ्कल्पतेऽन्नस्य
संक्लृप्त्यै प्राणाः सङ्कल्पन्ते प्राणानां संक्लृप्त्यै मन्त्राः
सङ्कल्पन्ते मन्त्राणां संक्लृप्त्यै कर्माणि सङ्कल्पन्ते कर्मणां
सक्लृप्त्यै लोकः सङ्कल्पते लोकस्य संक्लृप्त्यै सर्वं सङ्कल्पते
स एष सङ्कल्पः सङ्कल्पमुपास्स्वेति ॥ २ ॥

Tāni ha vā etāni saṅkalpaikāyanāni saṅkalpātmakāni saṅkalpe pratiṣṭhitāni samaklṛpatāṁ dyāvāpṛthivī samakalpetāṁ vāyuścākāśaṁ ca samakalpantāpaśca tejaśca teṣāṁ saṁklṛptyai varṣaṁ saṅkalpate varṣasya saṁklṛptyā annaṁ saṅkalpate'nnasya saṁklṛptyai prāṇāḥ saṅkalpante prāṇānāṁ saṁklṛptyai mantrāḥ saṅkalpante mantrāṇāṁ saṁklṛptyai karmāṇi saṅkalpante karmaṇāṁ saṁklṛptyai lokaḥ saṅkalpate lokasya saṁklṛptyai sarvaṁ saṅkalpate sa eṣa saṅkalpaḥ saṅkalpamupāssveti.

Tāni ha vai etāni, all these [i.e., mind, speech, name, mantra, and karma]; *saṅkalpa-ekāyanāni,* merge in saṅkalpa; *saṅkalpātmakāni,* rise from saṅkalpa; *saṅkalpe pratiṣṭhitāni,* supported by saṅkalpa; *dyāvāpṛthivī,* heaven and the earth; *samaklṛpatām,* will; *vāyuḥ ca ākāśam ca,* the air and the sky; *samakalpetām,* will; *āpaḥ ca tejaḥ ca,* water and fire; *samakalpanta,* will; *teṣām saṁklṛptyai,* through their will; *varṣam saṅkalpate,* rain wills; *varṣasya saṁklṛptyai,* because the rain wills; *annam saṅkalpate,* food wills; *annasya saṁklṛptyai,* because of the will of food; *prāṇāḥ saṅkalpante,* the prāṇas will; *prāṇānām saṁklṛptyai,* because of the will of the prāṇas; *mantrāḥ saṅkalpante,* the mantras will; *mantrāṇām saṁklṛptyai,* because the mantras will; *karmāṇi saṅkalpante,* the karmas will; *karmaṇām saṁklṛptyai,* because the karmas will; *lokaḥ saṅkalpate,* the heaven and other worlds will; *lokasya saṁklṛptyai,* because the worlds will; *sarvam saṅkalpate,* everything wills; *saḥ eṣaḥ,* this is the way; *saṅkalpaḥ,* will [works]; *saṅkalpam upāssva iti,* worship will.

2. All these things [mind, speech, name, etc.] merge in saṅkalpa, arise from saṅkalpa, and are supported

by saṅkalpa. [That is, the will decides the direction of everything you do. It is the soul of everything.] Heaven and earth will, and so do air, space, water, and fire. [That is, it is their will that determines their work.] Through their will the rain wills, and through the will of the rain, food wills. The will of food is the will of life. The will of life is the will of the mantras, and the will of the mantras is the will of all activities. The will of the activities is the will of the worlds, and the will of the worlds determines the will of everything. Such is the will. Worship this will.

Sanatkumāra says here that because of saṅkalpa, each of the forces of nature plays its role—as if each knows the duty it's supposed to perform and has taken a vow to do it. For instance, the earth remains steady—as if it decided long ago that it would remain firm and unmoving. The world goes on, nature goes on, society goes on—all due to this saṅkalpa, to the principle of each doing his or her own duty.

स यः सङ्कल्पं ब्रह्मेत्युपास्ते क्लृप्तान्वै स लोकान्ध्रुवान् ध्रुवः प्रतिष्ठितान्प्रतिष्ठितोऽव्यथमानानव्यथमानोऽभिसिध्यति यावत्सङ्कल्पस्य गतं तत्रास्य यथाकामचारो भवति यः सङ्कल्पं ब्रह्मेत्युपास्तेऽस्ति भगवः सङ्कल्पाद्भूय इति सङ्कल्पाद्वाव भूयोऽस्तीति तन्मे भगवान्ब्रवीत्विति ॥ ३ ॥
इति चतुर्थः खण्डः ॥ ४ ॥

Sa yaḥ saṅkalpaṁ brahmetyupāste klṛptānvai sa lokāndhruvān dhruvaḥ pratiṣṭhitānpratiṣṭhito'vyathamānānavyathamāno'bhisidhyati yāvatsaṅkalpasya gataṁ tatrāsya yathākāmacāro bhavati yaḥ saṅkalpaṁ brahmetyupāste'sti bhagavaḥ saṅkalpādbhūya iti saṅkalpādvāva bhūyo'stīti tanme bhagavānbravītviti. Iti caturthaḥ khaṇḍaḥ.

Saḥ yaḥ saṅkalpam brahma iti upāste, he who worships will-power as Brahman; *klṛptān vai saḥ lokān dhruvān,* the true worlds he wishes for; *dhruvaḥ,* being true himself; *pratiṣṭhitān,* the well-established [worlds]; *pratiṣṭhitaḥ,* [himself being] well-established; *avyathamānān,* [the worlds] free from pain; *avyathamānaḥ,* [himself being] free from pain; *abhisidhyati,* he attains; *yāvat saṅkalpasya gatam,* as far as will can go; *tatra,* that far; *asya yathā-kāmacāraḥ bhavati,* as he wishes he can go; *yaḥ saṅkalpam brahma iti upāste,* he who worships saṅkalpa as Brahman; *bhagavaḥ,* sir; *saṅkalpāt bhūyaḥ asti iti,* is there anything higher than saṅkalpa; *saṅkalpāt vāva bhūyaḥ asti iti,* there is certainly something higher than saṅkalpa; *bhagavān,* sir; *tat me bravītu iti,* please explain it to me. *Iti caturthaḥ khaṇḍaḥ,* here ends the fourth section.

3. 'One who worships saṅkalpa as Brahman can attain any world he wills. He becomes true and attains the world of truth. He is firmly established and also attains a world which is firmly established. He is free from pain and attains also a world free from pain. One who worships saṅkalpa as Brahman can

do what he pleases within the limits of saṅkalpa.' Nārada asked, 'Sir, is there anything higher than saṅkalpa?' 'Of course there is something higher than saṅkalpa,' replied Sanatkumāra. Nārada then said, 'Sir, please explain that to me.'

The will is the beginning and end of everything concerning the mind. Not only that—the will is the root of the earth, heaven, of all the worlds, of space, air, fire, water, food, life, the mantras, and work. The will is the origin and end of the phenomenal world. If you meditate on this, you learn the secret of progress in life.

But if you are a true seeker of Truth, you soon begin to feel that there must be something higher. This is divine discontent. And this is why Nārada asks Sanatkumāra if there is anything higher. Sanatkumāra takes him step by step, from a lower truth to a higher truth.

Section Five

चित्तं वाव सङ्कल्पाद्भूयो यदा वै चेतयतेऽथ सङ्कल्पयतेऽथ मनस्यत्यथ वाचमीरयति तामु नाम्नीरयति नाम्नि मन्त्रा एकं भवन्ति मन्त्रेषु कर्माणि॥ १॥

Cittaṁ vāva saṅkalpādbhūyo yadā vai cetayate'tha saṅkalpayate'tha manasyatyatha vācamīrayati tāmu nāmnīrayati nāmni mantrā ekaṁ bhavanti mantreṣu karmāṇi.

Cittam vāva saṅkalpāt bhūyaḥ, intelligence is certainly higher than saṅkalpa [will-power]; *yadā vai cetayate,* when one comprehends; *atha saṅkalpayate,* then one wills; *atha,* then; *manasyati,* he thinks; *atha,* then; *vācam īrayati,* he directs the organ of speech; *tām u nāmni īrayati,* he makes speech utter the name; *nāmni,* in the names; *mantrāḥ,* all the mantras; *ekam bhavanti,* are united; *mantreṣu karmāṇi,* the actions [are united] in the mantras.

1. Intelligence is certainly superior to will-power. A person first comprehends, and then he wills. Next he thinks it over again and again, and then he directs the organ of speech. Finally he makes the organ of speech utter the name. All the mantras then merge in the names, and all the actions merge in the mantras.

Higher than saṅkalpa is *citta.* Just as saṅkalpa is part of the mind, so also is citta. Śaṅkara says that here citta means intelligence. It is right understanding of what to do in a present situation in the light of past experience. You have in your mind your past experiences and your future plans, and according to that you weigh the pros and cons of your present condition and decide what to do. Citta is the power to judge what is good and bad, what is right and wrong, and then make a decision promptly and correctly. A person who has this intelligence never does things impulsively.

Saṅkalpa, or will, is good, but suppose you cannot discriminate and you apply your will to a wrong purpose. A foolish person may be very obstinate, but that kind of will-power will eventually land him in trouble. Our will must be guided by our intelligence.

You may have noticed that the order here is from gross to fine. First Sanatkumāra mentions words, which are gross; then the mind, which is finer; then saṅkalpa, which is more fine; and now citta, still finer. He does not reject the gross. The gross level is also truth, but it is a lower truth. Gradually he takes Nārada to the finest, the highest.

तानि ह वा एतानि चित्तैकायनानि चित्तात्मानि चित्ते प्रतिष्ठितानि तस्माद्यद्यपि बहुविदचित्तो भवति नायमस्तीत्येवैनमाहुर्यदयं वेद यद्वा अयं विद्वान्नेत्थमचित्तः स्यादित्यथ यद्यल्पविच्चित्तवान्भवति तस्मा एवोत शुश्रूषन्ते चित्तं ह्येवैषामेकायनं चित्तमात्मा चित्तं प्रतिष्ठा चित्त-मुपास्स्वेति ॥ २ ॥

Tāni ha vā etāni cittaikāyanāni cittātmāni citte pratiṣṭhitāni tasmādyadyapi bahuvidacitto bhavati nāya-mastītyevainamāhuryadayaṁ veda yadvā ayaṁ vidvān-netthamacittaḥ syādityatha yadyalpaviccittavānbhavati tasmā evota śuśrūṣante cittaṁ hyevaiṣāmekāyanaṁ cittamātmā cittaṁ pratiṣṭhā cittaṁupāssveti.

Tāni ha vai etāni, all these [saṅkalpa, mind, speech, etc.]; *citta-ekāyanāni,* merge in the citta [intelligence]; *cittātmāni,* citta is the self [of all these]; *citte pratiṣṭitāni,* they rest in citta; *tasmāt,* that is why; *yadi api,* even if; *bahuvit,* a person knows much; *acittaḥ bhavati,* but is dull [i.e., is lacking in true understanding]; *na ayam asti iti,* that person does not exist; *eva enam āhuḥ,* people say about him; *yat ayam veda,* no matter how much he knows; *yat vai ayam vidvān,* if he were really learned; *na ittham acittaḥ syāt iti,* he would not be foolish like this; *atha,* but; *yadi alpavit bhavati,* if there is a person without much knowledge; *cittavān,* [but] with intelligence; *tasmāi eva uta śuśrūṣante,* they would like to hear him speak; *eṣām,* of all these; *cittam hi eva ekāyanam,* intelligence is where they merge; *cittam ātmā,* intelligence is their soul; *cittam pratiṣṭhā,* intelligence is their support; *cittam upāssva iti,* worship intelligence.

2. All these [will-power, mind, etc.] merge in intelligence, are directed by intelligence, and are supported by intelligence. That is why, a person may be learned but if he is dull, people [ignore him and] say: 'He does not exist, no matter how much he seems to know. If he were really learned, he would not be so foolish.' On the other hand, if a person is not learned but he is intelligent, people will listen to him [with respect]. It is intelligence that governs all these. It is their soul and their support. Therefore, worship intelligence.

स यश्चित्तं ब्रह्मेत्युपास्ते चित्तान्वै स लोकान्ध्रुवान् ध्रुवः प्रतिष्ठितान्प्रतिष्ठितोऽव्यथमानानव्यथमानोऽभिसिध्यति यावच्चित्तस्य गतं तत्रास्य यथाकामचारो भवति यश्चित्तं ब्रह्मेत्युपास्तेऽस्ति भगवश्चित्ताद्भूय इति चित्ताद्वाव भूयोऽस्तीति तन्मे भगवान्ब्रवीत्विति ॥ ३ ॥ इति पञ्चमः खण्डः ॥ ५ ॥

Sa yaścittaṁ brahmetyupāste cittānvai sa lokāndhruvān dhruvaḥ pratiṣṭhitānpratiṣṭhito'vyathamānānavyathamāno'bhisidhyati yāvaccittasya gataṁ tatrāsya yathākāmacāro bhavati yaścittaṁ brahmetyupāste'sti bhagavaścittādbhūya iti cittādvāva bhūyo'stīti tanme bhagavānbravītviti. Iti pañcamaḥ khaṇḍaḥ.

Saḥ yaḥ, he who; *cittam brahma iti upāste,* worships intelligence as Brahman; *abhisidhyati,* he attains; *cittān vai lokān,* worlds of intelligence; *dhruvān,* [worlds that are] true; *dhruvaḥ,* being true himself; *pratiṣṭhitān,* the well-established [worlds]; *pratiṣṭhitaḥ,* [himself being] well-established; *avyathamānān,* [the worlds] free from pain; *avyathamānaḥ,* [himself being] free from pain; *yāvat cittasya gatam,* as far as intelligence can go; *tatra,* that far; *asya yathā-kāmacāraḥ bhavati,* as he wishes he can go; *yaḥ cittam brahma iti upāste,* he who worships intelligence as Brahman; *bhagavaḥ,* sir; *cittāt bhūyaḥ asti iti,* is there anything higher than intelligence; *cittāt vāva bhūyaḥ asti iti,* there is certainly something higher than intelligence; *bhaga-*

vān, sir; *tat me bravītu iti,* please explain it to me. *Iti pañcamaḥ khaṇḍaḥ,* here ends the fifth section.

3. 'One who worships intelligence as Brahman attains worlds of intelligence [i.e., things he regards as important]. He becomes true and attains the world of truth. He is firmly established and also attains a world which is firmly established. He is free from pain and also attains a world free from pain. One who worships intelligence as Brahman can do what he pleases within the limits of intelligence.' Nārada asked, 'Sir, is there anything higher than intelligence?' 'Of course there is something higher than intelligence,' replied Sanatkumāra. Nārada then said, 'Sir, please explain that to me.'

Section Six

ध्यानं वाव चित्ताद्भूयो ध्यायतीव पृथिवी ध्यायतीवान्तरिक्षं ध्यायतीव द्यौर्ध्यायन्तीवापो ध्यायन्तीव पर्वता ध्यायन्तीव देवमनुष्यास्तस्माद्य इह मनुष्याणां महत्तां प्राप्नुवन्ति ध्यानापादांशा इवैव ते भवन्त्यथ येऽल्पाः कलहिनः पिशुना उपवादिनस्तेऽथ ये प्रभवो ध्यानापादांशा इवैव ते भवन्ति ध्यानमुपास्स्वेति ॥ १ ॥

Dhyānaṁ vāva cittādbhūyo dhyāyatīva pṛthivī dhyāyatīvāntarikṣaṁ dhyāyatīva dyaurdhyāyantīvāpo dhyāyan-

tīva parvatā dhyāyantīva devamanuṣyāstasmādya iha manuṣyāṇāṁ mahattāṁ prāpnuvanti dhyānāpādāṁśā ivaiva te bhavantyatha ye'lpāḥ kalahinaḥ piśunā upavādinaste'tha ye prabhavo dhyānāpādāṁśā ivaiva te bhavanti dhyānamupāssveti.

Dhyānam vāva cittāt bhūyaḥ, meditation is certainly superior to intelligence; *dhyāyati iva pṛthivī,* the earth seems to be meditating; *antarikṣam dhyāyati iva,* the space between the earth and heaven seems to be meditating; *dyauḥ dhyāyati iva,* the heaven seems to be meditating; *āpaḥ dhyāyanti iva,* water seems to be meditating; *parvatāḥ dhyāyanti iva,* the mountains seem to be meditating; *deva-manuṣyāḥ dhyāyanti iva,* gods and human beings seem to be meditating; *tasmāt,* this is why; *ye,* those who; *iha,* in this world; *manuṣyāṇām,* among human beings; *mahattām prāpnuvanti,* attain greatness; *dhyānāpādāṁśāḥ iva eva te bhavanti,* they seem to enjoy the fruits of meditation; *atha,* but; *ye alpāḥ,* those who are small; *kalahinaḥ,* are quarrelsome; *piśunāḥ,* crooked; *upavādinaḥ,* those who love scandel-mongering; *atha,* but; *ye prabhavaḥ,* those who are great; *dhyānāpādāṁśāḥ iva eva te bhavanti,* they seem to enjoy the fruits of meditation; *dhyānam upāssva iti,* worship meditation.

1. Meditation is certainly superior to intelligence. The earth seems to be meditating. The space between the earth and heaven seems to be meditating. So also, heaven seems to be meditating. Water seems to be meditating. The mountains seem to be meditating. Gods and human beings also seem to be meditating.

This is why, those people in this world who attain greatness seem to enjoy the fruits of meditation. But there are people of small calibre. They are quarrelsome, crooked, and always finding fault with others. Those who are great, however, are so because of their habit of meditation. Therefore worship meditation.

According to Śaṅkara, *dhyāna* is an uninterrupted stream of thought directed towards some object. Thinking of some idea, you concentrate your mind on it without breaking the flow, without any interruption—like pouring oil from one vessel to another in a continuous stream. In the same way, you must fix your mind on God. You may meditate on him as something abstract, as an idea. Or, if that is difficult, you may meditate on him with some kind of form.

Sanatkumāra says here that everything seems to be meditating—the earth, the intermediate region, heaven, the mountains. Once Swami Vivekananda said: 'Look at the Himalayas. Does it not strike you that it is a yogi meditating?' Śaṅkara also compares the earth to a yogi sitting in meditation, firm and unmoving. As the earth is steady and fixed, so we also should be steady and fixed when we meditate.

Before Buddha attained illumination he vowed:

> *Ihāsane śuṣyatu me śarīraṁ tvagasthimāṁsaṁ*
> *pralayaṁ ca yātu;*
> *Aprāpya bodhiṁ bahukalpadurlabhāṁ naivāsa-*
> *nātkāyamataścaliṣyate.*

May my body shrivel up on this seat; may

> my skin, bones, and flesh disintegrate. Without attaining enlightenment, which is so hard to attain, I shall not leave this seat.

This is the sort of determination we must have.

If you can think of everything as meditating, then you also will be able to meditate. And those people who meditate attain greatness, because they constantly think of great things. Śaṅkara says that greatness comes through knowledge or wealth or some other thing. But in order to become great you must think in a great way, speak in a great way, and behave in a great way.

Suppose you cannot think in terms of being great. You condemn yourself and think, 'Oh, that is not for me.' This is not humility. It is foolishness. It is being small-minded, and it is condemned by the scriptures. Swami Vivekananda used to say, 'You may have faith in all the gods and goddesses, but if you do not have faith in yourself you will never achieve anything.'

Similarly, if you are jealous or speak ill of others, you will not be able to meditate on great things. And if you cannot meditate on great things, your nature will deteriorate. Someone once told Vidyasagar that a certain person was criticizing him. Vidyasagar said, 'I don't remember having helped him in any way, so why should he criticize me?' Sometimes you find that the very people who have received your help try to harm you. This is the nature of small-minded people.

Thinking shapes our character. If we meditate on noble things we become noble.

स यो ध्यानं ब्रह्मेत्युपास्ते यावद्ध्यानस्य गतं तत्रास्य यथाकामचारो भवति यो ध्यानं ब्रह्मेत्युपास्तेऽस्ति भगवो ध्यानाद्भूय इति ध्यानाद्वाव भूयोऽस्तीति तन्मे भगवान्ब्रवीत्विति॥ २॥ इति षष्ठः खण्डः॥ ६॥

Sa yo dhyānaṁ brahmetyupāste yāvaddhyānasya gataṁ tatrāsya yathākāmacāro bhavati yo dhyānaṁ brahmetyupāste'sti bhagavo dhyānādbhūya iti dhyānād-vāva bhūyo'stīti tanme bhagavānbravītviti. Iti ṣaṣṭhaḥ khaṇḍaḥ.

Saḥ yaḥ dhyānam brahma iti upāste, one who worships meditation as Brahman; *yāvat dhyānasya gatam,* as far as meditation can go; *tatra,* that far; *asya yathā-kāmacāraḥ bhavati,* as he wishes he can go; *yaḥ dhyānam brahma iti upāste,* he who worships meditation as Brahman; *bhagavaḥ,* sir; *dhyānāt bhūyaḥ asti iti,* is there anything higher than meditation; *dhyānāt vāva bhūyaḥ asti iti,* there is certainly something higher than meditation; *bhagavān,* sir; *tat me bravītu iti,* please explain it to me. *Iti ṣaṣṭhaḥ khaṇḍaḥ,* here ends the sixth section.

2. 'One who worships meditation as Brahman can do what he pleases within the limits of meditation.' Nārada asked, 'Sir, is there anything higher than

meditation?' 'Of course there is something higher than meditation,' replied Sanatkumāra. Nārada then said, 'Sir, please explain that to me.'

Section Seven

विज्ञानं वाव ध्यानाद्भूयो विज्ञानेन वा ऋग्वेदं विजानाति यजुर्वेदं सामवेदमाथर्वणं चतुर्थमितिहासपुराणं पञ्चमं वेदानां वेदं पित्र्यं राशिं दैवं निधिं वाकोवाक्यमेकायनं देवविद्यां ब्रह्मविद्यां भूतविद्यां क्षत्रविद्यां नक्षत्रविद्यां सर्पदेवजनविद्यां दिवं च पृथिवीं च वायुं चाकाशं चापश्च तेजश्च देवांश्च मनुष्यांश्च पशूंश्च वयांसि च तृणवनस्पतीञ्छ्वापदान्याकीटपतङ्गपिपीलिकं धर्मं चाधर्मं च सत्यं चानृतं च साधु चासाधु च हृदयज्ञं चाहृदयज्ञं चान्नं च रसं चेमं च लोकममुं च विज्ञानेनैव विजानाति विज्ञानमुपास्स्वेति॥ १ ॥

Vijñānaṁ vāva dhyānādbhūyo vijñānena vā ṛgvedaṁ vijānāti yajurvedaṁ sāmavedamātharvaṇaṁ caturthamitihāsapurāṇaṁ pañcamaṁ vedānāṁ vedaṁ pitryaṁ rāśiṁ daivaṁ nidhiṁ vākovākyamekāyanaṁ devavidyāṁ brahmavidyāṁ bhūtavidyāṁ kṣattravidyāṁ nakṣatravidyāṁ sarpadevajanavidyāṁ divaṁ ca pṛthivīṁ ca vāyuṁ cākāśaṁ cāpaśca tejaśca devāṁśca manuṣyāṁśca paśūṁśca vayāṁsi ca tṛṇavanaspatīñchvāpadānyākīṭapa-

taṅgapipīlikaṁ dharmaṁ cādharmaṁ ca satyaṁ cānṛtaṁ ca sādhu cāsādhu ca hṛdayajñaṁ cāhṛdayajñaṁ cānnaṁ ca rasaṁ cemaṁ ca lokamamuṁ ca vijñānenaiva vijānāti vijñānamupāssveti.

Vijñānam vāva dhyānāt bhūyaḥ, vijñāna [i.e., the practical application of knowledge] is certainly superior to meditation; *vijñānena vai vijānāti,* through vijñāna one knows; *ṛg vedam yajur vedam sāma vedam ātharvaṇam caturtham,* the Ṛg Veda, the Yajur Veda, the Sāma Veda, and the fourth, the Atharva Veda; *itihāsa purāṇam pañcamam,* history and the Purāṇas, as the fifth; *vedānām vedam,* grammar [lit., the Veda of the Vedas]; *pitryam,* rites offered out of respect to the ancestors; *rāśim,* mathematics; *daivam,* the science of meteors and other natural phenomena [and omens]; *nidhim,* the science of underground resources; *vākovākyam,* logic; *ekāyanam,* moral science; *deva-vidyām,* astrology; *brahma-vidyām,* knowledge of the Vedas; *bhūta-vidyām,* geology; *kṣattra-vidyām,* archery; *nakṣatra-vidyām,* astronomy; *sarpa [-vidyām],* snake-charming; *devajana-vidyām,* fine arts; *divam ca,* heaven; *pṛthivīm ca,* and the earth; *vāyum ca,* and air; *ākāśam ca,* and space; *āpaḥ ca,* and water; *tejaḥ ca,* and fire; *devān ca,* and the gods; *manuṣyān ca,* and human beings; *paśūn ca,* and animals; *vayāṁsi ca,* and birds; *tṛṇa-vanaspatīn,* creepers and big trees; *śvāpadāni,* animals of prey; *ākīṭa-pataṅga-pipīlikam,* worms, fleas, and ants; *dharmam ca adharmam ca,* merit and demerit; *satyam ca anṛtam ca,* and truth and untruth; *sādhu ca asādhu ca,* and good and evil; *hṛdayajñam ca ahṛdayajñam ca,* pleasant and unpleasant; *annam ca rasam ca,* food and water; *imam ca lokam amum ca,* this world and the other world; *vijñānena eva vijānāti,* one knows this through vijñāna; *vijñānam upāssva iti,* worship vijñāna.

1. Vijñāna [the practical application of knowledge] is certainly superior to meditation. Through vijñāna one knows the Ṛg Veda, the Yajur Veda, the Sāma Veda, and the fourth—the Atharva Veda; then the fifth—history and the Purāṇas; also, grammar, funeral rites, mathematics, the science of omens, the science of underground resources, logic, moral science, astrology, Vedic knowledge, the science of the elements, archery, astronomy, the science relating to snakes, plus music, dance, and other fine arts; also heaven and earth; air, space, water, and fire; the gods and human beings; cattle and birds; creepers and big trees; animals of prey as well as worms, fleas, and ants; merit and demerit; truth and untruth; good and evil; the pleasant and the unpleasant; food and water; and this world and the other world. One knows all this through vijñāna. Worship vijñāna.

Vijñāna is higher than dhyāna, meditation. What is vijñāna? It is knowledge of the meaning of the scriptures (*vjñānam śāstrārthaviṣayam jñānam*). There are so many scriptures, but suppose you are able to recite all of them from memory. That is not enough. You must understand the real purport of what each is saying and then put the teachings into practice.

Some people have one book that they read over and over again. It may be the Gītā or *The Gospel of Sri Ramakrishna* or something else. But each time they read it they find a new meaning, a new insight, in it.

When Swami Turiyananda was young he would read one verse at a time from the Gītā and spend the whole day, or the next several days, meditating on it. He would not go on to the next verse until he had realized the truth of the one he had just read. This is vijñāna, and this is why vijñāna is higher than meditation.

स यो विज्ञानं ब्रह्मेत्युपास्ते विज्ञानवतो वै स लोकान् ज्ञानवतोऽभिसिध्यति यावद्विज्ञानस्य गतं तत्रास्य यथाकामचारो भवति यो विज्ञानं ब्रह्मेत्युपास्तेऽस्ति भगवो विज्ञानाद्भूय इति विज्ञानाद्वाव भूयोऽस्तीति तन्मे भगवान्ब्रवीत्विति ॥ २ ॥ इति सप्तमः खण्डः ॥ ७ ॥

Sa yo vijñānaṁ brahmetyupāste vijñānavato vai sa lokān jñānavato'bhisidhyati yāvadvijñānasya gataṁ tatrāsya yathākāmacāro bhavati yo vijñānaṁ brahmetyu-pāste'sti bhagavo vijñānādbhūya iti vijñānādvāva bhūyo-'stīti tanme bhagavānbravītviti. Iti saptamaḥ khaṇḍaḥ.

Saḥ yaḥ, he who; *vijñānam brahma iti upāste,* worships vijñāna [i.e., the practical application of knowledge] as Brahman; *saḥ vai vijñānavataḥ jñānava-taḥ lokān abhisidhyati,* attains the vijñānamaya and jñānamaya worlds; *yāvat vijñānasya gatam,* as far as vijñāna goes; *tatra,* that far; *asya yathā-kāmacāraḥ bhavati,* as he wishes he can go; *yaḥ vijñānam brahma iti upāste,* he who worships vijñāna as Brahman; *bhagavaḥ,* sir; *vijñānāt bhūyaḥ asti iti,* is there anything higher than vijñāna; *vijñānāt vāva bhūyaḥ asti iti,* there is certainly something higher than vijñāna; *bhagavān,* sir; *tat me bravītu iti,* please explain it to me. *Iti saptamaḥ khaṇḍaḥ,* here ends the seventh section.

2. 'One who worships vijñāna as Brahman attains the vijñānamaya and jñānamaya worlds. One who worships vijñāna as Brahman can do what he pleases within the limits of vijñāna.' Nārada asked, 'Sir, is there anything higher than vijñāna?' 'Of course there is something higher than vijñāna,' replied Sanatkumāra. Nārada then said, 'Sir, please explain that to me.'

Section Eight

बलं वाव विज्ञानाद्भूयोऽपि ह शतं विज्ञानवतामेको बलवानाकम्पयते स यदा बली भवत्यथोत्थाता भवत्युत्तिष्ठन्परिचरिता भवति परिचरन्नुपसत्ता भवत्युपसीदन्द्रष्टा भवति श्रोता भवति मन्ता भवति बोद्धा भवति कर्ता भवति विज्ञाता भवति बलेन वै पृथिवी तिष्ठति बलेनान्तरिक्षं बलेन द्यौर्बलेन पर्वता बलेन देवमनुष्या बलेन पशवश्च वयांसि च तृणवनस्पतयः

श्वापदान्याकीटपतङ्गपिपीलिकं बलेन लोकस्तिष्ठति बलमुपास्स्वेति ॥ १ ॥

Balaṁ vāva vijñānādbhūyo'pi ha śataṁ vijñānavatā-meko balavānākampayate sa yadā balī bhavatyathotthātā bhavatyuttiṣṭhanparicaritā bhavati paricarannupasattā bhavatyupasīdandraṣṭā bhavati śrotā bhavati mantā bhavati boddhā bhavati kartā bhavati vijñātā bhavati balena vai pṛthivī tiṣṭhati balenāntarikṣaṁ balena dyaurbalena parvatā balena devamanuṣyā balena paśa-vaśca vayāṁsi ca tṛṇavanaspatayaḥ śvāpadānyākīṭa-pataṅgapipīlikaṁ balena lokastiṣṭhati balamupāssveti.

Balam vāva vijñānāt bhūyaḥ, strength is superior to understanding; *ekaḥ balavān,* one strong person; *api ha śatam vijñānavatām ākampayate,* can make even a hundred persons of understanding shake [with fear]; *yadā saḥ balī bhavati,* when a person is strong [he is full of enthusiasm]; *atha utthātā bhavati,* he is then up and about; *uttiṣṭhan,* being up; *paricaritā bhavati,* he looks after [his teacher]; *paricaran,* attending to the needs [of his teacher]; *upasattā bhavati,* he sits near [the teacher]; *upasīdan,* sitting near him; *draṣṭā bhavati,* he watches [what the teacher does]; *śrotā bhavati,* he listens [to what the teacher says]; *mantā bhavati,* [and] thinks it over; *boddhā bhavati,* he tries to understand the meaning; *kartā bhavati,* he does what he is supposed to do; *vijñātā bhavati,* he grasps the meaning [of what the teacher had said]; *balena vai pṛthivī tiṣṭhati,* through power the whole world is sustained; *balena antarikṣam,* through power, the interspace [is sustained]; *balena dyauḥ,* through power, heaven; *balena parvatāḥ,* through strength, the mountains; *balena deva-manuṣyāḥ,* through strength, gods and human beings; *balena paśavaḥ ca,* through strength, cattle; *vayāṁsi ca tṛṇa-vanaspatayaḥ,* and birds and creepers and big trees; *śvāpadāni,* animals of prey; *ākīṭa-pataṅga-pipīlikam,* worms, fleas, and ants; *balena lokaḥ tiṣṭhati,* through strength the whole world is sustained; *balam upāssva iti,* worship strength.

1. Strength is certainly superior to understanding. One strong person can make even a hundred people of understanding shake with fear. If a person is strong, he will be enthusiastic and up and about. He will then start serving his teacher, and while serving his teacher he will be close to him. While sitting close to the teacher, he will watch him and listen to what he says. Then he will think it over and try to understand. He will then act on it, and finally he will grasp the inner meaning. Strength supports the earth. It also supports the interspace, heaven, the mountains, gods and human beings, cattle, birds, creepers, and trees. It supports animals of prey as well as worms, fleas, and ants. It supports the whole world. Worship strength.

What is higher than understanding? Strength. You might remember that startling remark Swami Vivekananda made in the course of a lecture: 'You will reach heaven quicker by playing football than by reading the Gita.' Why do we play football? To be strong, to have strong muscles and a healthy body. How will you understand what Śrī Kṛṣṇa is saying unless you have a strong body and nerves? If you are weak, you can never grasp the real meaning of the Gītā. As the Muṇḍaka Upaniṣad (III.ii.4) says, '*Nāyamātmā balahīnena labhyaḥ*—This Self cannot be known by the weak.'

This, of course, does not mean just physical strength. Intellectual strength is also necessary—in fact, strength at all levels. Everyone follows a strong person. Gandhi was very strong-minded. If he made up his mind to do something, nothing on earth could make him change—even if he had to do it alone. He meant what he said, and that is why he commanded so much respect. It is very important to mean what you say and say what you mean. Weak people cannot do that.

Sanatkumāra says that in the presence of a strong man, a hundred men of understanding tremble. If you are strong you will be enterprising, but weak people are always vacillating. They never know their minds. A strong person will start acting immediately. He is never idle. If a person wants to gain anything materially, he has to work hard. How often does someone gain something by a fluke? And this is even more important if one is seeking the Truth. Lots of us say, 'Oh, when will I realize the Self?' But are we prepared to work hard to do it? In ancient days if people wanted to learn the Vedas they would have to go to a teacher and live with him. Besides attending to their studies, the students would serve the teacher. They would have many duties to perform. It was a difficult life.

There was a devotee who used to come with his classmates to Belur Math when Swami Brahmananda was there. He noticed that Swami Brahmananda would sometimes ask one of his disciples to bring him a glass of water, or do some other little service. This devotee always hoped that some day Swami Brahmananda would ask him to do something. Finally one day the postman came with a parcel for Swami Brahmananda, who wanted someone to unpack it for him. As if in answer to this devotee's prayers, Swami Brahmananda turned to him and said: 'Would you do me this favour? Take this parcel, unpack it, and bring me the contents. But look, be sure you don't tear the paper or cut the ropes with which it is tied.' So, with great care, the devotee did as he was asked.

Sri Ramakrishna was also like this—punctilious. If you are a seeker of Truth, you have to be correct in every detail. You may think that attaining Self-knowledge is only a matter of renunciation and practice of meditation and so on. But how can you meditate if your mind is not attentive to every detail?

Through service the teacher watches the student. He sees whether the student is careless or absent-minded or lazy. When you serve the teacher you become intimate, and if you are intimate, he will gladly share his knowledge with you. A good teacher is always looking for a good student, and he is happy when he finds a student who is attentive, humble, keen to learn, and who loves him.

Swami Nirvanananda was considered the best of Swami

Brahmananda's attendants. Swami Brahmananda was always surrounded by young people who loved him and wanted to serve him. But none could surpass Swami Nirvanananda because he would not wait for Swami Brahmananda to tell him what he needed. Swami Nirvanananda would anticipate his needs beforehand. Whether it was a cup of tea, a glass of water, or something to eat, it would be there before Swami Brahmananda would ask. Most of the time Swami Brahmananda would be on a high spiritual plane, forgetful of his physical needs. A good attendant had to know what he needed beforehand and provide it.

Religion is not just something intellectual. It is a transformation of the whole personality. The teacher is the mould, and you try to form yourself according to that mould. How? First you hear what the teacher says, and then you reason: 'Why did he say that? What did he mean by that?' Then you watch what he does. Very soon the truth of what the teacher says reveals itself to you. You realize what he is saying, and then you act accordingly.

This earth is an example of what strength can do. The earth sustains everything through its own strength. In fact, everything in nature is sustained by its own inherent strength. It is not strength borrowed from something else. Similarly, we must support ourselves by our own strength.

So Sanatkumāra says first you rise. That is to say, once you have decided to attain Self-knowledge, don't be idle. Begin immediately. As Swami Vivekananda said, 'Arise, awake, and stop not till the goal is reached.' If you meditate on strength as Brahman, you can do anything.

स यो बलं ब्रह्मेत्युपास्ते यावद्बलस्य गतं तत्रास्य यथाकामचारो भवति यो बलं ब्रह्मेत्युपास्तेऽस्ति भगवो बलाद्भूय इति बलाद्वाव भूयोऽस्तीति तन्मे भगवान्ब्रवीत्विति ॥ २ ॥ इत्यष्टमः खण्डः ॥ ८ ॥

Sa yo balaṁ brahmetyupāste yāvadbalasya gataṁ tatrāsya yathākāmacāro bhavati yo balaṁ brahmetyupāste'sti bhagavo balādbhūya iti balādvāva bhūyo'stīti tanme bhagavānbravītviti. Ityaṣṭamaḥ khaṇḍaḥ.

Saḥ yaḥ, he who; *balam brahma iti upāste,* worships strength as Brahman; *yāvat balasya gatam,* as far as strength goes; *tatra,* that far; *asya yathā-kāmacāraḥ bhavati,* as he wishes he can go; *yaḥ balam brahma iti upāste,* he who worships strength as Brahman; *bhagavaḥ,* sir; *balāt bhūyaḥ asti iti,* is there anything higher than strength; *balāt vāva bhūyaḥ asti iti,* there is certainly something higher than strength; *bhagavān,* sir; *tat me bravītu iti,* please explain it to me. *Iti aṣṭamaḥ khaṇḍaḥ,* here ends the eighth section.

2. 'One who worships strength as Brahman can do what he pleases within the limits of strength.' Nārada asked, 'Sir, is there anything higher than strength?' 'Of course there is something higher than strength,'

replied Sanatkumāra. Nārada then said, 'Sir, please explain that to me.'

Strength here means strength produced by food. If you starve, you become weak and then you do not understand the scriptures. Perhaps your teacher will ask you to recite something from the scriptures, but you won't be able to because of your weakness from fasting. A strong person, however, can please his teacher by his enthusiasm and service. He can also carry out his teacher's instructions to the latter's satisfaction. By virtue of his strength, he becomes an ideal person in all respects.

Section Nine

अन्नं वाव बलाद्भूयस्तस्माद्यद्यपि दश रात्रीर्नाश्नीयाद्यद्यु
ह जीवेदथवाद्रष्टाश्रोतामन्ताबोद्धाकर्ताविज्ञाता भवत्यथा-
न्नस्यायै द्रष्टा भवति श्रोता भवति मन्ता भवति बोद्धा
भवति कर्ता भवति विज्ञाता भवत्यन्नमुपास्स्वेति॥ १ ॥

Annaṁ vāva balādbhūyastasmādyadyapi daśa rātrīr-nāśnīyādyadyu ha jīvedathavādraṣṭāśrotāmantāboddhā-kartāvijñātā bhavatyathānnasyāyai draṣṭā bhavati śrotā bhavati mantā bhavati boddhā bhavati kartā bhavati vijñātā bhavatyannamupāssveti.

Annam vāva balāt bhūyaḥ, food is certainly superior to strength; *tasmāt,* that is why; *yadi api,* even if; *daśa rātrīḥ na aśnīyāt,* a person fasts for ten [days and] nights; *yadi u ha jīvet,* though he may live; *atha vā adraṣṭā,* he may not be able to see; *aśrotā,* or hear; *amantā,* think; *aboddhā,* understand; *akartā,* work; *avijñātā bhavati,* nor can he fully grasp [the meaning of what he is taught]; *atha,* but; *annasya āyai,* when he eats food; *draṣṭā bhavati,* he can see; *śrotā bhavati,* he can hear; *mantā bhavati,* he can think; *boddhā bhavati,* he can understand; *kartā bhavati,* he can work; *vijñātā bhavati,* he can grasp the meaning; *annam upāssva iti,* worship food.

1. Food is certainly superior to strength. This is why if a person fasts for ten days and nights, he may survive but he will not be able to see, hear, think, understand, work, or fully grasp the meaning of what he is taught. But if he eats food, he can then see, hear, think, understand, work, and fully grasp the meaning of the teachings. Therefore worship food.

Food creates strength. Suppose you fast for ten days or so. What will happen? It is possible you could die, but even if you don't, your sense organs will not function. You won't be able to see, hear, or think. If you went to a teacher you would not be able to learn anything from him.

But then if you resume eating, your organs and your mind would again start functioning. You could then study and serve the teacher and learn from him.

You would be able to understand what he says, and you could again make progress. So we see, everything depends on food.

स योऽन्नं ब्रह्मेत्युपास्तेऽन्नवतो वै स लोकान्पानवतोऽभिसिध्यति यावदन्नस्य गतं तत्रास्य यथाकामचारो भवति योऽन्नं ब्रह्मेत्युपास्तेऽस्ति भगवोऽन्नाद्भूय इत्यन्नाद्वाव भूयोऽस्तीति तन्मे भगवान्ब्रवीत्विति ॥ २ ॥ इति नवमः खण्डः ॥ ९ ॥

Sa yo'nnaṁ brahmetyupāste'nnavato vai sa lokān-pānavato'bhisidhyati yāvadannasya gataṁ tatrāsya yathākāmacāro bhavati yo'nnaṁ brahmetyupāste'sti bhagavo'nnādbhūya ityannādvāva bhūyo'stīti tanme bhagavānbravītviti. Iti navamaḥ khaṇḍaḥ.

Saḥ yaḥ, he who; *annam brahma iti upāste,* worships food as Brahman; *saḥ abhisidhyati,* he attains; *annavataḥ vai lokān pānavataḥ,* worlds full of food and drink; *yāvat annasya gatam,* as far as food goes; *tatra,* that far; *asya yathā-kāmacāraḥ bhavati,* as he wishes he can go; *yaḥ annam brahma iti upāste,* he who worships food as Brahman; *bhagavaḥ,* sir; *annāt bhūyaḥ asti iti,* is there anything higher than food; *annāt vāva bhūyaḥ asti iti,* there is certainly something higher than food; *bhagavān,* sir; *tat me bravītu iti,* please explain it to me. *Iti navamaḥ khaṇḍaḥ,* here ends the ninth section.

2. 'One who worships food as Brahman attains worlds full of food and drink. One who worships food as Brahman can do what he pleases within the limits of food.' Nārada asked, 'Sir, is there anything higher than food?' 'Of course there is something higher than food,' replied Sanatkumāra. Nārada then said, 'Sir, please explain that to me.'

Section Ten

आपो वावान्नाद्भूयस्तस्माद्यदा सुवृष्टिर्न भवति व्याधीयन्ते प्राणा अन्नं कनीयो भविष्यतीत्यथ यदा सुवृष्टिर्भवत्यानन्दिनः प्राणा भवन्त्यन्नं बहु भविष्यतीत्याप एवेमा मूर्ता येयं पृथिवी यदन्तरिक्षं यद्द्यौर्यत्पर्वता यद्देवमनुष्या यत्पशवश्च वयांसि च तृणवनस्पतयः श्वापदान्याकीटपतङ्गपिपीलिकमाप एवेमा मूर्ता अप उपास्स्वेति॥ १ ॥

Āpo vāvānnādbhūyastasmādyadā suvṛṣṭirna bhavati vyādhīyante prāṇā annaṁ kanīyo bhaviṣyatītyatha yadā suvṛṣṭirbhavatyānandinaḥ prāṇā bhavantyannaṁ bahu bhaviṣyatītyāpa evemā mūrtā yeyaṁ pṛthivī yadantarikṣaṁ yaddyauryatparvatā yaddevamanuṣyā yatpaśavaśca vayāṁsi ca tṛṇavanaspatayaḥ śvāpadānyākīṭapataṅga-pipīlikamāpa evemā mūrtā apa upāssveti.

Āpaḥ vāva annāt bhūyaḥ, water is certainly superior than food; *tasmāt,* this is why; *yadā suvṛṣṭiḥ na bhavati,* when there is not enough rain; *prāṇāḥ vyādhīyante,* people are anxious; *annam kanīyaḥ bhaviṣyati iti,* [thinking,] there will not be much food; *atha yadā suvṛṣṭiḥ bhavati,* then when it rains; *prāṇāḥ ānandinaḥ bhavanti,* people become happy; *annam bahu bhaviṣyati iti,* [thinking,] there will be much food; *āpaḥ eva imāḥ,* water is all this; *mūrtāḥ,* different forms; *yā iyam pṛthivī,* this earth; *yat antarikṣam,* this interspace; *yat dyauḥ,* this heaven; *yat parvatāḥ,* these mountains; *yat deva-manuṣyāḥ,* these gods and human beings; *yat paśavaḥ ca,* these cattle; *vayāṁsi ca,* and birds; *tṛṇa-vanaspatayaḥ,* and creepers and trees; *śvāpadāni,* animals of prey; *ākīṭa-pataṅga-pipīlikam,* worms, insects, and ants; *āpaḥ eva imāḥ mūrtāḥ,* these are all water in different forms; *apaḥ upāssva iti,* worship water.

1. Water is certainly superior to food. That is why if there is no rain, people worry and think, 'There will not be enough food.' But if there is a good rainfall, they are happy, thinking, 'There will be plenty of food.' All these are water in different forms: the earth, the interspace, heaven, the mountains, gods and human beings, cattle and birds, creepers and trees, animals of prey, worms, insects, and ants. All these are water in different forms. Therefore worship water.

Suppose one year there is very little rainfall. Everyone then becomes very worried. They say: 'What will happen to us? This is a bad year. The crops will fail and there will be a famine.' On the other hand, if there is good rain during the year, then there is a good harvest. People say, 'This year we will have plenty to eat.'

The bodies of all living beings are products of water and are dependent on water.

स योऽपो ब्रह्मेत्युपास्त आप्नोति सर्वान्कामां-स्तृप्तिमान्भवति यावदपां गतं तत्रास्य यथाकामचारो भवति योऽपो ब्रह्मेत्युपास्तेऽस्ति भगवोऽद्भ्यो भूय इत्यद्भ्यो वाव भूयोऽस्तीति तन्मे भगवान्ब्रवीत्विति ॥ २ ॥ इति दशमः खण्डः ॥ १० ॥

Sa yo'po brahmetyupāsta āpnoti sarvānkāmāṁstṛpti-mānbhavati yāvadapāṁ gataṁ tatrāsya yathākāmacāro bhavati yo'po brahmetyupāste'sti bhagavo'dbhyo bhūya ityadbhyo vāva bhūyo'stīti tanme bhagavānbravītviti. Iti daśamaḥ khaṇḍaḥ.

Saḥ yaḥ, he who; *apaḥ brahma iti upāste,* worships water as Brahman; *sarvān kāmān āpnoti,* gets all he wishes; *tṛptimān bhavati,* [and] he is happy; *yāvat apām gatam,* as far as water goes; *tatra,* that far; *asya yathā-kāmacāraḥ bhavati,* as he wishes he can go; *yaḥ apaḥ brahma iti upāste,* he who worships water as Brahman; *bhagavaḥ,* sir; *adbhyaḥ bhūyaḥ asti iti,* is there anything higher than water; *adbhyaḥ vāva bhūyaḥ asti iti,* there is certainly something higher than water; *bhagavān,* sir; *tat me bravītu iti,* please explain it to me. *Iti daśamaḥ khaṇḍaḥ,* here ends the tenth section.

2. 'One who worships water as Brahman gets all he desires and is happy. One who worships water as Brahman can do what he pleases within the limits of water.' Nārada asked, 'Sir, is there anything higher than water?' 'Of course there is something higher than water,' replied Sanatkumāra. Nārada then said, 'Sir, please explain that to me.'

The Upaniṣad says that if you worship water as Brahman all your desires are fulfilled and you become happy. You can also do whatever you please. This is an exaggeration, but the Upaniṣad is trying to entice you to understand the value of water.

Section Eleven

तेजो वावाद्भ्यो भूयस्तद्वा एतद्वायुमागृह्याकाशमभितपति तदाहुर्निशोचति नितपति वर्षिष्यति वा इति तेज एव तत्पूर्वं दर्शयित्वाथापः सृजते तदेतदूर्ध्वाभिश्च तिरश्चीभिश्च विद्युद्भिराह्रादाश्चरन्ति तस्मादाहुर्विद्योतते स्तनयति वर्षिष्यति वा इति तेज एव तत्पूर्वं दर्शयित्वाथापः सृजते तेज उपास्स्वेति॥ १ ॥

Tejo vāvādbhyo bhūyastadvā etadvāyumāgṛhyākāśamabhitapati tadāhurniśocati nitapati varṣiṣyati vā iti teja eva tatpūrvaṁ darśayitvāthāpaḥ sṛjate tadetadūrdhvābhiśca tiraścībhiśca vidyudbhirāhrādāścaranti tasmādāhurvidyotate stanayati varṣiṣyati vā iti teja eva tatpūrvaṁ darśayitvāthāpaḥ sṛjate teja upāssveti.

Tejaḥ vāva adbhyaḥ bhūyaḥ, fire is certainly superior to water; *tat vai etat,* that [fire]; *vāyum āgṛhya,* taking the support of air; *ākāśam abhitapati,* heats the sky; *tadā,* then; *āhuḥ,* people say; *niśocati,* it is very hot; *nitapati,* it is burning; *varṣiṣyati vai iti,* there will be rain; *tejaḥ eva tat,* there is fire; *pūrvam,* first; *darśayitvā,* showing; *atha apaḥ,* then water; *sṛjate,* creates; *tat etat,* that [fire]; *ūrdhvābhiḥ ca tiraścībhiḥ ca,* going upwards and sideways in an irregular way; *vidyudbhiḥ,* with lightning; *āhrādāḥ,* the roar of thunder; *caranti,* moves about; *tasmāt,* this is why; *āhuḥ,* people say; *vidyotate,* there is lightning; *stanayati,* there is thunder; *varṣiṣyati vai iti,* there will certainly be rain; *tejaḥ eva tat pūrvam darśayitvā,* first heat is seen; *atha apaḥ sṛjate,* then it creates water; *tejaḥ upāssva iti,* worship fire.

1. Fire [or, heat] is certainly better than water. That fire, taking air as its support, heats the sky. Then people say: 'It is very hot. The body is burning. It will rain soon.' Fire first produces these signs, and then creates the rain. This is why there is lightning going straight up or going sideways in a zigzag manner, and along with it thunder. This is why people say: 'There is lightning and thunder. It will rain soon.'

Tejas first produces these signs and then creates the rain. Worship tejas.

In Indian philosophy, there is no such thing as creation—that is, something created out of nothing. But there is manifestation. This universe is always there, only sometimes it is manifest and sometimes it is not. When it is not manifest it is in a seed form. But Brahman is the essence of everything. It is infinite Existence, and that Existence is Consciousness.

The first manifestation of Brahman is space. After that comes air and then fire. Water comes from fire, or energy. Finally, earth comes from water. Some things in this universe are gross, and some are subtle, but according to Indian philosophy all are by-products of earth, water, fire, air, and space. This universe is nothing but a permutation and combination of these five elements.

Tejas means fire, heat, or energy. Fire is superior to water in the sense that it is the cause, and the cause is always superior to the effect. Fire is said to take air as its support and then make the air motionless through its power. The heat then spreads through space. We all know that when the atmosphere becomes very hot, it will soon rain. Also, before it rains we often see lightning and hear the roar of thunder. This indicates that the atmosphere is surcharged with electricity. So it is said that fire is the cause of water. Fire manifests itself as water.

It is not that these elements are separate things.

They are all manifestations of Brahman; only the names and forms are different according to their manifestations.

स यस्तेजो ब्रह्मेत्युपास्ते तेजस्वी वै स तेजस्वतो लोकान्भास्वतोऽपहततमस्कानभिसिध्यति यावत्तेजसो गतं तत्रास्य यथाकामचारो भवति यस्तेजो ब्रह्मेत्युपास्तेऽस्ति भगवस्तेजसो भूय इति तेजसो वाव भूयोऽस्तीति तन्मे भगवान्ब्रवीत्विति ॥ २ ॥ इत्येकादशः खण्डः ॥ ११ ॥

Sa yastejo brahmetyupāste tejasvī vai sa tejasvato lokānbhāsvato'pahatatamaskānabhisidhyati yāvattejaso gataṁ tatrāsya yathākāmacāro bhavati yastejo brahmetyupāste'sti bhagavastejaso bhūya iti tejaso vāva bhūyo'stīti tanme bhagavānbravītviti. Ityekādaśaḥ khaṇḍaḥ.

Saḥ yaḥ, he who; *tejaḥ brahma iti upāste,* worships fire as Brahman; *saḥ vai tejasi,* he becomes energetic and bright; *abhisidhyati,* [and] attains; *tejasvataḥ bhāsvataḥ lokān,* worlds that are bright and shining; *apahatatamaskān,* and without a hint of darkness; *yāvat tejasaḥ gatam,* as far as tejas goes; *tatra,* that far; *asya yathā-kāmacāraḥ bhavati,* as he wishes he can go; *yaḥ tejaḥ brahma iti upāste,* he who worships fire as Brahman; *bhagavaḥ,* sir; *tejasaḥ bhūyaḥ asti iti,* is there anything higher than tejas; *tejasaḥ vāva bhūyaḥ asti iti,* there is certainly something higher than tejas; *bhagavān,* sir; *tat me bravītu iti,* please explain it to me. *Iti ekādaśaḥ khaṇḍaḥ,* here ends the eleventh section.

2. 'One who worships fire as Brahman becomes bright himself, and he attains worlds that are bright, shining, and without a hint of darkness. One who worships fire as Brahman can do what he pleases within the range of fire.' Nārada asked, 'Sir, is there anything higher than tejas?' 'Of course there is something higher than tejas,' replied Sanatkumāra. Nārada then said, 'Sir, please explain that to me.'

From ancient times there has been the practice of worshipping fire in different cultures all over the world. In India during the Vedic period people performed sacrifices to fire and always kept their fire burning. But among the religions of the world now, the Parsees are especially known for their worship of fire.

The Upaniṣad says that if you worship fire you become like fire—radiant, bright, strong, and shining. That is the Hindu idea. You choose some model, called an *iṣṭa.* My iṣṭa is my desired state of excellence. Suppose I choose Buddha as my iṣṭa. If I worship him and meditate on him, slowly my character will be changed and I will be transformed.

But fire does not just give radiance. Fire, or light, is also a symbol of knowledge as well as a symbol of purity. Fire is said to burn away all impurities. When you meditate on fire as a symbol of knowledge, you meditate on all that is good, bright, and radiant.

Slowly we are approaching Brahman. We are going to the source. Suppose we want to walk from Calcutta to Gangotri, the source of the Ganga. How do we do it? We follow the course of the river. Gradually, step by step, we leave Calcutta behind and go further and further north, until at last we find ourselves at Gangotri. In the same way, Sanatkumāra is taking Nārada step by step to the knowledge of the Self.

Section Twelve

आकाशो वाव तेजसो भूयानाकाशे वै सूर्याचन्द्र-
मसावुभौ विद्युन्नक्षत्राण्यग्निराकाशेनाह्वयत्याकाशेन शृणो-
त्याकाशेन प्रतिशृणोत्याकाशे रमत आकाशे न रमत
आकाशे जायत आकाशमभिजायत आकाशमुपा-
स्स्वेति ॥ १ ॥

Ākāśo vāva tejaso bhūyānākāśe vai sūryācandramasāvubhau vidyunnakṣatrāṇyagnirākāśenāhvayatyākāśena śṛṇotyākāśena pratiśṛṇotyākāśe ramata ākāśe na ramata ākāśe jāyata ākāśamabhijāyata ākāśamupāssveti.

Ākāśaḥ vāva tejasaḥ bhūyān, space is certainly superior to fire; *ākāśe vai,* within space; *sūryā-candramasau ubhau,* are both the sun and the moon; *vidyut,* lightning; *nakṣatrāṇi,* the stars; *agniḥ,* [and] fire; *ākāśena,* through space; *āhvayati,* one calls; *ākāśena śṛṇoti,* through space one hears; *ākāśena pratiśṛṇoti,* through space one hears what others are saying; *ākāśe ramate,* in space one enjoys; *ākāśe na ramate,* in space one suffers; *ākāśe jāyate,* in space one is born; *ākāśam abhijāyate,* [trees and plants] grow pointing to space; *ākāśam upāssva iti,* worship space.

1. Ākāśa [space] is certainly superior to fire. The sun and the moon are both within ākāśa, and so are lightning, the stars, and fire. Through ākāśa one person is able to speak to another. Through ākāśa one is able to hear. And through ākāśa one is able to hear what others are saying. In ākāśa one enjoys, and in ākāśa one suffers. A person is born in ākāśa, and plants and trees grow pointing to ākāśa. Worship ākāśa.

You may find what seem to be errors in every religion, because no religion can reveal the whole of the Ultimate Truth. No religion can exhaust God. It can reveal only one or two aspects of God. So we see here, Sanatkumāra is taking Nārada from a lower truth to a higher truth. He is showing how the cause is higher than the effect.

Suppose there is no such thing as space. Where would fire be? Or lightning? Or the sun or the moon or the stars? So space is higher than fire, or energy. Without space there would be no sound, and no one could speak to another. Nor could anyone be born or grow.

स य आकाशं ब्रह्मेत्युपास्त आकाशवतो वै स लोकान्प्रकाशवतोऽसम्बाधानुरुगायवतोऽभिसिध्यति यावदाकाशस्य गतं तत्रास्य यथाकामचारो भवति य आकाशं ब्रह्मेत्युपास्तेऽस्ति भगव आकाशाद्भूय इत्याकाशाद्वाव भूयोऽस्तीति तन्मे भगवान्ब्रवीत्विति ॥ २ ॥ इति द्वादशः खण्डः ॥ १२ ॥

Sa ya ākāśaṁ brahmetyupāsta ākāśavato vai sa lokānprakāśavato'sambādhānurugāyavato'bhisidhyati yāvadākāśasya gataṁ tatrāsya yathākāmacāro bhavati ya ākāśaṁ brahmetyupāste'sti bhagava ākāśādbhūya ityākāśādvāva bhūyo'stīti tanme bhagavānbravītviti. Iti dvādaśaḥ khaṇḍaḥ.

Saḥ yaḥ, he who; *ākāśam brahma iti upāste,* worships space as Brahman; *saḥ vai lokān,* he attains worlds; *ākāśavataḥ prakāśavataḥ,* that are spacious and shining; *asambādhān,* free from all hindrances; *urugāyavataḥ,* [and] extensive; *yāvat ākāśasya gatam,* as far as space goes; *tatra,* that far; *asya yathā-kāmacāraḥ bhavati,* as he wishes he can go; *yaḥ ākāśam brahma iti upāste,* he who worships space as Brahman; *bhagavaḥ,* sir; *ākāśāt bhūyaḥ asti iti,* is there anything higher than ākāśa; *ākāśāt vāva bhūyaḥ asti iti,* there is certainly something higher than ākāśa; *bhagavān,* sir; *tat me bravītu iti,* please explain it to me. *Iti dvādaśaḥ khaṇḍaḥ,* here ends the twelfth section.

2. 'One who worships ākāśa [space] as Brahman attains worlds that are spacious, shining, free from all drawbacks, and extensive. One who worships ākāśa as Brahman can do what he pleases within the range of ākāśa.' Nārada asked, 'Sir, is there anything higher than ākāśa?' 'Of course there is something higher than ākāśa,' replied Sanatkumāra. Nārada then said, 'Sir, please explain that to me.'

If you meditate on something vast, you become vast. Space is infinite, so when you meditate on space you gradually envelop the whole universe. You become so vast that you find there are no hurdles in your way.

Why do we practise meditation? One reason is to quicken our growth, our inner development. When we meditate on the deity we like most, we are, in fact, meditating on the qualities that deity embodies. Then gradually we find we are acquiring those same qualities.

There is a Sanskrit saying: 'As you think, so you are.' If you think you are good, then you will be good. But if you start thinking you are bad, you will soon discover that you are deteriorating. This is why we must meditate on that which is good and noble.

Again Nārada is not content. He asks if there is something higher. The student has to ask; otherwise, if he is not interested, there is no point in teaching him. The student must have the urge within himself to learn, and then he should question the teacher until his doubts are dispelled.

Section Thirteen

स्मरो वावाकाशाद्भूयस्तस्माद्यद्यपि बहव आसीरन्न स्मरन्तो नैव ते कञ्चन शृणुयुर्न मन्वीरन्न विजानीरन्यदा वाव ते स्मरेयुरथ शृणुयुरथ मन्वीरन्नथ विजानीरन्स्मरेण वै पुत्रान्विजानाति स्मरेण पशून्स्मरमुपास्स्वेति ॥ १ ॥

Smaro vāvākāśādbhūyastasmādyadyapi bahava āsīranna smaranto naiva te kañcana śṛṇuyurna manvīranna vijānīranyadā vāva te smareyuratha śṛṇuyuratha manvīrannatha vijānīransmareṇa vai putrānvijānāti smareṇa paśūnsmaramupāssveti.

Smaraḥ vāva ākāśāt bhūyaḥ, memory is certainly superior to ākāśa [space]; *tasmāt,* this is why; *yadi api,* even if; *bahavaḥ,* many people; *āsīran,* get together; *na smarantaḥ,* [but] they cannot remember; *te,* they; *na eva kañcana śṛṇuyuḥ,* cannot hear anything; *na manvīran,* nor think; *na vijānīran,* nor know; *yadā vāva te smareyuḥ,* but if they can remember; *atha śṛṇuyuḥ,* then they can hear; *atha manvīran,* then they can think; *atha vijānīran,* then they can know; *smareṇa vai,* by virtue of memory; *putrān vijānāti,* one knows one's children; *smareṇa paśūn,* by virtue of memory [one knows one's] animals; *smaram upāssva iti,* worship memory.

1. Memory is certainly superior to ākāśa [space]. This is why, if many people get together but their memory fails, then they cannot hear or think or know anything. But if they remember, they can then hear, think, and know. Through memory one knows one's children and animals. Therefore, worship memory.

Memory is the medium through which we learn. Without memory we cannot progress, because we cannot retain anything. Because we have the faculty of memory, we hear something, we understand it, and then we are prompted to action. Suppose someone tells me: 'Beware! There is a snake over there. Don't go that way.' If I cannot remember what that person has said, then I will go in that direction and be bitten by the snake.

When the guru gives us spiritual instructions, we have to hear it correctly, think over it and ponder it, and then meditate on it again and again. We must think deeply on it. Without memory we cannot do that.

स यः स्मरं ब्रह्मेत्युपास्ते यावत्स्मरस्य गतं तत्रास्य यथाकामचारो भवति यः स्मरं ब्रह्मेत्युपास्तेऽस्ति भगवः स्मराद्भूय इति स्मराद्वाव भूयोऽस्तीति तन्मे भगवान्ब्रवी-त्विति ॥ २ ॥ इति त्रयोदशः खण्डः ॥ १३ ॥

Sa yaḥ smaraṁ brahmetyupāste yāvatsmarasya gataṁ tatrāsya yathākāmacāro bhavati yaḥ smaraṁ brahmetyu-pāste'sti bhagavaḥ smarādbhūya iti smarādvāva bhūyo-'stīti tanme bhagavānbravītviti. Iti trayodaśaḥ khaṇḍaḥ.

Saḥ yaḥ, he who; *smaram brahma iti upāste,* worships memory as Brahman; *yāvat smarasya gatam,* as far as memory goes; *tatra,* that far; *asya yathā-kāmacāraḥ bhavati,* as he wishes he can go; *yaḥ smaram brahma iti upāste,* he who worships memory as Brahman; *bhagavaḥ,* sir; *smarāt bhūyaḥ asti iti,* is there anything higher than memory; *smarāt vāva bhūyaḥ asti iti,* there is certainly something higher than memory; *bhagavān,* sir; *tat me bravītu iti,* please explain it to me. *Iti trayodaśaḥ khaṇḍaḥ,* here ends the thirteenth section.

2. 'One who worships memory as Brahman has free movement as far as memory goes.' Nārada asked, 'Sir, is there anything higher than memory?' 'Of course there is something higher than memory,' replied Sanatkumāra. Nārada then said, 'Sir, please explain that to me.'

Sanatkumāra says to meditate on memory as Brahman. Even the lowest truth is Brahman. But we must not stop there. That is not the goal.

True knowledge is not a collection of information stored in our memory. True knowledge is attained through assimilation. We have to grasp it, absorb it. Knowledge has to become part and parcel of our being; otherwise we are like beasts of burden.

It is no use knowing the truth unless we act in the light of that truth. Until scholarship has made some impact on our character, it is nothing. Only when it makes us a new individual do we become truly enlightened.

Sri Ramakrishna used to give the example of a vulture. A vulture flies very high in the sky, but it is always looking down at the ground—looking for the dead body of some animal so that it can come down and eat the flesh. Similarly, merely going up won't do. That is to say, merely stuffing your mind with infomation is not enough. You have to use that information to overcome the obstacles in your life. That's what is meant.

Section Fourteen

आशा वाव स्मराद्भूयस्याशेद्धो वै स्मरो मन्त्रानधीते कर्माणि कुरुते पुत्रांश्च पशूंश्चेच्छत इमं च लोकममुं चेच्छत आशामुपास्स्वेति ॥ १ ॥

Āśā vāva smarādbhūyasyāśeddho vai smaro mantrā-nadhīte karmāṇi kurute putrāṁśca paśūṁścecchata imaṁ ca lokamamuṁ cecchata āśāmupāssveti.

Āśā vāva smarāt bhūyasī, hope is certainly superior to memory; *āśā-iddhaḥ vai,* fired by hope; *smaraḥ,* memory; *mantrān,* the mantras; *adhīte,* learns; *karmāṇi kurute,* performs the rituals; *putrān ca,* children; *paśūn ca,* and animals; *icchate,* he wishes for; *imam ca lokam amum ca,* this world and the other [world]; *icchate,* he wishes for; *āśām upāssva iti,* worship hope.

1. Hope is certainly better than memory. Hope inspires a person's memory, and one uses one's memory to learn the mantras and perform rituals. One then wishes for children and animals, and one also wishes to attain this world and the next. Therefore, worship hope.

Suppose there is something you want. You have not got it, but you hope to get it. This kind of desire can be helpful. Maybe you have money, children, and a good reputation, but you are not happy. You discover that any amount of material prosperity you attain does not give you peace of mind. You see many people who are very prosperous but unhappy. You then start yearning for spiritual enlightenment. This is called divine discontent. This discontent pushes you on and on to make progress. Without burning desire, you cannot attain anything in spiritual life.

स य आशां ब्रह्मेत्युपास्त आशयास्य सर्वे कामाः समृध्यन्त्यमोघा हास्याशिषो भवन्ति यावदाशाया गतं तत्रास्य यथाकामचारो भवति य आशां ब्रह्मेत्युपास्तेऽस्ति भगव आशाया भूय इत्याशाया वाव भूयोऽस्तीति तन्मे भगवान्ब्रवीत्विति ॥ २ ॥ इति चतुर्दशः खण्डः ॥ १४ ॥

Sa ya āśāṁ brahmetyupāsta āśayāsya sarve kāmāḥ samṛdhyantyamoghā hāsyāśiṣo bhavanti yāvadāśāyā gataṁ tatrāsya yathākāmacāro bhavati ya āśāṁ brahmetyupāste'sti bhagava āśāyā bhūya ityāśāyā vāva bhūyo'stīti tanme bhagavānbravītviti. Iti caturdaśaḥ khaṇḍaḥ.

Saḥ yaḥ, he who; *āśām brahma iti upāste,* worships hope as Brahman; *āśayā,* by that hope; *asya sarve kāmāḥ,* all his desires; *samṛdhyanti,* are fulfilled; *amoghāḥ,* without fail; *ha asya āśiṣaḥ bhavanti,* his desires are fulfilled; *yāvat āśāyāḥ gatam,* as far as hope goes; *tatra,* that far; *asya yathā-kāmacāraḥ bhavati,* as he wishes he can go; *yaḥ āśām brahma iti upāste,* he who worships hope as Brahman; *bhagavaḥ,* sir; *āśāyāḥ bhūyaḥ asti iti,* is there anything higher than hope; *āśāyāḥ vāva bhūyaḥ asti iti,* there is certainly something higher than hope; *bhagavān,* sir; *tat me bravītu iti,* please explain it to me. *Iti caturdaśaḥ khaṇḍaḥ,* here ends the fourteenth section.

2. 'One who worships hope as Brahman has all his desires fulfilled. He gets whatever he wants without fail. One who worships hope as Brahman has free movement as far as hope goes.' Nārada asked, 'Sir, is there anything higher than hope?' 'Of course there is something higher than hope,' replied Sanatkumāra. Nārada then said, 'Sir, please explain that to me.'

The message given here is that one must not lose heart. No doubt there are many difficulties in the way, but they can be overcome, and they are overcome given hope and courage. If you are trying to attain Self-realization, you have to have hope to the last moment.

Section Fifteen

प्राणो वाव आशाया भूयान्यथा वा अरा नाभौ समर्पिता एवमस्मिन्प्राणे सर्वं समर्पितं प्राणः प्राणेन याति प्राणः प्राणं ददाति प्राणाय ददाति प्राणो ह पिता प्राणो माता प्राणो भ्राता प्राणः स्वसा प्राण आचार्यः प्राणो ब्राह्मणः ॥ १ ॥

Prāṇo vāva āśāyā bhūyānyathā vā arā nābhau samarpitā evamasminprāṇe sarvaṁ samarpitaṁ prāṇaḥ prāṇena yāti prāṇaḥ prāṇaṁ dadāti prāṇāya dadāti prāṇo ha pitā prāṇo mātā prāṇo bhrātā prāṇaḥ svasā prāṇa ācāryaḥ prāṇo brāhmaṇaḥ.

Prāṇaḥ vāva āśāyāḥ bhūyān, prāṇa [the vital force] is certainly superior to hope; *yathā vai arāḥ,* just as the spokes; *nābhau samarpitāḥ,* are attached to the hub; *evam,* in the same way; *asmin prāṇe,* on this prāṇa; *sarvam,* all this; *samarpitam,* are resting; *prāṇaḥ prāṇena yāti,* prāṇa works by its own power; *prāṇaḥ prāṇam dadāti,* prāṇa gives prāṇa; *prāṇāya,* to prāṇa; *dadāti,* [and again] gives; *prāṇaḥ ha pitā,* prāṇa is the father; *prāṇaḥ mātā,* prāṇa is the mother;

prāṇaḥ bhrātā, prāṇa is the brother; *prāṇaḥ svasā,* prāṇa is the sister; *prāṇaḥ ācāryaḥ,* prāṇa is the teacher; *prāṇaḥ brāhmaṇaḥ,* prāṇa is the brāhmin.

1. Prāṇa [the vital force] is certainly superior to hope. Just as spokes on a wheel are attached to the hub, similarly everything rests on prāṇa. Prāṇa works through its own power [i.e., prāṇa is the means as well as the end]. Prāṇa gives prāṇa to prāṇa, and prāṇa directs prāṇa to prāṇa. Prāṇa is the father, prāṇa is the mother, prāṇa is the brother, prāṇa is the sister, prāṇa is the teacher, and prāṇa is the brāhmin.

Prāṇa, the vital force, is superior to hope. Suppose you are dead. Can hope do anything for you then? You must have life. If you are not living then there can be no hope, no memory—nothing.

The Upaniṣad says that prāṇa is the resting place of everything. It is like a wheel with its spokes. All the spokes are fixed on the hub of the wheel. Similarly, my mind and my organs are all fixed on prāṇa. My eyes are very powerful, but if I am dead they may still be intact but they cannot see.

Prāṇa functions on the individual level in you, in me, in plants and insects and animals. But we represent only a small portion of this life force, because prāṇa also functions on the cosmic level. On the cosmic level prāṇa is Hiraṇyagarbha, the first manifestation of Brahman. The whole cosmos is governed and activated by prāṇa. Brahman is beyond thought and speech, but when it becomes manifest as prāṇa then we see this cosmic process going on.

If I stop breathing my body and organs can no longer function, and eventually they disintegrate. Similarly, if the cosmic life force withdraws itself from this universe, everything comes to a halt. The sun does not shine; the air does not blow. The whole life process comes to a standstill.

We see so many beings around us. Someone is your mother, someone your father, someone your brother, someone your sister, but they are all prāṇa. Prāṇa is in the form of your mother. Prāṇa is in the form of your father, or your sister, or your teacher, and so on. Our family, society, the entire humanity, all living beings—all are prāṇa in different forms. Prāṇa takes various forms and then assumes different relationships.

स यदि पितरं वा मातरं वा भ्रातरं वा स्वसारं वाचार्यं वा ब्राह्मणं वा किञ्चिद्भृशमिव प्रत्याह धिक्त्वास्त्वित्येवैनमाहुः पितृहा वै त्वमसि मातृहा वै त्वमसि भ्रातृहा वै त्वमसि स्वसृहा वै त्वमस्याचार्यहा वै त्वमसि ब्राह्मणहा वै त्वमसीति॥ २॥

Sa yadi pitaraṁ vā mātaraṁ vā bhrātaraṁ vā svasāraṁ vācāryaṁ vā brāhmaṇaṁ vā kiñcidbhṛśamiva pratyāha dhiktvāstvityevainamāhuḥ pitṛhā vai tvamasi mātṛhā vai tvamasi bhrātṛhā vai tvamasi svasṛhā vai tvamasyācāryahā vai tvamasi brāhmaṇahā vai tvamasīti.

Saḥ yadi, if anyone; *pitaram vā mataram vā,* his father or mother; *bhrātaram vā svasāram vā,* or brother or sister; *ācāryam vā brāhmaṇam vā,* or teacher or a brāhmin; *kiñcit,* anything; *bhṛśam iva,* discourteously; *pratyāha,* answers; *dhik tvā astu iti,* shame on you; *enam eva āhuḥ,* [people] say to him; *pitṛhā vai tvam asi,* you have killed your father; *mātṛhā vai tvam asi,* you have killed your mother; *bhrātṛhā vai tvam asi,* you have killed your brother; *svasṛhā vai tvam asi,* you have killed your sister; *ācāryahā vai tvam asi,* you have killed your teacher; *brāhmaṇahā vai tvam asi iti,* you have killed a brāhmin.

2. If a person speaks rudely to his father, mother, brother, sister, teacher, or to a brāhmin, people say to him: 'Shame on you! You have murdered your father. You have murdered your mother. You have murdered your brother. You have murdered your sister. You have murdered your teacher. You have murdered a brāhmin.'

According to Śaṅkara, using the informal *tvam* (you) instead of the more formal *bhavān* would be such an offense. Here the Upaniṣad means that you should treat everyone with respect. Being disrespectful to people is as good as murdering them.

अथ यद्यप्येनानुत्क्रान्तप्राणाञ्छूलेन समासं व्यतिषन्दहेन्नैवैनं ब्रूयुः पितृहासीति न मातृहासीति न भ्रातृहासीति न स्वसृहासीति नाचार्यहासीति न ब्राह्मणहासीति ॥ ३ ॥

Atha yadyapyenānutkrāntaprāṇāñchūlena samāsaṁ vyatiṣandahennaivainaṁ brūyuḥ pitṛhāsīti na mātṛhāsīti na bhrātṛhāsīti na svasṛhāsīti nācāryahāsīti na brāhmaṇa-hāsīti.

Atha, but; *yadi api enān,* if even all these; *utkrāntaprāṇān,* when life has departed; *śūlena,* with the help of a spear; *vyatiṣan,* tears the bodies to pieces; *samāsam,* puts them in a pile; *dahet,* [and] burns them; *na eva enam brūyuḥ,* people will not say to him; *pitṛhā asi iti,* you killed your father; *na mātṛhā asi iti,* nor you killed your mother; *na bhrātṛhā asi iti,* nor you killed your brother; *na svasṛhā asi iti,* nor you killed your sister; *na ācāryahā asi iti,* nor you killed your teacher; *na brāhmaṇahā asi iti,* nor you killed a brāhmin.

3. But when they have died, if a person piles their bodies on a funeral pyre and burns them, piercing them with a spear [so that the body burns more quickly], no one will say to him, 'You have killed your father,' or 'You have killed your mother,' or 'You have killed your brother,' or 'You have killed your sister,' or 'You have killed your teacher,' or 'You have killed a brāhmin.'

Suppose you say something very rude to your father. People will say: 'Shame on you! You have killed your father.' But suppose your father has died. You will then have to burn or bury his body. Yet no one will scold you or blame you for doing something wrong, because prāṇa has left the body. This is the difference between prāṇa existing in the body and prāṇa not existing in the body.

प्राणो ह्येवैतानि सर्वाणि भवति स वा एष एवं पश्यन्नेवं मन्वान एवं विजानन्नतिवादी भवति तं चेद्ब्रूयुरतिवाद्यसीत्यतिवाद्यस्मीति ब्रूयान्नापह्नुवीत ॥ ४ ॥ इति पञ्चदशः खण्डः ॥ १५ ॥

Prāṇo hyevaitāni sarvāṇi bhavati sa vā eṣa evaṁ paśyannevaṁ manvāna evaṁ vijānannativādī bhavati taṁ cedbrūyurativādyasītyativādyasmīti brūyānnāpahnuvīta. Iti pañcadaśaḥ khaṇḍaḥ.

Prāṇaḥ hi eva etāni sarvāṇi bhavati, prāṇa is all this; *saḥ vai eṣaḥ,* he who; *evam,* thus; *paśyan,* seeing; *evam manvānaḥ,* thus considering; *evam vijānan,* thus knowing; *ativādī bhavati,* becomes a superior speaker; *cet,* if; *tam brūyuḥ,* anybody says to him; *ativādī asi iti,* you are a superior speaker; *ativādī asmi iti brūyān,* he will say, 'Yes I am a superior speaker'; *na apahnuvīta,* he will not deny it. *Iti pañcadaśaḥ khaṇḍaḥ,* here ends the fifteenth section.

4. It is prāṇa that is all this. He who sees thus, thinks thus, and knows thus becomes a superior speaker. If anyone says to him, 'You are a superior speaker,' he may say, 'Yes, I am a superior speaker.' He need not deny it.

Who is an *ativādī*? Here *ativādī* means 'a superior speaker.' It is one who has realized the Truth and has thereby acquired the ability to say nothing but the truth.

When a holy person speaks, his words make sense. There is a ring of truth about them. They are authoritative. Such a person is an *ativādī.* We all speak. We are speaking all the time. But for most of us our words are like the cawing of crows. Our words are just sounds. They make no sense. But when the speaker is a holy person, one who has realized God, who has seen the Truth face to face, everything he says is true.

If you have read Josephine McLeod's reminiscences of Swami Vivekananda, you will remember how she described the first time she heard Swamiji speak: 'He stood up and said something, and I thought, "Yes, this is true." Again he said something, and I thought, "Yes, this is true too." Yet again he said something and I said to myself, "This is also true." Whatever he said was true.' Such a person is an *ativādī.*

In one of the Upaniṣads we find a ṛṣi calling to humanity: 'Hear me, O children of immortal bliss. I have known the Truth. If you know it you overcome death.' It is this kind of speech, coming from a holy person, that draws and inspires people, and reveals a new path.

Section Sixteen

एष तु वा अतिवदति यः सत्येनातिवदति सोऽहं भगवः सत्येनातिवदानीति सत्यं त्वेव विजिज्ञासितव्यमिति सत्यं भगवो विजिज्ञास इति ॥ १ ॥ इति षोडशः खण्डः ॥ १६ ॥

Eṣa tu vā ativadati yaḥ satyenātivadati so'haṁ bhagavaḥ satyenātivadānīti satyaṁ tveva vijijñāsitavya-miti satyaṁ bhagavo vijijñāsa iti. Iti ṣoḍaśaḥ khaṇḍaḥ.

Eṣaḥ, this [person]; *tu,* but; *vai ativadati,* is truly an ativādī; *yaḥ,* who; *satyena ativadati,* who speaks of Truth after having known the Truth; *bhagavaḥ,* sir; *saḥ aham,* as I am that [i.e., one who is unhappy]; *satyena ativadāni iti,* I want to be an ativādī by knowing the Truth; *satyam tu eva vijijñāsitavyam iti,* but Truth must be thoroughly enquired into; *bhagavaḥ,* sir; *satyam vijijñāse iti,* I wish to thoroughly enquire into Truth. *Iti ṣoḍaśaḥ khaṇḍaḥ,* here ends the sixteenth section.

1. 'But a person must first know the Truth. Then he is truly an ativādī.' Nārada said, 'Sir, I want

to be an ativādī by knowing the Truth.' Sanatkumāra replied, 'But one must earnestly desire to know the Truth.' 'Sir, I earnestly desire to know the Truth,' Nārada said.

Hearing Sanatkumāra's words about prāṇa, Nārada concluded that prāṇa is everything, that it is the ultimate. Thinking he was now an ativādī, he kept quiet. He did not make any further enquiries.

Sanatkumāra understood, however, and told him: 'No, you do not know it yet. This is not the ultimate. This is not Brahman. Prāṇa is a manifestation of Brahman but not Brahman itself. In order to know Brahman one must know the Truth.' That is to say, one must know the meaning behind the words.

You may speak of God, but have you seen God yourself? If you have not seen him, if you have not realized him, what right have you got to talk about him? You are like a blind man trying to lead another blind man. Have you yourself realized the Truth?—that is the criterion. You must have direct experience of the Truth—not just some information you have picked up from books or from other people. It must be *a-parokṣa*—that is, not through another source. It must be direct, personal, immediate.

Nārada immediately understood his mistake and with great humility asked to learn the Truth. This spirit of humility is very important. As Sri Ramakrishna says, water cannot accumulate in a high place. It always runs down to a low place. Similarly, good qualities cannot remain in a proud person. They will soon run off. Only in a humble person can they be retained. If you are humble the teacher will be glad to teach you. So also, a good teacher will never say: 'I am supreme. I know everything.'

Section Seventeen

यदा वै विजानात्यथ सत्यं वदति नाविजानन्सत्यं वदति विजानन्नेव सत्यं वदति विज्ञानं त्वेव विजिज्ञासितव्यमिति विज्ञानं भगवो विजिज्ञास इति ॥ १ ॥
इति सप्तदशः खण्डः ॥ १७ ॥

Yadā vai vijānātyatha satyaṁ vadati nāvijānansatyaṁ vadati vijānanneva satyaṁ vadati vijñānaṁ tveva vijijñāsitavyamiti vijñānaṁ bhagavo vijijñāsa iti. Iti saptadaśaḥ khaṇḍaḥ.

Yadā, when; *vai vijānāti,* a person knows well; *atha,* then; *satyam vadati,* he speaks what he knows to be the Truth; *avijānan,* without knowing it well; *satyam na vadati,* he does not speak of Truth; *vijānan eva,* knowing it well; *satyam vadati,* one can speak of Truth; *vijñānam tu eva vijijñāsitavyam iti,* but one must seek knowledge in depth; *vijñānam bhagavaḥ vijijñāse iti,* sir, I seek knowledge in depth. *Iti saptadaśaḥ khaṇḍaḥ,* here ends the seventeenth section.

1. Sanatkumāra said: 'When a person knows for certain, then he can truly speak of the Truth. But without

knowing well, he cannot speak of the Truth. One who knows for certain speaks of Truth. But one must seek knowledge in depth.' Nārada said, 'Sir, I seek knowledge in depth.'

Sanatkumāra says that when you know the Truth, whatever you say is nothing but the truth. You cannot say anything that is not the truth.

Truth is Truth, and there is no compromise in it. Once you know this Truth, everything else is irrelevant. But what if that Truth is associated with names and forms? Is that Truth? The scriptures admit it as a relative truth. It is not, however, the Absolute Truth.

The Absolute Truth is called 'that' because it is beyond the reach of the sense organs. As regards the relative truth, it is called 'this', because it is within the reach of the sense organs.

The Absolute Truth is difficult to understand. For instance, the elements in their pure form are beyond the reach of the sense organs, so they are sometimes referred to as 'that', but they are not the Absolute Truth. Brahman is the Absolute Truth.

In this connection it is to be remembered that fire was said to be red, water white, and earth black. Though it was said that the colours alone were real, this is not 'real' from the standpoint of Absolute Truth. These colours are also attributes. This is why the Absolute Truth is difficult to understand. Knowing the Absolute Truth is *vijñāna.*

Section Eighteen

यदा वै मनुतेऽथ विजानाति नामत्वा विजानाति मत्वैव विजानाति मतिस्त्वेव विजिज्ञासितव्येति मतिं भगवो विजिज्ञास इति॥ १॥ इत्यष्टादशः खण्डः॥ १८॥

Yadā vai manute'tha vijānāti nāmatvā vijānāti matvaiva vijānāti matistveva vijijñāsitavyeti matiṁ bhagavo vijijñāsa iti. Ityaṣṭādaśaḥ khaṇḍaḥ.

Yadā vai manute, when one learns to think well; *atha vijānāti,* then one can know deeply; *amatvā,* without applying the mind; *na vijānāti,* one cannot know deeply; *matvā eva vijānāti,* a person knows deeply when he thinks deeply; *matiḥ tu eva vijijñāsitavya iti,* but one must want to know how to think well; *bhagavaḥ,* sir; *matim vijijñāse iti,* I want to know what this thinking is. *Iti aṣṭādaśaḥ khaṇḍaḥ,* here ends the eighteenth section.

1. Sanatkumāra said: 'When a person learns to think well, then he can know deeply. Without thinking well, one cannot know deeply. One knows for certain when one thinks deeply. But one must want to know how to think well.' Nārada replied, 'Sir, I want to know how to think well.'

How do we know something? We know it by applying our mind—that is, by concentrating our mind on it.

Swami Turiyananda used to say that if you continue reading the Gītā with a concentrated mind, then whenever you read it new meanings will unfold, meanings which you never suspected.

Sanatkumāra says that without applying your mind seriously, you will not understand what you are studying. At Belur Math, Swamiji used to have the monks debate on different issues. One person would say something, and another would contradict him. When two people debate about something, they both get excited and the heat rises. As one of the monks used to say, 'When there is some heat there will also be some light.' Debating is like churning milk. As you churn the milk the cream gradually begins to appear. So also, when there is a debate, truth gradually comes to the surface.

Suppose you have a thorn stuck in your foot. What do you do? As Sri Ramakrishna used to say, you take another thorn and use it to remove the first thorn. Then you throw away both. Similarly, you have to use your mind to go beyond the mind. Vedānta says that Truth is within you. But you must first hear about it from a teacher. Then you must reflect on it. Think over it again and again: 'What does this mean? How can I be one with Brahman?' You go on questioning, searching for the real meaning of the words. After that you must deeply meditate on it. Then only the real meaning dawns on you. It comes as if in a flash.

What else is this mind for? If we don't think, we are as good as dead. Human beings are superior to animals because we can think, argue, and question. All our great discoveries have come because of our power to think and reflect.

Śaṅkara gives a wonderful definition of reflection. He says it means having great love for the subject being considered.

Section Nineteen

यदा वै श्रद्दधात्यथ मनुते नाश्रद्दधन्मनुते श्रद्दधदेव मनुते श्रद्धा त्वेव विजिज्ञासितव्येति श्रद्धां भगवो विजिज्ञास इति॥ १॥ इत्येकोनविंशः खण्डः॥ १९॥

Yadā vai śraddadhātyatha manute nāśraddadhanmanute śraddadhadeva manute śraddhā tveva vijijñāsitavyeti śraddhāṁ bhagavo vijijñāsa iti. Ityekonaviṁśaḥ khaṇḍaḥ.

Yadā vai śraddadhāti, when a person has respect [for something or someone—or faith in something or someone]; *atha manute,* then he thinks deeply [of that thing or person]; *aśraddadhat,* if there is no respect; *na manute,* he does not think deeply; *śraddadhat eva manute,* one thinks deeply when one has respect; *śraddhā tu eva vijijñāsitavya iti,* but one must try to have this respect; *śraddhām bhagavaḥ vijijñāse iti,* sir, I want to have this respect. *Iti ekonaviṁśaḥ khaṇḍaḥ,* here ends the nineteenth section.

1. Sanatkumāra said: 'When a person has respect [for what he hears], then he gives due thought to it. Without this respect he attaches no importance to what he hears. One thinks deeply over something that one respects. But one must try to attain this respect.' Nārada replied, 'Sir, I want to have this respect.'

Reflecting is good, but one should do it with śraddhā, faith. Śraddhā also means respect. For instance, if my guru tells me something, I know it must be true because I know he will never mislead me.

When you go to a guru you should have faith in what he says. Then later you will get the confirmation of what he has taught you from within, and at that point your own mind becomes the guru. But to begin with you must have respect for what the guru says.

This does not mean, however, that you cannot ask him questions. You have every right to have things clarified. But if you say, 'Well, after all, this person knows nothing; he is just trying to fool me,' and so on, then you will never get anywhere. Rather, one must listen with an open mind, thinking, 'This person is held in high respect, so I will listen and I will study.'

Ramakrishna, for instance, made many statements which some of his disciples, such as Swami Vivekananda, had difficulty accepting, so they would question him and argue. And Ramakrishna would welcome their questions and arguments. Others would protest and say, 'When Ramakrishna has said something, why not accept it?' But Ramakrishna would reply, 'No, let them question.' It was because their enquiry was done with śraddhā, respect, and with a keen desire to know.

Suppose you don't have śraddhā. Then you would not care. You would not even give a moment's thought to finding out the Truth. Only when you have śraddhā can you go on thinking and reflecting on it.

Section Twenty

यदा वै निस्तिष्ठत्यथ श्रद्दधाति नानिस्तिष्ठञ्छ्रद्दधाति निस्तिष्ठन्नेव श्रद्दधाति निष्ठा त्वेव विजिज्ञासितव्येति निष्ठां भगवो विजिज्ञास इति ॥ १ ॥ इति विंशः खण्डः ॥ २० ॥

Yadā vai nistiṣṭhatyatha śraddadhāti nānistiṣṭhañ-chraddadhāti nistiṣṭhanneva śraddadhāti niṣṭhā tveva vijijñāsitavyeti niṣṭhāṁ bhagavo vijijñāsa iti. Iti viṁśaḥ khaṇḍaḥ.

Yadā vai nistiṣṭhati, when one is steady in one's service and devotion to one's teacher; *atha śraddadhāti,* then one has respect; *anistiṣṭhan,* where this steadiness and devotion is missing; *na śraddadhāti,* there is no respect; *nistiṣṭhan eva śraddadhāti,* a person has respect when he has this steadiness; *niṣṭhā tu eva vijijñāsitavya iti,* but one must be determined to have this steadiness and devotion; *bhagavaḥ niṣṭhām vijijñāse iti,* sir, I truly want this steadiness and devotion. *Iti viṁśaḥ khaṇḍaḥ,* here ends the twentieth section.

1. Sanatkumāra: 'When a person is steady and devoted to his teacher, then he has respect. Without being steady, one cannot have respect. One has steadiness when one has genuine respect and devotion. But one must seek this steadiness with great earnestness.' Nārada replied, 'I seek this steadiness.'

It is difficult to translate the word *niṣṭhā.* The closest word in English is probably 'steadiness.' For instance, you say you want to know something, but actually it is only a passing mood on your part. You really don't mean it. This is the opposite of steadiness. But if you really mean it, if you go on struggling to get that knowledge, no matter how difficult or frustrating it may be to acquire it, then this is niṣṭhā, steadiness.

Śaṅkara says that niṣṭhā comes from serving the guru with devotion. When you devotedly serve your teacher, your love for the subject of your enquiry grows stronger and stronger, and your conviction also grows stronger and stronger. You begin to think: 'Yes, there is such a thing as Self-realization. How else can I explain my teacher being so good, so kind, so affectionate, so selfless?' You find that your teacher is unfailing in his loyalty to the ideals which he professes, and slowly you are able to understand the real implication of the words *tyāga,* renunciation, *titikṣā,* forbearance, and so forth, because you see him putting them into practice. In this way you get firmness in your beliefs and steadiness in your practice.

Section Twenty-one

यदा वै करोत्यथ निस्तिष्ठति नाकृत्वा निस्तिष्ठति कृत्वैव निस्तिष्ठति कृतिस्त्वेव विजिज्ञासितव्येति कृतिं भगवो विजिज्ञास इति ॥ १ ॥ इत्येकविंशः खण्डः ॥ २१ ॥

Yadā vai karotyatha nistiṣṭhati nākṛtvā nistiṣṭhati kṛtvaiva nistiṣṭhati kṛtistveva vijijñāsitavyeti· kṛtiṁ bhagavo vijijñāsa iti. Ityekaviṁśaḥ khaṇḍaḥ.

Yadā vai karoti, when a person does his duty [i.e., when he practises self-restraint and concentration of the mind]; *atha nistiṣṭhati,* then he is steady; *akṛtvā,* without doing one's duty; *na nistiṣṭhati,* one cannot be steady; *kṛtvā eva nistiṣṭhati,* one becomes steady by doing one's duty; *kṛtiḥ tu eva vijijñāsitavya iti,* but one should know well the nature of duty; *bhagavaḥ kṛtim vijijñāse iti,* sir, I want to know the nature of duty. *Iti ekaviṁśaḥ khaṇḍaḥ,* here ends the twenty-first section.

1. Sanatkumāra said: 'When a person keeps doing his duty, he becomes steady. If one does not do one's duty, one cannot have steadiness. One attains steadiness by doing one's duty. But one should try

to know what duty means.' Nārada replied, 'Sir, I want to know about duty.'

Kṛtiḥ means 'application,' or 'repeated practice.' How do we get niṣṭhā, or steadiness? Śaṅkara says it comes through repeated practice of self-restraint and self-discipline—that is, through the control of the organs and the mind.

Section Twenty-two

यदा वै सुखं लभतेऽथ करोति नासुखं लब्ध्वा करोति सुखमेव लब्ध्वा करोति सुखं त्वेव विजिज्ञासितव्यमिति सुखं भगवो विजिज्ञास इति ॥ १ ॥ इति द्वाविंशः खण्डः ॥ २२ ॥

Yadā vai sukhaṁ labhate'tha karoti nāsukhaṁ labdhvā karoti sukhameva labdhvā karoti sukhaṁ tveva vijijñāsitavyamiti sukhaṁ bhagavo vijijñāsa iti. Iti dvāviṁśaḥ khaṇḍaḥ.

Yadā vai sukham labhate, when a person gets happiness; *atha karoti,* he then works; *asukham labdhvā,* without getting happiness; *na karoti,* he does not do his duty; *sukham eva labdhvā karoti,* one works by getting happiness; *sukham tu eva vijijñāsitavyam iti,* but one should try to understand the nature of this happiness; *bhagavaḥ sukham vijijñāse iti,* sir, I want to understand the nature of this happiness. *Iti dvādaśaḥ khaṇḍaḥ,* here ends the twenty-second section.

1. Sanatkumāra said: 'A person works when he gets happiness. He does not care to work if he does not get happiness. By getting happiness one does one's duty. But one must try to understand the true nature of this happiness.' Nārada replied, 'Sir, I want to know well the true nature of happiness.'

Section Twenty-three

यो वै भूमा तत्सुखं नाल्पे सुखमस्ति भूमैव सुखं
भूमा त्वेव विजिज्ञासितव्य इति भूमानं भगवो विजिज्ञास
इति॥ १ ॥ इति त्रयोविंशः खण्डः॥ २३ ॥

Yo vai bhūmā tatsukhaṁ nālpe sukhamasti bhūmaiva sukhaṁ bhūmā tveva vijijñāsitavya iti bhūmānaṁ bhagavo vijijñāsa iti. Iti trayoviṁśaḥ khaṇḍaḥ.

Yaḥ vai bhūmā, that which is infinite [lit., big, or the biggest]; *tat sukham,* that is happiness; *na alpe sukham asti,* there is no happiness in the finite [small]; *bhūmā eva sukham,* happiness is only in the infinite; *bhūmā tu eva vijijñāsitavyaḥ iti,* but one must try to understand the true nature of the infinite; *bhūmānam bhagavaḥ vijijñāse iti,* sir, I want to understand the true nature of the infinite. *Iti trayoviṁśaḥ khaṇḍaḥ,* here ends the twenty-third section.

1. Sanatkumāra said: 'That which is infinite is the source of happiness. There is no happiness in the finite. Happiness is only in the infinite. But one must try to understand what the infinite is.' Nārada replied, 'Sir, I want to clearly understand the infinite.'

If you attain *bhūmā,* then you have real happiness. What is bhūmā? It is Brahman. It is the biggest. It is infinite. Something is infinite when it is without any limitations in terms of time and space. Even our own lives are limited. We were born at a certain point in time and we shall live for a certain span of time. It may be for a hundred years or it may be less, but the body will not last forever.

Then why should we bother about God or Brahman or something that is said to be infinite? Because we want to be happy. Perhaps you are very fond of sweets and enjoy eating them. But when you have finished eating them your joy is gone. Moreover, if you eat too many then you become sick and are miserable. Only in the infinite is there real joy, real happiness, real peace—peace that is constant, always there, and never disturbed. As Sanatkumāra says, *'Na alpe sukham asti*—there is no happiness in that which is small, limited, or short-lived.'

Śaṅkara says, anything that is finite causes *tṛṣṇā,* thirst—that is, it increases your desire for more. Whatever you get, you desire still more. Suppose you possess the whole world; even then you would not be happy. Therefore that which is finite is *duḥkhabījam*—the seed of unhappiness.

As long as you are confined to the limited world of sense experience you can never be happy. You have to go beyond sense experience. When you attain the state of bhūmā you feel you have got everything you have ever wanted. As the Gītā says (VI.22): 'Attaining that, one does not regard anything to be higher.'

Section Twenty-four

यत्र नान्यत्पश्यति नान्यच्छृणोति नान्यद्विजानाति स भूमाथ यत्रान्यत्पश्यत्यन्यच्छृणोत्यन्यद्विजानाति तदल्पं यो वै भूमा तदमृतमथ यदल्पं तन्मर्त्यं स भगवः कस्मिन्प्रतिष्ठित इति स्वे महिम्नि यदि वा न महिम्नीति॥ १॥

Yatra nānyatpaśyati nānyacchṛṇoti nānyadvijānāti sa bhūmātha yatrānyatpaśyatyanyacchṛṇotyanyadvijānāti tadalpaṁ yo vai bhūmā tadamṛtamatha yadalpaṁ tanmartyaṁ sa bhagavaḥ kasminpratiṣṭhita iti sve mahimni yadi vā na mahimnīti.

Yatra, where; *na anyat paśyati,* one sees nothing else; *na anyat śṛṇoti,* hears nothing else; *na anyat vijānāti,* knows nothing about other things; *saḥ bhūmā,* that is bhūmā [the infinite]; *atha,* but; *yatra,* where; *anyat paśyati,* one sees something else; *anyat śṛṇoti,* hears something else; *anyat vijānāti,* knows of something else; *tat alpam,* that is small [finite]; *yaḥ vai bhūmā,* that which is infinite; *tat amṛtam,* that is immortal; *atha,* but; *yat alpam,* that which is finite; *tat martyam,* that is mortal; *bhagavaḥ,* sir; *kasmin saḥ pratiṣṭhitaḥ iti,* on what does that [bhūmā] rest; *sve mahimni,* on its own power; *yadi vā na mahimni iti,* or not even on that power.

1. Sanatkumāra said: 'Bhūmā [the infinite] is that in which one sees nothing else, hears nothing else, and knows [i.e., finds] nothing else. But alpa [the finite] is that in which one sees something else, hears something else, and knows something else. That which is infinite is immortal, and that which is finite is mortal.' Nārada asked, 'Sir, what does bhūmā rest on?' Sanatkumāra replied, 'It rests on its own power—or not even on that power [i.e., it depends on nothing else].'

At the level of bhūmā, the infinite, there is only bhūmā—nothing but bhūmā. And when you attain that level, you see nothing but bhūmā. If you see anything else, then you know at once it is *alpa,* finite.

Suppose you are alone in a room with a hundred mirrors. What will you see? Only yourself—the same self multiplied a hundred times. But if you attain the state of bhūmā, or Brahman, this is just the experience you will have. You will see yourself everywhere—the same Self in all beings.

We talk of love and compassion, but how can there

be love unless there is a feeling of oneness? When you have this feeling of oneness, then if someone is in pain, you are also in pain. True love is possible only when we realize that 'you' and 'I' are one and the same. This is the supreme experience.

Once at Dakshineswar two boatmen were having a quarrel and one of them started beating the other. Ramakrishna saw it from a distance and felt as if he were being beaten. Even the marks of the beating were seen on his body. Another day he saw someone walking on some grass, and he felt that the person was stepping on him.

When Ramakrishna had throat cancer he could hardly eat a thing. One day some of his disciples went to him and begged him to ask Mother Kali to cure him. Ramakrishna replied that he could not ask such a thing from her, that he depended totally on her will. But the disciples would not let him alone. They pleaded again and again: 'Do it for our sake.' They could not bear to see him suffer.

Finally Ramakrishna agreed to say something to the Mother. When the disciples came back to him later to ask if he had talked to the Mother, Ramakrishna said, 'I told Mother that I could not eat because of the pain in my throat, and I asked her to allow me to eat something.' 'What did she say?' they asked. Ramakrishna replied: 'She showed me all of you, and then she said, "But you are eating through so many mouths." I was ashamed and could not utter another word.'

There is a story about Ganesh and his mother Parvati. Once when Ganesh was playing with a cat, he became very rough and beat it. Later, when he went to his mother, he noticed wounds all over her body. Ganesh was alarmed and asked, 'Who has beaten you, Mother?' Parvati replied: 'Son, you have done this. You beat the cat, but I am also in the cat. If you hurt the cat you hurt me too.'

The Vedāntic idea is that the same Self is everywhere. It is the same consciousness. In some cases that consciousness is more manifest, and in other cases it is less, but it is the same Self permeating everything. From a tiny atom to the whole cosmos, it is all one. The difference is only in the degree of manifestation.

Where there is duality there is conflict, so we must beware of the finite. We must beware of limiting ourselves to our own body. That is the small 'I'. The body will die, and you think you will die. But if you are one with bhūmā, you are immortal.

Nārada is a very intelligent person. He asks: 'There is this bhūmā. But who or what supports it?' Sanatkumāra replies: 'Bhūmā is self-sufficient. It supports itself. In fact, there is nothing besides bhūmā to speak of supporting or not supporting. There is just one. If there are two things, then only does the question of supporting arise.'

गोअश्वमिह महिमेत्याचक्षते हस्तिहिरण्यं दासभार्यं क्षेत्राण्यायतनानीति नाहमेवं ब्रवीमि ब्रवीमीति होवाचान्यो ह्यन्यस्मिन्प्रतिष्ठित इति ॥ २ ॥ इति चतुर्विंशः खण्डः ॥ २४ ॥

Goaśvamiha mahimetyācakṣate hastihiraṇyaṁ dāsabhāryaṁ kṣetrāṇyāyatanānīti nāhamevaṁ bravīmi bravīmīti hovācānyo hyanyasminpratiṣṭhita iti. Iti caturviṁśaḥ khaṇḍaḥ.

Go-aśvam, cows and horses; *iha,* in this world; *mahimā iti ācakṣate,* are called the glory; *hasti-hiraṇyam,* elephants and gold; *dāsa-bhāryam,* servants and wives; *kṣetrāṇi āyatanāni iti,* farmlands and houses; *aham evam na bravīmi,* I am not speaking of this kind [of glory]; *anyaḥ hi anyasmin pratiṣṭhitaḥ iti,* something depending on something else; *bravīmi iti ha uvāca,* this is what I am saying. *Iti caturviṁśaḥ khaṇḍaḥ,* here ends the twenty-fourth section.

2. In this world it is said that cattle, horses, elephants, gold, servants, wives, farmlands, and houses are a person's glory. I do not mean this type of glory, for these things are not independent of each other. This is what I am talking about—

In those days in India if you had cattle and other animals, you were considered very rich because they supported you. They were a source of income. So also if you had gold or fields or other property.

In this type of situation, there are two separate things—you, the owner, and the things you own. One supports the other. But if there is only one, then the question of supporting does not arise. Who supports whom?

So Sanatkumāra tells Nārada, bhūmā is everything. It is one without a second, and it is self-sufficient.

Section Twenty-five

स एवाधस्तात्स उपरिष्टात्स पश्चात्स पुरस्तात्स दक्षिणतः स उत्तरतः स एवेदं सर्वमित्यथातोऽहङ्कारादेश एवाहमेवाधस्तादहमुपरिष्टादहं पश्चादहं पुरस्तादहं दक्षिणतोऽहमुत्तरतोऽहमेवेदं सर्वमिति ॥ १ ॥

Sa evādhastātsa upariṣṭātsa paścātsa purastātsa dakṣiṇataḥ sa uttarataḥ sa evedaṁ sarvamityathāto'haṅkārādeśa evāhamevādhastādahamupariṣṭādahaṁ paścādahaṁ purastādahaṁ dakṣiṇato'hamuttarato'hamevedaṁ sarvamiti.

Saḥ, that [bhūmā]; *eva adhastāt,* is down below; *saḥ upariṣṭāt,* that is up above; *saḥ paścāt,* that is behind; *saḥ purastāt,* that is in front; *saḥ dakṣiṇataḥ,* that is to the right; *saḥ uttarataḥ,* that is to the left; *saḥ eva idam sarvam iti,* it is truly all this; *atha ataḥ,* next; *ahaṅkāra ādeśaḥ eva,* the instruction regarding one's own identity; *aham eva adhastāt,* I am down below; *aham upariṣṭāt,* I am up above; *aham paścāt,* I am behind; *aham purastāt,* I am in front; *aham dakṣiṇataḥ,* I am to the right; *aham uttarataḥ,* I am to the left; *aham eva idam sarvam iti,* I am truly all this.

1. That bhūmā is below; it is above; it is behind; it is in front; it is to the right; it is to the left. All this is bhūmā. Now, as regards one's own identity: I am below; I am above; I am behind; I am in front; I am to the right; I am to the left. I am all this.

Our Self is the Self of all. Our Self is in the sky, in the air, in the water, in the tiny insect, and in the biggest animal. It is all-embracing, everywhere, in every being, in everything. It is Existence itself.

Imagine that the whole cosmos is a vast ocean, and in that ocean there are waves. Some of the waves are huge and some of them are very small, maybe only ripples. But it is the same water. Similarly, there is one Existence, but we see diversity. This diversity, however, is only in name and form. It is not real. Underlying the diversity is one Existence, and that Existence is our own Self.

This is not just an intellectual theory. There are great saints who have actually experienced this. They say, suppose you throw a stone into the middle of a lake. Immediately the water surrounding the spot where you have thrown the stone becomes disturbed.

Then gradually you discover that the entire mass of water is disturbed. Similarly, if someone is in pain somewhere, then you also are in pain.

You may have noticed that if you play a stringed instrument in a room where there are other stringed instruments, you will find that sounds are coming from the other instruments. The sound vibration from one will affect the others.

Swami Vivekananda had many such experiences. Once one of his brother disciples found him pacing back and forth outside his room at midnight. The brother disciple asked Swamiji why he was not sleeping, and Swamiji replied that he had suddenly woken up with the feeling that something terrible had just happened, that a great calamity had just happened somewhere. The next day when the newspaper arrived people found that there had been a terrible volcanic eruption that night in a certain place, and many people had died.

A great person has that kind of sensitivity, because he feels that there is just one heart, one mind, one consciousness. What you think, he thinks. If you are suffering, he can at once see it when he looks at you.

You may ask, 'Is it possible for me to identify myself with everything?' The scriptures say, 'Yes, it is possible.' Now you think of yourself as small, as *alpa*. You think you are an individual and separate from others. But when you identify yourself with the cosmos, you become bhūmā, infinite.

Swamiji once said, suppose you are a small drop of water in a cloud in the sky. Then one day it rains. You start falling towards the ocean, and you cry, 'Oh, I am lost, I am lost!' But what happens when you reach the ocean? You are no longer a tiny drop. You are one with the vast ocean.

It is the sense of separateness that makes us feel we are small. Then we become jealous of each other or afraid of others, and because of this we are unhappy. Vedānta says, when you have the feeling that you are one with the whole cosmos, that you alone exist, then you will be happy. It is all a question of how you think of yourself. The Upaniṣad says here to think: 'I am below. I am above. I am everywhere. I am everything.'

Many people have a hint of this experience at some time or other in their life. For instance, you may have seen someone in terrible pain. Maybe you didn't even know the person, yet at the very sight of that person's suffering, you felt that you were suffering. Though physically you were not affected, still you felt the pain. A human being's development towards this sense of oneness is the sign of real progress.

This is not to deny differences among us, however. Of course there are differences. Differences are accepted. They are natural. We would not like uniformity. But the differences are only minor details. Now we may think, 'I am short and that person is tall.' But when we begin to look at things as a whole, then we shall see that we are everywhere. Then we will think: 'Sometimes I am tall, and sometimes

I am short.' Instead of thinking, 'Some people are very bright and others are dull,' we will think: 'The bright person is me, and the dull person is also me. All are me in different forms.'

As long as you think you are separate from others, you will sometimes be good to others and sometimes be very selfish and not care about others. And even when you do something for others, you will do it only out of a temporary sense of pity. But when you feel your identity with others you never lose that feeling of oneness, and then there is never any room for selfishness.

Aham eva idam sarvam—I am all this. *Idam* means 'this.' It is this physical world, this empirical world. It is all that you see and feel. It is the world of sense experience. We think we know this world, but in reality we do not. You may say something is hard, but to me it may be soft. You may say something looks red, but I may see it as orange. This is the nature of this world. No two people have the same experience of it. Yet, the Upaniṣad says, behind this world of sense experience is bhūmā. It is the same Self everywhere, in different forms and with different names.

अथात आत्मादेश एवात्मैवाधस्तादात्मोपरिष्टादात्मा पश्चादात्मा पुरस्तादात्मा दक्षिणत आत्मोत्तरत आत्मैवेदं सर्वमिति स वा एष एवं पश्यन्नेवं मन्वान एवं

विजानन्नात्मरतिरात्मक्रीड आत्ममिथुन आत्मानन्दः स स्वराड् भवति तस्य सर्वेषु लोकेषु कामचारो भवति। अथ येऽन्यथातो विदुरन्यराजानस्ते क्षय्यलोका भवन्ति तेषां सर्वेषु लोकेष्वकामचारो भवति॥ २॥ इति पञ्चविंशः खण्डः॥ २५॥

Athāta ātmādeśa evātmaivādhastādātmopariṣṭādātmā paścādātmā purastādātmā dakṣiṇata ātmottarata ātmaivedaṁ sarvamiti sa vā eṣa evaṁ paśyannevaṁ manvāna evaṁ vijānannātmaratirātmakrīḍa ātmamithuna ātmānandaḥ sa svarāḍ bhavati tasya sarveṣu lokeṣu kāmacāro bhavati; Atha ye'nyathāto viduranyarājānaste kṣayyalokā bhavanti teṣāṁ sarveṣu lokeṣvakāmacāro bhavati. Iti pañcaviṁśaḥ khaṇḍaḥ.

Atha ataḥ, next; *ātmādeśaḥ eva,* the instruction regarding the Self; *ātmā eva adhastāt,* the Self is down below; *ātmā upariṣṭāt,* the Self is up above; *ātmā paścāt,* the Self is behind; *ātmā purastāt,* the Self is in front; *ātmā dakṣiṇataḥ,* the Self is to the right; *ātmā uttarataḥ,* the Self is to the left; *ātmā eva idam sarvam iti,* the Self is truly all this; *saḥ vai eṣaḥ,* that [worshipper] who; *evam paśyan,* sees in this way; *evam manvānaḥ,* thinks in this way; *evam vijānan,* knows in this way; *ātmaratiḥ,* has love for the Self; *ātmakrīḍah,* sports with the Self; *ātmamithunaḥ,* enjoys the company of the Self; *ātmānandaḥ,* has joy in the Self; *saḥ svarāṭ bhavati,* he becomes supreme [a sovereign]; *sarveṣu lokeṣu,* in all the worlds; *tasya kāmacāraḥ bhavati,* he can go about as he likes; *atha,* then; *ye,* those who; *anyatha ataḥ viduḥ,* know otherwise; *anyarājānaḥ,* are under the control of others; *te kṣayyalokāḥ bhavanti,* they live in worlds that are not permanent; *sarveṣu lokeṣu,* in all the worlds; *teṣām akāmacāraḥ bhavati,* he cannot move about as he likes. *Iti pañcaviṁśaḥ khaṇḍaḥ,* here ends the twenty-fifth section.

2. Next is the instruction on the Self: The Self is below; the Self is above; the Self is behind; the Self is in front; the Self is to the right; the Self is to the left. The Self is all this. He who sees in this way, thinks in this way, and knows in this way, has love for the Self, sports with the Self, enjoys the company of the Self, and has joy in the Self, he is supreme and can go about as he likes in all the worlds. But those who think otherwise are under the control of others. They cannot remain in the worlds they live in, nor can they move about in the worlds as they like [i.e., they are under many limitations].

The Upaniṣad says, you see yourself in all that exists. When you have the experience, 'I am infinite, I am one with all,' then there is no duality. You enjoy your own Self. Normally we look for friends so we can enjoy ourselves in their company. But when you realize bhūmā, you don't need any companions. You know that everything is within and not outside.

Now we are so dependent on things outside. If someone is harsh to us we feel bad, and if someone is good to us we are happy. Similarly, we may be addicted to cigarettes and are miserable if we don't get them. So our happiness always depends on external conditions. Where is our freedom? This is not freedom. We are simply beggars. A free soul, however, is always happy within himself. He is not bothered by external conditions.

Sri Ramakrishna was not dependent on anyone or anything. Once some servants came to him and told him that the owner of the temple garden said he must leave immediately. Sri Ramakrishna at once got up and started walking out of the temple compound, just as he was. He did not stop to pack anything or take a second look at his room. He simply started leaving. The owner happened to see him leaving, and asked: 'Sir, why are you leaving? I asked your nephew to leave, not you.' Then Sri Ramakrishna replied, 'Oh, you don't want me to leave?' and he immediately turned around and went back to his room as if nothing had happened.

Suppose you enjoy a certain kind of music, but another person does not care for it. Why does this happen? It is because that music evokes in you a certain feeling or emotion which it does not evoke in the other person. The enjoyment is not in the music. It is within you. So also, sometimes you may sit and daydream, thinking of a pilgrimage you took in the Himalayas long back. You go on thinking and enjoying the memories even though the Himalayas are no longer in front of you. The enjoyment is totally within you.

So when you realize your Self, you no longer need

the world outside. In fact, it no longer exists for you. You alone exist. Some people may say this is selfishness, but it is not. Rather, your self has expanded. It has become all-embracing. It has become bhūmā.

'Saḥ svarāṭ bhavati—he becomes a sovereign.' When you attain sovereignty you no longer identify yourself with the body. You feel yourself to be one with the entire cosmos. This is the goal of life—to realize that there is only One which appears as many, with different names and forms.

Section Twenty-six

तस्य ह वा एतस्यैवं पश्यत एवं मन्वानस्यैवं विजानत आत्मतः प्राण आत्मत आशात्मतः स्मर आत्मत आकाश आत्मतस्तेज आत्मत आप आत्मत आविर्भावतिरोभावावात्मतोऽन्नमात्मतो बलमात्मतो विज्ञानमात्मतो ध्यानमात्मतश्चित्तमात्मतः सङ्कल्प आत्मतो मन आत्मतो वागात्मतो नामात्मतो मन्त्राः आत्मतः कर्माण्यात्मत एवेदं सर्वमिति॥ १ ॥

Tasya ha vā etasyaivaṁ paśyata evaṁ manvānasyaivaṁ vijānata ātmataḥ prāṇa ātmata āśātmataḥ smara ātmata ākāśa ātmatasteja ātmata āpa ātmata āvirbhāva-tirobhāvāvātmato'nnamātmato balamātmato vijñāna-

mātmato dhyānamātmataścittamātmataḥ saṅkalpa ātmato mana ātmato vāgātmato nāmātmato mantrā ātmataḥ karmāṇyātmata evedaṁ sarvamiti.

Tasya ha vai etasya, of a person like this; *evam paśyataḥ,* who sees in this way; *evam manvānasya,* who thinks in this way; *evam vijānataḥ,* who has such knowledge; *ātmataḥ prāṇaḥ,* life [comes] from the Self; *ātmataḥ āśā,* hope [comes] from the Self; *ātmataḥ smaraḥ,* memory [comes] from the Self; *ātmataḥ ākāśaḥ,* space [comes] from the Self; *ātmataḥ tejaḥ,* fire [comes] from the Self; *ātmataḥ āpaḥ,* water [comes] from the Self; *ātmataḥ āvirbhāva-tirobhāvau,* birth and death [come] from the Self; *ātmataḥ annam,* food [comes] from the Self; *ātmataḥ balam,* strength [comes] from the Self; *ātmataḥ vijñānam,* knowledge in depth [comes] from the Self; *ātmataḥ dhyānam,* meditation [comes] from the Self; *ātmataḥ cittam,* the heart [comes] from the Self; *ātmataḥ saṅkalpaḥ,* resolution [comes] from the Self; *ātmataḥ manaḥ,* the mind [comes] from the Self; *ātmataḥ vāk,* speech [comes] from the Self; *ātmataḥ nāma,* name [comes] from the Self; *ātmataḥ mantrāḥ,* the mantras [comes] from the Self; *ātmataḥ karmāṇi,* all work [comes] from the Self; *ātmataḥ eva idam sarvam iti,* all this [comes] from the Self.

1. For a person like this who sees in this way, thinks in this way, and has this knowledge, everything comes from the Self: Life, hope, memory, space, fire, water, birth and death, food, strength, knowledge in depth, meditation, the heart, resolution, the mind,

speech, name, mantras, and all work—all this comes from the Self.

Just as waves rise from and fall back on the ocean, so also all these things—prāṇa, hope, memory, birth, death, happiness, unhappiness, etc.—come from the Self and go back to the Self. They are all within our own self.

Once we know the Self, the phenomenal world no longer exists for us.

तदेष श्लोकः

न पश्यो मृत्युं पश्यति न रोगं नोत दुःखताम्।
सर्वं ह पश्यः पश्यति सर्वमाप्नोति सर्वशः॥ इति॥

स एकधा भवति त्रिधा भवति पञ्चधा सप्तधा
नवधा चैव पुनश्चैकादशः स्मृतः शतं च दश चैकश्च
सहस्राणि च विंशतिराहारशुद्धौ सत्त्वशुद्धिः सत्त्वशुद्धौ
ध्रुवा स्मृतिः स्मृतिलम्भे सर्वग्रन्थीनां विप्रमोक्षस्तस्मै
मृदितकषायाय तमसस्पारं दर्शयति भगवान्सनत्कुमारस्तं
स्कन्द इत्याचक्षते तं स्कन्द इत्याचक्षते॥ २॥ इति
षड्विंशः खण्डः॥ २६॥ इति छान्दोग्योपनिषदि सप्तमो-
ऽध्यायः॥ ७॥

Tadeṣa ślokaḥ:

Na paśyo mṛtyuṁ paśyati na rogaṁ nota duḥkhatām;
Sarvaṁ ha paśyaḥ paśyati sarvamāpnoti sarvaśaḥ. Iti.

Sa ekadhā bhavati tridhā bhavati pañcadhā saptadhā navadhā caiva punaścaikādaśaḥ smṛtaḥ śataṁ ca daśa caikaśca sahasrāṇi ca viṁśatirāhāraśuddhau sattvaśuddhiḥ sattvaśuddhau dhruvā smṛtiḥ smṛtilambhe sarvagranthīnāṁ vipramokṣastasmai mṛditakaṣāyāya tamasaspāraṁ darśayati bhagavānsanatkumārastaṁ skanda ityācakṣate taṁ skanda ityācakṣate. Iti ṣaḍviṁśaḥ khaṇḍaḥ. Iti chāndogyopaniṣadi saptamo'dhyāyaḥ.

Tat eṣaḥ ślokaḥ, here is a verse on the subject; *paśyaḥ,* a person who sees thus [i.e., who knows the Self]; *mṛtyum na paśyati,* does not see death; *na rogam,* nor disease; *na uta duḥkhatam,* nor suffering; *paśyaḥ,* a person who sees thus; *sarvam ha paśyati,* sees everything; *sarvam āpnoti,* he obtains all; *sarvaśaḥ,* in every way.

Saḥ ekadhā bhavati, he is one [before the creation]; *tridhā bhavati,* [and] he is in three forms [fire, water, and earth]; *pañcadhā,* in five forms; *saptadhā,* in seven forms; *ca eva navadhā,* and in nine forms; *punaḥ ca,* also; *ekādaśaḥ smṛtaḥ,* he is thought of as having eleven forms; *śatam ca daśa ca,* and one hundred and ten forms; *ekaḥ ca sahasrāṇi ca viṁśatiḥ,* and also one thousand and twenty forms; *āhāra-śuddhau,* if the food is pure; *sattva-śuddhiḥ,* the mind is pure; *sattva-śuddhau,* if the mind is pure; *dhruvā smṛtiḥ,* the memory is strong and steady; *smṛtilambhe,* when the memory is good; *sarva-granthīnām,* from all bondages; *vipramokṣaḥ,* one is freed; *tasmai,* to him [to Nārada]; *mṛditakaṣāyāya,* who was free from all impurities; *bhagavān sanatkumāraḥ,* revered Sanatkumāra; *tamasaḥ pāram,* beyond darkness; *darśayati,* showed; *tam,* him [Sanatkumāra]; *skanda iti ācakṣate,* they refer to as 'Skanda' [the wise]; *tam,* him [Sanatkumāra]; *skanda iti ācakṣate,* they refer to as 'Skanda' [the wise]. *Iti ṣaḍviṁśaḥ khaṇḍaḥ,* here ends the twenty-sixth section. *Iti chāndogyopaniṣadi saptamaḥ adhyāyaḥ,* here ends the seventh chapter of the Chāndogya Upaniṣad.

2. Here is a verse on the subject: 'He who has realized the Self does not see death. For him there is no disease or sorrow. Such a seer sees everything [as it is] and also attains everything in whatever way [he wants].' He is one [i.e., before creation; but after creation], he is in three forms, five forms, seven forms, and nine forms. Then again, he is in eleven, a hundred and ten, and even a thousand and twenty forms. If one eats pure food, one's mind becomes pure. If the mind is pure, one's memory becomes strong and steady. If the memory is good, one becomes free from all bondages. The revered Sanatkumāra freed Nārada from all his shortcomings and led him beyond darkness [i.e., ignorance]. The wise say that Sanatkumāra is a man of perfect knowledge.

from death and disease. You see yourself everywhere and in everything. You are one but you are also many.

But how do you attain this knowledge? You have to have pure food. Pure food makes the body and mind pure, and you are then able to keep the mind under control. By controlling the mind, you are able to go beyond ignorance and become free from bondage. Like Sanatkumāra, you earn the title 'Skanda,' the wise one.

CHAPTER EIGHT

Section One

ॐ। अथ यदिदमस्मिन्ब्रह्मपुरे दहरं पुण्डरीकं वेश्म दहरोऽस्मिन्नन्तराकाशस्तस्मिन्यदन्तस्तदन्वेष्टव्यं तद्वाव विजिज्ञासितव्यमिति ॥ १ ॥

Om. Atha yadidamasminbrahmapure daharaṁ puṇḍarīkaṁ veśma daharo'sminnantarākāśastasminyadantastadanveṣṭavyaṁ tadvāva vijijñāsitavyamiti.

Atha, next; *asmin brahmapure,* in this city of Brahman [i.e., the body]; *yat idam daharam,* this small; *puṇḍarīkam,* lotus; *veśma,* an abode [i.e., the heart]; *asmin,* in this; *daharaḥ antarākāśaḥ,* is a small space; *tasmin yat antaḥ,* within that; *tat anveṣṭavyam,* one must seek that; *tat vāva vijijñāsitavyam iti,* one must earnestly desire to know that.

1. Om. This body is the city of Brahman. Within it is an abode in the shape of a lotus [i.e., the heart], and within that there is a small space. One must search within this space and earnestly desire to know what is there.

The scriptures try to help us know our real identity, because when we know that, we know we are all one with Brahman. But first we must have a pure mind. The mind becomes purified by living a good life and by practising self-restraint and truthfulness. It is in the pure mind that the Self reveals itself. The heart is said to be like a lotus, and in that lotus resides the Self—as if this is the home of the Self.

तं चेदब्रूयुर्यदिदमस्मिन्ब्रह्मपुरे दहरं पुण्डरीकं वेश्म दहरोऽस्मिन्नन्तराकाशः किं तदत्र विद्यते यदन्वेष्टव्यं यद्वाव विजिज्ञासितव्यमिति स ब्रूयात्॥ २ ॥

Taṁ cedbrūyuryadidamasminbrahmapure daharaṁ puṇḍarīkaṁ veśma daharo'sminnantarākāśaḥ kiṁ tadatra vidyate yadanveṣṭavyaṁ yadvāva vijijñāsitavyamiti sa brūyāt.

Cet, if; *tam,* to him [the teacher]; *brūyuḥ,* [the disciples] ask; *asmin brahmapure,* in this city of Brahman [i.e., the body]; *yat idam daharam,* this small; *puṇḍarīkam,* lotus; *veśma,* an abode [i.e., the heart]; *asmin,* in this; *daharaḥ antarākāśaḥ,* is a small space; *kim tat atra,* what is it that is there; *yat anveṣṭavyam,* which one must seek; *yat vāva vijijñāsitavyam iti,* which one must earnestly desire to know; *saḥ brūyāt,* he [the teacher] should reply.

2. If the disciples ask, 'This body is the city of Brahman; within it is an abode in the shape of a lotus [i.e., the heart], and within that there is a

small space; what is it that one must search for within this space, and what should one earnestly desire to know?'—the teacher should reply:

The disciples wanted to know what was within the heart. The teacher had said there is a space there. But is there anything within this space? If so, is it something very special? Why is it necessary that they should know about it? They asked, 'Should we investigate it?' The scriptures say, 'Yes, investigate it.'

यावान्वा अयमाकाशस्तावानेषोऽन्तर्हृदय आकाश उभे अस्मिन्द्यावापृथिवी अन्तरेव समाहिते उभावग्निश्च वायुश्च सूर्याचन्द्रमसावुभौ विद्युन्नक्षत्राणि यच्चास्येहास्ति यच्च नास्ति सर्वं तदस्मिन्समाहितमिति॥ ३ ॥

Yāvānvā ayamākāśastāvāneṣo'ntarhṛdaya ākāśa ubhe asmindyāvāpṛthivī antareva samāhite ubhāvagniśca vāyuśca sūryācandramasāvubhau vidyunnakṣatrāṇi yaccāsyehāsti yacca nāsti sarvaṁ tadasminsamāhitamiti.

Yāvān, as much as; *ayam ākāśaḥ,* this space; *tāvān,* so that much; *eṣaḥ antaḥ-hṛdaye ākāśe,* this space inside the heart; *ubhe,* both; *asmin,* in this; *dyāvā-pṛthivī,* heaven and earth; *antaḥ eva samāhite,* are resting deep within; *ubhau agniḥ ca vāyuḥ ca,* both fire and air; *sūryā-candramasau ubhau,* both the sun and the moon; *vidyut,* lightning; *nakṣatrāṇi,* the stars;

yat ca, whatever; *asya,* of it [of the self with the body]; *iha,* in this world; *asti,* exists; *yat ca na asti,* or whatever does not exist; *sarvam tat,* all that; *asmin samāhitam iti,* is resting within.

3. [The teacher replies:] 'The space in the heart is as big as the space outside. Heaven and earth are both within it, so also fire and air, the sun and the moon, lightning and the stars. Everything exists within that space in the embodied self—whatever it has or does not have.'

तं चेद्ब्रूयुरस्मिंश्चेदिदं ब्रह्मपुरे सर्वं समाहितं सर्वाणि
च भूतानि सर्वे च कामा यदैतज्जरा वाप्नोति प्रध्वंसते
वा किं ततोऽतिशिष्यत इति ॥ ४ ॥

Taṁ cedbrūyurasmiṁścedidaṁ brahmapure sarvaṁ samāhitaṁ sarvāṇi ca bhūtāni sarve ca kāmā yadaitajjarā vāpnoti pradhvaṁsate vā kiṁ tato'tiśiṣyata iti.

Cet, if; *tam,* to him [the teacher]; *brūyuḥ,* [the disciples] ask; *asmin brahmapure,* in this city of Brahman [i.e., the body]; *idam sarvam cet,* if all this; *samāhitam,* are lying; *sarvāṇi ca bhūtāni,* and all things; *sarve ca kāmāḥ,* and all desires [that people may have]; *yadā,* when; *etat,* this [body]; *jarā,* old age; *āpnoti vā,* attains; *pradhvaṁsate vā,* or it perishes; *kim,* what; *tataḥ,* then; *atiśiṣyate iti,* remains?

4. If the disciples ask the teacher, 'If in this body [brahmapura] are all this, all things, and all desires, is there anything left behind when the body gets old or perishes?'—

स ब्रूयान्नास्य जरयैतज्जीर्यति न वधेनास्य हन्यत एतत्सत्यं ब्रह्मपुरमस्मिन्कामाः समाहिता एष आत्मा-पहतपाप्मा विजरो विमृत्युर्विशोको विजिघत्सोऽपिपासः सत्यकामः सत्यसङ्कल्पो यथा ह्येवेह प्रजा अन्वाविशन्ति यथानुशासनं यं यमन्तमभिकामा भवन्ति यं जनपदं यं क्षेत्रभागं तं तमेवोपजीवन्ति ॥ ५ ॥

Sa brūyānnāsya jarayaitajjīryati na vadhenāsya hanyata etatsatyaṁ brahmapuramasminkāmāḥ samāhitā eṣa ātmāpahatapāpmā vijaro vimṛtyurviśoko vijighatso-'pipāsaḥ satyakāmaḥ satyasaṅkalpo yathā hyeveha prajā anvāviśanti yathānuśāsanaṁ yaṁ yamantamabhikāmā bhavanti yaṁ janapadaṁ yaṁ kṣetrabhāgaṁ taṁ tamevopajīvanti.

Saḥ, he [the teacher]; *brūyāt,* will say; *asya,* its [the body's]; *jarayā,* by old age; *etat,* this [i.e., the space within the heart—the Self]; *na jīryati,* is not affected; *vadhena asya na hanyate,* nor does it meet death by being killed; *etat,* this; *satyam brahmapuram,* city of Brahman is real; *asmin,* in this; *kāmāḥ,* all desires; *samāhitāḥ,* are contained; *eṣaḥ ātmā,* this Self; *apahatapāpmā,* is free from all sins [or, sorrows]; *vijaraḥ,* free from old age; *vimṛtyuḥ,* deathless; *viśokaḥ,* free from bereavement; *vijighatsaḥ,* without hunger; *apipāsaḥ,* without thirst; *satyakāmaḥ,* love of Truth; *satyasaṅkalpaḥ,* committed to Truth; *yathā,* like; *hi eva iha,* in this world; *prajāḥ,* people; *anu-āviśanti,* come and go; *yathā-anuśāsanam,* according to the law of the country; *yam yam,* whatever; *antam,* province; *abhikāmāḥ bhavanti,* they desire; *yam janapadam,* any village; *yam kṣetrabhāgam,* [or] any field; *tam tam eva,* that very [place]; *upajīvanti,* they enjoy.

5. —in reply the teacher will say: 'The body may decay due to old age, but the space within [i.e., brahmapura] never decays. Nor does it perish with the death of the body. This is the real abode of Brahman. All our desires are concentrated in it. It is the Self—free from all sins as well as from old age, death, bereavement, hunger, and thirst. It is the cause of love of Truth and the cause of dedication to Truth. If a person strictly follows whatever the ruler of the country commands, he may then get as a reward some land, or even an estate.'

The idea is that an ignorant person may get whatever he wants as the fruit of his actions, but he remains bound.

तद्यथेह कर्मजितो लोकः क्षीयत एवमेवामुत्र पुण्यजितो लोकः क्षीयते तद्य इहात्मानमननुविद्य व्रजन्त्येतांश्च सत्यान् कामांस्तेषां सर्वेषु लोकेष्वकामचारो भवत्यथ य इहात्मानमनुविद्य व्रजन्त्येतांश्च सत्यान्कामांस्तेषां सर्वेषु लोकेषु कामचारो भवति ॥ ६ ॥ इति प्रथमः खण्डः ॥ १ ॥

Tadyatheha karmajito lokaḥ kṣīyata evamevāmutra puṇyajito lokaḥ kṣīyate tadya ihātmānamananuvidya vrajantyetāṁśca satyān kāmāṁsteṣāṁ sarveṣu lokeṣvakāmacāro bhavatyatha ya ihātmānamanuvidya vrajantyetāṁśca satyānkāmāṁsteṣāṁ sarveṣu lokeṣu kāmacāro bhavati. Iti prathamaḥ khaṇḍaḥ.

Tat yathā, just as; *iha,* in this world; *karmajitaḥ,* results acquired according to one's efforts; *lokaḥ,* this world; *kṣīyate,* perishes; *evam eva,* similarly; *amutra;* in the other world; *puṇyajitaḥ,* what is earned by meritorious work [such as performing the Agnihotra and other sacrifices]; *lokaḥ,* heaven [or other worlds]; *kṣīyate,* perishes; *tat ye,* those; *iha,* in this world; *ātmānam ananuvidya,* without knowing the Self; *etān ca satyān kāmān,* and these worthwhile things; *vrajanti,* leave [this world]; *teṣām,* for them; *sarveṣu lokeṣu,* in all the worlds; *akāmacāraḥ bhavati,* there is bondage; *atha,* but; *ye,* those who; *iha,* in this world; *ātmānam anuvidya,* knowing the self; *etān ca satyān kāmān,* and these worthwhile things; *vrajanti,* leave this world; *teṣām,* for them; *sarveṣu lokeṣu,* in all the worlds;

kāmacāraḥ bhavati, they are free to go anywhere. *Iti prathamaḥ khaṇḍaḥ,* here ends the first section.

6. Everything perishes, whether it is something you have acquired through hard work in this world or it is a place in the other world which you have acquired through meritorious deeds. Those who leave this world without knowing the Self and the Truths which they should know are not free, no matter where they go. But those who leave this world after knowing the Self and the Truths which they should know are free, no matter where they are.

Section Two

स यदि पितृलोककामो भवति सङ्कल्पादेवास्य पितरः समुत्तिष्ठन्ति तेन पितृलोकेन सम्पन्नो महीयते ॥ १ ॥

Sa yadi pitṛlokakāmo bhavati saṅkalpādevāsya pitaraḥ samuttiṣṭhanti tena pitṛlokena sampanno mahīyate.

Yadi, if; *saḥ,* he [who has realized the Self and is free to go where he wants]; *pitṛlokakāmaḥ bhavati,* wishes for a place in the world of fathers; *pitaraḥ sam-ut-tiṣṭhanti,* the fathers appear; *asya saṅkalpāt eva,* through his wish; *tena pitṛlokena sampannaḥ,* joining his forefathers in that world; *mahīyate,* he becomes great.

1. If that person wishes to be in the company of his forefathers, they appear before him as he wishes. Joining his forefathers in that world, he becomes great.

अथ यदि मातृलोककामो भवति सङ्कल्पादेवास्य मातरः समुत्तिष्ठन्ति तेन मातृलोकेन सम्पन्नो महीयते ॥ २ ॥

Atha yadi mātṛlokakāmo bhavati saṅkalpādevāsya mātaraḥ samuttiṣṭhanti tena mātṛlokena sampanno mahīyate.

Atha, then; *yadi,* if; *mātṛlokakāmaḥ bhavati,* he wishes for a place in the world of mothers; *mātaraḥ sam-ut-tiṣṭhanti,* the mothers appear; *asya saṅkalpāt eva,* through his wish; *tena mātṛlokena sampannaḥ,* joining the mothers in that world; *mahīyate,* he becomes great.

2. Then if he wishes to be in the company of mothers, they appear before him as he wishes. Joining the mothers in that world, he becomes great.

अथ यदि भ्रातृलोककामो भवति सङ्कल्पादेवास्य भ्रातरः समुत्तिष्ठन्ति तेन भ्रातृलोकेन सम्पन्नो महीयते ॥ ३ ॥

Atha yadi bhrātṛlokakāmo bhavati saṅkalpādevāsya

bhrātaraḥ samuttiṣṭhanti tena bhrātṛlokena sampanno mahīyate.

Atha, then; *yadi,* if; *bhrātṛlokakāmaḥ bhavati,* he wishes for a place in the world of brothers; *bhrātaraḥ sam-ut-tiṣṭhanti,* brothers appear; *asya saṅkalpāt eva,* through his wish; *tena bhrātṛlokena sampannaḥ,* joining brothers in that world; *mahīyate,* he becomes great.

3. Then if he wishes to be in the company of brothers, they appear before him as he wishes. Joining the brothers in that world, he becomes great.

अथ यदि स्वसृलोककामो भवति सङ्कल्पादेवास्य स्वसारः समुत्तिष्ठन्ति तेन स्वसृलोकेन सम्पन्नो महीयते ॥ ४ ॥

Atha yadi svasṛlokakāmo bhavati saṅkalpādevāsya svasāraḥ samuttiṣṭhanti tena svasṛlokena sampanno mahīyate.

Atha, then; *yadi,* if; *svasṛlokakāmaḥ bhavati,* he wishes for a place in the world of sisters; *svasāraḥ sam-ut-tiṣṭhanti,* sisters appear; *asya saṅkalpāt eva,* through his wish; *tena svasṛlokena sampannaḥ,* joining the sisters in that world; *mahīyate,* he becomes great.

4. Then if he wishes to be in the company of sisters, they appear before him as he wishes. Joining the sisters in that world, he becomes great.

अथ यदि सखिलोककामो भवति सङ्कल्पादेवास्य सखायः समुत्तिष्ठन्ति तेन सखिलोकेन सम्पन्नो महीयते ॥ ५ ॥

Atha yadi sakhilokakāmo bhavati saṅkalpādevāsya sakhāyaḥ samuttiṣṭhanti tena sakhilokena sampanno mahīyate.

Atha, then; *yadi,* if; *sakhilokakāmaḥ bhavati,* he wishes for a place in the world of friends; *sakhāyaḥ sam-ut-tiṣṭhanti,* friends appear; *asya saṅkalpāt eva,* through his wish; *tena sakhilokena sampannaḥ,* joining friends in that world; *mahīyate,* he becomes great.

5. Then if he wishes to be in the company of friends, they appear before him as he wishes. Joining friends in that world, he becomes great.

अथ यदि गन्धमाल्यलोककामो भवति सङ्कल्पादेवास्य गन्धमाल्ये समुत्तिष्ठतस्तेन गन्धमाल्यलोकेन सम्पन्नो महीयते ॥ ६ ॥

Atha yadi gandhamālyalokakāmo bhavati saṅkalpādevāsya gandhamālye samuttiṣṭhatastena gandhamālyalokena sampanno mahīyate.

Atha, then; *yadi,* if; *gandhamālyalokakāmaḥ bhavati,* he wishes for a world of fragrant flower garlands; *gandhamālye sam-ut-tiṣṭhataḥ,* the fragrant flower garlands appear; *asya saṅkalpāt eva,* through his wish; *tena gandhamālyalokena sampannaḥ,* by having fragrant flower garlands in that world; *mahīyate,* he becomes great.

6. Then if he wishes for a world of fragrant flower garlands, they appear before him as he wishes. By having fragrant flower garlands in that world, he becomes great.

अथ यद्यन्नपानलोककामो भवति, सङ्कल्पादेवास्यान्नपाने समुत्तिष्ठतस्तेनान्नपानलोकेन, सम्पन्नो महीयते ॥ ७ ॥

Atha yadyannapānalokakāmo bhavati saṅkalpādevāsyānnapāne samuttiṣṭhatastenānnapānalokena sampanno mahīyate.

Atha, then; *yadi,* if; *annapānalokakāmaḥ bhavati,* he wishes for a world of food and drink; *annapāne sam-ut-tiṣṭhataḥ,* food and drink appear; *asya saṅkalpāt eva,* through his wish; *tena annapānalokena sampannaḥ,* by having food and drink in that world; *mahīyate,* he becomes great.

7. Then if he wishes for a world of food and drink, they appear before him as he wishes. By having food and drink in that world, he becomes great.

अथ यदि गीतवादित्रलोककामो भवति सङ्कल्पादेवास्य गीतवादित्रे समुत्तिष्ठतस्तेन गीतवादित्रलोकेन सम्पन्नो महीयते ॥ ८ ॥

Atha yadi gītavāditralokakāmo bhavati saṅkalpādevāsya gītavāditre samuttiṣṭhatastena gītavāditralokena sampanno mahīyate.

Atha, then; *yadi,* if; *gītavāditralokakāmaḥ bhavati,* he wishes for a world of music; *gītavāditre sam-ut-tiṣṭhataḥ,* music comes; *asya saṅkalpāt eva,* through his wish; *tena gītavāditralokena sampannaḥ,* by having music in that world; *mahīyate,* he becomes great.

8. Then if he wishes for a world of music, that world appears to him as he wishes. By enjoying music in that world, he becomes great.

अथ यदि स्त्रीलोककामो भवति सङ्कल्पादेवास्य स्त्रियः समुत्तिष्ठन्ति तेन स्त्रीलोकेन सम्पन्नो महीयते ॥ ९ ॥

Atha yadi strīlokakāmo bhavati saṅkalpādevāsya striyaḥ samuttiṣṭhanti tena strīlokena sampanno mahīyate.

Atha, then; *yadi,* if; *strīlokakāmaḥ bhavati,* he wishes for the company of women; *striyaḥ sam-ut-tiṣṭhanti,* women appear; *asya saṅkalpāt eva,* through his wish; *tena strīlokena sampannaḥ,* being with women in that world; *mahīyate,* he becomes great.

9. Then if he wishes for the company of women, they appear before him as he wishes. Being with women in that world, he becomes great.

यं यमन्तमभिकामो भवति यं कामं कामयते सोऽस्य सङ्कल्पादेव समुत्तिष्ठति तेन सम्पन्नो महीयते॥ १०॥ इति द्वितीयः खण्डः॥ २॥

Yaṁ yamantamabhikāmo bhavati yaṁ kāmaṁ kāmayate so'sya saṅkalpādeva samuttiṣṭhati tena sampanno mahīyate. Iti dvitīyaḥ khaṇḍaḥ.

Yam yam antam abhikāmaḥ bhavati, whatever province he wishes for; *yam kāmam kāmayate,* [and] whatever good thing he wishes to have; *saḥ sam-ut-tiṣṭhati,* that appears; *asya saṅkalpāt eva,* through his wish; *tena sampannaḥ,* by acquiring that; *mahīyate,* he becomes great. *Iti dvitīyaḥ khaṇḍaḥ,* here ends the second section.

10. Whatever province he wishes for, whatever good thing he wishes to have, it appears before him just as he wishes. By acquiring it, he becomes great.

Section Three

त इमे सत्याः कामा अनृतापिधानास्तेषां सत्यानां सतामनृतमपिधानं यो यो ह्यस्येतः प्रैति न तमिह दर्शनाय लभते॥ १ ॥

Ta ime satyāḥ kāmā anṛtāpidhānāsteṣāṁ satyānāṁ satāmanṛtamapidhānaṁ yo yo hyasyetaḥ praiti na tamiha darśanāya labhate.

Te ime, all these; *satyāḥ kāmāḥ,* true desires; *anṛtāpidhānāḥ,* with a false look; *teṣām satyānām satām,* of those true desires [resting in the Self]; *anṛtam apidhānam,* have a false look; *yaḥ yaḥ hi asya,* whoever of one's [relatives]; *itaḥ,* from this world; *praiti,* leaves; *tam,* he; *iha,* here [in this world]; *darśanāya na labhate,* cannot be seen again.

1. But all these true desires are under a false cover. Though they rest on the Self, they are all false. This is why if a relative dies, one does not see him again in this world.

अथ ये चास्येह जीवा ये च प्रेता यच्चान्यदिच्छन्न लभते सर्वं तदत्र गत्वा विन्दतेऽत्र ह्यस्यैते सत्याः

कामा अनृतापिधानास्तद्यथापि हिरण्यनिधिं निहितमक्षेत्रज्ञा उपर्युपरि सञ्चरन्तो न विन्देयुरेवमेवेमाः सर्वाः प्रजा अहरहर्गच्छन्त्य एतं ब्रह्मलोकं न विन्दन्त्यनृतेन हि प्रत्यूढाः ॥ २ ॥

Atha ye cāsyeha jīvā ye ca pretā yaccānyadicchanna labhate sarvaṁ tadatra gatvā vindate'tra hyasyaite satyāḥ kāmā anṛtāpidhānāstadyathāpi hiraṇyanidhiṁ nihitamakṣetrajñā uparyupari sañcaranto na vindeyurevamevemāḥ sarvāḥ prajā aharahargacchantya etaṁ brahmalokaṁ na vindantyanṛtena hi pratyūḍhāḥ.

Atha, further; *ye asya jīvāḥ ca,* those of his [i.e., the relatives of one who knows the Self] who are alive; *ye ca pretāḥ,* and those who are dead; *yat ca anyat,* and whatever else; *icchan,* one wishes for; *na labhate,* [but] does not get; *sarvam tat,* all that; *atra,* here; *gatvā,* going; *vindate,* one gets; *atra hi,* for here; *asya,* his; *ete satyāḥ kāmāḥ,* these true desires; *anṛtāpidhānāḥ,* with a false look; *tat yathā,* as; *akṣetrajñāḥ nihitam,* those who have no idea about what is hidden underground; *api hiraṇyanidhim,* though precious as gold; *upari-upari,* again and again; *sañcarantaḥ,* going over it; *na vindeyuḥ,* do not get it; *evam eva,* in this way; *imāḥ sarvāḥ prajāḥ,* all these beings; *ahaḥ ahaḥ,* daily; *gacchantyaḥ,* going; *etam brahmalokam,* to this world of Brahman; *na vindanti,* do not attain it; *hi,* because; *anṛtena,* by falsehood [i.e., ignorance]; *pratyūḍhāḥ,* they are covered.

2. Further, those of his relatives who are still alive and those who are dead, and also those things a person cannot get even if he wishes for them—all these he gets by going within his heart. All true desires of a person are in his heart, though they are hidden. It is like when there is gold hidden someplace underground and people who are ignorant of it walk over that spot again and again, knowing nothing about it. Similarly, all these beings go to Brahmaloka every day, and yet they know nothing about it because they are covered by ignorance.

Inside the heart is the whole universe. When we have *suṣupti,* dreamless sleep, we are then one with Brahman and one with the whole world. We are not conscious of it, however, because of our ignorance.

स वा एष आत्मा हृदि तस्यैतदेव निरुक्तं हृद्ययमिति
तस्माद्धृदयमहरहर्वा एवंवित्स्वर्गं लोकमेति॥ ३ ॥

Sa vā eṣa ātmā hṛdi tasyaitadeva niruktaṁ hṛdyayamiti tasmāddhṛdayamaharaharvā evaṁvitsvargaṁ lokameti.

Saḥ vai eṣaḥ, it is this; *ātmā hṛdi,* the Self in the heart; *tasya etat eva niruktam,* this is the meaning of it; *hṛdi + ayam iti,* 'it is in the heart'; *tasmāt,* therefore; *hṛdayam,* it is [known as] the heart; *evam vit,* one who knows this; *ahaḥ ahaḥ vai,* every day; *svargam lokam eti,* goes to the heavenly world.

3. The Self resides in the heart. The word *hṛdayam* is derived thus: *hrdi* + *ayam*—'it is in the heart.' Therefore the heart is called *hṛdayam.* One who knows thus goes daily to the heavenly world [i.e., in his dreamless sleep he is one with Brahman].

Where is the Self? It is within. Normally when we think of God, we look up in the sky or we go to a temple, thinking he is there. But in reality God is within us, in our own heart. The heart is the place where we experience the Self. It is the seat of Self-realization. So here the Upaniṣad says, for this reason we worship our own heart as Brahman.

Svarga loka normally means the 'heavenly world.' But here it means that we go into our own Self. We become one with the Self.

The word *hṛdayam* means *hṛdi* plus *ayam. Hṛdi* means 'in the heart,' and *ayam* means 'this'—that is, this Self, the Cosmic Self, which is the source of everything, is within the heart.

अथ य एष सम्प्रसादोऽस्माच्छरीरात्समुत्थाय परं ज्योतिरुपसम्पद्य स्वेन रूपेणाभिनिष्पद्यत एष आत्मेति होवाचैतदमृतमभयमेतद्ब्रह्मेति तस्य ह वा एतस्य ब्रह्मणो नाम सत्यमिति ॥ ४ ॥

Atha ya eṣa samprasādo'smāccharīrātsamutthāya paraṁ jyotirupasampadya svena rūpeṇābhiniṣpadyata eṣa ātmeti hovācaitadamṛtamabhayametadbrahmeti tasya ha vā etasya brahmaṇo nāma satyamiti.

Atha, then; *yaḥ eṣaḥ samprasādaḥ,* this [Self] which is the embodiment of happiness [from dreamless sleep]; *asmāt śarīrāt samutthāya,* emerging from the body; *param jyotiḥ upasampadya,* attaining the highest light; *svena rūpeṇa abhiniṣpadyate,* he assumes his real nature; *eṣaḥ ātmā,* this is the Self; *iti ha uvāca,* he [the teacher] said; *etat amṛtam,* this is immortal; *abhayam,* fearless; *etat brahma iti,* this is Brahman; *tasya ha vai etasya brahmaṇaḥ nāma satyam iti,* this Brahman is [also] called 'Truth.'

4. The teacher said: 'Then, this person, who is the embodiment of happiness, emerging from the body and attaining the highest light, assumes his real nature. This is the Self. It is immortal and also fearless. It is Brahman. Another name for Brahman is *satya,* Truth.'

When the self leaves the body during deep sleep, it assumes its real nature. What is that nature? Does it have any form? Not exactly. It attains its real nature as light.

Knowledge is very often associated with light. We sometimes repeat the prayer, *'Tamasaḥ mā jyotiḥ gamaya*—lead us from darkness to light.' That is to say, lead us from the darkness of ignorance to the light of knowledge.

When we are attached to the body, we are always trying to enjoy more and more sense objects. For that reason we are always disturbed and unhappy. There is no peace or calmness in us—no serenity. If you look at an image of Buddha, what do you see? His face is calm and peaceful. If you look at the face of any god or goddess you see that peace and serenity. That serenity is our very nature, but when we are attached to the body we rarely feel it. Sometimes we smile, but that smile often signifies more pain than pleasure. It is superficial. It does not come from within. Indian scriptures remind us again and again that everything is within. Strength, knowledge, joy—it is all within us.

When we know our true nature, we are no longer attached to the body, and it is nothing for us to leave it behind. Once Sarada Devi was in a state of ecstasy and saw herself outside her body. She thought to herself: 'How can I go back to such a body?' For people like her, leaving the body is a matter of choice. They can assume a body or reject it as they like. After a long time she persuaded herself to return to the body.

When you can overcome the delusion that you are the body, you can reject it. You then get back your true nature, as it were. You realize you are free, full of bliss, and enlightened. You are then immortal (*amṛtam*) and fearless (*abhayam*). You have conquered fear. So long as you feel you are the body, you have fear. One day you may fall sick and die—that fear is always haunting you. When you know you are Brahman, however, you know you will never die.

The Upaniṣad says Brahman is named *satya,* Truth. Truth is that which was true in the past, is now true in the present, and will be true in the future. This Self is Truth itself.

तानि ह वा एतानि त्रीण्यक्षराणि सतीयमिति तद्यत्सत्तदमृतमथ यत्ति तन्मर्त्यमथ यद्यं तेनोभे यच्छति यदनेनोभे यच्छति तस्माद्यमहरहर्वा एवंवित्स्वर्गं लोकमेति ॥५॥ इति तृतीयः खण्डः॥३॥

Tāni ha vā etāni trīṇyakṣarāṇi satīyamiti tadyatsattadamṛtamatha yatti tanmartyamatha yadyaṁ tenobhe yacchati yadanenobhe yacchati tasmādyamaharaharvā evaṁvitsvargaṁ lokameti. Iti tṛtīyaḥ khaṇḍaḥ.

Tāni ha vai etāni trīṇi akṣarāṇi, these are the three syllables; *sa tī yam iti,* 'sa', 'tī', and 'yam'; *tat yat sat,* that which is 'sat' [i.e., 'sa']; *tat amṛtam,* that is immortal; *atha,* then; *yat ti,* what is 'ti'; *tat martyam,* that is mortal; *atha,* then; *yat yam,* what is 'yam'; *tena ubhe yacchati,* both are controlled by it; *yat anena ubhe yacchati,* as both are controlled by it [i.e., by 'yam']; *tasmāt,* therefore; *yam,* it is 'yam'; *evamvit,* one who knows thus; *ahaḥ ahaḥ,* daily; *vai svargam lokam eti,* goes to the heavenly world [in deep sleep]. *Iti tṛtīyaḥ khaṇḍaḥ,* here ends the third section.

5. *Sa, tī,* and *yam*—these are the three syllables [which represent Brahman]. *Sa* stands for that which is immortal. *Ti* stands for that which is mortal. And *yam* stands for that which controls both the mortal and the immortal. As both [the mortal and the immortal] are controlled by it, it is called *yam.* The person who knows the significance of these three syllables enjoys divine bliss every day in dreamless sleep.

The Upaniṣad says there are three syllables that make up the word *satyam—sa, tī,* and *yam. Sa* stands for *sat. Sat* is derived from the root *as,* which means 'existence.' It is Existence Absolute, eternal. Here the Upaniṣad says, *sa* is that which is immortal and *ti* is that which is mortal. We have both immortal and mortal aspects to us. At the transcendental level we are immortal, but at the empirical, or phenomenal, level we are mortal. At the transcendental level there is no 'I' or 'you'. There is no duality at all. There is only one.

Where does this universe come from? It comes from that which is immortal. That is to say, the immortal becomes the mortal. The Absolute becomes the relative. The syllable *yam* stands for *saṁyama,* to control. It is the Self that controls both the relative and the Absolute.

Similarly, one who has realized his true nature has control of both the transcendental and the relative. He is always the same, everywhere—whether in the transcendental world, in samādhi, which is here called *sat,* or in the phenomenal world, *ti,* the world that is subject to change. That person is always conscious of his real identity.

Evamvit ahaḥ ahaḥ svargam lokam eti—one who knows this goes every day into heaven. That is to say, when we are in deep sleep we are in *svargaloka,* the world of peace. We are then one with the Self, resting on the Self. It's like a bird resting on its nest. It is happy and safe. But sometimes the bird has to go about after food. Similarly, when we wake up we have to be involved in this empirical world. Then there is diversity—no more unity.

Śaṅkara says that when even the syllables of *satyam,* which is the name of Brahman, are so significant, how great then must be the state that the word signifies. Similarly, even the idea 'I am Brahman' is so inspiring—what to speak of having the experience itself.

Suppose you have been hearing for a long time about Benaras but you have never been there. You have some idea about it and would love to go there. Even the word Benaras excites you. How thrilled you feel then when you at last get there.

From our experience of deep sleep we have some idea of what Brahman is like. We know, even from this brief experience, how wonderful it is to be one with the Self. But when we are firmly established in Brahman and our ignorance is gone, what a wonderful thing it is.

So, as Śaṅkara says, we have to go on meditating that we are one with Brahman, and gradually this meditation will lead us to the experience itself. The experience is what we need. We have to have that. Swami Vivekananda used to say that religion is realization. Suppose we go on talking about Brahman. This may help us and inspire us. It may even give us some impetus, but that's all. We must not stop there. Our goal is the experience.

Section Four

अथ य आत्मा स सेतुर्विधृतिरेषां लोकानामसम्भेदाय नैतं सेतुमहोरात्रे तरतो न जरा न मृत्युर्न शोको न सुकृतं न दुष्कृतं सर्वे पाप्मानोऽतो निवर्तन्तेऽपहतपाप्मा ह्येष ब्रह्मलोकः ॥ १ ॥

Atha ya ātmā sa seturvidhṛtireṣāṁ lokānāmasambhedāya naitaṁ setumahorātre tarato na jarā na mṛtyurna śoko na sukṛtaṁ na duṣkṛtaṁ sarve pāpmāno'to nivartante'pahatapāpmā hyeṣa brahmalokaḥ.

Atha, next; *yaḥ ātmā,* that Self; *saḥ,* it; *setuḥ,* [is like] a dam; *vidhṛtiḥ,* the support; *eṣām lokānām,* of these worlds; *asambhedāya,* for their protection [so that they may remain separate from one another]; *ahorātre,* day and night; *etam setum na tarataḥ,* cannot cross over this dam; *na jarā,* nor old age; *na mṛtyuḥ,* nor death; *na śokaḥ,* nor bereavement; *na sukṛtam,* nor good actions; *na duṣkṛtam,* nor bad actions; *sarve pāpmānaḥ,* all sins; *ataḥ nivartante,* turn away from it; *hi eṣaḥ brahmalokaḥ,* for this world of Brahman; *apahatapāpmā,* has no evil.

1. Next, this Self is like a dam. It supports the worlds and protects them from getting mixed up. Day and night cannot cross over this dam, nor can old age, death, bereavement, good actions, and bad actions. All sins turn away from it, for this Brahmaloka is free from evil.

In this world there are so many varieties of things, and each has its role to play. Human beings have their role to play; animals have theirs, and plants have theirs. The sun rises at a certain time. It never fails. Each thing is in its place, doing what it's supposed to be doing. There should be no mix-up. If there were a mix-up, there would be chaos. Who supervises all this so that everything is in its proper place? It is the Self.

The word *setu* usually means 'bridge,' but here it means a dam. Suppose you have a large river and you want to separate the water for some reason or other. You then erect a dam. This keeps the two sides apart and prevents them from mixing. Similarly, the Upaniṣad says, in this phenomenal world the Self acts as a dam so that everything functions as it should, without getting mixed up. The Self stands as a barrier, keeping each thing in its place. It is never failing. Day and night, sorrow, sin, the castes and stages of life, material things—animate or inanimate—whatever there is in the world of diversity, each plays its own role and cannot deviate from it because of the Self.

It is the Self that creates all the diversity—good, bad, rich, poor, educated, ignorant. There are so many kinds of people and so many kinds of plants, animals, and objects. The Self not only manifests all this diversity—it also maintains it. It does not want the diversity to disappear, because this diversity is necessary for the phenomenal world to go on.

But these divisions do not touch the Self. Nothing can affect it. It is the Master, controlling everything, but it is not controlled by anything. *Mṛtyu* (death), for instance, is so powerful. Everyone is subject to death, but it cannot overcome this dam, the Self. No blemish or impurity can even approach the Self. It is never affected by the good or bad that exists in the world. It is always the same—constant and pure.

The Self is also called here *brahma-loka.* The Self, the ātman, is Brahman. When you look at the world, you say, *'Sarvam khalu idam brahma'*—all this is Brahman. When you look inside, within you, you say, *'Aham brahmāsmi'*—I am Brahman, or *'Ayam ātmā brahma'*—this self is Brahman. It is the same Self, inside and outside.

Śaṅkara says that if you know you are the Self, you are not affected by anything. But how do you realize the Self? Śaṅkara says you realize it by brahmacarya, by continence and self-control.

तस्माद्वा एतं सेतुं तीर्त्वान्धः सन्ननन्धो भवति विद्धः सन्नविद्धो भवत्युपतापी सन्ननुपतापी भवति तस्माद्वा एतं सेतुं तीर्त्वापि नक्तमहरेवाभिनिष्पद्यते सकृद्विभातो ह्येवैष ब्रह्मलोकः ॥ २ ॥

Tasmādvā etaṁ setuṁ tīrtvāndhaḥ sannanandho bhavati viddhaḥ sannaviddho bhavatyupatāpī sannanupatāpī bhavati tasmādvā etaṁ setuṁ tīrtvāpi naktamaharevābhiniṣpadyate sakṛdvibhāto hyevaiṣa brahmalokaḥ.

Tasmāt, this is why; *vai etam setum tīrtvā,* when crossing this dam; *andhaḥ san,* if a person is blind; *anandhaḥ bhavati,* he behaves as if he is not blind; *viddhaḥ san,* if a person is hurt; *aviddhaḥ bhavati,* he behaves as if he is not hurt; *upatāpī san,* if a person is mentally upset; *anupatāpī bhavati,* he behaves as if he is not mentally upset; *tasmāt,* this is why; *vai etam setum tīrtvā,* when crossing this dam; *api naktam,* even night; *ahaḥ eva abhiniṣpadyate,* looks like day; *hi eva eṣaḥ brahmalokaḥ,* for this Brahmaloka; *sakṛt vibhātaḥ,* is always manifest.

2. Therefore, by crossing this dam, if you are blind you do not feel you are blind. Similarly, if you are hurt, you do not feel you are hurt, and if you are mentally upset, you no longer feel the sorrow. This is why if you cross this dam, even night will be like day, for this world of Brahman is always full of light.

Again and again the Upaniṣad stresses knowledge of the Self. Why? This knowledge is necessary for us to live in this world; otherwise we are not safe. We are vulnerable to all the forces of this phenomenal world. These forces may sweep us off our feet. Sri Ramakrishna used to say, 'Tie the knowledge of Advaita in the corner of your cloth and then go wherever you like.' That is, once we know we are the Self, nothing can affect us. We are like that dam, without any change. A person may be a householder or a monk—it doesn't matter. He is safe.

Here, the Upaniṣad says, you may be blind, but you do not feel you are blind. The blindness does not affect you. It affects the body, but you know you are not the body. Similarly, you may have some disease or illness in the body, but you do not feel you are ill. If you are conscious of the body then you will also be conscious of its limitations. Blindness is a limitation, so you will be conscious that you are blind. But the pure Self is not conditioned by anything. If you feel you are the Self you are not subject to the limitations of the body. This applies to the mind also.

Swami Turiyananda would now and then get carbuncles that would have to be removed by surgery. He would not let the doctor give him any anaesthetic, however. He would ask the doctor to give him a few minutes' warning, and he would meditate for a while. Then he would tell the doctor he was ready. The carbuncle might be large and require a long time for the surgery, but Swami Turiyananda would not show any sign of pain. How could he do it? He withdrew his mind from the body. It was as if the doctor was operating on someone else's body.

When Swami Shivananda was old he suffered from asthma. Sometimes he had no sleep at all during the night, but in the morning people would come and find him very cheerful. They would ask him, 'Sir, how are you?' and he would smile and say, 'I am fine.' Then he would say: 'Look, if you are asking about the body, then I will say this body is old and diseased. But by the grace of my Master, I know I am not this body, so I am not affected by it.'

Suppose there is something wrong with the shirt you are wearing. You would not think there is something wrong with you. You know you are independent of the shirt. Similarly, your body is just a covering, as it were. You are independent of your body.

The example the Upaniṣad gives of the dam is very apt. A dam stands supreme. Nothing can affect it. Similarly, if you know your true nature, you will stand firm like a rock even when waves of sorrow come and try to overwhelm you. Disease, poverty, humiliation—all kinds of misfortunes may come, but they will all be forced back without making any impression on you, as if there is a dam that stands between the world and your Self.

The scriptures are constantly reminding us that this is what we are missing. Why else should we care for Self-knowledge? All this is just to encourage us and to invite us to taste the bliss of Self-knowledge.

Lots of people say: 'What do you mean by Self-knowledge? I know who I am. What else should I know?' But do they know they are not the body? Do they know they cannot be affected by old age, disease, or death, or by poverty or misfortune? Most people are slaves of their circumstances. Only one who knows his real Self is free.

Most of our external conditions cannot be changed. They are not under our control. If it is summer it will be hot. Can you change it? No, but you can change yourself. Similarly, with other circumstances in our lives. Our attitude should be: 'Well, I don't care. I will face this problem. It can never affect my real Self.' When you have this attitude, you know you will not be cowed by adversities and external circumstances. This is the message of the Upaniṣads and also of the Gītā. In the Gītā Kṛṣṇa again and again talks about the *sthita-prajña,* the person of steady wisdom, who is firmly rooted in Self-knowledge, and whom nothing can sway.

When Alexander the Great came to India, he met a yogī and was so impressed with him that he wanted to bring him to Greece. Alexander tried in many ways to tempt the yogī to go to Greece, but nothing worked. Then Alexander threatened to kill him. The yogī just laughed and said: 'You have never told such a lie. You cannot kill me. You may kill the body, but I am not the body. I am the Self.'

The Upaniṣad says that when you know the Self, night and day are the same to you. It may appear to be night to others, but for you there is always light. You always have inner light. You always see yourself as Brahman. Śaṅkara says that the word *Brahmaloka* here means the state of Brahman. Whether you are blind or not, whether you are healthy or not, you are always conscious that you are Brahman. Not for a moment do you forget it.

तद्य एवैतं ब्रह्मलोकं ब्रह्मचर्येणानुविन्दन्ति तेषामेवैष ब्रह्मलोकस्तेषां सर्वेषु लोकेषु कामचारो भवति ॥ ३ ॥ इति चतुर्थः खण्डः ॥ ४ ॥

Tadya evaitaṁ brahmalokaṁ brahmacaryeṇānuvindanti teṣāmevaiṣa brahmalokasteṣāṁ sarveṣu lokeṣu kāmacāro bhavati. Iti caturthaḥ khaṇḍaḥ.

Tat ye, those who; *eva etam brahmalokam,* this Brahmaloka; *brahmacaryeṇa,* through the practice of brahmacarya; *anuvindanti,* attain; *teṣām eva,* for such people; *eṣaḥ brahmalokaḥ,* is this Brahmaloka; *teṣām,* for them; *sarveṣu lokeṣu,* to all the worlds; *kāmacāraḥ bhavati,* they can go as they like. *Iti caturthaḥ khaṇḍaḥ,* here ends the fourth section.

3. Those who attain this Brahmaloka through brahmacarya become the masters of Brahmaloka. They can visit all worlds as they like.

There is a wonderful statement in one of the scriptures that says scholars talk about sweets but they never taste them. That is to say, the scholars talk about things they know nothing about. The scholars, it says, get only *takra,* whey. But the yogīs are the ones who taste the *kṣīra,* the thickened, sweet milk. Unless you eat the kṣīra, how do you know what it is like? Similarly, you may talk very well about Brahman. What you say may sound very good. But unless you have the experience of Brahman, you can't understand what it is like.

Here the Upaniṣad says, how do you get this experience? Through brahmacarya, self-control. The word *brahmacarya* means *brahma carati*—that is, one who is always at the level of Brahman. The scriptures say there are two paths open to us—*śreyas,* the good, and *preyas,* the pleasant, the attractive. One who practises brahmacarya will reflect on these two and say: 'I shall not accept that which is merely attractive. I shall only have śreyas, that which is the highest.'

Religion does not come by magic. It comes through self-discipline, and that means a lot of hard work, sweat, and tears. You have to yearn for it and cry for it, saying, 'Oh when am I going to succeed?' Sri Ramakrishna would often have no sleep at night and no food for the whole day. Sometimes someone would have to force food into his mouth in order to get him to eat. He had no body consciousness. Moreover, he would never accept money.

The Upaniṣad says that if you practise brahmacarya you are free and everything is at your disposal. But, like Ramakrishna, your attitude is: 'I don't care for all this. I don't want anything in all these worlds. I want only Brahman.'

Vedānta says, you are free because you feel you are one with everything. Everything is within your grasp. There is no barrier between you and the world outside. Now there is a barrier. We want to see something because we think it is separate from us, outside of us. But when this idea of separation ceases, we feel we are everything.

Section Five

अथ यद्यज्ञ इत्याचक्षते ब्रह्मचर्यमेव तद्ब्रह्मचर्येण ह्येव यो ज्ञाता तं विन्दतेऽथ यदिष्टमित्याचक्षते ब्रह्मचर्यमेव तद्ब्रह्मचर्येण ह्येवेष्ट्वात्मानमनुविन्दते ॥ १ ॥

Atha yadyajña ityācakṣate brahmacaryameva tadbrahmacaryeṇa hyeva yo jñātā taṁ vindate'tha yadiṣṭamityācakṣate brahmacaryameva tadbrahmacaryeṇa hyeveṣṭvātmānamanuvindate.

Atha, then; *yat,* that which; *yajñaḥ iti ācakṣate,* is called 'yajña' [sacrifice]; *tat brahmacaryam eva,* that is brahmacarya; *hi,* because; *yaḥ jñātā,* one who knows this; *brahmacaryeṇa,* through brahmacarya; *tam vindate,* attains that [Brahmaloka]; *atha,* then; *yat iṣṭam iti ācakṣate,* that which is called 'iṣṭa' [worship]; *tat brahmacaryam eva,* that is brahmacarya; *hi,* because; *brahmacaryeṇa eva,* through brahmacarya; *iṣṭvā ātmānam anuvindate,* one attains the desired Self.

1. Then that which is known as *yajña* [sacrifice] is brahmacarya. This is because one who knows the Self attains Brahmaloka through brahmacarya. Again, that which is known as *iṣṭa* [worship] is brahmacarya, for the desired Self is attained through brahmacarya.

Whatever you do with the idea of self-restraint is brahmacarya. Worship is brahmacarya; fasting is brahmacarya; observing silence is brahmacarya. If you retire from the world and go to the forest, that also is brahmacarya. The whole idea is self-restraint. Many people observe silence for a certain length of time. Gandhiji, for instance, would observe absolute silence once a week. Some people may say this is silly, but it's not. Such observances bring strength.

Suppose something has provoked you and you are angry, but through strength of mind you get control of your emotions and you do not retaliate. Similarly, you may feel tempted to do something you shouldn't and you refuse to do it. Or you may see some good food and feel tempted to eat something that is bad for you, but then you restrain yourself. Self-control in any form is brahmacarya. It is brahmacarya because it ultimately leads to Self-realization and union with Brahman.

The Upaniṣad says here that the performance of a sacrifice is also brahmacarya because there are many restrictions imposed on the sacrificer. For instance, he cannot eat until he finishes the worship. The word for sacrifice is *yajña,* which comes from *yaḥ* and *jñaḥ,* 'one who knows'—that is, one who knows the Self.

Another reason why worship is called brahmacarya is that the worship is done to a particular deity (*iṣṭa*), and you must meditate on that deity. That is, you are wishing (*iṣ*) for that deity, or wishing for your union with that deity.

The only way to control the mind is through mental strength. According to Vedānta, strength is not outside. It is within. And self-control is the source of strength. First and foremost is brahmacarya. In fact, it is first and last. It's not that you practise self-control for some time and then you say, 'I don't need to observe this any more.' No, all through we need self-control. Gradually, however, it becomes natural. By constantly observing truthfulness, you find you are incapable of saying what is immoral or wrong.

अथ यत्सत्त्रायणमित्याचक्षते ब्रह्मचर्यमेव तद्ब्रह्मचर्येण ह्येव सत आत्मनस्त्राणं विन्दतेऽथ यन्मौनमित्याचक्षते ब्रह्मचर्यमेव तद्ब्रह्मचर्येण ह्येवात्मानमनुविद्य मनुते॥ २॥

Atha yatsattrāyaṇamityācakṣate brahmacaryameva tadbrahmacaryeṇa hyeva sata ātmanastrāṇaṁ vindate-'tha yanmaunamityācakṣate brahmacaryameva tadbrahmacaryeṇa hyevātmānamanuvidya manute.

Atha, then; *yat sattrāyaṇam iti ācakṣate,* that which is called a 'Sattrāyaṇa' [a long sacrifice]; *tat brahmacaryam eva,* that is brahmacarya; *hi,* for; *brahmacaryeṇa eva,* through brahmacarya; *sataḥ,* from Sat [i.e., the Cosmic Self]; *ātmanaḥ trāṇam vindate,* the individual self attains its liberation [union with the Cosmic Self]; *atha,* then; *yat maunam iti ācakṣate,* that which is called 'mauna' [silence]; *tat brahmacaryam eva,* that is brahmacarya; *hi,* for; *ātmānam anuvidya,* knowing the Self; *brahmacaryeṇa eva,* through brahmacarya; *manute,* one remains absorbed in thinking.

2. Then, that which is known as 'Sattrāyaṇa' [a sacrifice lasting a long time] is brahmacarya, for it is through brahmacarya that the individual self gets liberated [attains union with the Cosmic Self]. Then, that which is called 'mauna' [silence] is brahmacarya, for through brahmacarya one realizes the Self, and having realized the Self one remains absorbed in the thought of it.

There is a particular sacrifice called *Sattrāyaṇa,* which involves the services of many priests. It is a big affair. The Upaniṣad says it is considered brahmacarya to perform this Sattrāyaṇa sacrifice because through Existence (*sat*) a person gets protection (*trāṇa*) for oneself (*ātmana*). You always feel you are protected by Sat, so you are sure of yourself. In the same way, when you are practising brahmacarya, you know nothing is going to sway you from the vow you have taken.

As the Gītā says, the self is your own friend and it is also your own enemy. By practising brahmacarya you will gradually become stronger, and as you grow stronger you become fearless. A friend or relation who is supposed to be protecting you may fail you, but if you are protecting yourself you are safe.

Mauna, a vow of silence, is also a form of brahmacarya. We all know that when we are doing something serious we like to be quiet. We don't like to talk much, nor do we like our mind to be restless. We want to be able to fix our mind on what we are doing. Similarly, brahmacarya means that our mind is fixed on Brahman. We are in touch with Brahman, always reminding ourselves that we are not this body and not this mind. We are the Self. We are Brahman. So taking a vow of silence (*mauna*) means that a person contemplates, or meditates, (*manute*) on his identity with Brahman.

Śaṅkara says that this meditation on Brahman comes after seeking the help of the scriptures and the teacher. Both are necessary. The scriptures give you guidelines, but the teacher takes you by the hand and leads you to the goal.

अथ यदनाशकायनमित्याचक्षते ब्रह्मचर्यमेव तदेष ह्यात्मा न नश्यति यं ब्रह्मचर्येणानुविन्दतेऽथ यदरण्याय-नमित्याचक्षते ब्रह्मचर्यमेव तत्तदरश्च ह वै ण्यश्चार्णवौ ब्रह्मलोके तृतीयस्यामितो दिवि तदैरम्मदीयं सरस्त-दश्वत्थः सोमसवनस्तदपराजिता पूर्ब्रह्मणः प्रभुविमितं हिरण्मयम् ॥ ३ ॥

Atha yadanāśakāyanamityācakṣate brahmacaryameva tadeṣa hyātmā na naśyati yaṁ brahmacaryeṇānuvindate-'tha yadaraṇyāyanamityācakṣate brahmacaryameva tat-tadaraśca ha vai ṇyaścārṇavau brahmaloke tṛtīyasyāmito divi tadairammadīyaṁ sarastadaśvatthaḥ somasavanas-tadaparājitā pūrbrahmaṇaḥ prabhuvimitaṁ hiraṇmayam.

Atha, next; *yat anāśakāyanam iti ācakṣate,* that which is called 'anāśakāyana' [i.e., *anāśaka* + *ayana,* the path of fasting]; *tat brahmacaryam eva,* that is brahmacarya; *hi,* for; *eṣaḥ ātmā,* this Self; *yam brahmacaryeṇa anuvindate,* which one attains through brahmacarya; *na naśyati,* never perishes; *atha,* then; *yat araṇyāyanam iti ācakṣate,* that which is called 'araṇyāyana' [i.e., *araṇya* + *ayana,* life in the forest]; *tat brahmacaryam eva,* that is brahmacarya; *tat,* there; *araḥ ca ha vai ṇyaḥ ca,* Ara and Ṇya; *arṇavau,* are the two oceans; *brahmaloke,* in Brahmaloka; *tṛtīyasyām itaḥ divi,* in the third heaven from here [i.e., from the earth]; *tat,* [and] there; *airammadīyam saraḥ,* is a lake called 'Airammadīya'; *tat aśvatthaḥ,* [and] there is a peepal tree; *somasavanaḥ,* which exudes soma juice; *tat aparājitā pūḥ,* [and] there is the city Aparājitā [the 'Invincible']; *brahmaṇaḥ,* belonging to Brahmā; *prabhu-vimitam,* built specially by the Lord; *hiraṇmayam,* [a canopy] made of gold.

3. Then, that which is known as 'anāśakāyana' [the path of fasting] is brahmacarya, for through brahmacarya one attains the Self which is immortal. Then, that which is called 'araṇyāyana' [life in the forest] is brahmacarya. This is because in Brahmaloka, which

is the third world from the earth, there are two oceans called Ara and Ṇya. There also one finds a lake called Airammadīya [so-called because its waters are intoxicating], a peepal tree always exuding soma juice, a city called Aparājitā [the Invincible] belonging to Brahmā, and a canopy of gold specially made by the Lord.

When you practise brahmacarya, you are always moving on the plane of the Self. Fasting (*anāśakāyana*) is also called brahmacarya, because when you fast you attain (*ayana*) the Self that is protected (*anāśaka*).

So also, if you retire to the forest, that is brahmacarya. You say, 'I've had enough of this drama of life,' so you go and live in the forest to meditate on Brahman.

Then finally, by practising continence and self-control, you become transformed and you enter the realm of Brahman. In that world there is a vast lake which is filled with a sweet drink. When you taste that drink you are exhilarated. There is also a banyan tree from which streams of nectar flow. You are now in a world which is not meant for the weak. Only those with strong will-power, who have practised continence and self-control over the years, can enter this world. It is the world of bliss.

The Upaniṣad says this is the third world. The first world is this earth, the second is the intermediate region, and the third is this heaven. You are close to Brahman here, and you are happy and enjoy yourself.

तद्य एवैतावरं च ण्यं चार्णवौ ब्रह्मलोके ब्रह्मचर्येणानुविन्दन्ति तेषामेवैष ब्रह्मलोकस्तेषां सर्वेषु लोकेषु कामचारो भवति ॥ ४ ॥ इति पञ्चमः खण्डः ॥ ५ ॥

Tadya evaitāvaraṁ ca ṇyaṁ cārṇavau brahmaloke brahmacaryeṇānuvindanti teṣāmevaiṣa brahmalokas-teṣāṁ sarveṣu lokeṣu kāmacāro bhavati. Iti pañcamaḥ khaṇḍaḥ.

Tat ye, those who; *etau arṇavau,* these two oceans; *aram ca ṇyam ca,* Ara and Ṇya; *brahmaloke,* in Brahmaloka; *anuvindanti,* attain; *brahmacaryeṇa,* through brahmacarya; *teṣām eva,* for them; *eṣaḥ brahmalokaḥ,* is this Brahmaloka; *sarveṣu lokeṣu,* in all the worlds; *teṣām kāmacāraḥ bhavati,* they can go freely. *Iti pañcamaḥ khaṇḍaḥ,* here ends the fifth section.

4. When they attain through brahmacarya the two oceans, Ara and Ṇya, in Brahmaloka, that Brahmaloka is theirs, and they can then move freely in all the worlds.

Brahmaloka is not a physical region like this earth. It is a state of being. It is next to liberation. You are almost free there, but not quite.

Vedānta says there are four states. The first and the highest is when a person merges immediately into Brahman at the time of death. The next state is Brahmaloka. After that is Svargaloka, heaven. This is where people who have done good things go after death. They are very happy there, but they must eventually come back to earth.

The majority of people, however, fall into the fourth category. After death they must immediately come back to this world. They have desires, and in order to fulfil their desires they must have a body.

Section Six

अथ या एता हृदयस्य नाड्यस्ताः पिङ्गल-
स्याणिम्नस्तिष्ठन्ति शुक्लस्य नीलस्य पीतस्य लोहितस्येत्यसौ
वा आदित्यः पिङ्गल एष शुक्ल एष नील एष पीत
एष लोहितः ॥ १ ॥

Atha yā etā hṛdayasya nāḍyastāḥ piṅgalasyāṇimnas-tiṣṭhanti śuklasya nīlasya pītasya lohitasyetyasau vā ādityaḥ piṅgala eṣa śukla eṣa nīla eṣa pīta eṣa lohitaḥ.

Atha, then; *yaḥ etāḥ hṛdayasya nāḍyaḥ,* these veins which are in the heart; *tāḥ,* they; *piṅgalasya aṇimnaḥ tiṣṭhanti,* are filled with a very thin, tawny-coloured liquid; *śuklasya,* of white; *nīlasya,* of blue; *pītasya,* of yellow; *lohitasya iti,* of red; *asau vai ādityaḥ,* the sun there; *piṅgalaḥ,* is tawny; *eṣaḥ śuklaḥ,* it is white; *eṣaḥ nīlaḥ,* it is blue; *eṣaḥ pītaḥ,* it is yellow; *eṣaḥ lohitaḥ,* it is red.

1. Then these veins connected with the heart are each filled with a thin liquid, coloured reddish-yellow, white, blue, yellow, and red. The sun there also has these colours—reddish-yellow, white, blue, yellow, and red.

The heart is the place where one meditates on Brahman. The heart is said to be shaped like a lotus bud, and it also has some similarities to the sun. The sun emits its rays, which spread out in all directions. Similarly, the veins arise from the heart and spread out in all directions. These veins are filled with a very thin substance. This substance changes its colour, and along with it, the veins also change colour. Sometimes it is reddish-yellow, sometimes blue, sometimes white, etc. The sun changes its colour likewise.

तद्यथा महापथ आतत उभौ ग्रामौ गच्छतीमं चामुं चैवमेवैता आदित्यस्य रश्मय उभौ लोकौ गच्छन्तीमं चामुं चामुष्मादादित्यात्प्रतायन्ते ता आसु नाडीषु सृप्ता आभ्यो नाडीभ्यः प्रतायन्ते तेऽमुष्मिन्नादित्ये सृप्ताः ॥ २ ॥

Tadyathā mahāpatha ātata ubhau grāmau gacchatīmaṁ cāmuṁ caivamevaitā ādityasya raśmaya ubhau lokau gacchantīmaṁ cāmuṁ cāmuṣmādādityātpratāyante tā āsu nāḍīṣu sṛptā ābhyo nāḍībhyaḥ pratāyante te'muṣminnāditye sṛptāḥ.

Tat yathā, just as; *ātataḥ mahāpathaḥ,* a long and broad road; *ubhau grāmau gacchati,* connects two villages; *imam ca amum ca,* this one with that; *evam eva,* like that; *etāḥ ādityasya raśmayaḥ,* these rays [which are blue, yellow, etc.] of the sun; *ubhau lokau gacchanti,* connect two worlds; *imam ca amum ca,* this [the human body] with that [the sun]; *tāḥ,* these [rays]; *amuṣmāt ādityāt,* from the solar region; *pratāyante,* emerge; *āsu nāḍīṣu,* into these veins; *sṛptāḥ,* enter; *te,* these [rays]; *ābhyaḥ nāḍībhyaḥ pratāyante,* emerge from the veins; *te amuṣmin āditye sṛptāḥ,* [and] they go back into the solar region.

2. Just as a big, broad road connects one village with another one which is far-off, in the same way, the rays emerge from the sun and reach out to a person, connecting one with the other. After entering the veins of that person, they emerge from them and then go back into the sun.

How are the rays of the sun related to the veins of a human body? The Upaniṣad compares the rays to a big, wide road connecting two villages far away from each other. The rays of the sun go out and enter the veins of a human body, and then they return to the sun.

तद्यत्रैतत्सुप्तः समस्तः सम्प्रसन्नः स्वप्नं न विजानात्यासु तदा नाडीषु सृप्तो भवति तं न कश्चन पाप्मा स्पृशति तेजसा हि तदा सम्पन्नो भवति ॥ ३ ॥

Tadyatraitatsuptaḥ samastaḥ samprasannaḥ svapnaṁ na vijānātyāsu tadā nāḍīṣu sṛpto bhavati taṁ na kaścana pāpmā spṛśati tejasā hi tadā sampanno bhavati.

Tat yatra; then when; *etat suptaḥ,* a person is sleeping; *samastaḥ,* with all the organs quiet; *samprasannaḥ,* free from worry; *svapnam na vijānāti,* has no dreams; *tadā,* then; *āsu nāḍīṣu,* into the [blue, yellow, etc.] veins; *sṛptaḥ bhavati,* he enters; *tam,* him; *na kaścana pāpmā spṛśati,* no sin whatever can touch; *hi tadā,* for then; *tejasā sampannaḥ bhavati,* he is surrounded by the rays of the sun.

3. When a person is sound asleep, all his organs are inactive and quiet. He is free from all worries, and he does not have any dreams. The organs then disappear into the veins. No sin can affect him then, for the rays of the sun have surrounded him.

There are two kinds of sleep: one kind in which you have dreams, and another in which you have no dreams. The latter is called *suṣupti.*

In suṣupti all your organs merge within you, and this means you have no contact whatsoever with the world outside. The energy of the sun fills your veins, and your sense organs then remain inactive. As a result, there is no way anything good or bad can touch you or contaminate you. You are therefore in your true state—free and pure.

अथ यत्रैतदबलिमानं नीतो भवति तमभित आसीना आहुर्जानासि मां जानासि मामिति स यावदस्माच्छरीरा-दनुत्क्रान्तो भवति तावज्जानाति ॥ ४ ॥

Atha yatraitadabalimānaṁ nīto bhavati tamabhita āsīnā āhurjānāsi māṁ jānāsi māmiti sa yāvadasmāc-charīrādanutkrānto bhavati tāvajjānāti.

Atha, then; *yatra,* when; *etat,* a person; *abalimānam,* weakness; *nītaḥ bhavati,* is reduced to; *tam abhitaḥ,* around him; *āsīnāḥ,* those sitting; *āhuḥ,* say; *jānāsi mām jānāsi mām iti,* do you know me, do you know me; *saḥ,* he; *yāvat,* as long as; *asmāt śarīrāt,* from this body; *anutkrāntaḥ bhavati,* does not leave; *tāvat jānāti,* that long he knows [them].

4. Then when a person becomes weak, his relations sit around him and keep asking: 'Do you know me? Do you know me?' As long as he has not left the body, he is able to recognize them.

When a person is dying, he is surrounded by his relatives and friends, and they keep asking him: 'Do you know me? Do you recognize us?' As long as there is life left in his body he can recognize them. But when he has left the body, he cannot answer, because the body cannot speak without him.

अथ यत्रैतदस्माच्छरीरादुत्क्रामत्यथैतैरेव रश्मिभि-रूर्ध्वमाक्रमते स ओमिति वा होद्वा मीयते स यावत्क्षिप्येन्मनस्तावदादित्यं गच्छत्येतद्वै खलु लोकद्वारं विदुषां प्रपदनं निरोधोऽविदुषाम्॥ ५॥

Atha yatraitadasmāccharīrādutkrāmatyathaitaireva raśmibhirūrdhvamākramate sa omiti vā hodvā mīyate sa yāvatkṣipyenmanastāvadādityaṁ gacchatyetadvai khalu lokadvāraṁ viduṣāṁ prapadanaṁ nirodho'viduṣām.

Atha, then; *yatra,* when; *etat,* this [person]; *asmāt śarīrāt,* from this body; *utkrāmati,* leaves; *atha,* then; *etaiḥ eva raśmibhiḥ,* by these rays; *ūrdhvam ākramate,* is carried upward; *saḥ,* he; *om iti,* by meditating on Om; *vā ha ut mīyate,* he surely goes up; *vā,* or [i.e., otherwise not]; *yāvat,* in the time that; *manaḥ kṣipyet,* the mind moves; *tāvat,* in that time; *saḥ ādityam gacchati,* he goes to the realm of the sun; *etat vai,* that [sun]; *lokadvāram khalu,* is the gateway [to the world of Brahman]; *viduṣām prapadanam,* for those who know [this Om] it is the entrance; *nirodhaḥ aviduṣām,* for the ignorant, entry is barred.

5. Then when a person leaves the body, he goes upward with the help of these rays. If he dies while meditating on Om, his going up is assured; otherwise not. In the amount of time it takes his mind to move from one thought to another he can reach the realm of the sun. The sun is the gateway to

Brahmaloka. Those who know the meaning of Om and think of it at the time of death enter Brahmaloka, but those who are ignorant of it have no chance of entering.

What happens to a person when he dies? If he is a good person and has been meditating on Om, at the time of death he will try to meditate on Om in the heart. In Hinduism, it is the practice for religious people to die thinking of God. Here the Upaniṣad suggests meditation on Om.

Then when the dying person leaves the body, he quickly goes through the sun rays to the realm of the sun. How quickly? As quick as the mind can move. Suppose we think of someone who lives very close to us. Then we think of someone in England, or somewhere else far away. That is how fast the mind can move. Similarly, that is how fast it takes for a person to reach the sun.

The Upaniṣad says that the sun is the door to Brahmaloka. If you have meditated on your oneness with Om, then you go through this door to Brahmaloka. But what if a person is not religious and does not think of God or Om at the time of death? Then that door is closed for him. He cannot enter within.

Vedānta says, you are the architect of your own fate. A good person will have a good world to go to. And if he knows his true nature, he will go right to Brahmaloka. But those who still have desires are not free. They must stay in lower regions to wait for their rebirth.

तदेष श्लोकः। शतं चैका च हृदयस्य नाड्यस्तासां मूर्धानमभिनिःसृतैका। तयोर्ध्वमायन्नमृतत्वमेति विष्वङ्ङन्या उत्क्रमणे भवन्त्युत्क्रमणे भवन्ति॥ ६॥ इति षष्ठः खण्डः॥ ६॥

Tadeṣa ślokaḥ; Śataṁ caikā ca hṛdayasya nāḍyastāsāṁ mūrdhānamabhiniḥsṛtaikā; Tayordhvamāyannamṛtatvameti viṣvaṅṅanyā utkramaṇe bhavantyutkramaṇe bhavanti. Iti ṣaṣṭhaḥ khaṇḍaḥ.

Tat eṣaḥ ślokaḥ, there is a verse about this; *śatam ca ekā ca,* one hundred and one; *hṛdayasya nāḍyaḥ,* arteries of the heart; *tāsām ekā,* one of them; *mūrdhānam abhiniḥsṛtā,* extends to the top of the head; *tayā,* by that [artery]; *urdhvam āyan,* going up; *amṛtatvam eti,* one attains immortality; *anyāḥ,* as regards the others; *viṣvan utkramaṇe bhavanti utkramaṇe bhavanti,* they cause one to depart from the body in different directions, they cause one to depart. *Iti ṣaṣṭhaḥ khaṇḍaḥ,* here ends the sixth section.

6. There is a verse about this: There are a hundred and one arteries connected with the heart. One of them goes up to the top of the head. A person who goes up following this artery attains immortality. The other arteries go in different directions and cause one to depart from the body in other ways.

The Upaniṣad says, there are a hundred and one arteries, and one of these goes up to the crown of the head. That is the *sūrya nāḍī,* the passage to the sun, described in the previous verse. It goes from the heart to the top of the head. Those who depart from the body through this passage attain immortality—that is, liberation.

But what happens to other people? Those who depart through other passages must be reborn. They may be reborn as a human being, or they may be reborn as an animal, or even as an insect. But please note: It is the same Self that is a human being, an animal, and an insect. From an amoeba to the state of Brahman, it is the same Consciousness.

You may start as an amoeba, never mind. If you are Brahman, you are always Brahman, whether you have a good body or not. You may not know you are Brahman. But that does not change the fact that you are Brahman. You may think you are just an amoeba, because you identify yourself with an amoeba body. Similarly, you may think you are a dog because you have a dog body. Or you may think you are a human being because you are in a human body. But this is all ignorance. Your goal is to realize yourself as Brahman, and, no matter what kind of body you have now, some day you will reach that goal.

Section Seven

य आत्मापहतपाप्मा विजरो विमृत्युर्विशोको विजि-
घत्सोऽपिपासः सत्यकामः सत्यसङ्कल्पः सोऽन्वेष्टव्यः स
विजिज्ञासितव्यः स सर्वांश्च लोकानाप्नोति सर्वांश्च
कामान्यस्तमात्मानमनुविद्य विजानातीति ह प्रजापति-
रुवाच ॥ १ ॥

Ya ātmāpahatapāpmā vijaro vimṛtyurviśoko vijighatso'pipāsaḥ satyakāmaḥ satyasaṅkalpaḥ so'nveṣṭavyaḥ sa vijijñāsitavyaḥ sa sarvāṁśca lokānāpnoti sarvāṁśca kāmānyastamātmānamanuvidya vijānātīti ha prajāpatiruvāca.

Yaḥ ātmā apahatapāpmā, the Self is free from sin; *vijaraḥ,* free from the effects of age; *vimṛtyuḥ,* free from death; *viśokaḥ,* free from sorrow; *vijighatsaḥ,* free from hunger; *apipāsaḥ,* free from thirst; *satyakāmaḥ,* is the cause of desire for Truth; *satyasaṅkalpaḥ,* is the cause of commitment to Truth; *saḥ,* that; *anveṣṭavyaḥ,* has to be sought; *saḥ vijijñāsitavyaḥ,* that has to be thoroughly investigated; *saḥ,* a person; *sarvān ca lokān āpnoti,* attains all worlds; *sarvān ca kāmān,* and all desires; *yaḥ,* who; *tam ātmānam,* that Self; *anuvidya,* having learned; *vijānāti,* [and] knows it; *prajāpatiḥ iti ha uvāca,* Prajāpati once said.

1. Prajāpati once said: 'The Self is free from sin, free from old age, free from death, free from sorrow, and free from hunger and thirst. It is the cause of desire for Truth and for commitment to Truth. This Self has to be sought for and thoroughly known. The person who has sought for and known the Self attains all worlds and all desires.'

Again and again the Upaniṣads glorify Self-knowledge, but what is the nature of the Self, and how do we attain that knowledge? Here the Upaniṣad begins a story to answer this. Once Prajāpati, the creator, decided to teach people about the Self. He described the Self as *apahata-pāpmā,* free from sins, or blemishes (*pāpa*)—that is to say, it is pure. *Vijara*—it never ages, or decays. *Vimṛtyu*—it is free from death.

The body, of course, is subject to decay and it perishes. When you look at an old person you can tell at once that the body has decayed. It has become weak, and there are wrinkles and grey hair, and so on. Then gradually it must perish. That which has birth also has death. No matter when the body was born, it will eventually begin to fall apart and die. But the Self will never die.

Then Prajāpati says, the Self is *viśoka,* without sorrow, *vijighatsa,* not subject to hunger, and *apipāsa,* not subject to thirst. Besides this, the Self is *satyakāma* and *satyasaṅkalpa*—seeking the Truth and always rooted in Truth. That is to say, it is Truth itself. It is always one with Truth, so it can never deviate from Truth.

Saḥ anveṣṭavyaḥ—that has to be known. This is the purpose of life. Sri Ramakrishna used to say, 'To realize God is the goal of life.' The goal is not money, not power, not scholarship. It is nothing but God. *Saḥ vijijñāsitavyaḥ*—it has to be enquired about. You cannot sit back and wait for it to reveal itself to you. You must go and find someone to teach you about it. And when you have found a capable teacher, you must fall at his feet and beg him to teach you. Then you must ask again and again until your doubts are removed: 'Is it like this? Is it like that?' But you must go to someone who knows the Self. Can a blind man lead another blind man? If the teacher does not know the Self, how will you learn?

When you fulfil these conditions, what happens? You get everything you want. You become supreme. The Upaniṣad says, you conquer the whole universe. How? Because you realize you are the Self. And that Self is the Self of all that exists. You are everything. In this way too, all your desires are fulfilled.

Self-knowledge gives you the highest. You may have everything else—friends, relatives, great political power, money, scholarship, a high social standing—but if you do not have Self-knowledge, everything is useless.

Prajāpati has declared: 'This is the nature of the Self. And if you know the Self, you attain everything.' He has sent out an invitation, as it were: 'Come and learn from me.' Here, in order to teach the nature of the Self, and also to emphasize the need for self-discipline to attain Self-knowledge, the Upaniṣad introduces this story of Indra and Virocana coming to Prajāpati for knowledge of the Self.

तद्धोभये देवासुरा अनुबुबुधिरे ते होचुर्हन्त तमात्मानमन्विच्छामो यमात्मानमन्विष्य सर्वांश्च लोकानाप्नोति सर्वांश्च कामानितीन्द्रो हैव देवानामभिप्रवव्राज विरोचनोऽसुराणां तौ हासंविदानावेव समित्पाणी प्रजापतिसकाशमाजग्मतुः ॥ २ ॥

Taddhobhaye devāsurā anububudhire te hocurhanta tamātmānamanvicchāmo yamātmānamanviṣya sarvāṁś-ca lokānāpnoti sarvāṁśca kāmānitīndro haiva devā-nāmabhipravavrāja virocano'surāṇāṁ tau hāsaṁvidā-nāveva samitpāṇī prajāpatisakāśamājagmatuḥ.

Tat ha, that [what Prajāpati had said]; *ubhaye deva-asurāḥ,* both the gods and the demons; *anububu-dhire,* learned from what other people said; *te ha ucuḥ,* they said [among themselves]; *hanta tam ātmānam anvicchāmaḥ,* so let us search for the Self; *yam ātmānam,* that Self; *anviṣya,* by seeking; *sarvān ca lokān āpnoti,* a person attains all worlds; *sarvān ca kāmān iti,* and all desires; *indraḥ,* Indra; *ha eva devānām,* among all the gods; *abhipravrāja,* went [to Prajāpati]; *virocanaḥ asurānām,* [and] Virocana from among the asuras; *tau,* those two; *ha asaṁvidānau,* without letting each other know; *eva samitpāṇī,* with fuel in hand; *prajāpati-sakāśam,* to Prajāpati; *ājagma-tuḥ,* went.

2. Both the gods and the demons came to know from people what Prajāpati had said. They said, 'We shall search for that Self, by knowing which we can attain all the worlds and whatever things we desire.' With this object in view, Indra among the gods and Virocana among the demons went to Prajāpati, carrying fuel in their hands. But they did not let each other know their plans.

Indra is the chief of the gods and goddesses, and Virocana is the chief of the demons. Though Prajāpati is the grandparent of both of them, they are adversaries. Both Indra and Virocana heard from people what Prajāpati had said about the Self, and they were curious. They each decided to go to Prajāpati for instructions. As they often fought with one another, they never let each other know what they were doing. Everything was secret and confidential. But by chance both Indra and Virocana came to Prajāpati at the same time.

How did they go? Śaṅkara says they went with great humility. Both of them were rulers, yet they put aside their royal robes and regalia, and wore the simplest clothes. They also came *samitpāṇī,* 'with fuel in hand,' as an offering and as a sign of humility. Why? To show that they knew this knowledge to be superior even to rulership of the three worlds.

In the Kaṭha Upaniṣad, Yama told Naciketā he would give him anything he wanted instead of Naciketā's request for knowledge of the Self. Naciketā could have been ruler of the three worlds if he wanted, but he refused. He knew that Self-knowledge was greater.

तौ ह द्वात्रिंशतं वर्षाणि ब्रह्मचर्यमूषतुस्तौ ह प्रजापतिरुवाच किमिच्छन्तावववास्तमिति तौ होचतुर्य आत्मापहतपाप्मा विजरो विमृत्युर्विशोको विजिघत्सोऽपिपासः सत्यकामः सत्यसङ्कल्पः सोऽन्वेष्टव्यः स विजिज्ञासितव्यः स सर्वांश्च लोकानाप्नोति सर्वांश्च कामान्यस्तमात्मानमनुविद्य विजानातीति भगवतो वचो वेदयन्ते तमिच्छन्तावववास्तमिति ॥ ३ ॥

Tau ha dvātriṁśataṁ varṣāṇi brahmacaryamūṣatustau ha prajāpatiruvāca kimicchantāvavāstamiti tau hocaturya ātmāpahatapāpmā vijaro vimṛtyurviśoko vijighatso'pipāsaḥ satyakāmaḥ satyasaṅkalpaḥ so'nveṣṭavyaḥ sa vijijñāsitavyaḥ sa sarvāṁśca lokānāpnoti sarvāṁśca kāmānyastamātmānamanuvidya vijānātīti bhagavato vaco vedayante tamicchantāvavāstamiti.

Tau, those two; *ha dvātriṁśatam varṣāṇi,* for thirty-two years; *brahmacaryam ūṣatuḥ,* lived there practising strict self-control; *tau ha prajāpatiḥ uvāca,* Prajāpati said to them; *kim icchantau avāstam iti,* for what purpose have you stayed here; *tau ha ucatuḥ,* they said; *yaḥ ātmā apahatapāpmā,* the Self is free from sin; *vijaraḥ,* free from the effects of age; *vimṛtyuḥ,* free from death; *viśokaḥ,* free from sorrow; *vijighatsaḥ,* free from hunger; *apipāsaḥ,* free from thirst; *satyakāmaḥ,* is the cause of desire for Truth; *satyasaṅkalpaḥ,* is the cause of commitment to Truth; *saḥ,* that; *anveṣṭavyaḥ,* has to be sought; *saḥ vijijñāsitavyaḥ,* that has to be thoroughly investigated; *saḥ,* a person; *sarvān ca lokān āpnoti,* attains all worlds; *sarvān ca kāmān,* and all desires; *yaḥ,* who; *tam ātmānam,* that Self; *anuvidya,* having learned; *vijānāti iti,* [and] knows it; *bhagavataḥ,* sir; *vacaḥ vedayante,* this is your message; *tam icchantau,* wishing for that [knowledge of the Self]; *avāstam iti,* we have lived here.

3. Both of them spent thirty-two years there living as brahmacarins. One day Prajāpati said to them: 'For what purpose are you staying here?' They replied: '"The Self is free from sin, free from old age, free from death, free from sorrow, and free from hunger and thirst. It is the cause of desire for Truth and for commitment to Truth. This Self has to be sought for and thoroughly known. The person who has learned about the Self and known it attains all worlds and all desires."—Sir, this is your message. We wish to know that Self, and this is why we are here.'

Indra and Virocana heard that Prajāpati had said the Self was pure, undecaying, without death, and so on, and they decided to go and learn from him. But a student must first go through some disciplines and prepare himself to receive these instructions. So for thirty-two years they practised brahmacarya, living with Prajāpati. They served him with humility, forgetting all about their status as kings. And all that time, Prajāpati took no notice of them.

After thirty-two years, Prajāpati one day sent for them and asked: 'Why are you here? What do you want from me?' Indra and Virocana replied: 'We heard from people that you said the Self is without decay, without death, and without sorrow. We want to know that Self. This is why we have come to you. We have been living here the past thirty-two years because we want to know the Self.'

Śaṅkara says that previously Indra and Virocana were hostile to each other. But now they are humble and no longer jealous, and they have even become friendly. Why has their nature changed? Because they have practised brahmacarya, self-control.

Brahmacarya means *brahma carati,* one who moves around Brahman—that is, one who is always thinking of Brahman and trying to feel that he is Brahman. His whole life is centred around Brahman. Such a person lives a simple and austere life—with simple food, simple clothes, and so on. And he always practises self-restraint in everything he does. In Hinduism, self-restraint is the key to everything. If you want to achieve anything, even in secular life, you have to practise self-restraint.

तौ ह प्रजापतिरुवाच य एषोऽक्षिणि पुरुषो दृश्यत एष आत्मेति होवाचैतदमृतमभयमेतद्ब्रह्मेत्यथ योऽयं

भगवोऽप्सु परिख्यायते यश्चायमादर्शे कतम एष इत्येष
उ एवैषु सर्वेष्वन्तेषु परिख्यायत इति होवाच ॥ ४ ॥
इति सप्तमः खण्डः ॥ ७ ॥

Tau ha prajāpatiruvāca ya eṣo'kṣiṇi puruṣo dṛśyata eṣa ātmeti hovācaitadamṛtamabhayametadbrahmetyatha yo'yaṁ bhagavo'psu parikhyāyate yaścāyamādarśe katama eṣa ityeṣa u evaiṣu sarveṣvanteṣu parikhyāyata iti hovāca. Iti saptamaḥ khaṇḍaḥ.

Tau, to those two; *prajāpatiḥ ha uvāca,* Prajāpati said; *yaḥ eṣaḥ puruṣaḥ,* that person which; *akṣiṇi dṛśyate,* is seen in the eye; *eṣaḥ ātmā iti,* that is the Self; *ha uvāca,* [then] he said; *etat amṛtam,* that is immortal; *abhayam,* [and] fearless; *etat brahma iti,* that is Brahman; *atha,* then [they asked]; *bhagavaḥ,* Lord; *yaḥ ayam apsu parikhyāyate,* that which is seen in water; *yaḥ ca ayam ādarśe,* and that which is in a mirror; *katamaḥ eṣaḥ iti,* which is it; *eṣaḥ,* this [Self]; *u eva eṣu parikhyāyate,* is that which is seen; *sarveṣu anteṣu,* in all these; *iti ha uvāca,* he said. *Iti saptamaḥ khaṇḍaḥ,* here ends the seventh section.

4. Prajāpati said to those two, 'That which is seen in the eyes is the Self.' He also said: 'This Self is immortal and fearless. It is Brahman.' Then they asked: 'Lord, we see something when we look in water and again when we look in a mirror. Which

is it?' Prajāpati replied, 'The Self is seen in all these.'

According to Hindu philosophy, Supreme Knowledge is not meant for people whose minds are not pure. Though Indra and Virocana had been with Prajāpati for thirty-two years and they had made some progress towards purity, their minds were not yet pure enough to receive Self-knowledge. So Prajāpati's first instruction was neither here nor there. It didn't help them much.

To begin with, Prajāpati said the Self is in the eyes. We all know that if we stand in front of someone, we can see our own reflection on that person's eyes, and this is what Indra and Virocana thought Prajāpati meant. They said: 'We see a similar reflection when we look in water or in a mirror. We see ourselves reflected there. Which of these is the Self?' Prajāpati answered, 'The Self is in all these.'

Here Śaṅkara raises the question: What did he mean by this? Was he misleading them? No, he was not misleading them, because it is true the Self is everywhere and in everything. But a person has to search. They could take his statement literally, but that would be a mistake. He wanted them to ask questions and use their judgement. He knew they would not understand, however. They were not yet ready for the highest Truth. He felt they had to spend more time practising brahmacarya.

Section Eight

उदशराव आत्मानमवेक्ष्य यदात्मनो न विजानीथस्तन्मे प्रब्रूतमिति तौ होदशरावेऽवेक्षाञ्चक्राते तौ ह प्रजापतिरुवाच किं पश्यथ इति तौ होचतुः सर्वमेवेदमावां भगव आत्मानं पश्याव आ लोमभ्य आ नखेभ्यः प्रतिरूपमिति ॥ १ ॥

Udaśarāva ātmānamavekṣya yadātmano na vijānīthas-tanme prabrūtamiti tau hodaśarāve'vekṣāñcakrāte tau ha prajāpatiruvāca kiṁ paśyatha iti tau hocatuḥ sarvamevedamāvāṁ bhagava ātmānaṁ paśyāva ā lomabhya ā nakhebhyaḥ pratirūpamiti.

Udaśarāve ātmānam avekṣya, look at yourself in a vessel filled with water; *yat ātmanaḥ na vijānīthaḥ,* what you do not understand about the Self; *tat me prabrūtam iti,* tell me what it is; *tau ha udaśarāve avekṣāñcakrāte,* [then] they looked [at themselves] in the water; *tau ha prajāpatiḥ uvāca,* Prajāpati said to them; *kim paśyathaḥ iti,* what do you see; *tau ha ucatuḥ,* the two of them said; *āvām,* we both; *bhagavaḥ,* Lord; *sarvam eva idam ātmānam paśyāvaḥ,* see the whole of our self; *pratirūpam,* a reflection; *ālomabhyaḥ,* from the hair; *ānakhebhyaḥ,* to the nails.

1. [Prajāpati said:] 'Look at yourselves in a vessel full of water. If you have any doubts about the Self then let me know.' They then looked at themselves

in the water, and Prajāpati asked, 'What do you see?' They replied, 'We see the reflection of our whole self, including even our hair and nails.'

Prajāpati told them to bring a pan of water. They brought it, and he said: 'Look in the water. What do you see? If you have any doubt, if it is not clear to you exactly what I mean when I say the Self is in the water, then ask me.' A kind teacher is always ready to answer any question that a student may put. But instead of thinking and questioning, they simply said they saw the reflection of their own bodies—to the hair and the nails. When they even included the hair and nails, it should have been obvious to them that this could not be the Self.

In the Vedānta philosophy there is the illustration of the pole-star. How do you show someone the pole-star? First you draw that person's attention to a tree. Then you point to a big branch of the tree, and then to a smaller branch, and then to the pole-star beyond that. So you take the person step by step. This is what Prajāpati is trying to do. He is not trying to mislead them, but to take them from where they are, one step at a time.

तौ ह प्रजापतिरुवाच साध्वलङ्कृतौ सुवसनौ परिष्कृतौ भूत्वोदशरावेऽवेक्षेथामिति तौ ह साध्वलङ्कृतौ सुवसनौ परिष्कृतौ भूत्वोदशरावेऽवेक्षाञ्चक्राते तौ ह प्रजापतिरुवाच किं पश्यथ इति॥ २॥

Tau ha prajāpatiruvāca sādhvalaṅkṛtau suvasanau pariṣkṛtau bhūtvodaśarāve'vekṣethāmiti tau ha sādhvalaṅkṛtau suvasanau pariṣkṛtau bhūtvodaśarāve'vekṣāñcakrāte tau ha prajāpatiruvāca kiṁ paśyatha iti.

Tau ha prajāpatiḥ uvāca, Prajāpati said to them; *sādhu-alaṅkṛtau,* well-dressed; *suvasanau,* wearing fine clothes; *pariṣkṛtau bhūtvā,* having become neat and clean; *udaśarāve avekṣethām iti,* look into the vessel of water; *sādhu-alaṅkṛtau bhūtvā,* having become well-dressed; *suvasanau,* wearing fine clothes; *pariṣkṛtau,* neat and clean; *tau ha udaśarāve avekṣāñcakrāte,* they looked in the vessel of water; *tau ha prajāpatiḥ uvāca,* Prajāpati said to them; *kim paśyathaḥ iti,* what do you see?

2. Prajāpati said to them, 'After getting well-dressed and putting on fine clothes and making yourselves neat and clean, then look into the pan of water.' So the two of them got well-dressed in fine clothes, and made themselves neat and clean. Then they looked into the water. Prajāpati asked, 'What do you see?'

Now Prajāpati tells them to wash themselves and put on fine clothes and ornaments, and then look again into the pan of water. He was trying to raise a doubt in their minds. This is one way of teaching the Truth.

तौ होचतुर्यथैवेदमावां भगवः साध्वलङ्कृतौ सुवसनौ परिष्कृतौ स्व एवमेवेमौ भगवः साध्वलङ्कृतौ सुवसनौ परिष्कृतावित्येष आत्मेति होवाचैतदमृतमभयमेतद्ब्रह्मेति तौ ह शान्तहृदयौ प्रवव्रजतुः॥ ३ ॥

Tau hocaturyathaivedamāvāṁ bhagavaḥ sādhvalaṅkṛtau suvasanau pariṣkṛtau sva evamevemau bhagavaḥ sādhvalaṅkṛtau suvasanau pariṣkṛtāvityeṣa ātmeti hovācaitadamṛtamabhayametadbrahmeti tau ha śāntahṛdayau pravavrajatuḥ.

Tau ha ucatuḥ, they both said; *bhagavaḥ,* sir; *yathā eva,* just as; *idam āvām,* we two here; *sādhu-alaṅkṛtau,* well-dressed; *suvasanau,* wearing fine clothes; *pariṣkṛtau svaḥ,* are neat and clean; *evam eva,* like this; *bhagavaḥ,* lord; *imau,* these two [reflections]; *sādhu-alaṅkṛtau,* well-dressed; *suvasanau,* wearing fine clothes; *pariṣkṛtau iti,* neat and clean; *iti ha uvāca,* [Prajāpati] said; *eṣaḥ ātmā,* this is the Self; *etat amṛtam,* this is immortal; *abhayam,* fearless; *etat brahma iti,* this is Brahman; *tau,* both of them; *śāntahṛdayau pravavrajatuḥ,* left happy in mind.

3. The two of them said, 'Revered sir, just as we are well-dressed in fine clothes, and neat and clean, in the same way, these two reflections are well-dressed in fine clothes, and neat and clean.' Prajāpati said: 'That is the Self. It is immortal and fearless. It is Brahman.' The two of them left then, happy in mind.

Now Indra and Virocana see themselves with fine clothes and ornaments on. Just as it should have been obvious to them that the Self is not the body with its hair and nails, even more so it should be obvious that the Self is not the body with its fine clothes, as they were not wearing those clothes before. Prajāpati was trying to provoke them into thinking. Is the body with its fine clothes deathless and free from fear? If it is unchanging, why does it look different when you put on different clothes? But they went away very happy, thinking they had the answer.

Ordinarily our minds are wavering back and forth with doubts and indecision. That is the nature of the mind. But the Upaniṣad says Indra and Virocana went away *śāntahṛdaya,* with their minds at rest. That means without any doubt, without any question. It means they think they have received a satisfactory answer to their question, and the problem is solved.

तौ हान्वीक्ष्य प्रजापतिरुवाचानुपलभ्यात्मानमननुविद्य व्रजतो यतर एतदुपनिषदो भविष्यन्ति देवा वासुरा वा ते पराभविष्यन्तीति स ह शान्तहृदय एव विरोचनो-ऽसुराञ्जगाम तेभ्यो हैतामुपनिषदं प्रोवाचात्मैवेह महय्य आत्मा परिचर्य आत्मानमेवेह महयन्नात्मानं परिचरन्नुभौ लोकाववाप्नोतीमं चामुं चेति॥ ४॥

Tau hānvīkṣya prajāpatiruvācānupalabhyātmānamananuvidya vrajato yatara etadupaniṣado bhaviṣyanti devā vāsurā vā te parābhaviṣyantīti sa ha śāntahṛdaya eva virocano'surāñjagāma tebhyo haitāmupaniṣadaṁ provācātmaiveha mahayya ātmā paricarya ātmānameveha mahayannātmānaṁ paricarannubhau lokāvavāpnotīmaṁ cāmuṁ ceti.

Tau ha anu-īkṣya, having observed them; *prajāpatiḥ uvāca,* Prajāpati said; *anupalabhya ātmānam,* without realizing the Self; *ananuvidya,* without knowing; *vrajatah,* they have left; *yatare,* whoever among these two [gods or demons]; *etat upaniṣadaḥ bhaviṣyanti,* will understand this teaching this way; *devāḥ vā asurāḥ vā,* whether gods or demons; *te parābhaviṣyanti iti,* they will be destroyed; *saḥ ha virocanaḥ,* that Virocana; *śāntahṛdayaḥ eva,* with a happy mind; *asurān jagāma,* went to the demons; *tebhyaḥ,* to them; *etām upaniṣadam ha provāca,* explained the meaning of this upaniṣad; *ātmā eva ha iha mahayyaḥ,* the body is an object of worship in this world; *ātmā paricaryaḥ,* the body should be well taken care of; *ātmānam eva iha mahayan,* by treating the body with due respect in this world; *ātmānam paricaran,* by taking good care of it; *ubhau lokau,* both worlds; *imam ca amum ca,* this and the other; *āpnoti iti,* one attains.

4. Seeing them leave, Prajāpati said to himself: 'They are going without realizing or knowing anything about the Self. Anyone among them, whether a god or a demon, who will understand the teaching this way [thinking the body to be the Self] will be lost.' Virocana, the king of the demons, went back to the demons happy in mind and explained to them the upaniṣad:

'The body is the Self, and in this world it should be worshipped and taken care of. If the body is worshipped and well taken care of in this world, one attains both this world and the next.'

Prajāpati deplored the fact that they had left without asking for clarification. He was their teacher and well-wisher, and he was also their grandfather. He said: 'Poor children, they have gone away without knowing anything. They should have asked me, "When the body changes, does that mean the Self also changes?" But they did not ask any questions. Because they do not understand, they will fall away from the right path.'

Virocana went back to the demons and said: 'I have got the answer. The body is the Self.' Nourish this body, and look after it; eat, drink, and be merry; enjoy yourselves—this is the aim of life for a demon, that is, for a materialist. That which is gross, which can be perceived by the sense organs, that is the reality. And that which cannot be perceived is not real. This is the doctrine that Virocana preached.

The Upaniṣad uses the word *upaniṣad* to refer to what Virocana taught the demons, but it uses the word ironically. The word *upaniṣad* means *niḥśeṣa*—that is to say, it 'totally destroys' your ignorance. An Upaniṣad is supposed to give you Self-knowledge. But Virocana took the teaching to mean that the body was the Self. He thought that by worshipping and taking care of the body one would gain not only this world, but the other world also.

तस्मादप्यद्येहाददानमश्रद्दधानमयजमानमाहुरासुरो बते-
त्यसुराणां ह्येषोपनिषत्प्रेतस्य शरीरं भिक्षया वसने-
नालङ्कारेणेति संस्कुर्वन्त्येतेन ह्यमुं लोकं जेष्यन्तो
मन्यन्ते ॥ ५ ॥ इत्यष्टमः खण्डः ॥ ८ ॥

Tasmādapyadyehādadānamaśraddadhānamayajamānamāhurāsuro batetyasurāṇāṁ hyeṣopaniṣatpretasya śarīraṁ bhikṣayā vasanenālaṅkāreṇeti saṁskurvantyetena hyamuṁ lokaṁ jeṣyanto manyante. Ityaṣṭamaḥ khaṇḍaḥ.

Tasmāt, this is why; *api adya,* till today; *iha,* here in this world; *adadānam,* one incapable of giving anything in charity; *aśraddadhānam,* one who has no respect for others; *ayajamānam,* one who never performs a sacrifice; *āhuḥ,* they say; *āsuraḥ bata iti,* 'Oh, he is like a demon'; *asurānām hi eṣaḥ upaniṣat,* because this knowledge is suited for the demons; *pretasya,* of a dead person; *śarīram,* the body; *bhikṣayā,* with gifts [flowers, food, drink, etc.]; *vasanena,* with clothes; *alaṅkāreṇa,* with jewellery; *saṁskurvanti,* they decorate; *hi,* for; *etena,* in this way; *amum lokam,* the other world; *jeṣyantaḥ,* they will win; *manyante,* they think. *Iti aṣṭamaḥ khaṇḍaḥ,* here ends the eighth section.

5. This is why in this world even today people say, 'Oh, he is a demon,' if that person is devoid of the feeling of charity, has no respect for others, and never cares to perform a sacrifice, because the

demons have the idea that the body is the Self. When a person dies they decorate the body with all kinds of offerings, new clothes, and jewellery, for they think that by this, the person will conquer the other world.

Here the Upaniṣad says that there is a class of people who are not interested in self-discipline. They are the demons. They are only interested in sense pleasure, and they only believe in what can be perceived by the senses and what is present before them. They do not believe in God, and they are not interested in higher things. They are selfish and do not give anything in charity. They do not have faith in higher things, nor do they have respect for anything that is good—for good people or for good deeds. And they do not believe in sacrifice. Their attitude is: 'Why should I share what I have? I want everything for myself.'

What is the aim of their life? What is their ideal? Only that which concerns their body. The body is everything to them. Even when someone dies, they decorate the body with all kinds of things they like—flowers, garlands, fragrance, ornaments, silk clothes. Everything is done to make the body appear beautiful, as if a dead body is beautiful! They think if the body is properly decorated in this way, the deceased will look like a prince and will conquer heaven. They think the gods and goddesses will receive him as their ruler, and so on.

In ancient Egypt, when the Pharaohs died, their bodies

were treated with special ointments to preserve them. Then when they were put in their tombs, the bodies of their servants and attendants were also put there so they could look after them. Besides this, all the vessels and things the Pharaohs used were put in the tomb. Everything went with them.

The Hindu concept, however, is that the body will decay and perish, but the self is independent of the body. The self will never decay and never perish. It is a common experience that when a person dies, we see all his organs intact, but if we talk to him he does not answer. Why? Because the self has left the body.

The Upaniṣad does not mean to say that the body is not important. As a means to attain Self-knowledge it is important. It is a tool that we need for progress in our spiritual life and also in our mundane life. As the Muṇḍaka Upaniṣad says, *'Nāyamātmā balahīnena labhyaḥ*—this Self is not attained by one who has no strength.' If you have a weak, feeble body, then you cannot struggle or make sustained effort in any vocation—whether spiritual or secular. But when too much importance is given to the body, we forget that we are not the body, but the Self.

Section Nine

अथ हेन्द्रोऽप्राप्यैव देवानेतद्भयं ददर्श यथैव
खल्वयमस्मिञ्छरीरे साध्वलङ्कृते साध्वलङ्कृतो भवति

सुवसने सुवसनः परिष्कृते परिष्कृत एवमेवायमस्मिन्नन्धेऽन्धो भवति स्रामे स्रामः परिवृक्णे परिवृक्णोऽस्यैव शरीरस्य नाशमन्वेष नश्यति नाहमत्र भोग्यं पश्यामीति॥ १॥

Atha hendro'prāpyaiva devānetadbhayaṁ dadarśa yathaiva khalvayamasmiñcharīre sādhvalaṅkṛte sādhvalaṅkṛto bhavati suvasane suvasanaḥ pariṣkṛte pariṣkṛta evamevāyamasminnandhe'ndho bhavati srāme srāmaḥ parivṛkṇe parivṛkṇo'syaiva śarīrasya nāśamanveṣa naśyati nāhamatra bhogyaṁ paśyāmīti.

Atha, but; *indraḥ,* Indra, the king of the gods; *ha aprāpya eva,* even before getting back; *devān,* to the gods; *etat bhayam dadarśa,* saw this fear [i.e., doubt]; *yathā eva,* just as; *asmin śarīre sādhu-alaṅkṛte,* with this body being well decorated; *khalu ayam,* this [reflection of the body]; *sādhu-alaṅkṛtah bhavati,* is also well decorated; *suvasane suvasanaḥ,* when the body is in fine clothes, the reflection is wearing fine clothes; *pariṣkṛte pariṣkṛtaḥ,* when the body is neat and clean, the reflection is neat and clean; *evam eva,* like this; *asmin andhe,* if [the body] is blind; *ayam andhaḥ bhavati,* this [reflection] is of a blind person; *srāme srāmaḥ,* if the body is lame, the reflection is of a lame person; *parivṛkṇe parivṛkṇaḥ,* if the body is hurt, the reflection is of an injured body; *asya śarīrasya eva nāśam anu,* on the body's destruction; *eṣaḥ naśyati,* this [reflection] is destroyed; *aham atra bhogyam na paśyāmi iti,* I see nothing good in this.

1. But even before Indra returned to the gods, a

doubt arose in his mind: 'When the body is well decorated, the reflection is also well decorated. When the body is in fine clothes, the reflection is also in fine clothes. When the body is neat and clean, the reflection is also neat and clean. Again, suppose a person is blind. Then the reflection will show a blind body. Or if the body is lame, the reflection will show a lame body. Or if the body is hurt in some way, the reflection will show the same. Then again, if the body is destroyed, the reflection is gone. I don't see that anything good will come from this.'

Virocana was happy. He had no more doubts or questions. He liked the idea of the body being the Self. But what about Indra? Indra was a higher being. He was a god and was endowed with some spiritual qualities. Whereas Virocana thought Prajāpati was saying the body was the Self, Indra thought he was saying the reflection was the Self.

Indra also left Prajāpati and started to go back home, but then he was struck by a doubt: 'How can that reflection be my Self? It can't be. When I first looked at the reflection in the water it looked one way. Then when I put on fine clothes it looked another way. Suppose I lose a limb. The reflection will show that there is a limb missing. Whatever change there is in the body will show on the reflection. And if the body perishes, the reflection will be gone. But Prajāpati himself spoke of the Self as something constant, free from all defects, and immortal. It is something that does not change. What did Prajāpati mean when he said, "This is the Self"? Surely the reflection cannot be the Self. This answer does not satisfy me.'

स समित्पाणिः पुनरेयाय तं ह प्रजापतिरुवाच मघवन्यच्छान्तहृदयः प्राव्राजीः सार्धं विरोचनेन किमिच्छन्पुनरागम इति स होवाच यथैव खल्वयं भगवोऽस्मिञ्छरीरे साध्वलङ्कृते साध्वलङ्कृतो भवति सुवसने सुवसनः परिष्कृते परिष्कृत एवमेवायमस्मिन्नन्धेऽन्धो भवति स्रामे स्रामः परिवृक्णे परिवृक्णोऽस्यैव शरीरस्य नाशमन्वेष नश्यति नाहमत्र भोग्यं पश्यामीति ॥ २ ॥

Sa samitpāṇiḥ punareyāya taṁ ha prajāpatiruvāca maghavanyacchāntahṛdayaḥ prāvrājīḥ sārdhaṁ virocanena kimicchanpunarāgama iti sa hovāca yathaiva khalvayaṁ bhagavo'smiñcharīre sādhvalaṅkṛte sādhvalaṅkṛto bhavati suvasane suvasanaḥ pariṣkṛte pariṣkṛta evamevāyamasminnandhe'ndho bhavati srāme srāmaḥ parivṛkṇe parivṛkṇo'syaiva śarīrasya nāśamanveṣa naśyati nāhamatra bhogyaṁ paśyāmīti.

Saḥ, he [Indra]; *punaḥ eyāya,* again went back; *samitpāṇiḥ,* with fuel in hand; *tam,* to him; *prajāpatiḥ ha uvāca,* Prajāpati said; *maghavan,* O Maghavan [Indra]; *yat prāvrājīḥ,* you left; *śāntahṛdayaḥ,* satisfied; *sārdham virocanena,* along with Virocana; *kim icchan,* what do you want; *punaḥ āgamaḥ iti,* that you have come back again; *saḥ ha uvāca,* he [Indra] said;

bhagavaḥ, lord; *yathā eva,* just as; *asmin śarīre sādhu-alaṅkṛte,* with this body being well decorated; *khalu ayam,* this [reflection of the body]; *sādhu-alaṅkṛtah bhavati,* is also well decorated; *suvasane suvasanaḥ,* when the body is in fine clothes, the reflection is wearing fine clothes; *pariṣkṛte pariṣkṛtaḥ,* when the body is neat and clean, the reflection is neat and clean; *evam eva,* like this; *asmin andhe,* if [the body] is blind; *ayam andhaḥ bhavati,* this [reflection] is of a blind person; *srāme srāmaḥ,* if the body is lame, the reflection is of a lame person; *parivṛkṇe parivṛkṇaḥ,* if the body is hurt, the reflection is of an injured body; *asya śarīrasya eva nāśam anu,* on the body's destruction; *eṣaḥ naśyati,* this [reflection] is destroyed; *aham atra bhogyam na paśyāmi iti,* I see nothing good in this.

2. Indra returned with fuel in hand. Prajāpati asked: 'Indra, you left with Virocana happy in mind. What has made you come back?' Indra replied: 'Lord, when the body is well decorated, the reflection is also well decorated. When the body is in fine clothes, the reflection is also in fine clothes. When the body is neat and clean, the reflection is also neat and clean. Again, suppose a person is blind. Then the reflection will show a blind body. Or if the body is lame, the reflection will show a lame body. Or if the body is hurt in some way, the reflection will show the same. Then again, if the body is destroyed, the reflection is gone. I don't see anything good in this.'

Again Indra went to Prajāpati with fuel in hand as a symbol of surrender and humility. Śaṅkara makes a very significant comment here. The question is raised, 'Virocana went away satisfied, but why did Indra come back?' Śaṅkara says that we understand a thing according to our own level and inclination—according to our own nature.

Śaṅkara cites the example given in the Bṛhadāraṇyaka Upaniṣad of Prajāpati's instruction to the gods, humans, and asuras. To all of them Prajāpati gave the same instruction: he simply said, 'da.' The gods understood him to be saying *dāmyata,* be self-controlled. The human beings took it to mean *datta,* give in charity. And the asuras thought he was saying *dayadhvam,* be compassionate.

They all heard the same thing, but they interpreted it differently, according to their nature. The gods have the purest nature. They are the closest to Brahman. What is preventing them from being united with Brahman? Just a very thin layer of ignorance. They have to have a full measure of purity, and self-discipline is what leads to this purity. This is why they took the instruction to mean they should practise self-control.

The next are human beings. They are good, but they could be better. How? By practising selflessness. They should give whatever they can, share what they have with others, and not be selfish.

But the demons are not ready for self-control or charity. They are very cruel and passionate by nature. Therefore they took the instruction to mean that they should not be cruel, that they should have mercy on others.

These are the three characteristics we find among people. One kind of person needs to practise self-control; another kind, charity; and a third kind, mercy. It all depends on the level one is at.

Vedānta says you have to be ready to receive Self-knowledge. You have to be prepared. How a person understands the instructions is based on how much preparation he has had. Prajāpati was not trying to deceive Indra and Virocana. He was testing them, but he knew they were not prepared to receive Self-knowledge.

एवमेवैष मघवन्निति होवाचैतं त्वेव ते भूयो-
ऽनुव्याख्यास्यामि वसापराणि द्वात्रिंशतं वर्षाणीति स
हापराणि द्वात्रिंशतं वर्षाण्युवास तस्मै होवाच॥ ३॥ इति
नवमः खण्डः॥ ९॥

Evamevaiṣa maghavanniti hovācaitaṁ tveva te bhūyo-'nuvyākhyāsyāmi vasāparāṇi dvātriṁśataṁ varṣāṇīti sa hāparāṇi dvātriṁśataṁ varṣāṇyuvāsa tasmai hovāca. Iti navamaḥ khaṇḍaḥ.

Evam eva eṣaḥ, it is like that; *maghavan,* O Maghavan; *iti ha uvāca,* [Prajāpati] said; *etam tu eva bhūyaḥ anuvyākhyāsyāmi,* I will explain it once again; *te,* to you; *vasa,* stay here; *aparāṇi dvātriṁśatam,* another thirty-two; *varṣāṇi iti,* years; *saḥ,* he [Indra]; *ha aparāṇi dvātriṁśatam varṣāṇi,* for another thirty-two years; *uvāsa,* lived there; *tasmai ha uvāca,* [Prajāpati] said to him. *Iti navamaḥ khaṇḍaḥ,* here ends the ninth section.

3. Prajāpati said: 'Indra, it is so. I will explain the matter to you again. Stay here another thirty-two years.' Indra lived another thirty-two years there. Then Prajāpati said to him—

Prajāpati was obviously pleased that Indra had come back, but he wanted him to practise brahmacarya for another thirty-two years. Then he would again give him instructions.

Section Ten

य एष स्वप्ने महीयमानश्चरत्येष आत्मेति होवाचैतदमृतमभयमेतद्ब्रह्मेति स ह शान्तहृदयः प्रवव्राज स हाप्राप्यैव देवानेतद्भयं ददर्श तद्यद्यपीदं शरीरमन्धं भवत्यनन्धः स भवति यदि स्राममस्रामो नैवैषोऽस्य दोषेण दुष्यति ॥ १ ॥

Ya eṣa svapne mahīyamānaścaratyeṣa ātmeti hovācaitadamṛtamabhayametadbrahmeti sa ha śāntahṛdayaḥ pravavrāja sa hāprāpyaiva devānetadbhayaṁ dadarśa tadyadyapīdaṁ śarīramandhaṁ bhavatyanandhaḥ sa bhavati yadi srāmamasrāmo naivaiṣo'sya doṣeṇa duṣyati.

Yaḥ eṣaḥ, this [person] who; *svapne mahīyamānaḥ,* [appearing to be] worshipped in dreams; *carati,* goes about; *eṣaḥ ātmā,* this is the Self; *iti ha uvāca,* [Prajāpati] said; *etat amṛtam abhayam,* it is immortal and fearless; *etat brahma iti,* it is Brahman; *saḥ ha śāntahṛdayaḥ pravavrāja,* he left happy in mind; *ha aprāpya eva,* even before getting back; *devān,* to the gods; *etat bhayam dadarśa,* saw this fear [i.e., doubt]; *yadi api,* even if; *tat idam śarīram,* this body; *andham bhavati,* is blind; *saḥ anandhaḥ bhavati,* this [dream body] is not blind; *yadi srāmam asrāmaḥ,* if [the body] is lame, the [dream body] is not lame; *na eva eṣaḥ asya doṣeṇa duṣyati,* nor is this [dream body] affected by the defects [of the body].

1. 'That person who goes about being worshipped in dreams is the Self. It is immortal and fearless. It is Brahman.' Indra then left happy in mind. But even before he returned to the gods, a doubt arose in his mind: 'A person may be blind, but when he is dreaming he is not blind. He may be lame, but when he is dreaming he is not lame. There may be some defects in his body, but his dream body is not affected by them.'

Then after thirty-two years, Prajāpati said to Indra, 'When you are asleep you have dreams and you find yourself moving about, as if you are the ruler of all, as if you are very great and powerful. That self you experience in your dreams is your real Self. That is Brahman.'

Indra left satisfied, but on the way back home he began to think about what Prajāpati had said: 'When I saw the reflection in the water, it was just as my body was. If the body was decorated, the reflection also was decorated. That means if the body is blind, the reflection shows a blind body. But suppose I am blind and I am dreaming. At that time I can see so many things. So it is true, the condition of the body does not affect the Self. The Self is something different.'

न वधेनास्य हन्यते नास्य स्राम्येण स्रामो घ्नन्ति त्वेवैनं विच्छादयन्तीवाप्रियवेत्तेव भवत्यपि रोदितीव नाहमत्र भोग्यं पश्यामीति ॥ २ ॥

Na vadhenāsya hanyate nāsya srāmyeṇa srāmo ghnanti tvevainaṁ vicchādayantīvāpriyavetteva bhavatyapi roditīva nāhamatra bhogyaṁ paśyāmīti.

Asya vadhena na hanyate, [the dream body] is not killed when [the body] is killed; *na asya srāmyeṇa srāmaḥ,* nor is it lame with [the body's] lameness; *tu,* nevertheless; *enam eva ghnanti,* as if they are killing him; *vicchādayanti iva,* as if they are chasing him; *apriyavettā iva bhavati,* as if there is something unpleasant; *api roditi iva,* as if he is even weeping; *aham atra bhogyam na paśyāmi iti,* I see nothing good in this.

2. 'The body may be killed but the other is not killed. Nor is the dream body lame if the body is lame. Nevertheless, in dreams it may seem as if people are killing him; it may seem as if people are chasing him; it may seem as if there is something unpleasant. He may even seem to be weeping. I see nothing good in this.'

Indra continued to think about what Prajāpati had said. This is the nature of someone who has discrimination. And this is what Prajāpati expected him to do. In fact, Prajāpati would have been disappointed if Indra had not questioned what he had said. A good teacher is ready to give his knowledge, but the student also has to be ready. He has to be mentally alert and ask questions.

Indra thought: 'It is true, the dream-self is independent of the body. But I find that even in my dreams I am sometimes happy and sometimes unhappy. Sometimes I am in pain, and sometimes I am crying. And sometimes I even see myself being chased by someone and I am frightened. Prajāpati said the Self is free from fear, so how could this fear come? It should not happen. If the Self is subject to such limitations and unpleasant experiences, then it is not free and perfect. No, I cannot accept this answer.'

स समित्पाणिः पुनरेयाय तं ह प्रजापतिरुवाच मघवन्यच्छान्तहृदयः प्राव्राजीः किमिच्छन्पुनरागम इति

स होवाच तद्यद्यपीदं भगवः शरीरमन्धं भवत्यनन्धः
स भवति यदि स्राममस्रामो नैवैषोऽस्य दोषेण दुष्यति ॥ ३ ॥

Sa samitpāṇiḥ punareyāya taṁ ha prajāpatiruvāca maghavanyacchāntahṛdayaḥ prāvrājīḥ kimicchanpunarāgama iti sa hovāca tadyadyapīdaṁ bhagavaḥ śarīramandhaṁ bhavatyanandhaḥ sa bhavati yadi srāmamasrāmo naivaiṣo'sya doṣeṇa duṣyati.

Saḥ, he [Indra]; *punaḥ eyāya,* again went back; *samitpāṇiḥ,* with fuel in hand; *tam,* to him; *prajāpatiḥ ha uvāca,* Prajāpati said; *maghavan,* O Maghavan [Indra]; *yat prāvrājīḥ,* you left; *śāntahṛdayaḥ,* satisfied; *kim icchan,* what do you want; *punaḥ āgamaḥ iti,* that you have come back again; *saḥ ha uvāca,* he [Indra] said; *bhagavaḥ,* lord; *yadi api,* even if; *tat idam śarīram,* this body; *andham bhavati,* is blind; *saḥ anandhaḥ bhavati,* this [dream body] is not blind; *yadi srāmam asrāmaḥ,* if [the body] is lame, the [dream body] is not lame; *na eva eṣaḥ asya doṣena duṣyati,* nor is this [dream body] affected by the defects [of the body].

3. Indra returned with fuel in hand. Prajāpati asked: 'Indra, you left happy in mind. What has made you come back?' Indra replied: 'Lord, a person may be blind, but when he is dreaming he is not blind. He may be lame, but when he is dreaming he is not lame. There may be some defects in his body, but his dream body is not affected by them.'

Most of us think the body is everything. But the

idea of Vedānta is that we are independent of the body and the mind. The body and the mind are limitations. In reality, however, nothing can limit us. Our real Self is free and fearless. Prajāpati is happy that Indra has discovered this.

न वधेनास्य हन्यते नास्य स्राम्येण स्रामो घ्नन्ति त्वेवैनं विच्छादयन्तीवाप्रियवेत्तेव भवत्यपि रोदितीव नाहमत्र भोग्यं पश्यामीत्येवमेवैष मघवन्निति होवाचैतं त्वेव ते भूयोऽनुव्याख्यास्यामि वसापराणि द्वात्रिंशतं वर्षाणीति स हापराणि द्वात्रिंशतं वर्षाण्युवास तस्मै होवाच ॥ ४ ॥ इति दशमः खण्डः ॥ १० ॥

Na vadhenāsya hanyate nāsya srāmyeṇa srāmo ghnanti tvevainaṁ vicchādayantīvāpriyavetteva bhavatyapi roditīva nāhamatra bhogyaṁ paśyāmītyevamevaiṣa maghavanniti hovācaitaṁ tveva te bhūyo'nuvyākhyāsyāmi vasāparāṇi dvātriṁśataṁ varṣāṇīti sa hāparāṇi dvātriṁśataṁ varṣāṇyuvāsa tasmai hovāca. Iti daśamaḥ khaṇḍaḥ.

Asya vadhena na hanyate, [the dream body] is not killed when [the body] is killed; *na asya srāmyeṇa srāmaḥ,* nor is it lame with [the body's] lameness; *tu,* nevertheless; *enam eva ghnanti,* as if they are killing him; *vicchādayanti iva,* as if they are chasing him; *apriyavettā iva bhavati,* as if there is something unpleasant; *api roditi iva,* as if he is even weeping;

aham atra bhogyam na paśyāmi iti, I see nothing good in this; *evam eva eṣaḥ,* it is like that; *maghavan,* O Maghavan; *iti ha uvāca,* [Prajāpati] said; *etam tu eva bhūyaḥ anuvyākhyāsyāmi,* I will explain it once again; *te,* to you; *vasa,* stay here; *aparāṇi dvātriṁśatam,* another thirty-two; *varṣāṇi iti,* years; *saḥ,* he [Indra]; *ha aparāṇi dvātriṁśatam varṣāṇi,* for another thirty-two years; *uvāsa,* lived there; *tasmai ha uvāca,* [Prajāpati] said to him. *Iti daśamaḥ khaṇḍaḥ,* here ends the tenth section.

4. 'The body may be killed but the other is not killed. Nor is the dream body lame if the body is lame. Nevertheless, in dreams it may seem as if people are killing him; it may seem as if people are chasing him; it may seem as if there is something unpleasant. He may even seem to be weeping. I see nothing good in this.' Prajāpati said: 'Indra, it is so. I will explain the matter to you again. Stay here another thirty-two years.' Indra lived another thirty-two years there. Then Prajāpati said to him—

Indra says to Prajāpati, 'Sir, if your original statement is true that the Self is without any shortcomings and it never changes, then the dream self cannot be the real Self.' Prajāpati's first premise was that the Self was *apahatapāpmā,* without any limitations. *Pāpa* has a very comprehensive meaning. It is not just 'sin.' It may also mean weakness, shortcoming, or limitation.

So in the light of this premise Indra has come back.

Section Eleven

तद्यत्रैतत्सुप्तः समस्तः सम्प्रसन्नः स्वप्नं न विजानात्येष आत्मेति होवाचैतदमृतमभयमेतद्ब्रह्मेति स ह शान्तहृदयः प्रवव्राज स हाप्राप्यैव देवानेतद्भयं ददर्श नाह खल्वयमेवं सम्प्रत्यात्मानं जानात्ययमहमस्मीति नो एवेमानि भूतानि विनाशमेवापीतो भवति नाहमत्र भोग्यं पश्यामीति॥ १ ॥

Tadyatraitatsuptaḥ samastaḥ samprasannaḥ svapnaṁ na vijānātyeṣa ātmeti hovācaitadamṛtamabhayametad-brahmeti sa ha śāntahṛdayaḥ pravavrāja sa hāprāpyaiva devānetadbhayaṁ dadarśa nāha khalvayamevaṁ sampratyātmānaṁ jānātyayamahamasmīti no evemāni bhūtāni vināśamevāpīto bhavati nāhamatra bhogyaṁ paśyāmīti.

Yatra tat etat, when this [self]; *suptaḥ,* is sleeping; *samastaḥ,* all organs inactive; *samprasannaḥ,* free from worry; *svapnam na vijānāti,* does not have any dreams; *eṣaḥ ātmā,* this is the Self [free from sin]; *iti ha uvāca,* [Prajāpati] said; *etat amṛtam abhayam,* it is immortal and fearless; *etat brahma iti,* it is Brahman; *saḥ ha śāntahṛdayaḥ pravavrāja,* he [Indra] left happy in mind; *aprāpya eva devān,* but even before getting back to the gods; *saḥ etat bhayam dadarśa,* he saw this fear [i.e., difficulty]; *ayam,* this [self]; *nāha khalu samprati,* does not while [in deep sleep]; *evam,* in this way [i.e., as when awake]; *ātmānam jānāti,* know itself; *ayam aham asmi iti,* I am so-and-so; *na eva imāni bhūtāni,* nor even all these beings; *vināśam eva apītaḥ bhavati,* as if he becomes obliterated; *na aham atra bhogyam paśyāmi iti,* I don't see any good in this.

1. Prajāpati said: 'When the self is sleeping, with all its organs inactive, it is free from worry and has no dreams. This is what the Self is like [i.e., it is spotless]. It is immortal and fearless. It is Brahman.' Indra left happy in mind. But even before he got back to the gods, he was troubled by a doubt: 'When the self is in deep sleep, it is not able to recognize itself as "I am so-and-so," as it does when it is awake. Not only that, it does not even recognize beings around it. It is as if the self has been obliterated. I don't see that anything good will come from this.'

Next, Prajāpati told Indra about deep sleep. Normally when we are awake, our sense organs are outgoing, as if they are constantly searching for something. Then when we are dreaming, our body is at rest but our mind is not at rest. But if we have sound, dreamless sleep, our body, our organs, and our mind are all resting.

Prajāpati says: 'This is the Self [*Ātman*]. This is Brahman.' According to Vedānta, Ātman and Brahman are one and the same. When we use the word Ātman, we are referring to the Self within us. The word Brahman, means 'the biggest,' 'the greatest,' 'the ultimate.' There is nothing higher, nothing greater. Really speaking, we don't know what the ultimate is like. But we use the word Brahman to convey the idea of its uniqueness, that it is superior to everything.

What Prajāpati said seemed very convincing, and Indra left *śāntahṛdaya*—with his mind satisfied, with no more doubts. But as he was on his way back home, something began to trouble him. He thought: 'When I have dreamless sleep, why is it that I am not conscious of anything—even of myself? It's as if I have been annihilated and everything around me has disappeared. Why should this be?'

When Sri Ramakrishna used to have samādhi, he had no external consciousness and there was almost no sign of life in his body, but his face was beaming with joy. What is the difference between samādhi and deep sleep? In samādhi you have Self-knowledge. You know your real Self. And when your consciousness of the external world returns you are liberated. You have no more attachments or hankering after worldly pleasures. You are in a state of supreme bliss.

In suṣupti, deep sleep, all feelings, all experiences, all perceptions are temporarily wiped out. But when you wake up, you are the same person you were when you went to sleep. Your ignorance is still there, and there is no change in your outlook. You have the same attachments and fears, and you run after the same worldly pleasures that you did before you had deep sleep. Your bondage continues. That is the difference between the two.

Indra thought: 'In deep sleep it is as if I am annihilated. This could not be the Self.'

स समित्पाणिः पुनरेयाय तं ह प्रजापतिरुवाच मघवन्यच्छान्तहृदयः प्राव्राजीः किमिच्छन्पुनरागम इति स होवाच नाह खल्वयं भगव एवं सम्प्रत्यात्मानं जानात्ययमहमस्मीति नो एवेमानि भूतानि विनाशमेवापीतो भवति नाहमत्र भोग्यं पश्यामीति॥ २॥

Sa samitpāṇiḥ punareyāya taṁ ha prajāpatiruvāca maghavanyacchāntahṛdayaḥ prāvrājīḥ kimicchanpunarāgama iti sa hovāca nāha khalvayaṁ bhagava evaṁ sampratyātmānaṁ jānātyayamahamasmīti no evemāni bhūtāni vināśamevāpīto bhavati nāhamatra bhogyaṁ paśyāmīti.

Saḥ, he [Indra]; *punaḥ eyāya,* again went back; *samitpāṇiḥ,* with fuel in hand; *tam,* to him; *prajāpatiḥ ha uvāca,* Prajāpati said; *maghavan,* O Maghavan [Indra]; *yat prāvrājīḥ,* you left; *śāntahṛdayaḥ,* satisfied; *kim icchan,* what do you want; *punaḥ āgamaḥ iti,* that you have come back again; *saḥ ha uvāca,* he [Indra] said; *bhagavaḥ,* lord; *ayam,* this [self]; *nāha khalu samprati,* does not while [in deep sleep]; *evam,* in this way [i.e., as when awake]; *ātmānam jānāti,* know itself; *ayam aham asmi iti,* I am so-and-so; *na eva imāni bhūtāni,* nor even all these beings; *vināśam eva apītaḥ bhavati,* as if he becomes obliterated; *na aham atra bhogyam paśyāmi iti,* I don't see any good in this.

2. Indra returned with fuel in hand. Prajāpati asked: 'Indra, you left happy in mind. What has made you come back?' Indra replied: 'Lord, when the self is in deep sleep, it is not able to recognize itself as "I am so-and-so," as it does when it is awake. Not only that, it does not even recognize beings around it. It is as if the self has been obliterated. I don't see anything good coming from this.'

एवमेवैष मघवन्निति होवाचैतं त्वेव ते भूयोऽनुव्या-
ख्यास्यामि नो एवान्यत्रैतस्माद्वसापराणि पञ्च वर्षाणीति
स हापराणि पञ्च वर्षाण्युवास तान्येकशतं सम्पेदुरेतत्त-
द्यदाहुरेकशतं ह वै वर्षाणि मघवान्प्रजापतौ ब्रह्मचर्यमुवास
तस्मै होवाच॥ ३ ॥ इत्येकादशः खण्डः॥ ११ ॥

Evamevaiṣa maghavanniti hovācaitaṁ tveva te bhūyo-'nuvyākhyāsyāmi no evānyatraitasmādvasāparāṇi pañca varṣāṇīti sa hāparāṇi pañca varṣāṇyuvāsa tānyekaśataṁ sampeduretattadyadāhurekaśataṁ ha vai varṣāṇi maghavānprajāpatau brahmacaryamuvāsa tasmai hovāca. Ityekādaśaḥ khaṇḍaḥ.

Evam eva eṣaḥ, it is like that; *maghavan,* O Maghavan; *iti ha uvāca,* [Prajāpati] said; *etam tu eva bhūyaḥ anuvyākhyāsyāmi,* I will explain it once again; *te,* to you; *vasa,* stay here; *aparāṇi pañca,* another five; *varṣāṇi iti,* years; *saḥ,* he [Indra]; *ha aparāṇi pañca varṣāṇi,* for another five years; *uvāsa,* lived there; *tāni ekaśatam sampeduḥ,* one hundred and one [years] were completed; *etat tat yat āhuḥ,* this is what it is when people say; *maghavān prajāpatau brahmacaryam uvāsa,* Indra lived with Prajāpati practising brahmacārya; *ekaśatam ha vai varṣāṇi iti,* one hundred and one years; *tasmai ha uvāca,* [Prajāpati] said to him. *Iti ekādaśaḥ khaṇḍaḥ,* here ends the eleventh section.

3. Prajāpati said: 'Indra, it is so. I will explain the matter to you again. Stay here another five years.' Indra lived there another five years. The total time Indra spent thus was one hundred and one years. This is what sages refer to when they say, 'Indra lived with Prajāpati for one hundred and one years practising brahmacarya.' Then Prajāpati said to him—

For the third time Indra returned. Prajāpati must have been very pleased with this. If the student comes back again and again with questions, then naturally the teacher is pleased. He thinks: 'I have a very clever student. He wants to know, and I am happy to be able to help him.'

This time he asked Indra to practise brahmacarya for just five years, as he could see Indra was almost ready. So Indra practised austerities for a total of a hundred and one years. Śaṅkara says that the reason this story has been introduced here is to show how important Self-knowledge is—that there is nothing higher and more desirable than Self-knowledge.

The Indian scriptures are very clear: If you are mainly interested in acquiring money they say: 'All right, have money. But remember, it will only give you happiness for a while. Very soon you will discover what a bondage it is.' It is the same for other things—scholarship, political power, social standing, and so on. You may enjoy them if you want, but all the time you must know that they will not last long and they will not give you peace of mind.

The scriptures say that it is only through Self-knowledge that you will get happiness which is eternal, which is always yours. This is why Self-knowledge is considered to be the highest goal of life.

Section Twelve

मघवन्मर्त्यं वा इदं शरीरमात्तं मृत्युना तदस्यामृत-
स्याशरीरस्यात्मनोऽधिष्ठानमात्तो वै सशरीरः प्रियाप्रियाभ्यां
न वै सशरीरस्य सतः प्रियाप्रिययोरपहतिरस्त्यशरीरं वाव
सन्तं न प्रियाप्रिये स्पृशतः ॥ १ ॥

Maghavanmartyaṁ vā idaṁ śarīramāttaṁ mṛtyunā tadasyāmṛtasyāśarīrasyātmano'dhiṣṭhānamātto vai saśarīraḥ priyāpriyābhyāṁ na vai saśarīrasya sataḥ priyāpriyayorapahatirastyaśarīraṁ vāva santaṁ na priyāpriye spṛśataḥ.

Maghavan, O Maghavan [Indra]; *martyam vai idam śarīram,* this body is mortal [subject to death]; *āttam mṛtyunā,* it has been captured by death; *tat,* that [body]; *asya amṛtasya aśarīrasya ātmanaḥ adhiṣṭhānam,* is the foundation of this immortal and formless Self; *āttaḥ vai saśarīraḥ priya-apriyābhyām,* one who has a body is subject to good and evil; *saśarīrasya sataḥ,* for one who has a body; *priya-apriyayoḥ apahatiḥ na asti,* there is no end to good and evil; *aśarīram vāva santam,* but one who is without a body; *priya-apriye na spṛśataḥ,* is not touched by good and evil.

1. Indra, this body is mortal. It has been captured by death. Yet it is the base of the Self, which is immortal and formless. One who has a body is subject to both happiness and unhappiness. In fact, there is no end to happiness and unhappiness so long as one has a body. But when a person is free from the body, nothing good or bad can touch him.

Prajāpati now starts teaching Indra about the nature of the Self. He says the Self has no body and no form, yet somehow or other the Self has identified itself with the body. Why? Because of ignorance. But if the Self is supposed to be pure consciousness, pure knowledge, where has this ignorance come from? Can light and darkness coexist? Similarly, can knowledge and ignorance coexist? No.

There is, in fact, no ignorance at all in the Self. Yet, somehow or other, the formless Self identifies itself with the body and imagines that whatever happens to the body happens to it. It feels it is born when the body is born, and that it dies when the body dies. Vedānta says this ignorance is temporary and it can be removed.

Vedānta calls this ignorance *māyā.* Māyā is often translated as 'illusion,' but this is not quite correct. Swami Vivekananda calls it 'a statement of fact.' You cannot say it does not exist, but again you cannot say exactly what it is. It is *anirvacanīya,* indescribable.

Śaṅkara often uses the example of the rope and the snake to explain how māyā works. Suppose you are walking along a road on a dark night, and you suddenly see what you think is a snake lying across the road in front of you. You are frightened and you start yelling, 'Snake! Snake!' Then some people living nearby come running out of their homes with lights, and you discover it is not a snake after all. It is just a rope.

Another example given is that of the mirage. Suppose you are walking in a desert and you are very thirsty. In the distance you see a lake and you start walking towards it. You go on and on, but you never reach the water. Finally you realize it is just a mirage. It is all due to the effect of the sunrays on the sand. Another example is that of thinking you see silver where there is just a piece of mother-of-pearl. When you see the mother-of-pearl, you are convinced that you are seeing silver. So māyā is an error with a semblance of truth. Yet, Vedānta says, the mother-of-pearl never becomes silver, nor does the rope ever become a snake or the sand become water.

Māyā has two aspects—*āvaraṇa* and *vikṣepa. Āvaraṇa* means 'covering.' Māyā covers the rope and hides its real nature. *Vikṣepa* is the projecting power of māyā. It projects the appearance of a snake where there is just a rope. This is also called *adhyāsa,* superimposition.

Vedānta says this ignorance is just temporary. As soon as light comes, we see the rope rather than the snake. Similarly, as soon as knowledge is awakened in us, our false identification with the body is gone and we realize our true nature.

Prajāpati says to Indra, 'This body has been captured by death.' Here Śaṅkara asks: 'Why does Prajāpati say this? He says this so that we will try to get rid of our ignorance quickly.' If we are merely told that we are mortal and that some day we will die, we may say: 'Well, I will not die soon. I still have many years at my disposal to live as I like. I will enjoy myself as long as possible.' But if we are told that we are already in the grips of death, that death is already at our doorstep, that it has already conquered us, we will understand that there is no time to lose. We must attain Self-knowledge immediately.

The Hindu idea is that anything that has a beginning also has an end. Anything that is born must some day die. This is something we don't like to accept. When Yama asked King Yuddhiṣṭhira what the most amazing thing was, Yuddhiṣṭhira replied, 'The most amazing thing is that people see others dying all around them, but somehow or other they believe they will never die.' But the fact is, the moment we are born, the process of death begins. When we are born, death comes to us and says: 'Here I am. I am going to follow you like a shadow. Sooner or later you will be my victim, even if I have to wait a hundred years.'

Vedānta says, however, that the Self is never born and it never dies. It is immortal. Death is for the *śārīra*—that is, for one who feels he is a body. So also pleasure and pain. These changing conditions afflict only the person who identifies himself with the body. This empirical world is a world of sense experience, and it is always subject to change. One moment it is hot, the next moment it is cold. One moment there is pleasure, and the next there is pain. This is the way the world goes on, continuously.

But if you can get rid of the delusion that you are an embodied being, then you are no longer swayed by the changing conditions of life. You are always the same, always calm. And there is no question of pleasure and pain for you. They cannot touch you. Even if the body is affected, *you* are not affected.

Prajāpati says the body is the *adhiṣṭhānam,* the abode or resting place, of the Self. For the time being the Self chooses to live in this house. Though the Self is *amṛtam,* immortal, and *aśarīram,* without a body, it identifies itself with the body and thinks it is mortal. This fact of delusion has to be recognized. We cannot ignore it. But if delusion, or ignorance, were in the nature of the Self, how could we get rid of it? We couldn't. We would always be ignorant. But Vedānta says Knowledge is our true nature, only somehow or other that Knowledge is hidden.

How do we uncover that Knowledge? How do we remove our delusion and stop identifying ourself with the body? Śaṅkara says, first we must become free from desires. We identify ourself with the body because we have desires. For example, we want to eat something. How will we eat it if we do not have a body? For any sense desire we have, we must have a body to fulfil it. And as long as we have a body, we will sometimes have pleasure and sometimes have pain. We cannot always have pleasure. Along with pleasure comes pain. Then again, some of our desires will be fulfilled, but some of them will not. And if they are not fulfilled, we will be disappointed. Vedānta says, even the desire for liberation requires a body to fulfil it.

But when we attain Self-knowledge we realize a state where there is no such change. We then know our true nature, our real Self, which is never touched by the changing conditions of the world.

Then Śaṅkara says, if you want Self-knowledge you must go to a teacher. But not just any teacher. You must go to one who is himself free from desires—one who is a *paramahaṁsa.* The word *paramahaṁsa* literally means a swan. A swan is said to be able to separate milk from water. If there is milk mixed with water, it will drink only the milk and leave behind the water. So a teacher who is a paramahaṁsa has developed discrimination between the real and the unreal, the permanent and the impermanent. He rejects whatever is unreal, and accepts only that which is real and immortal. That is to say, he has no more desires for anything in this world.

What does such a teacher do? He shows you your real nature. Sri Ramakrishna used to explain this with the story of the tiger and the goats. Once a pregnant tigress was running after a flock of goats when she fell down exhausted and died. But as she died, she gave birth to a baby tiger. The baby tiger was adopted by the goats, and in course of time he began to eat grass and bleat just like them. All the while he thought he was a goat. Even when he grew up he never realized he was a tiger.

One day a big tiger came there and was about to spring on the flock when he noticed another tiger running away frightened and bleating like a goat. Disgusted, he ran and caught hold of the grass-eating tiger and said: 'What are you doing here with these goats? Shame on you! You are a tiger.' But the grass-eating tiger started crying and said: 'No, no, I am a goat. Let me go.' Then the big tiger dragged the other to a river and said: 'Look at your reflection in the water. You look just like me. You are not a goat. You are a tiger.' He then forced a piece of meat into the grass-eating tiger's mouth. Getting the taste of the meat, the grass-eating tiger started to roar.

So this is what the guru does. He removes our ignorance and tells us who we really are—*tat tvam asi,* thou art that.

अशरीरो वायुरभ्रं विद्युत्स्तनयित्नुरशरीराण्येतानि तद्यथैतान्यमुष्मादाकाशात्समुत्थाय परं ज्योतिरुपसम्पद्य स्वेन रूपेणाभिनिष्पद्यन्ते ॥ २ ॥

Aśarīro vāyurabhraṁ vidyutstanayitnuraśarīrāṇyetāni tadyathaitānyamuṣmādākāśātsamutthāya paraṁ jyotiru-pasampadya svena rūpeṇābhiniṣpadyante.

Aśarīraḥ vāyuḥ, air is formless; *abhram vidyut stanayitnuḥ,* light clouds, lightning, and thunder; *etāni,* all these; *aśarīrāṇi,* are formless; *tat yathā,* just as; *etāni,* all these; *amuṣmāt ākāśāt,* from the sky; *samutthāya,* arise; *param jyotiḥ upasampadya,* attain the great light [i.e., are exposed to the heat of the sun in summer]; *svena rūpeṇa abhiniṣpadyante,* appear in their respective forms [in the rainy season].

2. The air is formless. So also are clouds, lightning, and thunder. All these arise from the sky and assume their respective forms due to the heat of the sun.

Here the idea is that even though we don't see the Self, it is always within us. The Upaniṣad compares it with air, clouds, lightning, and thunder. In winter the sky is clear. There are very few clouds, and there are no strong winds or storms. But then as summer begins the temperature starts rising, and slowly the clouds gather. Then come the storms with their high winds and lightning and thunder.

Where were the clouds and lightning during winter? They were there, but they were not visible. We see them only when the conditions are right; otherwise they are in a latent form, one with the sky. They appear from the sky, and then they merge into the sun.

एवमेवैष सम्प्रसादोऽस्माच्छरीरात्समुत्थाय परं ज्योति-रुपसम्पद्य स्वेन रूपेणाभिनिष्पद्यते स उत्तमः पुरुषः स तत्र पर्येति जक्षत्क्रीडन्रममाणः स्त्रीभिर्वा यानैर्वा ज्ञातिभिर्वा नोपजनं स्मरन्निदं शरीरं स यथा प्रयोग्य आचरणे युक्त एवमेवायमस्मिञ्छरीरे प्राणो युक्तः ॥ ३ ॥

Evamevaiṣa samprasādo'smācchārīrātsamutthāya param jyotirupasampadya svena rūpeṇābhiniṣpadyate sa uttamaḥ puruṣaḥ sa tatra paryeti jakṣatkrīḍanramamāṇaḥ strībhirvā yānairvā jñātibhirvā nopajanaṁ smarannidaṁ śarīraṁ sa yathā prayogya ācaraṇe yukta evamevāyamasmiñcharīre prāṇo yuktaḥ.

Evam eva, just like that; *eṣaḥ samprasādaḥ,* this serene one [i.e., the individual self, after attaining Self-knowledge]; *asmāt śarīrāt,* from this body; *samutthāya,* arising; *param jyotiḥ,* the radiance of the Cosmic Self; *upasampadya,* attains; *svena rūpeṇa abhiniṣpadyate,* appears in his own form; *saḥ uttama puruṣaḥ,* this is the Supreme Being; *saḥ tatra paryeti,* he goes about; *jakṣat krīḍan ramamāṇaḥ,* eating, playing, and enjoying himself; *strībhiḥ vā,* with women; *yānaiḥ vā,* or in carriages; *jñātibhiḥ vā,* or with relatives; *na smaran,* not remembering; *upajānam idam śarīram,* this body in which he was born; *yathā,* just as; *saḥ prayogyaḥ,* an animal [a horse or bullock]; *ācaraṇe yuktaḥ,* is harnessed to a carriage [or chariot]; *evam eva,* like that; *ayam prāṇaḥ,* this life; *asmin śarīre yuktaḥ,* is harnessed to the body.

3. In the same way, the joyful self arises from the body and, attaining the light of the Cosmic Self, appears in his own form. This is the Paramātman, the Cosmic Self. He then freely moves about eating, playing, or enjoying himself with women, carriages, or relatives, not remembering at all the body in which he was born. Just as horses or bullocks are harnessed to carriages, similarly prāṇa [life] remains harnessed to the body [due to karma].

The question here is, who is the enjoyer? It is the self. This is something basic to Vedānta philosophy. The self is the master. The body is like a house, and the self is like the owner of the house. Just as the owner of a house can change his house at any time, so also, the self can change its body at any time.

Here the relationship of the self with the body is clearly brought out. The self is immortal and *aśarīra,* without a body. But, like lightning or clouds, the self is sometimes manifest in a form. With ordinary people the distinction between the self and the body is not noticeable, but with an enlightened person the distinction is quite conspicuous. In all his manners and his way of speaking, you see that the enlightened person is using his body as his instrument. He is always conscious that he is the self. He may be eating or drinking or talking or moving about like anyone else, but still you see there is a difference.

An ordinary person is not his own master. He is a slave to his body and mind. But a knower of the Self has conquered the body and the mind and can make them behave as he wants. He is merely the *draṣṭā,* the spectator. He sees the world going on with all its madness, and to him it is great fun, because he is totally unaffected and untouched.

Vedānta keeps trying to convince us of the fact that happiness is not outside. It is not dependent on any objective circumstances. It is all within. If happiness were dependent on external conditions then why doesn't the same thing give happiness to everyone? Some people are very happy if they get some sweets to eat. But there are other people who don't care for sweets at all. If the sweets were the source of happiness they should make everyone happy, but they don't. There are people who, in spite of seemingly unfavorable circumstances, are very happy. They know that they don't have to seek for happiness outside. They find it within.

But this is not to say a knower of the Self is cold and indifferent. Śaṅkara says, when you know your Self, when you know you are Brahman and that everything you see is nothing but Brahman, then you feel you are one with all. If others are happy, you are happy. If others are in pain, you are also in pain. Now we are separate from others because we think we are the body and we identify ourself with our body. Yet still we talk of love, compassion, of sharing the sorrows and sufferings of others. How can we share them? We can't. We may have pity on someone, but often that pity is accompanied by a sense of superiority. By showing pity we are often merely showing our arrogance.

This is why the Taittirīya Upaniṣad says that when you give someone something, give it with respect. You may give something to a beggar. He may be in rags. Never mind, he is God. You should feel grateful to him that he is accepting your offering. The Upaniṣad also says, if you cannot give with respect then it is better not to give at all. You will hurt the other person's self-respect. So whatever you give, give with love and humility. When you give something, you are giving it to your own Self, because you are everywhere—in the small, in the big, in a human being, and in an insect.

अथ यत्रैतदाकाशमनुविषण्णं चक्षुः स चाक्षुषः पुरुषो दर्शनाय चक्षुरथ यो वेदेदं जिघ्राणीति स आत्मा गन्धाय घ्राणमथ यो वेदेदमभिव्याहराणीति स आत्माभिव्याहाराय वागथ यो वेदेदं शृणवानीति स आत्मा श्रवणाय श्रोत्रम् ॥ ४ ॥

Atha yatraitadākāśamanuviṣaṇṇaṁ cakṣuḥ sa cākṣuṣaḥ puruṣo darśanāya cakṣuratha yo vededaṁ jighrāṇīti sa ātmā gandhāya ghrāṇamatha yo vededamabhivyāharāṇīti sa ātmābhivyāhārāya vāgatha yo vededaṁ śṛṇavānīti sa ātmā śravaṇāya śrotram.

Atha, then; *yatra etat cakṣuḥ,* where this organ of vision is; *ākāśam anuviṣaṇṇam,* lying inside the space [in the eye]; *saḥ cākṣuṣaḥ puruṣaḥ,* that is the deity presiding over the eye; *darśanāya cakṣuḥ,* the eye is the instrument of vision; *atha,* then; *yaḥ veda,* one who knows; *idam jighrāṇi iti,* I smell this; *saḥ ātmā,* that is the Self; *gandhāya ghrāṇam,* the organ of smell is the instrument of smelling; *atha,* then; *yaḥ veda,* one who knows; *idam abhivyāharāṇi iti,* I speak this; *saḥ ātmā,* that is the Self; *abhivyāhārāya vāk,* the organ of speech is the instrument of speaking; *atha,* then; *yaḥ veda,* one who knows; *idam śṛṇavāni iti,* I hear this; *saḥ ātmā,* that is the Self; *śravaṇāya śrotram,* the ear is the instrument of hearing.

4. Next, this organ of vision lies inside the space in the eyes. That is where the deity presiding over the eyes [i.e., the Self] is. The eye is the instrument through which the Self sees. Next, the one who knows 'I am smelling this' is the Self. The organ of smell is the instrument through which the Self smells. Next, the one who knows 'I am speaking this' is the Self. The organ of speech is the instrument through which the Self speaks. Next, the one who knows 'I hear this' is the Self. The organ of hearing is the instrument through which the Self hears.

The Upaniṣad is saying that the Self is within us, and that the Self makes use of the organs for its experience in this empirical world. 'I see, I hear, I speak'—who is this 'I'? When I say, 'I see,' do I mean the eyes are seeing something by their own power? No. The Self is behind the eyes, and the Self uses them for its own purpose. The eyes are not independent. When we die, all our organs may be intact, yet we won't be able to see or hear anything.

You may ask, 'How do I know that the Self is working through the organs?' Vedānta says, suppose you are absent-minded and are absorbed in thinking something. Someone may come and stand before you and say something, but you don't see him at all. Now who is it that is absorbed? It is the Self. The Self has withdrawn itself from the sense organs, and because of this they are not able to operate in the way they normally do.

Earlier Prajāpati had told Indra and Virocana that the person in the eyes is the Self. Indra took it to mean that his own reflection was the Self. But this is not what Prajāpati meant. He meant that there is a being within us who sees through the eyes and hears through the ears. He says that within the eye there is a space, and that is where the Self is. The Self is hiding there, as it were. Prajāpati uses the word *puruṣa* to refer to the Self. Here puruṣa does not mean 'male,' as it does in Bengali. The word *puruṣa* literally means *pure śayate*—that is, 'one who is lying,' or 'hidden' (*śayate*) 'in a place' (*pure*).

Who does the organ of smelling work for? The Self. All our organs are servants of the Self. The person in the eye uses the eye to see and the organ of smelling to smell. When the Self, the puruṣa, wants to speak, it uses the organ of speaking. And when it wants to hear, it uses the organ of hearing.

अथ यो वेदेदं मन्वानीति स आत्मा मनोऽस्य दैवं चक्षुः स वा एष एतेन दैवेन चक्षुषा मनसैतान्कामान्पश्यन्रमते य एते ब्रह्मलोके॥ ५॥

Atha yo vededaṁ manvānīti sa ātmā mano'sya daivaṁ cakṣuḥ sa vā eṣa etena daivena cakṣuṣā manasaitānkāmānpaśyanramate ya ete brahmaloke.

Atha, next; *yaḥ veda,* that which knows; *idam manvāni iti,* I am thinking this; *saḥ ātmā,* that is the Self; *manaḥ asya daivam cakṣuḥ,* the mind is its divine eye; *saḥ vai eṣaḥ,* that [Self]; *etena daivena cakṣuṣā manasā,* with the help of the divine mental eye; *etān kāmān paśyan ramate,* enjoys seeing the things it likes; *yaḥ ete brahmaloke,* those which are in Brahmaloka.

5. Then, it is the Self which knows 'I am thinking this.' The mind is its divine eye. The Self, now free, enjoys seeing everything it wants to see in Brahmaloka through its divine mental eye.

Next comes the mind. The mind is the principal organ. The Self works through the mind, and by means of the mind it works through the eyes, ears, and other organs.

You may remember the example given in the Kaṭha Upaniṣad: The Self is the master of the chariot, the mind is the charioteer, and the organs are the horses. The mind is directly responsible for keeping the organs under control.

The mind is called here the *daivam cakṣuḥ,* the divine eye, because the Self sees through the mind. The mind is extraordinary. One who is firmly established in Self-knowledge can enjoy whatever he wants mentally. And for such a person everything is Brahman and every place is Brahmaloka.

तं वा एतं देवा आत्मानमुपासते तस्मात्तेषां सर्वे च लोका आत्ताः सर्वे च कामाः स सर्वांश्च लोकानाप्नोति सर्वांश्च कामान्यस्तमात्मानमनुविद्य विजानातीति ह प्रजापतिरुवाच प्रजापतिरुवाच॥ ६॥ इति द्वादशः खण्डः॥ १२॥

Taṁ vā etaṁ devā ātmānamupāsate tasmātteṣāṁ sarve ca lokā āttāḥ sarve ca kāmāḥ sa sarvāṁśca lokānāpnoti sarvāṁśca kāmānyastamātmānamanuvidya vijānātīti ha prajāpatiruvāca prajāpatiruvāca. Iti dvādaśaḥ khaṇḍaḥ.

Tam vai etam devāḥ ātmānam upāsate, that is the Self which the gods worship; *tasmāt,* this is why; *sarve ca lokāḥ,* all the worlds; *teṣām āttāḥ,* are within the grasp of them [the gods]; *sarve ca kāmāḥ,* and all things they desire; *sarvān ca lokān,* all worlds; *sarvān ca kāmān,* and all things one desires; *āpnoti,* one attains; *yaḥ tam ātmānam anuvidya,* one who knows the Self; *vijānāti iti,* and has a direct, personal experience of it; *prajāpatiḥ ha uvāca prajāpatiḥ uvāca,* this is what Prajāpati taught. *Iti dvādaśaḥ khaṇḍaḥ,* here ends the twelfth section.

6. This Self is worshipped by the gods. This is why all worlds and all desirable things are within their grasp. One who fully understands and realizes this Self [with the help of teachers and the scriptures] is able to attain whatever worlds and whatever desirable things he wants. This is what Prajāpati taught Indra.

Here the Upaniṣad is praising Self-knowledge in order to tempt us to attain it. Earlier the Upaniṣad said, *'Na alpe sukham asti'*—there is no happiness in the finite, in what is small or limited. Only in *bhūmā,* the infinite, is there happiness. Bhūmā is infinite in terms of both time and space. Whatever is limited by time and space cannot give us peace and happiness.

Even the state of a god or goddess is a limitation, according to Hinduism. By virtue of the kind of life you have lived and the good things you have done, you may be elevated to the position of a god or goddess. But that position is only temporary. When your term expires, you are right back where you started from. The attainment of Self-knowledge, however, is different. When you realize your true Self, you realize a state that has always been yours.

Śaṅkara says the Upaniṣad does not mean to say that this state can be attained only by gods and goddesses. It is for human beings also. In fact, it is our very birthright.

The story of Indra and Virocana going to Prajāpati for Self-knowledge shows that we are all suffering from discontent. We are always seeking something, though we may not know exactly what it is. Even the gods and goddesses in heaven are not content. After many births they have attained the status of a god or goddess, and they seem to have everything they desire, yet still they are not satisfied.

This is why Indra went to Prajāpati and spent a hundred and one years practising austerities to get the knowledge of the Self. The Upaniṣad says again and again that Self-knowledge is the highest. If you attain that you attain everything.

Section Thirteen

श्यामाच्छबलं प्रपद्ये शबलाच्छ्यामं प्रपद्येऽश्व इव रोमाणि विधूय पापं चन्द्र इव राहोर्मुखात्प्रमुच्य धूत्वा शरीरमकृतं कृतात्मा ब्रह्मलोकमभिसम्भवामीत्यभि-सम्भवामीति॥ १॥ इति त्रयोदशः खण्डः॥ १३॥

Śyāmācchabalaṁ prapadye śabalācchyāmaṁ prapadye'śva iva romāṇi vidhūya pāpaṁ candra iva rāhormukhātpramucya dhūtvā śarīramakṛtaṁ kṛtātmā brahmalokamabhisambhavāmītyabhisambhavāmīti. Iti trayodaśaḥ khaṇḍaḥ.

Śyāmāt śabalam prapadye, from the dark may I attain the diverse; *śabalāt śyāmam prapadye,* from the diverse may I attain the dark; *aśvaḥ romāṇi iva,* as a horse [shakes] its fur; *pāpam vidhūya,* I will shake off any shortcomings [I have]; *candra iva rāhoḥ mukhāt pramucya,* as the moon gets free from the mouth of Rāhu; *dhūtvā śarīram,* laying down the body; *kṛtātmā,* having accomplished everything; *akṛtam,* eternal; *brahmalokam,* Brahmaloka; *abhisambhavāmi iti abhisambhavāmi iti,* I will attain, I will attain. *Iti trayodaśaḥ khaṇḍaḥ,* here ends the thirteeenth section.

1. From the dark may I attain the diverse. From the diverse may I attain the dark. Like a horse shaking its fur [to remove the dirt], I will shake off whatever spot I may have on my character. Like the moon freeing itself from the mouth of Rāhu [and regaining its brightness], I will, having accomplished everything, lay down this body and attain that eternal Brahmaloka.

This is a meditation mantra. It contains the essence of all that has been said before in this Upaniṣad.

There are two important words used here—*śyāma* and *śabala. Śyāma* means 'dark,' or 'black.' *Śyāmā* is the feminine form, and it is also a name of Mother Kālī. Śaṅkara says that *śyāma* is *gambhīraḥ varṇaḥ,* a deep colour—that is to say, it is not perceptible to our sense organs. When we say something is dark, it suggests that it is difficult to know. Mother Kālī is said to be dark because we really do not know what or who she is.

Here the word *śyāma* refers to Brahman, because Brahman also is difficult to know. Where do we realize Brahman? Within us, within the heart. *Śabala* means many-coloured, or with many forms. It stands for Brahmaloka. It is the multiplicity outside. The idea is, what is inside is also outside. The One becomes the many.

Suppose you enter a room where there are a hundred mirrors. What do you see? You see a hundred reflections of yourself. Or suppose the moon is shining above and there are many pots of water on the ground. In each pot there is a reflection of the moon, but there is in reality only one moon.

How do we realize this—that the One becomes the many? Through *cittaśuddhi,* purification of the mind. Your mind is like a mirror. If the mirror is clean you have a very clear reflection of yourself. But if there is dust and dirt on the mirror you cannot see your reflection very well. The Upaniṣad has again and again been emphasizing this need for purification of the mind. It is not something that is attained all of a sudden. It does not happen by a fluke. It comes only after years of hard struggle and self-discipline.

Two illustrations are given here in this verse. The first is about a horse. When a horse has dirt on his body, he wants to get rid of it. He does not like something unnatural sticking to his fur. What does he do? He shakes his body. So also, we have the dirt of ignorance, egotism, and other things clinging to our mind, but they are not part of our real nature and we must get rid of them. We must shake them off. How? Through discrimination: 'I am not this body, nor am I identified with anything the body is identified with, such as caste or country. These are all superimpositions. My real Self is always pure, without birth, without death.' When you practise this kind of discrimination, slowly the conviction grows on you that you are not the body, that you are the Self, separate from the body.

The second illustration is taken from the myth of the churning of the ocean. In ancient times the gods and the demons decided to churn the ocean to obtain the nectar of immortality so that they would never die. After much difficulty they managed to get the nectar, and then the gods tricked the demons and snatched it away so they could have it all for themselves.

When the nectar was being distributed among the gods, the sun and the moon noticed that Rāhu, a demon, was hiding among them and they shouted a warning. But it was too late. Rāhu was able to get a taste of the nectar just before his head was cut off. Thus the rest of his body perished but his head became immortal, and that head is forever chasing his enemies, the sun and the moon. When there is an eclipse of the moon, it is said that Rāhu has swallowed the moon. But because Rāhu has no body, the moon soon comes out from the bottom of his head and we again see the shining form of the moon.

The Upaniṣad says that it is as if we were all within the mouth of Rāhu. We have all been swallowed by ignorance, as it were. By nature we are the luminous Self, but the light of the Self has been covered by the darkness of ignorance. Somehow or other we have to free ourselves from the mouth of Rāhu and we will then regain our inherent splendour.

Vedānta says, if you are Brahman you have always been Brahman. It is not that you are attaining something new. When you realize Brahman, you realize what you have always been. It is like a prince kidnapped by some beggars when he is just a baby. As he grows up among the beggars, he behaves just like them. He never realizes he is a prince. But one day some people discover him and take him to the palace and tell him he is the prince. He was always the prince, only he did not know it.

There is a wonderful example told by Holy Mother. There was a large diamond lying on the ground near a bathing ghat. Everyone thought it was a piece of glass, and those who came to bathe there used to scrape the dirt off their feet by rubbing them on the diamond. One day a jeweller saw it and realized it was a diamond. Hadn't it always been a diamond? Similarly, you have always been Brahman, only you did not know it.

Vedānta says we have placed our own hands over

our eyes and we are saying: 'Help! I can't see anything. I am blind.' We have always been telling ourselves that we are worthless and good for nothing. Now we must reverse our thinking. We must tell ourselves that we are pure, free, and divine.

Vedānta does not claim it can perform any miracles. It does not have any strange, magical formulas. What Vedānta says is very simple and straightforward—*Tat tvam asi,* thou art that. Vedānta tries to awaken the power that is already lying dormant within us. And in how many different ways it tries. Śaṅkara says the scriptures are *ādaravati,* affectionate, like a mother. Perhaps you want to eat only sweets and nothing else, but the doctor has said you should not eat sweets. What does your mother do? She will go on coaxing you in different ways to eat what is good for you. Similarly, the Upaniṣad goes on coaxing us to attain Self-knowledge.

The Upaniṣad is telling us we are now mesmerized into thinking we are good for nothing, a sinner, a slave. We have to get out of the grips of this delusion, like the moon gets out of the mouth of Rāhu. We have to shake off this delusion, like the horse shaking off the dirt on its fur.

We then attain a state which is called *akṛtam,* uncreated. Whatever is created will be destroyed. If we build a house, then some day or other it will be destroyed. But that which is uncreated, which is not the effect of anything, is eternal. It will never come to an end. Self-knowledge is not something created in us. It is not a product. Nor is it the result of anything.

It was always there, always within us, only we did not know it.

Section Fourteen

आकाशो वै नाम नामरूपयोर्निर्वहिता ते यदन्तरा तद्ब्रह्म तदमृतं स आत्मा प्रजापतेः सभां वेश्म प्रपद्ये यशोऽहं भवामि ब्राह्मणानां यशो राज्ञां यशो विशां यशोऽहमनुप्रापत्सि स हाहं यशसां यशः श्येतमदत्कमदत्कं श्येतं लिन्दु माभिगां लिन्दु माभिगाम्॥ १ ॥ इति चतुर्दशः खण्डः ॥ १४ ॥

Ākāśo vai nāma nāmarūpayornirvahitā te yadantarā tadbrahma tadamṛtaṁ sa ātmā prajāpateḥ sabhāṁ veśma prapadye yaśo'haṁ bhavāmi brāhmaṇānāṁ yaśo rājñāṁ yaśo viśāṁ yaśo'hamanuprāpatsi sa hāhaṁ yaśasāṁ yaśaḥ śyetamadatkamadatkaṁ śyetaṁ lindu mābhigāṁ lindu mābhigām. Iti caturdaśaḥ khaṇḍaḥ.

Ākāśaḥ vai nāma, that which is described as 'space'; *nāmarūpayoḥ nirvahitā,* is manifest through names and forms; *te,* those [names and forms]; *yat antarā,* are within that; *tat brahma,* that is Brahman; *tat amṛtam,* that [Brahman] is immortal; *saḥ ātmā,* it is the Self [the inmost being in everyone]; *prapadye,* may I be able to enter; *sabhām veśma,* the court; *prajāpateḥ,* of Prajāpati; *aham bhavāmi yaśaḥ brāhmaṇānām,* may

I attain the fame of a brāhmin; *yaśaḥ rājñām,* the fame of a prince; *yaśaḥ viśam,* the fame of a merchant; *aham yaśaḥ anuprāpatsi,* I wish to have real fame; *saḥ ha aham yaśasām yaśaḥ,* I want to be famous among all famous people; *mā abhigām,* may I not be born again; *śyetam adatkam adatkam śyetam lindu,* so that I may not have a body covered with blood and dirt, and which is toothless yet always wanting to eat. *Iti caturdaśaḥ khaṇḍaḥ,* here ends the fourteenth section.

1. That which is described as space manifests names and forms. These names and forms are within Brahman. Brahman is immortal; it is the Self. May I attend the court of Prajāpati. May I attain the fame of a brāhmin, and also of a prince and a merchant. I wish to have real fame. I want to be famous among all famous people. May I not have to be born again and have a body covered with blood and dirt, which is toothless and at the same time always wanting to eat.

How do we meditate on the infinite? One way is to think of ākāśa, space. Sri Ramakrishna used to advise this also. If we can think we are one with the infinite, then slowly the consciousness that we are the body, that we are limited and bound, will go.

We must not make the mistake of thinking that Brahman and ākāśa are the same, however. They are by no means synonymous. Ākāśa is matter, and Brahman is not. Brahman is pure consciousness. But often we find that, just to give us some idea of what Brahman is like, ākāśa is used as an example. This is because we cannot see it or feel it, yet we know it is everywhere.

How do we identify something or someone? Only by mentioning its name and form. If we take away the names and forms, there is just one vast Existence. I am Existence. You are Existence. Everything is Existence, *Sat.* And this Sat is one and undivided. But as soon as we give something a form and a name, it becomes individualized. Then one individual becomes separate from another. The Upaniṣad says, that in which all these names and forms exist, and which is unattached and unaffected by them, is Brahman.

Section Fifteen

तद्धैतद्ब्रह्मा प्रजापतय उवाच प्रजापतिर्मनवे मनुः प्रजाभ्य आचार्यकुलाद्वेदमधीत्य यथाविधानं गुरोः कर्मातिशेषेणाभिसमावृत्य कुटुम्बे शुचौ देशे स्वाध्याय-मधीयानो धार्मिकान्विदधदात्मनि सर्वेन्द्रियाणि सम्प्रति-ष्ठाप्याहिंसन्सर्वभूतान्यन्यत्र तीर्थेभ्यः स खल्वेवं वर्तयन्यावदायुषं ब्रह्मलोकमभिसम्पद्यते न च पुनरावर्तते न च पुनरावर्तते॥१॥ इति पञ्चदशः खण्डः॥१५॥

इति छान्दोग्योपनिषद्यष्टमोऽध्यायः॥८॥

Taddhaitadbrahmā prajāpataya uvāca prajāpatirmanave manuḥ prajābhya ācāryakulādvedamadhītya yathāvidhānaṁ guroḥ karmātiśeṣeṇābhisamāvṛtya kuṭumbe śucau deśe svādhyāyamadhīyāno dhārmikānvidadhadātmani sarvendriyāṇi sampratiṣṭhāpyāhiṁsansarvabhūtānyanyatra tīrthebhyaḥ sa khalvevaṁ vartayanyāvadāyuṣaṁ brahmalokamabhisampadyate na ca punarāvartate na ca punarāvartate. Iti pañcadaśaḥ khaṇḍaḥ. Iti chāndogyopaniṣadyaṣṭamo'dhyāyaḥ.

Tat ha etat, this [knowledge of the Self, which has so long been discussed]; *brahmā prajāpataye uvāca,* Brahmā taught Prajāpati [i.e., to Kaśyapa]; *prajāpatiḥ manave,* Prajāpati [taught] Manu; *manuḥ prajābhyaḥ,* Manu [taught] his own children [i.e., to all human beings]; *yathā-vidhānam,* strictly according to the prescribed rules; *vedam adhītya,* studying the Vedas; *guroḥ karma atiśeṣena,* in the time he is free after serving the teacher; *abhisamāvṛtya ācāryakulāt,* after returning home from the teacher's house; *kutumbe,* he marries; *śucau deṣe,* in a holy place; *svādhyāyam adhīyānaḥ,* studying the scriptures regularly and as the occasion demands; *dhārmikān vidadhāt,* teaching his children and disciples to be truly religious; *ātmani sarvendriyāṇi sampratiṣṭhāpya,* withdrawing all organs into himself; *ahiṁsan sarvabhūtāni,* practising non-injury to all living beings; *anyatra tīrthebhyaḥ,* except at a holy place; *saḥ khalu evam vartayan,* he lives in this way; *yāvat āyuṣam,* to the end of his life; *brahmalokam abhisampadyate,* goes to Brahmaloka; *na ca punaḥ āvartate na ca punaḥ āvartate,* and he does not return, he does not return [to this world again]. *Iti pañcadaśaḥ khaṇḍaḥ,* here ends the fifteenth section. *Iti chāndogya upaniṣadi aṣṭamaḥ adhyāyaḥ,* here ends the eighth chapter of the Chāndogya Upaniṣad.

1. Brahmā taught this knowledge of the Self to Prajāpati, and Prajāpati taught it to Manu. Manu, in his turn, taught it to all human beings. A young man goes to live at his teacher's house and serves him, and when he is free he studies the Vedas in the prescribed manner. After finishing all his studies, he goes back home and marries. But he continues to study the scriptures in a sacred place. He also teaches his children and disciples in such a way that they will be religious. He keeps all his senses under control and avoids violence unless he is at a holy place. This is how he lives his whole life. Then after death he goes to Brahmaloka, and he is not born again, he is not born again.

The Chāndogya Upaniṣad has altogether eight chapters, the first five of them being devoted to karma (worship), and the last three being almost exclusively devoted to *ātmā-jñāna* (Self-knowledge). One may ask, 'Why waste so much space on worship?' The answer is that worship is necessary in order to attain *citta-śuddhi* (purification of the mind).

A pure mind is like a clean mirror. If you stand before a clean mirror, you can see yourself clearly. Similarly, when your mind is purified, the Self reveals itself to you. You then know that your self is the Self of all and you are one with all.

The Upaniṣad says here that as soon as you receive the sacred thread, you go and live with your teacher as a brahmacārin. You become part of his family. You serve him in various ways, and he teaches you all that you need to know. Though you must work hard serving the teacher and also studying the scriptures, in the long run you learn more from the way your teacher lives. He shows you what kind of person you have to be.

If the teacher is satisfied with your progress, he permits you to go back home. This permission is called *samāvartan*—a convocation, in common parlance. You may or may not go back home. If you return home, you may marry and raise a family. The scriptures tell you what sort of life you have to live there. As a householder, you have many obligations to fulfil, and you fulfil them as best you can, following the scriptures.

There are two kinds of brahmacārins: The *naiṣṭhika* brahmacārins never marry. They remain with the teacher and are life-long celibates. The *upakurvāṇa* brahmacārins live with the teacher for twelve years as celibates, and then they may return home and marry.

But no matter whether you remain with the teacher or you return home and become a householder, you are required to continue studying the scriptures. And you must study them according to the rules laid down about place and time. This is called *svadhyāya.*

Along with svadhyāya, you are also required to practise *ahiṁsā,* non-violence. The Upaniṣad says you must practise non-violence everywhere, the only exception being a place of pilgrimage. What does this mean? Here non-violence means not begging for food. All forms of violence are prohibited, including even begging. Begging becomes a form of violence when you beg of a person who is himself needy, almost a beggar. The Upaniṣad says you may beg in a holy place, but elsewhere you are forbidden to beg of a needy person. Begging from such a person is as bad as being violent.

ॐ आप्यायन्तु ममाङ्गानि वाक्प्राणश्चक्षुः श्रोत्रमथो बलमिन्द्रियाणि च सर्वाणि। सर्वं ब्रह्मौपनिषदं माऽहं ब्रह्म निराकुर्यां मा मा ब्रह्म निराकरोदनिराकरणमस्त्वनिराकरणं मेऽस्तु। तदात्मनि निरते य उपनिषत्सु धर्मास्ते मयि सन्तु ते मयि सन्तु।

ॐ शान्तिः शान्तिः शान्तिः॥

Om Āpyāyantu mamāṅgāni vākprāṇaścakṣuḥ śrotramatho balamindriyāṇi ca sarvāṇi; Sarvaṁ brahmaupaniṣadaṁ mā'haṁ brahma nirākuryāṁ mā mā brahma nirākarodanirākaraṇamastvanirākaraṇaṁ me'stu; Tadātmani nirate ya upaniṣatsu dharmāste mayi santu te mayi santu. Om Śāntiḥ Śāntiḥ Śāntiḥ.

May all my limbs grow strong, so also my breath, speech, eyes, ears, and all my organs. All is Brahman, of which the Upaniṣads speak. May I never turn away from Brahman. May Brahman never turn me away. Let there be no turning away, no turning away at least on my side. I am engaged in the study of the Self. The Upaniṣads speak of qualities that one must possess to succeed in such a study. May I acquire those qualities. Om Peace! Peace! Peace!